THE ULTIMATE
CLIFF

THE ULTIMATE
CLIFF

PETER LEWRY
& NIGEL GOODALL

SIMON &
SCHUSTER

First published in Great Britain by Simon & Schuster Ltd, 1996
A Viacom Company
Copyright © Peter Lewry and Nigel Goodall 1996

Simon & Schuster Ltd
West Garden Place
Kendal Street
London W2 2AQ

Simon & Schuster of Australia Pty Ltd
Sydney

A CIP catalogue record for this book is available from the British Library
ISBN 0-684-81696-2

Book interior by Design/Section, Frome
Printed and bound in Great Britain by Butler & Tanner Ltd, Frome and London

DEDICATION

To Simon and Sue
for all their help and encouragement over the years
PL

To Peggy, Julie and Sue
for all their enthusiasm and support through the years
NG

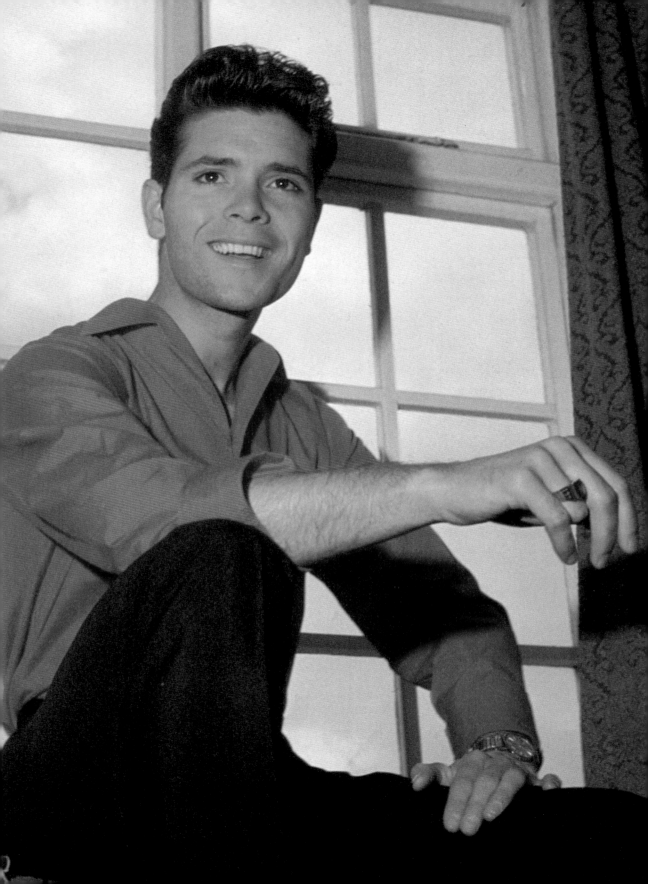

ACKNOWLEDGEMENTS

First of all, we would like to thank all of those individuals and organisations that have helped with this long term project. Without you, this book would have been arduous to complete: British Film Institute, National Sound Archives, Alliance Records, Time Life Music, Readers Digest, Evening Argus, Film Studios at Elstree, Pinewood, and Shepperton, Cheshunt School, Tracy Finch, Gill Reading, Bob Leal, Fiona Wilkins, Steve Dodds, and Nicky Chatterton. We are especially grateful and indebted to Sue Andrews, Tricia Hercoe, John McGoran, Christine Whitehead, Eileen Edwards, William Hooper, Mary Posner, Michael Wilson, and Ray and Colette Williams, for sharing their astute knowledge with us, and for graciously supplying photographs and memorabilia from their private collections.

Dozens of people have been supportive and helpful over the past several years including Bill Latham, David Bryce, Malcolm Smith, Roger Bruce, Peter Gormley, Gill Snow, Bruce Welch, Hank Marvin, Mike Read, Terri Anderson, Ken Townsend, Lou Swoffer, Richard Lee, Peter Vince, David Mackay, Tony Clarke, Malcolm Addey, Ruth Edge, Jenny Keen, Janet Lord, Dimitri Coryton, Jill Betts, Amanda Rabbs, Matt Duffy, Ashley Howe, Paul Moessl, Gerry Kitchingham, Ben Robbins, Keith Bessey, Stuart Booth, Rosie Anderson, Geoff Barker, Hanne Jordan, Tony Hoffman, Stuart Colman, Alan Beadle, Mike Evans, Andrew King, Margaret Sadler, Ashley Western, Julie Pettitt, Keith Allfrey, Harry de Louw, Stock Aitken and Waterman, Mike Gardner, Gerry Bron, Steve Maycock, Adrian McKinney, Mike Heatley, Ann Bush, Vanessa Burrows, Mike Sammes, Leanne Dearsley, John Hudson, Bob Morgan, Gary Scott, Clem Cattini, Mark Lewisohn, Peter Day, Carole Lewry, and of course, Cliff.

Special mention should also go to the many organisations who have provided tremendous help through the years including Cliff United, Dynamite International, Grapevine, Capitol Radio, EMI Records, EMI Music Archives, Polydor Records, See For Miles, The Hit Factory, numerous recording studios including Abbey Road, RG Jones, Eden, Mayfair, Air, and Sarm, selected regional newspapers including Worthing Herald, Sussex Express and Seaford Gazette, and of course, The Cliff Richard Organisation.

We'd be remiss if we didn't mention our editors Helen Gummer and Catherine Reed, and the other staff at our publishers, Simon & Schuster.

We sincerely thank you all.

CONTENTS

PART 4

THE PERFORMER

PART 5

COLLECTING CLIFF

PART 6

MISCELLANEA

FOREWORD

BY BRUCE WELCH

So here we are, a new year – 1996 – and as I move ever closer to the bus pass and pension book, my thoughts drift back thirty-eight years to the summer of 1958 in Soho, London. Hank Marvin and I were just sixteen years old, and we had just met a much older man (he was seventeen) who was to change our lives; his name was Cliff Richard. Little did we know then that we were destined to become inseparable for the next ten years. Together as a team, and as separate acts, we created a unique partnership that went on to make pop music history: Cliff and the Shadows.

Here in this book, *The Ultimate Cliff*, you can follow in amazing detail what Cliff has been doing these last thirty-eight years: the records, films, television shows, stage shows, tours, books and the people who helped him along the way. A real

trainspotter's delight!

Now I too will be able to flick through these pages and remind myself of so many great times that Cliff and the Shadows shared. I'm sure all Cliff fans will find this book a treasure trove of information that will keep them occupied over the years ahead. As for myself, it has been a privilege to have played a part in this superstar's story as a musician, songwriter and record producer.

As for the future, no doubt I will be able to eat out forever by telling the 'inside' story – and the chilling facts behind why my hair is grey and Cliff and Hank's isn't!

Enjoy the book.

Bruce Welch

January, 1996

PREFACE

When *Jack Good*, producer of the *Oh Boy* show introduced Cliff Richard to the teenage television viewers of Great Britain as 'the boy who's gonna rock the world' no one realised how enduring and appropriate that introduction would be, least of all Jack, who probably thought that it was unlikely that any rock 'n' roll performer could dominate the record charts and concert platform for more than a few years at the most because the music market was then, and is still today, so fragmented. For more than thirty-eight years, the sales of Cliff Richard records and concert tickets has *never* stopped.

There have probably been a larger number of books published on Cliff (including a couple written by us a few years ago) than on any other performer, with the exception of Elvis Presley. Why so many? Because the average Cliff Richard fan has an appetite to read *anything* on or about Cliff. Never before, however, has any one book contained as much information as the one you are now holding in your hands.

The Ultimate Cliff is separated into six parts to facilitate the location of facts. The portion devoted to Cliff's films is very comprehensive – more so than any previous book has devoted to the subject. For the first time ever, the cast and credit lists are complete, and the background information is probably the most detailed you'll ever find. And we doubt that the reader will ever find a more useful guide to Cliff's music career than is presented in that section. The discography is the most comprehensive ever published anywhere, the song title index details where every song appeared, and there's a fascinating but descriptive section on all Cliff's alternate takes ever released. The concert appearances, the tours, television and radio performances are again the most detailed that you could ever wish to find, and for collectors and 'trainspotters' worldwide, there's a whole section on collecting Cliff with detailed lists of the earliest memorabilia, such as bubblegum cards, magazine collectables and the rarer items. There's also a price guide to the most valuable Cliff records.

It's all here in one book, and that was our goal in writing *The Ultimate Cliff*: to provide a one-stop reference guide to Cliff Richard. We believe we've succeeded. Of course, we'll never be completely satisfied. There's so much to learn.

In a book of this nature, there is bound to be an occasional mistake or omission, although we've made every effort to eliminate such problems. If you spot a mistake or omission, or just want to enlighten us with new or updated material, please write to us. We would be particularly interested in rare, one-of-a-kind photos. If you know of any songs sung by Cliff in concert, but never recorded, send the information to us, documenting the place and date. Precise dates on early concert appearances are especially welcome. Complete foreign discographies from any country would also be greatly appreciated. We hope we'll have the opportunity to update this book some-time in the future and, with your support, we will.

We have put a lot of time and effort into this book, so we hope you enjoy it as much as we have putting it together.

Peter Lewry and Nigel Goodall.

PART 1

INTRODUCING CLIFF

INTRODUCTION

For most people of forty and under, British pop probably begins with the Beatles, and for those of us over that age, it probably begins with Cliff Richard and Marty Wilde – Britain's two biggest rock stars from 1958 through to the full onset of Beatlemania in the summer of 1963. The period really begins when two strands of American music came together in the British charts during January 1956. Bill Haley was at number one with 'Rock Around The Clock' – the first rock 'n' roll chart topper in the UK – while Lonnie Donegan was having a hit with his punked up version of an old Leadbelly tune, 'Rock Island Line'. But Lonnie Donegan's hit wasn't just a record, it was a way of life called 'skiffle'. Within six months there were skiffle groups, clubs, and even fashions.

Girls liked rock 'n' roll, and they particularly liked Elvis Presley. And skiffle gave boys an entry point into youth culture. Rock 'n' roll was modern and very American. A mix of contemporary, country and R&B styles, skiffle represented 1920's American folk blues and had been played in British clubs since the late 1940's. Donegan's hit was an afterthought that inspired two generations of British musicians. What we must remember though is that skiffle wasn't the *real* thing. The real thing was Elvis Presley.

The arrival of rock 'n' roll was considered as scandalous in the UK as it had been in the US. The music, like the Teds, became the focus of adult disapproval in the mid-fifties. Add to this a general fear of youth, and 'juvenile delinquency' had become the new big issue.

When Elvismania hit our shores, he became the king of rock 'n' roll both here and in America. Our answer was a young singer from Bermondsey called Tommy Steele, who became the first British rock star. A true phenomenon, he elicited screams and dominated front covers of magazines, singing cover versions, such as 'Singing The Blues', which was his biggest hit. Steele was discovered in a Soho coffee bar, the 2i's, which made Old Compton Street the mecca for every aspiring musician. Nearly all of the British rock 'n' rollers played there at one time or another – Cliff Richard, Adam Faith, Terry Dene, Hank Marvin and Bruce Welch. Some only occasionally, and others on a regular basis. The birth of British rock 'n' roll was that simple, and it went directly into the most famous pop film of the era, *Expresso Bongo*.

By the time the 2i's generation were ready to make records, they had to contend with an industry stuck in the early fifties. At that time, live performances were often undertaken as part of a variety show, with comic turns, jugglers, fire eaters, and an orchestra in the pit. And, despite Cliff's brave assertion in 'Move It', nobody thought that rock 'n' roll was here to stay. Although American was all powerful in terms of record sales, here in the UK sheet music was the thing. Singers were highlighted in front of groups and encouraged to dilute their pure rock action in favour of something more sedate which might appeal to the mums and dads. And – even more so than in

the States – the UK utilised the medium of television to spread the rock 'n' roll word. Following the *Six Five Special*, Jack Good delivered the perfect rock television concept in 1958 with *Oh Boy!* – no variety, no handicraft moments, no stupid presenters trying to be funny, just hard and fast music with melodramatic lighting. It made the first real British rockers, Marty Wilde and Cliff. We finally had our answer to Elvis. Audiences were now primed to ignite on contact with any authentic agent of American rock 'n' roll. Cliff looked right. He did a few of the necessary wiggles and that was it: he was the agent that the British fans had been waiting for, someone they could identify with. Cliff was the pioneer rock star who shrewdly widened his appeal with records and films for all ages. From 1959 through to 1963, Cliff dominated British pop with nineteen Top 5 records, seven number ones, and three smash movies. The boy who Jack Good said was 'gonna rock the world', did just that. For teenagers it was simply a case of 'let's go!' They heard the music, got goosebumps and were instantly hooked.

QUOTES

ABOUT CLIFF

'The most crude exhibitionism ever seen on TV. If we are expected to believe that Cliff Richard was acting naturally then consideration for medical treatment before it's too late may be advisable.'

– *New Musical Express*, 1958

'He is the artist with the second highest number of weeks spent in the British chart, only Elvis Presley is ahead of him, and should he continue he will necessarily pass Elvis. Cliff has the last laugh because he has no sell by date. He goes on and on.'

– Paul Gambaccini

'My first impression of Cliff was interesting because we'd never met him, we had seen him on the "Oh Boy!" show and we thought he was terrific. He had a great aura about him, a charisma.'

– Hank Marvin

'I'd never seen pink socks and pink shirt and black top, whatever he was wearing, or pink jacket, and I thought this is ridiculous. I'd been playing with people like Ronnie Scott and Tubby Hayes, and suddenly I was confronted with this pink-shirted whatever, and I thought, no this is … and then I saw the charts and that was it.'

– Jet Harris

'He's incredibly professional. He's got a great voice, great singing voice, great recording voice, it's that knack of whoever's listening to the record, it's as though he's singing purely to them.'

– Bruce Welch

'Usually when you hear a wonderful record you think yeah, he's got three chins or four eyes or he's missing a hand, something's wrong, you couldn't believe he looked any good at all. So I had to audition him, and when he turned up, there he was, looking absolutely normal.'

– Jack Good

'He was an imitation Elvis and he had that sexual projection that the early rockers had – a lot of swinging hips and suggestive movements and the rest of it, but by 1960 he was doing "Bachelor Boy" or "Living Doll" or whatever, and the whole thing had come very acceptable to the parents – very tame wasn't it?'

– Neil Spencer

'He's a nice, acceptable, good, clean-living lad. I don't know any rock 'n' roll singer that I've met would want to admit to that. He goes against all the unwritten laws of being a rock singer. He's clean cut, he's a nice lad, he looks healthy – all these things are not things that normally go to make up a successful rock singer, and Cliff's broken all the rules, and he's bigger than anybody. It's amazing.'

– Adam Faith

'If Cliff had to give up singing, he could always make a living as a dancer. He has a natural acting ability – there is never any display of temperament.'

– Peter Myers

'I have a little boy of three – if he grows up to behave like Cliff, then I shall be happy.'

– Ron Cass

'After Elvis you had very few people, in fact, I don't know of another act that has had a career as long as Cliff's, with as many hits.'

– Phil Everly

'I wanted to record with a legitimate orchestra of session musicians. "I'm Looking Out The Window" was one of a group of four songs recorded at the session, and I think we had it on the stocks some time before it was released. It was certainly a turning point for Cliff, whose broader talents became apparent when he did it.'

– Norrie Paramor

'His track record speaks for itself, every true professional should admire him.'

– Shakin' Stevens

'As Cliff Richard fans, we never thought the day would dawn when Cliff would want to work with us. It is a great honour for us that in the eighties he would want us to write a song for him.'

– Stock, Aitken and Waterman

'The ultimate professional, which is something very rare and extra special.'

– Dave Clark

'"I'll Love You Forever Today" is probably the most boring song Cliff has ever recorded. It's a shame really, because with his nice inoffensive way of singing, he has usually managed to lift even the most trivial of songs to a slightly higher commercial plane. But it would take a coal-heaver to do anything with this one – and he's certainly not that.'

– Penny Valentine, *Disc & Music Echo*

'He gets better and better as the years go on. Cliff has class. It is difficult to have show-biz without him!'

– Olivia Newton-John

'He is always in what's happening musically and for me that is the key ingredient for his continual success.'

– Elton John

'I consider myself lucky to have *met* Cliff, never mind working with him for ten years. He is a life enhancer.'

– Una Stubbs

QUOTES
FROM CLIFF

'I suppose I'm one of those people who went looking for fame and fortune.
I found it, but I also found it just wasn't enough. I was looking for something
else – and I found it in Christianity.'

'I never wanted to be a singer until I heard Elvis. When I heard Elvis, that was the inspiration I needed because he was unbelievable.'

'I just wanted to be a pop singer. I just wanted to put on my pink jacket, sing their songs, get all the glory and that was it.'

'People forget that I was once 18 and that I really was the first of the bad taste dressers! Until me, there was never anyone who came out wearing a puce jacket, luminous pink socks, pink tie, black trousers. I'm the one who invented all that.'

'Christianity gave me a sense of perspective. I realised that music wasn't the most important thing in my life. What matters is my relationship with God and my belief that, even though I don't deserve it, I will enter Heaven. Now, much as I want to live, I'm not scared of death.'

'I actually used to be a bit fat. I'd never even thought about it till one evening I was sitting watching *Coronation Street* on telly and Ena Sharples made a remark about that chubby Cliff Richard. I was horrified.'

'My mum still looks incredible for a 70 year old, so I suppose I've been lucky enough to inherit some of her genes. But tennis has helped a lot too. As a game it's very aerobic and whenever I can, I will book a pro and play for a couple of hours. And I eat well from a moderate and varied diet.'

'Olivia Newton-John is a lovely girl. I think the world of her and like her very much, but she's not a girlfriend.'

'People don't believe it, but I used to swear like a trooper.'

'What hurts is when my music is called bland and predictable. Name another artist who has sung with Elton John, Phil Everly, the Young Ones, Sarah Brightman and Aswad. If that's bland and predictable, then I need to revisit the dictionary.'

'No singer has managed to bridge the gap between pop and the theatre and I want to be the first to do so. But I'll never give up pop. I love it. Singing is the easiest thing for me next to getting out of bed. But I find acting very fulfilling.'

'I want to do so much in the acting field. I've made films, but I'm never happy with them once they are completed. I'd like to go for something completely different, like making a horror film, with me playing the Dracula-type lead. But television acting is hard for me, because you have so many distractions.'

'I left the normal world at 18. I wanted fame and fortune and I got it. I'll never understand to this day how some people chase it, get it, then reject it all and start complaining. Of course, I complain occasionally, but on the whole I'd rather be where I am than change anything.'

'A lot of people still don't think it's cool to like me.'

'I'm only in the business of making hits, and when the history books come out, when I'm dead and gone, that's what I'll have done.'

'I think it was the peak because I'd never ever sold as many records as quickly. "The Young Ones" was released as a single on the Friday, but prior to that we were being told that the advance orders were two hundred thousand. The advance orders were three hundred thousand and by Friday when it was released there were a million orders. By Monday morning it was a number one. And it's never happened to me since.'

'Logic tells me I can never top 1989 in terms of job satisfaction and achievement. "Mistletoe And Wine" launched me into the year that saw me playing to 150,000 people at Wembley and being named as the most popular male singer of the eighties by Independent Television audiences.'

'I never wanted to do anything but have hits. I'm unashamedly a hit maker. That's why I enjoy working with Stock, Aitken and Waterman, because that's exactly what they are too.'

'Everyone who makes a record at Christmas wants it to be a Number One.'

'The one country all other countries respect in pop music is England. They fear us. That's what makes the Eurovision so important.'

'I've performed behind the Iron Curtain before, of course. In the early sixties I was the first British pop performer to do so when I visited Poland. I've also played in Yugoslavia and Rumania.'

'I feel they didn't judge "Two A Penny" fairly as an artistic work. I think it's the best thing I've done on the screen. As for the message of Christianity, that seemed to embarrass them, but I don't think it should have done, after all, religion is an essential part of life.'

'We've made Take Me High for all the family. There's nothing in it that would be smutty or embarrassing. People can just go out and have a nice evening.'

'My relationship with Sue Barker resulted in a good many sleepless, anxious nights, and there were numerous instances when certain newspapers' distortion or fantasy caused embarrassment and sometimes real hurt.'

'To be a Christian and to have a wife would be difficult.'

'I suppose I'm a romantic at heart, but when I see what's happening around me, it puts me off marriage. I'm surrounded by people getting divorced. If I were to marry it'd be for life. But at the moment my life is as complete as anyone's can be. I don't think marriage would make it that much better. I'm surrounded by a lot of love, a lot of friends and I'm happier than I've ever been.'

'If marriage isn't in the pipeline for me, then I'm not going to worry about it. My life is very happy and fulfilled as it is.'

'I was the rage of my school because I looked like Elvis. I used to practise curling my lip the way he did. Elvis was the guy I wanted to be like. He was the greatest.'

'It's really hard to see me through other people's eyes. I guess if they were of an age when they can think back to "Summer Holiday" or "The Young Ones" they'll think of me in those terms. And if they're under 30, it'll be "Devil Woman" and "Miss You Nights". But I bet that all of them would think of me as a Christian, as someone who's stood up for what he believes. That's probably the thing that warms me most, that I've gained the respect of people regardless of whether they believe what I believe or not.'

'"Gee Whiz It's You" was released on the continent, because people there had asked for it, and when we got back from a tour there we discovered, much to our surprise, that it was in the charts here. Apparently, people in this country had heard it played over Radio Luxembourg and asked for it to be released here too.'

'When we first heard "Power To All Our Friends" we felt sure it was the obvious choice to go forward into the contest. But there were other good songs too. Like "Help It Along" which I thought was strong musically and which had been of tremendous use to me in my gospel act.'

'The Summer Holiday film was some of the happiest work I have ever done. We had a fantastic time over three or four months. All of us working on the film got along extremely well, and of course a lot of it was filmed in the gloriously sunny climate of Greece.'

'It's hard to follow a number one hit with another immediately afterwards, and I've only managed it once with "Travellin Light", the successor to "Living Doll". A good qualifier, I would have thought, for America's country charts.'

'Although I say it myself, I reckon "Move It" was the first real rock 'n' roll recording made outside of the USA. It's one of the few songs I've sung regularly since I first recorded it, and for me it never seems to date. I remember a punk band hearing it at an EMI function some years back. Dropping their image for a minute, the leader singer said "that's a great song, mate. Are you going to record it?" '

'It's one of the most unexpected occurrences in my life. I can't help thinking that I come from a council house in Cheshunt. I stayed up until midnight to hear it [Knighthood] confirmed on the late TV news. Some people go to extraordinary lengths to play tricks. It would have been embarrassing if it hadn't been true.'

'Who'd have thought it! A Knighthood. I suppose from now on I'll be known as Sir Cliff – but you can call me Cliff!'

CHRONOLOGY OF CLIFF
AND HIS ERA
1904–1996

In this section we have recorded a diary of major events between 1904 and 1996 relating to Cliff's life and career. As with most categories for Cliff this is considerable, however we have selected dates and events that are probably considered to be the most interesting and most important. We have also listed a number of events that are not connected directly with Cliff. They are included here because of their importance to the era.

1904–1939

23 December 1904 – Cliff's father, Rodger Oscar Webb, born.

13 August 1920 – Cliff's mother, Dorothy Marie Dazely, born.

8 January 1935 – Elvis Presley born in East Tupelo, Mississippi. Elvis was the biggest musical influence for a whole generation, including Cliff.

19 January 1939 – Phil Everly, youngest of the Everly Brothers, was born. The Everlys were musical heroes of Cliff's from the fifties. Some decades later, Cliff and Phil recorded a number of duets as well as performing them live on stage.

15 April 1939 – Reginald Smith (Marty Wilde) born. Marty was, along with Cliff, Britain's biggest rock star from 1958 through to 1960.

26 April 1939 – Rodger Oscar Webb and Dorothy Marie Dazely married in Asanol, India.

6 July 1939 – Terence Harris (Jet Harris) born.

1940s

9 February 1940 – Brian Bennett born.

23 June 1940 – Terence Nelhams (Adam Faith) born. Adam, along with Cliff, dominated the British pop charts from 1959 through to 1963.

14 October 1940 – Harry Rodger Webb (Cliff Richard) born in Lucknow, India.

17 April 1941 – Ronald Wycherley (Billy Fury) born. Fury was one of the biggest rock stars of pre-Beatles British rock with 29 Top 50 hits.

28 October 1941 – Brian Rankin (Hank Marvin) born.

2 November 1941 – Bruce Cripps (Bruce Welch) born.

16 June 1942 – John Rostill born.

2 March 1943 – Daniel Joseph Anthony Meehan (Tony Meehan) born.

27 May 1943 – Priscilla White (Cilla Black) born. Cilla was one of Britain's biggest female pop stars during Beatlemania.

1943 – Cliff's sister, Donella (Donna), born.

1945 – Cliff enrolled at the school attached to St Thomas's Church in Lucknow, India.

21 November 1947 – Cliff's sister, Jacqueline Ann (Jacqui), born.

21 August 1948 - The Webbs moved from Lucknow, India to Carshalton, Surrey, England and stayed with Cliff's grandparents at 47 Windborough Road.

September 1948 – Cliff enrolled at the Stanley Park Road Junior School.

26 September 1948 – Olivia Newton-John born in Cambridge. Olivia was 'the girl who sang with Cliff', and went on to gain fame in both country and rock music.

October 1949 – The Webbs move from Carshalton to

Waltham Cross, Hertfordshire and stayed with Cliff's aunt and her family.

1950s

January 1950 – Rodger Webb began work for the Eastwoods Ltd.

February 1950 – Cliff's third sister, Joan, born.

11 April 1951 – The Webbs moved from Waltham Cross to Cheshunt and obtained a three-bedroom council house at Hargreaves Close.

May 1951 – Rodger and Dorothy Webb began work for Thorn Electrical Industries.

September 1952 – Cliff is enrolled at Cheshunt Secondary Modern School after failing his eleven plus.

February 1954 – Cliff joined the school drama society, and made his acting debut in 'The Price Of Perfection'.

12 April 1954 – Bill Haley & His Comets recorded 'Rock Around The Clock' in New York.

5 July 1954 – Elvis Presley's first commercial recording session at Sun Records. The first song put on tape was 'Harbour Lights' followed by 'I Love You Because'. 'That's All Right (Mama)' was recorded that evening, which became his first single.

September 1955 – Cliff played Ratty in the school production of 'The Wind In the Willows'.

12 November 1955 – 'Rock Around the Clock' by Bill Haley & His Comets was number one on Record Mirror's singles chart for six weeks.

10 January 1956 – Elvis's first RCA recording session took place in Nashville. The first song put on tape was 'I Got A Woman' followed by 'Heartbreak Hotel' and 'Money Honey'.

May 1956 – On a Saturday afternoon, Cliff hears 'Heartbreak Hotel' by Elvis for the first time from a car radio.

14 July 1956 – Cliff and friends, calling themselves the Quintones, appeared at the Holy Trinity Youth Club dance at Waltham Cross.

3 March 1956 - Cliff attends Bill Haley's concert at the Regal Edmonton.

15 November 1956 – Elvis Presley's first film *Love Me Tender* released.

August 1957 – Cliff obtained a summer job picking tomatoes at a local garden nursery.

19 September 1957 – Cliff is enlisted to the Dick Teague Skiffle Group.

1957 – Cliff began working at Atlas Lamps as a credit control clerk.

17 October 1957 – Elvis's third film *Jailhouse Rock* premiered at Loew's State Theatre in Memphis.

March 1958 – Cliff and the Drifters made their first cabaret appearance at the Forty Hill Badminton Club Annual Dinner and Dance.

24 March 1958 – Elvis Presley inducted into the US Army.

6 April 1958 – The Railroaders, a group that included Hank Marvin and Bruce Welch, came third in a talent show at the Edmonton Regal.

8 April 1958 – The Railroaders disbanded, but Hank and Bruce formed a new group with Pete Chester calling themselves the Chesternuts.

Mid April 1958 – Columbia release 'Teenage Love' by the Chesternuts, who make regular appearances at the famous '2i's' Coffee Bar in Soho, where they eventually meet Cliff.

April 1958 – Cliff and the Drifters play together at the 2i's Coffee Bar in Soho for two weeks.

3 May 1958 – Cliff and the Drifters 'Direct from the famous Soho 2i's Coffee Bar' made a concert appearance at the Regal Ballroom in Ripley, their biggest engagement so far, and their first outside London and Hertfordshire. Support was a 'top twenty record session', plus Keith Freer and his Dixielanders.

25 May 1958 – Cliff and the Drifters attend Jerry Lee Lewis' concert at the Kilburn State Theatre and afterwards met him in his dressing room.

Early June 1958 – Cliff and the Drifters recorded 'Lawdy Miss Clawdy' and 'Breathless' for demo purposes at a small studio above the HMV record shop in Oxford Street. They left with the original tape.

15 June 1958 – Marty Wilde appeared on the first *Oh Boy!* TV show. Produced by Jack Good, the programme was telecast live from the Hackney Empire.

June 1958 – Cliff and the Drifters made an appearance on the Gaumont Teenage Show at Shepherds Bush. It was the first Cliff performance that caused frenzied screaming from the audience.

14 June 1958 – Cliff and the Drifters returned to the Gaumont Theatre at Shepherds Bush as special guests on a talent show. Agent George Ganjou was in the audience, who would later bring them to the attention of record producer Norrie Paramor.

6 July 1958 – Cliff and the Drifters played the Astoria Cinema in Ware sharing the bill with a Kim Novak film.

24 July 1958 – Cliff's first commercial recording session at Abbey Road studios. The first song put on tape was 'Schoolboy Crush' followed by 'Move It'.

9 August 1958 – Norrie Paramor signs Cliff to Columbia Records.

29 August 1958 – DB 4178 'Schoolboy Crush'/'Move It' is Cliff's first commercial record release.

7 September 1958 – Cliff's first rehearsal for the *Oh Boy!* TV show.

13 September 1958 – Cliff made his television debut on *Oh Boy!* singing 'Move It' and 'Don't Bug Me Baby'. The show was transmitted live from the Empire Theatre in Hackney.

September 1958 – Hank Marvin and Bruce Welch enlisted to the Drifters replacing Ken Pavey and Norman Mitcham on guitars.

22 September 1958 – Elvis Presley and his Army unit left the Military Ocean Terminal in Brooklyn aboard the USS General Randall for Bremerhaven, West Germany, arriving there on 1 October 1958.

5 October 1958 – Cliff and the Drifters' first tour opened at the Victoria Hall in Hanley. The Kalin Twins were top of the bill.

25 October 1958 – On the day that Cliff made his

BBC radio debut on 'Saturday Club', Franklin Boyd took over John Foster's role as Cliff's manager.

November 1958 – Jet Harris from the Vipers enlisted to the Drifters replacing Ian Samwell.

14 November 1958 – First Cliff recording session to include the Drifters at Abbey Road studios in London. 'Livin' Lovin' Doll' and 'Mean Streak' were recorded at the session.

17 November – Cliff and the Drifters made their debut on the variety circuit at the Metropolitan Theatre in Edgware Road, London.

26 November 1958 – Bill Fury's first commercial recording session at Decca's West Hampstead studios. The first song put on tape was 'Maybe Tomorrow' followed by 'Gonna Type Me A Letter'.

December 1958 – Cliff began filming *Serious Charge*.

January 1959 – Franklin Boyd and John Foster let out of their managerial roles. Tito Burns became Cliff's new manager. Drummer Tony Meehan from Adam Faith's backing group the Worried Men joined the Drifters, replacing Terry Smart.

30 January 1959 – DB 4263 'Feeling' Fine'/'Don't Be A Fool With Love' is the Drifters' first record release.

9–10 February 1959 – Cliff made his first live recordings before invited audiences at Abbey Road studios. The sessions were taped for his first LP *Cliff*.

February 1959 – Cliff won the Best New Singer award in the *New Musical Express* annual readers' poll.

February 1959 – Norrie Paramor signs the Drifters to Columbia Records.

April 1959 – Adam Faith made his first appearance on the *Six-Five Special* TV show.

May 1959 – *Serious Charge* released.

July 1959 – The Drifters change their name to the Shadows.

10 July 1959 – DB 4306 'Living Doll'/'Apron Strings' was released. Cliff's first number one single.

October 1959 – Theatre Royal in Dublin dropped the curtain midway through Billy Fury's act because his suggestive gyrations were 'downright disgusting'.

9 October 1959 – Cliff voted Top British Male Singer in the *New Musical Express* readers' poll. 'Living Doll' was voted Disc of the Year.

17 October–28 November 1959 – 'Travellin' Light' was number one on *Record Mirror*'s UK singles' chart for seven weeks.

26 October 1959 – Cliff made his first live broadcast on Radio Luxembourg.

1 November 1959 – Cliff and the Shadows made their debut on *Sunday Night at the London Palladium* for ATV – then the biggest entertainment show on British television.

4 December 1959 – Adam Faith's 'What's Do You Want' made number one on the UK singles' chart.

December 1959 – Marty Wilde and Joyce Baker, one of the Vernon Girls, are married. The Vernon Girls were regulars of the *Oh Boy!* show. Some decades later they would reform to appear on Cliff's *Event* at Wembley Stadium.

6 December 1959 – Cliff voted the King of Rock 'n' Roll on Radio Luxembourg's 'Swoon Club'.

December 1959 – Cliff and the Shadows appeared in their first pantomime *Babes In The Wood* at the Stockton Globe.

28 December 1959 – Cliff voted Best British Male Vocalist of the Year on the TV's *Cool For Cats* pop programme.

1960s

17 January 1960 – Cliff and the Shadows' second appearance on *Sunday Night at the London Palladium* watched by nineteen million people – the largest television audience for a light entertainment show in Britain.

21 January 1960 – Cliff and the Shadows made their national American television debut on *The Pat Boone Show*.

22 January 1960 – Cliff and the Shadows began a six week American tour with 'The Biggest Show of Stars 1960' package tour.

February 1960 – Cliff won the Top British Male Singer award in the annual *New Musical Express* readers' poll.

5 March 1960 – Elvis Presley discharged from the US Army.

15 March 1960 – *Expresso Bongo* premiered in New York.

April 1960 – Adam Faith's first film *Beat Girl* released.

May 1960 – Cliff bought his parents a corner house at 2 Colne Road in Winchmore Hill, North London for £7,000.

23 May 1960 – Columbia Records invited selected fans to choose Cliff's next single. 'Please Don't Tease' was chosen.

June 1960 – Peter Gormley officially became the Shadows' manager.

7 July 1960 – Cliff and the Shadows began a thirteen week Sunday night series, 'Me And My Shadows', on Radio Luxembourg.

6 August 1960 – 'Please Don't Tease' was number one for two weeks on *Record Mirror*'s UK singles' chart.

12 August 1960 – Cliff bought a red Thunderbird convertible with white top.

20 August–24 September 1960 – the Shadows took over number one from Cliff for six weeks with 'Apache' on *Record Mirror*'s UK singles' chart.

16 September 1960 – DB 4506 'Nine Times Out Of Ten' was released to advance orders of 180,000 – then the biggest advance order for any record.

1 October 1960 – Cliff and the Shadows appeared on *Oh Boy!*

28 October 1960 – Cliff won the Top British Male Singer award in the *New Musical Express* readers' poll.

30 October 1960 – Cliff and the Shadows made a concert appearance at his old school, Cheshunt Secondary Modern.

30 October–25 December 1960 – Elvis's 'It's Now or Never' was number one in the UK singles' chart for eight weeks – the longest of any Presley single.

20 November 1960 – Cliff made his debut on the BBC Home Service.

January 1961 – Norrie Paramor signs Helen Shapiro to Columbia Records. She was Britain's first teenage female pop star at the age of fourteen.

February 1961 – The Beatles made their debut appearance at the Cavern Club in Liverpool. Within a few years they would dominate the pop charts, threatening Cliff's position as Britain's number one hitmaker.

1 March 1961 – Peter Gormley officially became Cliff's personal and professional manager, replacing Tito Burns.

15 March 1961 – Cliff and the Shadows made a concert appearance at the Johannesburg Coliseum. It was the first Cliff concert to be recorded.

7 April 1961 – DC 756 'Gee Whiz It's You' was Cliff's first European single to chart in Britain.

8 April 1961 – Cliff made his debut appearance on the panel of *Juke Box Jury*.

May 1961 – Cliff's father, Rodger Webb died at the age of fifty-six.

20 May 1961 – Cliff and the Shadows made their first appearance on 'Thank Your Lucky Stars'.

12 June 1961 – Cliff bought his mother a blue Hillman Automatic.

7 October 1961 – Cliff and the Shadows made a television appearance on *Thank Your Lucky Stars*.

14 October 1961 – Cliff's 21st birthday.

19 October 1961 – Cliff and the Shadows made their first concert tour of Australia.

October 1961 – Brian Bennett replaced Tony Meehan in the Shadows. Bennett had previously played drums for Marty Wilde's backing group the Wildcats.

1 December 1961 – Cliff voted Top British Male Singer in the *New Musical Express* readers' poll. He came second to Elvis Presley in the World Male Singer section.

December 1961 – Cliff won the Variety Club of Great Britain's Show Business Personality of the Year award.

13 December 1961 – *The Young Ones* premiered in London.

20 January 1962 – 'The Young Ones' was number one on *Record Mirror*'s UK singles chart – the only single of any Cliff song to enter the chart at number one.

February 1962 – Cliff won the Top British Male Singer award in the annual readers' poll organised by the *New Musical Express*.

15 March 1962 – Cliff and the Shadows appeared at the Eton College Missions Youth Club in Hackney in the presence of Princess Margaret and the Earl of Snowdon.

March 1962 – Bill Fury collapsed during his UK tour due to exhaustion.

13 April 1962 – The Shadows became the first British group awarded a gold disc.

15 April 1962 – Jet Harris made his last appearance with Cliff and the Shadows at the annual *New Musical Express* Poll Winners' Concert at Wembley.

22 April 1962 – Brian 'Licorice' Locking replaced Jet Harris and made his first appearance with the Shadows, backing Cliff at the Queens Theatre in Blackpool. Locking, like Brian Bennett, had previously played with Marty Wilde's backing group the Wildcats.

23 April 1962 – Bruce Welch collapsed on stage at a concert at the Queen's Theatre in Blackpool, with a septic throat.

27 April 1962 – Jet Harris signed a record deal with Decca.

10 May 1962 – 'I'm Looking Out The Window'/'Do You Wanna Dance' is Cliff's first double-sided hit.

18 May 1962 – Cliff and the Shadows signed to the Leslie Grade Organisation and formed Shad-Rich music publishing.

27 May 1962 – Cliff began filming *Summer Holiday* in Greece.

June 1962 – Billy Fury's first film *Play It Cool* released.

6 June 1962 – The Beatles' first recording session took place at Abbey Road studios in North London. The first song to be taped was 'Besame Mucho', followed by 'Love Me Do'; 'PS I Love You'; and 'Ask Me Why'.

July 1962 – Cliff and the Shadows' *Holiday Carnival* summer season opened at the ABC Blackpool.

28 August 1962 – Cliff and the Shadows made their first appearance on the *Billy Cotton Show*.

October 1962 – 'The Young Ones' released in America as 'It's Wonderful To Be Young'.

5 October 1962 – Parlophone 45-R 4949 'Love Me Do'/'PS I Love You' became the first commercial record release by the Beatles.

29 October 1962 – Cliff and the Shadows appeared in the Royal Variety Performance in the presence of Her Majesty The Queen.

31 October 1962 – Elvis's eleventh film *Girls! Girls! Girls!* was premiered in Honolulu, Hawaii.

30 November 1962 – Cliff voted Top British Male Singer in the *New Musical Express* readers' poll. 'The Young Ones' was third Best British Disc Of The Year.

15–29 December 1962 – RCA 8100 Elvis Presley's 'Return To Sender' was number one on *Record Mirror*'s UK singles' chart for Christmas.

3 January 1963 – 'The Next Time'/'Bachelor Boy' became Cliff's second double-sided hit to reach number one on the UK singles chart.

10 January 1963 – *Summer Holiday* premiered simultaneously in London and South Africa.

10 February 1963 – Cliff bought his mother a Chevrolet.

11 February 1963 – Cliff and the Shadows appeared at a charity concert in Nairobi organised by the Kenyan leader, Tom Mboya. The Beatles' first album recording session took place at Abbey Road studios in London. Ten new songs for *Please Please Me* were recorded between 10am and 10.45pm.

20 February 1963 – Cliff and the Shadows became the first artists to have four songs from one film (*Summer Holiday*) in the UK top thirty singles' chart.

24 February 1963 – Cliff and the Shadows made an appearance on *The Billy Cotton Band Show*.

8 March 1963 – 'Summer Holiday' was number one on the UK singles' chart.

20 April 1963 – 'Serious Charge' re-released.

21 April 1963 – Cliff and the Shadows made an appearance at the annual *New Musical Express* poll winners' concert at Wembley.

22 April 1963 – Cliff taped his first television special for BBC.

1 June 1963 – Cliff and the Shadows began their sixteen week summer season at the ABC in Blackpool.

July 1963 – Cilla Black signed to the Parlophone label.

2 August 1963 – Cliff was voted Most Promising Singer by readers of the American teen magazine, *16*.

10 August 1963 – Cliff and the Shadows appeared on the 100th edition of *Thank Your Lucky Stars*.

23 August 1963 – 'Lucky Lips' was No. 69 on the Billboard's Top 100 chart – the first of Cliff's songs to chart in America.

20 October 1963 – Cliff appeared on the Ed Sullivan TV show in New York.

3 November 1963 – Licorice Locking made his final appearance with the Shadows on *Sunday Night at The London Palladium*.

25 December 1963 – John Rostill replaced Licorice Locking and made his debut with Cliff and the Shadows in the ATV Spectacular *Sounds and Sweet Airs*.

January 1964 – Marty Wilde, Joe Brown, Susan Maughan and Freddie and the Dreamers appeared in the film *What A Crazy World*.

May 1964 – Olivia Newton-John's first single 'Till You Say You'll Be Mine' recorded at Decca's West Hampstead studios.

2 July 1964 – *Wonderful Life* premiered in London.

6 July 1964 – The Beatles' first film, *A Hard Day's Night* premiered at the London Pavilion.

August 1964 – Cliff and the Shadows opened their summer season at ABC Great Yarmouth.

2 November 1964 – Cliff and the Shadows appeared in the Royal Variety Show at the London Palladium in the presence of Her Majesty, The Queen.

22 December 1964 – Cliff and the Shadows' second pantomime *Aladdin and His Wonderful Lamp* opened at the London Palladium. The last performance took place on 10 March 1965.

January 1965 – The Shadows' film *Rhythm and Greens* released.

June 1965 – Cliff and the Shadows taped three television specials for ATV. The specials aired on 15, 22 and 29 September.

11 August 1965 – The Beatles' second film, *Help*, premiered in New York.

15 August 1965 – The Beatles broke the record for a single performance at a concert at Shea Stadium in New York. The attendance totalled 55,600 people, the largest audience for a pop concert.

27 August 1965 – Elvis Presley met the Beatles at his Perugia Way mansion in Bel Air.

2 September 1965 – Cliff and the Shadows gave a charity concert for the rebuilding of the Milton Keynes Church.

11 October 1965 – Cliff and the Shadows made their first concert appearance in Poland at the Roma Theatre, Warsaw.

26 October 1965 – The Beatles received their MBE's at Buckingham Palace.

4 December 1965 – Cliff and the Shadows gave a charity concert in Cheshunt at Cliff's old school.

10 December 1965 – Cliff is voted Top British Male Singer in the *New Musical Express* readers' annual poll.

25 December 1965 – Cliff, the Shadows and Frank Ifield appeared in *Cliff Richard's Christmas Cheer* on BBC Television.

31 January 1966 – Cliff and the Shadows made their cabaret debut at the Talk Of The Town in London.

4 March 1966 – John Lennon remarked that the Beatles were more popular than Jesus Christ during their US tour. Beatles records were burned on bonfires in several US cities, and radio stations were banned from playing them.

3 April 1966 – Cliff and the Shadows appeared at the *Daily Express Record Star Show* at the Empire Pool, Wembley.

April 1966 – Cliff attended the 25th Anniversary of the Abbey Christian Community service at the Royal Albert Hall in London.

30 April 1966 – Cliff and the Shadows made an appearance at the *New Musical Express* Poll Winners' concert.

27 May 1966 – Cliff began filming *Finders Keepers* at Pinewood Studios.

16 June 1966 – Cliff made an appearance at the Billy Graham Crusade staged at Earls Court in London, proclaiming that he was a Christian. He took part in the evening meeting, singing 'It Is No Secret', a traditional gospel song originally recorded by Elvis.

18 June 1966 – Cliff's mother, Dorothy Webb, married Derek Bodkin.

24 June 1966 – The Official Cliff Richard Fan Club run by Jan Vane with 42,000 members was closed down by Cliff as he was due to begin a three-year divinity course, leaving his career behind. In the following months his retirement plans were denied as Cliff decided on an equal mix of music and religion.

3 July 1966 – Cliff made a radio appeal to raise funds for the Westminster Homes for elderly people.

15 July 1966 – DB 7968 'Visions', recorded without the Shadows, released.

29 August 1966 – The Beatles played their final concert in San Francisco. They were disillusioned, tired and exhausted of touring.

9 October 1966 – Cliff compered and topped the bill at *Sunday Night at The London Palladium*.

22 October 1966 – Cliff appeared at the Royal Albert Hall with the Archbishop of York and the Bishop of Coventry.

7 December 1966 – Cliff appeared on *Cinema* discussing his film career.

8 December 1966 – *Finders Keepers* premiered in London.

12 December 1966 – *Thunderbirds Are Go* premiered in London.

December 1966 – Cliff and the Shadows' third pantomime *Cinderella* opened at the London Palladium.

January 1967 – Cliff appeared on the *Five To Ten* religious programme.

14 February 1967 – *Disc and Music Echo* voted Cliff Best Dressed Male Star.

1 May 1967 – Elvis Presley and Priscilla Beaulieu married at the Aladdin Hotel in Las Vegas.

May 1967 – Cliff began filming *Two A Penny* at Pinewood.

1 June 1967 – Parlophone PMC/PCS 7016 *Sergeant Pepper's Lonely Hearts Club Band* was number one for the Beatles on the UK album chart.

9 July 1967 – Cliff appeared with Billy Graham on the religious programme *Looking For An Answer*.

16 July 1967 – Cliff discussed religion with Paul Jones on *Looking For An Answer*.

19 August 1967 – Adam Faith and Jackie Irving are married at Caxton Hall. Jackie had previously been romantically linked with Cliff.

27 August 1967 – The Beatles' manager, Brian Epstein, aged thirty-two, was found dead at his London home from a drugs overdose. Some years later it began to be suggested that the pressure and stress of running the Beatles empire had become too much and that his untimely death might not have been accidental. All of the Beatles were shocked by the news. John Lennon said 'he was one of us'.

23 September 1967 – Cliff voted Top Male Singer in the *Melody Maker* reader's poll.

21 October 1967 – Cliff's first religious LP, *Good News*, released.

4 November 1967 – 'All My Love' became Cliff's 40th single.

6 December 1967 – Cliff confirmed as a member of the Church of England by Graham Leonard, the Bishop of Willesden, at St Paul's Church in Finchley, North London.

25 December 1967 – Cliff and the Shadows appeared in a Christmas Day presentation of *Aladdin* for Rediffusion TV.

1 January 1968 – The Shadows made their first West End appearance without Cliff at the Talk of the Town.

1 February 1968 – Elvis Presley's daughter, Lisa Marie, is born in Memphis, Tennessee.

February 1968 – Cliff began filming *A Matter Of Diamonds*, a drama for ATV.

14 February 1968 – Cliff was again voted Best Dressed Male Star by readers of *Disc And Music Echo*.

5 March 1968 – Cliff appeared on the *Cilla Black Show* and sang the songs short-listed for the Eurovision Song Contest.

15 March 1968 – DB 8376 'Congratulations' released as the song chosen by 170,000 viewers for Britain's entry for the Eurovision Song Contest.

April 1968 – Cliff's straight acting debut in *A Matter Of Diamonds* is screened on the ITV network.

6 April 1968 – 'Congratulations' came second in the Eurovision Song Contest staged at the Royal Albert Hall, London.

25 April 1968 – The Shadows began a season of shows at the London Palladium with Tom Jones.

2 May 1968 – Bruce Welch was sued for divorce by his wife Ann, who cited Olivia Newton-John as the other woman.

4 May 1968 – Cliff and the Shadows appeared on the 50th edition of the *Saturday Club* radio show on BBC.

12 May 1968 – Cliff and the Shadows made an appearance on the 16th NME Poll Winners concert at the Empire Pool, Wembley.

13 May 1968 – Cliff started a four-week season of cabaret shows at London's Talk of the Town without the Shadows.

20 June 1968 – *Two A Penny* premiered in London.

27 June 1968 – Elvis Presley taped his first television special at the NBC Burbank studios in California. The TV special aired in the US on 3 December 1968, and in the UK on 31 December 1969.

17 July 1968 – The Beatles' *Yellow Submarine* premiered at the London Pavilion.

19 September 1968 – Cliff began a twelve-week season of *The Autumn Show* at the London Palladium.

September 1968 – 'Established 1958' LP released to commemorate Cliff and the Shadows' tenth year.

1 December 1968 – Cliff introduced *Songs Of Praise* from the Holy Trinity Church in Manchester.

14 December 1968 – Cliff's Palladium season ends, and the Shadows disband.

13 January 1969 – Elvis Presley's first recording sessions in Memphis since leaving Sun Records in 1955.

15 January 1969 – Cliff and the Settlers gave a charity concert for the homeless starving refugees of Biafra.

January 1969 – Cliff began filming *Life With Johnny* for Tyne Tees Television. A series of six modern day parables.

11 June 1969 – Cliff goes to Israel for three weeks in the Holy Land making the film *His Land* for Billy Graham's Worldwide Films.

31 July–31 August 1969 – Elvis Presley's first Las Vegas appearance since 1956 and first live appearance since 1961.

October 1969 – The Shadows reformed with Hank Marvin, Brian Bennett, John Rostill and Alan Hawkshaw.

10 December 1969 – Cliff appeared at a special gala midnight performance at the London Palladium in aid of the Royal Society for the Prevention of Cruelty to Animals.

27 December 1969 – *The Young Ones* became the first Cliff Richard film to be shown on television.

1970s

January 1970 – Cliff began his thirteen-week television series *It's Cliff Richard* with Hank Marvin and Una Stubbs.

January 1970 – Cliff won the Songwriters Guild of Great Britain award for The Most Outstanding Service to Music in 1969.

14 February 1970 – Cliff won the Mr Valentine award from *Disc and Music Echo*. He was also voted Best Dressed Male Star, second Best British Singer, and third Best World Singer.

6 April 1970 – Cliff began a week's engagement of cabaret performances at the Batley Variety Club.

10 April 1970 – The Beatles officially disbanded.

3 May 1970 – Cliff is voted second British Male Singer, second British Vocal Personality, and third World Male Singer in the NME readers' poll.

8 May 1970 – The Beatles last album, *Let It Be*, released.

11 May 1970 – Cliff made his drama debut in *Five Finger Exercise* at Bromley New Theatre.

13 June 1970 – Cliff made a guest appearance at the Bratislavia Song Festival in Czechoslovakia.

11 July 1970 – Cliff began a South African tour lecturing at the invitation of the Bishop of Natal.

9 August 1970 – Hank Marvin and Bruce Welch team up with John Farrar to form Marvin, Welch & Farrar.

18 September 1970 – Jimi Hendrix found dead in London from a drugs overdose.

9 October 1970 – Cliff received the National Viewers and Listeners' Association annual award for Outstanding Contribution to Religious Broadcasting and Light Entertainment.

24 December 1970 – BBC TV aired a *Cliff Richard Special* with Hank Marvin and Una Stubbs.

2 January 1971 – Cliff began his second *It's Cliff Richard* series on BBC with Hank Marvin and Una Stubbs.

February 1971 – Marvin, Welch & Farrar debut LP released.

April 1971 – Olivia Newton-John's second single, 'If Not For You' released. The Bob Dylan song was produced by Bruce Welch & John Farrar.

17 May 1971 – Cliff opened a week's run in *The Potting Shed* at Sadlers Wells Theatre in London.

13 June 1971 – Cliff appeared in a charity concert to aid the dependents of singer Dickie Valentine.

5 July 1971 – Cliff received Ivor Novello Award for outstanding service to British music at the Festival of the Rose d'Or in France.

1 August 1971 – The Concert For Bangladesh organised by George Harrison took place at Madison Square Garden in New York.

30 August 1971 – Cliff filmed *Getaway With Cliff* special for BBC-1 with Olivia Newton-John, Hank Marvin, Bruce Welch and John Farrar.

11–30 October 1971 – Cliff appeared at the London Palladium with Olivia Newton-John and Marvin, Welch and Farrar – a show which broke all previous attendance records.

17 November 1971 – Cliff began a British tour at the Gloucester ABC with Olivia Newton-John and Marvin, Welch and Farrar.

November 1971 – 'Sing A Song of Freedom' was banned in South Africa.

11 December 1971 – Cliff took part in a carol concert at the Royal Festival Hall in London.

11 March 1972 – Cliff gave a religious concert for Tear Fund at New Century Hall in Manchester.

14 April 1972 – The *Sun* presented Cliff with its Top Male Pop Personality award for the third year running.

2 September 1972 – *The Case* a comedy thriller starring Cliff, Olivia Newton-John, and Tim Brooke-Taylor screened on BBC-2.

2 December 1972 – DB 8957 'A Brand New Song' released – the first of any Cliff single in the UK not to chart.

6 December 1972 – Cliff gave a charity concert for the Arts Centre Group.

11–23 December 1972 – Cliff appeared at the Batley Variety Club in Yorkshire.

January 1973 – Cliff appeared on Cilla Black's television series over six weeks, performing the songs entered for the Eurovision Song Contest. 'Power to all our Friends' was the winning entry, and was placed third at the contest in Luxembourg in April.

14 January 1973 – Elvis Presley's second television special *Aloha From Hawaii* was telecast worldwide via satellite from Honolulu in Hawaii, and became the most watched TV special of all time with an estimated audience of one billion.

April 1973 – David Essex's first film *That'll Be The Day* released.

June 1973 – Cliff began filming *Take Me High* in Birmingham.

27 August 1973 – Cliff made an appearance at Spree 73 concert staged at Earl's Court in London.

1 September 1973 – Cliff appeared at Wembley Stadium with Johnny Cash and Billy Graham.

November 1973 – *Take Me High* premiered in London.

26 November 1973 – John Rostill found dead from electrocution in his home studio.

June 1974 – *Help It Along* LP released in aid of Tear Fund.

3–12 July 1974 – Cliff played Bottom in Cheshunt School Dramatic Society's production of *A Midsummer-Night's Dream*.

August 1974 – *It's Cliff Richard* series screened on BBC-1.

October 1974 – *Stardust* the sequel to *That'll Be The Day* released. The film starred David Essex and Adam Faith.

27 October 1974 – The Shadows reformed to appear with Cliff in a charity concert at the London Palladium.

November 1974 – Cliff toured Britain.

8 January 1975 – Elvis Presley's 40th birthday.

25 January 1975 – Cliff appeared in The Name of Jesus concert at the Royal Albert Hall in London.

22 March 1975 – The Shadows won second place with 'Let Me Be The One' in the Eurovision Song Contest.

5 June 1975 – Cliff gave a charity concert for the dependents of two Manchester policemen who died on duty outside the Granada TV studios during riots.

8 June 1975 – Cliff received a gold disc presentation for *The Cliff Richard Story*, a six-record box set from World Records.

6 September 1975 – *It's Cliff and Friends* screened on BBC-1.

September 1975 – 'Honky Tonk Angel' became the second Cliff single in the UK not to chart.

28 February 1976 – 'Miss You Nights' became the first Cliff single to chart in the UK since 'You Keep Me Hangin On' in July 1974.

23 April 1975 – 'Devil Woman' released – it made number 9 in the British Charts.

May 1976 – *I'm Nearly Famous* LP released, which went to number 5 on the album charts.

1 October 1976 – Cliff began a gospel tour for the Tear Fund organisation.

October 1976 – 'Devil Woman' was number six on the Billboard Top 100 chart – the highest position of any Cliff song in the US.

22 November 1976 – Cliff made a concert appearance with the Brian Bennett Band at the Royal Albert Hall in London.

February 1977 – The Shadows' *Twenty Golden Greats* was number one for six weeks on the UK album chart – the first of any Shadows LP for nine years.

May 1977 – The Shadows played a Twenty Golden Dates tour in the UK.

29 May 1977 – London Weekend screen *Finders Keepers* – the only time the film has been seen on British television.

6 June 1977 – Cliff took part at a Youth Rally during the Queen's Silver Jubilee celebration at Windsor Great Park.

16 August 1977 – Elvis Presley is found dead by girl-friend Ginger Alden at approximately 2.30 pm in Elvis's bathroom on the second floor of his Graceland mansion.

18 October 1977 – The British Phonographic Institute named Cliff as Best British Male Solo Artist.

28 October 1977 – Cliff received the Gold Badge Award from the Songwriters' Guild of Great Britain.

November 1977 – *Small Corners* released – an album of religious songs.

27 February–11 March 1978 – Cliff and the Shadows appeared at the London Palladium in a two-week season of reunion concerts that celebrated their 20th anniversary.

16 June 1978 – Olivia Newton-John's second film *Grease* opened in the US. Her first film had been as a member of the Tomorrow group formed to appear in the film of the same name in 1970.

9–10 October 1978 – Cliff gave two concerts in celebration of Tear Fund's tenth anniversary.

1 February 1979 – Cliff received a gold replica of the key to the Manchester Square officers of EMI to commemorate their 21st year together.

13 February 1979 – Cliff and the Shadows received an award for their twenty-one years as major British recording artists from *Music Week*.

10 June 1979 – Cliff talked about his Christian faith at a theatre in Liverpool.

5 July 1979 – Variety Club of Great Britain honoured Cliff for his twenty-one years in show business.

25 August 1979 – 'We Don't Talk Anymore' was at number one on the UK singles chart for four weeks – his first chart topper since 'Congratulations' in 1968.

26 August 1979 – Cliff made an appearance at the Greenbelt Festival.

September 1979 – Norrie Paramor died. Paramor was Columbia A&R man whose productions for Cliff, the Shadows, Helen Shapiro and Adam Faith totally shaped pre-Beatles British rock.

4 October 1979 – Cliff and Kate Bush appeared with the London Symphony Orchestra at the Royal Albert Hall in aid of the LSO's 75th Birthday Appeal.

2 December 1979 – Cliff took part in a charity concert to aid the International Year of the Child.

18 December 1979 – Cliff gave a charity concert for the International Year of the Child.

1980s

6 February 1980 – Cliff topped the bill at a special tribute concert to Norrie Paramor at the Fairfield Hall, Croydon. The Duchess of Kent attended.

27 February 1980 – Cliff won the *Nationwide* Golden Award for Best Family Entertainer.

27 March 1980 – Cliff made an appearance at the Sing Good News event at London's Royal Albert Hall.

15 April 1980 – Cliff taped an appearance for the *Pop Gospel* television show.

July 1980 – Olivia Newton-John's third film, *Xanadu* released.

23 July 1980 – Cliff received his OBE at Buckingham Palace.

14 October 1980 – Cliff began five nights of concerts at London's Apollo Theatre. BBC filmed the opening night.

October 1980 – 'Suddenly' a duet with Olivia Newton-John released. The song appeared on the soundtrack of Olivia's film *Xanadu*.

8 December 1980 – John Lennon shot at the Dakota apartment buildings in New York by Mark David Chapman. Lennon was dead on arrival at the Roosevelt Hospital.

16 January 1981 – Cliff appeared at the twenty-fifth birthday celebrations of the *Crusade* evangelical magazine with Billy Graham.

18 January 1981 – Cliff began rehearsals for his gospel tour.

27 January 1981 – Cliff filmed footage for his *A Little In Love* video at Farningham in Kent. David Mallett produced.

9 February 1981 – Bill Haley found dead at his home in Texas.

14 February 1981 – Cliff attended a Crusaders meeting at Central Hall in Westminster, London.

16 February 1981 – Cliff began tour rehearsals at Shepperton studios.

24 February 1981 – Cliff received the *Daily Mirror* readers' award for Outstanding Music Personality of the Year.

March 1981 – *The Young Ones* became the first Cliff Richard film to be released on video.

1 May 1981 – Cliff's Hammersmith Odeon concert filmed by BBC TV for the four-part *Cliff* documentary.

May 1981 – Cliff voted Top Pop Star in the *Sunday Telegraph* readers' poll.

3 May 1981 – BBC filmed footage of Cliff performing at the Hard Rock Café in London for their *Cliff* documentary. The Fantoms backed Cliff on 'D In Love'.

May 1981 – Viewers of Noel Edmonds *Swap Shop* television show voted Cliff Top Pop Star.

May 1981 – *TV Times* presented an award to Cliff for Most Exciting Male Singer on Television.

June 1981 – *Love Songs* was number one on the UK album chart.

24 July 1981 – Cliff filmed footage for his *Wired For Sound* video at Milton Keynes shopping centre.

August 1981 – Cliff appeared at the Greenbelt festival.

16 November 1981 – Cliff made a guest appearance at the Tear Fund Gala Night at the Royal Albert Hall, London.

23 November 1981 – Cliff appeared on the Royal Variety Command Performance.

31 March 1982 – Cliff launched an appeal in London for children's hospitals.

10 July 1982 – Cliff's US tour opened in San Francisco.

27 September 1982 – Cliff filmed a Christmas record token commercial for EMI.

10 October 1982 – Cliff began his European tour in Hanover.

23 November 1982 – Cliff appeared in concert at the Royal Albert Hall, London with the London Philharmonic Orchestra on their 50th anniversary. The concert was filmed by the BBC and recorded by EMI.

23 December 1982 – Cliff made an appearance on Top Of The Pops singing 'Little Town'.

13 January 1983 – *Cliff In Kenya* premiered at the

BAFTA cinema in London.

20 January 1983 – Cliff began a six-night engagement at Blazers Nightclub in Windsor.

28 January 1983 – Bill Fury died at the age of forty-two.

19 February 1983 – 'She Means Nothing To Me' a duet with Phil Everly released.

19 July 1983 – Cliff filmed the *Never Say Die* video.

27 August 1983 – Cliff made an appearance at the Greenbelt Christian Festival.

23 September 1983 – The Everly Brothers reunion concert took place at the Royal Albert Hall in London.

12 December 1983 – Cliff made his debut as a tennis player at his first Pro-Celebrity Tennis Tournament at Brighton.

13 June 1984 – Cliff attended Mission to London, a Christian evening at Queen's Park Rangers football ground in West London.

2–5 July 1984 – Cliff and the Shadows appeared together in concert at Wembley Arena and the Birmingham NEC.

7 September 1984 – Cliff began a British gospel tour at the Southampton Gaumont.

8 October 1984 – Cliff began a six-night engagement at Blazers Nightclub, Windsor.

27–28 October 1984 – Cliff appeared on Perth's Channel 7 *Telethon* while on tour in Australia.

15 December 1984 – Cliff's second Pro-Celebrity Tennis Tournament took place at the Brighton Centre.

17 June 1985 – Cliff filmed the *She's So Beautiful* video in the Lake District. Ken Russell produced.

9 July 1985 – Cliff began his UK gospel tour at Harrogate Conference Centre.

13 July 1985 – The Live Aid concert took place at Wembley Stadium and at the JFK Stadium in Philadelphia.

24–27 July 1985 – Cliff had laryngitis and cancelled the opening shows on his gospel tour – the first time he had ever cancelled concerts for health reasons.

4, 5, 7 October 1985 – Cliff had laryngitis again and postponed the opening concerts of his European tour.

21 December 1985 – Cliff's third annual Pro-Celebrity Tennis Tournament took place at the Brighton Centre.

31 December 1985 – Fifties American rock star, Ricky Nelson and his band were killed when his aircraft crashed near De Kalb in Texas.

10 January 1986 – Drummer Graham Jarvis's funeral is attended by Cliff at Beckingham Crematorium.

30 January 1986 – Cliff and the Young Ones filmed the *Living Doll* video for Comic Relief.

26 February 1986 – Cliff received Top Singer award from *TV Times* magazine.

7 April 1986 – Royal preview of *Time – The Musical* occurred at London's Dominion Theatre for cancer research in the presence of the Duchess of Kent.

9 April 1986 – Dave Clark's *Time – The Musical* opened at the Dominion in London, with Cliff as Rock Star, Chris, and Laurence Olivier as Time Lord.

April 1986 – 'Living Doll' with the Young Ones was number one on the UK singles chart – the only single of Cliff's to return to number one with a new version.

16 November 1986 – *Cliff From The Hip* filmed at the London Hippodrome before an audience of fan club members.

11 April 1987 – Cliff gave his last performance in *Time* prior to a special matinee-only performance given on 14 April in honour of Laurence Olivier.

7 May 1987 – Cliff filmed footage for his *My Pretty One* video at Albert Wharf, London.

31 May 1987 – Cliff began tour rehearsals at Wimbledon Theatre.

6 June 1987 – Cliff renewed his contract with EMI.

8 June 1987 – Cliff gave a special concert at Wimbledon Theatre.

15 June 1987 – Cliff took part in *It's A Royal Knockout* with Prince Edward and the Duchess of York at Alton Towers.

15 September – *Remember Me* video filmed.

25 September 1987 – Cliff gave three tour 'break-in' performances at the Wimbledon Theatre.

2 November 1987 – 'Remember Me' released – the first Cliff CD single.

26 November 1987 – Cliff appeared in the Royal Variety Performance at the London Palladium.

12 December 1987 – Cliff broke the record for a single performance at a concert in Birmingham (NEC). The box-office receipts totalled £500,000.

19 December 1987 – Cliff's Pro-Celebrity Tennis Tournament at the Brighton Centre closed with a performance of carol singing.

25 January 1988 – Cliff gave a performance at the Australian Royal Command Performance attended by Prince Charles and Princess Diana. Part of the country's bicentennial celebrations.

14 April 1988 – Cliff appeared in part of a special performance of *Time* in aid of the Terence Higgins Trust.

16 April 1988 – The last public performance of *Time*. The show closed due to legal problems.

27 August 1988 – Cliff made an appearance at the Greenbelt festival.

22 September 1988 – Cliff presented 'Search For a Star' tennis awards at Bisham Abbey.

5 October 1988 – Cliff opened his 30th Anniversary tour at the Hammersmith Odeon, London.

8 October 1988 – Cliff filmed the video for 'Mistletoe And Wine' at the Albert Wharf Studio in London.

10 December 1988 – 'Mistletoe And Wine' was number one on the UK singles chart.

13 December 1988 – Cliff gave a charity concert for the Great Ormond Street Hospital for Children.

17 December 1988 – Cliff's Pro-Celebrity Tennis Tournament at Brighton raised £150,000 for the 'Search For A Star' scheme.

20 December 1988 – Cliff made an appearance at the Save The Children concert at the Royal Albert Hall in London.

8 February 1989 – Cliff and the Shadows were honoured at a 30th Anniversary Luncheon in aid of the Nordoff-Robbins Music Therapy Centre.

16 February 1989 – Cliff received the Lifetime Achievement award from the BPI.

18–22 April 1988 – Cliff appeared at Caeser's Palace in Luton.

25 April 1989 – Cliff began a five-night engagement at the Savvas Club in Usk, Wales.

2 May 1989 – Cliff began a twelve-night engagement at Blazers Nightclub in Windsor.

30 May 1989 – Cliff became the first artist to release his 100th single. 'The Best Of Me' reached number two on the UK singles chart.

6 June 1989 – Lord Olivier died.

16–17 June 1989 – The Event, at Wembley Stadium, played to Cliff's biggest-ever audience of 144,000 over two nights.

19 July 1989 – Cliff's gospel tour opened at City Hall in Newcastle.

1 September 1989 – Cliff filmed the video for 'I Just Don't have the Heart' at 'K' stage, Shepperton Studios.

30 October 1989 – *Stronger* LP launched at the Trocadero in London.

20 November 1989 – Cliff received the Lifetime Achievement Diamond Award in Antwerp.

7 December 1989 – Cliff turned on the Christmas lights of Weybridge Traders Association at Bowman's Garage.

16 December 1989 – Tickets for Cliff's annual Pro-Celebrity Tennis Tournament at Brighton were sold out within two days.

19 December 1989 – Cliff made an appearance at the Royal Albert Hall for the Joy To The World concert.

1990–1996

4 January 1990 – Cliff filmed *Stronger Than That* video at Shepperton Studios.

15 January 1990 – Cliff gave a charity concert with Rick Wakeman and Justin Hayward for Leukemia Research at the Queen Elizabeth Hall in London.

26–27 June 1990 – Cliff rehearsed with the Shadows for their Knebworth concert appearance on 30 June.

19 July 1990 – Cliff made an appearance at the London Palladium for the Queen Mother's 90th Birthday concert.

17 September 1990 – Cliff began a six-night engagement at the Savvas Club in Usk, Wales.

25 September 1990 – Cliff filmed the *Saviours Day* video at Durdle Dor in Dorset.

14 October 1990 – Cliff's fiftieth birthday.

1 November 1990 – From A Distance tour opened at the National Exhibition Centre in Birmingham.

5 November 1990 – *From A Distance: The Event* Live double album released.

7 November 1990 – Cliff celebrated his 50th birthday with an after-show party backstage at the NEC Birmingham.

12 November 1990 – Cliff turned on the Christmas lights in London's Oxford Street.

23 November 1990 – Cliff appeared on *Children in Need*.

8 December 1990 – Cliff linked up with the *Coronation Street* tribute from Wembley Arena during his From A Distance tour.

29 December 1990 – 'Saviours Day' was the Christmas number one on the UK singles chart.

14 May 1991 – Cliff and Olivia Newton-John hosted the World Music Awards in Monte Carlo.

2 September 1991 – 'More To Life' – the theme from the new BBC series *Trainer* released.

16 September 1991 – Cliff appeared for six-nights at the Savvas Club in Wales.

22 September 1991 – Cliff began rehearsals for his Australian tour which opened in Perth on 9 November, and finished in Sydney on 30 November.

18 November 1991 – Cliff's first traditional Christmas album *Together* released.

24 November 1991 – Freddie Mercury died from Aids at his London home.

17 December 1991 – Cliff performed in Joy To The World concert at the Royal Albert Hall in London.

28 January 1992 – Cliff attended the premiere of Jack Good's musical *Good Rockin' Tonight*. Timothy Whitnall played Cliff.

28 February 1992 – Cliff sang a duet, 'Goodnight Girl' with Wet Wet Wet on the *Wogan* show.

20 March 1992 – Cliff was invited on to the stage of Wembley Arena to sing 'Goodnight Girl' with Wet Wet Wet.

23 June 1992 – Cliff made an appearance at the Sammy Davis Jnr tribute concert at the Royal Albert Hall.

28 June 1992 – Cliff performed 'Move It' on the roof of BBC's Broadcasting House to open National Music day.

October 1992 – Cliff started his Access All Areas tour at Birmingham NEC.

19 December 1992 – Cliff's Pro-Celebrity Tennis Tournament moved from the Brighton Centre to the National Indoor Arena at Birmingham.

30 April 1993 – *Cliff Richard: The Album*, and *Access All Areas* video were simultaneously at number one in the UK album and video charts.

11 May 1993 – Cliff filmed the video for *Human Work of Art* at the Rainbow Theatre, Finsbury Park in London.

28 June 1993 – Cliff taped the duet 'This Love' with Tammy Wynette at RG Jones studios in Wimbledon.

1 July 1993 – Cliff recorded a book of Bible stories at RG Jones studios in Wimbledon.

15 July 1993 – Cliff and Bill Latham appeared at Glastonbury Abbey as part of the An Evening with Cliff Richard tour.

29 August 1993 – Cliff gave a performance at the 20th anniversary of the Greenbelt Festival.

15 September 1993 – Cliff filmed for Cilla Black's anniversary TV special.

26 September 1993 – Cliff made an appearance at Michael Ball's charity show at London's Dominion.

28 September 1993 – Cliff filmed footage for his *Never Let Go* video at Black Island Studios in London.

14 November 1993 – *The Story So Far* home video released.

24 December 1993 – An extended version of *The Story So Far* shown on the South Bank Show.

21–24 February 1994 – Press launches for the *Heathcliff* musical took place in London, Birmingham, Sheffield, Aberdeen and Glasgow.

21 March 1994 – *Heathcliff* recording session in the Penthouse Suite at Abbey Road studios with Cliff, Tim Rice and John Farrar.

13 May 1994 – Postponement of the *Heathcliff* musical was announced, due to rehearsals being behind schedule. The show would now be replaced with The Hit List tour in which Cliff would perform all of his Top 5 hits.

24 May 1994 – Cliff filmed for Cilla Black's *Surprise Surprise*.

2 June 1994 – Cliff filmed for EMI's centenary anniversary video.

14 July 1994 – Cliff gave a charity performance at Byfleet Village Hall to raise funds for repairs to the local church.

19 July 1994 – Cliff made an appearance at Roy Castle's Train of Hope concert staged at the Liverpool Empire.

8 September 1994 – Cliff and Bill Latham attended the funeral of Roy Castle.

3 October 1994 – *The Hit List* CD and video released.

15 October 1994 – Cliff began rehearsals for The Hit List tour at Bray studios.

10 November 1994 – Cliff switched on the Christmas Lights at Birmingham.

18 November 1994 – The Hit List tour opened at Wembley Arena.

28 November 1994 – 'All I Have To Do Is Dream', a duet with Phil Everly released.

17 June 1995 – Cliff arrived home from vacation in Portugal and was met by the Press at the airport following the announcement of his knighthood.

18 June 1995 – Cliff held a party in celebration of his knighthood for the staff of the Cliff Richard Organisation, his sisters and mum, and a handful of close friends.

29 June 1995 – Cliff made an appearance at a private charity event arranged by British Airways in Weybridge, Surrey.

23 July 1995 – Cliff gave a charity concert appearance at the London Palladium *For The Love of Roy (Castle)* with the Merseybeats, Joe Brown, P J Proby and Jimmy Tarbuck.

9 October 1995 – 'Misunderstood Man', the first song from *Heathcliff* released.

17 October 1995 – Cliff played a forty-minute unplugged set at the Headfirst Charity staged at Coutts & Co, London, hosted by Cheryl Baker.

25 October 1995 – The formal investiture of Cliff Richard as Knight Bachelor took place at 10.30am in Buckingham Palace.

30 October 1995 – The *Songs From Heathcliff* album released.

16 November 1995 – Cliff made a guest appearance with Hank Marvin during his Hank Plays Cliff tour at the Royal Albert Hall in London.

20 November 1995 – Cliff topped the bill at the Royal Variety Performance that took place at London's Dominion Theatre. His set lasted for over thirty minutes and included duets with Olivia Newton-John ('Had To Be') and Hank Marvin ('Move It').

27 November 1995 – 'Had To Be', the duet with Olivia Newton-John released as the second single from *Songs From Heathcliff* album.

9 December 1995 – Cliff and Hank Marvin made an appearance at the Diamond Awards Festival in Antwerp, Belgium.

16 December 1995 – Cliff's annual pro-celebrity tennis tournament took place at the National Indoor Arena in Birmingham.

4 March 1996 – Localpost UK Ltd issued two commemorative Cliff Richard postage stamps bearing images of Cliff in his portrayal of Heathcliff.

5 May 1996 – Cliff gave a charity concert appearance in a Gala Variety Show at the Wimbledon Theatre in aid of the Princess Alice Hospice.

6 June 1996 – Cliff attends the opening night of *Summer Holiday The Musical* at the Opera House in Blackpool. The role of Don, immortalised by Cliff in the original film is played by Darren Day.

PART 2

THE PEOPLE

THE PEOPLE

IN CLIFF'S LIFE

ACTORS, ACTRESSES, BIT PARTS, STAND-INS, PRODUCERS & DIRECTORS

Geoffrey Bayldon played Alec Fitch in *Two A Penny*. Geoffrey became a household name for his role as Catweazle in the children's television series of the same name.

Stanley Black was the musical director who worked on the orchestrations for three of Cliff's movies, *The Young Ones*, *Summer Holiday* and *Wonderful Life*.

Paul Birrell was the stand-in for Richard O'Sullivan in *The Young Ones*.

Wilfred Brambell played the part of verger in Cliff's first film *Serious Charge*. Wilfred became a household name in the sixties for his role as Albert Steptoe in the television series, and film version of *Steptoe & Son*. He was also seen as Paul McCartney's grandfather in the Beatles' first film *A Hard Day's Night* in 1964.

Ron Cass, with Peter Myers, wrote the original story and screenplay for *The Young Ones*, *Summer Holiday* and *Wonderful Life*, as well as composing a number of songs for each film.

George Cole played Bert Jackson in *Take Me High*. George later went on to become a household name by playing Arthur Daly in the popular television series *Minder*.

Jim Collier, who directed Cliff in *Two A Penny*, and wrote and directed *His Land* went on to make more films for Worldwide including *The Hiding Place*, *Joni*, *Caught* and *The Prodigal* before he died in 1991 aged sixty-two. His last film was *China Cry*.

Jess Conrad had one of his first acting roles in Cliff's first film *Serious Charge*. Conrad recorded four singles as a pop singer before concentrating on acting and singing in films and stage musicals.

Darren Day, star of West End musicals *Copacabana* and *Great Expectations*, played Cliff's role of Don in *Summer Holiday – The Musical* which opened at the Opera House in Blackpool on 6 June 1996 for a 25-week season before transferring to the West End.

Yolande Donlan played Dixie Collins in *Expresso Bongo*. She had previously appeared in *Tarzan And The Lost Safari* and was married to the producer-director of *Expresso Bongo*, Val Guest.

Frank Dunlop is the director of Cliff's musical production of *Heathcliff*. He is one of the most experienced directors in Great Britain, having hundreds of premiere performances in major theatres across the UK and in America. He served as an Associate Director of the National Theatre from 1967 to 1971, founded the Young Vic in 1969, and was Director of the Edinburgh International Festival for eight years from 1983 to 1991.

Sidney J Furie who directed Cliff in *The Young Ones* and *Wonderful Life* went on to direct Michael Caine in

The Ipcress File, Diana Ross's first film *Lady Sings The Blues*, and *Superman 4* with Christopher Reeve.

Nigel Goodwin who played a small bit part as Fitch's assistant in *Two A Penny* went on to travel the world encouraging Christian artists. He is supported by the Genesis Trust.

Val Guest produced and directed Cliff in his seconf film *Expresso Bongo*. He went on to direct the films *Casino Royale*, *When Dinosaurs Ruled The World*, *Confessions of A Window Cleaner* and *The Boys In Blue*.

Susan Hampshire played Jenny, Cliff's leading lady in *Wonderful Life*. Susan had also had a bit part in Cliff's second film *Expresso Bongo* playing Cynthia, the same part she had in the stage version.

Gerald Harper had a small bit part as GPO personnel Watts in *The Young Ones*. Harper later became a familiar face to television viewers through appearances in various drama productions.

Kenneth Harper was the producer who took the idea of a Cliff Richard musical to Associated British Picture Corporation at Elstree and ended up producing four of Cliff's films. Harper had previously worked as an independent film producer on such films as *Far Better, Far Worse* with Dirk Bogarde, *Yield To The Night* with Diana Dors, and Sean Connery's first film *Action Of The Tiger*. He later married Pamela Hart, one of the dancers in *Summer Holiday*.

Laurence Harvey played Johnny Jackson, Cliff's manager in *Expresso Bongo*. His previous screen performances in *The Truth About Women*, *The Silent Enemy*, and *Room At The Top* had made him a major box office star of the fifties and sixties.

Melvyn Hayes appeared in three of Cliff's movies; *The Young Ones*, *Summer Holiday* and *Wonderful Life*. He went on to act in the situation comedy series *It Ain't Half Hot Mum*. Cliff and Melvyn became good friends through working together on those early musicals.

Alan Haynes was the stand-in for Teddy Green in *The Young Ones*.

Ronald Hines played Sam, Debbie Watling's father in *Take Me High*. Ronald later played in a number of situation comedies.

Helen Hobson was chosen to play the part of Cathy in Cliff's musical production of *Heathcliff*. She had previously appeared in the West End productions of *Chess*, *Les Miserables* and *Aspects of Love*. More recently she played the part of Mrs Walker in the European premiere of *Tommy*, and as Clara in the London premiere of *Passion* starring alongside Michael Ball.

Noel Howlett played Mr Peters in Cliff's first film *Serious Charge*. Noel later played the role of the headmaster in the comedy television series *Please Sir*.

David Kossoff played a small bit part as the magistrate in *Summer Holiday*. David had worked with Cliff previously in the *Stars In Your Eyes* show at the London Palladium. An Academy award winning actor, Kossoff later played Alf Larkin in the situation comedy series *The Larkins* and appeared in *Conspiracy Of Hearts* and *A Kid For Two Farthings*.

John Le Mesurier played the part of Mr X in *Finders Keepers*. John became known for his role in the comedy television series, and feature film of *Dad's Army*.

Ron Moody played the part of Orlando in *Summer Holiday*. Moody gained international fame for his portrayal of Fagin in the screen version of Lionel Bart's musical *Oliver*.

Robert Morley played Hamilton Black (Cliff's father) in *The Young Ones* and Colonel Roberts in *Finders Keepers*. Robert made his film debut in Hollywood in 1937 with *Mario Antoinette* and has since appeared in countless films including *The Doctor's Dilemma*, *Oscar Wilde* and *The Battle of the Sexes*.

Peggy Mount who played Mrs Bragg in *Finders Keepers* first gained fame in the situation comedy television series

The Larkins with David Kossoff.

Peter Myers wrote the original story and screenplay for *The Young Ones*, *Summer Holiday* and *Wonderful Life* with Ronald Cass.

Richard O'Sullivan played Ernest in *The Young Ones*, and Edward in *Wonderful Life*. As well as being one of the regular faces in the Cliff movies, Richard later played in the very popular situation comedy series and feature film of *Man About The House*.

Gerald Paris was the stand-in for Cliff in *The Young Ones*.

Lauri Peters, Cliff's leading lady in *Summer Holiday* left films to study classical theatre, and work as a stage actress. She later became a journalist, a photographer and a novelist.

Anthony Quayle played Howard Phillips in Cliff's first film *Serious Charge*. He had previously been seen in *Ice Cold In Alex*. He went on to make *The Guns of Navarone* which became the blockbuster movie of 1962, and the top grossing film of that year.

Andrew Ray who played the part of Cliff's brother, Larry Thompson, in *Serious Charge* went on to work in theatre, films, and television. He has appeared in *Crown Matrimonial*, *Edward And Mrs Simpson* and *Tales Of The Unexpected*.

Herbert Ross who first worked with Cliff on the dance routines in *The Young Ones* left theatrical choreography to become a film director. Among his films are *Play It Again Sam*, *Funny Lady*, *The Sunshine Boys*, *The Turning Point*, *The Goodbye Girl*, *Pennies From Heaven*, *Flashdance* and *Footloose*.

John Sagar was the stand-in for Melvyn Hayes in *The Young Ones*.

The Shadows appeared as themselves in *The Young Ones*, *Summer Holiday*, *Wonderful Life* and *Finders Keepers*.

Pat Shaw was the stand-in for Carole Gray in *The Young Ones*.

Sylvia Sims played the part of stripper and Laurence Harvey's girlfriend, Maisie King, in *Expresso Bongo*. She had previously been seen in *Ice Cold In Alex*, and later went on to become well known for her comedy roles on the big screen.

Peter Yates who directed Cliff in *Summer Holiday* went on to make the films *One Way Pendulum*, *Bullitt*, *The Deep* and *The Dresser*.

ENGINEERS

Addey, Malcolm – Malcolm Addey engineered nearly all of Cliff's sessions from 1958 until 1966. He now lives in New York where he runs a successful company.

Asker-Brown, Damien – Second Engineer at the 'Living Doll' recording session in 1986.

Barrett, John – Assistant engineer on the 'I'm Nearly Famous' sessions.

Bendall, Hayden – Worked alongside Tony Clark on most of the sessions in the seventies.

Bessey, Keith – Sound engineer on numerous live recordings including *Dressed For The Occasion* and *From a Distance: The Event*. More recently, Keith introduced his own remastering sound system, BRP, on the *Hit List* and *Cliff At The Movies* albums.

Black, Robin – Worked on just one session – the recording of 'Everybody's Got A Crisis In Their Life'.

Boddicker, Michael – Engineered the 'Wired For Sound' recordings.

Bown, Peter – Engineer at Abbey Road studios where he worked on much of Cliff's fifties and early sixties output.

Bruce, Stuart – One of the engineers during the recording of *Cliff Richard The Album*.

Churchyard, Steve – Air Recording Studios engineer during 1982 sessions.

Clark, Tony – Engineer who worked on most of Cliff's seventies output. Also worked with Olivia Newton-John.

Cook, Steve – Assistant engineer on the 'Now You See Me…' sessions.

Duguid, Wally – Worked with Cliff in 1989.

Eltham, Stuart – Abbey Road engineer who worked on much of Cliff's fifties and early sixties output.

Epps, Stuart – Engineer at The 'Sol' Studies when Cliff and Elton John recorded together.

Greasley, Andrew – Assistant engineer during 1991 sessions.

Hewitt, Karen – Engineer at PWL Studios during Cliff's sessions.

Hofer, David – Engineer working along with Wally Duguid in 1989.

Holman, David J. – Worked on the Olivia Newton-John vocal sessions for 'Suddenly'.

Houison, Rod – Worked at Eden Studios and engineered the Cliff/Phil Everly track 'She Means Nothing To Me'.

Howe, Ashley – 'I'm No Hero' was one of the sessions Howe worked on.

Hudson, John – Engineer at Mayfair Studios where Cliff recorded in 1983.

Jarrett, Mike – Engineer along with Tony Clark and Allan Rouse on some mid-seventies sessions.

Johnson, Jimmy – Assistant to Malcolm Addey on the Blackpool sessions in 1963.

Kane, Alan – Assistant Engineer in 1964 on some 'Wonderful Life' sessions.

Kanelle, Carb – Engineer on the 'Living Doll' recording session in 1986.

Kitchingham, Gerry – RG Jones Studios engineer who worked with Cliff from 1986.

Kurlander, John – Engineer on the 1982 Royal Albert Hall live recordings.

Laico, Frank – Engineer at the studios in New York where Cliff recorded in August 1964.

Langham, Richard – Engineer who worked on some Abbey Road sessions for Cliff.

Litle, Ian – Worked along with Michael Boddicker in 1981.

Logie, Godwin – Engineer at The Lighthouse Studio where Cliff and Aswad recorded.

Luch, Richard – Abbey Road engineer who worked throughout the sixties in Cliff sessions.

McHutchon, Graham – Engineer on the live recordings for *The Kendrick Collection*.

McKenna, Mick – Live engineer who, along with Keith Bessey, was responsible for *The Event* recordings.

Newell, Norman – Engineered the backing tracks only for the *Oh Boy!* album in 1958.

Oliver, Matthew – Second engineer on the 'Everybody's Got A Crisis…' session.

Porter, Chris – Engineer on the 1985 'Born to Rock and Roll' session.

Quested, Roger – Engineered the single 'Honky-Tonk Angel' in 1974.

Richards, Tony – Assistant to John Walker during the eighties.

Robbins, Ben – Engineer at RG Jones Recording Studios. Along with Gerry Kitchingham has worked on nearly all of Cliff's sessions since 1986.

Ross-Trevor, Mike – Engineer at the Hit Factory when Cliff recorded 'I Still Believe In You'.

Rouse, Allan – Engineer on the occasional sessions in the mid-seventies. Worked alongside Tony Clark.

Scott, Ken – Worked alongside Malcolm Addey on the 1964 'Aladdin' sessions.

Smith, Norman – Abbey Road engineer who worked on much of Cliff's fifties and early sixties output.

Summerhayes, Tim – Engineered the Greenbelt live recordings in 1979.

Thomason, Mort – Engineer at the Nashville Columbia Studios where Cliff recorded.

Townsend, Ken – Engineered the live session at the ABC Theatre, Kingston in 1962. Until recently he was manager of Abbey Road Studios.

Vince, Peter – When Malcolm Addey left Abbey Road the job of engineering Cliff's sessions went to Peter Vince. He still works at Abbey Road.

Walker, John – Worked on many Cliff sessions throughout 1981 and 1982.

Yoyo – Engineer at PWL Studios where 'I Just Don't Have The Heart' was recorded.

MANAGERS, AGENTS & PROMOTERS

Benjamin, Louis – Louis, with Leslie Grade, promoted some of the *Cliff Richard Show* seasons at the London Palladium. Benjamin had a long and successful theatre management history and was Chairman of Pye Records.

Boyd, Franklin – Cliff's manager from October 1958 to January 1959.

Bruce, Roger – Roger has been Cliff's Personal Assistant since leaving 'Time' as Company Manager in 1988.

Browne, Amanda – Admin staff member at the Cliff Richard Organisation.

Bryce, David – David is Cliff's professional and recording manager. Was previously with Saville Artists and has been associated with Cliff's career since the early years.

Burns, Tito – Cliff's manager from February 1959 after Franklin Boyd and John Foster were dismissed by Cliff's father. Burns had a long career in show business as a performer, agent and manager.

Bush, Mel – Tour promoter who has been promoting concerts since 1960 working with such acts as The Eagles, Queen, The Beach Boys, Paul McCartney, Led Zeppelin, and David Essex. *The Event* was his first promotion with Cliff, and he has promoted all Cliff's British tours since.

Conlin, Mike – Mike was Cliff's road manager in the early sixties. After leaving Cliff around 1964, Mike worked with Frank Ifield.

Delfont, Bernard – Bernard, with brother Leslie Grade, and Leslie A MacDonnell promoted Cliff's pantomimes and *Cliff Richard Show* seasons at the London Palladium. He had a long and successful career history in theatre, films, television, and music, and was joint managing director of the Talk of the Town – another venue where Cliff and the Shadows appeared.

Foster, John – Cliff's first manager. 1958–1959. John now works organising promotional and corporate entertainment from his home in Northumberland.

Ganjou, George – Agent who signed Cliff and the Drifters to his agency after watching their act at the Gaumont Theatre in Shepherds Bush in 1958. George continued to manage variety acts until 1982. He died in 1988 aged eighty-seven.

Gormley, Peter – Cliff's personal manager from March 1961. Peter came to Britain from Australia at the end of 1959, and had been appointed as the Shadows' manager in July 1960. He would later look after the careers of Frank Ifield and Olivia Newton-John. Peter is now retired and spends his summers in Weybridge and his winters in Australia.

Grade, Leslie – Agent who signed Cliff to his Grade Organisation in the early sixties. Grade's agency became one of the most powerful theatrical agencies in the world later acquired by the EMI Group. Through Elstree Films, Leslie was instrument with Kenneth Harper for Cliff's motion pictures of the early sixties.

Hellyer, Bob – Bob is the technical crew member for the Cliff Richard Organisation responsible for lighting design and operation for Cliff's concert tours.

Howes, Arthur – Tour promoter of Cliff's early package tours.

King, Ron – Ron retired as Cliff's Personal Assistant in July 1988.

Latham, Bill – Cliff's best friend and management member of the Cliff Richard Organisation. Bill is respon-sible for Cliff's Christian and charity involvements, and all press and media matters. He is also director of the Cliff Richard Charitable Trust, Master of Ceremonies at the annual pro-celebrity tennis tournaments and host on Cliff's gospel tours.

MacDonnell, Leslie A – With Leslie Grade promoted Cliff's pantomimes *Aladdin* and *Cinderella*, and the *Cliff Richard Shows* at the London Palladium.

Norfield, Colin – Colin is the sound man of the Cliff Richard Organisation working to ensure that sound settings and levels are correctly mixed and balanced during Cliff's concert appearances.

Peasgood, Rita – Admin staff member at the Cliff Richard Organisation.

Sanders, Diane – Another admin member at the Cliff Richard Organisation.

Saville Artists – Tour promoters who were involved with promoting Cliff's tours.

Seymour, John – John is the production manager, set designer and general handyman at the Cliff Richard Organisation.

Smith, Malcolm – Malcolm directs all of Cliff's financial and business affairs in his managerial role at the Cliff Richard Organisation.

Snow, Gill – Cliff and Bill's secretary who works at the Cliff Richard Organisation dealing with the massive daily postbag, and answering the scores of telephone callers wanting information.

MUSICIANS

Aitken, Matt – Producer who played guitar on the 'Band Aid II' single and keyboards on 'Just Don't Have The Heart'.

Applebaum, Stan – Conducted the orchestra on Cliff's 1964 New York sessions.

Arch, Dave – Played piano on 'I Still Believe In You'.

Asprey, Ronnie – Saxaphone player on 'Never Say Die'.

Aswad – Sang and played all the instruments on the duet 'Share A Dream'.

Batt, Mike – Producer and creator of the Wombles, Mike Batt produced and played keyboards during the recording of 'Please Don't Fall In Love'.

Beauchemin, Derek – Played keyboards on the Greenbelt live recording of 'Yes He Lives'.

Beavis, Ray – Member of the brass section on the Knebworth recordings in 1990.

Beachill, Peter – One of the players in the brass section on *Cliff Richard The Album*.

Bennett, Brian – Drummer with the Shadows since the departure of Tony Meehan in 1962. As well as his work with Cliff and the Shadows Brian has composed music for many TV series, most notably *The Ruth Rendell Mysteries* and also released several solo albums.

Bernard Ebbinghouse Orchestra, The – Orchestra who first worked with Cliff on the *Listen To Cliff* album and on a number of other projects in the sixties.

Bertles, Bob – Saxophone player on the early seventies recordings that produced the *31st Of February Street* album.

Bishop, Dave – Saxophone player who worked with Cliff on the road and in the studio in the nineties.

Boddicker, Michael – Played synthesisers on 'I'm No Hero'.

Bremner, Billy – Lead, acoustic and tremolo guitar on 'She Means Nothing To Me'.

Britten, Terry – Guitarist on nearly all of Cliff's sessions in the seventies.

Carr, Tony – Percussionist on early eighties sessions.

Castle, Barry – Arranged the horns on 'Mistletoe And Wine'.

Cattini, Clem – Drummer who worked on some seventies sessions. Now tours as drummer with the Tornadoes.

Christopher, Dave – Guitarist during the reunion concerts in 1978.

Clark, John – Guitarist who has worked with Cliff in the studio and on the road since the early eighties.

Clarke, Frank – Bass player on Cliff's first session in 1958.

Collins, Mel – Saxophone player on early eighties sessions.

Colman, Stuart – Producer and bass guitarist on the Cliff and the Young Ones version of 'Living Doll' and also the Phil Everly/Cliff duet 'She Means Nothing To Me'.

Cooke, Dave – Songwriter and keyboard player who worked on a number of sessions in the eighties and also on the occasional gospel tour (see also Producers).

Cooper, Ray – Percussionist best known for his work with Elton John.

Cottle, Richard – Played keyboards on 'Healing Love'.

Cozens, Jim – Composer of and guitarist on 'Everybody's Got A Crisis In Their Life'.

Croft, David – Played guitar on the charity release 'Everybody's Got A Crisis In Their Life'.

Cunliffe, Dave – Provided the strings on the *Together With Cliff Richard* album.

David, John – Guitarist on the Phil Everly/Cliff duets.

Davis, Snake – Saxophone player on 'Little Mistreater' and 'I Need Love'.

Dobson, Martin – Worked on the 'Rock and Roll Juvenile' sessions playing saxophone.

Drover, Martin – Provided the brass accompaniment on *Rock And Roll Juvenile* album.

Dunne, Paul – Guitarist on 'More To Life'.

Earle, John – Member of the brass section on the Knebworth recordings in 1990.

Eaton, Chris – Composer of the Christmas number one single 'Saviour's Day' and played keyboards on 'Under Your Spell'.

Edwards, John – Bass player on 'Born To Rock And Roll'.

Farrar, John – Guitarist and songwriter who worked with Cliff and Tim Rice on the Heathcliff project.

Fenn, Rick – Acoustic guitarist on the Cliff/Sheila Walsh tracks.

Fletcher, Guy – Songwriter who played keyboards on 'Baby You're Dynamite'.

Flowers, Herbie – Best known for his work with the group Sky Herbie Flowers played bass on Cliff's 'Rock And Roll Juvenile' sessions.

Ford, George – Bass player in the late seventies.

Ford, Martyn – Conducted the orchestra on the single 'Little Town'.

Foster, Mo – Bass player on the re-union concerts in 1978 and ocassional studio sessions.

Fry, Tristran – Percussionist with Sky who also worked on the *Rock And Roll Juvenile* recordings.

Furst, Jerry – Harmonica player whose only session with Cliff was for 'Evergreen Tree'.

Gardener, Simon – One of the players in the brass section on *Cliff Richard The Album*.

Gee, Mickey – Played lead guitar on 'She Means Nothing To Me'. Also worked with Shakin' Stevens throughout the eighties.

Glennie-Smith, Nick – Played synthesisers on *I'm No Hero* album.

Goss, Luke – Drums on 'Band Aid II' single.

Gower, Chris – Member of the brass section on the Knebworth recordings in 1990.

Gray, Steve – Percussionist on *Dressed For The Ocassion* recordings.

Greasley, Andrew – Additional strings on 'Hold Us Together'.

Greene, Ed – Drummer at the Los Angeles studio where 'Suddenly' was recorded.

Griffiths, Mark – Bass player on the road and in the studio during the eighties.

Guard, Barrie – Percussionist on some of Cliff's early seventies sessions.

Hall, Cliff – Worked with the Shadows and played keyboards for Cliff in the early seventies.

Hanson, Dick – Member of the brass section of the Knebworth recordings in 1990.

Harris, Jet – Bass player with the Shadows. Went on to record a number of hit singles with Tony Meehan in the sixties including 'Diamonds' and 'Scarlett O'Hara'.

Hart, Paul – Played violin on 'Little Town'.

Hawkshaw, Alan – Keyboard player in the studio and on tour during the early seventies.

Haworth, Bryn – The slide guitar maestro on the 'Rock And Roll Juvenile' sessions.

Hay, Jerry – Bass player who worked on the 'Born To Rock And Roll' session only.

Hayward, Justin – Member of the Moody Blues who played guitar on the *Everybody's Got A Crisis In Their Life* release.

Hewson, Richard – Arranger and conductor who worked on a number of sessions in the eighties and nineties. Most notably on the *Dressed For The Ocassion* recordings.

Houison, Rod – As well as engineering the Cliff/Phil Everly duet he also played percussion.

Huntley, Gordon – Responsible for the steel guitar work on *31st Of February Street*.

Jarvis, Graham – Drummer with Cliff's touring and studio band throughout the late seventies and eighties.

Jenner, Mart – Guitarist who worked with Cliff in the studios and on the road throughout the eighties.

John, Elton – Recorded 'Slow Rivers' as a duet with Cliff in 1984.

Johnston, Davey – Long-time guitarist with Elton John who worked on the 'Slow Rivers' session.

Jones, Alan – Bass player on many of Cliff's seventies and eighties releases. Alan also worked as a member of the Shadows.

Kershaw, Nik – Played guitar on and composed a track for the 1993 release *Cliff Richard The Album*.

Knopfler, Mark – Lead guitarist with British supergroup Dire Straits who worked on one session in 1982 for Cliff.

Lauri, Steve – Studio and live guitarist in the eighties and nineties.

Lee, Adrian – Played keyboards on 'Moving In'.

Les Reed Orchestra, The – Orchestra featured on the *Kinda Latin* album.

Lewes, Brian – Played guitar during the 1974 Far East tour and on the subsequent *Japan Tour* album.

Livesy, Billy – Played keyboards on the *Rock And Roll Juvenile* sessions.

Locking, Brian – Bass player in the Shadows from April 1962 until the end of 1963.

Mackay, Duncan – Played keyboards on the *Green Light* album sessions.

Macrae, Dave – Keyboard player on *31st Of February Street*.

Mandell, Fred – Keyboard player on 'Slow Rivers'.

Marvin, Hank – Lead guitarist with the Shadows. Now lives in Australia.

Mattacks, David – Drummer on early eighties sessions.

May, Peter – Drummer in Cliff's live band and also works on occasional studio sessions for Cliff.

McDaniel, David – Played bass at the Los Angeles studio where the Cliff/Olivia duet 'Suddenly' was recorded.

Meehan, Tony – Drummer with the Shadows in the late fifties and early sixties.

Mercer, Chris – Provided the brass accompaniment on *Rock and Roll Juvenile* album.

Mike Leander Orchestra, The – First session for Cliff was the *Tracks And Grooves* album in 1967 and also worked on the *Two A Penny* soundtrack.

Mike Vickers Orchestra, The – Orchestra who worked on *Sincerely Cliff* and *Tracks and Grooves* albums.

Mitham, Norman – Played guitar on Cliff's demo recordings in early 1958.

Moessl, Paul – Producer and Cliff's musical director. Responsible for all Cliff's recordings since 'Mistletoe And Wine'.

Moran, Mike – Keyboard player on the Greenbelt festival recording of 'Yes He Lives'.

Murray, Graham – Guitarist during the reunion concerts in 1978.

Norrie Paramor Orchestra, The – Worked on most of Cliff's recordings in the sixties and early seventies where orchestral backing was required.

Paramor, Norrie – Played piano on a couple of Cliff

tracks in the early sixties (see also Producers).

Parks, Alan – Keyboard player who also worked with the Shadows.

Pask, Andy – Bass player on a couple of mid-eighties sessions.

Paul Jones, John – Bass player who appeared on the 'Congratulations' EP.

Pavey, Ken – Played drums on Cliff's demo recordings in early 1958.

Peek, Kevin – Guitarist who, along with Terry Britten, worked for Cliff in the seventies.

Piggott, Steve – Keyboard and bass player on session for *Cliff Richard – The Album*.

Pruess, Craig – Producer who also played various instruments on many of Cliff's sessions in the eighties (see also Producers).

Ralph Carmichael Orchestra, The – The only sessions this orchestra worked on were for the religious album and soundtrack of *His Land* in the late sixties.

Rea, Chris – Played guitar on the 'Band Aid II' single.

Reg Guest Orchestra, The – Orchestra featured on the *Kinda Latin* album.

Renwick, Tim – Guitarist on the 1986 'Living Doll' session.

Ricotti, Frank – Along with Brian Bennett he provided the percussion work on 'Every Face Tells A Story' and also worked on some sessions in the nineties.

Roberts, Bill – One of many guitarists who worked on sessions in the early eighties.

Rostill, John – Bass player with the Shadows from late 1963.

Samwell, Ian – Guitarist and songwriter. Worked on Cliff's first session in 1958 and also composed 'Move It' and several other early hits for Cliff.

Shear, Ernie – Lead guitarist on Cliff's first session in 1958. Famous for the instantly recognizable intro to 'Move It'.

Sheppard, Adrian – Conducted orchestra on Cliff's 1964 Nashville sessions.

Sidwell, Steve – Trumpet player during the From A Distance tour in 1990.

Skellern, Peter – Well known musician and composer who worked with Cliff in the early eighties on 'Now You See Me, Now You Don't'.

Smart, Terry – Drummer on Cliff's first session in 1958 and throughout the year.

Smith, Mike – Along with Rick Wakeman Mike played keyboard on a 1989 charity record.

Spencer, Trevor – Played drums for Cliff throughout the seventies and eighties.

Spinetti, Henry – Drummer on the 30th Anniversary tour in 1988.

Squire, Billy – Worked on the 1985 'Born To Rock And Roll' session playing lead guitar.

Stanley Black Orchestra, The – Orchestra who worked on *The Young Ones* and *Summer Holiday* films and accompanying soundtrack releases.

Stewart, Dave – Keyboard player who worked on one session in 1985 for Cliff.

Stock, Mike – Producer who also played keyboards on 'Just Don't Have The Heart' and 'Do They Know It's Christmas'.

Stroud, Steve – Bass player in Cliff's live band and

also used frequently on Cliff's studio sessions in the eighties and nineties.

Talbot, Jamie – One of the players in the brass section of *Cliff Richard The Album*.

Tarney, Alan – Multi-talented instrumentalist who worked on many sessions for Cliff including 'I'm Nearly Famous', 'Green Light', 'I'm No Hero' and played nearly every instrument on the 'Always Guaranteed' sessions. (See also producers)

Tibble, Howard – Drummer on the 1986 'Living Doll' session.

Todd, Graham – One of many keyboard players who have worked with Cliff during the seventies.

Wakeman, Rick – Respected keyboardist who worked on charity record in 1989.

Wallis, Gary – Provided additional percussion during the recording of *Cliff Richard The Album*.

Watkins, Derek – Part of the brass section on *Together With Cliff Richard*.

Welch, Bruce – Along with Hank Marvin guitarist

Bruce Welch is one of the founder members of the Shadows. Credited with turning Cliff's career around in the mid-seventies when he produced the *I'm Nearly Famous* album.

Westwood, Paul – Played bass at the Cliff/Elton John session and also worked on the recording of 'Now You See Me, Now You Don't'.

Wetton, John – Bass player.

White, Snowy – Guitarist on the Greenbelt live recording of 'Yes He Lives'.

Wickens, Paul – Keyboard player on 'Born To Rock and Roll'.

Williams, Terry – Drummer on the Phil Everly/Cliff duet 'She Means Nothing To Me'.

Wingfield, Pete – Keyboard player on the 1986 'Living Doll' session. Has also worked with the Everly Brothers on their recent tours.

Wonder, Stevie – This multi-instrumentalist and singer provided all the musical accompaniment on 'She's So Beautiful'.

PARTICIPANTS IN CLIFF'S PRO-CELEBRITY TENNIS TOURNAMENTS

The players have included Sue Barker, Hank Marvin, Sue Mappin, Trevor Eve, Anne Hobbs, Mike Read, Jo Durie, Sara Gomer, Terry Wogan, Annabel Croft, Mike Yarwood, Julie Salmon, Virginia Wade, Shakin' Stevens, Peter Cook, Sebastian Coe, Ronnie Corbett, Emlyn Hughes, Elton John, Aled Jones, Jimmy Tarbuck, Roy Castle, Jason Donovan, Clare Wood, Jeremy Irons, Paul Daniels, Bruce Forsyth, Amanda Barrie, Alvin Stardust, Bill Roache, Des O'Connor, Gloria Hunniford, Frank Bruno, Jeremy Bates, Jasper Carrott, Tommy Cannon, Bobby Ball, Roger Taylor, Tim Rice, Brian Conley, Mr Motivator, Chris Bailey, Michael Barrymore, Greg Rusedski, Michael Ball, David Lloyd, Suzanne Dando and Cliff, of course.

Umpires have included Jeremy Shales, Bob Jenkins, Gerry Armstrong, Georgina Clark, and Mike Sertin.

Master of Ceremonies is always Bill Latham while hosts and guests have included Gerald Williams, Mike Read, Jimmy Hill, Sue Mappin, Michael Ball, Roy Barraclough, Rosemary Ford, Nick Owen, Jeremy Bates, Chris Bailey and John Feaver.

PEOPLE A–Z

A

Abbott, Judith – Organising member of the Grapevine fan club which was founded in September 1978 and has a worldwide membership.

Andrews, Sue – Avid British Cliff fan and photographer who has taken hundreds of pictures of Cliff, many of which have been published in books, magazines and on the official Cliff calendars. Sue donates proceeds from the sale of her pictures to Cliff's charitable trust.

B

Barrows, Cliff – Has been a member of the Billy Graham Organisation since the start of the evangelist's ministry. Barrows filmed *His Land* with Cliff in 1969.

Bart, Lionel – Writer and composer. Lionel wrote 'Living Doll', 'No Turning Back' and 'Mad About You' for Cliff's first film *Serious Charge*. He later went on to write some very successful stage musicals; *Fings Ain't Wot They Used T'be*, *Blitz!*, *Maggie May* and *Oliver!* which was later turned into a blockbusting movie with Ron Moody, Oliver Reed and Mark Lester. The new stage version opened with Jonathan Pryce playing Fagin at the London Palladium in 1994.

Bennett, Roy – Composer who with Sid Tepper composed forty-three songs for Elvis to sing in his motion pictures. Cliff also sang a number of their songs in his movies as well, including 'When The Girl In Your Arms Is The Girl In Your Heart' in *The Young Ones*.

Bloomstein, Rex – Director of *The Story So Far* home video and the extended version used in the *South Bank Show* on Christmas Eve, 24 December 1994.

Bodkin, Derek – Cliff's former chauffeur who married and divorced Cliff's mother. Dorothy still uses the Bodkin surname.

Bulley, Terence – Director of the *From A Distance: The Event* video shot at Wembley Stadium on June 16 and 17, 1989, during Cliff's Event concerts.

C

Capes, Geoff – British strong man who was Cliff's guest at the launch of his *Stronger* album.

Cassidy, David – American pop idol who took over the part of 'The Rock Star, Chris Wilder' from Cliff in Dave Clark's *Time – The Musical* at the London Dominion.

Chester, Jo – With Adrian Hopkins, runs Cliff's official merchandising company known as Chester-Hopkins Merchandising. Previously known as Adrian Hopkins Merchandising, and Theatre Franchise UK Ltd.

Chipperfield, Chips – Produced the *Together with Cliff Richard* Christmas home video.

Clark, Dave – Drummer and leader of the Dave Clark Five whose twenty-five hits during the sixties sold in excess of fifty million records. Clark later devised, created, co-wrote the music and lyrics, and produced *Time – The Musical* with Cliff in the lead role as 'The Rock Star, Chris Wilder'. Cliff remained in the show for one year.

Conway, Russ – Signed to Columbia Records, Russ had a string of hits in the early sixties including 'Side Saddle', 'Roulette', 'China Tea' and 'Lesson One'. He shared top billing with Cliff at the London Palladium for the *Stars In Your Eyes* show. His last top thirty hit was in 1962.

Cutteridge, Nigel – Producer of Radio 2 documentary *The Cliff Richard Story*. Narrated by Mike Read, the programme was broadcast in six parts.

D

Davies, Freddie 'Parrot Face' – Comedian who appeared on Cliff's show at the London Palladium, who had become one of Britain's best-known and funniest comedians created by his highly original style and infectious personality.

De Louw, Harry – Avid Dutch Cliff fan since 1958, who teamed up with Anton Husmann to run the International Cliff Richard Movement. Harry is also the editor of *Dynamite International*.

Devis, Pamela – Choreographer who worked with Cliff on many occasions. Pamela was dance director for *Sunday Night At The London Palladium* and has produced dance routines for the film *Up Jumped A Swagman* with Frank Ifield.

Douglas, Jack – Comedian who played 'The Baron' in Cliff's *Cinderella* pantomime at the London Palladium.

Duffet, Diana – Organising member of the Grapevine fan club that was founded in September 1978.

E

Edwards, Eileen – Avid British Cliff fan and tennis umpire who has been the line judge at every one of Cliff's pro-celebrity tennis tournaments. Eileen contributes regular Cliff articles to fan clubs around the world and writes her own column in *Dynamite International*.

Elsbury, Gordon – Directed the *Together With Cliff Richard* Christmas home video.

Everly, Phil – One of the Everly Brothers who with brother Don had a string of hits in the fities and sixties, split up, and then got back together years later for a reunion concert at the Royal Albert Hall in London. Cliff and Phil recorded 'She Means Nothing To Me', 'When Will I Be Loved', and one of the Everly hits 'All I Have To Do Is Dream'.

F

Faith, Adam – Pop singer who was discovered at the '2i's' coffee bar and had a string of hits in the early sixties with his backing group the Roulettes before

concentrating on acting in the theatre, on television and in films. In 1971, he took the title role in the series *Budgie* before returning to the music business to manage Leo Sayer, and produce for Roger Daltry. He appeared in the films *Stardust*, and *McVicar* and writes a newspaper financial column. He also starred in the popular drama series *Love Hurts* with Zoe Wanamaker.

Farrar, John – John has composed all the music for Cliff's *Heathcliff* album and musical. Farrar first achieved international acclaim as writer of Olivia Newton-John's biggest hits, including *You're The One I Want*, *Hopelessly Devoted To You*, *Have You Never Been Mellow*, and *Magic* – all of Olivia's favourites. He has been Olivia's producer since 1971, and also produced the Cliff and Olivia duet *Suddenly* for the film *Xanadu* in 1980.

G

Gilmore, Peter – Actor who was married to Una Stubbs played 'The Prince' in Cliff's *Cinderella* pantomime. Peter went on to become familiar with television audiences in the popular drama series *The Onedin Line*.

Good, Jack – Producer of the *Oh Boy!* TV show, and recognised for 'inventing Cliff Richard'. His auto-biographical musical *Good Rockin' Tonight*, which features Timothy Whitnall as Cliff, opened in 1991 and played to packed houses for its entire run in London's West End.

Graham, Billy – Evangelist who met Cliff in 1966 during the Billy Graham crusade at Earls Court in London, and has remained friends with Cliff ever since. Graham gained fame with his mission crusades across the world preaching the message of God's love and forgiveness. He later formed Worldwide Films and produced two films with Cliff: *Two A Penny* and *His Land*.

H

Henney, Jimmy – Master of Ceremonies on the *Oh Boy!* TV show in 1958, and hosted the *Oh Boy!* section of Cliff's Event concerts at Wembley Stadium in June 1989.

Hercoe, Tricia – Avid British Cliff fan and photographer who travels all over the world to take pictures of Cliff. Tricia has had her pictures published in numerous books and magazines, and donates proceeds from the sale of her photos to Cliff's charitable trust.

Hillier, David G – Directed the *Cliff And The Shadows Together* home video in 1984.

Hopkins, Adrian – With Jo Chester runs Cliff's official merchandising company Chester-Hopkins Merchandising, previously known as Adrian Hopkins Merchandising, and Theatre Franchise UK Ltd.

Hooper, William – Avid British Cliff fan and collector who writes his own column and compiles the Cliff pop polls for 'Dynamite International'. William is also the editor of the 'Constantly Cliff' magazine.

Husmann, Anton – Avid Dutch Cliff fan and founder of the International Cliff Richard Movement and its publication 'Dynamite International' which he named after his favourite Cliff song.

J

John, Elton – Singer and songwriter who has recorded and sung with Cliff on stage as well as playing tennis in one of Cliff's pro-celebrity tournaments. Elton is a big Cliff Richard fan, and friend.

Johnson, Janet – Founder of the 'Cliff Richard Fan Club UK' which operated from Winchmore Hill in North London and was independent of the International Cliff Richard Movement and its affiliated clubs and meeting houses.

Jones, Paul – Singer who performs with the Blues Band and as a solo artist, which is reflected in his radio work on *Sing Gospel* and *Rhythm and Blues*. In the sixties, Paul was the lead singer with Manfred Mann before embarking on an acting career which included his role opposite Jean Shrimpton in *Privilege*. Paul is the reader on the audio version of Steve Turner's book *Cliff – The Biography*.

K

Kalin, Hal and Herb – Brothers who performed in the late fifties as The Kalin Twins and still do. Cliff's first tour in 1958 was as a supporting act on a package that was headlined by the Kalins. They reunited with Cliff for the *Oh Boy!* section of The Event in June 1989 at Wembley Stadium.

Kent, Cindy – Vocalist with the Settlers who played some of Cliff's first gospel concerts, and starred with Cliff in the religious television series *Life With Johnny*. She later became a broadcaster and consultant in media and communication skills.

Knight, Albert J – Albert was Director and Company Secretary of the Grade Organisation combining his admin duties with theatre production. He produced Cliff's *Aladdin* and *Cinderella* pantomimes as well as some of Cliff's other seasonal shows at the London Palladium.

Knight, Amanda – Cliff's product and marketing manager for EMI Records UK in London.

L

Large, Eddie – Part of the comedy duo, Little and Large, who appeared on the *Cliff Richard Show* at the London Palladium before gaining fame with his partner, Syd Little, on their own *Little And Large* television series.

Leyland, Richard – Produced the footage of Cliff's two concert appearances at Wembley Stadium which later became *From A Distance – The Event* home video and television specials.

Little, Syd – One half of the comedy duo, Little And Large who made one of their early appearances on Cliff's show at the London Palladium before gaining fame with his partner Eddie Large on their own *Little And Large* television series.

Lordon, Jerry – Songwriter who had seventeen chart

entries as a composer including 'A Girl Like You' for Cliff, 'Wonderful Land' for the Shadows, and 'Diamonds' for Jet Harris & Tony Meehan.

Lloyd, Hugh – Comedy actor who with Terry Scott became a familiar face and name to television viewers in the situation comedy series *Hugh And I*. Both Hugh and Terry played the ugly sisters in Cliff's *Cinderella* pantomime.

M

Mappin, Sue – Former tennis player. Sue organises all of Cliff's pro-celebrity tennis tournaments.

Martin, Bill – Composer with Phil Coulter of 'Congratulations' which Cliff recorded in 1968 for the Eurovision Song Contest. Martin and Coulter went on to write all the Bay City Rollers hits, as well as 'Surround Yourself With Sorrow' for Cilla Black.

Martin, Ray – Host of his own Australian television chat show *Ray Martin Presents* which Cliff has often appeared on during his Australian tours.

O

O'Connor, Des – Singer and comedian who toured with Cliff in the early days. Des went on to become a household name with his many television appearances and later had his own TV show. He recently played tennis in one of Cliff's pro-celebrity tournaments that took place in Brighton.

Owen, Veronica – Organising member of the Grapevine fan club which was founded in September 1978. The club is operated from Colchester.

R

Read, Mike – Gained fame as a household name broadcaster on Radio 1 and as host of *Pop Quiz*. Cliff and Mike are close friends, and the Cliff Richard Organisation are Mike's professional management.

Reid, John – Elton John's manager who was instrumental in releasing Cliff's *I'm Nearly Famous* album and 'Devil Woman' single on Rocket Records in the US.

Rice, Tim – Composer with Andrew Lloyd Webber of some of the most successful West End musicals including *Evita*, *Jesus Christ Superstar*, *Chess*, and *Joseph And His Amazing Technicolor Dreamcoat*. Rice and Webber also composed the song *It's Easy For You* which Elvis Presley recorded in 1976. His Oscar-winning contribution to Disney's *Aladdin* as writer of *A Whole New World* followed his role as lyricist on *The Lion King* and represents his most recent career highlights which also includes teaming up with John Farrar to compose the music for Cliff's *Heathcliff* album and musical.

S

Scott, Terry – Comedy actor who with Hugh Lloyd gained fame with television viewers in the situation comedy series *Hugh And I*. Terry played one of the ugly sisters in Cliff's *Cinderella* pantomime at the London Palladium. Hugh played the other ugly sister.

Shapiro, Helen – Singer signed by Norrie Paramor to Columbia Records in the early sixties who had a number one hit with her first single 'Walkin Back To Happiness'. Helen has worked with Cliff on one of his gospel tours and has since recorded a duet with Cliff.

Simmons, Cyril – Music publisher who commissioned songwriters Sid Tepper and Roy Bennett to write three songs for Cliff's motion picture *The Young Ones* in the same way they had been writing songs for two of Elvis's movies – to order from early drafts of the scripts.

Smith, Chrissie – Produced the *Cliff And The Shadows Together 1984* home video.

Smith, Martin R – Produced Cliff's *Hit List* and *Hit List Live* home videos.

Smith, Paul – Produced *The Story So Far* home video and the extended version for the *South Bank Show* that was shown on Christmas Eve, 24 December 1994.

Steel, Pippa – Actress who played *Cinderella* in Cliff's pantomime at the London Palladium, and escorted Cliff to the premiere of his film *Finders Keepers*. Pippa's first film *Stranger In The House* with James Mason was completed shortly before *Cinderella*.

Sullivan, Ed – Ed Sullivan hosted his own show that became America's longest running variety series. Cliff and the Shadows appeared on the programme several times during their various visits to the US.

T

Teague, Dick – Founder member of the Dick Teague Skiffle group which Cliff joined in September 1957.

Tepper, Sid – Composer who with Roy Bennett wrote forty-three songs for Elvis' motion pictures and a number of songs for Cliff including 'Travellin' Light', and 'The Young Ones'.

V

Vane, Jan – Founder of the first official Cliff Richard fan club which she operated from 1958 to around 1960/61 from her home in Romford, Essex.

W

Wainer, Cherry – Cherry was the South African who played the Hammond organ music on Cliff's first *Oh Boy!* appearance in September 1958 and had coached him in the art of holding a microphone. Cliff and Cherry became close friends.

Whitehead, Christine – Founder and editor of 'Cliff United', a Christian based organisation and quarterly magazine that supports Cliff's Christian and secular activities. Christine is also the editor of a training publication, and member of the Chartered Institute of Journalists.

Williams, Ray and Colette – Cliff Super-fans whose collection of Cliff memorabilia is probably the largest in the world.

Wilde, Marty – One of Britain's earliest rock 'n' roll singers who appeared on the first national broadcast of the *Oh Boy!* TV show in 1958. Marty had a string of hits in the late fifties as he continued to appear with Cliff and others on *Oh Boy!* Marty continues to record and play live dates in between producing and songwriting for his daughter Kim.

PHOTOGRAPHERS
THAT HAVE TAKEN PICTURES OF CLIFF

Sue Andrews	Brian Aris
Joan Batten	Paolo Battigelli
Willie Christie	Mary Corbett
Paul Cox	Andy Earl
Samantha Esplin	Martin Evans
Simon Fowler	Marty Fresco
Lisa Gray	Frank Griffin
Tricia Hercoe	Dezo Hoffman

Hanne Jordan	Vera Knook
Ken Lambert	Mary Liprino
Gered Mankowitz	John McGoran
Doug McKenzie	Caron Merrick
Denisa Nova	Philip Offerenshaw
Mike Owen	Ken Palmer
Adrian Pope	Bent K Rasmussen
Trevor Rodgers	Rebecca Swearingen
Mogens Troiesen	Peter Vernon
Christine Whitehead	Theresa Wassif
Richard Young	

PRODUCERS

Aitken, Mike – Along with Mike Stock and Pete Waterman produced a string of hit records in the eighties including 'I Just Don't Have The Heart' for Cliff.

Aswad – Produced just one track – 'Share A Dream' (see also Musicians).

Barratt, Bob – Produced some soundtrack recordings for the film and album *Wonderful Life*.

Batt, Mike – Produced just one session that included 'Please Don't Fall In Love' (see also Musicians).

Bessey, Keith – As well as engineering many of Cliff's sessions Bessey also turned his hand to production, working on the occasional session in the eighties and nineties.

Britten, Terry – One of the many producers who worked on sessions for Cliff throughout the eighties.

Collins, Peter – Produced the single 'Born To Rock And Roll' in 1985.

Colman, Stuart – Well-known producer, musician and

disc jockey who produced Cliff on two tracks – 'Living Doll' and 'She Means Nothing To Me' (see also Musicians).

Cooke, Dave – Songwriter and keyboard player who produced a couple of sessions for Cliff (see also Musicians).

Cozens, Jim – Producer of the charity single 'Everybody's Got A Crisis In Their Lives'.

Croft, David – Produced the charity single along with Jim Cozens.

Dudgeon, Gus – Elton John's producer who worked on the 'Slow Rivers' recording.

Farrar, John – Composer and musician who also produced the 'Suddenly' session in Los Angeles (see also Musicians).

Hewson, Richard – Along with Cliff he produced the *Dressed For The Occasion* recordings.

Hopkins, Doug – Produced just one session, the live recording of 'Yes He Lives' at the Greenbelt Festival in 1979.

Kershaw, Nik – Along with Cliff and Paul Moessl he produced 'Healing Love' in 1992 (see also Musicians and Vocalists).

Lee, John – Produced the vocal overdub sessions for *When In Rome* at the EMI Studios in Lisbon, Portugal in 1965.

Lloyd-Webber, Andrew – The duet between Cliff and Sarah Brightman, 'All I Ask Of You', was produced by Andrew Lloyd-Webber.

MacKay, David – Took over the role of producer from Norrie Paramor in the early seventies. 'A Brand New Song' was the first track he produced.

Moessl, Paul – Paul first worked with Cliff on the 'Mistletoe And Wine' recording session in 1988 and he worked constantly with Cliff on all his albums and single releases throughout the nineties. He also works on stage acting as Cliff's Musical Director (see also Musicians).

Morgan, Bob – Produced the highly successful 'New York' and, along with Billy Sherril, the Nashville sessions in 1964.

Moroder, Giorgio – Famous producer who has worked with Donna Summer among others and who produced the Janet Jackson/Cliff single 'Two To The Power'.

Paramor, David – Produced one session in the sixties for Cliff.

Paramor, Norrie – Cliff's producer from 1958 up to the early seventies. As well as producing Cliff he was also musical arranger on many of the sessions (see also Musicians).

Pruess, Craig – Regular producer who worked with Cliff throughout the eighties and into the nineties.

Rhodes, Burt – Produced *The Kendrick Collection*.

Richard, Cliff – Starting in the late eighties Cliff began to produce many of his own recordings.

Schroeder, J – Produced the successful group of sessions recorded in New York.

Sherrill, Billy – Famed country producer who worked with Cliff during his Nashville sessions.

Stock, Mike – Along with Matt Aitken and Pete Waterman produced a string of hit records in the eighties including 'I Just Don't Have The Heart' for Cliff.

Tarney, Alan – Multi-talented instrumentalist and producer who worked on many of Cliff's sessions in the eighties (see also Musicians).

Tew, Tony – Produced just one session, the live recording of 'Yes He Lives' at the Greenbelt Festival in 1979.

Vince, Peter – Engineer who also produced a handful of sessions for Cliff in 1969.

Waterman, Pete – Pete Waterman, of the hit-making trio at PWL, produced Cliff's first dance hit, 'I Just Don't Have The Heart'. Waterman also appeared with Cliff at the Event concerts in 1989.

Welch, Bruce – In the mid-seventies Bruce produced the albums *I'm Nearly Famous* and *Every Face Tells A Story*, two of the most important releases in Cliff's career. Worked on a couple of other sessions in the eighties and nineties (see also Musicians).

Wonder, Stevie – Motown singer who produced 'She's So Beautiful' for Cliff in the eighties.

TOUR PERSONNEL & COMPANIES

Adrian Hopkins Promotions – Tour Merchandisers

Agyei, Steve – Dancer – From a Distance tour

Aiken Promotions – Tour promoters – Ireland

Air Artists – Inflatables used during 1990 tours

Barnett, Michael – Concert promoter – Australia

Benji – Dancer – From A Distance tour

Bray Studios – Rehearsal Studios used extensively in the eighties for concert tour rehearsals

Bray, Debbie – Tour assistant on Hit List tour

Brilliant Constructions – Stage construction company used during the Hit List tour

Brittania Row Productions – Sound equipment

Bruce, Roger – Cliff's personal assistant during his tours

Bryce, David – Professional manager

Bush, Ann – Tour co-ordinator

Bush, Mel – Concert promoter for The Event and has promoted every Cliff concert tour since.

Bush, Zena – Tour co-ordinator

Chantelle – Dancer – From A Distance tour

Chester Hopkins International – Tour merchandisers

Cleaver, Robin – Dancer – From A Distance tour

Complex Sound – Sound equipment

Concert Haul – Truck rental

Concert Productions – Lighting equipment

Cream – Famous design company responsible for tour brochure designs in the seventies and eighties

Creative Technology – Video screens used during From A Distance tour

Danielle, Jane – Dancer – 1979

Design Room, The – Tour brochure design company

Easby, Sandra – Dancer – 1979

Eat To The Beat – Catering company used during the Access All Areas tour in 1992

Eat Your Hearts Out – Catering company on 1987 World tour

Fenny, Adrienn – Tour manager on 1983 Australian tour

Fusion – Tour merchandisers on the Silver tour in mid-eighties

Gormley Management – Personal Management

Guard, Marty – Stage equipment on From A Distance tour

Haggar, Derek – Technician on Hit List tour

Haynes, Stacy – Associate choreographer on From A Distance tour

Hellyer, Bob – Lighting designer on the tours

Howes, Arthur – Concert promoter in the fifties and sixties

Hurrell, Frazer – Dancer – From A Distance tour

Jalland, Dawn – Dancer – From A Distance tour

James, John – Monitor engineer on From A Distance tour

Jands/ACT – Sound and lighting – Australia

Jarrett, Eddie – Tour promoter – worked for Saville Artists

Jem Smoke Machine Company – Provided smoke machines for the Access All Areas and From A Distance tours

Jepsen, Stig – European tour manager – 1987 World tour

Jones, Derek – Vari*Lite operator

Juke Box Services – Suppliers of juke box for Hit List tour 1994

Kendall, Chrissy – Dancer – 1979

King, Ron – Cliff's personal assistant in the early eighties – worked for Saville Artists (See also C.R.O.)

Lasermation – Lasers

Laserpoint Communications Ltd – Laser equipment suppliers

Lynn, Tim – Stage special effects on From A Distance tour

Lythgoe, Nigel – Dance sequence arranger – 1979

Martin, Bill – Production manager on Access All Areas tour 1992

Maxwell, Paul – Tour merchandise – works for Chester Hopkins International

McCartney, Billy – Production manager – Australia 1983

Mel Bush Organisation, The – Concert promoters

Messer, Timothy E. – Tour manager for North American tour 1981

Millar, Drew – Dancer – From A Distance tour

Norfield, Colin – Live sound engineer

Parkinson, Dick – Production co-ordinator for The Event and tour manager for The Hit List tour

Pincis, Harvey – Tour brochure design – 1987 World tour

RDE Stage and Lighting Systems – Tour stage and lighting systems

Redburn Transfer – Truck rental company

Roland (UK) Ltd – Stage equipment

Rowe, Bill – Tour director – Australia 1983

Samuleson Concert Productions – Lighting equipment

Saville Artists Associates – Concert promoters

Seymour, John – Stage design and production

Shelton, Simon – Choreographer for The Event and From A Distance tours

Shirvell, Charles – Dancer – From A Distance tour

Show Presentation Services – Video relay services

Smith, Dennis – Concert promoter – Australia

Smith, Holly – Dancer – 1979

Snakatak – Catering company

Supermick Lights – Lighting company used in the mid-eighties including the Silver and Rock Connection tours

Sutherland, Colin – Stage technician – 1990 tours

Tasco Communictions – Lighting, starlites and rigging for 1987 World tour

Theatre Franchise UK Ltd – Merchandisers

TNT – Trucking – Australia

Twin Sounds – Concert productions

Upfront Productions – Rigging

Vari*Lite Europe – Lighting equipment

Wadsworth, Carol – Dancer – From A Distance tour

Worrall, Alex – Dancer – From A Distance tour

Worsoe, Arne – European concert promoters – 1987 World tour

Zarkowski Designs – Brochure design for the Hit List tour

VOCALISTS & VOCAL GROUPS

All Souls Orchestra, The – Worked with Cliff during the recording on The Kendrick Collection.

Andrews, Anthony – Appeared in the film *Take Me High* duetting with Cliff on the track 'Why'.

Aswad – 'Share A Dream', a duet with Cliff, appeared on the *Stronger* album.

Baley, Audrey – Appeared on the 'This Was My Special Day' single in 1964.

Barrows, Cliff – Appeared on the *His Land* album and also the film.

Batt, Mike – Supplied backing vocals on the 'Please Don't Fall In Love' single (see also Producers).

Bayliss, Steve – One of the back-up vocalists on the Access All Areas tour.

Bell, Madelaine – Vocalist on the *Rock 'n' Roll Juvenile* sessions.

Breakaways, The – Vocals on the *Live At The Talk Of The Town* recordings in 1968.

Brightman, Sara – Duetted with Cliff on the single 'All I Ask Of You'.

Britten, Terry – Vocals on the *31st Of February Street* release (see also Musicians).

Bryson, Ann – One of the many artists who supplied backing vocals on the charity record 'Everybody's Got A Crisis In Their Lives'.

Butler, Stephen – Back-up vocalists on the Access All Areas tour.

Calver, Stuart – Supplied vocals for Cliff in the seventies and eighties.

Carroll, Pat – Featured along with Olivia Newton-John on the 1972 live album.

Clark, John – Supplied back-up vocals during recent tours (see also Musicians).

Clark, Mick – One of many vocalists who worked on the *Together With Cliff Richard* Christmas album.

Clark, Pat – Soprano who worked on the *Good News* album in the late sixties.

Corona Children, The – Worked on a couple of tracks on the *Finders Keepers* soundtrack album.

Croft, Jill – Back-up vocalist on the charity record 'Everybody's Got A Crisis In Their Lives'.

Dallas Boys, The – Appeared with Cliff at the Event concerts in 1989. Sang in their own right and also backed Cliff on several numbers.

De Sykes, Stephanie – Singer who supplied backing vocals on the charity record 'Everybody's Got A Crisis In Their Lives'.

Dee, Kiki – Singer who sang back-up vocals on the Elton John/Cliff duet 'Slow Rivers'.

Edmonson, Adrian – Member of the Young Ones comedy team who recorded a comic version of 'Living Doll' with Cliff.

Everly, Phil – Phil Everly recorded a number of tracks with Cliff as well as appearing on stage with him. The old Everly Brothers track 'Dream' was released as a single featuring Cliff and Phil.

Farrar, John – Early seventies vocalist with Cliff (see also Musicians).

Fenton, Adam – Provided backing vocals on the charity record 'Everybody's Got A Crisis In Their Lives'.

Fletcher, Guy – Songwriter who provided backing vocals on 'Baby You're Dynamite'.

Ford, Rosemarie – During the Always Guaranteed tour Rosemarie Ford provided back-up vocals and also danced.

Frame, Grazina – Duetted with Cliff in the film and on the album from *The Young Ones*.

Gibb, Robin – Worked on the 'Live-In World' single.

Harding, Tony – Supplied vocals for Cliff in the seventies and eighties.

Harley, Steve – Cockney Rebel lead singer provided backing vocals on the anti-heroin single 'Live-In World'.

Hawker, Jean – Provided backing vocals on *31st Of February Street*.

Hayward, Justin – Ex-Moody Blue who supplied backing vocals on the charity record 'Everybody's Got A Crisis In Their Lives'.

Herron, Ian – Another artist who supplied backing vocals on the charity record 'Everybody's Got A Crisis In Their Lives'.

Howarth, Peter – Back-up vocalists with Cliff in the eighties and nineties.

Jackson, Gillian – One of the back-up vocalists on the Access All Areas tour.

Jackson, Janet – Duetted with Cliff on 'Two To The Power'.

James, Tank – Supplied backing vocals on the charity record 'Everybody's Got A Crisis In Their Lives'.

John, Elton – Duetted with Cliff on the single 'Slow Rivers'.

Johnson, Holly – Ex-Frankie Goes To Hollywood lead singer who worked on the 'Live-In World' single.

Jordanaires, The – Best known for their work with Elvis Presley the Jordanaires worked with Cliff during his Nashville sessions.

Kalin Twins, The – Appeared with Cliff at The Event performing their hit single 'When'.

Kershaw, Nik – Backing vocalist on 'Healing Love' (see also Musicians).

Ladybirds, The – All girl vocal group who worked on TV and Radio shows with Cliff in the sixties.

Lee, Jackie – Duetted with Cliff on the *Cinderella* album.

London Community Gospel Choir, The – Vocals on the 'Peace In Our Time' track.

Marvin, Hank – Recorded a couple of duets with Cliff as well as providing vocal backing as part of the Shadows (see also Musicians).

Mastersingers, The – This group of music teachers sang a cappella with Cliff on the tracks that made up the Carol Singers EP.

Mather, Stuart – Back-up singer on 'Born To Rock 'n' Roll' in 1985.

May, Peter – Provided back-up vocals during recent tours (see also Musicians).

Mayall, Rik – Member of the Young Ones comedy team who recorded a comic version of 'Living Doll' with Cliff.

McKenna, Mae – Vocalist on 'Just Don't Have The Heart' along with Miriam Stockley.

Mezek, Alexander – Sang a duet with Cliff on 'To A Friend'.

Mike Sammes Singers, The – This well known vocal group worked with Cliff throughout the fifties and sixties. As well as on record they provided vocals for some of the movies.

Moessl, Paul – Provided back-up vocals during recent tours (see also Musicians).

Morgan, Julie – Back-up vocalist on 'Everybody's Got A Crisis In Their Lives'.

Morgan, Sonia – One of the singers at The Event concerts in 1989.

Morrison, Van – Duetted with Cliff on 'Whenever God Shines His Light'.

Mullins, Mick – Worked with Cliff in the eighties and nineties. Appeared at The Event concerts.

Murrell, Keith – Worked with Cliff in the eighties and nineties and also appeared at The Event concerts.

Newton-John, Olivia – A star in her own right Olivia recorded a number of tracks with Cliff including material on the *Songs From Heathcliff* album as well as touring in the early seventies on his show.

Niles, Tessa – One of the singers at The Event concerts in 1989 and also worked on *Cliff Richard The Album*.

Noble, Bob – Provided back-up vocals during recent tours (see also Musicians).

O'Connor, Hazel – Eighties pop singer who sang back-up on the 'Live-In World' single.

Palethorpe, Joan – Appeared on the 'This Was My Special Day' single in 1964.

Parfitt, Marietta – Rick Parfitt's wife who supplied backing vocals on the charity record 'Everybody's Got A Crisis In Their Lives'.

Peacock, Anna – Appeared on several tracks recorded in the mid-seventies.

Perrin, Nigel – Appeared on the track 'Little Town', recorded in 1982.

Perry, John – Vocalist who worked on many seventies sessions with Cliff.

Planer, Nigel – Member of the Young Ones comedy team who recorded a comic version of 'Living Doll' with Cliff.

Rivers, Tony – Supplied vocals for Cliff in the seventies and eighties, most notably on the *I'm Nearly Famous* album.

Ryan, Christopher – Member of the Young Ones comedy team who recorded a comic version of 'Living Doll' with Cliff.

Settlers, The – Recorded several tracks with Cliff in the late sixties, all remain unreleased.

Shapiro, Helen – Cliff recorded a duet with Helen Shapiro released on her album.

Smith, Mike – Back-up vocalist on the charity record 'Everybody's Got A Crisis In Their Lives'.

Solomon, Diane – Singer who supplied backing vocals on the charity record 'Everybody's Got A Crisis In Their Lives'.

Squire, Billy – Vocalist on the 1985 recording 'Born To Rock 'n' Roll' (see also Musicians).

Stardust, Alvin – Alvin supplied backing vocals on 'Everybody's Got A Crisis In Their Lives'.

Stockley, Miriam – Backing vocals on 'Just Don't Have The Heart'.

Stroud, Steve – Provided back-up vocals during recent tours (see also Musicians).

Stubbs, Una – Appeared on the 'This Was My Special Day' single in 1964.

Tarney, Alan – As well as producer and musician Tarney provided vocals on many of Cliff's seventies and eighties material (see also Musicians and Producers).

Thompson, Anthony – One of many vocalists who worked on the *Together With Cliff Richard* Christmas album.

Vernon Girls, The – Appeared with Cliff at The Event concerts in 1989. Sang in their own right and also backed Cliff on several numbers.

Walmsley, Judith – One of the back-up vocalists on the Access All Areas tour.

Walsh, Sheila – Duetted with Cliff on 'Driftin'.

Wayne, Carl – Sixties singer who was one of many back-up vocalists on 'Everybody's Got A Crisis In Their Lives'.

Welch, Bruce – Supplied backing vocals throughout the fifties, sixties and into the nineties on various album projects (see also Musicians).

Wetton, John – Back-up vocalist on the charity record 'Everybody's Got A Crisis In Their Lives'.

Wilde, Kim – Marty Wilde's pop singer daughter provided vocals on the anti-heroin single 'Live-In World'.

Wynette, Tammy – Recently recorded a duet with Cliff, 'This Love', for her album.

Zorian, Joanne – Another back-up vocalist on 'Everybody's Got A Crisis In Their Lives'.

WOMEN IN CLIFF'S LIFE

Barker, Sue – Former professional tennis player who retired from tennis in 1984 although she is still associated with the game through her work as a presenter and commentator. Sue became linked romantically with Cliff in the eighties as his girlfriend. The possibility of

marriage was regularly rumoured and reported in the national press during their relationship.

Black, Cilla – Singer and television personality who was discovered by the Beatles manager Brian Epstein, and produced four records by George Martin. She had a string of hits in the sixties and made a couple of movies before starting her own television series *Cilla*. She currently hosts *Surprise Surprise* and *Blind Date*. She is an honorary member of the London and Surrey fan club. Cliff and Cilla are close friends.

Costa, Carol – Former wife of Jet Harris who became romantically involved with Cliff during his early career.

Hunniford, Gloria – Radio and television personality. Cliff and Gloria are close friends.

Irving, Jackie – Dancer who became one of Cliff's earliest girlfriends. They met while working together on one of Cliff's summer seasons. She later went on to become one of Lionel Blair's dancers before she married Adam Faith in 1967.

Newton-John, Olivia – Olivia first gained fame as the girl who sang with Cliff on television and at his concerts. After her first international hit 'If Not For You', she had a string of hits in America including 'Let Me Be There' and 'If You Love Me Let Me Know', and she starred in the films *Grease* and *Xanadu*. She recorded a number of duets with Cliff including the hit 'Suddenly' and became the only female artist in the US to have had seven movie songs on Billboard's Top 40 chart. Cliff and Olivia are close friends. Most recently, Olivia duetted with Cliff on a selection of songs on his *Heathcliff* album.

Norris, Jay – Cliff's English teacher at Cheshunt Secondary Modern. She took early retirement from teaching in 1982. Cliff and Jay are very close friends.

Parfitt, Maria – Former wife of Status Quo's Rick Parfitt. Cliff and Maria are close friends.

Stubbs, Una – Actress who played Sandy in *Summer Holiday*, and Barbara in *Wonderful Life*, and Princess Balroubadour in *Aladdin And His Wonderful Lamp*. In 1970, she joined the Young Vic and became a nationally-known stage actress. On television she became a familiar and well known face in *Till Death Us Do Part* and *Worzel Gummidge* as well as being a regular guest on *Give Us a Clue* and *It's Cliff Richard*. She worked with Cliff for ten years, and became romantically involved with him during the shooting of *Wonderful Life*. Una is an honorary member of the London and Surrey fan club.

Webb, Donna – Cliff's sister lives in Ware and is married to Terry Goulden. They have two adopted children, Ty and Emma.

Webb (Bodkin), Dorothy Marie – Cliff's mother lives in a granny annex connected to her daughter Joan's property. She is often seen at Cliff's concerts.

Webb, Joan – Cliff's youngest sister lives in Broxbourne, Hertfordshire with her husband David Pilgrim. She is often seen at Cliff's concerts looking after guests backstage.

Webb, Jacqui – Cliff's sister lives in Norfolk with her husband Peter Harrison. She has five children, the youngest of which is four. Jacqui became a grandmother in 1992.

Wicks, Delia – Cliff's first girlfriend did a lot of television commercials in the early sixties for Signal Toothpaste, Quality Street, and Martini. She then joined the Black and White Minstrel Show until she married in 1970. She is now divorced.

PART 3

THE MUSIC

SONGS A–Z

In this section we have listed every song Cliff is known to have recorded or is thought to have recorded, as well as several songs sung in concert, or on Radio Luxembourg, that have not appeared on record. Each entry also includes a recording date, the first issue, and composer credits where known. Following each song entry, we have listed every Cliff single, EP, album, and video on which the song appears.

A

A BRAND NEW SONG

(Barry/Williams)

Recorded: 11 October 1972

Singles:

A BRAND NEW SONG/The Old
Accordion

A FOREVER KIND OF LOVE

(Keller/Goffin)

Recorded: 12 July 1962

EPs:

A Forever Kind Of Love

LPs:

The EP Collection

A GIRL IN EVERY PORT

(Myers/Cass)

Recorded: 20 May 1964

EPs:

Wonderful Life No. 2

LPs:

Wonderful Life

Videos:

Wonderful Life

A GIRL LIKE YOU

(Lordan)

Recorded: 28 January 1961

Singles:

A GIRL LIKE YOU/Now's The
Time To Fall In Love

EPs:

Cliff's Hit Parade

LPs:

Cliff's Hit Album

40 Golden Greats

20 Original Greats

Cliff In The 60s

The Best of Cliff Richard And
The Shadows

The Rock 'n' Roll Era: Cliff
Richard 1958–1963

The Hit List

Videos:

The Hit List Live

A HEART WILL BREAK

(Tarney/Spencer)

Recorded: May/June 1980

LPs:

I'm No Hero

ALGY THE PICCADILLY JOHNNY

(Norris)

Recorded: 9 August 1961

LPs:

The Young Ones

Videos:

The Young Ones

A LITTLE IMAGINATION

(Myers/Cass)

Recorded: 22 April 1964

EPs:

Wonderful Life No. 2

LPs:

Wonderful Life

Videos:

Wonderful Life

A LITTLE IN LOVE

(Tarney)

Recorded: May/June 1980

Singles:

A LITTLE IN LOVE/Keep On
Looking

LPs:

I'm No Hero

Love Songs

Private Collection

30th Anniversary Picture
Collection

Videos:

The Video Connection

Private Collection

A MATTER OF MOMENTS

(Welch)

Recorded: 10 November 1963

Singles:

On The Beach/A MATTER OF
MOMENTS

EPs:

Wonderful Life No. 2

LPs:

Wonderful Life

More Hits By Cliff

Videos:

Wonderful Life

A MIGHTY LONELY MAN

(Curtis)

Recorded: 30 January 1961

LPs:

21 Today

How Wonderful To Know

AND ME (I'M ON THE OUTSIDE NOW)

(Leander/Richard)

Recorded: 8 March 1968

LPs:

Two A Penny

ANYONE SWEETER THAN YOU

(Unknown)

Recorded: Unknown date

Radio Luxembourg performance

A SAD SONG WITH A HAPPY SOUL

(Unknown)

Recorded: 1 June 1970

Not Released

A SPOONFUL OF SUGAR

(Unknown)

Recorded: 18 November 1965

Not Released

A SWINGIN AFFAIR
(Myers/Cass)
Recorded: 26 August 1962
LPs:
Summer Holiday
Videos:
Summer Holiday

A TEENAGER IN LOVE
(Unknown)
Recorded: 4 May 1959
Not Released

A THOUSAND CONVERSATIONS
(Marvin/Welch)
Recorded: 24 August 1971
Singles:
Sing A Song Of Freedom/A
THOUSAND CONVERSATIONS

A VOICE IN THE WILDERNESS
(Paramor/Lewis)
Recorded: 20 December 1959
Singles:
A VOICE IN THE WILDERNESS/
Don't Be Mad At Me
EPs:
Expresso Bongo
LPs:
Cliff's Hit Album
20 Original Greats
Love Songs
One Hour Of Cliff Richard
Rock On With Cliff Richard
30th Anniversary Picture
Collection
The Best Of Cliff Richard And
The Shadows
The Rock 'n' Roll Era: Cliff Richard
1958–1963
The Hit List
Videos:
The Hit List
The Hit List Live

ABRAHAM, MARTIN AND JOHN
(Holler)
Recorded: 22 September 1969
LPs:
Tracks 'n' Grooves

AGAIN
(Cochran/Newman)
Recorded: 19 August 1964
LPs:
Cliff Richard
All My Love

**AIN'T NOTHING BUT A
HOUSE PARTY**
(Thomas/Fisher)
Recorded: 30 May 1968
LPs:
Live At The Talk Of The Town

ALL AT ONCE
(Myers/Cass)
Recorded: 26 August 1962
EPs:
More Hits From Summer Holiday
LPs:
Summer Holiday
Videos:
Summer Holiday

ALL BY MYSELF
(Unknown)
No known recording, but sung
in concert

ALL FOR ONE
(Myers/Cass)
Recorded: 9 August 1961
LPs:
The Young Ones
Videos:
The Young Ones

ALL GLORY LAUD AND HONOUR
(Neale - Arranged Paramor)
Recorded: 4 May 1967
LPs:
Good News
Hymns And Inspirational Songs

ALL I ASK OF YOU
(Webber/Hart)
Recorded: 6 August 1986
Singles:
ALL I ASK OF YOU/Phantom Of
The Opera Overture
ALL I ASK OF YOU/Phantom Of
The Opera Overture/Only You
LPs:
Private Collection

ALL I DO IS DREAM OF YOU
(Freed/Brown)
Recorded: 4 May 1961
EPs:
Dream
LPs:
The EP Collection

ALL I HAVE TO DO IS DREAM
(Boudleaux/Bryant)
Recorded: 1 May 1981
Singles:
ALL I HAVE TO DO IS
DREAM/Miss You Nights
ALL I HAVE TO DO IS
DREAM/Miss You Nights/
When Will I Be Loved/Tribute
To The Legends (Medley)
ALL I HAVE TO DO IS
DREAM/Miss You Nights/True
Love Ways/Party Megamix
Videos:
The Hit List Live

ALL IN THE APRIL EVENING
(Unknown)
Recorded: 28 April 1967

Not released, but sung in concert

ALL I WANT

(Unknown)

No known recording but sung in concert

ALL KINDS OF PEOPLE

(Myers/Cass)

Recorded: 22 April 1964

EPs:

Hits From Wonderful Life

LPs:

Wonderful Life

Videos:

Wonderful Life

ALL MY LOVE

(Arduini/Callander)

Recorded: 5 October 1967

Singles:

ALL MY LOVE/Sweet Little Jesus Boy

LPs:

The Best Of Cliff

Live At The Talk Of The Town

40 Golden Greats

All My Love

Cliff In The 60s

30th Anniversary Picture Collection

The Best Of Cliff Richard And The Shadows

ALL OF A SUDDEN (MY HEART SINGS)

(Rome/Jamblan/Herpin)

Recorded: 17 July 1964

LPs:

Love Is Forever

Everybody Needs Somebody

ALL SHOOK UP

(Blackwell/Presley)

Recorded: 4 March 1978

LPs:

Thank You Very Much

Videos:

Thank You Very Much

ALL THE TIME YOU NEED

(Eaton)

Recorded: August 1988

Singles:

Silhouettes/The Winner/ALL THE TIME YOU NEED

LPs:

From A Distance The Event

Live And Guaranteed

Videos:

Live and Guaranteed 1988

ALMOST LIKE BEING IN LOVE

(Lerner/Loewe)

Recorded: 11 January 1961

EPs:

Listen To Cliff No. 2

LPs:

Listen To Cliff

ALRIGHT, IT'S ALRIGHT

(Allison/Sills)

Recorded: 1 December 1975

LPs:

I'm Nearly Famous

ALWAYS

(Berlin)

Recorded: 16/17 June 1989

LPs:

From A Distance The Event

Videos:

From A Distance The Event

ALWAYS

(Britten)

Recorded: 6 July 1968

LPs:

Sincerely Cliff Richard

ALWAYS GUARANTEED

(Tarney)

Recorded: September 1986

LPs:

Always Guaranteed

Live And Guaranteed

Videos:

Live And Guaranteed 1988

AMAZING GRACE

(Traditional - Arranged Guard)

Recorded: September 1973

LPs:

Help It Along

Japan Tour

Hymns And Inspirational Songs

AMOR, AMOR, AMOR

(Mendez/Ruiz)

Recorded: 28 April 1963

LPs:

When In Spain

ANGEL

(Tepper/Bennett)

Recorded: August 1964

Singles:

ANGEL/Razzle Dazzle

EPs:

Angel

LPs:

Cliff Richard

ANNABELLA UMBRELLA

(Avons/Spiro)

Recorded: 12 February 1971

Singles:

Silvery Rain/ANNABELLA UMBRELLA/Time Flies

ANOTHER CHRISTMAS DAY

(Richard)

Recorded: April 1987

Singles:

Remember Me/ANOTHER

CHRISTMAS DAY
Remember Me/ANOTHER
  CHRISTMAS DAY/Brave New
  World
Remember Me/ANOTHER
  CHRISTMAS DAY/Some People
ANOTHER CHRISTMAS DAY/
  Engraved Message from Cliff
  (Always Guaranteed Box Set
  only)

ANOTHER TEAR FALLS
(Unknown)
No known recording, but sung
  in concert

ANTI-BROTHERHOOD OF MAN
(Cole)
Recorded: 26/27 May 1973
LPs:
  Take Me High

ANYONE WHO HAD A HEART
(Unknown)
No known recording, but sung
  in concert

ANYTHING I CAN DO
(Tarney)
Recorded: May/June 1980
LPs:
  I'm No Hero

APRON STRINGS
(Weiss/Schroeder)
Recorded: 25 May 1959
Singles:
  Living Doll/APRON STRINGS
EPs:
  Cliff No. 1
LPs:
  Cliff
  Rock On With Cliff Richard

A WORLD OF DIFFERENCE
(Unknown)
No known recording but sung by
  Cliff during the party held after
  the 1985 Live-Aid Concert

ARE YOU ONLY FOOLING ME
(Froggatt)
Recorded: 22 September 1969
LPs:
  Tracks 'n' Grooves

ARRIVEDERCI ROMA
(Garinei/Giovannini/Rascel)
Recorded: 2/3 October 1964
EPs:
  Hits From When In Rome
LPs:
  When In Rome

**AS I WALK INTO THE MORNING
OF YOUR LIFE**
(Brooks)
Recorded: 2 July 1968
LPs:
  Tracks 'n' Grooves

AS TIME GOES BY
(Hupfeld)
Recorded: 10 September 1959
EPs:
  Cliff Sings No. 3
LPs:
  Cliff Sings

AS WONDERFUL AS YOU
(Unknown)
Recorded: 15 April 1965
Not released

ASHES TO ASHES
(Cole)
Recorded: 27 December 1972
Singles:
  Help It Along/Tomorrow Rising/

Days Of Love/ASHES TO
  ASHES

AT THE TOP
(Singer)
Recorded: 16/17 June 1989
LPs:
  From A Distance The Event
AWAY IN A MANGER
(Traditional)
Videos:
  Christmas With Cliff Richard

B

**BABY I COULD BE SO
GOOD AT LOVING YOU**
(Clifford)
Recorded: 1 July 1968
LPs:
  Sincerely Cliff Richard

BABY I DON'T CARE
(Leiber/Stoller)
Recorded: 9 February 1959
EPs:
  Cliff No. 1
LPs:
  Cliff

BABY IT'S YOU
(David/Bacharach/Williams)
Recorded: 15 January 1967
LPs:
  Don't Stop Me Now

BABY YOU'RE DYNAMITE
(Fletcher/Flett)
Recorded: August 1983
Singles:
  BABY YOU'RE DYNAMITE/Ocean
    Deep
  BABY YOU'RE DYNAMITE/Ocean
    Deep/BABY YOU'RE DYNAMITE
    (Extended Mix)

LPs:

Silver

From The Heart

Videos:

The Video Connection

BACHELOR BOY

(Richard/Welch)

Recorded: 16 November 1962

Singles:

The Next Time/BACHELOR BOY

EPs:

Hits From Summer Holiday

LPs:

Summer Holiday

More Hits By Cliff

Live In Japan

Japan Tour

40 Golden Greats

From The Heart

Cliff In The 60s

The Best Of Cliff Richard And

The Shadows

The Rock 'n' Roll Era: Cliff Richard

1958–1963

The Hit List

Videos:

Summer Holiday

Rock In Australia

Cliff And The Shadows Together

1984

The Story So Far

The Hit List

The Hit List Live

BACK IN VAUDEVILLE

(Unknown)

Recorded: 7-12 March 1983

B side of foreign release

**BANG BANG (MY BABY
SHOT ME DOWN)**

(Bono)

Recorded: 10 October 1968

LPs:

Tracks 'n' Grooves

BE BOP A LULA

(Vincent/Davis)

Recorded: 10 February 1959

LPs:

Cliff

Rock 'n' roll Silver

The Rock Connection

BE IN MY HEART

(Perry)

Recorded: January 1982

LPs:

Now You See Me Now You Don't

The Winner

BE WITH ME ALWAYS

(Rice/Farrar)

Recorded: 1995

LPs:

Songs From Heathcliff

**BEAT OUT DAT RHYTHM
ON A DRUM**

(Hammerstein II/Bizet)

Recorded: 11 January 1961

EPs:

Listen To Cliff No. 2

LPs:

Listen To Cliff

One Hour Of Cliff Richard

BETTER DAY

(Tarney)

Recorded: March-May 1989

LPs:

Stronger

BETTER THAN I KNOW MYSELF

(Cooke/MacKenzie)

Recorded: May/July 1981

LPs:

Wired For Sound

Walking In The Light

BIG NEWS

(Richard/Conlin/Cass)

Recorded: 16 November 1962

LPs:

Summer Holiday

Videos:

Summer Holiday

BIG SHIP

(Froggatt)

Recorded: 22 April 1969

Singles:

BIG SHIP/She's Leaving You

LPs:

The Best Of Cliff Volume 2

BILDER VON DIR

(Ferris/Hertha)

Recorded: 25 April 1967

Singles:

Ein Girl Wie Du/BILDER VON DIR

LPs:

When In Germany Volume 2

BIN VERLIEBT

(Samwell/Fleming)

Recorded: 5 December 1960

Singles:

BIN VERLIEBT/Die Stimme Der

Liebe

BIRD DOG

(Bryant/Boudleaux)

Recorded: 16/17 June 1989

Singles:

Saviours Day/The 'Oh Boy'

Medley

Saviours Day/The 'Oh Boy'

Medley/Where Are You

LPs:

From A Distance The Event

Videos:

From A Distance The Event

**BLAME IT ON THE
BOSSA NOVA**

(Weil/Mann)

Recorded: 7 October 1965

LPs:

Kinda Latin

The Best of Cliff Richard And
The Shadows

BLOWIN' IN THE WIND

(Dylan)

Recorded: 22 October 1965

LPs:

Kinda Latin

BLUE MOON

(Rodgers/Hart)

Recorded: 17 November 1960

Singles:

What'D I Say/BLUE MOON

EPs:

Listen To Cliff

LPs:

Listen To Cliff

The Best Of Cliff Richard And
The Shadows

From A Distance The Event

Videos:

From A Distance The Event

BLUE SUEDE SHOES

(Perkins)

Recorded: 7 September 1959

EPs:

Cliff Sings No. 1

LPs:

Cliff Sings

Videos:

The Story So Far

BLUE TURNS TO GREY

(Richard/Jagger)

Recorded: 17 January 1966

Singles:

BLUE TURNS TO GREY/

Somebody Loses

LPs:

The Best Of Cliff

40 Golden Greats

One Hour Of Cliff Richard

BLUEBERRY HILL

(Lewis/Stock/Rose)

Recorded: 17 May 1962

EPs:

Time For Cliff And The Shadows

LPs:

32 Minutes And 17 Seconds

It'll Be Me

One Hour Of Cliff Richard

BONIE MORONIE

(Shury/Kipner)

Recorded: 7/8 October 1974

LPs:

Japan Tour

BOOK OF LOVE

(Davis/Malone/Patrick)

Recorded: 16/17 June 1989

LPs:

From A Distance The Event

**BOOM BOOM (THAT'S
HOW MY HEART BEATS)**

(Mills)

Recorded: 14 April 1965

EPs:

Take Four

LPs:

The EP Collection

BORN TO ROCK 'N' ROLL

(Clark/Soames/Daniels)

Recorded: 25 August 1965

Singles:

BORN TO ROCK 'N' ROLL/Law Of
The Universe

LPs:

Silver

The Rock Connection

Time

My Kinda Life

BOUM

(Trenet)

Recorded: 5 August 1963

EPs:

When In France

LPs:

When In France

The EP Collection

BRAVE NEW WORLD

(Unknown)

Recorded: April 1987

Singles:

Remember Me/Another
Christmas Day/BRAVE NEW
WORLD

BREATHLESS

(Unknown)

Recorded: Mid 1958

Not released

BROKEN DOLL

(Goulden/Hacon)

Recorded: May/July 1981

LPs:

Wired For Sound

BROTHER TO BROTHER

(Moessl/Glen)

Recorded: May/June 1992

LPs:

The Album

BRUMBURGER DUET

(Cole)

Recorded: May 1973

LPs:

Take Me High

Videos:

Take Me High

BRUMBURGER FINALE

(Cole)

Recorded: September 1973

LPs:

Take Me High

Videos:

Take Me High

BULANGE DOWNPOWER

(Richard)

Recorded: May/June 1992

Singles:

I Still Believe In You/BULANGE
DOWNPOWER

I Still Believe In You/BULANGE
DOWNPOWER/There's No
Power In Pity

BURN ON

(Unknown)

Recorded: 2 February 1988

LPs:

The Kendrick Collection

C

CANCION DE ORFEO

(Bonfa/Peretti/Creator/Weiss)

Recorded: 29 April 1963

LPs:

When In Spain

CAN IT BE TRUE

(Brother William)

Recorded: 20 February 1970

LPs:

About That Man

Carols

CAN'T HELP MYSELF

(Unknown)

No known recording, but sung
in concert

CAN'T LET YOU GO

(Unknown)

Recorded: October 1972

LPs:

Live In Japan

**CAN'T TAKE THE
HURT ANYMORE**

(Andrew)

Recorded: 11 July 1977

Singles:

CAN'T TAKE THE HURT
ANYMORE/Needing A Friend

LPs:

Green Light

Love Songs

CAPTAIN GINJAH

(Leigh/Baston)

Recorded: 9 August 1961

LPs:

The Young Ones

Videos:

The Young Ones

CARINA

(Testa/Poes)

Recorded: 2 October 1964

LPs:

When In Rome

CARNIVAL

(Bonfa/Peretti/Creator/Weiss)

Recorded: 6 December 1962

EPs:

Holiday Carnival

LPs:

The EP Collection

CARRIE

(Britten/Robertson)

Recorded: January 1979

Singles:

CARRIE/Moving In

Healing Love/Yesterday's
Memories/CARRIE

Healing Love/CARRIE/Daddy's
Home/Some People

LPs:

Rock 'n' Roll Juvenile

Love Songs

Dressed For The Occasion

Private Collection

30th Anniversary Picture
Collection

The Best Of Cliff Richard And
The Shadows

My Kinda Life

The Hit List

Videos:

The Video Connection

Private Collection

The Hit List Live

CASA SENZA FINESTRE

(Testa/Pockriss)

Recorded: 2 October 1964

LPs:

When In Rome

CATCH ME

(Teper/Bennett)

Recorded: 9 September 1960

EPs:

Cliff Richard No. 1

LPs:

21 Today

How Wonderful To Know

CAUSE I BELIEVE IN LOVING

(Unknown)

Recorded: 5 March 1971

Not released

CELEBRATE

(Unknown)

Recorded: 11 January 1969

Not released

CELESTIAL HOUSES

(Britten)

Recorded: September 1973

Singles:

Take Me High/CELESTIAL
HOUSES

LPs:

Help It Along

C'EST SI BON

(Betti/Horner)

Recorded: 5 August 1963

EPs:

When In France

LPs:

When In France

CHANTILLY LACE

(Richardson)

Recorded: 7/8 October 1974

LPs:

Japan Tour

From A Distance The Event

CHASER

(Unknown)

Recorded: September 1973

Not released

**CHE COSA DEL FARAI
MIO AMOUR**

(Pallavicini/De Ponti)

Recorded: 2 October 1964

LPs:

When In Rome

CHI LO SA

(Unknown)

Recorded: 24 February 1969

Singles:

Non Dimenticare Chi Ti Ama/
CHI LO SA

CHIM CHIM CHEREE

(Unknown)

Recorded: 18 November 1965

Not released

CHOPPIN' 'N' CHANGIN'

(Samwell)

Recorded: 24 June 1960

EPs:

Me And My Shadows No. 2

LPs:

Me And My Shadows

CHOOSING WHEN IT'S TOO LATE

(Rice/Farrar)

Recorded: 1995

LPs:

Songs From Heathcliff

CHRISTMAS ALPHABET

(Kaye/Loman)

Recorded: June/July 1991

LPs:

Together

Videos:

Together

CHRISTMAS NEVER COMES

(Field)

Recorded: June/July 1991

LPs:

Together

Videos:

Together

CITIES MAY FALL

(Britten/Robertson)

Recorded: January 1979

LPs:

Rock 'n' Roll Juvenile

CLEAR BLUE SKIES

(Cooke/Turner)

Recorded: March-May 1989

LPs:

Stronger

CLOSE TO CATHY

(Goodman/Shuman)

Recorded: 17 November 1965

LPs:

Two A Penny

CLOSER TO YOU

(Unknown)

Recorded: January 1982

Not released

CLOUDY

(Simon/Woodley)

Recorded: 11 October 1967

LPs:

Two A Penny

C'MON EVERYBODY

(Capehart/Cochran)

Recorded: 16/17 June 1989

Singles:

Saviours Day/THE OH BOY
MEDLEY

Saviours Day/THE OH BOY
MEDLEY/Where Are You

LPs:

From A Distance The Event

Videos:

From A Distance The Event

COME BACK BILLIE JO

(Murray/Macauley)

Recorded: 27 December 1972

Singles:

Power To All Our Friends/COME
BACK BILLIE JO

Il Faut Chanter La Vie/COME
 BACK BILLIE JO
Todor El Poder A Los Amigos/
 COME BACK BILLIE JO

COME CLOSER TO ME

(Stewart/Farres)
Recorded: 22 October 1965
LPs:
 Kinda Latin

COME PRIMA

(Panzeri/Di Paola/Taccani)
Recorded: 2 October 1964
EPs:
 Hits From When In Rome
LPs:
 When In Rome

COME SUNDAY

(Marvin/Welch/Bennett/Rostill)
Recorded: 14 October 1966
EPs:
 Cinderella
LPs:
 Cinderella

COMPASSION ROAD

(Unknown)
Recorded: 2/3 December 1968
Not released

CONCERTO D'AUTUMNO

(Danpa/Bargoni)
Recorded: 2 October 1964
LPs:
 When In Rome

CONCERTO

(Gordoni/Hertha)
Recorded: 25 November 1970
LPs:
 Ich Traume Deine Traume

CONCRETE AND CLAY

(Moeller/Parker)
Recorded: 22 October 1965
LPs:
 Kinda Latin

CONGRATULATIONS

(Martin/Coulter)
Recorded: 3 February 1968
Singles:
 CONGRATULATIONS/High 'n' Dry
 Never Let Go/
  CONGRATULATIONS
 Never Let Go/
  CONGRATULATIONS/The
  Young Ones/You've Got Me
  Wondering
EPs:
 Congratulations
LPs:
 The Best Of Cliff
 Live At The Talk Of The Town
 40 Golden Greats
 Live In Japan
 Japan Tour
 From The Heart
 The Best Of Cliff Richard And
  The Shadows
 30th Anniversary Picture
  Collection
 The Hit List
Videos:
 Cliff And The Shadows Together
  1984
 The Story So Far
 The Hit List
 The Hit List Live

CONSTANTLY

(Seracini/Julien)
Recorded: 17 November 1963
Singles:
 CONSTANTLY/True True Lovin'
EPs:
 A Forever Kind Of Love
LPs:

 More Hits By Cliff
 Japan Tour
 40 Golden Greats
 Love Songs
 The Best Of Cliff Richard And
  The Shadows
 The Hit List
Videos:
 The Hit List
 The Hit List Live

COS I LOVE THAT
ROCK 'N' ROLL

(Tarney)
Recorded: May/July 1981
LPs:
 Wired For Sound

COUNT ME OUT

(Britten/Welch)
Recorded: 15 January 1978
Singles:
 We Don't Talk Anymore/COUNT
  ME OUT
LPs:
 Green Light

CROCODILE ROCK

(John/Taupin)
Recorded: 7/8 October 1974

LPs:
Japan Tour

D

'D' IN LOVE
(Tepper/Bennett)
Recorded: 9 September 1960
Singles:
I Love You/D IN LOVE
LPs:
One Hour Of Cliff Richard

DADDY'S HOME
(Sheppard/Miller)
Recorded: May 1981
Singles:
DADDY'S HOME/Shakin' All Over
Healing Love/Carrie/DADDY'S
HOME/Some People
LPs:
Wired For Sound
Private Collection
30th Anniversary Picture
Collection
The Hit List
Videos:
The Video Connection
Private Collection
From A Distance The Event
Access All Areas
The Hit List Live

DA DO RON RON
(Spector/Greenwich/Barry)
Bootleg LPs:
Imagine (live version, 1965)

DANCE THE NIGHT AWAY
(Unknown)
No known recording, but sung
in concert

DANCING SHOES
(Welch/Marvin)

Recorded: 5 May 1962
Singles:
Summer Holiday/DANCING
SHOES
EPs:
Hits From Summer Holiday
LPs:
Summer Holiday
More Hits By Cliff
Japan Tour
20 Original Greats
One Hour Of Cliff Richard
Rock On With Cliff Richard
The Best Of Cliff Richard And
The Shadows
Videos:
Summer Holiday

DANNY
(Weisman/Wise)
Recorded: 10 February 1959
LPs:
Cliff

DAS GIRL VON NEBENAN
(Rosemeier/Jacobi)
Recorded: 24 November 1970
Singles:
Ich Traume Deine Traume/DAS
GIRL VON NEBENAN
LPs:
Ich Traume Deine Traume

DAS GLUCK IST ROSAROT
(Olden/Relin)
Recorded: 10 November 1966
Singles:
DAS GLUCK IST ROSAROT/Was
Kann Ich Tun

**DAS IST DIE FRAGE ALLER
FRAGEN**
(Lieber/Stoller/Blecher)
Recorded: 10 October 1964

Singles:
DAS IST DIE FRAGE ALLER
FRAGEN/Nur Mit Dir
LPs:
Seine Grossen Erfolgen

DAY BY DAY
(Schwartz)
Recorded: September 1973
LPs:
Help It Along
Hymns And Inspirational Songs
One Hour Of Cliff Richard

DEEP PURPLE
(Unknown)
Recorded: 10 May 1965
Not released

DIE LIEBE IST IMMER NUR HEUT
(Richard/Collier/Hertha)
Recorded: 20 November 1968
LPs:
Heir Ist Cliff

DEINE AUGEN TRAUMEN MARY
(Marvin/Bennett/Relin)
Recorded: 27 November 1968
LPs:
Heir Ist Cliff

DER MANN NEBEN DIR
(Westlake/Relin)
Recorded: 25 November 1970
LPs:
Ich Traume Deine Traume

DEVIL WOMAN
(Britten/Holmes)
Recorded: 8 September 1975
Singles:
DEVIL WOMAN/Love On
Human Work Of Art/DEVIL
WOMAN/Ragged/Free

LPs:
  I'm Nearly Famous
  40 Golden Greats
  It's A Small World
  Thank You Very Much
  Dressed For The Occasion
  From The Heart
  30th Anniversary Picture
  Collection
  The Best Of Cliff Richard And
    The Shadows
  My Kinda Life
  The Hit List
  Live And Guaranteed
Videos:
  Thank You Very Much
  The Video Connection
  Rock in Australia
  Live And Guaranteed 1988
  Access All Areas
  The Story So Far

DICITENCELLO VUIE

(Kalmanoff/Ward/Fusco/
  Val/Dale/Falvo)
Recorded: 2 October 1964
EPs:
  Hits From When In Rome
LPs:
  When In Rome

DID HE JUMP OR WAS
HE PUSHED

(Unknown)
No known recording, but sung
  in concert

DIE STIMME DER LIEBE

(Richard/Collier/Hertha)
Recorded: 5 December 1960
Singles:
  Bin Verliebt/DIE STIMME DER
    LIEBE

DIM DIM THE LIGHTS

(Unknown)
Recorded: 7 March 1962
Not released. Also unreleased
  Radio Luxembourg
    performance

DISCOVERING

(Eaton)
Recorded: January 1982
Singles:
  Where Do We Go From Here/
    DISCOVERING
LPs:
  Now You See Me Now You Don't
  The Winner

DIZZY MISS LIZZY

(Williams)
Recorded: 19 October 1966
LPs:
  Don't Stop Me Now

DOIN' FINE

(Britten)
Recorded: July 1978
LPs:
  Rock 'n' Roll Juvenile

DO THEY KNOW
IT'S CHRISTMAS

(Ure/Geldof)
Recorded: 3/4 December 1989
Singles:
  DO THEY KNOW IT'S CHRISTMAS
LPs:
  Now That's What I Call Christmas
  It's Christmas Time

DO WHAT YOU GOTTA DO

(Unknown)
Recorded: 12 January 1977
Not released

DO YOU REMEMBER

(Welch/Marvin)
Recorded: 1 November 1963
EPs:
  Wonderful Life No. 1
  Congratulations
LPs:
  Wonderful Life
Videos:
  Wonderful Life

DO YOU WANNA DANCE

(Freeman)
Recorded: 19 December 1961
Singles:
  I'm Looking Out The Window/DO
    YOU WANNA DANCE
EPs:
  Cliff's Hits
LPs:
  Cliff's Hit Album
  40 Golden Greats
  Live In Japan
  Japan Tour
  Thank You Very Much
  20 Original Greats
  Rock On With Cliff Richard
  The Best Of Cliff Richard And
    The Shadows
  The Rock 'n' Roll Era: Cliff Richard
    1958–1963
  Knebworth The Album
  The Hit List
Videos:
  Cliff And The Shadows Together
    1984
  Thank You Very Much
  From A Distance The Event
  The Hit List
  The Hit List Live

DONNA

(Valens)
Recorded: 9 February 1959

EPs:

Cliff No. 2

LPs:

Cliff

Rock 'n' Roll Silver

The Rock Connection

From The Heart

Videos:

Rock In Australia

DON'T

(Lieber/Stoller)

Recorded: 19 October 1966

LPs:

Don't Stop Me Now

DON'T ASK ME TO BE FRIENDS

(Keller/Goffin)

Recorded: 5 October 1967

LPs:

Tracks 'n' Grooves

DON'T BE MAD AT ME

(Tepper/Bennett)

Recorded: 18 November 1959

Singles:

A Voice In The Wilderness/DON'T
BE MAD AT ME

DON'T BLAME ME

(Unknown)

Recorded: 8/9 January 1969

Not released

DON'T BUG ME BABY

(Luallen/Bragg)

Recorded: 10 February 1959

EPs:

Cliff No. 2

LPs:

Cliff

DON'T FORGET TO CATCH ME

(Marvin/Welch/Bennett)

Recorded: 31 May 1968

Singles:

DON'T FORGET TO CATCH ME/
What's More (I Don't Need Her)

LPs:

Established 1958

DON'T LET TONIGHT EVER END

(Simoni/Libano/Shane)

Recorded: 2 July 1968

LPs:

Tracks 'n' Grooves

DON'T MAKE PROMISES

(Hardin)

Recorded: 15 January 1967

LPs:

Don't Stop Me Now

DON'T MEET THE BAND

(Richard/Welch)

Recorded: October 1974

LPs:

Japan Tour

DON'T MOVE AWAY

(Avon/Spiro)

Recorded: 16 November 1970

Singles:

Sunny Honey Girl/DON'T MOVE
AWAY/I Was Only Fooling Myself

Had To Be (album version)/Had
To Be (instrumental)/I DON'T
MOVE AWAY

DON'T TALK TO HIM

(Richard/Welch)

Recorded: 13 October 1963

Singles:

DON'T TALK TO HIM/Say You're
Mine

EPs:

Cliff Sings Don't Talk To Him

LPs:

More Hits By Cliff

When In Rome

Japan Tour

40 Golden Greats

20 Original Greats

Love Songs

The Best Of Cliff Richard And
The Shadows

The Rock 'n' Roll Era: Cliff Richard
1958–1963

The Hit List

Videos:

Cliff And The Shadows Together
1984

The Hit List Live

DON'T TURN THE LIGHT OUT

(Fletcher/Flett)

Recorded: 7 September 1976

LPs:

Every Face Tells A Story

DOWN THE LINE

(Orbison)

Recorded: 9 February 1959

EPs:

Cliff No. 1

LPs:

Cliff

Videos:

The Story So Far

DREAM

(Mercer)

Recorded: 4 May 1961

EPs:

Dream

DREAM TOMORROW

(Rice/Farrar)

Recorded:

LPs:

Songs From Heathcliff

DREAMIN'

(Tarney/Sayer)

Recorded: May/June 1980

Singles:
DREAMIN'/Dynamite
LPs:
I'm No Hero
30th Anniversary Picture
Collection
The Best Of Cliff Richard And
The Shadows
Private Collection
Videos:
The Video Connection
Rock In Australia
Private Collection
From A Distance The Event
The Hit List Live

DREIZEHN AUF EIN DUTZEND
(Unknown)
Recorded: 20 November 1968
Foreign release

DRIFTING
(Woolley/Darlow)
Recorded: 1982/1983
Singles:
DRIFTING/It's Lonely When The
Lights Go Out (Sheila Walsh)

DRIVING
(Cole)
Recorded: 26 May 1973
LPs:
Take Me High
Videos:
Take Me High

DU BIST MEIN
ERSTER GEDANKE
(Roig/Rodriguez/Siegell)
Recorded: 13 May 1966
Singles:
DU BIST MEIN ERSTER
GEDANKE/Was Ist Dabei
LPs:
Seine Grossen Erfolgen

DU DU GEFALST MIR SO
(McGuire/Sparks)
Recorded: 21 January 1970
Singles:
DU DU GEFALST MIR SO/Lieben
Kann Man Einmal Nur
LPs:
When In Germany Volume 2
Seine Grossen Erfolgen

DU FRAGST MICH
IMMER WIEDER
(Muller/Verner)
Recorded: 24 November 1970
LPs:
Ich Traume Deine Traume

DYNAMITE
(Samwell)
Recorded: 6 September 1959
Singles:
Travellin' Light/DYNAMITE
Dreamin'/DYNAMITE
LPs:
Cliff In Japan
Rock 'n' Roll Silver
The Rock Connection
Rock On With Cliff Richard
The Best Of Cliff Richard And
The Shadows

E

EARLY IN THE MORNING
(Darin/Harris)
Recorded: 21 October 1958
LPs:
Oh Boy!

EARLY IN THE MORNING
(Leander/Seago)
Recorded: 2 May 1969
LPs:
Live In Japan
Japan Tour

Tracks 'n' Grooves

EASE ALONG
(Tarney/Spencer)
Recorded: 9 January 1977
LPs:
Green Light

EIN GIRL WIE DU
(Poll/Meizer)
Recorded: 25 April 1967
Singles:
EIN GIRL WIE DU/Bilder Von Dir
LPs:
When In Germany Volume 2

EIN SONNTAG MIT MARIE
(Marvin/Bradtke)
Recorded: 27 September 1967
Singles:
Es Ist Nicht Gut, Allein Zu Sein/
EIN SONNTAG MIT MARIE
LPs:
When In Germany Volume 2
Seine Grossen Erfolgen

EIN SPIEL OHNE GRENZEN
(Volauvent/Hertha)
Recorded:
Singles:
Gut, Dass Es Freunde Gibt/EIN
SPIEL OHNE GRENZEN
LPs:
Ich Traume Deine Traume

EMBRACEABLE YOU
(Gershwin/Gershwin)
Recorded: 10 September 1959
EPs:
Cliff Sings No. 3
LPs:
Cliff Sings

EMPTY CHAIRS
(Maclean)

Recorded: 28 April 1972

Singles:

Living In Harmony/EMPTY CHAIRS

END OF THE SHOW
(THANK YOU VERY MUCH)

(Wilson/Jakobson)

Recorded: March 1978

LPs:

Thank You Very Much

Videos:

Thank You Very Much

ES GEHOREN ZWEI ZUM
GLUCKLICHSEIN

(Mize/Allen/Olden)

Recorded: 24 June 1974

Singles:

ES GEHOREN ZWEI ZUM
GLUCKLICHSEIN/Liebesleid

LPs:

When In Germany Volume 2

ES IST NICHT GUT,
ALLEIN ZU SEIN

(Niessen/Strom)

Recorded: 28 September

Singles:

ES IST NICHT GUT, ALLEIN ZU
SEIN/Ein Sonntag mit Marie

LPs:

When In Germany Volume 2

ES KONNTE SCHON
MORGEN SEIN

(Galety/Hertha)

Recorded: 15 April 1965

Singles:

Es War Keine So Wunderbar Wie
Du/ES KONNTE SCHON
MORGEN SEIN

ES WAR KEINE SO
WUNDERBAR WIE DU

(Marvin/Welch/Rostill/Bennett/

Blecher)

Recorded: 15 April 1965

Singles:

ES WAR KEINE SO WUNDERBAR
WIE DU/Es Konnte Schon
Morgen Sein

LPs:

Seine Grossen Erfolge

ESO BESO

(Sherman/Sherman)

Recorded: 7 October 1965

LPs:

Kinda Latin

EVENING COMES

(Marvin/Welch/Bennett/Rostill)

Recorded: 15 October 1964

EPs:

Cliff's Hits From Aladdin And His
Wonderful Lamp

LPs:

Aladdin And His Wonderful Lamp

EVERGREEN TREE

(Schroeder/Gold)

Recorded: 16 March 1960

EPs:

Me And My Shadows No. 1

LPs:

Me And My Shadows

Cliff In Japan

EVERY FACE TELLS A STORY
(IT NEVER TELLS A LIE)

(Allison/Sills)

Recorded: 18 September 1976

LPs:

Every Face Tells A Story

Walking In The Light

EVERYBODY KNOWS

(Tarney)

Recorded: March-May 1989

LPs:

Stronger

EVERYBODY'S GOT A
CRISIS IN THEIR LIFE

(Cozens)

Recorded: 5 February 1989

Singles:

EVERYBODY'S GOT A CRISIS IN
THEIR LIFE

EVERYMAN

(Tarney)

Recorded: May/June 1980

LPs:

I'm No Hero

Videos:

Christmas With Cliff Richard

EVERYONE NEEDS
SOMEONE TO LOVE

(Bacharach/David)

Recorded: August 1964

EPs:

Love Is Forever

LPs:

Love Is Forever

Everybody Needs Somebody

F

FABULOUS

(Unknown)

No known recording, but sung

in concert

FALL IN LOVE WITH YOU

(Samwell)

Recorded: 18 November 1959

Singles:

FALL IN LOVE WITH YOU/Willie
And The Hand Jive

EPs:

Cliff's Silver Discs

LPs:

Cliff's Hit Album

40 Golden Greats

20 Original Greats

Love Songs

The Best Of Cliff Richard And
The Shadows

The Rock 'n' Roll Era: Cliff Richard
1958-1963

The Hit List

Videos:

The Story So Far

The Hit List

The Hit List Live

FALLIN' IN LUV

(Britten/Robertson)

Recorded: July 1978

LPs:

Rock 'n' Roll Juvenile

FALLING IN LOVE WITH LOVE

(Rodgers/Hart)

Recorded: 5 December 1961

EPs:

Cliff Sings Don't Talk To Him

LPs:

32 Minutes And 17 Seconds

It'll Be Me

FIESTA

(Marvin/Welch/Bennett/Rostill)

LPs:

Finders Keepers

FIFTY TEARS FOR EVERY KISS

(Bella)

Recorded: 30 January 1961

EPs:

Cliff Richard No. 2

LPs:

21 Today

How Wonderful To Know

FIGHTER/THIEF IN THE NIGHT

(Kendrick/Field)

Recorded: 2 February 1988

LPs:

The Kendrick Collection

Walking In The Light

Now You See Me Now You Don't

Dressed For The Occasion

From A Distance The Event

The Winner

Videos:

Rock In Australia

Live And Guaranteed 1988

When The Music Stops

From A Distance The Event

Christmas With Cliff Richard

FINDERS KEEPERS

(Marvin/Welch/Bennett/Rostill)

Recorded: 26 April 1966

Singles:

In The Country/FINDERS KEEPERS

LPs:

Finders Keepers

Cliff In Japan

The Best Of Cliff Richard And
The Shadows

FIRE AND RAIN

(Taylor)

Recorded: September 1973

LPs:

Help It Along

One Hour Of Cliff Richard

FIRESIDE SONG

(Richard)

Recorded: 12 February 1974

LPs:

The 31st of February Street

Japan Tour

FIRST DATE

(John/Battle)

Recorded: January 1982

LPs:

Now You See Me Now You Don't

FIRST LESSON IN LOVE

(Chester/Welch)

Recorded: 13 October 1960

EPs:

Listen To Cliff No. 2

LPs:

Listen To Cliff

FLESH AND BLOOD

(Unknown)

No known recording, but sung
in concert

FLY ME TO THE MOON

(Howard)

Recorded: 7 October 1965

EPs:

Love Is Forever

LPs:

Love Is Forever

Kinda Latin

Everybody Needs Somebody

The Best Of Cliff Richard And
The Shadows

FLYING MACHINE

(Hultgreen)

Recorded: 20 March 1971

Singles:

FLYING MACHINE/Pigeon

LPs:

The Best of Cliff Volume 2

THE MUSIC   SONGS A-Z

Live In Japan

FOODS WISDOM

(Unknown)

No known recording, but sung
in concert

**FOR EMILY WHENEVER
I MAY FIND HER**

(Simon)

Recorded: 11 October 1967

LPs:

Sincerely Cliff Richard

FOR YOU FOR ME

(Welch/Richard)

Recorded: 4 April 1962

EPs:

Holiday Carnival

FOREVER

(Tarney)

Recorded: September 1986

LPs:

Always Guaranteed

FOREVER YOU WILL BE MINE

(Tarney)

Recorded: March-May 1989

LPs:

Stronger

FORGIVE ME

(Unknown)

Recorded: 8/9 January 1969

Not released

FORTY DAYS

(Berry)

Recorded: 4 July 1961

EPs:

Cliff Richard No. 1

LPs:

21 Today

How Wonderful To Know

FRAGEN

(Richard/Collier/Blecher)

LPs:

Heir Ist Cliff

FREE

(MacKenzie)

Singles:

Human Work Of Art/Devil
Woman/Ragged/FREE

Videos:

Access All Areas

FREE MY SOUL

(Britten)

Recorded: 11 January 1978

LPs:

Green Light

FRENESI

(Dominguez)

Recorded: 28 April 1963

EPs:

Cliff Palladium Successes

LPs:

When In Spain

FRIENDS

(Marvin/Welch/Bennett/Rostill)

Recorded: 21 October 1964

EPs:

Cliff's Hits From Aladdin And His
Wonderful Lamp

LPs:

Aladdin And His Wonderful Lamp

FROM A DISTANCE

(Gold)

Recorded: 16/17 June 1989

Singles:

FROM A DISTANCE/Lindsay
Jane II

FROM A DISTANCE/I Could Easily
Fall

FROM A DISTANCE/Lindsay

Jane II/Wired For Sound

LPs:

From A Distance The Event

The Winner

Videos:

From A Distance The Event

When The Music Stops

Access All Areas

FROM THIS DAY ON

(Unknown)

Not released

FRONT PAGE

(John/Battle)

Recorded: May/June 1983

LPs:

Silver

G

GALADRIEL

(Marvin/Farrar)

Recorded: 23 November 1982

Singles:

True Love Ways/GALADRIEL

LPs:

Dressed For The Occasion

GEE BUT IT'S LONESOME

(Unknown)

Recorded: 20 December 1959

Not released

GEE WHIZ IT'S YOU

(Marvin/Sanwell)

Recorded: 17 March 1960

Singles:

GEE WHIZ IT'S YOU/I Cannot Find
A True Love

All I Have To Do Is Dream/Miss
You Nights/When Will I Be
Loved/TRIBUTE TO THE
LEGENDS MEDLEY

All I Have To Do Is Dream/Miss

You Nights/True Love Ways/
PARTY MEGAMIX
EPs:
Me And My Shadows No. 3
LPs:
Me And My Shadows
40 Golden Greats
20 Original Greats
Rock On With Cliff Richard
One Hour Of Cliff Richard
The Rock 'n' Roll Era: Cliff Richard
1958–1963
The Hit List
Videos:
The Hit List
The Hit List Live

**GEH DEINEN WEG
NICHT SO ALLEIN**
(Marvin/Blecher)
Recorded: 31 October 1968
LPs:
Heir Ist Cliff

GET BACK
(Lennon/McCartney)
Recorded: October 1974
LPs:
Japan Tour

GET READY
(Unknown)
No known recording, but sung
in concert

GET IT RIGHT NEXT TIME
(Unknown)
No known recording, but sung
in concert

**GET ON BOARD
LITTLE CHILDREN**
(Traditional - Arranged Leander)
Recorded: 27 April 1967
LPs:

Good News

GETTIN' THE FEELIN'
(Unknown)
Recorded: 14 January 1978
Not released

GIRL ON THE BUS
(Rostill)
Recorded: 29 May 1968
LPs:
Established 1958

**GIRL YOU'LL BE A
WOMAN SOON**
(Diamond)
Recorded: 11 February 1968
Singles:
I'll Love You Forever Today/GIRL
YOU'LL BE A WOMAN SOON
Ah Quelle Histoire/GIRL YOU'LL
BE A WOMAN SOON
LPs:
The Best Of Cliff
Live At The Talk Of The Town

**GIVE ALL YOUR LOVE
TO THE LORD**
(Unknown)
No known recording, but sung
in concert

GIVE A LITTLE BIT MORE
(Hodge/Hill)
Recorded: May/June 1980
LPs:
I'm No Hero

**GIVE ME BACK THAT OLD
FAMILIAR FEELING**
(Graham)
Recorded: 11 February 1974
LPs:
The 31st Of February Street
Japan Tour

GIVE ME LOVE YOUR WAY
(Tarney Spencer)
Recorded: 7 September 1976
LPs:
Every Face Tells A Story

GLAUB NUR MIR
(Taylor/Relin)
Recorded: 27 October 1965
Singles:
Nur Bei Dir Bin Ich Zu Haus/
GLAUB NUR MIR

GO WHERE I SEND THEE
(Traditional - Arranged Leander)
Recorded: 27 April 1967
LPs:
Good News

**GOD REST YE MERRY
GENTLEMEN**
(Arranged. Keating)
Recorded: 10 September 1967
EPs:
Carol Singers
LPs:
Carols

GOING AWAY
(Foggatt)
Recorded: 11 October 1972
LPs:
The 31st Of February Street

GOIN' HOME
(Herring)
Recorded: 17 January 1977
LPs:
Small Corners

GOOD GOLLY MISS MOLLY
(Blackwell/Marascalco/Martinez)
Recorded: 5 February 1967
LPs:
Don't Stop Me Now

The Best Of Cliff Richard And
   The Shadows
From A Distance The Event
Videos:
From A Distance The Event

GOOD NEWS
(Traditional – Arranged
   Leander)
Recorded: 13 May 1967
LPs:
Good News
One Hour Of Cliff Richard

GOOD OLD ROCK 'N' ROLL
Recorded: 7/8 October 1974
LPs:
Japan Tour

GOOD ON THE SALLY ARMY
(Shiers)
Recorded: 19 January 1977
Singles:
Yes He Lives/GOOD ON THE
   SALLY ARMY
LPs:
Small Corners

GOOD TIMES (BETTER TIMES)
(Lordan/Cook/Greenaway)
Recorded: 31 January 1969
Singles:
GOOD TIMES/Occasional Rain
LPs:
The Best Of Cliff Volume 2

**GOODBYE SAM, HELLO
SAMANTHA**
(Murray/Callender/Stephens)
Recorded: 12 March 1970
Singles:
GOODBYE SAM, HELLO
   SAMANTHA/You Can Never Tell
LPs:
The Best Of Cliff Volume 2

40 Golden Greats
Live In Japan
Japan Tour
The Best Of Cliff Richard And
   The Shadows

**GOODBYE SAM
DAS IST DIE LIEBE**
(Murray/Callender/Stephens/
   Schauble)
Recorded: 29 June 1970
Foreign release

GOT A FUNNY FEELING
(Marvin/Welch)
Recorded: 19 April 1961
Singles:
When The Girl In Your Arms
   (Is The Girl In Your Heart)/GOT
   A FUNNY FEELING
EPs:
Hits From The Young Ones
LPs:
The Young Ones
One Hour Of Cliff Richard
Videos:
The Young Ones

GOT TO GET YOU INTO MY LIFE
(Unknown)
No known recording, but sung
   in concert

GREAT BALLS OF FIRE
(Blackwell/Hammer)
Recorded: September 1972
LPs:
Live in Japan

GREEN LIGHT
(Tarney)
Recorded: 17 April 1978
Singles:
GREEN LIGHT/Imagine Love

LPs:
Green Light
Dressed For The Occasion
From The Heart
Private Collection
The Hit List

GRETNA GREEN
(Olden/Hertha)
Foreign release

GUITAR MAN
(Hubbard)
No known recording, but sung
   in concert

GYPSY BUNDLE
(Rice/Farrar)
Recorded: 1995
LPs:
Songs From Heathcliff

GUT DASS ES FREUNDE GIBT
(Fletcher/Flett/Kunze)
Recorded: 21 March 1973
Singles:
GUT DASS ES FREUNDE GIBT/
   Ein Spiel Ohne Grenzen
LPs:
Seine Grossen Erfolge

H

HAD TO BE
(Rice/Farrar)
Recorded: 1995
Singles:
HAD TO BE (album version)/HAD
   TO BE (live)/Interview
HAD TO BE (album version)/HAD
   TO BE (instrumental)/Don't
   Move Away
LPs:
Songs From Heathcliff

HANDLE MY HEART WITH LOVE
(Daniels/Thomson)
Recorded: May/June 1992
LPs:
  The Album
Videos:
  Access All Areas

HANG ON TO A DREAM
(Hardin)
Recorded: 15 January 1967
LPs:
  Don't Stop Me Now
  Cliff In Japan

**HANG UP MY ROCK
AND ROLL SHOES**
(Unknown)
Unreleased Radio Luxembourg
  recording

(YOU KEEP ME) HANGIN' ON
(Mize/Allen)
Recorded: 11 February 1973
Singles:
  (YOU KEEP ME) HANGIN' ON/
  Love Is Here
LPs:
  Japan Tour
  40 Golden Greats
  30th Anniversary Picture
  Collection

HAPPY BIRTHDAY TO YOU
(Hill)
Recorded: 28 July 1961
LPs:
  21 Today

HAPPY WORLD
(Unknown)
Recorded: 11 January 1969
Not Released

**HAVE A LITTLE TALK
WITH MYSELF**
(Unknown)
Recorded: October 1972
LPs:
  Live In Japan

**HAVE A SMILE FOR
EVERYONE YOU MEET**
(Rule/Cunningham/Brennan)
Recorded: 9 August 1961
LPs:
  The Young Ones
Videos:
  The Young Ones

**HAVE I TOLD YOU LATELY
THAT I LOVE YOU**
(Wiseman)
Recorded: 10 May 1965
LPs:
  Love Is Forever
  Everybody Needs Somebody
  The Best Of Cliff Richard And
  The Shadows

**HAVE YOURSELF A MERRY
LITTLE CHRISTMAS**
(Martin/Blane)
Recorded: June/July 1991

LPs:
  Together
Videos:
  Together

HAVIN' FUN
(Marvin/Welch/Bennett/Rostill)
Recorded: 15 October 1964
EPs:
  Cliff's Hits From Aladdin And His
  Wonderful Lamp
LPs:
  Aladdin And His Wonderful Lamp

HEALING LOVE
(Kershaw/Morgan)
Recorded: October 1992
Singles:
  HEALING LOVE/Yesterday's
  Memories/Carrie
  HEALING LOVE/Carrie/Daddy's
  Home/Some People
LPs:
  The Album
Videos:
  The Story So Far

HEART USER
(Britten/Shifrin)
Recorded: July 1984
Singles:
  HEART USER/I Will Follow You
  HEART USER/I Will Follow You/
  HEART USER (extended mix)
LPs:
  The Rock Collection
  Private Collection
  From The Heart

HEARTBEAT
(Montgomery/Petty)
Recorded: 15 January 1967
LPs:
  Don't Stop Me Now

HEARTBREAK HOTEL

(Axton/Durden/Presley)

No known recording, but sung
in concert

HELP

(Lennon/McCartney)

Recorded: 2/3 December 1968

Not released

HELP IT ALONG

(Neil)

Recorded: 28 December 1972

Singles:

HELP IT ALONG/Tomorrow
Rising/Days Of Love/Ashes
To Ashes

LPs:

Help It Along

HERE COMES SUMMER

(Keller)

Recorded: 6 September 1959

EPs:

Cliff Sings No. 1

LPs:

Cliff Sings

Videos:

The Story So Far

HERE (SO DOGGONE BLUE)

(Tarney)

Recorded: May/June 1980

LPs:

I'm No Hero

HE'S EVERYTHING TO ME

(Carmichael)

Recorded: Date Unknown

LPs:

His Land

Videos:

His Land

HE'S GOT THE WHOLE WORLD

(Unknown)

Bootleg LPs:

Imagine (live version, 1968)

HEY DOCTOR MAN

(Marvin/Welch/Bennett/Rostill)

Recorded: 16 November 1966

EPs:

Cinderella

LPs:

Cinderella

HEY EVERYBODY

(Unknown)

Unreleased Radio Luxembourg
recording

HEY MISTER

(Tarney)

Recorded: March-May 1989

Singles:

Lean On You/HEY MISTER

Lean On You/HEY MISTER/Lean
On You (extended mix)

HEY MR DREAM MAKER

(Tarney/Welch)

Recorded: 18 September 1976

Singles:

HEY MR DREAM MAKER/No One
Waits

LPs:

Every Face Tells A Story

Videos:

The Video Connection

HEY WATCHA SAY

(Herring/Ward/Ward)

Recorded: 19 January 1977

LPs:

Small Corners

HIGH CLASS BABY

(Samwell)

Recorded: 3 October 1958

Singles:

HIGH CLASS BABY/My Feet Hit
The Ground

The Best Of Me/Move It/Lindsay
Jane/HIGH CLASS BABY

LPs:

The Rock 'n' Roll Era: Cliff Richard
1958–1963

Rock On With Cliff Richard

The Best Of Cliff Richard And
The Shadows

HIGH 'N' DRY

(Cook/Greenaway)

Recorded: 2 February 1968

Singles:

Congratulations/HIGH 'N' DRY

Que Buena Suerte/HIGH 'N' DRY

EPs:

Congratulations

HIGH SCHOOL CONFIDENTIAL

(Lewis/Hargrave)

Recorded: 21 October 1958

LPs:

Oh Boy

HIGHER GROUND

(Traditional – Arranged Mackay)

Recorded: September 1973

LPs:

Help It Along

Japan Tour

Hymns And Inspirational Songs

HIS LAND

(Carmichael)

Recorded: Date Unknown

LPs:

His Land

Videos:

His Land

HIS LATEST FLAME
(Pomus/Shuman)
Recorded: 7/8 October 1974
LPs:
Japan Tour

HIS LOVE COVERS YOUR SIN
(Unknown)
No known recording, but sung
in concert

HITCHIN A RIDE
(Unknown)
Bootleg LPs:
Imagine (live version, 1970)

HOLD ON
(Tarney)
Recorded: May/June 1980
Singles:
Wired For Sound/HOLD ON
LPs:
Silver

HOLD ON
(Britten/Shifrin)
Recorded: May/June 1983
LPs:
Silver

HOLD US TOGETHER
(Richard/Moessl)
Recorded: May/June 1992
LPs:
The Album

HOME
(Myers/Cass)
Recorded: 22 April 1964
EPs:
Hits From Wonderful Life
LPs:
Wonderful Life
Videos:
Wonderful Life

HOMEWARD BOUND
(Simon)
Recorded: 19 October 1966
LPs:
Don't Stop Me Now

HONKY TONK ANGEL
(Seals/Rice)
Recorded: 20 June 1974
Singles:
HONKY TONK ANGEL/(Wouldn't
You Know It) Got Myself A Girl

HOT SHOT
(Britten/Robertson)
Recorded: January 1979
Singles:
HOT SHOT/Walking In The Light
LPs:
Rock 'n' Roll Juvenile
My Kinda Life

HOUSE WITHOUT WINDOWS
(Tobias/Pockriss)
Recorded: 24 July 1964
LPs:
Cliff Richard
When In Rome
All My Love

HOW GREAT THOU ART
(Hine)
No known recording, but sung
in concert

HOW LONG IS FOREVER
(McDevitt/Douglas)
Recorded: 5 December 1961
LPs:
32 Minutes And 17 Seconds
It'll Be Me

HOW TO HANDLE A WOMAN
(Unknown)
Recorded: March 1983

Not released

HOW WONDERFUL TO KNOW
(D'Esposito/Goell)
Recorded: 30 January 1961
EPs:
Cliff Richard No. 1
LPs:
21 Today
How Wonderful To Know

HUMAN WORK OF ART
(Leeson/Vale)
Recorded: May/June 1992
Singles:
HUMAN WORK OF ART/Ragged
HUMAN WORK OF ART/Move It/
Never Even Thought
HUMAN WORK OF ART/Devil
Woman/Ragged/Free
LPs:
The Album
Videos:
Access All Areas
The Story So Far

I

I AIN'T GOT TIME ANYMORE
(Leander/Seago)
Recorded: 12 March 1970
Singles:
I AIN'T GOT TIME ANYMORE/
Monday Comes Too Soon
LPs:
The Best Of Cliff Volume 2

I CANNOT FIND A TRUE LOVE
(Samwell)
Recorded: 30 March 1960
Singles:
Gee Whiz It's You/I CANNOT
FIND A TRUE LOVE
EPs:
Me And My Shadows No. 1

LPs:

Me And My Shadows

I CAN'T ASK FOR ANY
MORE THAN YOU

(Gold/Denne)

Recorded: 8 September 1975

Singles:

I CAN'T ASK FOR ANYTHING
MORE THAN YOU/Junior
Cowboy

LPs:

I'm Nearly Famous

40 Golden Greats

I COULD EASILY FALL
(IN LOVE WITH YOU)

(Marvin/Welch/Bennett/Rostill)

Recorded: 15 October 1964

Singles:

I COULD EASILY FALL (IN LOVE
WITH YOU)/I'm In Love With You
From A Distance/I COULD EASILY
FALL (IN LOVE WITH YOU)

EPs:

Cliff's Hits From Aladdin And His
Wonderful Lamp

LPs:

Aladdin And His Wonderful Lamp

More Hits By Cliff

40 Golden Greats

Love Songs

20 Original Greats

One Hour Of Cliff Richard

The Best Of Cliff Richard And
The Shadows

The Hit List

Videos:

Cliff And The Shadows Together
1984

From A Distance The Event

ICH KANN TREU SEIN

(Diamond/Maat)

Singles:

Man Gratuliert Mir/ICH KANN
TREU SEIN

LPs:

When In Germany Volume 2

ICH TRAUME DEINE TRAUME

(Olden/Hertha)

Singles:

ICH TRAUME DEINE TRAUME/
Das Girl Von Nebenan

LPs:

Sein Grossen Erfolgen

Ich Traume Deine Traume

I DON'T KNOW

(Samwell)

Recorded: 15 March 1960

EPs:

Me And My Shadows No. 3

LPs:

Me And My Shadows

I DON'T KNOW WHY

(Turk/Ahlert)

Recorded: 10 September 1959

EPs:

Cliff Sings No. 4

LPs:

Cliff Sings

I DON'T LOVE YOU ISABELLA

(Rice/Farrar)

Recorded: 1995

Singles:

The Wedding/Sleep Of The Good
(live)/I DON'T LOVE YOU
ISABELLA/I DON'T LOVE
YOU ISABELLA (instrumental)

LPs:

Songs From Heathcliff

I DON'T WANNA LOVE YOU

(Mann/Weil)

Recorded: August 1964

LPs:

Cliff Richard

All My Love

IF EVER I WOULD LEAVE YOU

(Loew/Lerner)

LPs:

Live At The Talk Of The Town

I FOUND A ROSE

(Tepper/Bennett)

Recorded: 12 December 1962

LPs:

Love Is Forever

Everybody Needs Somebody

IF YOU WALKED AWAY

(Pomeranz)

Recorded: 2 December 1975

LPs:

I'm Nearly Famous

I GET THE FEELIN'

(Diamond)

Recorded: 24 April 1967

Singles:

I'll Come Running/I Got The
Feelin'

I GOT A FEELING

(Night)

Recorded: 9 February 1959

EPs:

Cliff No. 1

LPs:

Cliff

I GOTTA KNOW

(Williams/Evans)

Recorded: 6 September 1959

EPs:

Cliff Sings No. 1

LPs:

Cliff Sings

I GOT A WOMAN
(Charles)
Recorded: 7 March 1962
Not released

I JUST DON'T HAVE THE HEART
(Stock/Aitken/Waterman)
Recorded: 1989
Singles:
I JUST DON'T HAVE THE HEART/
Wide Open Space
I JUST DON'T HAVE THE HEART/
Wide Open Space/I JUST
DON'T HAVE THE HEART
(instrumental)
LPs:
Stronger
The Hit List
Videos:
From A Distance The Event
The Story So Far
The Hit List

I LIVE FOR YOU
(Chester/Marvin)
Recorded: 1 April 1960
LPs:
Listen To Cliff

I LOVE
(Wall/Wild)
Recorded: 19 January 1977
LPs:
Small Corners

I LOVE THE WAY YOU ARE
(Unknown)
Not released

I LOVE YOU
(Welch)
Recorded: 9 September 1960
Singles:
I LOVE YOU/D' In Love
This New Year/I LOVE YOU/
Scarlet Ribbons/We Don't Talk
Anymore
EPs:
Cliff's Hit Parade
LPs:
Cliff's Hit Album
From The Heart
Cliff In The 60s
The Rock 'n' Roll Era: Cliff Richard
1958–1963
The Best Of Cliff Richard And
The Shadows
The Story So Far
The Hit List
Videos:
Cliff And The Shadows Together
1984
Together
The Hit List Live

I LOVE YOU SO
(Samwell/Harris/Richard)
Recorded: 17 March 1960
EPs:
Me And My Shadows No. 3
LPs:
Me And My Shadows

I'M IN LOVE WITH YOU
(Marvin/Welch/Bennett/Rostill)
Singles:
I Could Easily Fall (In Love With
You)/I'M IN LOVE WITH YOU
LPs:
Aladdin And His Wonderful Lamp

I'M WALKING THE BLUES
(Tepper/Bennett)
Recorded:
EPs:
Time For Cliff And The
Shadows
LPs:
32 Minutes And 17 Seconds
It'll Be Me
One Hour Of Cliff Richard

I NEED LOVE
(Wilson)
Recorded: June 1991
LPs:
The Album

IN THE BLEAK MID-WINTER
(Holst)
Recorded: 10 September 1967
EPs:
Carol Singers
LPs:
Carols
Videos:
Christmas With Cliff Richard

I ONLY CAME TO SAY GOODBYE
(Grant/Guthrie)
Recorded: 17 November 1963
EPs:
Angel
LPs:
Cliff Richard
All My Love

I ONLY HAVE EYES FOR YOU
(Dubin/Warren)
Recorded: 28 December 1962
EPs:
Love Songs
LPs:
The EP Collection

I ONLY KNOW I LOVE YOU

(Unknown)

Not released

I ONLY LIVE TO LOVE YOU

(Unknown)

Not released

I SAW HER STANDING THERE

(Lennon/McCartney)

Recorded: 21 September 1966

LPs:

Don't Stop Me Now

I SAW THE LIGHT

(Unknown)

No known recording, but sung
    in concert

I STILL BELIEVE IN YOU

(Pomeranz/Pitchford)

Recorded: 14 September 1992

Singles:

I STILL BELIEVE IN YOU/Bulange
    Downpour

I STILL BELIEVE IN YOU/Bulange
    Downpour/There's No Power
    In Pity

I STILL BELIEVE IN YOU/
    Remember (When Two Worlds
    Drift Apart – French
    adaptation)/Ocean Deep

LPs:

The Album

Videos:

Access All Areas

I STILL SEND HER FLOWERS

(Unknown)

Not released

I'VE GOT GOD

(Unknown)

No known recording, but sung
    in concert

I'VE JUST REALISED

(Unknown)

No known recording, but sung
    in concert

I WAKE UP CRYING

(Bacharach/David)

Recorded: 4 December 1961

LPs:

32 Minutes And 17 Seconds

It'll Be Me

I WALK ALONE

(Unknown)

LPs:

Love Is Forever

I WANT TO HOLD YOUR HAND

(Lennon/McCartney)

No known recording, but sung
    in concert

I WANT YOU TO KNOW

(Bartholomew/Domino)

Recorded: 4 March 1961

LPs:

Listen To Cliff

I WAS ONLY FOOLING MYSELF

(Unknown)

Recorded: 16 November 1970

Singles:

Sunny Honey Girl/Don't Move
    Away/I WAS ONLY FOOLING
    MYSELF

I WHO HAVE NOTHING

(Unknown)

Recorded: 5 March 1971

Not released

I WILL ARISE AND GO

(Unknown)

Recorded: 11 January 1969

Not released

I WILL FOLLOW YOU

(Richard)

Recorded: 24 June 1984

Singles:

Heart User/I WILL FOLLOW YOU

Heart User/I WILL FOLLOW YOU/
    Heart User (extended mix)

LPs:

Mission England Volume 2

It's A Small World

I WISH WE'D ALL BEEN READY

(Norman)

LPs:

Small Corners

Live And Guaranteed

Videos:

Christmas With Cliff Richard

Live And Guaranteed 1988

**I WISH YOU'D CHANGE
YOUR MIND**

(Britten)

Recorded: 4 December 1975

LPs:

I'm Nearly Famous

I WONDER

(Richard/Marvin)

Recorded: 8 March 1963

Singles:

Lucky Lips/I WONDER

EPs:

Cliff's Lucky Lips

I'D JUST BE FOOL ENOUGH

(Endsley)

Recorded: 1 June 1967

LPs:

Tracks 'n' Grooves

IDLE GOSSIP

(Meyer/Huddleston)

Recorded: 17 November 1960

EPs:

Listen To Cliff No. 2

LPs:

Listen To Cliff

IF EVER I SHOULD LEAVE YOU

(Loewe/Lerner)

Recorded: 30 May 1968

LPs:

Live At The Talk Of The Town

IF I DO

(Unknown)

Recorded: 24 October 1968

Not released

IF I GIVE MY HEART TO YOU

(Crane/Jacobs/Brewster)

EPs:

Look In My Eyes Maria

LPs:

The EP Collection

IL FAUT CHANTER LA VIE

(Fletcher/Flett/Jourdan)

Recorded: 23 March 1973

Singles:

IL FAUT CHANTER LA VIE/Come
Back Billie Joe

LPs:

When In France

IL MONDO ET TONDO

(Unknown)

Recorded: 3 May 1968

Italian release

I'LL BE BACK

(Lennon/McCartney)

Recorded: 19 September 1966

LPs:

Don't Stop Me Now

I'LL BE WAITING

(Unknown)

Not released

I'LL COME RUNNING

(Diamond)

Recorded: 24 April 1967

Singles:

I'LL COME RUNNING/I Get The
Feelin'

LPs:

Cliff In Japan

The Best Of Cliff

**I'LL LOVE YOU
FOREVER TODAY**

(Richard/Collier)

Recorded: 1 July 1967

Singles:

I'LL LOVE YOU FOREVER TODAY/
Girl You'll Be A Woman Soon

LPs:

Two A Penny

The Best Of Cliff Volume 2

Videos:

Two A Penny

I'LL MAKE IT ALL UP TO YOU

(Rich)

Recorded: 24 April 1967

LPs:

Tracks 'n' Grooves

**I'LL MEND YOUR
BROKEN HEART**

(Everly)

Recorded: 5 October 1982

LPs:

Phil Everly

I'LL SEE YOU IN MY DREAMS

(Kahn/Jones)

Recorded: 4 May 1961

EPs:

Dream

I'LL STRING ALONG WITH YOU

(Dubin/Warren)

Recorded: 9 September 1959

EPs:

Cliff Sings No. 3

LPs:

Cliff Sings

I'LL TRY

(Twitty/Nance)

Recorded: 21 October 1958

LPs:

Oh Boy!

I'LL WALK ALONE

(Cahn/Styne)

Recorded: 10 June 1965

LPs:

Love Is Forever

Everybody Needs Somebody

I'M 21 TODAY

(Traditional)

No known recording, but sung
in concert

I'M AFRAID TO GO HOME

(Geld/Udell)

Recorded: 24 July 1964

Singles:

The Twelfth Of Never/I'M AFRAID
TO GO HOME

EPs:

Why Don't They Understand

I'M ALIVE

(Ballard Jnr)

No known recording, but sung
in concert

I'M GONNA GET YOU

(Harris/Marvin/Samwell)

Recorded: 30 March 1960

EPs:

Me And My Shadows No. 1

LPs:
Me And My Shadows

I'M IN LOVE AGAIN
(Domino/Bartholomew)
Unreleased Radio Luxembourg
recording

**I'M IN LOVE WITH
MY TELEVISION**
(Unknown)
Videos:
The Story So Far

I'M IN LOVE WITH YOU
(Marvin/Welch/Bennett/Rostill)
Recorded: 15 October 1964
Singles:
I Could Easily Fall/I'M IN LOVE
WITH YOU
LPs:
Aladdin And His Wonderful Lamp

I'M IN THE MOOD FOR LOVE
(McHugh/Fields)
Recorded: 6 December 1962
EPs:
Love Songs
LPs:
Love Songs

**I'M LOOKING OUT
THE WINDOW**
(Niles)
Recorded: 11 December 1961
Singles:
I'M LOOKING OUT THE WINDOW/
Do You Wanna Dance
EPs:
Cliff's Hits
LPs:
Cliff's Hit Album
40 Golden Greats
Cliff In The 60s
30th Anniversary Picture

Collection
The Best Of Cliff Richard And
The Shadows
The Rock 'n' Roll Era: Cliff Richard
1958–1963
Videos:
The Story So Far
The Hit List

I'M NEARLY FAMOUS
(Allison/Sills)
Recorded: 2 December 1975
LPs:
I'm Nearly Famous
From The Heart
Videos:
Rock In Australia

I'M NO HERO
(Tarney/Spencer)
Recorded: May/June 1980
LPs:
I'm No Hero

I'M NOT GETTING MARRIED
(Hammond/Hazlewood)
Recorded: 31 January 1968
LPs:
Sincerely Cliff Richard

I'M ON MY WAY
(Tepper/Bennett)
Recorded: 18 January 1962
LPs:
32 Minutes And 17 Seconds
It'll Be Me

I'M THE LONELY ONE
(Mills)
Recorded: 23 November 1963
Singles:
I'M THE LONELY ONE/Watch
What You Do With My Baby
EPs:
Cliff's Palladium Successes

LPs:
More Hits By Cliff
20 Original Greats
Cliff In The 60s
30th Anniversary Picture
Collection

I'M WALKIN'
(Domino/Bartholomew)
Recorded: 8 September 1959
EPs:
Cliff Sings No. 2
LPs:
Cliff Sings

I'M WILLING TO LEARN
(Wise/Weisman)
Recorded: 24 June 1960
EPs:
Me And My Shadows No. 3
LPs:
Me And My Shadows

IMMAGINA UN GIORNO
(Unknown)
Singles:
IMMAGINA UN GIORNO/Oh No No

IMAGINE LOVE
(Tarney/Lordan)
Recorded: 30 March 1970
Singles:
Green Light/IMAGINE LOVE

IN THE COUNTRY
(Marvin/Welch/Bennett/Rostill)
Recorded: 16 November 1966
Singles:
IN THE COUNTRY/Finders
Keepers
All I Have To Do Is Dream/Miss
You Nights/True Love Ways/
PARTY MEGAMIX
LPs:
Cinderella

The Best Of Cliff
Japan Tour
40 Golden Greats
20 Original Greats
The Best Of Cliff Richard And
The Shadows
30th Anniversary Picture Collection
From A Distance The Event

IN THE NIGHT
(Bowkett)
Recorded: May/June 1980
LPs:
I'm No Hero

IN THE PAST
(Cahill)
Recorded: 2 July 1968
LPs:
Sincerely Cliff Richard

IN THE STARS
(Myers/Cass)
Recorded: 22 April 1964
EPs:
Wonderful Life No. 2
LPs:
Wonderful Life
Videos:
Wonderful Life

INDIFFERENCE
(Unknown)
Recorded: 30 June 1970
Not released

**INTO EACH LIFE SOME
RAIN MUST FALL**
(Roberts/Fisher)
Recorded: 10 May 1965
LPs:
Finders Keepers

IS THERE AN ANSWER
(Unknown)

Recorded: 24 March 1969
Not released

**IT CAME UPON THE
MIDNIGHT CLEAR**
(Unknown)
Recorded: 10 September 1967
Not released

**IT COULD ALREADY
BE TOMORROW**
(Unknown)
Not released

**IT HAS TO BE YOU,
IT HAD TO BE ME**
(Cooke/Field)
Recorded: January 1982
LPs:
Now You See Me Now You Don't
It's a Small World

IT IS NO SECRET
(Hamblen)
Recorded: 3 May 1967
LPs:
Good News
Hymns And Inspirational Songs
One Hour Of Cliff Richard
Videos:
The Story So Far

IT'LL BE ME
(Clement)
Recorded: 17 May 1962
Singles:
IT'LL BE ME/Since I Lost You
EPs:
Cliff's Hits
LPs:
32 Minutes and 17 Seconds
More Hits By Cliff
It'll Be Me
40 Golden Greats
Rock 'n' Roll Silver

Rock On With Cliff Richard
The Best of Cliff Richard And
The Shadows
The Rock 'n' Roll Era: Cliff Richard
1958–1963
The Hit List
The Hit List Live

IT'LL BE ME BABE
(Marvin/Farrar)
Recorded: 8 September 1976
LPs:
Every Face Tells A Story

IT MUST BE LOVE
(Unknown)
No known recording, but sung
in concert

IT'S ALL IN THE GAME
(Sigman/Dawes)
Recorded: 28 December 1962
Singles:
IT'S ALL IN THE GAME/Your Eyes
Tell On You
EPs:
Cliff's Lucky Lips
LPs:
More Hits By Cliff
40 Golden Greats
Love Songs
The Best Of Cliff Richard And
The Shadows
The Rock 'n' Roll Era: Cliff Richard
1958–1963
The Hit List
Videos:
Cliff And The Shadows Together
1984
Access All Areas

IT'S ALL OVER
(Everly)
Recorded: 11 October 1966

Singles:

IT'S ALL OVER/Why Wasn't I Born
Rich?

LPs:

The Best Of Cliff

Cliff In The 60s

The Best Of Cliff Richard And
The Shadows

IT'S IN EVERY ONE OF US

(Pomeranz)

Recorded: 10/11 June 1985

Singles:

IT'S IN EVERY ONE OF US/Alone
(instrumental)/IT'S IN EVERY
ONE OF US (choral version)

IT'S IN EVERY ONE OF US/IT'S IN
EVERY ONE OF US
(instrumental)/Alone

LPs:

Time

IT'S MY PARTY

(Crane/Gluck/Gold)

Recorded: 16/17 June 1989

LPs:

From A Distance The Event

IT'S NO USE PRETENDING

(Allison/Sills)

Recorded: 10 December 1975

LPs:

I'm Nearly Famous

IT'S NOT FOR ME TO SAY

(Stillman/Allen)

Recorded: 17 July 1964

LPs:

Cliff Richard

IT'S ONLY MAKE BELIEVE

(Unknown)

Not released

IT'S ONLY ME YOU'VE LEFT BEHIND

(Marvin/Farrar)

Recorded: 27 January 1975

Singles:

IT'S ONLY ME YOU'VE LEFT
BEHIND/You're The One

IT'S ONLY MONEY

(Cole)

Recorded: 26/27 May 1973

LPs:

Take Me High

Videos:

Take Me High

IT'S WONDERFUL TO BE YOUNG

(Bacharach/David)

Recorded: 11 August 1962

Singles:

IT'S WONDERFUL TO BE YOUNG

EPs:

A Forever Kind Of Love

IT'S YOU

(Chester/Welch)

Recorded: 28 July 1960

LPs:

Listen To Cliff

I'VE GOT CONFIDENCE

(Crouch)

Recorded: September 1973

Not released

I'VE GOT NEWS FOR YOU

(Stonehill)

Recorded: 17 January 1977

LPs:

Small Corners

I'VE SAID TOO MANY THINGS

(Marvin/Welch/Bennett/Rostill)

Recorded: 17 October 1964

LPs:

Aladdin And His Wonderful Lamp

I WANT YOU TO KNOW

(Bartholomew/Domino)

LPs:

Me And My Shadows

I WISH YOU'D CHANGE YOUR MIND

(Britten)

Recorded: 4 December 1975

LPs:

I'm Nearly Famous

I WILL FOLLOW YOU

(Unknown)

Singles:

Heart User/I WILL FOLLOW YOU

I WISH WE'D ALL BEEN READY

(Norman)

Recorded: 19 January 1977

LPs:

Small Corners

J

JAILHOUSE ROCK

(Lieber/Stoller)

Recorded: October 1972

LPs:

Live In Japan

J'ATTENDRAI

(Poterat/Olivieri)

Recorded: 6 August 1963

EPs:

When In France

LPs:

When In France

The EP Collection

JE SUIS FORMIDABLE

(Richard/Collier)

Recorded: 21 February 1969
LPs:
  When In France

JERUSALEM, JERUSALEM
  (Shemer – English Lyrics Newell)
  Recorded: Date Unknown
LPs:
  His Land
Videos:
  His Land

JESUS
  (Hamburger/Darjean)
  Recorded: 14 December 1971
Singles:
  JESUS/Mr Cloud
LPs:
  The Best Of Cliff Volume 2
  Help It Along
  Japan Tour

**JESUS ADDRESSES THE
CROWD ON THE HILLSIDE:**
MATTHEW 5: 1-17; 21-28; 38-48.
MATTHEW 6: 19-34. MATTHEW 7:
1-8; 13, 14: 24-29
  Recorded: 20 February 1970
LPs:
  About That Man

JESUS, CALL YOUR LAMBS
  (Unknown)
  Recorded: 1992/1993
LPs:
  Portrait

**JESUS IS BETRAYED
AND ARRESTED:**
LUKE 22: 1-6. JOHN 13: 1-19.
LUKE 22: 33, 34; 39-51; 54-62
  Recorded: 20 February 1970
LPs:
  About That Man

JESUS IS THE ANSWER
  (Crouch/Crouch)
Videos:
  Christmas With Cliff Richard

JESUS IS MY KIND OF PEOPLE
  (Weatherly)
LPs:
  Japan Tour
  Live At Spre-e

JESUS LOVES YOU
  (Richard)
  Recorded: September 1973
LPs:
  Help It Along

**JESUS RECRUITS HIS HELPERS
AND HEALS THE SICK:**
MARK 1: 12-2: 12
  Recorded: 20 February 1970
LPs:
  About That Man

JE T'AIME TOUJOURS CE JOUR
  (Richard/Collier)
LPs:
  When In France

JOANNA
  (Eaton)
  Recorded: March-May 1989
Singles:
  Stronger Than That/JOANNA
  Stronger Than That/JOANNA/
    Stronger Than That (extended
    mix)
LPs:
  Stronger
Videos:
  From A Distance The Event

**JOHN THE BAPTIST
POINTS OUT JESUS:**
JOHN 1: 19-51

Recorded: 20 February 1970
LPs:
  About That Man

JOHNNY
  (Unknown)
  Recorded: 8/9 January 1969
  Not released

JOHNNY WAKE UP TO REALITY
  (Unknown)
  Recorded: 8/9 January 1969
  Not released

JOIN THE BAND
  (Cole)
  Recorded: September 1973
LPs:
  Take Me High
Videos:
  Take Me High

JOSEPH
  (Britten)
  Recorded: 8 September 1976
LPs:
  Small Corners
  Carols

JOSHUAH
  (Lee/Arthurs)
  Recorded: 9 August 1961
LPs:
  The Young Ones
Videos:
  The Young Ones

JUNIOR COWBOY
  (Allison/Sills)
  Recorded: 4 December 1975
Singles:
  I Can't Ask For Anything More
    Than You/JUNIOR COWBOY
LPs:
  I'm Nearly Famous

JUST A CLOSER WALK WITH THEE

(Traditional – Arranged
  Ebbinghouse)
Recorded: 3 May 1967
LPs:
Good News
Hymns And Inspirational Songs

JUST A LITTLE BIT TOO LATE

(Marvin)
Recorded: 4 April 1965
Singles:
On My Word/JUST A LITTLE BIT
  TOO LATE

JUST ANOTHER GUY

(Diamond)
Recorded: August 1964
Singles:
The Minute You're Gone/JUST
  ANOTHER GUY

JUST DANCE

(Myers/Cass)
LPs:
The Young Ones
Videos:
The Young Ones

K

KANSAS CITY

(Unknown)
Unreleased Radio Luxembourg
  recording

KEEP ME WARM

(Tarney)
Recorded: March-May 1989
LPs:
Stronger

KEEP ME WHERE LOVE IS

(Collier/Carmichael)

Recorded: Date Unknown
LPs:
His Land
Videos:
His Land

KEEP ON LOOKING

(Tarney)
Recorded: 8 July 1980
Singles:
A Little In Love/KEEP ON
  LOOKING

KEEP ON KNOCKING

(Unknown)
No known recording, but sung
  in concert

KING CREOLE

(Lieber/Stoller)
Recorded: 21 October 1958
LPs:
Oh Boy!

KISS

(Gillespie/Newman)
LPs:
Cliff Richard

KISSES SWEETER THAN WINE

(Unknown)
Not released

KLEINE TAUBE

(Fletcher/Flett/Kunze)
Recorded: 23 August 1971
Singles:
Wenn Du Lachst, Lacht Das
  Gluck/KLEINE TAUBE
LPs:
When In Germany Volume 2

L

LA BALLADE DE BALTIMORE

(Riviere/Maryland)
Recorded: 2 June 1971
Singles:
LA BALLADE DE BALTIMORE/
  L'Amandier Sauvage
LPs:
When In France

LA GONAVE

(Richard)
Recorded: 24 June 1984
Singles:
Mistletoe And Wine/Marmaduke/
  Little Town/LA GONAVE
LPs:
The Rock Connection
It's A Small World
From The Heart

LA LA LA LA LA

(Paul)
Recorded: 11 October 1966
EPs:
La La La La La
LPs:
Cliff In Japan
Live At The Talk Of The Town
The EP Collection

LA LA LA SONG

(Marvin/Welch/Bennett/Rostill)
Recorded: 28 April 1966

LPs:

Finders Keepers

LA MER

(Trenet)

Recorded: 5 August 1963

EPs:

When In France

LPs:

When In France

The EP Collection

LADY CAME FROM BALTIMORE

(Hardin)

Recorded: 30 May 1968

LPs:

Live At The Talk Of The Town

L'AMANDIER SAUVAGE

(Dousset/Bonnes)

Recorded: 2 June 1971

Singles:

La Ballade De Baltimore/

L'AMANDIER SAUVAGE

LPs:

When In France

LAMP OF LOVE

(Tepper/Bennett)

Recorded: 30 March 1960

EPs:

Me And My Shadows No. 2

LPs:

Me And My Shadows

LANGUAGE OF LOVE

(Britten/Robertson)

Recorded: January 1979

LPs:

Rock 'n' Roll Juvenile

My Kinda Life

**LASS UNS SCHNELL
VERGESSEN**

(Goffin/Keller/Olden)

Recorded: 24 November 1970

LPs:

Ich Traume Deine Traume

LAWDY MISS CLAWDY

(Price)

Recorded: Mid-1958

Not Released

LEAN ON YOU

(Tarney)

Recorded: March-May 1989

Singles:

LEAN ON YOU/Hey Mister

LEAN ON YOU/Hey Mister/LEAN

ON YOU (extended mix)

LPs:

Stronger

My Kinda Life

**LEARNING HOW TO
ROCK 'N' ROLL**

(McCulloch)

Recorded: July 1984

LPs:

The Rock Connection

Videos:

Rock In Australia

LEAVE MY WOMAN ALONE

(Charles)

Recorded: 10 October 1968

Singles:

The Joy Of Living/LEAVE MY

WOMAN ALONE/Boogatoo

LEFT OUT AGAIN

(Chester)

Recorded: 16 March 1960

EPs:

Me And My Shadows No. 2

LPs:

Me And My Shadows

**LEGATA AD UN GRANELLO
DI SABBIA**

(Marchetti/Fidenco)

Recorded: 2 October 1964

LPs:

When In Rome

LESSONS IN LOVE

(Soloway/Wolfe)

Recorded: 11 August 1961

EPs:

Hits From The Young Ones

LPs:

The Young Ones

Videos:

The Young Ones

LET THE GOOD TIMES ROLL

(Unknown)

Unreleased Radio Luxembourg

recording

LET US TAKE YOU FOR A RIDE

(Myers/Cass)

LPs:

Summer Holiday

Videos:

Summer Holiday

LET'S HAVE A PARTY

(Robinson)

Recorded: 16/17 June 1989

Singles:

Saviours Day/Oh Boy! Medley

Saviours Day/Oh Boy! Medley/

Where Are You

LPs:

From A Distance The Event

LET'S MAKE A MEMORY

(Crompton)

Recorded: 4 December 1961

Singles:

Rote Lippen Sol Man Kussen/

LET'S MAKE A MEMORY

LPs:

32 Minutes And 17 Seconds

Cliff In Japan

It'll Be Me

LET'S STICK TOGETHER

(Unknown)

Not released

**LIEBEN KANN MAN
EINMAL NUR**

(Last/Relin)

Singles:

Du, Du Gefalst Mir Sol/LIEBEN
KANN MAN EINMAL NUR

LPs:

When In Germany Volume 2

LIEBESLEID

(Lordan/Franklin/Olden)

Recorded: 24 June 1974

Singles:

Es Gehoren Zwei Zum
Glucklichsein/LIEBESLEID

LPs:

When In Germany Volume 2

LIES AND KISSES

(Hunter/Heard/Boulanger)

Recorded: 19 August 1964

EPs:

Take Four

LIFE

(Cole)

Recorded: 26/27 May 1973

LPs:

Take Me High

Videos:

Take Me High

LINDSAY JANE

(Richard)

Recorded: March-May 1989

Singles:

The Best Of Me/Move It/

LINDSAY JANE

The Best Of Me/Move It/LINDSAY
JANE/High Class Baby

LINDSAY JANE II

(Richard)

Recorded: July 1990

Singles:

From A Distance/LINDSAY JANE II

From A Distance/LINDSAY JANE
II/Wired For Sound

LITTLE BITTY PRETTY ONE

(Byrd)

Recorded: May/June 1983

LPs:

Rock 'n' Roll Silver

LITTLE MISTREATER

(Wilson/Gorrie/Pigott)

Recorded: June 1991

LPs:

The Album

Videos:

Access All Areas

The Story So Far

LITTLE RAG DOLL

(Leander)

Recorded: 11 February 1968

EPs:

Congratulations

LPs:

The EP Collection

LITTLE THINGS MEAN A LOT

(Stutz/Lindeman)

Recorded: 9 September 1959

EPs:

Cliff Sings No. 4

LPs:

Cliff Sings

LITTLE TOWN

(Traditional-Arranged Eaton)

Recorded: January 1982

Singles:

LITTLE TOWN/Love And A Helping
Hand/You Me And Jesus

Mistletoe And Wine/Marmaduke/
LITTLE TOWN

Mistletoe And Wine/Marmaduke/
LITTLE TOWN/La Gonave

LPs:

Now You See Me Now You Don't

Carols

Private Collection

30th Anniversary Picture
Collection

Together

LIVE-IN WORLD

(Unknown)

Recorded: 7 September 1986

Singles:

LIVE-IN WORLD/unknown

LIVIN' LOVIN' DOLL

(May/Gustard)

Recorded: 14 November 1958

Singles:

LIVIN' LOVIN' DOLL/Steady With
You

LPs:

The Best Of Cliff Richard And
The Shadows

LIVING DOLL

(Bart)

Recorded: 28 April 1959

Singles:

LIVING DOLL/Apron Strings

LIVING DOLL (with The Young
Ones)/Happy

LIVING DOLL (with The Young
Ones)/Happy/Disco Funk Get
Up Get Down

Peace In Our Time (7" remix)/
Peace In Our Time (Gospel
mix)/LIVING DOLL/Peace In

Our Time (instrumental)

EPs:

Serious Charge

LPs:

Cliff's Hit Album

The Young Ones

Live In Japan

Cliff In Japan

40 Golden Greats

From The Heart

30th Anniversary Picture
Collection

Rock On With Cliff Richard

The Best Of Cliff Richard And
The Shadows

Utterly Utterly Live

The Rock 'n' Roll Era: Cliff Richard
1958–1963

The Hit List

Live And Guaranteed

Videos:

Serious Charge

The Young Ones

Rock In Australia

Cliff And The Shadows Together
1984

Live And Guaranteed 1988

When The Music Stops

Access All Areas

The Story So Far

The Hit List

The Hit List Live

LIVING IN HARMONY

(Tarney/Spencer)

Recorded: 4 July 1972

Singles:

LIVING IN HARMONY/Empty
Chairs

LPs:

Live in Japan

30th Anniversary Picture
Collection

LOCKED INSIDE YOUR PRISON

(Headly)

Recorded: May/June 1983

LPs:

Silver

LONDON IST NICHT WEIT

(Marvin/Bradtke)

Recorded: 15 March 1968

Singles:

LONDON IST NICHT WEIT/Mrs
Emily Jones

LPs:

When In Germany Volume 2

LONDON'S NOT TOO FAR

(Marvin)

Recorded: 8 March 1968

LPs:

Sincerely Cliff

Live At The Talk Of The Town

LONELY GIRL

(Leander/Richard)

Recorded: 8 March 1968

LPs:

Two A Penny

Videos:

Two A Penny

LONG AGO (AND FAR AWAY)

(Gershwin/Kern)

Recorded: 10 June 1965

LPs:

Love Is Forever

Everybody Needs Somebody

LONG LONG TIME

(White)

Recorded: 13 February 1974

LPs:

The 31st Of February Street

LONG TALL SALLY

(Johnson/Penniman/Blackwell)

Bootleg LPs:

Imagine (live version, 1965)

LOOK BEFORE YOU LOVE

(Arnold/Morrow/Martin)

Recorded: 10 May 1965

Singles:

The Time In Between/LOOK
BEFORE YOU LOVE

EPs:

Wind Me Up

LOOK DON'T TOUCH

(Unknown)

Cliff At The Movies

LOOK HOMEWARD ANGEL

(Gold)

Recorded: 17 July 1964

LPs:

Love Is Forever

Everybody Needs Somebody

LOOK IN MY EYES MARIA

(Bacharach/David)

Recorded: 19 August 1964

EPs:

Look In My Eyes Maria

LPs:

The EP Collection

LORD I LOVE YOU

(Unknown)

No known recording, but sung
in concert

LOST IN A LONELY WORLD

(Eaton)

Recorded: May/July 1981

LPs:

Wired For Sound

Walking In The Light

LOVE

(Paramor/Lewis)
Recorded: 8 September 1959
EPs:
Expresso Bongo
Videos:
Expresso Bongo
Thank You Very Much
The Story So Far

LOVE AND A HELPING HAND

(Richard)
Recorded: June 1982
Singles:
Little Town/LOVE AND A HELPING
HAND/You Me And Jesus
LPs:
Walking In The Light

LOVE IS ENOUGH

(Moore)
Recorded: 27 January 1975
Singles:
Miss You Nights/LOVE IS ENOUGH

LOVE IS HERE

(Lordan/Franklin)
Recorded: 13 February 1974
Singles:
(You Keep Me) Hangin' On/LOVE
IS HERE

LOVE IS LIKE A CRESCENDO

(Unknown)
Recorded: 22 September 1969
Not released

LOVE IS MORE THAN WORDS

(Unknown)
Recorded: 2/3 December 1968
Not released

LOVE IS THE STRONGEST EMOTION

(Leeson/Vale)
Recorded: May/June 1992
LPs:
The Album
Videos:
Access All Areas

LOVE LETTERS

(Heyman/Young)
Recorded: 11 December 1961
EPs:
Love Songs
LPs:
The EP Collection

LOVE NEVER GIVES UP

LPs:
Dick Saunders 10th Annual Rally

LOVE ON (SHINE ON)

(Richard)
Recorded: 25 March 1976
Singles:
Devil Woman/LOVE ON
(SHINE ON)
Videos:
Access All Areas

LOVE'S SALVATION

(Richard/Moesel)
Recorded: May/June 1992
LPs:
The Album

LOVE STEALER

(Wainman/Myhill)
Recorded: May/June 1983
LPs:
Silver
Videos:
Rock In Australia

LOVE, TRUTH AND EMILY STONE

(Marvin/Lordan)
Recorded: 29 July 1969
LPs:
Tracks 'n' Grooves

LOVE YA

(Richard)
Recorded: April 1987

Singles:

My Pretty One/LOVE YA

My Pretty One/LOVE YA/Under
the Gun

LOVER

(Rodgers/Hart)

Recorded: 11 January 1961

EPs:

Listen To Cliff

LPs:

Listen To Cliff

LOVERS

(Newbury)

Recorded: 4 December 1975

LPs:

I'm Nearly Famous

LOVERS AND FRIENDS

(Trott/Sweet)

Recorded: July 1984

LPs:

The Rock Connection

Videos:

Rock In Australia

LOVING ME LORD FOREVER

(Unknown)

No known recording, but sung
in concert

LUCILLE

(Penniman/Collins)

Recorded: May/June 1983

Singles:

Never Say Die/LUCILLE

LPs:

Live in Japan

Rock 'n' Roll Silver

The Rock Connection

My Kinda Life

Videos:

Rock In Australia

LUCKY LIPS

(Lieber/Stoller)

Recorded: 8 March 1963

Singles:

LUCKY LIPS/I Wonder

EPs:

Cliff's Lucky Lips

LPs:

More Hits By Cliff

Cliff In Japan

40 Golden Greats

20 Original Greats

Cliff In The 60s

The Best Of Cliff Richard And
The Shadows

The Rock 'n' Roll Era: Cliff Richard
1958–1963

The Hit List

Videos:

Cliff And The Shadows Together
1984

The Hit List

The Hit List Live

M

MAD ABOUT YOU

(Bart)

Recorded: 28 April 1959

EPs:

Serious Charge

Videos:

Serious Charge

MAGIC IS THE MOONLIGHT

(Pasquale/Grever)

Recorded: 17 July 1964

LPs:

Cliff Richard

All My Love

**MAKE EVERYDAY A
CARNIVAL DAY**

(Marvin/Welch/Bennett/Rostill)

Recorded: 17 October 1964

LPs:

Aladdin And His Wonderful Lamp

MAKE IT EASY ON YOURSELF

(Bacharach/David)

Recorded: October 1974

LPs:

Japan Tour

MAKE ME NEW

(Unknown)

No known recording, but sung
in concert

MAKIN' HISTORY

(Griffiths/Lyle)

Recorded: May/June 1983

LPs:

Rock 'n' Roll Silver

The Rock Connection

MAMBO

(Black)

Recorded: 9 August 1961

LPs:

The Young Ones

Videos:

The Young Ones

MAN GRATULIERT MIR

(Martin/Coulter/Lambert/
Fleming)

Recorded: 9 April 1968

Singles:

MAN GRATULIERT MIR/Ich Kann
Treu Sein

LPs:

When In Germany Volume 2

Seine Grosen Erfolgen

MARKED WITH DEATH

(Rice/Farrar)

Recorded: 1995

LPs:

Songs From Healthcliff

MARIA
(Sondheim/Bernstein)
Recorded: 23 June 1964
EPs:
Look Into My Eyes Maria
LPs:
The EP Collection

MARIA NINGUEM
(Moore/Lyra)
Recorded: 2 October 1964
LPs:
When In Rome

MARIA NO MAS
(Salina/Lyra)
Recorded: 1 May 1963
LPs:
When In Spain

MARIANNE
(Endrigo/Feltz)
Recorded: 2 July 1968
Singles:
MARIANNE/Mr Nice
LPs:
The Best Of Cliff Volume 2
Hier Ist Cliff

MARMADUKE
(Tarney/Spencer)
Recorded: August 1988
Singles:
Mistletoe And Wine/
MARMADUKE
Mistletoe And Wine/
MARMADUKE/Little Town
Mistletoe And Wine/
MARMADUKE/Little Town/
La Gonave
Mistletoe And Wine/
MARMADUKE/True Love Ways

MARY WHAT YOU GONNA NAME THAT PRETTY LITTLE BABY
(King)
Recorded: 27 April 1967
LPs:
Good News
Carols

MAY THE GOOD LORD BLESS AND KEEP YOU
(Wilson)
Recorded: 3 May 1967
LPs:
Good News
Hymns And Inspirational Songs

MAYBE SOMEDAY
(Klevatt/Fialka)
Recorded: 23 November 1982
LPs:
Dressed For The Occasion

ME LO DIJO ADELA
(Portal)
Recorded: 30 April 1963
LPs:
When In Spain

ME AND MY SHADOWS
Unreleased Radio Luxembourg recording

MEAN STREAK
(Ralph/Samwell/Seener)
Recorded: 14 November 1958
Singles:
MEAN STREAK/Never Mind
LPs:
20 Original Greats
Rock On With Cliff Richard
The Rock 'n' Roll Era: Cliff Richard 1958–1963

MEAN WOMAN BLUES
(Demetrius)

Recorded: 7 September 1959
EPs:
Cliff Sings No. 2
LPs:
Cliff Sings

MEDITATION
(Jobim/Gimbel/Mendonca)
Recorded: 4 October 1965
LPs:
Kinda Latin

MEMORIES LINGER ON
(Chester/Welch)
Recorded: 28 July 1960
LPs:
Listen To Cliff

MICHELLE
(Unknown)
Recorded: 20 September 1960
Not released

MIDNIGHT BLUE
(Cole)
Recorded: 28/29 May 1973
LPs:
Take Me High
Videos:
Take Me High

MISS YOU NIGHTS
(Townsend)
Recorded: 9 September 1975
Singles:
MISS YOU NIGHTS/Love Is Enough
We Should Be Together/MISS YOU NIGHTS
We Should Be Together/ MISS YOU NIGHTS/Mistletoe And Wine
All I Have To Do Is Dream/ MISS YOU NIGHTS
All I Have To Do Is Dream/ MISS YOU NIGHTS/When Will I Be

Loved/Tribute To The Legends
All I Have To Do Is Dream/MISS
   YOU NIGHTS/True Love Ways/
   Party Megamix
MISS YOU NIGHTS (A cappella
   version)/Engraved Message
   from Cliff
(From A Distance – The Event
   Box Set only)
LPs:
   I'm Nearly Famous
   40 Golden Greats
   Thank You Very Much
   Love Songs
   Dressed For The Occasion
   From The Heart
   The Best Of Cliff Richard And
     The Shadows
   30th Anniversary Picture
     Collection
   The Hit List
   Live And Guaranteed
Videos:
   Thank You Very Much
   The Video Connection
   We Don't Talk Anymore/Miss
     You Nights
   Rock In Australia
   Live And Guaranteed 1988
   When The Music Stops
   From A Distance The Event
   Access All Areas
   The Story So Far
   The Hit List Live

MISTLETOE AND WINE
(Strachan/Stewart/Poole)
Recorded: June/July 1988
Singles:
   MISTLETOE AND WINE/
     Marmaduke
   MISTLETOE AND WINE/
     Marmaduke/Little Town
   MISTLETOE AND WINE/
     Marmaduke/Little Town/

La Gonave
MISTLETOE AND WINE/
   Marmaduke/True Love Ways
We Should Be Together/Miss
   You Nights/- MISTLETOE AND
   WINE
EPs:
   Christmas EP
LPs:
   Private Collection
   30th Anniversary Picture
     Collection
   Together
   Access All Areas
   The Hit List
Videos:
   Private Collection
   When The Music Stops
   Access All Areas
   The Story So Far
   The Hit List
   The Hit List Live

MISUNDERSTOOD MAN
(Rice/Farrar)
Recorded: 1995
Singles:
   MISUNDERSTOOD MAN (edit)/
     MISUNDERSTOOD MAN
     (instrumental)/
     MISUNDERSTOOD MAN
LPs:
   Songs From Healthcliff

**MOBILE ALABAMA SCHOOL
LEAVING HULLABALOO**
(Unknown)
Recorded: 11 July 1977
Not released

MONDAY COMES TOO SOON
(Unknown)
Recorded: 12 March 1970
Singles:
   I Ain't Got Time Anymore/

MONDAY COMES TOO SOON

MONDAY THRU FRIDAY
(Britten)
Recorded: July 1978
LPs:
   Rock 'n' Roll Juvenile
   My Kinda Life
Videos:
   Access All Areas

MONEY
(Unknown)
No known recording, but sung
   in concert

MOONLIGHT BAY
(Madden/Wenrich)
Recorded: 12 December 1962
EPs:
   Holiday Carnival
LPs:
   The EP Collection

MOON RIVER
(Unknown)
No known recording but sang in
   concert

MORE TO LIFE
(May/Read)
Recorded: June 1992
Singles:
   MORE TO LIFE/Mo's Theme
   (instrumental)
LPs:
   The Winner

MOVE IT
(Samwell)
Recorded: 24 July 1958
Singles:
   Schoolboy Crush/MOVE IT
   MOVE IT/Schoolboy Crush
   The Best Of Me/MOVE IT/

Lindsay Jane
The Best Of Me/MOVE IT/
   Lindsay Jane/High Class Baby
Human Work Of Art/MOVE IT/
   Never Even Thought
EPs:
Cliff No. 2
LPs:
Cliff
Cliff's Hit Album
Live In Japan
Don't Stop Me Now
Cliff In Japan
40 Golden Greats
Thank You Very Much
Rock 'n' Roll Silver
20 Original Greats
Rock On With Cliff Richard
The Best Of Cliff Richard And
   The Shadows
From The Heart
30th Anniversary Picture
   Collection
The Rock 'n' Roll Era: Cliff Richard
   1958–1963
From A Distance The Event
The Hit List
Videos:
Thank You Very Much
Cliff And The Shadows Together
   1984
From A Distance The Event
Access All Areas
The Story So Far
The Hit List
The Hit List Live

MOVING IN
(Richard)
Recorded: 26 October 1979
Singles:
Carrie/MOVING IN
LPs:
It's A Small World

MR BUSINESSMAN
(Stevens)
Recorded: September 1973
LPs:
Help It Along
One Hour Of Cliff Richard

MR CLOUD
(Fletcher/Flett)
Recorded: 28 April 1971
Singles:
Jesus/MR CLOUD

MR NICE
(Britten)
Recorded: 1 July 1968
Singles:
Marianne/MR NICE

MR NIEMAND
(Richard)
LPs:
Heir Ist Cliff

MRS EMILY JONES
(Parks/Flemming)
Recorded: 28 September 1967
Singles:
London Ist Nicht Weit/MRS
   EMILY JONES
LPs:
When In Germany Volume 2

MUDDY WATER
(Unknown)
Recorded: 11 January 1977
Not released

MUMBLIN' MOSIE
(Otis)
Recorded: 28 January 1961
Singles:
Theme For A Dream/MUMBLIN'
   MOSIE

MUST BE LOVE
(Britten)
Recorded: 9 September 1976
LPs:
Every Face Tells A Story

MY BABE
(Dixon/Stone)
Recorded: 9 February 1958
EPs:
Cliff No. 1
LPs:
Cliff
Don't Stop Me Now

MY BLUE HEAVEN
(Whiting/Donaldson)
Recorded: 19 April 1961
LPs:
21 Today
How Wonderful To Know

MY COLOURING BOOK
(Ebb/Kander)
Recorded: 23 June 1964
EPs:
Love Is Forever
LPs:
Love Is Forever
Everybody Needs Somebody

MY FEET HIT THE GROUND
(Samwell/Seener)
Recorded: 3 October 1958
Singles:
High Class Baby/MY FEET HIT
   THE GROUND
LPs:
Rock On With Cliff Richard

MY FOOLISH HEART
(Washington/Young)
Recorded: 10 June 1965
LPs:
Love Is Forever

Everybody Needs Somebody

MY HEAD GOES AROUND
(Goddard)
Recorded: 22 April 1969
LPs:
Tracks 'n' Grooves

MY HEART IS AN OPEN BOOK
(Pockriss/David)
Recorded: 19 August 1964
EPs:
Take Four
LPs:
The EP Collection

MY KINDA LIFE
(East)
Recorded: 10 January 1977

Singles:
MY KINDA LIFE/Nothing Left For
Me To Say
LPs:
Every Face Tells A Story
40 Golden Greats
The Best Of Cliff Richard And
The Shadows
My Kinda Life
Videos:
The Video Connection
Access All Areas
The Story So Far

MY LUCK WON'T CHANGE
(Britten/Robertson)
Recorded: January 1979
LPs:
Rock 'n' Roll Juvenile

MY ONE AND ONLY LOVE
(Unknown)
No known recording, but sung
in concert

MY PRETTY ONE
(Tarney)
Recorded: September 1986
Singles:
MY PRETTY ONE/Love Ya
MY PRETTY ONE/Love Ya/Under
The Gun
LPs:
Always Guaranteed
30th Anniversary Picture
Collection
Private Collection
Videos:
Always Guaranteed
Private Collection

MY SOUL IS MY WITNESS

(Unknown)

No known recording, but sung
  in concert

MY WAY

(Marvin/Welch/Bennet/Rostill)

Recorded: October 1972

LPs:

Live In Japan

N

**NARRATION AND
HALLELUJAH CHORUS**

(Handell-Arranged Carmichael)

LPs:

His Land

Videos:

His Land

**NEBEN DIR WIRD'S
KEINE GEBEN**

(Leander/Raschek)

Recorded: 25 November 1970

LPs:

Ich Traume Deine Traume

NEEDING A FRIEND

Recorded: 11 July 1977

Singles:

Can't Take The Hurt Anymore/
  NEEDING A FRIEND

NEL BLU DIPINTO DI BLU

(Modungno/Migliacci)

Recorded: 2 October 1964

EPs

When In Rome

LPs:

When In Rome

**NEVER BE ANYONE ELSE BUT
YOU**

(Knight)

Recorded: May/June 1983

LPs:

Rock 'n' Roll Silver

The Rock Connection

NEVER EVEN THOUGHT

(Head)

Recorded: 12 January 1978

Singles:

Human Work of Art/Move It/
  NEVER EVEN THOUGHT

LPs:

Green Light

My Kinda Life

**NEVER KNEW WHAT
LOVE COULD DO**

(Marvin/Rostill/Bennet)

Recorded: 21 September 1966

EPs:

La La La La La

NEVER LET GO

(Wilson/Gorrie)

Recorded: May/June 1992

Singles:

NEVER LET GO/Congratulations

NEVER LET GO/Congratulations/
  The Young Ones/You've Got
  Me Wondering

LPs:

The Album

NEVER MIND

(Samwell)

Recorded: 9 March 1959

Singles:

Mean Streak/NEVER MIND

LPs:

Rock On With Cliff Richard

**NEVER SAY DIE (GIVE
A LITTLE BIT MORE)**

(Britten/Shifrin)

Recorded: 21/22 May 1983

Singles:

NEVER SAY DIE/Lucille

LPs:

Silver

Private Collection

Videos:

The Video Connection

Private Collection

NIGHT TIME GIRL

(Unknown)

No known recording, but sung
  in concert

NINE TIMES OUT OF TEN

(Hall/Blackwell)

Recorded: 15 March 1960

Singles:

NINE TIMES OUT OF TEN/
  Thinking Of Our Love

EPs:

Cliff's Silver Discs

LPs:

Cliff's Hit Album

40 Golden Greats

20 Original Greats

Rock On With Cliff Richard

Cliff In The 60s

The Best Of Cliff Richard And
  The Shadows

The Rock 'n' Roll Era: Cliff Richard
  1958-1963

The Hit List

Videos:

The Hit List

The Hit List Live

NO MATTER WHAT

(Ashby)

Recorded: 25 February 1974

LPs:

The 31st Of February Street

NO NAME NO FAME

(Unknown)

Recorded: 2 May 1969
Not released

NO ONE SEEMS TO CARE
(Unknown)
Recorded: 2/3 December 1968
Not released

NO ONE WAITS
(Richard/Sherwood)
Recorded: 17 September 1976
Singles:
Hey Mr Dream Maker/NO ONE
WAITS

NO TURNING BACK
(Bart)
Recorded: 28 April 1959
EPs:
Serious Charge
Videos:
Serious Charge

NON DIMENTICARE CHI TI AMA
Recorded: 24 February 1969
Singles:
NON DIMENTICARE CHI TI AMA/
Chi Lo Sa

NON L'ASCOLTARE
(Richard/Welch/Cassia)
Recorded: 2 October 1964
LPs:
When In Rome

NOT BY MIGHT
(Unknown)
No known recording, but sung
in concert

**NOT THE WAY THAT IT
SHOULD BE**
(Marvin/Welch/Bennett)
Recorded: 10 June 1968
LPs:

Established 1958

NOTE IN A BOTTLE
(Unknown)
Recorded: 24 October 1968
Not released

NOTHING'S IMPOSSIBLE
(Myers/Cass)
Recorded: 9 August 1961
LPs:
The Young Ones
Videos:
The Young Ones

NOTHING LEFT FOR ME TO SAY
(Richard)
Recorded: 22 September 1976
Singles:
My Kinda Life/NOTHING LEFT
FOR ME TO SAY
LPs:
From The Heart

NOTHING TO REMIND ME
(Richard)
Recorded: 11 February 1973
LPs:
The 31st Of February Street

NOW I'VE DONE IT
(Unknown)
Recorded: 8/9 January 1969
Not released

NOW THAT YOU KNOW ME
(Unknown)
Recorded: January 1982
Not released

**NOW YOU SEE ME,
NOW YOU DON'T**
(John/Turner)
Recorded: January 1982
LPs:

Now You See Me, Now You Don't

NOWHERE MAN
(Lennon/McCartney)
Recorded: 11 January 1969
Not released

**NOW'S THE TIME TO
FALL IN LOVE**
(Welch/Chester)
Recorded: 20 September 1960
Singles:
A Girl Like You/NOW'S THE TIME
TO FALL IN LOVE

NUR BEI DIR BIN ICH ZU HAUS
(Tally/Siegel)
Recorded: 27 October 1965
Singles:
NUR BEI DIR BIN ICH ZU HAUS/
Glaub Nur Mir

NUR MIT DIR
(Marvin/Welch/Richard/Bradtke)
Recorded: 10 October 1964
Singles:
Das Ist Die Frage Aller Fragen/
NUR MIT DIR

O
—

**O COME ALL YE FAITHFUL
(VENITE)**
(Traditional-Arranged Eaton)
Recorded: June/July 1991
LPs:
Together
Videos:
Together

O LITTLE TOWN OF BETHLEHEM
(Traditional)
Recorded: 10 September 1967
EPs:
Carol Singers

LPs:
Carols
Videos:
Christmas With Cliff Richard

O MIO SIGNORE
(Vianello/Mogol)
Recorded: 2 October 1964
LPs:
When In Rome

OCCASIONAL RAIN
(Richey/Richey)
Recorded: 6 July 1968
Singles:
Good Time/OCCASIONAL RAIN

OCEAN DEEP
(Trott/Sweet)
Recorded: May/June 1983
Singles:
Baby You're Dynamite/OCEAN
DEEP
Baby You're Dynamite/OCEAN
DEEP/Baby You're Dynamite
(Extended Mix)
OCEAN DEEP/Baby You're
Dynamite
I Still Believe In You/Remember
(When Two World's Drift
Apart)/OCEAN DEEP
LPs:
Silver
From The Heart
Private Collection
Videos:
Rock In Australia

OH BOY!
(Petty)
Recorded: 16/17 June 1989
Singles:
Saviours Day/OH BOY! MEDLEY
Saviours Day/OH BOY!
MEDLEY/Where Are You

LPs:
From A Distance The Event
Videos:
From A Distance The Event

OH NO, DON'T LET GO
(Tarney)
Recorded: May/July 1981
LPs:
Wired for Sound

OH NO NO
Singles:
Immagina Un Giorno/OH NO NO

OH SENORITA
(Marvin/Welch/Bennett/Rostill)
Recorded: 26 April 1966
LPs:
Finders Keepers

ONLY ANGEL
(Williams)
Recorded: May/June 1992
LPs:
The Album

ON MY WORD
(Taylor)
Recorded: 19 August 1964
Singles:
ON MY WORD/Just A Little Bit
Too Late
EPs:
Angel
LPs:
The Best Of Cliff

ON THE BEACH
(Welch/Marvin/Richard)
Recorded: 5 November 1963
Singles:
ON THE BEACH/A Matter Of
Moments
EPs:

Hits From Wonderful Life
LPs:
Wonderful Life
More Hits By Cliff
Japan Tour
Cliff In Japan
40 Golden Greats
20 Original Hits
Cliff In The 60s
The Best Of Cliff Richard And
The Shadows
Knebworth The Album
Videos:
Wonderful Life
Cliff And The Shadows Together
1984
Access All Areas
The Story So Far

ONCE IN A WHILE
(Tarney)
Recorded: May/July 1981
LPs:
Wired For Sound

ONCE UPON A TIME
(Tarney)
Recorded: September 1986
LPs:
Always Guaranteed

ONE FINE DAY
(King/Goffin)
Recorded: 11 October 1966
LPs:
Don't Stop Me Now

ONE NIGHT
(Tarney)
Recorded: September 1986
LPs:
Always Guaranteed

ONE NOTE SAMBA
(Hendricks/Jobim)

Recorded: 22 October 1965
LPs:
Kinda Latin

ONE TIME LOVER MAN
(Richard)
Recorded: April 1987
Singles:
Some People/ONE TIME LOVER
MAN
Some People/ONE TIME LOVER
MAN/Reunion Of The Heart

ONLY YOU
Recorded: 6 August 1986
Singles:
All I Ask Of You/Phantom Of The
Opera Overture/ONLY YOU

OOH LA LA
(Rostill/Volauvent)
Recorded: 31 May 1968
LPs:
Established 1958
Heir Ist Cliff

OUR DAY WILL COME
(Hillard/Garson)
Recorded: 4 October 1965
LPs:
Kinda Latin

**OUR LOVE COULD BE SO
REAL**
(Richard)
Recorded: 12 February 1974
LPs:
The 31st Of February Street

OUR STORY BOOK
(Crane/Kingsbury)
Recorded: 24 April 1967
Singles:
The Day I Met Marie/OUR STORY
BOOK

OUTSIDER
(Tepper/Bennett)
Recorded: 30 January 1961
LPs:
21 Today
How Wonderful To Know

OVER IN BETHLEHEM
(Carmichael)
Recorded: Date Unknown
LPs:
His Land
Videos:
His Land

OVER YOU
(Cooke/Richard)
Recorded: July 1984
LPs:
The Rock Connection

P
—

PAELLA
(Marvin/Welch/Bennett/Rostill)
Recorded: 30 April 1966
LPs:
Finders Keepers

PARADISE LOST
(Loring/Rodgers)
Recorded: 19 August 1964
LPs:
Love Is Forever
Everybody Needs Somebody

PART OF ME
(Unknown)
Not released

PARTY DOLL
(Unknown)
No known recording, but sung
in concert

PARTY MEGAMIX
(Various)
Singles:
All I Have To Do Is Dream/Miss
You Nights/True Love Ways/
PARTY MEGAMIX

PEACE AND QUIET
(Marvin/Welch/Bennett/Rostill)
Recorded: 16 November 1966
EPs:
Cinderella
LPs:
Cinderella

PEACE IN OUR TIME
(Sinfield/Hill)
Recorded: May/June 1992
Singles:
PEACE IN OUR TIME/Somebody
Loves You
PEACE IN OUR TIME (Extended
Mix)/Somebody Loves You/
That's All Right
PEACE IN OUR TIME (7" Remix)/
PEACE IN OUR TIME (Gospel
Mix)/Living Doll/PEACE IN OUR
TIME (Instrumental)
LPs:
The Album
The Winner
Videos:
Access All Areas

PENTECOST
(Unknown)
Recorded: 21 January 1970
Not released

PER UN BACIO D'AMOR
(Bertini/Ravasini)
Recorded: 2 October 1964
LPs:
When In Rome

PERFIDIA

(Dominquez)

Recorded: 21 December 1962

LPs:

When In Spain

Cliff Richard

All My Love

PERHAPS PERHAPS PERHAPS

(Unknown)

EPs:

Cliff's Palladium Successes

LPs:

When In Spain

PER UN BACIO D'AMORE

(Unknown)

LPs:

When In Rome

PIGEON

(Fletcher/Flett)

Recorded: 12 February 1971

Singles:

Flying Machine/PIGEON

PLEASE DON'T FALL IN LOVE

(Batt)

Recorded: March 1983

Singles:

PLEASE DON'T FALL IN LOVE/
Too Close To Heaven

LPs:

Silver

Private Collection

30th Anniversary Picture
Collection

The Best Of Cliff Richard And
The Shadows

Videos:

The Video Connection

Private Collection

PLEASE DON'T TEASE

(Welch/Chester)

Recorded: 25 March 1960

Singles:

PLEASE DON'T TEASE/Where Is
My Heart?

Please Remember Me/PLEASE
DON'T TEASE

EPs:

Cliff's Silver Discs

LPs:

Cliff's Hit Album

40 Golden Greats

Thank You Very Much

From The Heart

Rock On With Cliff Richard

The Best Of Cliff Richard And

The Shadows

The Rock 'n' Roll Era: Cliff Richard
1958–1963

The Hit List

Videos:

Cliff And The Shadows Together
1984

Access All Areas

The Hit List

The Hit List Live

PLEASE REMEMBER ME

(Loggins/Woodley)

Recorded: 10 January 1977

Singles:
 PLEASE REMEMBER ME/Please
  Don't Tease
LPs:
 Green Light

POINTED TOE SHOES
 (Perkins)
 Recorded: 7 September 1959
EPs:
 Cliff Sings No. 2
LPs:
 Cliff Sings

POOR BOY
 (McEntire)
 Recorded: 19 April 1961
EPs:
 Cliff Richard No. 2
LPs:
 21 Today
 How Wonderful To Know

POSTMARK HEAVEN
 (Unknown)
 Recorded: 22 September 1969
 Not released

POVERTY
 (Marvin/Welch/Bennett/Rostill)
 Recorded: 9 November 1966
LPs:
 Cinderella

POWER TO ALL OUR FRIENDS
 (Fletcher/Flett)
 Recorded: 28 December 1972
Singles:
 POWER TO ALL OUR FRIENDS/
  Come Back Billie Jo
LPs:
 Japan Tour
 40 Golden Greats
 30th Anniversary Picture
  Collection

The Best Of Cliff Richard And
 The Shadows
The Hit List
Videos:
 Cliff And The Shadows Together
  1984
 The Hit List
 The Hit List Live

PRAISE MY SOUL
THE KING OF HEAVEN
 (Unknown)
 Recorded: 4 May 1967
 Not released

PROUD MARY
 (Fogarty)
 No known recording, but sung
  in concert

PUNCH AND JUDY
 (D'Abo)
 Recorded: 11 February 1968
LPs:
 Sincerely Cliff Richard

PUT MY MIND AT EASE
 (Diamond)
 Recorded: 1 June 1967
LPs:
 Tracks 'n' Grooves

Q

QUANDO QUANDO QUANDO
 (Testa/Renis)
 Recorded: 7 October 1965
LPs:
 Kinda Latin

QUE BUENA SUERTE
 (Unknown)
 Recorded: 23 April 1968
Singles:
 QUE BUENA SUERTE/High And Dry

QUELLE HISTOIRE JE SUIS
MILLIONAIRE
 (Martin/Coulter/Salvet)
 Recorded: 23 April 1968
 Foreign release

QUESTIONS
 (Richard/Collier)
 Recorded: 1 July 1967
LPs:
 Two A Penny
Videos:
 Two a Penny

QUIEN SERA
 (Ruiz)
 Recorded: 29 April 1963
LPs:
 When In Spain

QUIET NIGHT OF QUIET STARS
 (Jobim/Lees)
 Recorded: 4 October 1965
LPs:
 Kinda Latin

QUIZAS, QUIZAS, QUIZAS
 (Farres)
 Recorded: 29 April 1963
LPs:
 When In Spain

R

RAGGED
 (Trott/Elswood)
 Recorded: May/June 1992
Singles:
 Human Work Of Art/RAGGED
 Human Work Of Art/Devil
  Woman/RAGGED/Free

RAIN CLOUD
 (Unknown)
 Recorded: 30 June 1960

Not released

RATTLER

(Woodley)

Recorded: 8 March 1968

LPs:

Two A Penny

RAVE ON

(West/Tilghman/Petty)

No known recording, but sung
in concert

RAZZLE DAZZLE

(Calhoun)

Recorded: 12 July 1962

Singles:

Angel/RAZZLE DAZZLE

LPs:

Cliff Richard

All My Love

The Best Of Cliff Richard And
The Shadows

READY TEDDY

(Marascalco/Blackwell)

Recorded: 10 February 1959

EPs:

Cliff No. 2

LPs:

Cliff

The Best Of Cliff Richard And
The Shadows

REALLY WALTZING

(Myers/Cass)

Recorded: 22 November 1962

EPs:

More Hits From Summer Holiday

LPs:

Summer Holiday

Videos:

Summer Holiday

RED RUBBER BALL

(Simon/Woodley)

Recorded: 1 June 1967

LPs:

Two A Penny

REELIN' AND ROCKIN'

(Berry)

Recorded: 12 July 1962

LPs:

Cliff Richard

All My Love

The Best Of Cliff Richard And
The Shadows

REFLECTIONS

(Richard/Craddock)

Recorded: 29 July 1969

Singles:

Throw Down A Line/
REFLECTIONS

LPs:

About That Man

RELEVE MON DEFI

(Richard/Collier)

Recorded: 21 February 1968

LPs:

When In France

**REMEMBER (WHEN TWO
WORLDS DRIFT APART)**

(Barbelivien/Stills)

Recorded: 1/2 February 1992

Singles:

I Still Believe In You/REMEMBER
(WHEN TWO WORLDS DRIFT
APART)/Ocean Deep

LPs:

My Kinda Life

REMEMBER ME

(Tarney)

Recorded: September 1986

Singles:

REMEMBER ME/Another
Christmas Day

REMEMBER ME/Another
Christmas Day/Brave New
World

LPs:

Always Guaranteed

Private Collection

Live And Guaranteed

Videos:

Always Guaranteed

Live And Guaranteed 1988

Private Collection

From A Distance The Event

REUNION OF THE HEART

(Pope)

Recorded: April 1987

Singles:

Some People/One Time Lover
Man/REUNION OF THE HEART

LPs:

The Winner

RIP IT UP

(Unknown)

No known recording, but sung
in concert

**ROCK 'N' ROLL IS
HERE TO STAY**

(White)

Recorded: 16/17 June 1989

LPs:

From A Distance The Event

Videos:

From A Distance The Event

ROCK 'N' ROLL JUVENILE

(Richard)

Recorded: 24 January 1979

LPs:

Rock 'n' Roll Juvenile

It's A Small World

ROCK AND ROLL MUSIC

(Berry)

No known recording, but sung
  in concert

ROCKIN' ROBIN

(Thomas)

Recorded: 21 October 1958

LPs:

Oh Boy!

ROSEILEA COME BACK TO ME

Unreleased Radio Luxembourg
  recording

**ROTE LIPPEN SOL MAN
KUSSEN**

(Lieber/Hans/Bradtke)

Recorded: 11 August 1963

Singles:

ROTE LIPPEN SOL MAN
  KUSSEN/Let's Make A Memory

LPs:

Seine Grossen Erfolgen

ROVING GAMBLER

(Unknown)

Recorded: 7 March 1962

Not released

RUN FOR SHELTER

(Unknown)

Recorded: 28 April 1971

Not released

RUN TO THE DOOR

(Knight)

Recorded: 20 September 1966

LPs:

Finders Keepers

S

SAG NO ZU IHM

(Richard/Welch/Blecher)

Recorded: 20 March 1964

Singles:

Zuviel Allein/SAG NO ZU IHM

LPs:

Seine Grossen Erfolgen

SAM

(Murray/Callander)

Recorded: 18 April 1969

LPs:

Sincerely Cliff Richard

**SATURDAY NIGHT AT THE
WHIRL**

(Unknown)

Recorded: 12 February 1974

Not released

SAVE MY SOUL

(Unknown)

Recorded: 7 March 1962

Not released

SAVE THE LAST DANCE FOR ME

(Pomus/Shuman)

Recorded: 19 October 1966

LPs:

Don't Stop Me Now

The Best Of Cliff Richard And
  The Shadows

SAVIOUR'S DAY

(Eaton)

Recorded: July 1990

Singles:

SAVIOURS DAY/Oh Boy! Medley

SAVIOURS DAY/Oh Boy! Medley/
  Where Are You

LPs:

From A Distance The Event

Together

The Hit List

Videos:

From A Distance The Event

Together

The Story So Far

The Hit List

The Hit List Live

SAY YOU DON'T MIND

(Tarney)

Recorded: May/July 1981

LPs:

Wired For Sound

SAY YOU'RE MINE

(Meehan/Rodgers)

Recorded: 6 August 1963

Singles:

Don't Talk To Him/SAY YOU'RE
  MINE

EPs:

Cliff Sings Don't Talk To Him

SCARLET RIBBONS

(Danzig/Segal)

Recorded: June/July 1991

Singles:

This New Year/SCARLET
  RIBBONS

This New Year/SCARLET
  RIBBONS/We Don't Talk
  Anymore

This New Year/I Love You/
  SCARLET RIBBONS/We Don't
  Talk Anymore

LPs:

Together

Videos:

Together

SCHON WIE EIN TRAUM

(Unknown)

Recorded: 10 April 1961

Singles:

SCHON WIE EIN TRAUM/Vreneli

SCHOOLBOY CRUSH

(Schroeder/Gilbert)

Recorded: 24 July 1958

Singles:
SCHOOLBOY CRUSH/Move It
Move It/SCHOOLBOY CRUSH

SCI-FI

(Britten/Robertson)
Recorded: July 1978
LPs:
Rock 'n' Roll Juvenile

SEA CRUISE

(Vincent/Smith)
Recorded: 16/17 June 1989
LPs:
From A Distance The Event
Videos:
From A Distance The Event

SECRET LOVE

(Webster/Fain)
Recorded: 5 December 1961
EPs:
Love Songs
LPs:
The EP Collection

SEEING IS BELIEVING

(West/Spreen)
Recorded: 11 January 1969
Not released

SENTIMENTAL JOURNEY

(Green/Brown/Homer)
Recorded: 11 January 1961
LPs:
Listen To Cliff

SEVEN DAYS TO A HOLIDAY

(Myers/Cass)
Recorded: 22 November 1962
EPs:
More Hits From Summer Holiday
LPs:
Summer Holiday

Videos:
Summer Holiday

SHAKE, RATTLE AND ROLL

(Calhoun)
Recorded: 16/17 June 1989
LPs:
From A Distance The Event
Videos:
From A Distance The Event

SHAKIN' ALL OVER

(Heath)
Recorded: 1 May 1981
Singles:
Daddy's Home/SHAKIN' ALL OVER

SHAME ON YOU

(Welch/Marvin/Jacobson)
Recorded: 11 July 1961
LPs:
21 Today
How Wonderful To Know

SHARE A DREAM

(Osborne/Trott/Sweet)
Recorded: August 1988
LPs:
Stronger
From A Distance The Event

SHE MEANS NOTHING TO ME

(David)
Recorded: 5 October 1982
Singles:
SHE MEANS NOTHING TO ME/
A Man And A Woman (Phil
Everly)
LPs:
Phil Everly
The Rock Connection
Private Collection

SHE NEEDS HIM MORE THAN ME

(Marvin/Welch/Bennett/Rostill)
Recorded: 17 October 1966
EPs:
Cinderella
LPs:
Cinderella

SHE'S A GYPSY

(Bryant/Dempsey)
Recorded: 18 April 1978
LPs:
Green Light
From The Heart

SHE'S GONE

(Marvin/Harris)
Recorded: 17 March 1960
EPs:
Me And My Shadows No. 1
LPs:
Me And My Shadows

SHE'S LEAVING YOU

(Bennett)
Recorded: 30 April 1969
Singles:
Big Ship/SHE'S LEAVING YOU

SHE'S SO BEAUTIFUL

(Poulsen)
Recorded: 20/21 December 1984
Singles:
SHE'S SO BEAUTIFUL/SHE'S SO
BEAUTIFUL (instrumental)
SHE'S SO BEAUTIFUL/SHE'S SO
BEAUTIFUL (extended mix)
LPs:
Time
Private Collection
Videos:
Private Collection

SHINE JESUS SHINE

(Unknown)

Recorded: 2 February 1988

LPs:

The Kendrick Collection

SHIPS THAT PASS IN THE NIGHT

(Unknown)

Recorded: 10 January 1977

Not released

SHOOM LLAMA BOOM BOOM

(Roker/Littlewood/Bradtke)

Recorded: 28 November 1968

LPs:

Heir Ist Cliff

SHOOTING FROM THE HEART

(Giles/Greenaway)

Recorded: July 1984

Singles:

SHOOTING FROM THE HEART/
Small World

LPs:

The Rock Connection

Videos:

Rock In Australia

SHOOTING STAR

(Marvin/Rostill/Bennett)

Recorded: 5 May 1966

EPs:

Thunderbirds Are Go

Videos:

Thunderbirds Are Go

SHOUT

(The Isley Brothers)

Recorded: 5 February 1967

LPs:

Don't Stop Me Now

Cliff In Japan

Live At The Talk Of The Town

SICK AND TIRED

(Unknown)

Unreleased Radio Luxembourg
recording

SILENT NIGHT

(Traditional-Arranged Richard/
Moessl)

Recorded: June/July 1991

LPs:

Together

Videos:

Christmas With Cliff Richard

Together

SILHOUETTES

(Slay/Crewe)

Recorded: 16/17 June 1989

Singles:

SILHOUETTES/The Winner

SILHOUETTES/The Winner/All
The Time You Need

LPs:

From A Distance The Event

Videos:

From A Distance The Event

Access All Areas

SILVER'S HOME TONIGHT

(Pruess/Reilly)

Recorded: May/June 1983

LPs:

Silver

SILVERY RAIN

(Marvin)

Recorded: 17 November 1970

Singles:

SILVERY RAIN/Annabella
Umbrella/Time Flies

LPs:

The Best Of Cliff Volume 2

Help It Along

Live In Japan

Videos:

Access All Areas

SINCE I LOST YOU

(Unknown)

Recorded: 19 December 1961

Singles:

It'll Be Me/SINCE I LOST YOU

EPs:

Cliff's Hits

SING A SONG OF FREEDOM

(Fletcher/Flett)

Recorded: 24 August 1971

Singles:

SING A SONG OF FREEDOM/A
Thousand Conservations

LPs:

The Best Of Cliff Volume 2

Help It Along

Live In Japan

Japan Tour

40 Golden Greats

One Hour Of Cliff Richard

30th Anniversary Picture
Collection

SLOW RIVERS

(John/Taupin)

Recorded: 15 May 1984

Singles:

SLOW RIVERS/Billy And The Kids

SLOW RIVERS/Billy And The
Kids/Lord Of The Flies

LPs:

Private Collection

SMALL WORLD

(Richard)

Recorded: 24 June 1984

Singles:

Shooting From The Heart/SMALL
WORLD

LPs:

It's A Small World

Videos:
 The Story So Far

SO I'VE BEEN TOLD
 (Welch)
 Recorded: 18 December 1961
EPs:
 Time For Cliff And The Shadows
LPs:
 32 Minutes and 17 Seconds
 It'll Be Me

SOLAMENTE UNA VEZ
 (Lara)
 Recorded: 29 April 1963
LPs:
 When In Spain

SOLITARY MAN
 (Diamond)
 Recorded: 11 October 1966
EPs:
 La La La La La
LPs:
 The EP Collection

SO LONG
 (Arnold/Martin/Morrow)
 Recorded: 18 April 1969
Singles:
 With the Eyes Of A Child/SO LONG

SOFTLY AS I LEAVE YOU
 (Shaper/De Vita)
 Recorded: 23 November 1982
LPs:
 Dressed For The Occasion

SOME OF THESE DAYS
 (Brooks)
 Recorded: 12 December 1962
EPs:
 Holiday Carnival

SOME PEOPLE
 (Tarney)
 Recorded: September 1986
Singles:
 SOME PEOPLE/One Time Lover
  Man
 SOME PEOPLE/One Time Lover
  Man/Reunion Of The Heart
 Remember Me/Another
  Christmas Day/SOME PEOPLE
 Healing Love/Carrie/Daddy's
  Home/SOME PEOPLE
LPs:
 Always Guaranteed
 Private Collection
 30th Anniversary Picture
  Collection
 From A Distance The Event
 The Hit List
 Live And Guaranteed
Videos:
 Always Guaranteed
 Live And Guaranteed 1988
 Private Collection
 From A Distance The Event
 Access All Areas
 The Story So Far
 The Hit List Live

SOMEBODY LOSES
 (Tepper/Bennett)
 Recorded: 17 January 1966
Singles:
 Blue Turns To Grey/SOMEBODY
  LOSES

SOMEBODY TOUCHED ME
 (Ertegun)
 Recorded: 21 October 1958
LPs:
 Oh Boy!

SOMEDAY (YOU'LL WANT
ME TO WANT YOU)
 (Hodges)

 Recorded: 10 May 1965
EPs:
 Love Is Forever
LPs:
 Love Is Forever

SOMEBODY LOVES YOU
 (Wilson)
 Recorded: June 1991
Singles:
 Peace In Our Time/SOMEBODY
  LOVES YOU
 Peace In Our Time/SOMEBODY
  LOVES YOU/That's All Right

SOMETHING GOOD
 (Rodgers/Hammerstein II)
 Recorded: 30 May 1968
LPs:
 Live At The Talk Of The Town

SOMEWHERE
 (Unknown)
 Not released

SOMEWHERE ALONG THE WAY

(Gallop/Adams)

Recorded: 9 September 1959

EPs:

Cliff Sings No. 4

LPs:

Cliff Sings

SOMEWHERE BY THE SEA

(Marvin/Welch/Bennett/Rostill)

Recorded: 5 June 1968

LPs:

Established 1958

SONG FOR SARAH

(Stonehill)

Videos:

Christmas With Cliff Richard

The Story So Far

SON OF GOD

(Unknown)

No known recording, but sung
in concert

SON OF THUNDER

(Jenner/Perry)

Recorded: September 1981

LPs:

Now You See Me, Now You Don't

SOONER OR LATER

(Unknown)

Recorded: 18 November 1965

Not released

SOUL DEEP

(Unknown)

No known recording, but sung
in concert

SPANISH HARLEM

(Lieber/Spector)

Recorded: 4 December 1961

EPs:

Cliff Sings Don't Talk To Him

LPs:

32 Minutes And 17 Seconds

Cliff In Japan

It'll Be Me

One Hour Of Cliff Richard

The Best Of Cliff Richard And
The Shadows

SPIDER MAN

(Britten)

Recorded: 7 September 1976

LPs:

Every Face Tells A Story

STAR OF HOPE

(Unknown)

Recorded: 3 May 1967

Not released

START ALL OVER AGAIN

(Britten/Robertson)

Recorded: 14 January 1978

LPs:

Green Light

STEADY WITH YOU

(Samwell)

Recorded: 19 November 1958

Singles:

Livin' Lovin' Doll/STEADY WITH
YOU

**STELL MICH DEINEN
ELTERN VOR**

(Marvin/Bennett/Fleming)

Recorded: 27 November 1968

LPs:

Heir Ist Cliff

STERNEGOLD (ALL MY LOVE)

Recorded: 15 March 1968

Foreign release

STORY OHNE HAPPY END

(Rostill/Relin)

Recorded: 28 November 1968

LPs:

Heir Ist Cliff

STRANGER IN TOWN

(Myers/Cass)

Recorded: 26 August 1962

EPs:

More Hits From Summer Holiday

LPs:

Summer Holiday

Videos:

Summer Holiday

STREETS OF LONDON

(McTell)

Recorded: September 1973

Not released

STRONGER THAN THAT

(Tarney)

Recorded: March-May 1989

Singles:

STRONGER THAN THAT/Joanna

STRONGER THAN THAT/Joanna/
STRONGER THAN THAT
(extended mix)

LPs:

Stronger

Videos:

From A Distance The Event

SUCH IS THE MYSTERY

(Dawson/Read)

Recorded: 3 December 1975

LPs:

I'm Nearly Famous

Walking In The Light

The Winner

SUDDENLY

(Farrar)

Recorded: March 1980

Singles:
SUDDENLY/You Made Me Love
You (Olivia Newton-John)
LPs:
Xanadu
Private Collection
Videos:
Xanadu
The Story So Far

SUMMER HOLIDAY
(Welch/Bennett)
Recorded: 5 May 1962
Singles:
SUMMER HOLIDAY/Dancing Shoes
EPs:
Hits From Summer Holiday
LPs:
Summer Holiday
More Hits By Cliff
Cliff In Japan
40 Golden Greats
Cliff In The 60s
From The Heart
The Best Of Cliff Richard And
The Shadows
30th Anniversary Picture
Collection
The Rock 'n' Roll Era: Cliff Richard
1958-1963
From A Distance The Event
The Hit List
Videos:
Summer Holiday
Thank You Very Much
Cliff And The Shadows Together
1984
Rock In Australia
The Video Connection
From A Distance The Event
Access All Areas
The Story So Far
The Hit List
The Hit List Live

SUMMER RAIN
(Eaton)
Recorded: May/July 1981
LPs:
Wired For Sound

SUNNY HONEY GIRL
(Cook/Greenaway/Goodison/
Hiller)
Recorded: 16 November 1970
Singles:
SUNNY HONEY GIRL/Don't Move
Away/I Was Only Fooling Myself
LPs:
The Best Of Cliff Volume 2
Live In Japan

SWAY
(Gimbel/Ruiz)
Recorded: 17 July 1964
LPs:
When In Spain
Cliff Richard
All My Love
The Best Of Cliff Richard And
The Shadows

SWEET AND GENTLE
(Thorn/Portal)
EPs:
Take Four
LPs:
When In Spain

SWEET DREAMS
(Unknown)
Not released

SWEET LITTLE JESUS BOY
(MacGimsey)
Recorded: 28 April 1967
Singles:
All My Love/SWEET LITTLE
JESUS BOY

LPs:
About That Man
Carols
Videos:
Christmas With Cliff Richard

SWEET LOVING WAYS
(Unknown)
Recorded: 16 August 1973
Not released

T

TAKE A LOOK AROUND
(Unknown)
Recorded: 17 November 1970
Not released

TAKE ACTION
(Britten)
Recorded: 30 April 1969
LPs:
Sincerely Cliff Richard

TAKE ANOTHER LOOK
(Tarney)
Recorded: May/June 1980
LPs:
I'm No Hero

TAKE GOOD CARE OF HER
(Kent/Warren)
Recorded: 18 April 1969
LPs:
Sincerely Cliff Richard

TAKE ME BACK
(Unknown)
No known recording, but sung
in concert

TAKE ME HIGH
(Cole)
Recorded: 28/29 May 1973

Singles:

TAKE ME HIGH/Celestial

Houses

LPs:

Take Me High

Japan Tour

The Best Of Cliff Richard And

The Shadows

Videos:

Take Me High

TAKE ME TO THE LEADER

(Unknown)

Not released

TAKE ME WHERE I WANNA GO

(Unknown)

Recorded: January 1982

Not released

TAKE MY HAND,
PRECIOUS LORD

(Dorsey)

Recorded: 3 May 1967

LPs:

Good News

Hymns And Inspirational Songs

TAKE SPECIAL CARE

(Welch/Martin)

Recorded: 1 May 1962

LPs:

Cliff Richard

All My Love

TE QUIRO DIJESTE

(Grever)

Recorded: 30 April 1963

LPs:

When In Spain

TEA FOR TWO

(Youmans/Caesar)

Recorded: 4 July 1961

LPs:

21 Today

How Wonderful To Know

TEDDY BEAR

(Mann/Lowe)

Recorded: May/June 1983

LPs:

Rock 'n' Roll Silver

Videos:

The Story So Far

TELL ME

(Chester/Welch)

Recorded: 30 March 1960

EPs:

Me And My Shadows No. 3

LPs:

Me And My Shadows

TEENAGERS ROMANCE

(Unknown)

Unreleased Radio Luxembourg

recording

TEMPTATION

(Brown/Freed)

Recorded: 17 November 1960

LPs:

Listen To Cliff

TE QUIERO DIJISTE

(Grever)

LPs:

When In Spain

THAT'LL BE THE DAY

(Holly/Petty)

Recorded: 10 February 1959

LPs:

Cliff

THAT'S ALL RIGHT (MAMA)

(Crudup)

Singles:

Peace In Our Time/Somebody

Loves You/THAT'S ALL RIGHT

Videos:

Access All Areas

THAT'S MY DESIRE

(Kresa/Loveday)

Recorded: 9 September 1959

EPs:

Cliff Sings No. 4

LPs:

Cliff Sings

THAT'S WHAT LOVE IS

(Unknown)

Recorded: 2/3 December 1968

Not released

THAT'S WHY I LOVE YOU

(Gold/Garfin)

Recorded: 22 September 1976

Singles:

When Two Worlds Drift Apart/

THAT'S WHY I LOVE YOU

THE BELLMAN'S SPEECH

(Unknown)

LPs:

The Hunting Of The Snark

THE ANTI BROTHERHOOD
OF MAN

(Cole)

LPs:

Take Me High

Videos:

Take Me High

THE BEST OF ME

(Lubbock/Foster/Marx)

Recorded: March-May 1989

Singles:

THE BEST OF ME/Move It/

Lindsay Jane

THE BEST OF ME/Move It/
    Lindsay Jane/High Class Baby
LPs:
  Stronger
  The Hit List
Videos:
  From a Distance The Event
  The Hit List
  The Hit List Live

**THE BIRTH OF JOHN THE
BAPTIST AND THE BIRTH
OF JESUS:**
LUKE 1: 5-38; 57-66; 80.
  LUKE 2: 1-20
  Recorded: 20 February 1970
LPs:
  About That Man

THE CARNIVAL'S JUST FOR ME
  (Unknown)
  Recorded: 24 March 1969
  Not released

THE CHRISTMAS SONG
  (Torme/Wells)
  Recorded: June/July 1991
LPs:
  Together
Videos:
  Together

THE DAY I MET MARIE
  (Marvin)
  Recorded: 1 June 1967
Singles:
  THE DAY I MET MARIE/Our Story
    Book
LPs:
  The Best Of Cliff
  Live In Japan
  Japan Tour
  Live At The Talk Of The Town
  40 Golden Greats
  Thank You Very Much
  Love Songs
  Cliff In The 60s

From The Heart
The Best Of Cliff Richard And
  The Shadows
Videos:
  Thank You Very Much
  Cliff And The Shadows Together
    1984

THE DAYS OF LOVE
  (Hawkshaw/Wright)
  Recorded: 27 December 1972
Singles:
  Help It Along/Tomorrow Rising/
    THE DAYS OF LOVE/Ashes To
    Ashes

THE DREAMS I DREAM
  (Marvin)
  Recorded: 8 March 1968
LPs:
  Established 1958
  Live At The Talk Of The Town

THE FELLOW NEXT TO ME

(Unknown)

Recorded: 8/9 January 1969

Not released

THE FIRST EASTER – THE EMPTY TOMB:

LUKE 24: 1-12. JOHN 20: 19-20.
LUKE 24: 44-48. MATTHEW 28: 18-20

Recorded: 20 February 1970

LPs:

About That Man

THE GAME

(Cole)

Recorded: 26/27 May 1973

LPs:

Take Me High

Videos:

Take Me High

THE GIRL CAN'T HELP IT

(Troup)

Recorded: 11 October 1967

LPs:

Tracks 'n' Grooves

Live In Japan

From A Distance The Event

Videos:

From A Distance The Event

THE GIRL FROM IPANEMA

(Jobim/Gimbel/DeMoraes)

Recorded: 4 October 1965

LPs:

Kinda Latin

THE GLORY OF LOVE

Recorded: 16/17 June 1989

LPs:

From A Distance The Event

Videos:

From A Distance The Event

THE GOLDEN DAYS ARE OVER

(Britten/Shifrin)

Recorded: May/June 1983

LPs:

Silver

THE HOLLY AND THE IVY

Recorded: 10 September 1967

EPs:

Christmas EP

THE HUNT

(Marvin/Welch/Bennett/Rostill)

Recorded: 11 November 1966

LPs:

Cinderella

THE JOY OF LIVING

(Marvin/Ferris)

Recorded: 7 January 1970

Singles:

THE JOY OF LIVING/Leave My Woman Alone/Boogatoo

LPs:

The Best Of Cliff Volume 2

THE KING OF LOVE MY SHEPHERD IS

(Traditional - Arranged Paramor)

Recorded: 4 May 1967

LPs:

Good News

Hymns And Inspirational Songs

THE KING'S PLACE

(Marvin/Welch/Bennett/Rostill)

Recorded: 9 November 1966

LPs:

Cinderella

THE LADY CAME FROM BALTIMORE

(Hardin)

Recorded: 30 May 1968

LPs:

Live At The Talk Of The Town

THE LEAVING

(Sedgwick)

Recorded: 13 February 1974

LPs:

The 31st Of February Street

THE LETTER

(Unknown)

Recorded: 11 October 1967

Not released

THE LONG WAY HOME

(Unknown)

Not released

THE LOOK OF LOVE

(Bacharach/David)

Videos:

Thank You Very Much

THE LORD'S MY SHEPHERD

Recorded: 1967

LPs:

Hymns And Inspirational Songs

THE MINUTE YOU'RE GONE

(Gately)

Recorded: 25 August 1964

Singles:

THE MINUTE YOU'RE GONE/Just Another Guy

EPs:

Angel

LPs:

The Best Of Cliff

Live In Japan

Cliff In Japan

Love Songs

40 Golden Greats

From The Heart

The Best Of Cliff Richard And The Shadows

30th Anniversary Picture
   Collection
The Hit List
Videos:
   The Hit List
   The Hit List Live

THE 23RD PSALM

(Irvine – Arranged Paramor)
Recorded: 4 May 1967
LPs:
   Good News

THE NEW 23RD

(Carmichael)
Recorded: Date Unknown
LPs:
   His Land
   Hymns And Inspirational Songs
Videos:
   His Land

THE NEXT TIME

(Kaye/Springer)
Recorded: 10 May 1962
Singles:
   THE NEXT TIME/Bachelor Boy
EPs:
   Hits From Summer Holiday
LPs:
   Summer Holiday
   More Hits By Cliff
   40 Golden Greats
   Love Songs
   30th Anniversary Picture
      Collection
   From The Heart
   The Best Of Cliff Richard And
      The Shadows
   The Rock 'n' Roll Era: Cliff Richard
      1958-1963
   The Hit List
Videos:
   Summer Holiday
   The Hit List

The Hit List Live

THE NIGHT

(Marvin/Richard)
Recorded: 5 October 1965
Singles:
   Wind Me Up/THE NIGHT
EPs:
   Wind Me Up

THE NIGHT IS SO LONELY

(Vincent/Simmons)
Recorded: 4 July 1961
EPs:
   Cliff Richard No. 2
LPs:
   21 Today
   How Wonderful To Know

THE OLD ACCORDION

(Froggatt)
Recorded: 9 September 1971
Singles:
   A Brand New Day/THE OLD
      ACCORDION

THE ONLY WAY OUT

(Martinez)
Recorded: January 1982
Singles:
   THE ONLY WAY OUT/Under The
      Influence
LPs:
   Now You See Me, Now You Don't
   Private Collection
   It's A Small World
Videos:
   Rock In Australia
   Private Collection
   The Best Of Cliff Richard And
      The Shadows

THE ROCK THAT DOESN'T ROLL

(Norman)
Recorded: January 1982

Videos:
   Christmas With Cliff Richard

THE SHAPE I'M IN TONIGHT

(Unknown)
No known recording, but sung
   in concert

THE SHRINE ON THE
SECOND FLOOR

(Heneker/More/Norman)
Recorded: 19 October 1959
EPs:
   Expresso Bongo
LPs:
   The EP Collection

THE SINGER

(Froggatt)
Recorded: 11 October 1972
LPs:
   The 31st Of February Street

THE SLEEP OF THE GOOD

(Rice/Farrar)
Recorded:1995
Singles:
   The Wedding/SLEEP OF THE
      GOOD (live)/I Don't Love You
      Isabella/I Don't Love You
      Isabella (instrumental)
LPs:
   Songs From Heathcliff

THE SNAKE AND THE
BOOKWORM

(Pomus/Shuman)
Recorded: 6 September 1959
EPs:
   Cliff Sings No. 1
LPs:
   Cliff Sings

**THE SONG FROM
MOULIN ROUGE**

(Unknown)

Not released

**THE SOUND OF THE
CANDYMAN'S TRUMPET**

(Hazzard)

Recorded: 3 February 1968

EPs:

Congratulations

**THE SUN AIN'T GONNA
SHINE ANYMORE**

(Gaudio/Crewe)

Recorded: October 1974

LPs:

Japan Tour

**THE 31ST OF FEBRUARY
STREET CLOSING**

(Richard)

Recorded: 25 February 1974

LPs:

The 31st Of February Street

**THE 31ST OF FEBRUARY
STREET OPENING**

(Richard)

Recorded: 25 February 1974

LPs:

The 31st Of February Street

THE TIME IN BETWEEN

(Aber/Jones/Brown)

Recorded: 10 May 1965

Singles:

THE TIME IN BETWEEN/Look
Before You Love

EPs:

Wind Me Up

LPs:

The Best Of Cliff

THE TOUCH OF YOUR LIPS

(Noble)

Recorded: 10 September 1959

EPs:

Cliff Sings No. 3

LPs:

Cliff Sings

**THE TRIAL OF JESUS, HIS
EXECUTION AND DEATH:**
LUKE 22: 66-71. JOHN 18: 28-19:
19. LUKE 23: 39-46; 50-56

Recorded: 20 February 1970

LPs:

About That Man

THE TWELFTH OF NEVER

(Livingston/Webster)

Recorded: 23 June 1964

Singles:

THE TWELFTH OF NEVER/I'm
Afraid To Go Home

EPs:

Why Don't They Understand

LPs:

More Hits By Cliff

Love Songs

Cliff In The 60s

The Best Of Cliff Richard And
The Shadows

Videos:

Cliff And The Shadows Together
1984

**THE VISIT OF THE WISE MEN
AND THE ESCAPE INTO EGYPT:**
MATTHEW 2: 1-23

Recorded: 20 February 1970

LPs:

About That Man

THE WATER IS WIDE

(Traditional – Arranged Richard/
Pruess)

Recorded: 21/22 September
1981

LPs:

Now You See Me Now You Don't

From The Heart

THE WEDDING

(Rice/Farrar)

Recorded: 1995

Singles:

THE WEDDING/Sleep Of The
Good (live)/I Don't Love You
Isabella/I Don't Love You
Isabella (instrumental)

THE WINNER

(Richard/Cooke)

Recorded: December 1989

Singles:

Silhouettes/THE WINNER

Silhouettes/THE WINNER/All The
Time You Need

LPs:

The Winner

THE WORD IS LOVE

(Cole)

Recorded: 28/29 May 1973

LPs:

Take Me High

Videos:

Take Me High

THE YOUNG ONES

(Tepper/Bennett)

Recorded: 11 August 1961

Singles:

THE YOUNG ONES/We Say Yeah

Never Let Go/Congratulations/
THE YOUNG ONES/You've Got
Me Wondering

EPs:

Hits From The Young Ones

LPs:

The Young Ones

Cliff's Hit Album
Live in Japan
Cliff In Japan
Thank You Very Much
40 Golden Greats
From The Heart
30th Anniversary Picture
   Collection
Cliff In The 60s
The Best Of Cliff Richard And
   The Shadows
The Rock 'n' Roll Era: Cliff Richard
   1958–1963
From A Distance The Event
The Hit List
Live and Guaranteed
Videos:
   The Young Ones
   Thank You Very Much
   Cliff And The Shadows Together
      1984
   Live and Guaranteed 1988
   The Video Connection
   Access All Areas
   The Story So Far
   The Hit List
   The Hit List Live

**THEME FROM A
SUMMER PLACE**
   (Discant/Steiner)
LPs:
   Love Is Forever
   Everybody Needs Somebody
   The Best Of Cliff Richard And
      The Shadows

THEME FOR A DREAM
   (Garson/Shuman)
   Recorded: 28 January 1961
Singles:
   THEME FOR A DREAM/Mumblin'
      Mosie
EPs:
   Cliff's Hit Parade

LPs:
   Cliff's Hit Album
   40 Golden Greats
   Love Songs
   20 Original Greats
   Rock On With Cliff Richard
   30th Anniversary Picture
      Collection
   The Best Of Cliff Richard And
      The Shadows
   The Rock 'n' Roll Era: Cliff Richard
      1958–1963
   The Hit List
Videos:
   The Hit List
   The Hit List Live

**THERE IS A GREEN
HILL FAR AWAY**
   (Unknown)
   Recorded: 4 May 1967
   Not released

THERE'S GOTTA BE A WAY
   (Marvin/Welch/Bennett/Rostill)
   Recorded: 17 October 1965
LPs:
   Aladdin And His Wonderful Lamp

THERE'S NO POWER IN PITY
   (Richard)
   Recorded: May/June 1992
Singles:
   I Still Believe In You/Bulange
      Downpour/THERE'S NO
      POWER IN PITY

THERE YOU GO AGAIN
   (Richard)
   Recorded: 13 February 1974
LPs:
   The 31st Of February Street

THIEF IN THE NIGHT
   (Field)

Recorded: January 1982
LPs:
   Now You See Me, Now You Don't
   From A Distance The Event
   Live And Guaranteed
   The Winner
Videos:
   From A Distance The Event

THINGS WE SAID TODAY
   (Lennon/McCartney)
   Recorded: 11 October 1966
EPs:
   La La La La La
LPs:
   The EP Collection

THINKING OF OUR LOVE
   (Welch/Marvin)
   Recorded: 15 March 1960
Singles:
   Nine Times Out Of Ten/THINKING
      OF OUR LOVE

THIS DAY
   (Marvin/Welch/Bennett/Rostill)
   Recorded: 4 June 1966
LPs:
   Finders Keepers

THIS IS MY KIND OF LOVE
   (Unknown)
   Recorded: 11 January 1969
   Not released

THIS LOVE
   (Unknown)
   Recorded: Unknown Date
LPs:
   Without Walls (Tammy Wynette)

THIS NEW YEAR
   (Eaton)
   Recorded: June/July 1991

Singles:

THIS NEW YEAR/Scarlet Ribbons

THIS NEW YEAR/Scarlet
Ribbons/We Don't Talk
Anymore

THIS NEW YEAR/I Love You/
Scarlet Ribbons/We Don't Talk
Anymore

LPs:

Together

Videos:

Together

THIS TIME NOW

(Tarney)

Recorded: September 1986

LPs:

Always Guaranteed

THIS WAS MY SPECIAL DAY

(Marvin/Welch/Bennett/Rostill)

Recorded: 16 October 1964

Singles:

THIS WAS MY SPECIAL DAY/I'm
Feeling Oh So Lovely

LPs:

Aladdin and His Wonderful Lamp

THROUGH THE EYE
OF A NEEDLE

(Bacharach/David)

Recorded: August 1964

LPs:

Love Is Forever

Everybody Needs Somebody

THROW DOWN A LINE

(Marvin)

Recorded: 2 May 1969

Singles:

THROW DOWN A LINE/Reflections

LPs:

The Best of Cliff Volume 2

40 Golden Greats

The Best Of Cliff Richard And

The Shadows

30th Anniversary Picture
Collection

TILL WINTER FOLLOWS SPRING

(Unknown)

Recorded: 11 January 1969

Not released

TIME

(Merchant)

Recorded: 20 September 1966

LPs:

Sincerely Cliff Richard

TIME DRAGS BY

(Marvin/Welch/Bennett/Rostill)

Recorded: 26 April 1966

Singles:

TIME DRAGS BY/ The La La La
Song

LPs:

Finders Keepers

The Best Of Cliff

20 Original Greats

Cliff In The 60s

The Best Of Cliff Richard And
The Shadows

TIME FLIES

(Bennett/Hawker)

Recorded: 30 April 1969

Singles:

Silvery Rain/Annabella
Umbrella/TIME FLIES

TINKLE TINKLE TINKLE

(Woods)

Recorded: 9 August 1961

LPs:

The Young Ones

Videos:

The Young Ones

TINY PLANET

(Richard)

Recorded: 24 June 1984

LPs:

It's A Small World

TO A FRIEND

(Mezek/Dumbatze)

Recorded: 1990

Singles:

TO A FRIEND/Strong Is The
Current

TO PROVE MY LOVE FOR YOU

(Wolf/Raleigh)

Recorded: 30 January 1961

LPs:

21 Today

How Wonderful To Know

TODOR EL PODER
A LOS AMIGOS

(Unknown)

Recorded: 23 March 1973

Singles:

TODOR EL PODER A LOS
AMIGOS/Come Back
Billie Joe

TOMORROW RISING

(Hawker/Bennett)

Recorded: 28 December 1972

Singles:

Help It Along/TOMORROW
RISING/The Days Of
Love/Ashes To Ashes

TOO CLOSE TO HEAVEN

(Batt)

Recorded: March 1983

Singles:

Please Don't Fall In Love/TOO
CLOSE TO HEAVEN

TOO LATE TO SAY GOODBYE

(Unknown)

Recorded: 6 September 1976

Not released

TOO MUCH

(Rosenberg/Weinman)

Recorded: 10 February 1959

EPs:

Cliff No. 2

LPs:

Cliff

TOUGH ENOUGH

(Otis)

Recorded: 28 January 1961

EPs:

Cliff Richard No. 1

LPs:

21 Today

Rock On With Cliff Richard

How Wonderful To Know

TRAVELLIN' LIGHT

(Tepper/Bennett)

Recorded: 25 July 1959

Singles:

TRAVELLIN' LIGHT/Dynamite

EPs:

Cliff's Silver Discs

LPs:

Cliff's Hit Album

The 31st Of February Street

Japan Tour

40 Golden Greats

One Hour Of Cliff Richard

Rock On With Cliff Richard

From The Heart

The Best Of Cliff Richard And

The Shadows

30th Anniversary Picture

Collection

The Rock 'n' Roll Era: Cliff Richard

1958–1963

The Hit List

Videos:

The Story So Far

The Hit List

The Hit List Live

TREASURE OF LOVE

(Shapiro/Stallman)

Recorded: 23 November 1982

LPs:

Dressed For The Occasion

**TRIBUTE TO THE LEGENDS
(MEDLEY)**

(Various)

Recorded: Unknown Date

Singles:

All I Have To Do Is Dream/Miss

You Nights/When Will I Be

Loved/TRIBUTE TO THE

LEGENDS

TRUE LOVE WAYS

(Petty/Holly)

Recorded: 23 November 1982

Singles:

TRUE LOVE WAYS/Galadriel

Mistletoe And Wine/Marmaduke/

TRUE LOVE WAYS

All I Have To Do Is Dream/Miss

You Nights/TRUE LOVE WAYS/

Party Megamix

LPs:

Dressed For The Occasion

Private Collection

30th Anniversary Picture

Collection

The Best Of Cliff Richard And

The Shadows

**TRUE LOVE WILL COME
TO YOU**

(Chester/Welch)

Recorded: 13 October 1960

EPs:

Listen To Cliff

LPs:

Listen To Cliff

TRUE TRUE LOVIN'

(Welch)

Recorded: 26 March 1964

Singles:

Constantly/TRUE TRUE

LOVIN'

EPs:

A Forever Kind Of Love

TRY A SMILE

(Perry)

Recorded: 6 September 1976

LPs:
    Every Face Tells A Story

TURN AROUND
    (Tepper/Bennett)
    Recorded: 18 January 1962
LPs:
    32 Minutes And 17 Seconds
    It'll Be Me

TURN IT INTO CASH
    (Unknown)
    Recorded: 11 January 1969
    Not released

TURN ME LOOSE
    (Unknown)
Videos:
    Thank You Very Much
    The Story So Far

TUS BESOS
    (Newman)
    Recorded: 28 April 1963
LPs:
    When In Spain

TUTTI FRUTTI
    (LaBostrie/Penniman)
    Recorded: May/June 1983
LPs:
    Rock 'n' Roll Silver

TV HOP
    (Endsley)
    Recorded: 21 October 1958
LPs:
    Oh Boy!

TWELVE DAYS OF CHRISTMAS
    (Traditional)
    Recorded: 10 September 1967
EPs:
    Christmas EP

TWENTY FOUR HOURS FROM TULSA
    (Unknown)
    No known recording, but sung
        in concert

TWENTY FLIGHT ROCK
    (Fairchild/Cochran)
    Recorded: 6 September 1959
EPs:
    Cliff Sings No. 2
LPs:
    Cliff Sings

TWIST AND SHOUT
    (Russell/Medley)
    Recorded: 1 July 1967
LPs:
    Cliff In Japan
    Two A Penny
Videos:
    Two A Penny

TWIST IM BLUT
    (Russell/Medley)
    Recorded: 20 November 1968
LPs:
    Hier Ist Cliff

TWO A PENNY
    (Richard)
    Recorded: 1 July 1967
LPs:
    Two A Penny
Videos:
    Two A Penny

TWO HEARTS
    (Tarney)
    Recorded: September 1986
Singles:
    TWO HEARTS/Yesterday Today
        Forever
    TWO HEARTS/Yesterday Today
        Forever/Wild Geese

LPs:
    Always Guaranteed
    Private Collection
    My Kinda Life
    Live And Guaranteed
Videos:
    Always Guaranteed
    Live And Guaranteed 1988
    Private Collection
    From A Distance The Event

TWO TO THE POWER
    (Kipner)
    Recorded: 26 April 1984
Singles:
    TWO TO THE POWER/Rock And
        Roll
    TWO TO THE POWER/Rock And
        Roll/Don't Mess Up This Good
        Thing

U

UFO
    (Norman)
LPs:
    Live And Guaranteed
Videos:
    Live And Guaranteed 1988

UMBARELLA
    (Avon/Spiro/Henbourg)
    Recorded: 24 November 1970
LPs:
    Ich Traume Deine Traume

UNCHAINED MELODY
    (North/Zaret)
    Recorded: 4 March 1961
EPs:
    Listen To Cliff No. 2
LPs:
    Listen To Cliff
    One Hour Of Cliff Richard

UNDER LOCK AND KEY

(Britten)

Recorded: 9 January 1978

LPs:

Green Light

UNDER THE GUN

(Rushing/Martin)

Recorded: April 1987

Singles:

My Pretty One/Love Ya/UNDER
THE GUN

LPs:

The Winner

Videos:

Rock In Australia

UNDER THE INFLUENCE

(Hewitt)

Recorded: January 1982

Singles:

The Only Way Out/UNDER THE
INFLUENCE

LPs:

Walking In The Light

UNDER YOUR SPELL

(Eaton)

Recorded: September 1986

LPs:

Always Guaranteed

**UNTIL THE RIGHT ONE
COMES ALONG**

(Unknown)

Not released

UNTO US A CHILD IS BORN

(Arranged. Keating)

Recorded: 10 September 1967

LPs:

Carols

UP IN CANADA

(Norman)

Recorded: 17 January 1977

LPs:

Small Corners

From The Heart

Videos:

Thank You Very Much

UP IN THE WORLD

(Ward)

Recorded: 24 September 1976

LPs:

Love Songs

Dressed For The Occasion

Every Face Tells A Story

From The Heart

V

VAUDEVILLE ROUTINE

(Various)

Recorded: 9 August 1961

LPs:

The Young Ones

Videos:

The Young Ones

VAYA CON DIOS

(Jamboa/Russell/James/Pepper)

Recorded: 30 April 1962

LPs:

When In Spain

**VENITE (O COME ALL
YE FAITHFUL)**

(Traditional-Arranged Eaton)

Recorded: June/July 1991

LPs:

Together

Videos:

Together

VISIONS

(Ferris)

Recorded: 4 October 1965

Singles:

VISIONS/What Would I Do

LPs:

The Best Of Cliff

Japan Tour

Cliff In Japan

Live At The Talk Of The Town

40 Golden Greats

Love Songs

Cliff In The 60s

The Best Of Cliff Richard And
The Shadows

From The Heart

30th Anniversary Picture
Collection

Videos:

Cliff And The Shadows Together
1984

VRENELI

(Lindt/Thorn/Horn)

Recorded: 10 April 1961

Singles:

Schon Wie Ein Traum/VRENELI

W

WAKE UP LITTLE SUSIE

(Unknown)

Bootleg LPs:

Imagine (live version, 1970)

WAKE UP, WAKE UP

(Cook/Greenaway)

Recorded: 8 March 1968

LPs:

Two A Penny

Cliff In Japan

**WALK ON BY/THE LOOK
OF LOVE**

(Unknown)

LPs:

Live in Japan 72

WALK RIGHT IN

(Unknown)

Unreleased Radio Luxembourg
recording

WALKING IN THE LIGHT

(Britten)

Recorded: July 1978

Singles:

Hot Shot/WALKING IN THE LIGHT

LPs:

Walking In The Light

WAS IST DABEI

(Jones/Aber/Relin)

Recorded: 13 May 1966

Singles:

Du Bist Mein Erster Gedanke/
WAS IST DABEI

WASHERWOMAN

(Marvin/Welch/Bennett/Rostill)

Recorded: 28 April 1966

LPs:

Finders Keepers

WAS KANN ICH TUN

(Welch/Marvin/Walker)

Singles:

Das Gluck Ist Rosarot/WAS
KANN ICH TUN

**WATCH WHAT YOU DO
WITH MY BABY**

(Giant/Baum/Kaye)

Recorded: 23 November 1963

Singles:

I'm The Lonely One/WATCH
WHAT YOU DO WITH MY BABY

EPs:

Cliff's Palladium Successes

WE ALL HAVE OUR DREAMS

(Unknown)

No known recording, but sung

in concert

WE BEING MANY

(Unknown)

Recorded: Unknown Date

LPs:

Nothing But The Best (Helen
Shapiro)

WE CAN WORK IT OUT

(Lennon/McCartney)

No known recording, but sung
in concert

WE DON'T TALK ANYMORE

(Tarney)

Recorded: January 1979
29 May 1979

Singles:

WE DON'T TALK ANYMORE/
Count Me Out

This New Year/Scarlet Ribbons/
WE DON'T TALK ANYMORE

This New Year/I Love You/
Scarlet Ribbons/WE DON'T
TALK ANYMORE

LPs:

Rock 'n' Roll Juvenile

Love Songs

Dressed For The Occasion

From The Heart

30th Anniversary Picture
Collection

Private Collection

The Best Of Cliff Richard And
The Shadows

From A Distance The Event

My Kinda Life

The Hit List

Live And Guaranteed

Videos:

We Don't Talk Anymore/Miss You
Nights

Cliff And The Shadows Together
1984

Rock In Australia

The Video Connection

Live And Guaranteed 1988

Private Collection

From A Distance The Event

Access All Areas

The Story So Far

The Hit List

The Hit List Live

WE HAD IT MADE

(Sugar/Hall)

Not released

WE HAVE IT MADE

(Sugar/Hall)

Recorded: 24 June 1960

EPs:

Me And My Shadows No. 2

LPs:

Me And My Shadows

WE KISS IN THE SHADOW

(Rodgers/Hammerstein)

Recorded: 17 November 1960

LPs:

Listen To Cliff

WE LOVE A MOVIE

(Myers/Cass)

Recorded: 20 May 1964

EPs:

Hits From Wonderful Life

LPs:

Wonderful Life

Videos:

Wonderful Life

WE SAY YEAH

(Gormley/Welch/Marvin)

Recorded: 28 July 1961

Singles:

The Young Ones/WE SAY YEAH

EPs:

Hits From The Young Ones

LPs:
  The Young Ones
  Cliff In Japan
  20 Original Greats
  One Hour Of Cliff Richard
  Rock On With Cliff Richard
Videos:
  The Young Ones
  Thank You Very Much

WE SHALL BE CHANGED
  (Traditional – Arranged Leander)
  Recorded: 27 April 1967
LPs:
  Good News

WE SHOULD BE TOGETHER
  (Roberts)
  Recorded: June/July 1991
Singles:
  WE SHOULD BE TOGETHER/Miss
    You Nights
  WE SHOULD BE TOGETHER/Miss
    You Nights/Mistletoe And Wine
EPs:
  Christmas EP
LPs:
  Together
Videos:
  Together

**WENN DU LACHST, LACHT
DAS GLUCK**
  (Stephens/Reed/Werner)
  Recorded: 24 November 1970
Singles:
  WENN DU LACHST, LACHT DAS
    GLUCK/Kleine Taube
LPs:
  When In Germany Volume 2
  Seine Grossen Erfolge
  Ich Traume Deine Traume

WE'RE ALL ONE
  (Haworth)

Videos:
  Christmas With Cliff Richard

WERE YOU THERE
  (Unknown)
  Recorded: 28 April 1967
  Not released

**WHAT A FRIEND WE
HAVE IN JESUS**
  (Scriven/Converse – Arranged
    Paramor)
  Recorded: 28 April 1967
LPs:
  Good News
  Hymns And Inspirational Songs

WHAT A SILLY THING TO DO
  (Britten)
  Recorded: 1 July 1968
LPs:
  Tracks 'n' Grooves

WHAT IS THERE TO SAY
  (Unknown)
  Not released

WHAT THE WORLD NEEDS NOW
  (Unknown)
  No known recording, but sung
    in concert

**WHAT WOULD I DO (FOR THE
LOVE OF A GIRL)**
  (Unknown)
  Recorded: 22 May 1966
Singles:
  Visions/WHAT WOULD I DO (FOR
    THE LOVE OF A GIRL)

WHATCHA GONNA DO ABOUT IT
  (Unknown)
  Recorded: 4 April 1965
  Unreleased

**WHAT DO YOU KNOW, WE'VE
GOT A SHOW**
  (Myers/Cass)
  Recorded: 9 August 1961
LPs:
  The Young Ones
Videos:
  The Young Ones

WHAT'D I SAY
  (Charles)
  Recorded: 4 March 1961
Singles:
  WHAT'D I SAY/Blue Moon
EPs:
  Listen To Cliff
LPs:
  Listen To Cliff
  Cliff In Japan

**WHAT'S BEHIND THE
EYES OF MARY**
  (Marvin/Bennett)
  Recorded: 2 July 1968

LPs:

Established 1958

WHAT'S LOVE GOT
TO DO WITH IT

(Unknown)

No known recording, but Cliff
sang a line of the song during his
'Access All Areas' tour in 1992

WHAT'S MORE I DON'T
NEED HER

(Fletcher/Flett)

Recorded: 8 March 1968

Singles:

Don't Forget To Catch Me/
WHAT'S MORE (I DON'T
NEED HER)

LPs:

Live At The Talk Of The Town

WHAT'VE I GOTTA DO

(Welch/Marvin)

Recorded: 9 August 1963

EPs:

Wonderful Life No. 1

LPs:

Wonderful Life

Videos:

Wonderful Life

WHEN

(Reardon/Evans)

Recorded: 16/17 June 1989

LPs:

From A Distance The Event

Videos:

From A Distance The Event

WHENEVER GOD SHINES
HIS LIGHT

(Morrison)

Recorded: 20 February 1989

Singles:

WHENEVER GOD SHINES HIS

LIGHT (single version)/I'd Love
To Write Another Song/
WHENEVER GOD SHINES HIS
LIGHT (album version)

WHEN I FIND YOU

(Cambell)

Recorded: 22 April 1969

LPs:

Sincerely Cliff Richard

WHEN I GROW TOO
OLD TO DREAM

(Hammersmith II/Romberg)

Recorded: 12 May 1961

EPs:

Dream

LPs:

The EP Collection

WHEN I SURVEY THE
WONDROUS CROSS

(Miller – Arranged Paramor)

Recorded: 28 April 1967

LPs:

Good News

Small Corners

Hymns And Inspirational Songs

WHEN I'M 64

(Lennon/McCartney)

Recorded: 30 May 1968

LPs:

Live At The Talk Of The Town

Videos:

Thank You Very Much

WHEN MY DREAMBOAT
COMES HOME

(Friend/Franklin)

Recorded: 17 May 1962

EPs:

Time For Cliff And The Shadows

LPs:

32 Minutes And 17 Seconds

It'll Be Me

One Hour Of Cliff Richard

WHEN THE GIRL IN YOUR ARMS

(Tepper/Bennett)

Recorded: 30 January 1961

Singles:

WHEN THE GIRL IN YOUR ARMS/
Got A Funny Feeling

EPs:

Cliff's Hit Parade

LPs:

The Young Ones

Cliff's Hit Album

40 Golden Greats

20 Original Greats

Love Songs

The Best Of Cliff Richard And
The Shadows

The Rock 'n' Roll Era: Cliff Richard
1958–1963

The Hit List

Videos:

The Young Ones

The Hit List

The Hit List Live

WHEN TWO WORLDS
DRIFT APART

(Sills)

Recorded: 7 September 1976

Singles:

WHEN TWO WORLDS DRIFT
APART/That's Why I Love You

I Still Believe In You/Remember
(WHEN TWO WORLDS DRIFT
APART – French Adaptation)/
Ocean Deep

LPs:

Every Face Tells A Story

Love Songs

WHEN WILL I BE LOVED

(Everly)

Recorded: May 1981

Singles:

All I Have To Do Is Dream/Miss
  You Nights/WHEN WILL I BE
  LOVED/Tribute To The Legends
Videos:
  The Hit List Live

WHEN YOU ARE THERE
  (Unknown)
  Recorded: 22 September 1969
  Not released

WHEN YOU THOUGHT OF ME
  (Rice/Farrar)
  Recorded: 1995
  LPs:
  Songs From Heathcliff

WHERE DID THE SUMMER GO
  (Geid/Udel)
  Recorded: 20 September 1960
  LPs:
  Finders Keepers

**WHERE DID YOU GET
THAT HAT**
  (Rolmaz)
  Recorded: 9 August 1961
  LPs:
  The Young Ones
  Videos:
  The Young Ones

WHERE DO WE GO FROM HERE
  (Eaton)
  Recorded: January 1982
  Singles:
  WHERE DO WE GO FROM HERE/
    Discovering
  LPs:
  Now You See Me, Now You Don't
  It's A Small World
  Videos:
  Private Collection

WHERE IS MY HEART
  (Tepper/Bennett)
  Recorded: 30 March 1960
  Singles:
  Please Don't Tease/WHERE IS
    MY HEART

WHERE IS THAT MAN
  (Richard/Winter/Jones/Fyffe/
    Srodzinski/Kent)
  Recorded: 20 February 1970
  LPs:
  About That Man

WHERE IS THE MAN
  (Unknown)
  Recorded: 8/9 January 1969
  Not released

WHERE IS YOUR HEART
  (Auric/Engvick)
  Recorded: 24 July 1964
  EPs:
  Look In My Eyes Maria

WHERE THE FOUR WINDS BLOW
  (Batchelor/Roberts)
  Recorded: 6 December 1962
  EPs:
  Why Don't They Understand
  LPs:
  The EP Collection

WHERE YOU ARE
  (Richard/Cooke)
  Recorded: September 1989
  Singles:
  Saviours Day/The Oh Boy
    Medley/WHERE YOU ARE
  LPs:
  Songs Of Life
  Mission 89
  The Winner
  Videos:
  Rock In Australia

WHILE SHEPHERDS WATCHED
  (Arranged Keating)
  Recorded: 10 September 1967
  EPs:
  Carol Singers
  LPs:
  Carols

WHILE SHE'S YOUNG
  (Britten/Christie)
  Recorded: 13 January 1978
  LPs:
  Green Light

WHISPERING MY LOVE
  (Unknown)
  No known recording, but sung
    in concert

WHITE CHRISTMAS
  (Berlin)
  Recorded: June/July 1991
  LPs:
  Together
  Videos:
  Together

WHO ARE WE TO SAY
  (Kosloff/Pray)
  Recorded: 11 December 1961
  EPs:
  Cliff Sings Don't Talk To Him
  LPs:
  32 Minutes And 17 Seconds
  It'll Be Me

WHO'S IN LOVE
  (Tarney)
  Recorded: March-May 1989
  LPs:
  Stronger

**WHOLE LOTTA SHAKIN'
GOIN' ON**
  (Williams/David)

Recorded: 10 February 1959
LPs:
Cliff
The Best Of Cliff Richard And
The Shadows
Videos:
The Story So Far

WHO'S GONNA TAKE YOU HOME

(Unknown)
Not released

WHY

(Cole)
Recorded: 3-6 September 1973
LPs:
Take Me High
Videos:
Take Me High

WHY DO FOOLS FALL IN LOVE

(Unknown)
No known recording, but sung
in concert

WHY DON'T THEY UNDERSTAND

(Menderson/Fishman)
Recorded: 24 July 1964
EPs:
Why Don't They Understand

WHY ME LORD

(Kristofferson)
Recorded: 18/19 January 1977
LPs:
Small Corners

WHY SHOULD THE DEVIL HAVE ALL THE GOOD MUSIC

(Norman)
Recorded: 17 January 1977
LPs:
Small Corners
Thank You Very Much

Walking In The Light
Videos:
Thank You Very Much
The Story So Far

WHY WASN'T I BORN RICH

(Marvin/Welch/Bennett/Rostill)
Recorded: 19 November 1966
Singles:
It's All Over/WHY WASN'T I BORN
RICH
LPs:
Cinderella

WIDE OPEN SPACE

(Walmesley/Abbot)
Recorded: March-May 1989
Singles:
I Just Don't Have The Heart/WIDE
OPEN SPACE
I Just Don't Have The Heart/WIDE
OPEN SPACE/I Just Don't
Have The Heart (instrumental)

WILD GEESE

(Trott/Sweet)
Recorded: April 1987
Singles:
Two Hearts/Yesterday Today/
Forever/WILD GEESE
LPs:
The Winner

WILL YOU LOVE ME TOMORROW

(King/Goffin)
Recorded: 10 October 1968
LPs:
Sincerely Cliff Richard

WILLIE AND THE HAND JIVE

(Otis)
Recorded: 18 November 1959
Singles:
Fall In Love With You/WILLIE AND

THE HAND JIVE
LPs:
Thank You Very Much
The Rock Connection
20 Original Greats
Rock On With Cliff Richard
Videos:
Thank You Very Much
Access All Areas
The Story So Far

WILLIE DID THE CHA CHA

(Otis)
Unreleased Radio Luxembourg
recording

WIND ME UP (LET ME GO)

(Talley/Montgomery)
Recorded: 24 August 1964
Singles:
WIND ME UP/The Night
EPs:
Wind Me Up
LPs:
The Best Of Cliff
40 Golden Greats
The Best Of Cliff Richard And
The Shadows
30th Anniversary Picture
Collection
The Hit List
Videos:
The Hit List
The Hit List Live

WINNING

(Cole)
Recorded: 26/27 May 1973
LPs:
Take Me High
Japan Tour
Videos:
Take Me High

WIRED FOR SOUND

(Tarney/Robertson)

Recorded: May/July 1981

Singles:

WIRED FOR SOUND/Hold On

From A Distance/Lindsay Jane II/
WIRED FOR SOUND

LPs:

Wired For Sound

Private Collection

30th Anniversary Picture
Collection

The Best Of Cliff Richard And
The Shadows

The Hit List

Videos:

The Video Connection

Rock In Australia

Private Collection

From A Distance The Event

When The Music Stops

Access All Areas

The Story So Far

The Hit List

The Hit List Live

WITH THE EYES OF A CHILD

(Fletcher/Flett)

Recorded: 29 July 1969

Singles:

WITH THE EYES OF A CHILD/So
Long

LPs:

Best Of Cliff Volume 2

One Hour Of Cliff Richard

WITHOUT YOU

(Richard/Marvin/Welch)

Recorded: 11 July 1961

LPs:

21 Today

How Wonderful To Know

WONDERFUL LIFE

(Welch/Bennett)

Recorded: 5 November 1963

EPs:

Wonderful Life No. 1

LPs:

Wonderful Life

The Best Of Cliff Richard And
The Shadows

Videos:

Wonderful Life

WONDERFUL TO BE YOUNG

(Unknown)

Recorded: 11 August 1962

Canadian single

WONDERFUL WORLD

(Flett/Fletcher/Loose)

Recorded: 2 February 1968

Singles:

Zartliche Sekunden/WONDERFUL
WORLD

EPs:

Congratulations

LPs:

Hier Ist Cliff

WORDS

(Gibb)

Recorded: 13 May 1967

Bootleg LPs:

Imagine (live version, 1969)

WORKING AFTER SCHOOL

(Abrams/Medley)

Recorded: 1 April 1960

LPs:

Me And My Shadows

**WOULDN'T IT BE NICE (IF OUR
DREAMS CAME TRUE)**

(Marvin/Welch/Bennett/Rostill)

Recorded: 11 November 1966

LPs:

Cinderella

**WOULDN'T YOU KNOW IT
(GOT MYSELF A GIRL)**

(Tarney/Spencer)

Recorded: 29 May 1975

Singles:

Honky Tony Angel/WOULDN'T
YOU KNOW IT (GOT MYSELF
A GIRL)

Y

Y'ARRIVA

(Welch/Marvin)

Recorded: 11 July 1961

EPs:

Cliff Richard No. 2

LPs:

21 Today

How Wonderful To Know

YEAR AFTER YEAR

(Unknown)

No known recording, but sung
in concert

YES HE LIVES

(Britten)

Recorded: 18/19 January 1977

Singles:

YES HE LIVES/Good On The
Sally Army

LPs:

Small Corners

Greenbelt Live 1979

Videos:

Thank You Very Much

YESTERDAY'S MEMORIES

(Richard/Cooke)

Recorded: Unknown Date

Singles:

Healing Love/YESTERDAY'S
MEMORIES/Carrie

YESTERDAY, TODAY, FOREVER

(Richard)

Recorded: September 1973

Singles:

Two Hearts/YESTERDAY TODAY FOREVER

Two Hearts/YESTERDAY TODAY FOREVER/Wild Geese

LPs:

Help It Along

The Winner

YOU

(Unknown)

Recorded: 12 February 1974

Not released

YOU AND I

(Welch/Marvin)

Recorded: 1 April 1960

EPs:

Me And My Shadows No. 1

LPs:

Me And My Shadows

YOU AND ME

(Unknown)

Recorded: 11 February 1974

Not released

YOU BELONG TO MY HEART

(Gilbert/Lara)

Recorded: 17 July 1964

LPs:

Cliff Richard

All My Love

YOU CAN'T GET TO HEAVEN BY LIVIN' LIKE HELL

(Paxton)

Recorded: 18/19 January 1977

Videos:

Christmas With Cliff Richard

YOU CAN NEVER TELL

(Marvin)

Recorded: 24 October 1968

Singles:

Goodbye Sam, Hello Samantha/ YOU CAN NEVER TELL

YOU DON'T KNOW

(Spriggs)

Recorded: 18 December 1961

EPs:

Time For Cliff And The Shadows

LPs:

32 Minutes And 17 Seconds

It'll Be Me

YOU GOT ME WONDERING

(Britten)

Recorded: 10 September 1976

LPs:

Every Face Tells a Story

YOU GOTTA TELL ME

(Williams)

Recorded: 11 October 1966

LPs:

Don't Stop Me Now

YOU GOT WHAT IT TAKES

(Unknown)

No known recording, but sung in concert

YOU HELD MY HAND

(Unknown)

Recorded: 8/9 January 1969

Not released

YOU KNOW THAT I LOVE YOU

(Britten)

Recorded: July 1978

LPs:

Rock 'n' Roll Juvenile

YOU, ME AND JESUS

(Richard)

Recorded: January 1982

Singles:

Little Town/Love And A Helping Hand/YOU, ME AND JESUS

LPs:

Walking In The Light

YOU MOVE HEAVEN

(Moessl/Glenn)

Recorded: May/June 1992

LPs:

The Album

YOU WILL NEVER KNOW

(Kerr/Osborne)

Recorded: 12 February 1974

LPs:

The 31st Of February Street

YOU'LL WANT ME

(Cook/Greenaway)

Recorded: 31 January 1969

LPs:

Sincerely Cliff Richard

YOU NEED A LIGHT

(Unknown)

No known recording, but sung in concert

YOUNG LOVE

(Joyner/Cartey)

Unreleased Radio Luxembourg recording

YOUNG LOVE

(Tarney)

Recorded: May/July 1981

LPs:

Wired For Sound

YOUR EYES TELL ON YOU

(Martin)

Recorded: 10 April 1963
Singles:
　It's All In The Game/YOUR EYES
　　TELL ON YOU
EPs:
　Cliff's Lucky Lips

YOUR HEART'S NOT
IN YOUR LOVE
(Sedaka/Bayer)
Recorded: 22 September 1969
LPs:
　Tracks 'n' Groves

YOUTH AND EXPERIENCE
(Myers/Cass)
Recorded: 20 May 1964
LPs:
　Wonderful Life
Videos:
　Wonderful Life

YOU'RE JUST THE
ONE TO DO IT
(Otis/Blackwell)
Recorded: 16 March 1960
EPs:
　Me And My Shadows No. 2
LPs:
　Me And My Shadows

YOU'RE THE ONE
(Tarney/Spencer)
Recorded: 29 January 1975

Singles:
　It's Only Me You've Left Behind/
　　YOU'RE THE ONE

YOURS
(Unknown)
Recorded: 13 May 1966
Foreign release

YOU'VE GOT ME WONDERING
(Britten)
Recorded: 10 September 1976
Singles:
　Never Let Go/Congratulations/
　　The Young Ones/YOU'VE GOT
　　ME WONDERING
LPs:
　Every Face Tells A Story
　Walking In The Light
　My Kinda Life

YOU'VE GOT TO GIVE ME
ALL YOUR LOVIN'
(Gold/Denne)
Recorded: 1 December 1975
LPs:
　I'm Nearly Famous

YOU'VE LOST THAT
LOVIN' FEELING
(Mann/Weil/Spector)
Recorded: October 1974
LPs:
　Japan Tour

YOU WERE MEANT FOR ME
(Unknown)
Unreleased Radio Luxembourg
　recording

Z

ZARTLICHE SEKUNDEN
(Marvin/Welch/Bennett/Hertha)
Recorded: 28 November 1968
Singles:
　ZARTICHE SEKUNDEN/Wonderful
　　World
LPs:
　Heir Ist Cliff

ZIP-A-DEE-DOO-DAH
(Unknown)
Recorded: 18 November 1965
Not released

ZUM HEIRATEN BIN ICH
KEIN TYP
(Hammond/Hazlewood/Bradtke)
Recorded: 25 November 1970
LPs:
　Ich Traume Deine Traume

ZUVIEL ALLEIN
(Gorden/Hertha)
Recorded: 20 March 1964
Singles:
　ZUVIEL ALLEIN/Sag No Zu Ihm

DISCOGRAPHY

Cliff's recorded output has, obviously, been the major part of his career and, spanning five decades, his records have appeared on nearly every type of recorded media from 78 rpm records through to the CD single, limited edition 12-inch single to the picture and/or shaped discs. His first seven singles were available on both the 78 rpm format and the less popular, at the time, 45 rpm format. From March 1960 all his singles would appear as 45s only.

By the eighties and nineties a single did not just find release as a standard 7-inch 45 rpm release. There would be a flood of limited editions, sometimes as many as six or seven different issues would be made available – an expensive time for the collector who wanted every possible format! Many of these special editions featured extras such as advent calendars, posters or photographs and on many of the CD singles, tracks were included that would not be available elsewhere, even on the vinyl and cassette issues of the single.

Although widely available in foreign countries as early as the sixties, picture bags for Cliff's singles only appeared in the UK in the seventies. Many of these featured live action photographs, although there were some with studio portrait shots. By the mid-eighties this became the norm for singles.

Then, in the nineties, record companies realised they could sell the same song twice! And the 2-CD set appeared, on which the first single would be released with the lead track and maybe two or three others. The following week would see the release of part 2 with the same lead track plus one or two different tracks, forcing collectors to purchase both if they wanted a complete collection. Often the extra tracks would be live recordings or tracks that failed to find release on albums – although recently the trend has moved towards instrumental, album versions, edits and extended versions of songs appearing as bonuses. With the demise of vinyl it is likely that future singles will only appear on CD or cassette.

Between 1958 and 1968 Cliff released forty-six extended play albums. These normally featured four tracks and all appeared in picture sleeves. Of these forty-six releases many were lifted from albums, i.e. *Me and My Shadows, Cliff sings, Listen To Cliff,* and *The Young Ones.* There were several though that contained material unavailable elsewhere.

Many of Cliff's early albums were released in both the mono and stereo formats, and in some cases different versions of a track appeared, either intentionally or by accident, and these can be found in the Alternate Versions section of this book. It must be remembered that in those early days the mono issues of albums and extended plays were given priority and stereo was considered secondary. As a result the stereo issues are much harder to find today.

Throughout the world many different albums were released that featured different combinations of tracks along with alternate artwork, and companies such as Readers Digest and World Records in the UK released a number of boxed sets covering his entire career. This also applied to singles, as countries would often put out their own singles, combining tracks lifted from albums.

The following discography details all the UK releases listed chronologically, and is split up into sections covering 78 rpm and 45 rpm singles, extended play albums, albums, compact discs, box sets, cassettes, 12-inch singles, limited editions miscellaneous releases and bootlegs.

SINGLES – 78 rpm

Schoolboy Crush/Move It
DB 4178 August 1958

High Class Baby/My Feet Hit The Ground
DB 4203 November 1958

Livin' Lovin' Doll/Steady With You
DB 4249 January 1959

Mean Streak/Never Mind
DB 4290 April 1959

Living Doll/Apron Strings
DB 4306 July 1959

Travellin' Light/Dynamite
DB 4351 October 1959

A Voice In The Wilderness/Don't Be Mad At Me
DB 4398 January 1960

SINGLES – 45 rpm

Move It/Schoolboy Crush
DB 4178 August 1958

High Class Baby/My Feet Hit The Ground
DB 4203 November 1958

Livin' Lovin' Doll/Steady With You
DB 4249 January 1959

Mean Streak/Never Mind
DB 4290 April 1959

Living Doll/Apron Strings
DB 4306 July 1959

Travellin' Light/Dynamite
DB 4351 October 1959

A Voice In The Wilderness/Don't Be Mad At Me
DB 4398 January 1960

Fall In Love With You/Willie And The Hand Jive
DB 4431 March 1960

Please Don't Tease/Where Is My Heart?
DB 4479 June 1960

Nine Times Out Of Ten/Thinking Of Our Love
DB 4506 September 1960

I Love You/'D' In Love
DB 4547 November 1960

Theme For A Dream/Mumblin' Mosie
DB 4593 February 1961

Gee Whiz It's You/I Cannot Find A True Love
DC 756 March 1961

A Girl Like You/Now's The Time To Fall In Love
DB 4667 June 1961

When The Girl In Your Arms (Is The Girl In Your Heart)/Got A Funny Feeling
DB 4716 October 1961

What'd I Say/Blue Moon
DC 758 1961

The Young Ones/We Say Yeah
DB 4761 January 1962

I'm Looking Out The Window/Do You Wanna Dance
DB 4828 May 1962

It'll Be Me/Since I Lost You
DB 4886 August 1962

The Next Time/Bachelor Boy
DB 4950 November 1962

Summer Holiday/Dancing Shoes
DB 4977 February 1963

Lucky Lips/I Wonder
DB 7034 May 1963

It's All In The Game/Your Eyes Tell On You
DB 7089 August 1963

Don't Talk To Him/Say You're Mine
DB 7150 November 1963

I'm The Lonely One/Watch What You Do With My Baby
DB 7203 January 1964

Constantly/True True Lovin'
DB 7272 April 1964

On The Beach/A Matter Of Moments
DB 7305 June 1964

The Twelth Of Never/I'm Afraid To Go Home
DB 7372 October 1964

I Could Easily Fall (In Love With You)/I'm In Love With You
DB 7420 December 1964

This Was My Special Day/I'm Feeling Oh So Lonely
DB 7435 December 1964

The Minute You're Gone/Just Another Guy
DB 7496 March 1965

Angel/Razzle Dazzle
DC 762 May 1965

On My Word/Just A Little Bit Too Late
DB 7596 June 1965

The Time In Between/Look Before You Love
DB 7660 August 1965

Wind Me Up/The Night
DB 7745 October 1965

Blue Turns To Grey/Somebody Loses
DB 7866 March 1966

Visions/What Would I Do (For The Love Of A Girl)
DB 7968 July 1966

Time Drags By/The La La La Song
DB 8017 October 1966

In The Country/Finders Keepers
DB 8094 December 1966

It's All Over/Why Wasn't I Born Rich?
DB 8150 March 1967

I'll Come Running/I Get The Feelin'
DB 8210 June 1967

The Day I Met Marie/Our Story Book
DB 8245 August 1967

All My Love/Sweet Little Jesus Boy
DB 8293 November 1967

Congratulations/High 'n' Dry
DB 8376 March 1968

I'll Love You Forever Today/Girl You'll Be A Woman Soon
DB 8437 June 1968

Marianne/Mr Nice
DB 8476 September 1968

Don't Forget To Catch Me/What's More (I Don't Need Her)
DB 8503 November 1968

Good Times (Better Times)/Occasional Rain
DB 8548 February 1969

Big Ship/She's Leaving You
DB 8581 May 1969

Throw Down A Line (with Hank Marvin)**/Reflections**
DB 8615 September 1969

With The Eyes Of A Child/So Long
DB 8648 November 1969

The Joy Of Living (with Hank Marvin)**/Leave My Woman Alone/Boogatoo** (Hank Marvin)
DB 8657 February 1970

Goodbye Sam Hello Samantha/You Can Never Tell
DB 8685 June 1970

I Ain't Got Time Anymore/Monday Comes Too Soon
DB 8708 August 1970

Sunny Honey Girl/Don't Move Away (with Olivia Newton-John)**/I Was Only Fooling Myself**
DB 8747 January 1971

Silvery Rain/Annabella Umbrella/Time Flies
DB 8774 April 1971

Flying Machine/Pigeon
DB 8797 July 1971

Sing A Song Of Freedom/A Thousand Conversations
DB 8836 November 1971

Jesus/Mr Cloud
DB 8864 March 1972

Living In Harmony/Empty Chairs
DB 8917 August 1972

A Brand New Song/The Old Accordion
DB 8957 December 1972

Power To All Our Friends/Come Back Billie Jo
EMI 2012 March 1973

Help It Along/Tomorrow Rising/The Days Of Love/Ashes To Ashes
EMI 2022 May 1973

Take Me High/Celestial Houses
EMI 2088 November 1973

(You Keep Me) Hangin' On/Love Is Here
EMI 2150 March 1975

It's Only Me You've Left Behind/You're The One
EMI 2279 March 1975

Honky Tonk Angel/(Wouldn't You Know It) Got Myself A Girl
EMI 2344 September 1975

Miss You Nights/Love Enough
EMI 2376 February 1976

Devil Woman/Love On (Shine On)
EMI 2485 May 1976

I Can't Ask For Anything More Than You/Junior Cowboy
EMI 2499 August 1976

Hey Mr Dream Maker/No One Waits
EMI 2559 November 1976

My Kinda Life/Nothing Left For Me To Say
EMI 2584 February 1977

When Two Worlds Drift Apart/That's Why I Love You
EMI 2663 June 1977

Yes! He Lives/Good On The Sally Army
EMI 2730 January 1978

Please Remember Me/Please Don't Tease
EMI 2832 July 1978

Can't Take The Hurt Anymore/Needing A Friend
EMI 2885 November 1978

Green Light/Imagine Love
EMI 2920 March 1979

We Don't Talk Anymore/Count Me Out
EMI 2675 July 1979

Hot Shot/Walking In The Light
EMI 5003 November 1979

Carrie/Moving In
EMI 5006 February 1980

Dreamin'/Dynamite
EMI 5095 August 1980

Suddenly (with Olivia Newton-John)**/You Made Me Love You** (Olivia Newton-John)
JET 7002 October 1980

A Little In Love/Keep On Looking
EMI 5123 January 1981

Wired For Sound/Hold On
EMI 5221 August 1981

Daddy's Home/Shakin' All Over
EMI 5251 November 1981

The Only Way Out/Under The Influence
EMI 5318 July 1982

Where Do We Go From Here?/Discovering
EMI 5341 September 1982

Little Town/Love And A Helping Hand/You, Me And Jesus
EMI 5348 November 1982

She Means Nothing To Me (with Phil Everly)**/A Man And A Woman** (Phil Everly)
Capitol CL 276 January 1983

True Love Ways/Galadriel
EMI 5385 April 1983

Drifting (with Sheila Walsh)**/It's Lonely When The Lights Go Out** (Sheila Walsh)
DJM SHEIL 1 May 1983

Never Say Die/Lucille
EMI 5415 August 1983

Please Don't Fall In Love/Too Close To Heaven
EMI 5437 November 1983

Baby You're Dynamite/Ocean Deep
EMI 5457 March 1984

Ocean Deep/Baby You're Dynamite
EMI 5457 May 1984

Two To The Power (with Janet Jackson)**/Rock And Roll** (Janet Jackson)
A & M AM 210 September 1984

Shooting From The Heart/Small World
Rich 1 October 1984

Heart User/I Will Follow You
Rich 2 January 1985

She's So Beautiful/She's So Beautiful (instrumental)
EMI 5531 September 1985

It's In Every One Of Us/Alone (instrumental)
EMI 5537 November 1985

Living Doll (with The Young Ones and Hank Marvin)**/(All The Little Flowers Are) Happy**
WEA YZ65P March 1986

Born To Rock And Roll/Law Of The Universe
EMI 5545 May 1986

All I Ask Of You (with Sarah Brightman)**/Phantom Of The Opera Overture Act II** (Royal Philharmonic Orchestra)
Polydor POPSX 802 September 1985

Slow Rivers (with Elton John)**/Billy And The Kids** (Elton John)
Rocket EJS 13 November 1986

My Pretty One/Love Ya/Under The Gun
EM 4 June 1987

Some People/One Time Lover Man
EM 18 August 1987

Remember Me/Another Christmas Day
EM 31 October 1987

Two Hearts/Yesterday, Today, Forever
EM 42 February 1988

Mistletoe And Wine/Marmaduke
EM 78 November 1988

The Best Of Me/Move It/Lindsay Jane
EM 92 May 1989

I Just Don't Have The Heart/Wide Open Space
EM 101 August 1989

Lean On You/Hey Mister
EM 105 October 1989

Whenever God Shines His Light (with Van Morrison)/
I'd Love To Write Another Song (Van Morrison)
POLYDOR VANS2 December 1989

Stronger Than That/Joanna
EM 129 February 1990

Silhouettes/The Winner
EM 152 August 1990

From A Distance/Lindsay Jane II
EM 155 October 1990

Saviour's Day/The Oh Boy Medley
XMAS 90 November 1990

More To Life/Mo's Theme (instrumental)
EM 205 September 1991

We Should Be Together/Miss You Nights (Live
Version)
XMAS G91 – cassette single November 1991
(see also page 160)

This New Year (Edit)/**Scarlet Ribbons**
EMS 218 – features special engraved autograph
etched onto disc December 1991

I Still Believe In You/Bulange Downpour
EM 255 November 1992

Peace In Our Time/Somebody Loves You
EM 265 March 1993

Human Work Of Art/Ragged
EM 267 June 1993

Never Let Go/Congratulations
EMP 281 – Includes poster September 1993

Healing Love (7" Harding & Curnow Mis)/**Yesterday's
Memories/Carrie**
EM 294 December 1993

All I Have To Do Is Dream (with Phil Everly)/**Miss
You Nights**
EM 359 November 1994

Misunderstood Man/Misunderstood Man
(instrumental)
EM 394 9 October 1995

SINGLES – 12-inch

Never Say Die (extended version)/**Lucille**
EMI 12EMI 5415 August 1983

Baby You're Dynamite (extended version)/**Baby
You're Dynamite** (7" version)/**Ocean Deep**
12EMI 5457 March 1984

Two To The Power (with Janet Jackson)/**Rock And
Roll** (Janet Jackson)/**Don't Mess Up This Good Thing**
(Janet Jackson)
A & M AMX 210 September 1984

Heart User (extended mix)/**I Will Follow You**
EMI 12 Rich 2 January 1985

She's So Beautiful (extended mix)/**She's So Beautiful**
12EMI 5531 September 1985

It's In Every One Of Us/Alone (instrumental)/**It's In
Every One Of Us** (choral version)
EMI 12EMI 5537 November 1985

Living Doll (with The Young Ones and Hank
Marvin)/**(All The Little Flowers Are) Happy**
WEA YZ65T March 1986

Born To Rock And Roll (Special extended mix)/**Born
To Rock and Roll/Law Of The Universe**
EMI 12EMI 5545 May 1986

All I Ask Of Your (with Sarah Brightman)/**Phantom Of
The Opera Overture Act II** (Royal Philharmonic
Orchestra)/**Only You**
Polydor POPSX 802 September 1986

Slow Rivers (with Elton John)/**Billy And The Kids**
(Elton John)/**Lord Of The Flies** (Elton John)
Rocket EJS 13-12 November 1986

My Pretty One (extended mix)/**Love Ya/Under The Gun**
12EM 4 June 1987

My Pretty One (extended mix)/**Love Ya/Under
The Gun**
12EM 4 – with poster June 1987

Some People (extended version)/**One Time Lover
Man/Reunion Of The Heart**
12EM 18 August 1987

**Remember Me/Another Christmas Day/Brave
New World**
12EMP 31 October 1987

**Remember Me/Another Christmas Day/Brave
New World**
12EM 31 – poster cover October 1987

Two Hearts (extended version)/**Yesterday, Today,
Forever/Wild Geese**
12EM 42 February 1988

Two Hearts (extended version)/**Yesterday, Today,
Forever/Wild Geese**
12 EMG 42 – gatefold single with Valentine's card
February 1988

Mistletoe and Wine/Marmaduke/Little Town
12EM 78 November 1988

Mistletoe and Wine/Marmaduke/Little Town
12EMX 78 – with advent calendar November 1988

**The Best Of Me/Move It/Lindsay Jane/High
Class Baby**
12EM 92 May 1989

**I Just Don't Have The Heart/Wide Open Space/
I Just Don't Have The Heart** (instrumental)
12EMX 101 August 1989

I Just Don't Have The Heart/Wide Open Space/I Just Don't Have The Heart (instrumental)
12EMP 101 – with poster cover August 1989

Lean On You (extended mix)**/Lean On You/Hey Mister**
12EM 105 October 1989

Whenever God Shines His Light (album version)(with Van Morrison)**/Cry For Home** (Van Morrison)**/I'd Love To Write Another Song** (Van Morrison)
Polydor VANX2 December 1989

Stronger Than That (extended mix)**/Joanna/Stronger Than That**
12EM 129 February 1990

Stronger Than That (incl. signed print)**/Joanna/Stronger Than That**
12EMP 129 – poster bag February 1990

Silhouettes/The Winner/All The Time You Need
12EM 152 August 1990

From A Distance/Lindsay Jane II/Wired For Sound
(Live)
12EMP 155 – poster bag October 1990

Saviour's Day/The Oh Boy Medley/Where You Are
12XMAS 90 November 1990

This New Year/Scarlet Ribbons (12" remix)**/We Don't Talk Anymore** (remix 1991)
12EMP 218 – includes special free calendar poster December 1991

SINGLES – CD

Remember Me/Some People/Another Christmas Day/Remember Me (12" version)
CDEM 31 October 1987

Two Hearts/Yesterday, Today, Forever/Two Hearts (extended version)**/Wild Geese**
CDEMG 42 February 1988

Mistletoe And Wine/Marmaduke/Little Town/La Gonave
CDEM 78 – with Christmas card November 1988

The Best Of Me/Move It/Lindsay Jane/High Class Baby
CDEMS 92 – 100th single with special gold embossed sleeve May 1989

I Just Don't Have The Heart/Wide Open Space/I Just Don't Have The Heart (instrumental)
CDEM 101 August 1989

Lean On You (extended mix)**/Lean On You/Hey Mister**
CDEM 105 October 1989

Whenever God Shines His Light (7" version)**/I'd Love To Write Another Song** (Van Morrison)**/Whenever God Shines His Light** (album version)
VANCD2 December 1989

Stronger Than That (extended version)**/Joanna/Stronger Than That**
CDEM 129 February 1990

Silhouettes/The Winner/All The Time You Need
CDEM 152 August 1990

From A Distance/Lindsay Jane II/Wired For Sound
CDEM 155 October 1990

Saviour's Day/The Oh Boy Medley/Where You Are
CDXMAS 90 November 1990

More To Life/Mo's Theme (instrumental)
CDEM 205 September 1991

We Should Be Together/Miss You Nights (live version)**/Mistletoe And Wine**
CDXMAS 91 November 1991

This New Year/I Love You/Scarlet Ribbons (12" remix)**/We Don't Talk Anymore** (remix 1991)
CDEM 218 December 1991

I Still Believe In You/Bulange Downpour/There's No Power In Pity
CDEMS 255 November 1992

I Still Believe In You/Remember (When Two Worlds Drift Apart – French adaptation**)/Ocean Deep**
CDEM 255 – second CD single to complete special set November 1992

Peace In Our Time (Extended Mix)**/Somebody Loves You/That's All Right** (Live)
CDEMS 265 March 1993

Peace In Our Time (7" remix)**/Peace In Our Time** (Gospel mix)**/Living Doll** (Live version)**/Peace In Our Time** (Instrumental)
CDEM 265 – second CD single to complete special set March 1993

Human Work Of Art/Move It (Live version)**/Never Even Thought**
CDEMS 267 June 1993

Human Work Of Art/Devil Woman/Ragged Free (Live version)
CDEMS 267 – second CD single to complete special set June 1993

Never Let Go/Congratulations/The Young Ones/You've Got Me Wondering
CDEMS 281 – collectors box with three prints September 1993

Never Let Go/Congratulations/The Young Ones/You've Got Me Wondering
CDEM 281 September 1993

Healing Love/Carrie/Daddy's Home/Some People
CDEM 294

All I Have To Do Is Dream (with Phil Everly)**/Miss You Nights/When Will I Be Loved** (with Phil Everly)**/Tribute To The Legends** (medley)
CDEMS 359 November 1994

All I Have To Do Is Dream (with Phil Everly)**/Miss You Nights/True Love Ways/Party Megamix**
CDEMS 359 – second CD single to complete special set November 1994

Misunderstood Man (Edit)**/Misunderstood Man** (Instrumental)**/Misunderstood Man**
CDEM 394 October 1995

Had To Be (with Olivia Newton John)**/Had To Be** (live, with Olivia Newton John)**/Interview with John Cavanagh**
CDEMS 410 November 1995

Had To Be (Instrumental)**/Don't Move Away** (with Olivia Newton John)
CDEMS 410 – second CD single to complete special set November 1995

The Wedding (with Helen Hobson)**/Sleep Of The Good** (live)**/I Do Not Love You Isabella** (with Olivia Newton-John and Kristina Nichols)**/I Do Not Love You Isabella** (instrumental)
CDEM 422 March 1996

SINGLES – CASSETTE & SPECIAL/LIMITED EDITIONS

Drifting (with Sheila Walsh)**/It's Lonely When The Lights Go Out** (Sheila Walsh)
DJM SHEIL 100 – Picture disc May 1983

Shooting From The Heart/Small World
RICHP 1 – Heart-shaped picture disc November 1984

Living Doll (with The Young Ones and Hank Marvin)**/(All The Little Flowers Are) Happy** (The Young Ones)
WEA YZ65 – Picture disc March 1986

Slow Rivers (with Elton John)**/Billy And The Kids** (Elton John)
Rocket EJSP 13 – Picture disc November 1986

My Pretty One/Love Ya
EMG 4 – gatefold sleeve June 1987

Some People/One Time Lover Man
EMG 18 – gatefold sleeve August 1987

Some People/One Time Lover Man
EMP 18 – Cliff shaped picture disc August 1987

Two Hearts/Yesterday, Today, Forever
EMP 42 – double heart shaped picture disc
February 1988

Mistletoe And Wine/Marmaduke
EMP 78 – 7" poster bag with calendar November
1988

Mistletoe And Wine/Marmaduke/True Love Ways
EMS 78 – Special 7" December 1988

I Just Don't Have The Heart/Wide Open Space/I Just Don't Have The Heart (instrumental)
TCEM 101 – cassette single August 1989

Lean On You/Hey Mister/Lean On You (extended mix)
EMPD 105 – 7" picture disc October 1989

Lean On You/Hey Mister/Lean On You (extended mix)
TCEM 105 – cassette single October 1989

Stronger Than That/Joanna
TCEM 129 – cassette single February 1990

Stronger Than That/Joanna
EMS 129 – postcard pack February 1990

Silhouettes/The Winner
EMS 152 – special package including free print
August 1990

Silhouettes/The Winner/All The Time You Need
TCEM 152 – cassette single August 1990

From A Distance/I Could Easily Fall (In Love With You) (Live)
EMPD 155 – limited edition 7" picture disc
featuring alternative B-side October 1990

From A Distance/Lindsay Jane II
TCEM 155 – cassette single October 1990

Saviour's Day/The Oh Boy Medley
XMASP 90 – Decade pack includes five photos
from five decades November 1990

Saviour's Day/The Oh Boy Medley
TCXMASP 90 – cassette single November 1990

More To Life/Mo's Theme (instrumental)
TCEM 205 – cassette single September 1991

We Should Be Together/Miss You Nights
(live version)
XMASG 91 – 7" souvenir edition in gatefold sleeve
November 1991

We Should Be Together/Mistletoe And Wine/ Twelve Days Of Christmas/The Holly And The Ivy
XMAS 91 – Christmas EP inserts into 7" gatefold
sleeve December 1991

This New Year/Scarlet Ribbons
TCEM 218 – cassette single December 1991

I Still Believe In You/Bulange Downpour
TCEM 255 – cassette single November 1992

Peace In Our Time/Somebody Loves You
TCEM 265 – cassette single March 1993

Human Work Of Art/Ragged
TCEM 267 June 1993

Never Let Go/Congratulations
TCEM 281 – cassette single September 1993

Healing Love/Yesterday's Memories/Carrie
TCEM 294 – cassette single November 1994

All I Have To Do Is Dream/Miss You Nights
TCEM 359 – cassette single November 1994

Misunderstood Man/Misunderstood Man
(Instrumental)
TCEM 394 cassette single October 1995

Had To Be/Had To Be (Instrumental)
TCEM 410 – cassette single November 1995

The Wedding/I Do Not Love You Isabella (with Olivia Newton John and Kristina Nichols)
TCEM 422 – cassette single March 1996

EXTENDED PLAY ALBUMS

Serious Charge
SEG 7895 May 1959
Side 1: Living Doll/No Turning Back
Side 2: Mad About You/Chincilla (Drifters)
The soundtrack of Cliff's first feature film. The EP contained three tracks from Cliff and one performed by the Drifters.

Cliff No. 1
SEG 7903 June 1959
Side 1: Apron Strings/My Babe/Down The Line
Side 2: I Gotta Feeling/Baby I Don't Care/Jet Black (Drifters)
The first of two EPs which lifted tracks from the debut Cliff album. Along with the five Cliff tracks is one vocal by the Drifters.

Cliff No. 1
ESG 7754 June 1959
Stereo issue with same tracks as above.

Cliff No. 2
SEG 7910 July 1959
Side 1: Donna/Move It/Ready Teddy
Side 2: Too Much/Don't Bug Me Baby/Driftin' (Drifters)
The second EP taken from the Cliff album and as with No. 1 it also featured a vocal track by the Drifters.

Cliff No. 2
ESG 7769 July 1959
Stereo issue with same tracks as above.

Expresso Bongo
SEG 7971 January 1960
Side 1: Love/A Voice In The Wilderness
Side 2: The Shrine On The Second Floor/Bongo Blues (Shadows)
Cliff's second film provided the tracks for this EP which, again, included a Shadows instrumental.

Expresso Bongo
ESG 7783 January 1960
Stereo issue with same tracks as above.

Cliff Sings No. 1
SEG 7979 February 1960
Side 1: Here Comes Summer/I Gotta Know
Side 2: Blue Suede Shoes/The Snake And The Bookworm
Cliff's second album was a mix of rock and orchestral ballads and this first EP taken from the album featured four of the rock 'n' roll cuts.

Cliff Sings No. 1
ESG 7788 February 1960
Stereo issue with same tracks as above.

Cliff Sings No. 2
SEG 7987 March 1960
Side 1: Twenty Flight Rock/Pointed Toe Shoes
Side 2: Mean Woman Blues/I'm Walkin'
The second EP from the Cliff Sings album also featured four rock 'n' roll tracks.

Cliff Sings No. 2
ESG 7794 March 1960
Stereo issue with same tracks as above.

Cliff Sings No. 3
SEG 8005 June 1960
Side 1: I'll String Along With You/Embraceable You
Side 2: As Times Goes By/The Touch Of Your Lips

Four of the orchestral ballads made up this third selection from Cliff Sings.

Cliff Sings No. 3
ESG 7808 June 1960
Stereo issue with same tracks as above.

Cliff Sings No. 4
SEG 8021 September 1960
Side 1: I Don't Know Why/Little Things Mean A Lot
Side 2: Somewhere Along The Way/That's My Desire
These four ballads completed the transfer of the Cliff Sings album onto EP.

Cliff Sings No. 4
ESG 7816 September 1960
Stereo issue with same tracks as above.

Cliff's Silver Discs
SEG 8050 December 1960
Side 1: Please Don't Tease/Fall In Love With You
Side 2: Nine Times Out Of Ten/Travellin' Light
By 1960 Cliff had earned enough awards to justify a Silver Discs EP.

Me And My Shadows No. 1
SEG 8065/ESG 7837 February 1961
Side 1: I'm Gonna Get You/You And I/I Cannot Find A
    True Love
Side 2: Evergreen Tree/She's Gone
As with Cliff Sings this, and the next two EPs, contained all the material featured on the Me And My Shadows album.

Me And My Shadows No. 1
ESG 7837 February 1961
Stereo issue with same tracks as above.

Me And My Shadows No. 2
SEG 8071 March 1961
Side 1: Left Out Again/You're Just The One To Do It/
    Lamp Of Love
Side 2: Choppin' And Changin'/We Have It Made
The second EP to feature material from Me And My Shadows.

Me And My Shadows No. 2
ESG 7841 March 1961
Stereo issue with same tracks as above.

Me And My Shadows No. 3
SEG 8078 April 1961
Side 1: Tell Me/Gee Whiz It's You/I'm Willing To Learn
Side 2: I Love You So/I Don't Know
This third EP collected up the remaining Me and My Shadows tracks.

Me And My Shadows No. 3
ESG 7843 April 1961
Stereo issue with same tracks as above.

Listen To Cliff
SEG 8105 October 1961
Side 1: What'd I Say/True Love Will Come To You
Side 2: Blue Moon/Lover
As with Cliff Sings the Listen To Cliff set also featured standards and, along with the rocker What I'd Say, three made it onto this release.

Listen To Cliff
ESG 7858 October 1961
Stereo issue with same tracks as above.

Dream
SEG 8119 November 1961
Side 1: Dream/All I Do Is Dream Of You
Side 2: I'll See You In My Dreams/When I Grow Too
    Old To Dream
This EP featured four tracks that all had a theme to them and contained material unavailable elsewhere at the time of release.

Dream
ESG 7867 November 1961
Stereo issue with same tracks as above.

Listen To Cliff No. 2
SEG 8126 December 1961
Side 1: Unchained Melody/First Lesson In Love/Idle
    Gossip

Side 2: Almost Like Being In Love/Beat Out Dat
   Rhythm On A Drum
Five more standards from the Listen To Cliff album

Listen To Cliff No. 2
ESG 7870 December 1961
Stereo issue with same tracks as above.

Cliff's Hit Parade
SEG 8133 February 1962
Side 1: I Love You/Theme For A Dream
Side 2: A Girl Like You/When The Girl In Your Arms
   (Is The Girl In Your Heart)
As with Cliff's Silver Discs this EP rounded up four
recent chart successes.

Cliff Richard No. 1
SEG 8151 April 1962
Side 1: Forty Days/Catch Me
Side 2: How Wonderful To Know/Tough Enough
Four tracks lifted from the 21 Today album made up
this 1962 release

Hits From The Young Ones
SEG 8159 May 1962
Side 1: The Young Ones/Got A Funny Feeling
Side 2: Lessons In Love/We Say Yeah
As the title suggests this contained the four biggest and
best tracks from Cliff's third film.

Cliff Richard No. 2
SEG 8168 June 1962
Side 1: Fifty Tears For Every Kiss/The Night Is
   So Lonely
Side 2: Poor Boy/Y' Arriva
Four more 21 Today songs formed this mid-1962
EP release

Cliff's Hits
SEG 8203 November 1962
Side 1: It'll Be Me/Since I Lost You
Side 2: Do You Want To Dance/I'm Looking Out
   The Window
Another collection of recent hits made this EP
exceptional value for money.

Time For Cliff And The Shadows
SEG 8228 March 1963
Side 1: So I've Been Told/I'm Walking The Blues/
   When My Dreamboat Comes Home
Side 2: Blueberry Hill/You Don't Know
This five-track EP was made up of material from the
32 Minutes and 17 Seconds album

Time For Cliff And The Shadows
ESG 7887 March 1963
Stereo issue with same tracks as above.

Holiday Carnival

SEG 8246 May 1963

Side 1: Carnival/Moonlight Bay

Side 2: Some Of These Days/For You For Me

These four tracks were brought together for first-time release on EP.

Holiday Carnival

ESG 7892 May 1963

Stereo issue with same tracks as above.

Hits From Summer Holiday

SEG 8250 June 1963

Side 1: Summer Holiday/The Next Time

Side 2: Dancing Shoes/Bachelor Boy

As with the Young Ones EP this brought together the best of the movie songs from Summer Holiday and contained two of Cliff's biggest hits.

Hits From Summer Holiday

ESG 7896 June 1963

Stereo issue with same tracks as above.

More Hits From Summer Holiday

SEG 8263 September 1963

Side 1: Seven Days To A Holiday/Stranger In Town

Side 2: Really Waltzing/All At Once

Four more soundtrack songs lifted from the album.

More Hits From Summer Holiday

ESG 7898 September 1963

Stereo issue with same tracks as above.

Cliff's Lucky Lips

SEG 8269 October 1963

Side 1: It's All In The Game/Your Eyes Tell On You

Side 2: Lucky Lips/I Wonder

Both sides of two recent singles made up the contents of this popular 1963 release.

Love Songs

SEG 8272 November 1963

Side 1: I'm In The Mood For Love/Secret Love

Side 2: Love Letters/I Only Have Eyes For You

A selection of well known love songs aimed at a wider audience made this EP popular with old and young alike.

Love Songs

ESG 7900 November 1963

Stereo issue with same tracks as above.

When In France

SEG 8290 February 1964

Side 1: La Ber/Boum

Side 2: J'Attendrai/C'est Si Bon

The first foreign language EP was a collection of French standards.

Cliff Sings Don't Talk To Him

SEG 8299 March 1964

Side 1: Don't Talk To Him/Say You're Mine

Side 2: Spanish Harlem/Who Are We To Say/Falling In Love With Love

The recent hit, Don't Talk To Him, was the lead track on this EP. The remaining four tracks were taken from 32 Minutes and 17 Seconds.

Cliff's Palladium Successes

SEG 8320 May 1964

Side 1: I'm The Lonely One/Watch What You Do With My Baby

Side 2: Perhaps Perhaps Perhaps/Frenesi

Throughout the years Cliff appeared at many London Palladium seasons and this EP gathered four of the popular tracks performed during these appearances.

Wonderful Life No. 1

SEG 8338 August 1964

Side 1: Wonderful Life/Do You Remember

Side 2: What've I Gotta Do/Walkin' (Shadows)

Cliff's fifth film and the first of three EPs to include material taken from the album. As with many of the earlier EPs it also included an instrumental by the Shadows.

Wonderful Life No. 1

ESG 7902 August 1964

Stereo issue with same tracks as above.

A Forever Kind Of Love

SEG 8347 September 1964

Side 1: A Forever Kind Of Love/It's Wonderful To Be Young

Side 2: Constantly/True True Lovin'

With the inclusion of It's Wonderful To Be Young, the American title of the Young Ones film, and the recent hit Constantly this became a popular EP.

Wonderful Life No. 2

SEG 8354 October 1964

Side 1: A Matter Of Moments/Girl In Every Port

Side 2: A Little Imagination/In The Stars

The second EP lifted from the soundtrack album.

Wonderful Life No. 2

ESG 7903 October 1964

Stereo issue with same tracks as above.

Hits From Wonderful Life

SEG 8376 December 1964

Side 1: On The Beach/We Love A Movie

Side 2: Home/All Kinds Of People

This third EP lifted from the Wonderful Life album had an advantage, sales wise, as it contained the hit On The Beach

Hits From Wonderful Life

ESG 7906 December 1964

Stereo issue with same tracks as above.

Why Don't They Understand

SEG 8384 February 1965

Side 1: Why Don't They Understand/Where The Four Winds Blow

Side 2: The Twelfth Of Never/I'm Afraid To Go Home

This 1965 EP contained a recent hit single and three otherwise unavailable tracks.

Cliff's Hits From Aladdin And His Wonderful Lamp

SEG 8395 March 1965

Side 1: Havin' Fun/Evening Comes

Side 2: Friends/I Could Easily Fall (In Love With You)

These four tracks were taken from the cast/soundtrack album of Cliff's first pantomime Aladdin and featured the hit single I Could Easily Fall.

Look In My Eyes Maria

SEG 8405 May 1965

Side 1: Look In My Eyes Maria/Where Is Your Heart

Side 2: Maria/If I Give My Heart To You

The West Side Story hit song Maria was one of the highlights of this romantic EP.

Angel

SEG 8444 September 1965

Side 1: Angel/I Only Came To Say Goodbye

Side 2: On My Word/The Minute You're Gone

This EP contained some material recorded in the States during Cliff's Nashville/New York recording sessions.

Take Four

SEG 8450 October 1965

Side 1: Boom Boom (That's How My Heart Sings)/My Heart Is An Open Book

Side 2: Lies And Kisses/Sweet And Gentle

Four unrelated tracks formed this 1965 EP release.

Wind Me Up

SEG 8474 February 1966

Side 1: Wind Me Up/The Night

Side 2: The Time In Between/Look Before You Love

As with the Lucky Lips EP back in 1963 both sides of two recent singles were utilised on this collection.

Hits From When In Rome

SEG 8478 April 1966

Side 1: Come Prima (For The First Time)/Nel Blu Di Pinto Di Blu (Volare)

Side 2: Dicitencello Vuie (Just Say I Love Her)/Arrivederci Roma

Four of the popular Italian standards were taken from the When In Rome album to make up this EP.

Love Is Forever

SEG 8488 April 1966

Side 1: My Colouring Book/Fly Me To The Moon

Side 2: Someday/Everyone Needs Someone To Love

Well known standards made up this selection lifted from the Love Is Forever album.

Thunderbirds Are Go

SEG 8510 December 1966

Side 1: Shooting Star/Lady Penelope (Shadows)

Side 2: Thunderbirds Theme (Shadows)/Zero X
Theme (Shadows)

Only one Cliff track featured on this EP the rest being Shadows instrumentals. All four were taken from the Thunderbirds Are Go soundtrack which featured puppets of Cliff and the Shadows.

La La La La La

SEG 8517 December 1966

Side 1: La La La La La/Solitary Man

Side 2: Things We Said Today/Never Knew What
Love Could Do

This 1966 EP included tracks written by Lennon/McCartney and Neil Diamond.

Cinderella

SEG 8527 May 1967

Side 1: Come Sunday/Peace And Quiet

Side 2: She Needs Him More Than Me/Hey
Doctor Man

As with Aladdin these tracks were taken from the Cinderella cast/soundtrack release. Unlike Aladdin this featured no hit singles.

Carol Singers

SEG 8533 November 1967

Side 1: God Rest Ye Merry Gentlemen/In The Bleak
Midwinter/Unto Us A Boy Is Born

Side 2: While Shepherds Watched/O Little Town of
Bethlehem

A collection of traditional carols, performed a cappella, made up this festive EP.

Congratulations

SEG 8540 April 1968

Side 1: Congratulations/Wonderful World/Do You
Remember

Side 2: High And Dry/The Sound Of The Candyman's
Trumpet/Little Rag Doll

These six tracks were the songs Cliff performed on the Cilla Black Show for selection as the British entry in the Eurovision Song Contest. The winning entry, Congratulations, made this a popular EP.

Christmas EP

XMAS 91 December 1991

Side 1: We Should Be Together/Mistletoe And Wine

Side 2: Twelve Days Of Christmas/The Holly And
The Ivy

Released as a special limited edition this EP featured Cliff's current single along with two unreleased tracks from the sessions that produced the Carol Singers EP back in 1967.

ALBUMS

Cliff

Mono SX 1147 April 1959

Side 1: Apron Strings/My Babe/Down The Line/I Got
A Feeling/Jet Black (Drifters)/Baby I Don't Care/
Donna/Move It

Side 2: Ready Teddy/Too Much/Don't Bug Me Baby/
Driftin' (Drifters)/That'll Be The Day/Be Bop A Lula
(Drifters)/Danny/Whole Lotta Shakin' Goin' On

Cliff's first album consisted of sixteen tracks recorded

live before a specially invited audience at Abbey Road Studios. Cliff spent 32 weeks on the charts reaching a high of number 4.

Cliff Sings

Mono SX 1192 November 1959

Side 1: Blue Suede Shoes/The Snake And The Bookworm/I Gotta Know/Here Comes Summer/I'll String Along With You/Embraceable You/As Times Goes By/The Touch Of Your Lips

Side 2: Twenty Flight Rock/Pointed Toe Shoes/Mean Woman Blues/I'm Walking/I Don't Know Why/Little Things Mean A Lot/Somewhere Along The Way/ That's My Desire

Cliff's second album was a mix of rock 'n' roll tracks and well known standards aimed at a wider audience. Cliff Sings reached number 2 and stayed on the charts for 36 weeks.

Me And My Shadows

Mono SX 1261 October 1960

Side 1: I'm Gonna Get You/You And I/I Cannot Find a True Love/Evergreen Tree/She's Gone/Left Out Again/You're Just The One To Do It/Lamp Of Love

Side 2: Choppin' and Changin'/We Have It Made/Tell Me/Gee Whiz It's You/I Love You So/I'm Willing To Learn/I Don't Know/Working After School

The first real British rock 'n' roll album and a great mix of slow and uptempo tracks. Spent 33 weeks on the charts reaching the number 2 position.

Me And My Shadows

Stereo SCX 3330 October 1960

Stereo issue with same tracks as above, although certain titles are different versions. See Alternate Versions section, pages 196-7.

Listen To Cliff

Mono SX 1320 May 1961

Side 1: What'd I Say/Blue Moon/True Love Will Come To You/Lover/Unchained Melody/Idle Gossip/First Lesson In Love/Almost Like Being In Love

Side 2: Beat Out Dat Rhythm On a Drum/Memories Linger On/Temptation/I Live For You/Sentimental Journey/I Want You To Know/We Kiss In A

Shadow/It's You

As with Cliff Sings this album mixed well known standards with some rock 'n' roll material and spent 28 weeks on the charts peaking at number 2.

Listen To Cliff

Stereo SCX 3375 May 1961

Stereo issue with same tracks as above, although certain titles are different versions. See Alternate Versions section, pages 196-7.

21 Today

Mono SX 1368 October 1961

Side 1: Happy Birthday To You/Forty Days/Catch Me/ How Wonderful To Know/Tough Enough/Fifty Tears For Every Kiss/The Night Is So Lonely/Poor Boy

Side 2: Y'Arriva/Outside/Tea For Two/To Prove My Love For You/Without You/A Mighty Lonely Man/ My Blue Heaven/Shame On You

Released the month of Cliff's 21st birthday 21 Today, like his previous releases, continued the successful formula of mixing standards with new material. Cliff's first number one album spending 16 weeks on the charts.

21 Today

Stereo SCX 3409 October 1961

Stereo issue with same tracks as above.

The Young Ones

Mono SX 1384 December 1961

Side 1: Friday Night/Got A Funny Feeling/Peace Pipe (Shadows)/Nothing's Impossible/The Young Ones/ All For One/Lessons In Love

Side 2: No One For Me But Nicki/What Do You Know We've Got A Show – Vaudeville Routine/When The Girl In Your Arms (Is The Girl In Your Heart)/Just Dance-Mood Mambo/The Savage (Shadows)/We Say Yeah

All fourteen songs from Cliff's third film, The Young Ones, made up this album which spent an incredible 42 weeks on the charts peaking at number one.

The Young Ones

Stereo SCX 3397 December 1961

Stereo issue with same tracks as above.

32 Minutes And 17 Seconds With Cliff Richard

Mono SX 1431 October 1962

Side 1: It'll Be Me/So I've Been Told/How Long Is
Forever/I'm Walking The Blues/Turn Around/
Blueberry Hill/Let's Make A Memory

Side 2: When My Dreamboat Comes Home/I'm On My
Way/Spanish Harlem/You Don't Know/Falling In Love
With Love/Who Are We To Say/I Wake Up Cryin'

The title, 32 Minutes And 17 Seconds ..., was also the running time of this set of mainly well-known standards that
reached number 3 while spending 21 weeks in the charts.

32 Minutes And 17 Seconds With Cliff Richard

Stereo SCX 3436 October 1962

Stereo issue with same tracks as above.

Summer Holiday

Mono SX 1472 January 1963

Side 1: Seven Days To A Holiday/Summer Holiday/
Let Us Take You For A Ride/Les Girls (Shadows)/
Round And Round (Shadows)/Foot Tapper
(Shadows)/Stranger In Town/Orlando's Mime

Side 2: Bachelor Boy/A Swingin' Affair/Really
Waltzing/All At Once/Dancing Shoes/Yugoslav
Wedding/The Next Time/Big News

The soundtrack album from Cliff's third, and most
successful film, featured all sixteen tracks from the film.
This became Cliff's third number one album with 36
weeks on the charts.

Summer Holiday

Stereo SCX 3462 January 1963

Stereo issue with same tracks as above.

Cliff's Hit Album

Mono SX 1512 July 1963

Side 1: Move It/Living Doll/Travellin' Light/A Voice In
The Wilderness/Fall In Love With You/Please Don't
Tease/Nine Times Out Of Ten

Side 2: I Love You/Theme For A Dream/A Girl Like
You/When The Girl In Your Arms/The Young Ones/
I'm Looking Out The Window/Do You Wanna Dance

Fourteen top ten hits were included on this LP. Cliff's
Hit Album just failed to reach the top spot peaking at
number 2 with a run of 19 weeks on the charts.

Cliff's Hit Album

Stereo SCX 1512 July 1963

Stereo issue with same tracks as above.

When In Spain

Mono SX 1541 September 1963

Side 1: Perfidia/Amor, Amor, Amor/Frenesi/Solamente
Una Vez/Vaya Con Dios/Me Lo Dijo Adela

Side 2: Maria No Mas/Tus Besos/Quizás, Quizás,
Quizás/Te Quiero Dijiste/Canción De Orfeo/Quien
Sera

Cliff's first album of foreign language recordings, taped
during a run of sessions held in Barcelona in early 1963,
only reached number 8 on the charts, probably due to
the limited appeal of this type of recording. When In
Spain spent 10 weeks on the charts.

When In Spain

Stereo SCX 3488 September 1963

Stereo issue with same tracks as above.

Wonderful Life

Mono SX 1628 July 1964

Side 1: Wonderful Life/A Girl In Every Port/Walkin'
(Shadows)/Home/A Little Imagination/On The
Beach/In The Stars

Side 2: We Love A Movie/Do You Remember/What've
I Gotta Do/Theme For Young Lovers (Shadows)/All
Kinds Of People/A Matter Of Moments/Youth And
Experience

This was the soundtrack to Cliff's fifth film. All fourteen
movie songs were included. Wonderful Life stayed on
the charts for a total of 23 weeks peaking at number 2.

Wonderful Life

Stereo SCX 3515 July 1964

Stereo issue with same tracks as above.

Aladdin And His Wonderful Lamp

Mono SX 1676 December 1964

Side 1: Emperor Theme (Orchestra)/Chinese Street
Scene (Orchestra)/Me Oh My (Shadows)/I Could
Easily Fall (In Love With You)/Little Priness
(Shadows)/This Was My Special Day/I'm In Love
With You/There's Gotta Be A Way/Ballet: (Rubies,

Emeralds, Sapphires, Diamonds) (Orchestra)
Side 2: Dance Of The Warriors (Orchestra)/Friends/
Dragon Dance (Orchestra)/Genie With The Light
Brown Lamp (Shadows)/Make Ev'ry Day A Carnival
Day/Widow Twankey's Song (Orchestra)/I'm Feeling
Oh So Lonely (Orchestra)/I've Said Too Many Things/
Evening Comes/Havin' Fun

This cast album from the Aladdin pantomime contained a
mix of Cliff, Shadows solos and orchestral tracks. Aladdin
only reached number 13 with 5 weeks on the charts.

Aladdin And His Wonderful Lamp
Stereo SCX 3522 December 1964
Stereo issue with same tracks as above.

Cliff Richard
Mono SX 1709 April 1965
Side 1: Angel/Sway/I Only Came To Say Goodbye/
Take Special Care/Magic Is The Moonlight/House
Without Windows/Razzle Dazzle
Side 2: I Don't Wanna Love You/It's Not For Me To
Say/You Belong To My Heart/Again/Perfidia/Kiss/
Reelin' And Rockin'

Featuring material recorded over several months and
at various studios, including Nashville and Abbey Road,
this was the first Cliff album not to feature his picture
on the cover. Five weeks on the charts and a high of
number nine.

Cliff Richard
Stereo SCX 3456 April 1965
Stereo issue with same tracks as above.

More Hits By Cliff
Mono SX 1737 July 1965
Side 1: It'll Be Me/The Next Time/Bachelor Boy/
Summer Holiday/Dancing Shoes/Lucky Lips/It's All
In The Game
Side 2: Don't Talk To Him/I'm The Lonely One/
Constantly/On The Beach/A Matter Of Moments/
The Twelfth Of Never/I Could Easily Fall (In Love
With You)

This second compilation, containing fourteen recent
hits, only managed to reach number twenty on the
charts and spent just one week on the charts.

More Hits By Cliff
Stereo SCX 3555 July 1965
Stereo issue with same tracks as above.

When In Rome
Mono SX 1762 August 1965
Side 1: Come Prima/Nel Blu Dipinto Di Blu/Concerto
D'Autumno/O Mio Signore/Maria Ningeum/Non
L'Ascoltare/Dicitencello Vuie
Side 2: Arrivederci Roma/Carina/Legata Ad Un
Granello Di Sabbia/Casa Senza Finestre/Che Cosa
Del Farai Mio Amour/Per Un Bacio D'Amore

Cliff's second foreign language collection, this time
recorded in Lisbon, was the first album that failed to
chart.

Love Is Forever
Mono SX 1769 November 1965
Side 1: Everyone Needs Someone To Love/Long Ago
(And Far Away)/All Of A Sudden (My Heart Sings)/
Have I Told You Lately That I Love You/Fly Me To
The Moon/A Summer Place/I Found A Rose
Side 2: My Foolish Heart/Through The Eye Of A
Needle/My Colouring Book/I Walk Alone/Someday
(You'll Want Me To Want You)/Paradise Lost/Look
Homeward Angel

More well-known standards made up this fourteen-track
set that spent one week on the charts stalling at
number nineteen.

Love Is Forever
Stereo SCX 3569 November 1965
Stereo issue with same tracks as above.

Kinda Latin
Mono SX 6039 May 1966
Side 1: Blame It On The Bossa Nova/Blowing In The
Wind/Quiet Nights Of Quiet Stars/Eso Beso/The
Girl From Ipanema/One Note Samba
Side 2: Fly Me To The Moon/Our Day Will Come/
Quando, Quando, Quando/Come Closer To Me/
Meditation/Concrete And Clay

Latin influenced material, recorded during three Abbey
Road sessions in October 1965, scraped into the top
ten spending twelve weeks on the charts.

Kinda Latin

Stereo SCX 6039 May 1966

Stereo issue with same tracks as above.

Finders Keepers

Mono SX 6079 December 1966

Side 1: Finders Keepers/Time Drags By/
Washerwoman/La La La Song/My Way (Shadows)/
Oh Senorita/Spanish Music/Fiesta (Shadows)

Side 2: This Day/Paella/Finders Keepers/My Way/
Paella/Fiesta (Shadows)/Run To The Door/Where
Did The Summer Go/Into Each Life Some Rain
Must Fall

Fourteen tracks from Cliff's Finders Keepers film plus
an additional three bonus tracks made up this 1966
release. Eighteen weeks in the charts and a high of
number 6.

Finders Keepers

Stereo SCX 6079 December 1966

Stereo issue with same tracks as above.

Cinderella

Mono SX 6103 January 1967

Side 1: Welcome To Stoneybroke/Why Wasn't I Born
Rich/Peace And Quiet/The Flyder And The Spy
(Shadows)/Poverty/The Hunt/In The Country

Side 2: Come Sunday/Dare I Love Him Like I Do/If
Our Dreams Come True/Autumn/The King's Place/
Peace And Quiet/She Needs Him More Than Me/
Hey Doctor Man

Cinderella, Cliff's second pantomime cast album, was
Cliff's lowest charting album so far, reaching number
30 and spending six weeks on the charts.

Cinderella

Stereo SCX 6103 January 1967

Stereo issue with same tracks as above.

Don't Stop Me Now

Mono SX 6133 April 1967

Side 1: Shout/One Fine Day/I'll Be Back/Heartbeat/I
Saw Her Standing There/Hang On To A Dream/You
Gotta Tell Me/Homeward Bound

Side 2: Good Golly Miss Molly/Don't Make Promises/
Move It/Dizzy Miss Lizzy/Baby It's You/My Babe/
Save The Last Dance For Me

Don't Stop Me Now contained a selection of tracks
written by varied writers including Lennon & McCartney,
Simon & Garfunkel and Little Richard. Nine weeks on
the charts and a high of twenty-three was the best this
album could achieve.

Don't Stop Me Now

Stereo SCX 6133 April 1967

Stereo issue with same tracks as above.

Good News

Mono SX 6167 October 1967

Side 1: Good News/It Is No Secret/We Shall Be
Changed/23rd Psalm/Go Where I Send Thee/What
A Friend We Have In Jesus/All Glory Laud And
Honour

Side 2: Just A Closer Walk With Thee/The King Of
Love My Shepherd Is/Mary What You Gonna Name
That Pretty Little Baby/When I Survey The
Wondrous Cross/Take My Hand Precious Lord/Get
On Board Little Children/May The Good Lord Bless
And Keep You

Good News was Cliff's first gospel album. Maybe a
reflection of this type of material the album only
reached number 37 with a one week stay on the charts.

Good News

Stereo SCX 6167 October 1967

Stereo issue with same tracks as above.

Cliff In Japan

Mono SX 6244 May 1968

Side 1: Shout/I'll Come Running/The Minute You're
Gone/On The Beach/Hang On To A Dream/Spanish
Harlem/Finders Keepers/Visions/Move It

Side 2: Living Doll/La La La La La/Twist And Shout/
Evergreen Tree/What'd I Say/Dynamite/Medley:
Let's Make A Memory, The Young Ones, Lucky Lips,
Summer Holiday, We Say Yeah

Recorded during Cliff's 1967 Far-East tour this selection
of hits and recent material was Cliff's first real live
recording album. Two weeks on the charts and a high of
twenty-nine.

Cliff In Japan

Stereo SCX 6244 May 1968

Stereo issue with same tracks as above.

Two A Penny

Mono SX 6262 August 1968

Side 1: Two A Penny/I'll Love You Forever Today/
Questions/Long Is The Night (instrumental)/Lonely
Girl/And Me (I'm On The Outside Now)/Daybreak
(instrumental)

Side 2: Twist And Shout/Celeste (instrumental)/Wake
Up Wake Up/Cloudy/Red Rubber Ball/Close To
Cathy/Rattler

Fourteen tracks, including instrumentals, made up this
soundtrack album that failed to make any impression on
the charts.

Two A Penny

Stereo SCX 6262 August 1968

Stereo issue with same tracks as above.

Established 1958

Mono SX 6282 September 1968

Side 1: Don't Forget To Catch Me/Voyage To The
Bottom Of The Bath (Shadows)/Not The Way That
It Should Be/Poem/The Dreams I Dream/The
Average Life Of A Daily Man (Shadows)/
Somewhere By The Sea

Side 2: Banana Man (Shadows)/Girl On The Bus/The
Magical Mrs Clamps (Shadows)/Ooh La La/Here I
Go Again Loving You (Shadows)/What's Behind The
Eyes Of Mary/Maggie's Samba (Shadows)

To celebrate their ten years together this album
contained seven tracks each by Cliff and the Shadows
and was released in a gatefold sleeve. The album just
scraped in to the top thirty with a run of only four weeks
on the charts.

Established 1958

Stereo SCX 6282 September 1968

Stereo issue with same tracks as above.

The Best Of Cliff

Mono SX 6343 June 1969

Side 1: The Minute You're Gone/On My Word/The

Time In Between/Wind Me Up (Let Me Go)/Blue
Turns To Grey/Visions/Time Drags By

Side 2: In The Country/It's All Over/I'll Come Running/
The Day I Met Marie/All My Love/Congratulations/
Girl You'll Be A Woman Soon

Another fourteen-track compilation of recent hits that
included his first number one single for many years,
Congratulations. Cliff's first top five album since
Wonderful Life, with a run of seventeen weeks on
the charts.

The Best Of Cliff

Stereo SCX 6343 June 1969

Stereo issue with same tracks as above.

Sincerely Cliff Richard

Mono SX 6357 October 1969

Side 1: In The Past/Always/Will You Love Me
Tomorrow/You'll Want Me/I'm Not Getting Married/
Time/For Emily Whenever I May Find Her

Side 2: Baby I Could Be So Good At Loving You/
Sam/London's Not Too Far/Take Action/Take Good
Care Of Her/When I Find You/Punch And Judy

Recorded at various sessions over a fifteen-month
period Sincerely Cliff Richard is a mixed bag of
recordings. Sincerely reached number 24 and spent
three weeks on the chart.

Sincerely Cliff Richard

Stereo SCX 6357 October 1969

Stereo issue with same tracks as above.

Cliff Live At The Talk Of The Town

Regal SRS 5031 July 1970

Side 1: Introduction/Congratulations/Shout/All My
Love/Ain't Nothing But A House Party/Something
Good/If Ever I Should Leave You/Girl You'll Be A
Woman Soon/Hank's Medley/London's Not Too Far/
The Dreams That I Dream/The Day I Met Marie

Side 2: La La La La La/A Taste Of Honey/The Lady
Came From Baltimore/When I'm 64/What's More I
Don't Need Her/Bows and Fanfare/Congratulations/
Visions/Finale: Congratulations

In the late sixties and early seventies Cliff made many
cabaret appearances at the Talk Of The Town and this

recording, from May 1968, failed to chart despite the inclusion of several new tracks.

About That Man

SCX 6408 October 1970

Side 1: The Birth Of John The Baptist/Sweet Little Jesus Boy/The Visit Of The Wise Men And The Escape Into Egypt/John The Baptist Points Out Jesus/Jesus Recruits His Helpers And Heals The Sick/Where Is That Man

Side 2: Jesus Addresses The Crowd On The Hillside/ Can It Be True/Jesus Is Betrayed And Arrested/ The Trial Of Jesus/His Execution And Death/The First Easter – The Empty Tomb/Reflections

Cliff's second gospel collection featured Bible readings interspersed with a few songs. Again, possibly due to the material and limited appeal, this album failed to chart.

His Land

SCX 6443 November 1970

Side 1: Ezekiel's Vision/Dry Bones/His Land/ Jerusalem Jerusalem/The New 23rd

Side 2: His Land/Hava Nagila/Over In Bethelehem/ Keep Me Where Love Is/He's Everything To Me/ Narration And Hallelujah Chorus

The His Land film provided the material for this collection of gospel material. Once again limited appeal was the cause of its chart failure.

Tracks And Grooves

SCX 6435 November 1970

Side 1: Early In The Morning/As I Walk Into The Morning Of Your Life/Love Truth And Emily Stone/ My Head Goes Around/Put My Mind At Ease/ Abraham, Martin And John/The Girl Can't Help It/ Bang Bang (My Baby Shot Me Down)

Side 2: I'll Make It All Up To You/I'd Just Be Fool Enough/Don't Let Tonight Ever End/What A Silly Thing To Do/Your Heart's Not In Your Love/Don't Ask Me To Be Friends/Are You Only Fooling Me

As with Sincerely this album combined tracks recorded over a fifteen-month period and included several songs that had been recent hits for other artists. Tracks And Grooves spent just two weeks on the charts and stalled at number 37.

The Best Of Cliff Volume Two

SCX 6519 November 1972

Side 1: Goodbye Sam, Hello Samantha/Marianne/ Thrown Down A Line/Jesus/Sunny Honey Girl/I Ain't Got Time Anymore/Flying Machine

Side 2: Sing A Song Of Freedom/With The Eyes Of A Child/Good Times (Better Times)/I'll Love You Forever Today/The Joy Of Living/Silvery Rain/ Big Ship

The second volume in the Best Of Cliff series, collecting together fourteen recent singles, was a weaker selection than its predecessor as shown by its two-week run and a high of number 49.

Take Me High

EMI EMC 3016 December 1973

Side 1: It's Only Money/Midnight Blue/Hover/Why/ Life/Driving/The Game/Brumburger Duet

Side 2: Take Me High/The Anti-Brotherhood Of Man/ Winning/Driving/Join The Band/The Word Is Love/ Brumburger (Finale)

Take Me High featured all fifteen numbers from what was his last movie appearance. Several of the tracks were instrumentals. Take Me High had a four-week stay on the charts reaching number 41.

Help It Along

EMI EMA 768 June 1974

Side 1: Day By Day/Celestial Houses/Jesus/Silvery Rain/Jesus Loves You/Fire And Rain

Side 2: Yesterday Today Forever/Mr Businessman/ Help It Along/Amazing Grace/Higher Ground/Sing A Song Of Freedom

Another live-in-the-studio recording, this time featuring mainly gospel and inspirational tracks. Released in a gatefold sleeve the album failed to achieve any chart action.

The 31st Of February Street

EMI EMC 3048 November 1974

Side 1: 31st Of February Street Opening/Give Me Back That Old Familiar Feeling/The Leaving/ Travellin' Light/There You Go Again/Nothing To Remind Me/Our Love Could Be So Real

Side 2: No Matter What/Fireside Song/Going Away/

Long Long Time/You Will Never Know/The Singer/
31st Of February Street Closing

31st Of February Street can be seen as Cliff's first
concept album and included a re-working of his earlier
hit Travellin' Light. Strangely it failed to create any
interest chartwise.

I'm Nearly Famous

EMI EMC 3122 May 1976

Side 1: I Can't Ask For Any More Than You/It's No Use
Pretending/I'm Nearly Famous/Lovers/Junior
Cowboy/Miss You Nights

Side 2: I Wish You'd Change Your Mind/Devil Woman/
Such Is The Mystery/You've Got To Give Me All
Your Lovin'/If You Walked Away/Alright It's Alright

All the songs were recorded at Abbey Road Studios
and were produced by Bruce Welch. Always credited
as the album that turned Cliff's career around in the
mid-seventies it managed a high of number 5 and
spent 21 weeks on the charts.

Every Face Tells A Story

EMI EMC 3172 March 1977

Side 1: My Kinda Life/Must Be Love/When Two
Worlds Drift Apart/You Got Me Wondering/Every
Face Tells A Story (It Never Tells A Lie)/Try A Smile

Side 2: Hey Mr Dream Maker/Give Me Love Your Way/
Don't Turn The Light Out/It'll Be Me Babe/Up In The
World/Spider Man

Another mid-seventies collection of strong material that
carried on the Cliff renaissance with a ten-week run on
the charts peaking at number 8.

40 Golden Greats

EMI EMTVS 6/TCEMTVS 6/CDEMTV 6 September
1977

Side 1: Move It/Living Doll/Travellin' Light/Fall In Love
With You/Please Don't Tease/Nine Times Out Of
Ten/Theme For A Dream/Gee Whiz It's You/When
The Girl In Your Arms (Is The Girl In Your Heart)/A
Girl Like You

Side 2: The Young Ones/Do You Wanna Dance/I'm
Looking Out The Window/It'll Be Me/Bachelor Boy/
The Next Time/Summer Holiday/Lucky Lips/It's All
In The Game/Don't Talk To Him

Side 3: Constantly/On The Beach/I Could Easily Fall
(In Love With You)/The Minute You're Gone/Wind
Me Up (Let Me Go)/Visions/Blue Turns To Grey/In
The Country/The Day I Met Marie/All My Love

Side 4: Congratulations/Throw Down A Line/Goodbye
Sam, Hello Samantha/Sing A Song Of Freedom/
Power To All Our Friends/(You Keep Me) Hangin' On/
Miss You Nights/Devil Woman/I Can't Ask For
Anymore Than You/My Kinda Life

Released in a gatefold sleeve and supported with heavy
promotion this 40-track greatest hits package became
Cliff's first number one album since Summer Holiday in
1963. It went on to spend 19 weeks in the charts.

Small Corners

EMI EMC 3219 February 1978

Side 1: Why Should The Devil Have All The Good
Music/I Love/Why Me Lord/I've Got News For You/
Hey Watcha Say/I Wish We'd All Been Ready

Side 2: Joseph/Good On The Sally Army/Going Home/
Up In Canada/Yes He Lives/When I Survey The
Wondrous Cross

A collection of what was now termed rock-gospel and a very strong collection that only managed to reach number 33 with a five-week residence in the charts.

Green Light

EMI EMC 3231 September 1978

Side 1: Green Light/Under Lock And Key/She's A Gypsy/Count Me Out/Please Remember Me/Never Even Thought

Side 2: Free My Soul/Start All Over Again/While She's Young/Can't Take The Hurt Anymore/Ease Along

Reaching only 25 in the charts with a three-week stay did not do this album justice. One of the last albums to be recorded at Abbey Road, Green Light was a strong collection of contemporary material.

Thank You Very Much

EMI EMTV 15 February 1979

Side 1: The Young Ones/Do You Wanna Dance/The Day I Met Marie/Shadoogie (Shadows)/Atlantis (Shadows)/Nivram (Shadows)/Apache (Shadows)/Please Don't Tease/Miss You Nights

Side 2: Move It/Willie And The Hand Jive/All Shook Up/Devil Woman/Why Should The Devil Have All The Good Music/End Of The Show

Taped during Cliff and the Shadows reunion concerts at the Palladium. A mix of early hits, Shadows instrumentals and recent hits this album couldn't fail and hit a high of number 5 spending twelve weeks on the charts.

Rock And Roll Juvenile

EMI EMC 3307/TCEMC 3307 September 1979

Side 1: Monday Thru Friday/Doin' Fine/Cities May Fall/You Know That I Love You/My Luck Won't Change/Rock 'n' Roll Juvenile

Side 2: Sci Fi/Fallin' In Luv/Carrie/Hot Shot/Language Of Love/We Don't Talk Anymore

With backing tracks recorded in France and the vocals laid down at Abbey Road this album, Cliff's favourite, reached number 3 and had a 22-week stay on the charts, helped by the successful We Don't Talk Anymore which was added to the track listing at the last moment.

I'm No Hero

EMI EMA 796 September 1980

Side 1: Take Another Look/Anything I Can Do/A Little In Love/Here (So Doggone Blue)/Give A Little Bit More

Side 2: In The Night/I'm No Hero/Dreamin'/A Heart Will Break/Everyman

A new studio, Riverside, was used for the I'm No Hero recordings and the resulting album achieved an eleven-week run with a high of number 4.

Love Songs

EMTV 27/TCEMTV 27/CDEMTV 27 July 1981

Side 1: Miss You Nights/Constantly/Up In The World/Carrie/A Voice In The Wilderness/The Twelfth Of Never/I Could Easily Fall (In Love With You)/The Day I Met Marie/Can't Take The Hurt Anymore/A Little In Love

Side 2: The Minute You're Gone/Visions/When Two Worlds Drift Apart/The Next Time/It's All In The Game/Don't Talk To Him/When The Girl In Your Arms (Is The Girl In Your Heart)/Theme For A Dream/Fall In Love With You/We Don't Talk Anymore

A TV promoted album of twenty of Cliff's best love songs. With the help of TV advertising the album spent an incredible 43 weeks on the charts and reached the top spot

Wired For Sound

EMC 3377/TCEMI 5221 September 1981

Side 1: Wired For Sound/Once In A While/Better Than I Know Myself/Oh No Don't Let Go/'Cos I Love That Rock And Roll

Side 2: Broken Doll/Lost In A Lonely World/Summer Rain/Young Love/Say You Don't Mind/Daddy's Home

The successful accompanying video for the Wired For Sound single helped this album achieve its top 4 position and 25-week run on the charts.

Now You See Me Now You Don't

EMC 3415/TCEMC 3415 August 1982

Side 1: The Only Way Out/First Date/Thief In The Night/Where Do We Go From Here/Son Of Thunder/Little Town

Side 2: It Has To Be You It Has To Be Me/The Water Is Wide/Now You See Me Now You Don't/Be In My Heart/Discovering

A modern collection of gospel and inspirational recordings taped in 1982 at the Strawberry Studios gave Cliff his second consecutive top 4 album with a fourteen-week chart run.

Dressed For The Occasion

EMC 3432/TCEMC 3432 May 1983

Side 1: Green Light/We Don't Talk Anymore/True Love Ways/Softly As I Leave You/Carrie/Miss You Nights

Side 2: Galadriel/Maybe Someday/Thief In The Night/ Up In The World/Treasure Of Love/Devil Woman

Backed by the London Philharmonic Orchestra and recorded live at the Royal Albert Hall in London Dressed For The Occasion spent seventeen weeks on the charts reaching number 7.

Silver/Rock And Roll Silver

EMC 1077871 October 1983

Side 1: Silver's Home Tonight/Hold On/Never Say Die (Give A Little Bit More)/Front Page/Ocean Deep

Side 2: Locked Inside Your Prison/Please Don't Fall In Love/Baby You're Dynamite/The Golden Days Are Over/Love Stealer

Side 3: Makin' History/Move It/Donna/Teddy Bear/ It'll Be Me

Side 4: Lucille/Little Bitty Pretty One/There'll Never Be Anyone Else But You/Be Bop A Lula/Tutti Frutti

Released as a boxed set this two record set featured one album of new material and a second album of re-recorded rock 'n' roll classics. The Silver album was later re-issued as a single album. Twenty-four weeks on the chart and a high of number 7.

The Rock Connection

Clif 2/TCCLIF 2 November 1984

Side 1: Heart User/Willie And The Hand Jive/Lovers And Friends/Never Be Anyone Else But You/La Gonave/Over You/Shooting From The Heart

Side 2: Learning How To Rock and Roll/Lucille/Be Bop A Lula/Donna/Dynamite/She Means Nothing To Me/Makin' History

Offering some new material this album also included a couple of tracks from the previous set. The inclusion of the hit single She Means Nothing To Me (with Phil

Everly) made the Rock Connection a strong album but it failed to enter the top forty stalling at number 43 with only five weeks on the charts.

20 Original Greats

EMI CRS1 July 1984

Side 1: On The Beach/Do You Wanna Dance/Lucky Lips/Don't Talk To Him/A Voice In The Wilderness/ A Girl Like You/Fall In Love With You/Gee Whiz Its You/Mean Streak/In The Country

Side 2: Move It/Nine Times Out Of Ten/Dancing Shoes/Theme For A Dream/Willie And The Hand Jive/I'm The Lonely One/When The Girl In Your Arms (Is The Girl In Your Heart)/Time Drags By/ I Could Easily Fall/We Say Yeah

A collection of 20 hits covering the fifties and sixties. The album failed to chart.

Always Guaranteed

EMD 1004/TCEMD 1004 September 1987

Side 1: One Night/Once Upon A Time/Some People/ Forever/Two Hearts

Side 2: Under Your Spell/This Time Now/My Pretty One/Remember Me/Always Guaranteed

Recorded at RG Jones in Wimbledon this was Cliff's most successful album up to this point and during its 25-week run achieved a top five position.

Private Collection

CRTV 30/TCCRTV 30 November 1988

Side 1: Some People/Wired For Sound/All I Ask Of You/Carrie/Remember Me/True Love Ways/ Dreamin'/Green Light/She Means Nothing To Me/ Heart User/A Little In Love/Daddy's Home

Side 2: We Don't Talk Anymore/Never Say Die/The Only Way Out/Suddenly/Slow Rivers/Please Don't Fall In Love/Little Town/My Pretty One/Ocean Deep/ She's So Beautiful/Two Hearts/Mistletoe And Wine

A collection of Cliff's favourite recordings from the seventies and eighties made up this two-record set released in a gatefold sleeve. Another number one album with 22 weeks on the charts.

Stronger

EMD 1012/TCEMD 1012 October 1989

Side 1: Stronger Than That/Who's In Love/The Best Of Me/Clear Blue Skies/Keep Me Warm/Lean On You
Side 2: I Just Don't Have The Heart/Joanna/Everybody Knows/Share A Dream/Better Day/Forever You Will Be Mine

Stronger featured a mixture of tracks from the dance style of Just Don't Have The Heart to the reggae influenced Stare A Dream with a mix of rock and ballads along the way. Stronger also included Cliff's 100th single The Best Of Me and the album reached a high of number 7.

From A Distance – The Event

CRTV 31/TCCRTV 31 November 1990
Side 1: Oh Boy Medley/Zing Went The Strings Of My Heart (Dallas Boys)/Always/When (Kalin Twins)/The Glory Of Love
Side 2: Hoots Mon (Oh Boy Band)/Don't Look Now (Vernon Girls)/The Girl Can't Help It/Sea Cruise/Oh Boy Medley
Side 3: From A Distance/Some People/We Don't Talk Anymore/Shake Rattle And Roll/Silhouettes/Move It/Summer Holiday/The Young Ones
Side 4: In The Country/Good Golly Miss Molly/Fighter/Thief In The Night/Share A Dream/All The Time You Need/Saviour's Day

Recorded during the successful Event Concerts in 1989 this double album, issued in a gatefold sleeve, included material from the Oh Boy part of the show along with highlights from Cliff's own set. From A Distance – The Event peaked at number three.

Together With Cliff Richard

EMD 1028/TCEMD 1028 November 1991
Side 1: Have Yourself A Merry Little Christmas/Venite (O Come All Ye Faithful)/We Should Be Together/Mistletoe And Wine/Christmas Never Comes/Christmas Alphabet
Side 2: Saviour's Day/The Christmas Song (Merry Christmas To You)/Little Town/Scarlet Ribbons/Silent Night/White Christmas/This New Year

Cliff's first album of seasonal material was a mix of Christmas standards and contemporary material that included his two Christmas number ones, Mistletoe And Wine and Saviours Day. Together With Cliff Richard reached number ten in the album chart.

My Kinda Life (French Import)

EMD 1034/TCEMD 1034 May 1992
Side 1: Born To Rock 'n' Roll/Hot Shot/Devil Woman/Remember/Carrie/Lean On You/We Don't Talk Anymore
Side 2: Monday Thru Friday/Lucille/You've Got Me Wondering/Never Even Thought/Two Hearts/Language Of Love/My Kinda Life

Originally a French only release copies found their way into UK outlets. The content was mainly seventies material with additional overdubbed instrumental work to give them a nineties feel. Two of the tracks, Carrie and Remember had new vocals recorded, the latter being re-worked with French lyrics. As an import there was no chart action in this country.

Cliff Richard – The Album
TCEMD 1043 April 1993
Side 1: Peace In Our Time/Love's Salvation/I Still Believe In You/Love Is The Strongest Emotion/Only Angel/Handle My Heart With Love/Little Mistreater
Side 2: You Move Heaven/I Need Love/Hold Us Together/Never Let Go/Human Work Of Art/ Healing Love/Brother To Brother

Cliff Richard The Album, recorded in mid to late 1992 contained the hit singles I Still Believe In You and Peace in Our Time and included some very strong material produced by Bruce Welch and Gerry Kitchingham. The Album is the latest Cliff album to reach the coveted number one spot.

COMPACT DISCS

Cliff
CZ 1 1987
Same selections as SX 1147

Cliff Sings
80417 2 / CDEMC 3628 1992
Same selections as SX 1192

Me And My Shadows
80417 2 / CDEMC 3628 1992
Same selections as SX 1261

Listen To Cliff
80420 2 / CDEMC 3629 1992
Same selections as SCX 3375

21 Today
80420 2 / CDEMC 3629 1992
Same selections as SCX 3409

The Young Ones
MFP 6020 June 1988
Same selections as SX 1384

32 Minutes And 17 Seconds With Cliff Richard
80423 2 / CDEMC 3630 June 1988
Same selections as SCX 3436

Summer Holiday
MFP 6021 June 1988
Same selections as SX 1472

When In Spain
80423 2 / CDEMC 3630 1992
Same selections as SCX 3488

Wonderful Life
80426 2 / CDEMC 3631 1992
Same selections as SCX 3513

Aladdin And His Wonderful Lamp
80426 2 / CDEMC 3631 1992
Same selections as SCX 3522

Cliff Richard
80429 2 / CDEMC 3632 1992
Same selections as SCX 3456

When In Rome
80429 2 / CDEMC 3632 1992
Same selections as SX 1762

Love Is Forever
80432 2 / CDEMC 3633 1992
Same selections as SCX 3569

Kinda Latin
80432 2 / CDEMC 3633 1992
Same selections as SCX 6039

Finders Keepers
80435 2 / CDEMC 3634 1992
Same selections as SCX 6079

Cinderella

805352 / CDEMC 3634 1992

Same selections as SCX 6103

Don't Stop Me Now

80438 2 / CDEMC 3635 1992

Same selections as SCX 6133

Good News

80438 2 / CDEMC 3635 1992

Same selections as SCX 6167

Cliff In Japan

80441 2 / CDEMC 3636 1992

Same selections as SCX 6244

Two A Penny

80441 2 / CDEMC 3636 1992

Same selections as SCX 6262

Established 1958

80450 2 / CDEMC 3637 1992

Same selections as SCX 6282

The Best Of Cliff

80450 2 / CDEMC 3637 1992

Same selections as SCX 6343

Sincerely Cliff Richard

80444 2 / CDEMC 3638 1992

Same selections as SCX 6357

Cliff Live At The Talk Of The Town

80444 2 / CDEMC 3638 1992

Same selections as SRS 5031

About That Man

80482 2 / CDEMC 3639 1992

Same selections as SCX 6408

His Land

80482 2 / CDEMC 3639 1992

Same selections as SCX 6443

Tracks And Grooves

80485 / CDEMC 3640 1993

Same selections as SCX 6435

The Best Of Cliff Volume Two

80485 / CDEMC 3640 1993

Same selections as SCX 6519

Take Me High

80488 2 / CDEMC 3641 1993

Same selections as EMC 3016

Help It Along

80488 2 / CDEMC 3641 1993

Same selections as EMA 768

The 31st Of February Street

80491 2 / CDEMC 3642 1993

Same selections as EMC 3048

I'm Nearly Famous

80491 2 / CDEMC 3642 1993

Same selections as EMC 3122

Every Face Tells A Story

80494 2 / CDEMC 3643 1993

Same selections as EMC 3172

40 Golden Greats

CDEMTV 6 1989

Same selections as EMTVS 6

Small Corners

80494 2 / CDEMC 3643 1993

Same selections as EMC 3219

Green Light

80496 2 / CDEMC 3644 1993

Same selections as EMC 3231

Thank You Very Much

MFP 41 5677 1 1985

Same selections as EMTV 15

Thank You Very Much
80496 2 / CDEMC 3644 1993
Same selections as EMTV 15

Rock 'n' Roll Juvenile
CZ 188 1989
Same selections as EMC 3307

I'm No Hero
Fame FA 3148 June 1988
Same selections as EMA 796

Love Songs
CDP 7 48049 2 1987
Same selections as EMTV 27

Wired For Sound
Fame FA 3159 November 1988
Same selections as EMC 3377

Now You See Me Now You Don't
CDP 7 48276 2 1987
Same selections as EMC 3415

Dressed For The Ocassion
CZ 187 1989
Same selections as EMC 3432

Silver
CDP 7 46008 2 1983
Same selections as EMC 1077871 except Front
    Page/Makin' History/Teddy Bear/Tutti Frutti
    are omitted

Silver
80499 2 / CDEMC 3645 1993
As above

The Rock Connection
80499 2 / CDEMC 3645 1993
Same selections as Cliff 2

Always Guaranteed
CDEMD 1004 1987
Same selections as EMD 1004

Private Collection
CDCRTV 30 1988
Same selections as CRTV 30 except Slow
    River/Remember Me/Green Light/Heart User/
    Two Hearts

Stronger
CDEMD 1012 1989
Same selections as EMD 1012

From A Distance – The Event
CDCRTV 31 1990
Same selections as CRTV 31 except The Glory Of
    Love/Hoots Mon/Summer Holiday/In The Country/
    Good Golly Miss Molly omitted

Together With Cliff Richard
CDEMD 1028 1991
Same selections as EMD 1028

My Kinda Life (French Import)
CDEMD 1034 1992
Same selections as EMD 1034

Cliff Richard – The Album
CDEMD 1043 1993
Same selections as EMD 1012

The Hit List
CDEMTVD 84 November 1994
Move It/Living Doll/Travellin' Light/A Voice In The
    Wilderness/Fall In Love With You/Please Don't
    Tease/Nine Times Out Of Ten/I Love You/Theme
    For A Dream/Gee Whiz It's You/A Girl Like You/
    When The Girl In Your Arms Is The Girl In Your
    Heart/The Young Ones/Do You Wanna Dance/It'll
    Be Me/The Next Time/Bachelor Boy/Summer
    Holiday/Lucky Lips/It's All In The Game/Don't Talk
    To Him/Constantly/The Minute You're Gone/Wind
    Me Up (Let Me Go)/Congratulations/Power To All
    Our Friends/We Don't Talk Anymore/Carrie/Wired
    For Sound/Daddy's Home/Some People/Mistletoe
    And Wine/The Best Of Me/I Just Don't Have The
    Heart/Saviours Day/Miss You Nights/Green Light
This 1994 compilation contained every top five single

from 1958 to 1992. Miss You Nights and Green Light were added as bonus tracks.

Songs From Heathcliff

CDEMD 1091 October 1995

Misunderstood Man/The Sleep Of The Good/Gipsy Bundle/Had To Be/When You Thought Of Me/ Dream Tomorrow/I Don't Love You Isabella/ Choosing/When It's Too Late/Marked With Death/Be With Me Always

This album, as the title suggests, featured songs from the musical Heathcliff.

Cliff At The Movies 1959–1974

CD EMD 1096 July 1996

No Turning Back/Living Doll/Mad About You/Love/A Voice In The Wilderness/The Shrine On The Second Floor/Friday Night/Got A Funny Feeling/Nothing's Impossible/The Young Ones/Lessons In Love/When The Girl In Your Arms/We Say Yeah/(It's) Wonderful To Be Young/Outsider/Seven Days To A Holiday/Summer Holiday/Let Us Take You For A Ride/A Stranger In Town/Bachelor Boy/Swinging Affair/Dancing Shoes/The Next Time/Big News/Wonderful Life/A Girl In Every Port/A Little Imagination/On The Beach/Do You Remember/Look Don't Touch/In The Stars/What've I Gotta Do/A Matter Of Moments/Wonderful Life/Shooting Star/Finders Keepers/Time Drags By/Washerwoman/La La La Song/Oh Senorita/This Day/Paella/Two A Penny/Twist and Shout/I'll Love You Forever Today/Questions/It's Only Money/Midnight Blue/The Game/Brumburger Duet/Take Me High/The Anti-Brotherhood Of Man/Winning/The Young Ones/ Lessons In Love/Bachelor Boy/Summer Holiday.

This 1996 compilation contains the best of Cliff's movie performances including eleven alternate versions and one previously unreleased track. Compiled and coordinated by the authors of this book, this 2 CD set was lavishly packaged in a slip box with a 40 page booklet and picture discs.

BOX SETS

Silver

EMC 1077871 October 1983

Side 1: Silver's Home Tonight/Hold On/Never Say Die (Give A Little Bit More)/Front Page/Ocean Deep

Side 2: Locked Inside Your Prison/Please Don't Fall In Love/Baby You're Dynamite/The Golden Days Are Over/Love Stealer

Rock And Roll Silver

Side 1: Makin' History/Move It/Donna/Teddy Bear/It'll Be Me

Side 2: Lucille/Little Bitty Pretty One/There'll Never Be Anyone Else But You/Be Bop A Lula/Tutti Frutti

The above two albums were released as a limited edition box set that included a booklet.

Always Guaranteed: The Album Box Set

EMDB 1004 September 1987

Side 1: One Night/Once Upon A Time/Some People/ Forever/Two Hearts

Side 2: Under Your Spell/This Time Now/My Pretty One/Remember Me/Always Guaranteed

Limited edition box set featuring the same tracks as the album. The set included a large colour poster, calendar, autographed colour print, four colour postcards plus a 7" single including Another Christmas Day and an engraved message from Cliff.

From A Distance – The Event

The Album Box Set

CRTVB 31 December 1990

Side 1: Oh Boy Medley/Zing Went The Strings Of My Heart (Dallas Boys)/Always/When (Kalin Twins)/The Glory Of Love

Side 2: Hoots Mon (Oh Boy Band)/Don't Look Now (Vernon Girls)/The Girl Can't Help It/Sea Cruise/Oh Boy Medley

Side 3: From A Distance/Some People/We Don't Talk Anymore/Shake Rattle And Roll/Silhouettes/Move It/Summer Holiday/The Young Ones

Side 4: In The Country/Good Golly Miss Molly/ Fighter/Thief In The Night/Share A Dream/All The

Time You Need/Saviour's Day

Limited edition box set that included six exclusive prints, giant poster with lyrics, plus engraved 7" single including a cappella version of Miss You Nights. The CD version did not contain the following titles: The Glory Of Love/Hoots Mon/Summer Holiday/In The Country/Good Golly Miss Molly. Also available on CD (CDCRTVB 31) and Cassette (TCCRTVB 31)

MISCELLANEOUS RELEASES & SELECTED RE-ISSUES

Oh Boy

Parlophone PMC1072 (Mono) December 1958

Cliff sings: At The TV Hop/Rockin' Robin/High School Confidential/King Creole/I'll Try/Early In The Morning/Somebody Touched Me

How Wonderful To Know

World Record Club (S)T 643 1966

Side 1: Forty Days/Catch Me/How Wonderful To Know/Tough Enough/Fifty Tears For Every Kiss/The Night Is So Lonely/Poor Boy

Side 2: Y'Arriva/Outsider/Tea For Two/To Prove My Love For You/Without You/A Mighty Lonely Man/My Blue Heaven/Shame On You

Re-issue of **21 Today**

Cliff Live In Japan '72

EMI/ODEON EOP 93077 B 1972

Side 1: Backscratcher/Can't Let You Go/Have A Little Talk With Myself/Sunny Honey Girl/The Minute You're Gone/Flying Machine/The Day I Met Marie

Side 2: Silvery Rain/My Way/Move It/Living In Harmony/Walk On By – The Look Of Love/Early In The Morning/Goodbye Sam Hello Samantha

Side 3: Living Doll/Bachelor Boy/The Young Ones/Congratulations/Rock 'n' Roll Medley/Sing A Song Of Freedom

Side 4: The Rise And Fall Of Flingel Bunt/Mr Sun/Apache/Lonesome Mole/Tiny Robin/A Thousand Conversations/Bye Bye Love/Something/Keep The Customer Satisfied

Side 4 featured Marvin & Farrar only

Japan Tour '74

EMI/TOSHIBA EMS-67037-38 1974

Side 1: Winning/Do You Want Dance/(You Keep Me) Hangin' On/Make It Easy On Yourself/The Sun Ain't Gonna Shine Anymore/Get Back/Fireside Song

Side 2: Travellin' Light/Give Me Back That Old Familiar Feeling/Early In The Morning/Take Me High/Hit Medley

Side 3: Constantly/You've Lost That Lovin' Feelin'/Gospel Medley/Don't Talk To Him/Bachelor Boy

Side 4: Don't Meet The Band/Rock Medley/High Ground/Sing A Song Of Freedom/Visions/Power To All Our Friends

It'll Be Me

Regal Starline SRS 5011 1968

Side 1: It'll Be Me/So I've Been Told/How Long Is Forever/I'm Walking/The Blues/Turn Around/Blueberry Hill/Let's Make A Memory

Side 2: When My Dreamboat Comes Home/I'm On My Way/Spanish Harlem/You Don't Know/Falling In Love With Love/Who Are We To Say/I Wake Up Cryin'

Re-issue of **32 Minutes And 17 Seconds**

All My Love

Music For Pleasure MFP 1420 1970

Side 1: Sway/I Only Came To Say Goodbye/Take Special Care/Magic In The Moonlight/House Without Windows/Razzle Dazzle

Side 2: All My Love/I Don't Wanna Love You/You Belong To My Heart/Again/Perfidia/Reelin' 'n' Rockin'

Re-issue of **Cliff Richard** with additional title track

The Cliff Richard Story

World Record Club SM 255–260 1974

6-LP set including booklet

(Also available on cassette: World Record Club (CSM 255–260))

RECORD 1

Side 1: Move It/High Class Baby/Livin' Lovin' Doll/Never Mind/Mean Streak/Living Doll/Travellin' Light/A Voice In The Wilderness

Side 2: Love/The Shrine On The Second Floor/Fall In Love With You/Willie And The Hand Jive/Please Don't Tease/Apache (the Shadows)/Nine TimesOut Of Ten

RECORD 2

Side 1: Man Of Mystery (the Shadows)/I Love You/
F.B.I. (the Shadows)/Theme For A Dream/Gee Whiz
It's You/The Frightened City (the Shadows)/A Girl
Like You

Side 2: Kon-Tiki (the Shadows)/When The Girl In Your
Arms Is The Girl In Your Heart/The Savage (the
Shadows)/The Young Ones/Lessons In Love/We
Say Yeah/Wonderful Land (the Shadows)

RECORD 3

Side 1: Do You Want To Dance?/I'm Looking Out The
Window/Guitar Tango (the Shadows)/It'll Be Me/
The Next Time/Bachelor Boy/Dance On (the
Shadows)

Side 2: Summer Holiday/Foot-Tapper (the Shadows)/
All At Once/Dancing Shoes/Lucky Lips/Atlantis (the
Shadows)/It's All In The Game

RECORD 4

Side 1: Don't Talk To Him/Geronimo (the Shadows)/
I'm The Lonely One/Theme For Young Lovers (the
Shadows)/Constantly/The Rise And Fall Of Flingel

Bunt (the Shadows)/On The Beach

Side 2: Wonderful Life/The Twelfth Of Never/I Could
Easily Fall (In Love With You)/Genie With The Light
Brown Lamp (the Shadows)/Mary-Anne (the
Shadows)/The Minute You're Gone/On My Word

RECORD 5

Side 1: Stingray (the Shadows)/Don't Make My Baby
Blue (the Shadows)/Wind Me Up (Let Me Go)/The
War Lord (the Shadows)/Blue Turns To Grey/
Visions/Time Drags By

Side 2: Finders Keepers/In The Country/It's All Over/
The Day I Met Marie/All My Love/Congratulations/
Good Times (Better Times)

RECORD 6

Side 1: Big Ship/Throw Down A Line/With The Eyes
Of A Child/Goodbye Sam, Hello Samantha/The Joy
Of Living/Annabella Umbrella/Flying Machine

Side 2: Sing A Song Of Freedom/Living In Harmony/A
Brand New Song/Power To All Our Friends/Help It
Along/Tomorrow Rising/Take Me High

Cliff Richard

World Record Club STP 1051 1974

Side 1: I'll String Along With You/The Touch Of Your
Lips/Temptation/We Kiss In A Shadow/Long Ago
(And Far Away)/I'll Walk Alone

Side 2: Come Closer To Me/Maria/All I Do Is Dream
Of You/I'll See You In My Dreams/When I Grow Too
Old To Dream/Dream

It'll Be Me

Sounds Superb SPR 90018 1974

Side 1: It'll Be Me/So I've Been Told/How Long Is
Forever/I'm Walking/The Blues/Turn Around/
Blueberry Hill/Let's Make A Memory

Side 2: When My Dreamboat Comes Home/I'm On My
Way/Spanish Harlem/You Don't Know/Falling In Love
With Love/Who Are We To Say/I Wake Up Cryin'

2nd Re-issue of **32 Minutes And 17 Seconds**

Dick Saunders' 10th Annual Rally

Echo ECR008 September 1975

Includes one Cliff track – Love Never Gives Up

The Music And Life Of Cliff Richard

EMI TC EXSP 1601 1975

Six-cassette box set featuring music and interviews with Cliff, Olivia Newton-John, Brian Bennett, Cilla Black etc.

CASSETTE 1

Side 1: Intro – Power To All Our Friends/Schoolboy Crush/Move It/High Class Baby/Livin' Lovin' Doll/ Mean Streak/Living Doll/Travellin' Light/A Voice In The Wilderness/Lover

Side 2: Saturday Dance/Apache/Be-Bop-A-Lula/Willie And The Hand Jive/Fall In Love With You/She's Gone/Please Don't Tease/Chinchilla/Made About You/Love/Reprise – Power To All Our Friends

CASSETTE 2

Side 1: Intro – Power To All Our Friends/The Shrine On The Second Floor/Nine Times Out Of Ten/ Working After School/Evergreen Tree/I Love You/ Theme For A Dream/A Girl Like You/Without You/ When The Girl In Your Arms.

Side 2: The Young Ones/All For One/I'm Looking Out The Window/Do You Want To Dance/It'll Be Me/Spanish Harlem/Kon-Tiki/When My Dreamboat Comes In/The Next Time/Reprise – Power To All Our Friends.

CASSETTE 3

Side 1: Intro – Power To All Our Friends/Bachelor Boy/Summer Holiday/Dancing Shoes/Lucky Lips/ It's All In The Game/Maria No Mas/Don't Talk To Him/I'm The Lonely One/Constantly (L'Edera)/ Wonderful Life

Side 2: On The Beach/A Matter Of Moments/The Twelfth Of Never/I Could Easily Fall (In Love With You)/The Minute You're Gone/On My Word/Good Golly Miss Molly/The Time In Between/Reprise – Power To All Our Friends

CASSETTE 4

Side 1: Intro – Power To All Our Friends/Casa Senza Finestre (House Without Windows)/Wind Me Up (Let Me Go)/Jesus/23rd Pslam/Good News/Blue Turns To Grey/Through The Eye Of A Needle/Visions

Side 2: Time Drags By/Why Wasn't I Born Rich/In The Country/It's All Over/Good Vibrations (The Beach Boys)/Finders Keepers/Dynamite/Dizzy Miss Lizzy/ Baby It's You/Reprise – Power To All Our Friends

CASSETTE 5

Side 1: Intro – Power To All Our Friends/I'll Come Running'/The Day I Met Marie/Congratulations/ Early In The Morning/Let's Make A Memory/ Marianne/Two A Penny/I'll Love You Forever Today/ Big Ship/Always

Side 2: Throw Down A Line/With The Eyes Of A Child/ The Joy Of Living/Goodbye Sam, Hello Samantha/ If Not For You (Olivia Newton-John)/Sunny Honey Girl/Don't Move Away/I Ain't Got Time Anymore/ Reprise – Power To All Our Friends

CASSETTE 6

Side 1: Intro – Power To All Our Friends/As I Walk Into The Morning Of Your Life/Where Is That Man/Living In Harmony/Silvery Rain/Flying Machine/Sing A Song Of Freedom/Step Inside Love (Cilla Black)/ Jesus

Side 2: The New 23rd/A Brand New Song/Power To All Our Friends/Take Me High/Help It Along/The Joy Of Living/(You Keep Me) Hangin' On/It's Only Me You've Left Behind/Reprise – Power To All Our Friends

Everybody Needs Someone To Love

Sounds Superb SPR 90070 1975

Side 1: Everyone Needs Someone To Love/Long Ago (And Far Away)/All Of A Sudden (My Heart Sings)/ Have I Told You Lately That I Love You/Fly Me To The Moon/A Summer Place/I Found A Rose

Side 2: My Foolish Heart/Through The Eye Of A Needle/My Colouring Book/I Walk Alone/Someday (You'll Want Me To Want You)/Paradise Lost/Look Homeward Angel

Re-issue of **Love Is Forever**

Greenbelt Live

MRT 1001 November 1979

Cliff features on one track – Yes He Lives

The Cliff Richard Songbook

World Record Club ALBUM 26 1980

Six-LP set (Also available on cassette: World Record Club CASSETTE 26)

Tracks Unknown

Rock On With Cliff Richard

Music For Pleasure MFP 50467 February 1980

Side 1: Move It/High Class Baby/My Feet Hit The Ground/Mean Streak/Living Doll/Apron Strings/Travellin' Light/Dynamite

Side 2: Willie And The Hand Jive/A Voice In The Wilderness/Please Don't Tease/Gee Whiz It's You/Theme For A Dream/It'll Be Me/We Say Yeah/Do You Want To Dance

Phil Everly

Capitol EST 27670 1983

Features Cliff on two tracks – She Means Nothing To Me and I'll Mend Your Broken Heart

The Best Of Cliff Richard And the Shadows

Readers Digest 1984

RECORD 1 (Cliff's Golden Hits)

Side 1: Move It/Living Doll/Travellin' Light/A Girl Like You/Bachelor Boy/Lucky Lips/It's All In The Game

Side 2: Don't Talk To Him/Constantly/The Minute You're Gone/Wind Me Up (Let Me Go)/Congratulations/Throw Down A Line/Goodbye Sam, Hello Samantha

RECORD 2 (the Shadows Golden Hits)

Side 1: Apache/Man Of Mystery/The Savage/F.B.I./The Frightened City/Kon-Tiki/Wonderful Land

Side 2: Dance On/Foot Tapper/Shindig/Geronimo/Atlantis/The Rise And Fall Of Flingel Bunt/Theme For Young Lovers

RECORD 3 (Rockin' With Cliff And the Shadows)

Side 1: High Class Baby/Reelin' And Rockin'/River Deep, Mountain High (the Shadows)/Whole Lotta Shakin' Goin' On/Livin' Lovin' Doll/Bony Moronie (the Shadows)/Good Golly Miss Molly

Side 2: Ready Teddy/Please Don't Tease/Dynamite/Cathy's Clown (the Shadows)/Nine Times Out Of Ten/Razzle Dazzle/It'll Be Me/Riders In The Sky (the Shadows)

RECORD 4 (With Love – From Cliff And the Shadows)

Side 1: All My Love/Miss You Nights/God Only Knows (the Shadows)/The Next Time/The Day I Met Marie/The Most Beautiful Girl (the Shadows)/It's All Over/When The Girl In Your Arms Is The Girl In Your Heart

Side 2: Theme For A Dream/Bright Eyes (the Shadows)/I Love You/Don't Make My Baby Blue (the Shadows)/The Twelfth of Never/Visions/True Love Ways

RECORD 5 (Hits From Movies And Shows)

Side 1: Summer Holiday/Theme from 'The War Lord' (the Shadows)/I Could Easily Fall (In Love With You)/Don't Cry For Me Argentina (the Shadows)/Wonderful Life/Cavatina (the Shadows)/On The Beach

Side 2: The Young Ones/You're The One That I Want (the Shadows)/A Voice In The Wilderness/Genie With The Light Brown Lamp (the Shadows)/Finders Keepers/Take Me High/Time Drags By

RECORD 6 (Put On Your Dancing Shoes)

Side 1: Dancing Shoes/The Rumble (the Shadows)/Blame It On The Bossa Nova/Chattanooga Choo Choo (the Shadows)/Fall In Love With You/Johnny B. Goode (the Shadows)/Tennessee Waltz (the Shadows)

Side 2: Rhythm And Greens (the Shadows)/Save The Last Dance For Me/Guitar Tango (the Shadows)/Do You Want To Dance/Walk Don't Run (the Shadows)/In The Country/Good Vibrations (the Shadows)

RECORD 7 (Memories Are Made of Hits)

Side 1: Perfidia (the Shadows)/Fly Me To The Moon/Maria Elena (the Shadows)/Theme For 'A Summer Place'/Brazil (the Shadows)/Tonight (the Shadows)/Sway

Side 2: I'm Looking Out The Window/Stardust (the Shadows)/Blues Moon/The Breeze And I (the Shadows)/Spanish Harlem/Have I Told You Lately That I Love You/Temptation (the Shadows)

RECORD 8 (Today's Great Hits)

Side 1: Power To All Our Friends/Wired For Sound/Baker Street (the Shadows)/Dreamin'/Please Don't Fall In Love/The Only Way Out

Side 2: Devil Woman/Let Me Be The One (the Shadows)/My Linda Life/Rodrigo's Guitar Concerto De Aranjuez (the Shadows)/Carrie/We Don't Talk Anymore

Cliff In The '60s

Music For Pleasure 41 56564 1984

Side 1: Nine Times Out Of Ten/I Love You/A Girl Like You/The Young Ones/I'm Lookin' Out The Window/

Bachelor Boy/Summer Holiday
Side 2: Lucky Lips/I'm The Lonely One/On The
Beach/The Twelfth Of Never/Visions/Time Drags
By/It's All Over/All My Love/The Day I Met Marie

20 Original Greats – Cliff And The Shadows

EMI CRS 1 July 1984

Side 1: On The Beach/Do You Want To Dance/Lucky
Lips/Don't Talk To Him/A Voice In The Wilderness/
A Girl Like You/Fall In Love With You/Gee Whiz It's
You/Mean Streak/In The County

Side 2: Move It/Nine Times Out Of Ten/Dancing
Shoes/Theme For A Dream/Willie And The Hand
Jive/I'm The Lonely One/When The Girl In Your
Arms Is The Girl In Your Heart/Time Drags By/I
Could Easily Fall (In Love With You)/We Say Yeah

(Also available on CD (CDP 7 92421 1))

Walking In The Light

MYRR 1176 1984

Side 1: Better Than I Know Myself/Such Is The
Mystery/Every Face Tells A Story/Love And A
Helping Hand/You Got Me Wondering/Walking In
The Light

Side 2: Why Should The Devil Have All The Good
Music/Under The Influence/Lost In A Lonely World/
You Me And Jesus/Thief In The Night

(Also available on CD (MYRC 1176) and cassette
(MC 1176))

Hymns And Inspirational Songs

WRDR 3017 1985

Side 1: What A Friend We Have In Jesus/Higher
Ground/Day By Day/The King Of Love My Shepherd
Is/All Glory Laud And Honour/When I Survey The
Wondrous Cross

Side 2: Just A Closer Walk With Thee/Take My Hand
Precious Lord/Amazing Grace/The 23rd Psalm/It Is
No Secret/May The Good Lord Bless And Keep You

(Also available on cassette (WRD C 3017))

It's A Small World

MYRR 1209 1985

Side 1: Tiny Planet/Small World/Devil Woman/Moving
In/It Has To Be You, It Has To Be Me

Side 2: La Gonave/I Will Follow You/The Only Way Out/
Rock 'n' Roll Juvenile/Where Do We Go From Here

(Also available on CD (MYRCD 1209) and cassette
(MYRC 1209))

From The Heart

TELLY 28 1985

Two-LP set in gatefold sleeve

Available by mail-order only

Side 1: Livin' Doll/Please Don't Tease/Travellin' Light/
Bachelor Boy/I Love You/The Next Time/The Young
Ones/Summer Holiday

Side 2: The Day I Met Marie/Visions/Congratulations/
The Minute You're Gone/Move It (Live)/Green Light/
I'm Nearly Famous/Miss You Nights

Side 3: Up In The World/She's A Gypsy/Baby You're
Dynamite/Heart User/The Water Is Wide/Devil
Woman

Side 4: We Don't Talk Anymore/Donna/La Gonave/
Nothing Left For Me To Say/Up In Canada/Ocean
deep

'Time' The Album

EMI AMPM 1 May 1986

Contains three Cliff tracks – Born To Rock 'n' Roll/She's
So Beautiful/It's In Everyone Of Us

The Hunting Of The Snark

Adventure SNARK 1 November 1986

Cliff guests on one track – The Bellman's Speech

An Hour Of Cliff Richard

Music Of Pleasure 41 8122 4 1986

I Could Easily Fall (In Love With You)/Gee Whiz It's
You/Travellin' Light/Unchained Melody/Beat Out
Dat Rhythm On A Drum/Blueberry Hill/Got A Funny
Feeling/Spanish Harlem/It Is No Secret/We Say
Yeah/Day By Day/Dancing Shoes/Blue Turns To
Grey/A Voice In The Winderness/When My
Dreamboat Comes Home/'D' In Love/I'm Walkin'
The Blues/Fire And Rain/With The Eyes Of A Child/
Good News/Sing A Song Of Freedom/My
Businessman

Mission England volume 2

WSTR 9661 March 1986

Features a live version of I Will Follow You

Utterly, Utterly Live

WEA WX51 April 1986

Includes a live version of Living Doll with the Young Ones

Rock On With Cliff Richard

Music For Pleasure CD-MFP 6005 1987

Move It/High Class Baby/My Feet Hit The Ground/
Livin' Lovin' Doll/Mean Streak/Never Mind/Apron
Strings/Dynamite/Blue Suede Shoes/Twenty Flight
Rock/Mean Woman Blues/Willie And The Hand Jive/
Please Don't Tease/Nine Times Out Of Ten/'D' In
Love/Mumblin' Mosie/Gee Whiz It's You/What'd I
Say/Got A Funny Feeling/Forty Day/Tough Enough/
We Say Yeah/Do You Want To Dance/It'll Be Me/
Dancing Shoes

30th Anniversary Picture Record Collection

SMPLC1

Side 1: Move It/Livin' Doll/Travellin' Light/Voice In
The Wilderness/Theme For A Dream/The Young
Ones/I'm Looking Out The Window/The Next Time/
Summer Holiday

Side 2: I'm The Lonely One/The Minute You're Gone/
Wind Me Up/Visions/In The Country/All My Love/
Congratulations/Throw Down A Line/Sing A Song
Of Freedom

Side 3: Living In Harmony/Power To All Our Friends/
(You Keep Me) Hanging On/Miss You Nights/Devil
Woman/We Don't Talk Anymore/Carrie/Dreamin'

Side 4: A Little In Love/Wired For Sound/Daddy's
Home/Little Town/True Love Ways/Please Don't
Fall In Love/Some People/My Pretty One/Mistletoe
And Wine

Carols

Word WRDR 3034 1988

Side 1: Little Town/In The Bleak Mid-Winter/Sweet
Little Jesus Boy/While Shepherds Watched/Mary
What You Gonna Call That Little Baby Boy

Side 2: Joseph/God Rest Ye Merry Gentlemen/Unto
Us A Child Is Born/Can It Be True/O Little Town

Of Bethlehem

(Also available on cassette (WRDC 3034))

Small Corners

Word WRDR 3036 1988

Side 1: Why Should The Devil Have All The Good
Music/I Love/Why Me Lord/I've Got News For You/
Hey Watcha Say/I Wish We'd All Been Ready

Side 2: Joseph/Good On The Sally Army/Going Home/
Up In Canada/Yes He Lives/When I Survey The
Wondrous Cross

(Also available on CD (WRDD 3036) and cassette
(WRDC 3036))

Re-issue of the **EMI** release

The EP Collection

See For Miles SEE 280 1989

Side 1: Look In My Eyes, Maria/If I Give My Heart To
You/Maria/Secret Love/Love Letters/I Only Have
Eyes For You/All I Do Is Dream Of You/When I Grow
Too Old To Dream/My Heart Is An Open Book/
Boom Boom (That's How My Heart Beats)

Side 2: Moonlight Bay/A Forever Kind Of Love/La Mer/
J'Attendrai/The Shrine On The Second Floor/Where
The Four Winds Blow/Solitary Man/Things We Said
Today/Carnival/Little Rag Doll

(Also available on CD (SEE CD280))

The Kendrick Collection

Langham LANGR 003 June 1989

Cliff appears on three tracks – Burn On/Fighter/Shine
Jesus Shine

Songs Of Life

WORD WSTR 9710 December 1989

Includes one track by Cliff – Where You Are

Alexander Mezek

LD 1791 1990

Cliff duets on two tracks – Prijatelju (To A Friend) and
Vodna Pot (Watered Way)

The Rock 'n' Roll Era: Cliff Richard 1958–1963

Time-Life Music RRC-E08 1990

Living Doll/Move It/Do You Wanna Dance/Fall In Love

With You/Voice In The Wilderness/Travellin' Light/
The Young Ones/High Class Baby/A Girl Like You/
Mean Streak/Please Don't Tease/I Love You/The
Next Time/When The Girl In Your Arms Is The Girl
In Your Heart/Gee Whiz It's You/Nine Times Out of
Ten/Lucky Lips/ Bachelor Boy/It's All In The Game/
It'll Be Me/Theme For A Dream/I'm Looking Out
The Window/Don't Talk To Him/Summer Holiday

Knebworth – The Album

Polydor 843 921–1 August 1990

Features two tracks taken from Cliff and the Shadows
appearance at Knebworth – On The Beach/Do You
Wanna Dance

The Cliff Richard Collection

EMI CDP 7 98087 1992

This five-CD set released only in Australia contained the
following CDs:

STRONGER

Stronger Than That/Who's In Love/The Best Of Me/
Clear Blue Skies/Keep Me Warm/Lean On You/I
Just Don't Have The Heart/Joanna/Everybody
Knows/Share A Dream/Better Day/Forever You
Will Be Mine

LOVE SONGS

Miss You Nights/Constantly/Up In The World/Carrie/
A Voice In The Wilderness/The Twelfth Of Never/I
Could Easily Fall (In Love With You)/The Day I Met
Marie/Can't Take The Hurt Anymore/A Little In
Love/The Minute You're Gone/Visions/When Two
Worlds Drift Apart/The Next Time/It's All In The
Game/Don't Talk To Him/When The Girl In Your
Arms (Is The Girl In Your Heart)/Theme For A
Dream/Fall In Love With You/We Don't Talk Anymore

ME AND MY SHADOWS

I'm Gonna Get You/You And I/I Cannot Find A True
Love/Evergreen Tree/She's Gone/Left Out Again/
You're Just The One To Do It/Lamp Of Love/
Choppin' And Changin'/We Have It Made/Tell Me/
Gee Whiz It's You/I Love You So/I'm Willing To
Learn/I Don't Know/Working After School

CLIFF

Bachelor Boy/Don't Talk To Him/Fireside Song/It's A
Small World/I Will Follow You/La Gonave/Lindsay

Jane/Lindsay Jane II/Love And A Helping Hand/Love
On (Shine On)/Love Ya/Moving On/No One Waits/
Nothing Left For Me To Say/Nothing To Remind
Me/One Time Lover Man/Rock 'n' Roll Juvenile/
The Winner/There You Go Again/Where You Are/
Yesterday, Today, Forever/You, Me And Jesus

INTERVIEW

An interview with Tim Rice. Recorded at Abbey Road in
June 1991

The Winner

Alliance ALD 020 April 1995

The Winner/Wild Geese/Such Is The Mystery/Reunion
Of The Heart/Discovering/More To Life/Peace In
Our Time/Under The Gun/Yesterday, Today,
Forever/Where You Are/Be In My Heart/Fighter/
Thief In The Night/From A Distance

Hymns And Inspirational Songs

Alliance ALD 022 April 1995

CD and cassette featuring same tracks as the Word issue

It's A Small World

Alliance ALD 023 April 1995

CD and cassette featuring same tracks as the Word issue

Walking In The Light

Alliance ALD 024 April 1995

CD and cassette featuring same tracks as the Word issue

Carols

Alliance ALD 025 October 1995

CD and cassette featuring same tracks as the Word
issue with the addition of Saviours Day and Silent Night

Nothing But The Best

ICCD 13530 1995

Cliff appears on one track, We Being Many, on this
Helen Spapiro release

Without Walls

EPIC 474 800–2 1995

Cliff duets with Tammy Wynette on This Love

Live at SPRE-E

Key Records KL021 1973

Cliff's contribution to this album is – Jesus Is My Kind Of People

Don't Hide Your Heart

Bird 165 1985

Cliff duets with Sheila Walsh on Jesus Call Your Lambs

Live And Guaranteed

SAV 49113753 March 1995

This CD came with the Sound And Vision double pack and contained the following live tracks: Remember Me/Always Guaranteed/Two Hearts/Devil Woman/ All The Time You Need/Living Doll/The Young Ones/ Miss You Nights/Some People/UFO/Thief In The Night/I Wish We'd All Been Ready/We Don't Talk Anymore

Move It/Schoolboy Crush

PR 061

High Class Baby/My Feet Hit The Ground

PR 062

Livin' Lovin' Doll/Steady With You

PR 063

Never Mind/Mean Streak

PR 064

No Turning Back/Mad About You

PR 065

Living Doll/Apron Strings

PR 066

Dynamite/Travellin' Light

PR 067

Down The Line/Baby I Don't Care

PR 068

Ready Teddy/That'll Be The Day

PR 069

I Gotta Know/Blue Suede Shoes

PR 070

Mean Woman Blues/Twenty Flight Rock

PR 071

Whole Lotta Shakin' Goin' On/I'm Walking

PR 072

The above twelve singles were available as photodiscs

The Hit List

Catalogue No. unknown 1995

Up In Canada/Move It/Living Doll/The Young Ones/ Do You Want To Dance/Bachelor Boy/Summer Holiday/Don't Talk To Him/We Don't Talk Anymore/ Daddy's Home/Some People/The Best Of Me/Miss You Nights/Dreamin'/Devil Woman/A Little In Love/ I Still Believe In You/All I Have To Do Is Dream

This is the Canadian Hit List release with a completely different track listing to the UK version

Hank Plays Cliff

Polygram CD 529426-2 November 1995

This Hank Marvin release features guest vocals from Cliff on five-tracks – Move It/Carrie/I Could Easily Fall/ Travellin' Light/In The Country.

Cliff provides mainly backing vocals except on Move It. (Also available on cassette (MC 529426-4))

FOREIGN LANGUAGE RELEASES

GERMAN

Bin verliebt/Die Stimme der Liebe

C21703 January 1961

Schön wie ein Traum/Vreneli

C21843 June 1961

Rote Lippen sol man küssen/Let's make a memory

C22563 August 1963

Zuviel allein/Sag 'no' zu ihm
C22707 March 1964

Das ist die Frage aller Fragen/Nur mit dir
C22811 October 1964

Es war keine so wunderbar wie du/Es könnte schon morgen sein
C22962 April 1965

Nur bei dir bin ich zu Haus/Glaub nur mir
C23103 October 1965

Du bist mein erster Gedanke/Was ist dabei
C23211 June 1966

Das Glück ist rosarot/Was kann ich tun
C23371 November 1966

Ein girl wie du/Bilder von dir
C23510 May 1967

Es ist nicht gut, allein zu sein/Ein sonntag mit Marie
C23611 October 1967

Man gratuliert mir/Ich kann treu sein
C23776 April 1968

London is nicht weit/Mrs Emily Jones
C23777 July 1968

Zärtliche Sekunden/Wonderful World
1C006-28032 February 1969

Du, du gefälst mir so/Lieben kann man einmal nur
1C006-04364 February 1970

Goodbye Sam, (Das ist die Liebe)/Kein Zug nach Gretna Green
1C006-04523 June 1970

Ich träume deine Traume/Das girl von nebenan
1C006-04706 December 1970

Wenn du lachst, lacht das Glück/Kleine Taube
1C006-04903 June 1971

Gut, dass es Freunde gibt/Ein Spiel ohne Grenzen
1C006-05315 April 1973

Es gehören zwei zum Glücklichsein/Liebesleid
1C006-05609 July 1974

Heir Ist Cliff
SHZE261 May 1969
Side 1: Twist im Blut/Zärtliche Sekunden/Shoom Llama boom boom/Story ohne happy end/ Wonderful World/Marianne/Geh' deinen Weg nicht so allein
Side 2: Stell'mich deinen Eltern vor/Ooh-la-la/Deine Augen träumen Mary/Mr Niemand/Die Liebe ist immer nur heut/Fragen

Ich Träume Deine Träume
1C062-04639 December 1970
Side 1: Du fragst mich immer weider/Ein Spiel ohne Grenzen/Ich träume deine träume/Wenn du lachst, lacht dus Glück/Lass uns schnell vergessen/ Goodbye Sam, (Das ist die Liebe)
Side 2: Zum heiraten bin ich kein Typ/Umbarella/Das girl von nebenan/Neben dir wird's keine geben/Der Mann neben dir/Concerto

When In Germany volume 1
Side 1: Bin verliebt/Die Stimme der Liebe/Schön wie ein Traum/Vreneli/Zuviel allein/Sag 'no' zu ihm/Das ist die Frage aller Fragen/Nur mit dir
Side 2: Es war keine so wunderbar wie du/Es könnte schon morgen sein/Nur bei dir bin ich zu Haus/ Glaub nur mir/Du bist mein erster Gedanke/Was ist dabei/Das Glück ist rosarot/Was kann ich tun

When In Germany volume 2
Side 1: Ein girl wie du/Bilder von dir/Es ist nicht gut allein zu sein/Ein sonntag mit Marie/Man gratuliert mir/Ich kann treu sein/Mrs Emily Jones/London ist nicht weit
Side 2: Du, du gefalst mir so/Lieben kann man einmal nur/Kein zug nach Gretna Green/Das ist die liebe/

Kleine taube/Wenn du lachst, lacht das gluck/Es gehoren zwei zum glucklichsein/Liebesleid

Seine Grossen Erfolgen

EMI 538-7 98016-2 (CD) 1992

Gut das es Freunde gibt/Wenn du lachst, lacht das Gluck/Ich traume deine traume/Goodbye Sam, (Das ist die Liebe)/Sag 'no' zu ihm/Man gratuliert mir/Rote lippen sol man kussen/Du, du gefalst mir so/Ein sonntag mit Marie/Das ist die Frage aller Fragen/Es war keine so wunderbar wie du/Du bist mein erster Gedanke

FRENCH

Ah, quelle histoire/Girl You'll Be A Woman Soon

CF 155 May 1968

La ballade de Baltimore/L'amandier sauvage

2C006-04841 June 1971

If faut chanter la vie/Come Back Billie Joe

2C006-05324 April 1973

When In France

SEG 8290 February 1964

Side 1: La Mer/Boum

Side 2: J'attendrai/C'est ci bon

When In France

Columbia 4C062-06234 October 1976

Side 1: La Mer/Boum/J'attendrai/C'est ci bon/Ah, quelle histoire/Je suis formidable

Side 2: Je t'aime toujours ce jour/releve mon defi/La ballade de Baltimore/L'amandier sauvage/Il faut chanter la vie

ITALIAN

Immagina un giorno/Oh, no, no

SCMQ 7075 October 1967

Non dimenticare chi ti ama/Chi Lo Sa

3C006-04056

Hits From When In Rome

SEG 8478 April 1966

Side 1: Come Prima (For The First Time)/Nel Blu Di Pinto Di Blu (Volare)

Side 2: Dicitencello Vuie (Just Say I Love Her)/ Arrivederci Roma

When In Rome

Mono SX 1762 August 1965

Side 1: Come Prima/Nel Blu Dipinto Di Blu/Concerto D'Autumno/O Mio Signore/Maria Ninguem/Non L'Ascoltare

Side 2: Dicitencello Vuie/Arrivederci Roma/Carina/ Legata Ad Un Granello Di Sabbia/Casa Senza Finestre/Che Cosa Del Farai Mio Amour/Per Un Bacio D'Amore

SPANISH

Que Buena Suerte/High And Dry

PL 63198 May 1968

Todor El Poder A Los Amigos/Come Back Billie Joe

1J006-05340

When In Spain

Mono SX 1541 Stereo SCX 3488 September 1963

Side 1: Perfidia/Amor, Amor, Amor/Frenesi/ Solamente Una Vez/Vaya Con Dios/Me Lo Dijo Adela

Side 2: Maria No Mas/Tus Besos/Quizás, Quizás, Quizás/Te Quiero Dijiste/Canción De Orfeo/ Quien Sera

BOOTLEGS

Many of the following bootlegs only contained material previously available as B-sides or foreign releases and many also contained Shadows tracks. Unfortunately we have been unable to determine which tracks are previously unavailable or un-released on these releases. Under each entry is a brief comment about the contents, where known.

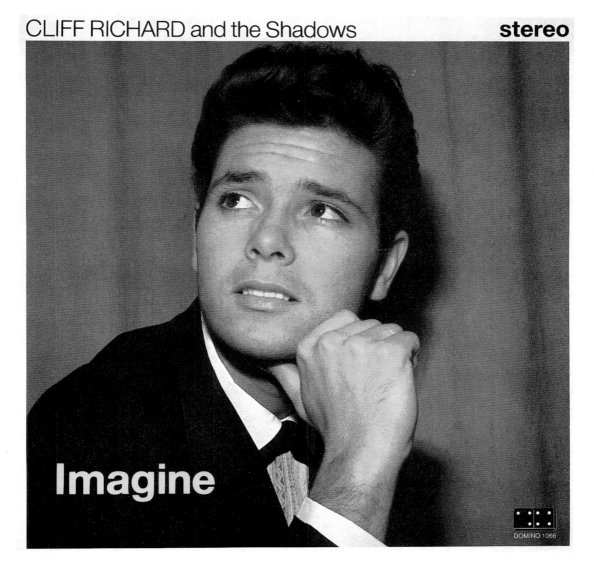

CLIFF RICHARD and the Shadows — stereo — Imagine — DOMINO 1066

Outtakes

LPMS MARVIN 5883

Side 1: 6-24-36/Blue Suede Shoes/Some Are Lonely/Congratulations (Spanish)/Alentejo/Now's The Time To Fall In Love

Side 2: Dynamite/I Want To Know/I Love You So Much/The Wild Roses/As I Walk Into The Morning Of Your Life/Ghost Riders In The Sky

A selection of alternate, foreign and instrumentals make up this 10-inch Cliff/Shadows bootleg.

Collectors Choice

SHOWAD RECORDS LMPS 5885

Side 1: It's Only Me You've Left Behind/Fender Bender/Wouldn't You Know It (Got Myself A Girl)/Rusk/Perhaps, Perhaps, Perhaps/Run Billy Run

Side 2: Equinoxe (Part V)/Don't Be Mad At Me/Song Of Yesterday/I Wonder/Sweet Saturday Night/Where Is My Heart

Again this 10-inch release features both Cliff and Shadows material.

Now And Then

SHOWAD RECORDS LMPS 5885/2

Side 1: Sweet Little Jesus Boy/It'll Be Me Babe/Love De Luxe/Todo, El Poder A Los Amigos/Spot The Ball

Side 2: A Thousand Conversations/The Shady Lady/Frenesi/Please Mr Please/Celestial Houses/The Fourth Man

Released as a 10-inch album this is another mix of Cliff and Shadows tracks.

Cliff And The Shadows 'Live On Stage'

DYNAMITE RECORDS 141040

Side 1: All Day/Heartbreak Hotel/I Saw The Light/Do You Want To Dance/Dynamite/'D' In Love/Turn Me Loose/Shakin' All Over

Side 2: Please Don't Tease/Stood Up/The Rock That Doesn't Roll/Me And My Shadows/Save My Soul/Sweeter Than You/Walk Right In/Greensleeves/Sweet Molly Malone/I Gotta Woman

This mixture of radio and TV broadcasts covers the fifties through to the eighties.

Christmas Greetings

DYNAMITE RECORDS 141040/2

Side 1: Jingle Bell Time/Santa Claus Is Coming To Town/Winter Wonderland/Jingle Bells/White Christmas/Good News/Carnival/Summer Holiday/Moonlight Bay/Sweet Little Jesus Boy

Side 2: It Came Upon The Midnight Clear/I Saw Three Ships/Silent Night/God Rest Ye Merry Gentlemen/Take Me Where I Wanna Go/How Great Thou Art/We Believe In Loving/See What You've Done/You Can't Get To Heaven/The Outlaw

Some of the Christmas material on this release is taken from a 1968 BBC Radio broadcast.

By Special Request

CRESCENT RECORDS TS-54535

Side 1: Honky Tonk Angel/Little Rag Doll/Sternengold/Maria/If I Give My Heart To You/It's Wonderful To Be Young/Elevenis

Side 2: Since I Lost You/Secret Love/Thinking Of Our Love/'D' In Love/Things We Said Today/Save The Last Dance For Me/Where Is Your Heart

Another collection of Cliff and Shadows material.

Delivery Has To Be This Week!!

MARVIN SP 002

Side 1: Move It/Don't Talk To Him/Please Don't Tease/It's All In The Game/Lucky Lips/Wonderful Land/The Dear Hunter/FBI/Living Doll/Bachelor Boy/Summer Holiday

Side 2: The Young Ones/I Love You/The Day I Met Marie/The Twelfth Of Never/Congratulations/Let Me Be The One/Power To All Our Friends/On The Beach/I Could Easily Fall/Do You Want To Dance

These tracks are lifted from the Cliff and the Shadows Together video from 1984.

Cliff Richard And The Shadows 'Have A Party'

GOLD STAR LPMS 1075

Side 1: Love Never Gives Up/Evening Comes/Let's Have A Party/Jointy Jump/Sinnerman/The Trouble With Me Is You/Back In Vaudevile/The Guitar Man

Side 2: That's Why I Love You/Trombone/FBI/Bongo Blues/The Shrine On The Second Floor/Chase Side Shoot/Bye Bye Love/Soul Deep

B-sides and film versions along with tracks from Jet Harris, Brian Bennett and the Shadows make up this bootleg album.

Move It

AR 30035

Side 1: Move It/Schoolboy Crush/My Feet Hit The Ground/High Class Baby/Livin' Lovin' Doll/Steady With You/Never Mind

Side 2: Mean Streak/Living Doll/Apron Strings/No Turning Back/Mad About You/Dynamite/Travelling Light

No details available for this release.

Ready Teddy

AR 31036

Side 1: Twenty Flight Rock/Pointed Toe Shoes/Mean Woman Blues/I'm Walkin'/Blue Suede Shoes/The Snake And The Bookworm/I Gotta Know

Side 2: Down The Line/I Got A Feeling'/Baby I Don't Care/Ready Teddy/Don't Bug Me Baby/That'll Be The Day/Whole Lotta Shakin' Goin On

No details available for this release.

All Round Trading

DLP 2-783

This double album contains both Move It and Ready Teddy as listed above.

Imagine

DOMINO 1066

Side 1: Imagine Love/Clearing Skies/Long Tall Sally/ Da Do Ron Ron/Love Enough/Congratulations/ Strike A Light/Words

Side 2: You Are The One/He's Got The Whole World/ Hitchin' A Ride/Wake Up Little Suzie/Janine/Love Is Here/Needing A Friend/Pegasus

Another collection of B-sides, tracks by Brian Bennet and Marvin, Welsh & Farrar and unissued live recordings make up this bootleg which also features a colourful sleeve with many rare pictures of Cliff.

FLEXI-DISCS

Cliff's Rock Party

Label/Number: Rainbow Records

Date: Unknown

Blue vinyl flexi given away with 'Boyfriend' magazine.

Cliff Richards Personal Message To You

Label/Number: Rainbow Records

Date: 1963

Flexi given away with 'Serenade' magazine.

Music From America

Label/Number: Rainbow Records

Date: 1960

Flexi given away with *Rainbow* magazine.

Star Souvenir Greetings

Label/Number: New Spotlight/208 Radio Luxembourg

Date: Unknown

Flexi featuring Cliff and other artists.

The Sound Of The Stars

Label/Number: Lyntone LYN-996

Date: 1967

Flexi given away with *Disc* and *Music Echo* that featured

Cliff along with other artists including the Shadows.

The Cliff Richard Story

Label/Number: Lyntone LYNSF-1218

Date: 1973

Flexi sampler given to promote the World records box set The Cliff Richard Story. Included an interview.

Best Of Cliff Richard And The Shadows

Label/Number: Lyntone LYN 14745

Date: Unknown

Details unknown

Cliff Richard Talks To You (SPREE 1973)

Label/Number: SHOL 1560

Date: 1973

Details unknown

Welcome To The Cliff Richard Fan Club UK ... Love Cliff

Label/Number: Unknown

Date: 1988

7" transparent flexi with dark blue lettering and a picture of Cliff. Issued with 30th anniversary newsletter.

Interview With Mike Read

Label/Number: No Number

Date: 1992

Flexi disc included with the Access All Areas tour brochure in 1992.

PROMOS

I'm The Lonely One/I Only Have Eyes For You

EPIC 5-9670 Radio Station Copy

Heartbeat/It's All Over

EPIC 5-10178 Radio Station Copy

Finders Keepers

PSR-304 1967

EMI one-sided promo

Nothing To Remind Me/The Leaving
PSR-368 1967
EMI promo

Every Face Tells A Story
PSR-410 1977
EMI sampler used to promote Cliff's Every Face Tells
A Story album featuring selected tracks from
the album.

40 Greatest Hits
PSR-414/5 1977
EMI double sampler used to promote the album.
Featured brief excerpts of each of the forty tracks.

Singles sampler
PSLP-350 1982
EMI issued this sampler to promote the re-issue of
fourteen of Cliff's singles. The singles were released in
new picture sleeves. The sampler featured excerpts
from Move It/Living Doll/Travellin' Light/Please Don't
Tease/The Young Ones/The Next Time/Bachelor
Boy/Congratulations/Summer Holiday/Wind Me
Up/Miss You Nights/Devil Woman/We Don't Talk
Anymore/Dynamite

Dressed For The Occasion
PSLP-372 1983
This EMI promo, for radio use, was banded for airplay.

It's Wonderful To Be Young/The Young Ones
DOT DGT-029-X 1962
An American promo single. It's Wonderful To Be Young
was the American title of the film The Young Ones.

Two A Penny (Interview single)
World Wide PR-1 1968

Two A Penny/I'll Love You Forever Today
Light L-601 1968

We Don't Talk Anymore
EMI SPRO-9252 1979
American promo single featuring long and short versions
of the song. The long version, a disco remix, appeared

in Holland on a 12" single and eventually saw release in
the UK.

It's All In The Game
EPIC ST5-26089 1961
Juke-box issue

Two A Penny
UNIEP-001 1968

Gee Whiz It's You/I Cannot Find A True Love
DC-756 1961
Export single

What'd I Say/Blue Moon
DC-758 1963
Export single

Razzle Dazzle/Angel
DC-762 1966
Export single

This Was My Special Day/I'm Feeling Oh So Lovely
DB-7435 1965
This single was withdrawn

Together (with Cliff Richard)
CDPROMO 1
Excerpts from the TOGETHER album plus a special
message from Cliff

Hit List Ballads
DJ only megamix on double 12" set

All I Have To Do Is Dream
12EMDJ359
12" promo

Never Let Go
CDEM-DJ-281
Radio promo CD in picture sleeve

Heathcliff Press Pack
This promotional pack featured the album *Songs From
Heathcliff*, the single *The Wedding* and a short video

that included Cliff, Tim Rice, Frank Dunlop and John Farrar talking about the Heathcliff musical and featuring excerpts from some of the songs.

RARIETIES

Breathless/Lawdy Miss Clawdy
HMV private recording of two tracks Cliff and the Drifters recorded at the HMV shop in London.

Who's Gonna Take You Home/Let's Stick Together
Two unreleased tracks that turned up on a 7" acetate. Possibly recorded in 1959.

We Had It Made
7" and 10" EMIDISC acetates of track from Me And My Shadows. It is unknown if this is an alternate version or was released on the album.

Cliff Richard Interview
1962

This very rare metal master disc contains an interview with Cliff by Bill McChord, recorded in Houston, Texas in 1962.

Summer Holiday
1962

This Elstree private pressing featured original soundtrack versions and was made as a souvenir for the stars and crew who worked on the film.

Wonderful Life
1963

Another Elstree private pressing featuring original soundtrack versions and made as a souvenir for the stars and crew who worked on the film.

Deep Purple
A 2 minute 10 second 7" acetate featuring an unreleased track recorded in 1965.

We Don't Talk Anymore/Count Me Out
EMI 2975 1979

This rare mis-pressing plays Bohemian Rhapsody by Queen on the B-side instead of Count Me Out.

ALTERNATE VERSIONS
THEIR DIFFERENCES & WHERE
THEY APPEAR ON RECORD

A Voice In The Wilderness
Slightly slower than the single release with slight differences in the lyrics.
  Available on the stereo issue of EXPRESSO BONGO EP (ESG 7783)

Choppin' 'n' Changin'
Slower, guitar more prominent and slight lyrical differences.

Available on stereo issue of ME AND MY SHADOWS
LP (SCX 3330) and stereo issue of ME AND MY
SHADOWS No. 2 EP (ESG 7841)

Dynamite

Faster rhythm and slightly different backing.
Available on 20 ROCK AND ROLL HITS (EMI 1
C064-07145)

I Gotta Know

Different backing especially in the lead guitar, slight
lyric changes and faster.
Available on stereo issue of CLIFF SINGS No. 1 EP
(ESG 7788)

I Love You So

Lead guitar missing.
Available on stereo issue of ME AND MY SHADOWS
LP (SCX 3330) and stereo issue of ME AND MY
SHADOWS No. 3 EP (ESG 7843)

I'm Willing To Learn

Different lead guitar.
Available on stereo issue of ME AND MY SHADOWS
LP (SCX 3330) and stereo issue of ME AND MY
SHADOWS No. 3 EP (ESG 7843)

I Want You to Know

Starts immediately with the vocals and has slightly
different backing, particularly on the lead guitar.
Available on stereo issue of LISTEN TO CLIFF LP
(SCX 3375)

Tell Me

Vocal arrangement different.
Available on stereo issue of ME AND MY SHADOWS
LP (SCX 3330) and stereo issue of ME AND MY
SHADOWS No. 3 EP (ESG 7843)

The Snake And The Bookworm

Different lead guitar
Available on stereo issue of CLIFF SINGS No. 1 EP
(ESG 7788)

The Young Ones

Addition of orchestral strings.
Available on the single release of THE YOUNG ONES
(DB 4761) and on both the mono and stereo
issues of CLIFF'S HIT ALBUM (SX 1512/SCX 1512)

True Love Will Come To You

Instrumental break twice as long.
Available on the stereo issue of LISTEN TO CLIFF NO
1 EP (ESG 7858) and the stereo issue of LISTEN
TO CLIFF LP (SCX 3375)

We Have It Made

Backing tracks differ.
Available on stereo issue of ME AND MY SHADOWS
LP (SCX 3330) and stereo issue of ME AND MY
SHADOWS No. 2 EP (ESG 7841)

What'd I Say

Different backing tracks.
Available on the South African 78 rpm single
(DSA 393)

CHART FACTS

SINGLES THAT REACHED NUMBER 1 IN THE UK

Livin' Doll (1959)
Travellin' Light (1959)
Please Don't Tease (1960)
I Love You (1960)
The Young Ones (1962)
The Next Time (1962)
Summer Holiday (1963)
The Minute You're Gone (1965)
Congratulations (1968)
We Don't Talk Anymore (1979)
Living Doll (1986)
Mistletoe And Wine (1988)
Saviours Day (1990)

EPs THAT REACHED NUMBER 1 IN THE UK

Expresso Bongo (1960)
Cliff's Silver Discs (1960)
Holiday Carnival (1963)

ALBUMS THAT REACHED NUMBER 1 IN THE UK

21 Today (1961)
The Young Ones (1961)
Summer Holiday (1963)
40 Golden Greats (1977)
Love Songs (1981)
Private Collection (1988)
Cliff Richard – The Album (1993)

SINGLES THAT REACHED THE TOP 10 IN THE UK

Move It (1958)
High Class Baby (1958)
Mean Streak (1959)
Living Doll (1959)
Travellin' Light (1959)
A Voice In The Wilderness (1960)
Fall In Love With You (1960)
Please Don't Tease (1960)
Nine Times Out Of Ten (1960)
I Love You (1960)
Theme For A Dream (1961)
Gee Whiz It's You (1961)
A Girl Like You (1961)
When The Girl In Your Arms Is The Girl In Your Heart (1961)
The Young Ones (1962)
I'm Looking Out The Window/Do You Want To Dance (1962)
It'll Be Me (1962)
The Next Time/Bachelor Boy (1962)
Summer Holiday (1963)
Lucky Lips (1963)
It's All In The Game (1963)
Don't Talk To Him (1963)
I'm The Lonely One (1964)
Constantly (1964)
On The Beach (1964)
The Twelfth Of Never (1964)
I Could Easily Fall (In Love With You) (1964)
The Minute You're Gone (1965)
Wind Me Up (1965)
Visions (1966)
Time Drags By (1966)
In The Country (1966)
It's All Over (1967)
The Day I Met Marie (1967)
All My Love (1967)
Congratulations (1968)
Big Ship (1969)
Throw Down A Line (1969)
Goodbye Sam, Hello Samantha (1970)
Power To All Our Friends (1973)
Devil Woman (1976)
We Don't Talk Anymore (1979)
Carrie (1980)
Dreamin' (1980)
Wired For Sound (1981)
Daddy's Home (1981)
The Only Way Out (1982)
She Means Nothing To Me (1983)
True Love Ways (1983)
Please Don't Fall In Love (1983)
Living Doll (w. The Young Ones) (1986)
All I Ask Of You (1986)

Cliff Sings (1959)
Me And My Shadows (1960)
Listen To Cliff (1961)
21 Today (1961)
The Young Ones (1961)
32 Minutes And 17 Seconds (1962)
Summer Holiday (1963)
Cliff's Hit Album (1963)
When In Spain (1963)
Wonderful Life (1964)
Cliff Richard (1965)
Kinda Latin (1966)
Finders Keepers (1966)
Best Of Cliff (1969)
I'm Nearly Famous (1976)
Every Face Tells A Story (1977)
40 Golden Greats (1977)
Thank You Very Much (1979)
Rock 'n' Roll Juvenile (1979)
I'm No Hero (1980)
Love Songs (1981)
Wired For Sound (1981)
Now You See Me, Now You
   Don't (1982)
Dressed For The Occasion (1983)
Silver (1983)
Always Guaranteed (1987)
Private Collection (1988)
Stronger (1989)
From A Distance – The Event
   (1990)
Together With Cliff Richard (1991)
Cliff Richard – The Album (1993)

My Pretty One (1987)
Some People (1987)
Mistletoe And Wine (1988)
The Best Of Me (1989)
I Just Don't Have The Heart (1989)
Silhouettes (1990)
Saviours Day (1990)
We Should Be Together (1991)
I Still Believe In You (1992)

EPs THAT REACHED
THE TOP 10 IN THE UK

Cliff Sings No. 1 (1959)
Expresso Bongo (1960)
Cliff Sings No. 2 (1960)
Cliff Sings No. 3 (1960)

Cliff's Silver Discs (1960)
Me And My Shadows No. 1 (1961)
Me And My Shadows No. 2 (1961)
Me And My Shadows No. 3 (1961)
Dream (1961)
Cliff's Hit Parade (1962)
Holiday Carnival (1963)
Hits From The Film 'Summer
   Holiday' (1963)
Love Songs (1963)
Wonderful Life No. 1 (1964)
Take Four (1965)

ALBUMS THAT REACHED
THE TOP 10 IN THE UK

Cliff (1959)

SINGLES THAT FAILED
TO REACH THE TOP 40

A Brand New Song/The Old
   Accordion (1972)
It's Only Me You've Left Behind/
   You're The One (1975)
Honky Tonk Angel/Wouldn't You
   Know It (1975)
When Two Worlds Drift Apart/That's

Why I Love You (1977)

Yes He Lives/Good On The Sally Army (1978)

Please Remember Me/Please Don't Tease (1978)

Can't Take The Hurt Anymore/Needing A Friend (1978)

Green Light/Imagine Love (1979)

Hot Shot/Walking In The Light (1979)

Where Do We Go From Here/ Discovering (1982)

Drifting/It's Lonely When The Lights Go Out (1983)

Two To The Power/Rock 'n' Roll (1984)

Shooting From The Heart/Small World (1984)

Heart User/I Will Follow You (1985)

It's In Everyone Of Us/Alone (1985)

Slow Rivers/Billy And The Kids (1986)

EPs THAT FAILED TO REACH THE TOP 40

Serious Charge (1959)

Cliff No. 1 (1959)

Cliff No. 2 (1959)

Cliff Sings No. 4 (1960)

Listen To Cliff No. 2 (1961)

Time For Cliff Richard And The Shadows (1963)

More Hits From 'Summer Holiday' (1963)

When In France (1964)

Cliff's Palladium Successes (1964)

A Forever Kind Of Love (1964)

Wonderful Life No. 2 (1964)

Hits From 'Wonderful Life' (1964)

Why Don't They Understand (1965)

Angel (1965)

Wind Me Up (1966)

Hits From 'When In Rome' (1966)

Love Is Forever (1966)

Thunderbirds Are Go (1966)

La, La, La, La, La (1966)

Cinderella (1967)

ALBUMS THAT FAILED TO REACH THE TOP 40

When In Rome (1965)

Two A Penny (1968)

About That Man (1970)

His Land (1970)

The Best Of Cliff Volume 2 (1972)

Take Me High (1973)

Help It Along (1974)

31st Of February Street (1974)

The Rock Connection (1984)

CLIFF'S HITS IN THE UNITED STATES

Living Doll (1959)

Lucky Lips (1963)

It's All In The Game (1963)

Devil Woman (1976)

We Don't Talk Anymore (1979)

Carrie (1980)

Dreamin' (1980)

Suddenly (1980)

A Little In Love (1980)

Give A Little Bit More (1981)

Daddy's Home (1982)

NUMBER 1 RECORDS IN OTHER COUNTRIES

AUSTRALIA
  The Young Ones
  It'll Be Me
  Summer Holiday
  We Don't Talk Anymore
  Living Doll (w. The Young Ones)

BELGIUM
  The Young Ones
  The Next Time
  Lucky Lips
  Don't Talk To Him
  Congratulations
  Dreamin'

CANADA
  Bachelor Boy
  It's All In The Game

DENMARK
  The Young Ones
  Summer Holiday
  Congratulations

GERMANY
  Lucky Lips
  Don't Talk To Him
  Congratulations

We Don't Talk Anymore

HONG KONG
It's All In The Game
Lucky Lips
We Don't Talk Anymore

INDIA
Please Don't Tease
The Young Ones
It'll Be Me
The Next Time
Summer Holiday
It's All In The Game
Lucky Lips
Don't Talk To Him
I Could Easily Fall In Love
   With You
The Minute You're Gone
Wind Me Up
Congratulations

IRELAND
The Young Ones
The Next Time
Summer Holiday
Don't Talk To Him
Congratulations
We Don't Talk Anymore

ISRAEL
The Next Time
Summer Holiday
Bachelor Boy
It's All In The Game
Lucky Lips
Don't Talk To Him
Congratulations
Power To All Our Friends

JAPAN
The Young Ones
Bachelor Boy
Summer Holiday
On The Beach

Congratulations
A Little In Love

LEBANON
Congratulations

LUXEMBOURG
Power To All Our Friends

MALAYSIA
I Could Easily Fall In Love
   With You
The Minute You're Gone
Wind Me Up
Congratulations

MALTA
We Don't Talk Anymore

NETHERLANDS
Please Don't Tease
I Love You
A Girl Like You
When The Girl In Your Arms
The Young Ones
Do You Want To Dance
Bachelor Boy
Summer Holiday
Lucky Lips
Congratulations
Power To All Our Friends
Living Doll (w. The Young Ones)

NEW ZEALAND
Please Don't Tease
Theme For A Dream
The Young Ones
Bachelor Boy
It's All In The Game
Don't Talk To Him
Living Doll (w. The Young Ones)

NORWAY
Please Don't Tease
When The Girl In Your Arms

Summer Holiday
Lucky Lips
Don't Talk To Him
Congratulations

THE PHILIPPINES
Constantly
On The Beach
I Just Don't Have The Heart

SINGAPORE
I Could Easily Fall In Love
   With You
The Minute You're Gone
Congratulations

SOUTH AFRICA
'D' In Love
Theme For A Dream
A Girl Like You
The Young Ones
It'll Be Me
Bachelor Boy
Lucky Lips
It's All In The Game
I Could Easily Fall In Love
   With You
Wind Me Up
Congratulations
All I Ask Of You

SPAIN
Congratulations

SWEDEN
Bachelor Boy
Lucky Lips
Congratulations
Power To All Our Friends

SWITZERLAND
Lucky Lips
Congratulations
We Don't Talk Anymore

THE HIT LISTS
1959–1990

15 AUGUST 1959

1.	LIVING DOLL	Cliff Richard
2.	DREAM LOVER	Bobby Darin
3.	BATTLE OF NEW ORLEANS	Lonnie Donegan
4.	LIPSTICK ON YOUR COLLAR	Connie Francis
5.	BIG HUNK OF LOVE	Elvis Presley
6.	A TEENAGER IN LOVE	Marty Wilde
7.	LONELY BOY	Paul Anka
8.	ROULETTE	Russ Conway
9.	HEART OF A MAN	Frankie Vaughan
10.	ONLY SIXTEEN	Craig Douglas

11 AUGUST 1960

1.	PLEASE DON'T TEASE	Cliff Richard
2.	SHAKING ALL OVER	Johnny Kidd & The Pirates
3.	APACHE	The Shadows
4.	MESS OF BLUES	Elvis Presley
5.	GOOD TIMIN'	Jimmy Jones
6.	BECAUSE THEY'RE YOUNG	Duanne Eddy
7.	WHEN WILL I BE LOVED	Everly Brothers
8.	ITSY BITSY TEENY WEENY YELLOW POLKA DOT BIKINI	Bryan Hyland
9.	LOOK FOR A STAR	Gary Mills
10.	AIN'T MISBEHAVIN'	Tommy Bruce

29 DECEMBER 1960

1.	I LOVE YOU	Cliff Richard
2.	IT'S NOW OR NEVER	Elvis Presley
3.	STRAWBERRY FAIR	Anthony Newley
4.	LITTLE DONKEY	Nina & Frederick
5.	SAVE THE LAST DANCE FOR ME	The Drifters
6.	POETRY IN MOTION	Johnny Tillotson
7.	LONELY PUP (IN A CHRISTMAS SHOP)	Adam Faith
8.	ROCKING GOOSE	Johnny & The Hurricanes
9.	MAN OF MYSTERY/THE STRANGER	The Shadows
10.	MY HEART HAS A MIND OF IT'S OWN	Connie Francis

20 JULY 1961

1.	TEMPTATION	Everly Brothers
2.	RUNAWAY	Del Shannon
3.	A GIRL LIKE YOU	Cliff Richard
4.	HELLO MARY LOU	Ricky Nelson
5.	WELL I ASK YOU	Eden Kane
6.	PASADENA	Temperance Seven
7.	HALFWAY TO PARADISE	Billy Fury
8.	BUT I DO	Clarence 'Frogman' Henry
9.	YOU DON'T KNOW	Helen Shapiro
10.	RUNNING SCARED	Roy Orbison

15 FEBRUARY 1962

1.	THE YOUNG ONES	Cliff Richard
2.	ROCK-A-HULA BABY	Elvis Presley
3.	FORGET ME NOT	Eden Kane
4.	LET'S TWIST AGAIN	Chubby Checker
5.	WALK ON BY	Leroy Van Dyke
6.	RUN TO HIM	Bobby Vee
7.	STRANGER ON THE SHORE	Acker Bilk
8.	HAPPY BIRTHDAY SWEET SIXTEEN	Neil Sedaka
9.	CRYIN' IN THE RAIN	Everly Brothers
10.	I'D NEVER FIND ANOTHER YOU	Billy Fury

10 JANUARY 1963

1.	THE NEXT TIME/BACHELOR BOY	Cliff Richard
2.	RETURN TO SENDER	Elvis Presley
3.	DANCE ON	The Shadows
4.	DANCE WITH THE GUITAR MAN	Duane Eddy
5.	LOVESICK BLUES	Frank Ifield
6.	IT ONLY TOOK A MINUTE	Joe Brown
7.	SUN ARISE	Rolf Harris
8.	GO AWAY LITTLE GIRL	Mark Wynter
9.	BOBBY'S GIRL	Susan Maughan
10.	LIKE I DO	Maureen Evans

14 MARCH 1963

1.	SUMMER HOLIDAY	Cliff Richard
2.	PLEASE PLEASE ME	The Beatles
3.	THAT'S WHAT LOVE WILL DO	Joe Brown
4.	LIKE I'VE NEVER BEEN GONE	Billy Fury

5. THE NIGHT HAS A THOUSAND
   EYES   Bobby Vee
6. ISLAND OF DREAMS   The Springfields
7. WAYWARD WIND   Frank Ifield
8. HEY PAULA   Paul and Paula
9. FOOT TAPPER   The Shadows
10. TELL HIM   Billie Davis

26 SEPTEMBER 1963
1. SHE LOVES YOU   The Beatles
2. IT'S ALL IN THE GAME   Cliff Richard
3. I WANT TO STAY HERE   Steve and Eydie
4. APPLEJACK   Jet Harris & Tony
                              Meehan
5. JUST LIKE EDDIE   Heinz
6. I'LL NEVER GET OVER YOU   Johnny Kidd &
                              The Pirates
7. DO YOU LOVE ME   Brian Poole &
                              The Tremeloes

8. IF I HAD A HAMMER   Trini Lopez
9. THEN HE KISSED ME   The Crystals
10. WISHING   Buddy Holly

15 APRIL 1965
1. THE MINUTE YOU'RE GONE   Cliff Richard
2. CONCRETE AND CLAY   Unit Four Plus Two
3. FOR YOUR LOVE   The Yardbirds
4. CATCH THE WIND   Donovan
5. HERE COMES THE NIGHT   Them
6. THE LAST TIME   The Rolling
                              Stones
7. STOP IN THE NAME OF LOVE   The Supremes
8. I CAN'T EXPLAIN   The Who
9. THE TIMES THEY ARE
    A-CHANGIN   Bob Dylan
10. POP GO THE WORKERS   The Barron
                              Knights

10 APRIL 1968
1. CONGRATULATIONS   Cliff Richard
2. DELILAH   Tom Jones
3. WHAT A WONDERFUL WORLD   Louis Armstrong
4. LADY MADONNA   The Beatles
5. IF I ONLY HAD TIME   John Rowles
6. (SITTIN' ON) THE DOCK OF
    THE BAY   Otis Redding
7. SIMON SAYS   1910 Fruitgum Co
8. STEP INSIDE LOVE   Cilla Black
9. IF I WERE A CARPENTER   The Four Tops
10. JENNIFER ECCLES   The Hollies

1 SEPTEMBER 1979
1. WE DON'T TALK ANYMORE   Cliff Richard
2. DON'T LIKE MONDAYS   The Boomtown
                              Rats
3. BANG BANG   B A Robertson
4. ANGEL EYES   Roxy Music
5. AFTER THE LOVE HAS GONE   Earth Wind & Fire
6. GANGSTERS   The Specials
7. DUKE OF EARL   Darts
8. MONEY   Flying Lizards
9. REASONS TO BE CHEERFUL   Ian Dury & The
                              Blockheads
10. OOH WHAT A LIFE   Gibson Brothers

26 DECEMBER 1981

1. DON'T YOU WANT ME — Human League
2. DADDY'S HOME — Cliff Richard
3. ONE OF US — Abba
4. ANT RAP — Adam & The Ants
5. THE LAND OF MAKE BELIEVE — Bucks Fizz
6. IT MUST BE LOVE — Madness
7. WEDDING BELLS — Godley & Creme
8. ROCK 'N' ROLL — Status Quo
9. MIRROR MIRROR — Dollar
10. I'LL FIND MY WAY HOME — Jon & Vangelis

10 DECEMBER 1988

1. MISTLETOE & WINE — Cliff Richard
2. ESPECIALLY FOR YOU — Kylie Minogue & Jason Donovan
3. SUDDENLY — Angry Anderson
4. CAT AMONG THE PIGEONS/ SILENT NIGHT — Bros
5. THE FIRST TIME — Robin Beck
6. TWO HEARTS — Phil Collins
7. CRACKERS INTERNATIONAL (EP) — Erasure
8. TAKE ME TO YOUR HEART — Rick Astley
9. SMOOTH CRIMINAL — Michael Jackson
10. MISSING YOU — Chris De Burgh

29 DECEMBER 1990

1. SAVIOUR'S DAY — Cliff Richard
2. ICE ICE BABY — Vanilla Ice
3. YOU'VE LOST THAT LOVING FEELING — Righteous Brothers
4. SADNESS PART I — Enigma
5. GREASE MEGAMIX — John Travolta & Olivia Newton-John
6. ALL TOGETHER NOW — Farm
7. JUSTIFY MY LOVE — Madonna
8. MARY HAD A LITTLE BOY — Snap!
9. PRAY — MC Hammer
10. UNBELIEVABLE — EMF

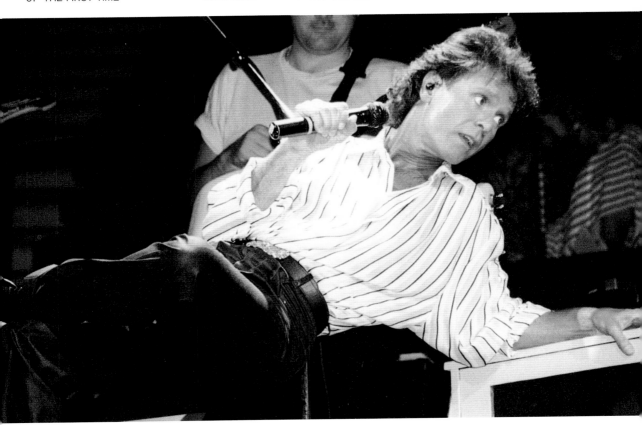

ALTERNATE TITLES

Many countries released their own compilations and also re-issued albums with different titles. Below we have listed some of the more unusual (with their equivalent title if known).

On Your Mark … Get Set … Let's Go (21 Today)
In A Mod Mood
Cliff Richard & Doris Day
Cliff Richard & Jim Reeves
Cliff's Birthday Party
Latin A La Cliff
Brand New Cliff
Shout (Don't Stop Me Now)
Cliff Sings For The Young Ones
Our Friends
Edition 2000
Gigantes De La Cancion
Asi Canta En Espanol
Pioneros Del Rock
Time To Rock
Cliff And The Shadows '65
Dance With Cliff Richard
Do You Want To Dance With Cliff Richard
Music Melody
The Teenage Story (The Young Ones)
On The Beach (Wonderful Life)
Cliff Sings Hits From His Movies
Vacasiones De Verano (Summer Holiday)
Cuando En Espana (When In Spain)
Maria No Mas (When In Spain)
Rock Turbulento Vol. 1 (Cliff)
Latino! (When In Spain)
Something Old, Something New
Mr Dreammaker
To My Italian Friends
Ascoltare Cliff Richard
Per Un Bacio D'Amour

SALES FIGURES – SINGLES

(Estimated/Approximate)

Move It	1,269,483
High Class Baby	270,140
Livin' Lovin' Doll	92,886
Mean Streak	186,161
Living Doll	1,855,555
Travellin' Light	1,588,747
A Voice In The Wilderness	1,092,893
Fall In Love With You	1,114,865
Please Don't Tease	1,590,462
Nine Times Out Of Ten	1,031,892
I Love You	1,413,756
Theme For A Dream	1,049,669
Gee Whiz It's You	1,053,874
A Girl Like You	1,203,874
When The Girl In Your Arms …	1,017,495
The Young Ones	2,555,555
I'm Looking Out The Window	1,036,847
It'll Be Me	1,131,982
The Next Time	2,002,103
Summer Holiday	1,590,462
Lucky Lips	1,219,708
It's All In The Game	1,092,883
Don't Talk To Him	1,002,288
I'm The Lonely One	731,982
Constantly	934,880
On The Beach	914,880
The Twelfth Of Never	521,341
I Could Easily Fall	1,521,880
The Minute You're Gone	1,237,036
On My Word	257,440
The Time In Between	156,090
Wind Me Up	1,194,808
Blue Turns To Grey	404,921
Visions	502,998
Time Drags By	312,998
In The Country	554,708
It's All Over	250,831
I'll Come Running	101,054
The Day I Met Marie	401,421
All My Love	536,186
Congratulations	2,258,677
I'll Love Your Forever Today	82,309
Marianne	116,090
Don't Forget To Catch Me	121,193
Good Times, Better Times	165,390
Big Ship	257,891

Throw Down A Line	281,026	Two To The Power	10,000
With The Eyes Of A Child	133,312	Shooting From The Heart	18,917
The Joy Of Living	109,745	Heart User	32,788
Goodbye Sam, Hello Samantha	402,053	She's So Beautiful	238,777
I Ain't Got Time Anymore	84,835	It's In Every One Of Us	31,691
Sunny Honey Girl	123,848	Living Doll	1,500,000
Silvery Rain	65,979	Born To Rock 'n' Roll	26,157
Flying Machine	85,345	All I Ask Of You	600,000
Sing A Song Of Freedom	211,889	Slow Rivers	100,000
Jesus	65,521	My Pretty One	225,843
Living In Harmony	137,440	Some People	617,836
A Brand New Song	12,502	Remember Me	115,941
Power Too All Our Friends	1,023,813	Two Hearts	34,564
Help It Along	44,837	Mistletoe And Wine	973,279
Take Me High	172,033	The Best Of Me	750,000
Hanging On	135,319		

It's Only Me You've Left Behind 10,214
Honky Tonk Angel 1,012
Miss You Nights 180,377
Devil Woman 2,356,862
I Can't Ask For Anything More 184,410
Hey Mr Dream Maker 156,356
My Kinda Life 209,466
When Two Worlds Drift Apart 67,325
Yes He Lives 23,219
Please Remember Me 34,745
Can't Take The Hurt Anymore 12,195
Green Light 32,991
We Don't Talk Anymore 2,753,880
Hot Shot 64,222
Carrie 1,297,798
Dreamin' 1,461,596
Suddenly 402,812
A Little In Love 461,587
Wired For Sound 629,067
Daddy's Home 1,000,419
The Only Way Out 320,313
Where Do We Go From Here 43,180
Little Town 240,440
She Means Nothing To Me 163,741
True Love Way 255,002
Drifting 31,866
Never Say Die 233,728
Please Don't Fall In Love 341,475
Baby You're Dynamite 101,666

SONGS CLIFF SANG WITH NO KNOWN RECORDING

'ALL BY MYSELF' (Gospel tour, 1987)

'ANGEL EYES' (Wogan TV show, 1992)

'ANOTHER TEAR FALLS' (in concert, 1988)

'ANYONE SWEETER THAN YOU' (Radio Luxembourg, 1960–1961)

'AWAY IN A MANGER' (Christmas TV show, 1980)

'A WORLD OF DIFFERENCE' (Gospel tour, 1985)

'CAN'T HELP MYSELF' (in concert, 1974)

'DANCE THE NIGHT AWAY' (in concert, 1974)

'DID HE JUMP OR WAS HE PUSHED' (while on European tour 1979)

'FABULOUS' (in concert, 1988)

'FLESH AND BLOOD' (Gospel tour, 1991)

'FOOLS WISDOM' (Tear Fund tour, 1981)

'GET READY' (in concert, 1971)

'GET IT RIGHT NEXT TIME' (while on tour in 1988)

'GIVE ALL YOUR LOVE TO THE LORD' (in concert, 1973)

'GOT TO GET YOU INTO MY LIFE' (in concert, 1973)

'GUITAR MAN' (in concert, 1973)

'HANG ON TO MY ROCK 'N' ROLL SHOES' (Radio Luxembourg, 1960)

'HEARTBREAK HOTEL' (while on tour in the US, 1981)

'HEY EVERYBODY' (Radio Luxembourg, 1960–1961)

'HIS LOVE COVERS YOUR SIN' (Gospel tour, 1985)

'HOW GREAT THOU ART' (Best of British Gospel
  Rock concert, South Africa, 1980)

'I SAW THE LIGHT' (in concert, 1970)

'I'VE GOT GOD' (in concert, 1972)

'I'VE JUST REALISED' (in concert, 1974)

'I WANT TO HOLD YOUR HAND' (in concert, 1971)

'I'M 21 TODAY' (Cliff's Birthday Night At Apollo,
  London 1980)

'I'M ALIVE' (Gospel tour, 1987)

'I'M IN LOVE WITH MY TELEVISION' (Gospel
  tour,1993)

'IT MUST BE LOVE' (in concert in the 1970s)

'IT'S ME AND I'M IN LOVE AGAIN' (Radio
  Luxembourg, 1960)

'JESUS IS THE ANSWER' (Christmas TV Show, 1980)

'KANSAS CITY' (Radio Luxembourg, 1960–1961)

'KEEP ON KNOCKING' (in concert, 1972)

'LET THE GOOD TIMES ROLL' (Radio Luxembourg,
  1960–1961)

'LORD I LOVE YOU' (Gospel tour, 1983)

'LOVING ME LORD FOREVER' (Tear Fund tour, 1981)

'MAKE ME NEW' (Gospel tour, 1991)

'ME AND MY SHADOWS' (Radio Luxembourg,
  1960–1961)

'MONEY' (Gospel tour, 1987)

'MOON RIVER' (on tour, 1964)

'MY ONE AND ONLY LOVE' (in cabaret, 1966)

'MY SOUL IS MY WITNESS' (Gospel tour 1991)

'NIGHT TIME GIRL' (Tear Fund concert, 1979)

'NOT BY NIGHT' (Gospel tour, 1985)

'PARTY DOLL' (while on tour in 1990)

'PROUD MARY' (in concert, 1970)

'RAVE ON' (in concert, 1972)

'RIP IT UP' (in concert, 1972)

'ROCK 'N' ROLL MUSIC' (in concert, 1970)

'ROSEILEA COME BACK TO ME' (Radio Luxembourg,
  1960–1961)

'SICK AND TIRED' (Radio Luxembourg, 1960–1961)

'SONG FOR SARAH' (Christmas TV show, 1980)

'SON OF GOD' (Gospel tour, 1983)

'SOUL DEEP' (in concert, 1970)

'TAKE ME BACK' (Gospel tour, 1985)

'TEENAGERS ROMANCE' (Radio Luxembourg,
  1960–1961)

'THE ROCK THAT DOESN'T ROLL' (Christmas TV
  Show, 1980)

'THE SHAPE I'M IN TONIGHT' (in concert, 1979)

'THREE COOL CATS' (Oh Boy! TV show,
  1958–1959)

'TURN ME LOOSE' (Oh Boy! TV show, 1958–1959)

'TWENTY FOUR HOURS FROM TULSA' (On tour, 1964)

'WALK RIGHT IN' (Radio Luxembourg, 1960–1961)

'WE ALL HAVE OUR DREAMS' (in concert, 1978)

'WE CAN WORK IT OUT' (in concert, 1971)

'WE'RE ALL ONE' (Christmas TV show, 1980)

'WHAT THE WORLD NEEDS NOW' (in concert, 1972)

'WHAT'S LOVE GOT TO DO WITH IT'
  (while on tour in 1990)

'WHISPERING MY LOVE' (Gospel tour, 1983)

'WILLIE DID THE CHA CHA' (Radio Luxembourg,
  1960–1961)

'YEAR AFTER YEAR' (Gospel tour, 1985)

'YOU GOT WHAT IT TAKES' (in concert, 1974)

'YOU NEED A LIGHT' (Gospel tour, 1983)

'YOUNG LOVE' (Radio Luxembourg, 1960–1961)

'YOU WERE MEANT FOR ME' (Radio Luxembourg,
  1960–1961)

UNRELEASED SONGS

'Cause I Believe In Loving – Unreleased track dating from an early 1971 session.

A Sad Song With A Happy Soul – One of three unreleased songs recorded in June 1970.

A Spoonful Of Sugar – Recorded for inclusion on a Disney project.

A Teenager In Love – Marty Wilde had a hit with this song that Cliff recorded in the late 1950s.

All In The April Evening – An unreleased track from the Good News sessions.

As Wonderful As You – One of two unissued tracks from a 1965 session of German recordings.

Breathless – From Cliff's first acetate.

Can It Be True – Recorded with the Settlers for a possible album project.

Celebrate – An unreleased track recorded with the Settlers and probably recorded for an album project.

Chaser – From the live Help It Along sessions in 1973.

Chim Chim Cheree – Recorded for inclusion on a Disney project.

Closer To You – From the Now

You See Me, Now You Don't session in 1981.

Compassion Road – The first of many unreleased tracks from late 1968-early 1969 recorded with the Settlers and probably recorded for an album project.

Deep Purple – Recorded by a variety of artists over the years Cliff's version dates back to 1965.

Dim Dim The Lights – A live recording from 1962.

Do What You Gotta Do – A track that originates from the Green Light sessions.

Don't Blame Me – An unreleased track recorded with the Settlers and probably recorded for an album project.

Don't Bug Me Baby – Recorded in October 1958 during the session for Cliff's second single and possibly a contender for the follow-up to Move It.

Forgive Me – An unreleased track recorded with the Settlers and probably recorded for an album project.

From This Day On – Another 1962 recording that may have been recorded for album or EP release.

Gee But It's Lonesome – Another track that may have been recorded for single release.

Gettin' The Feelin' – A track that

originates from the Green Light sessions.

Happy World – An unreleased track recorded with the Settlers and probably recorded for an album project.

Help – An unreleased track recorded with the Settlers and probably recorded for an album project.

How To Handle A Woman – An unusual title from 1983.

I Love The Way You Are – A 1965 recording that may have been recorded for issue on album.

I Only Live To Love You – From an October 1967 session.

I Still Send Her Flowers – Another 1965 track that may have been an album contender.

I Was Only Fooling Myself – From a June 1970 session from which no material was released.

I Who Have Nothing – This could be the same track that Cilla Black had a hit with.

I Will Arise And Go – An unreleased track recorded with the Settlers and probably recorded for an album project.

I'll Be Waiting – A 1962 recording.

I've Got Confidence – A gospel track that Elvis also recorded. Cliff's version comes from 1973.

If I Do – One of two unissued tracks from an October 1968 session.

Indifference – One of only two tracks recorded in another June 1970 session and both unreleased.

Is There An Answer – Recorded with the Settlers for a possible album project.

It Came Upon A Midnight Clear – An unreleased track from the Carol Singers sessions.

It Could Already Be Tomorrow – Second unissued track from a 1965 session of German recordings.

It's Only Make Believe – Well-known song recorded during the live debut album sessions.

Johnny – An unreleased track recorded with the Settlers and probably recorded for an album project.

Johnny Wake Up To Reality – An unreleased track recorded with the Settlers and probably recorded for an album project.

Just A Little Bit Too Late – Possible A or B side recording from 1964.

Kisses Sweeter Than Wine – The second unissued song taped during the live debut album sessions.

Lawdy Miss Clawdy – From Cliff's first private acetate.

One Night – A version of the Presley classic from the taping of the live debut album sessions in 1959.

Love Is Like A Crescendo – Recorded in September 1969 during the Tracks And Grooves sessions.

Love Is More Than Words – An unreleased track recorded with the Settlers and probably recorded for an album project.

Michelle – Not the Beatles classic but a track recorded in the early sixties.

Mobile Alabama School Leaving Hullabaloo – This unusual title originated from the Green Light sessions in 1977-78.

Muddy Water – A track that originates from the Green Light sessions.

No Name No Fame – An unissued track dating back to 1969.

No One Seems To Care – An unreleased track recorded with the Settlers and probably recorded for an album project.

Note In A Bottle – The second unissued track from the October 1968 session.

Now I've Done It – Recorded with the Settlers for a possible album project.

Now That You Know Me – From the Now You See Me, Now You Don't session in 1982.

Nowhere Man – An unreleased track recorded with the Settlers and probably recorded for an album project.

Part Of Me – A track that originates from the Every Face Tells A Story sessions.

Pentecost – This 1969 title suggests a gospel recording.

Postmark Heaven – Another 1969 gospel track.

Praise My Soul The King Of Heaven – An unreleased track from the Good News sessions.

Rain Cloud – The second unreleased track from the June 1970 session.

Rovin' Gambler – From the 1962 live recordings.

Run For Shelter – A possible single track recorded at the same time as Empty Chairs.

Saturday Night At The Whirl – Recorded during the 31st Of February sessions.

Save My Soul – From the 1962 live recordings.

Seeing Is Believing – Recorded with the Settlers for a possible album project.

Ships That Pass In The Night – A track that originates from the Green Light sessions.

Small World – Recorded with the Settlers for a possible album project. May be same track Cliff recorded later in his career.

Sooner Or Later – Recorded at the same time as the Disney tracks.

Star Of Hope – An unreleased track from the Good News sessions.

Streets Of London – Probably The Ralph McTell track that Cliff recorded live in 1973.

Sweet Loving Ways – Recorded during the sessions for Take Me High it is unclear if this track was a contender for the film.

Take A Look Around – From the same session as Silvery Rain.

Take Me To The Leader – From the Now You See Me, Now You Don't session in 1981.

Take Me Where I Wanna Go – From the Now You See Me, Now You Don't session in 1982.

That's What Love Is – An unreleased track recorded with the Settlers and probably recorded for an album project.

The Carnival's Just For Me – An unreleased track recorded with the Settlers and probably recorded for an album project.

The Fellow Next To Me – Recorded with the Settlers for a possible album project.

The Letter – Probably the well known Motown track recorded by Smokey Robinson and the Miracles around the same time.

The Long Way Home – A possible album track from 1968.

The Rock That Doesn't Roll – From the Now You See Me, Now You Don't session in 1982.

The Song From Moulin Rouge – A well-known standard that originates from 1964.

There Is A Green Hill Far Away – An unreleased track from the Good News sessions.

This Is My Kind Of Love – Recorded with the Settlers for a possible album project.

Till Winter Follows Spring – An unreleased track recorded with the Settlers and probably recorded for an album project.

Too Late To Say Goodbye – A track that originates from the Every Face Tells A Story sessions.

Turn It Into Cash – An unreleased track recorded with the Settlers and probably recorded for an album project.

Until The Right One Comes Along – From the Listen To Cliff sessions.

Were You There – An unreleased track from the Good News sessions.

What Is There To Say – Recorded during the soundtrack sessions for The Young Ones. It is unknown if this track was a contender for the film or album.

When You Are There – Possibly another unissued 1969 gospel track.

Where Is The Man – An unreleased track recorded with the Settlers and probably recorded for an album project.

Words – An unreleased track from the Good News sessions. It is unknown if this is the Bee Gees hit or another gospel recording.

You And Me – Recorded during the 31st Of February album sessions.

You Can't Get To Heaven By Living Like Hell – An unissued gospel recording from the Small Corners sessions.

You Held My Hand – An unreleased track recorded with the Settlers and probably recorded for an album project.

Zip-A-Dee-Doo-Dah – Recorded for inclusion on a Disney project.

GOSPEL, CHRISTMAS & INSPIRATIONAL TRACKS

23rd Psalm
(Good News – 1967)

All Glory Laud And Honour
(Good News – 1967)

Amazing Grace
(Help It Along – 1974)

Another Christmas Day
(Single – 1987)

Be In My Heart
(Now You See Me, Now You Don't – 1982)

Can It Be True
(About That Man – 1970)

Celestial Houses
(Help It Along – 1974)

Christmas Never Comes
(Together With Cliff Richard – 1991)

Christmas Alphabet
(Together With Cliff Richard – 1991)

Day By Day
(Help It Along – 1974)

Discovering
(Now You See Me, Now You Don't – 1982)

Dry Bones
(His Land – 1970)

Ezekiel's Vision
(His Land – 1970)

Fire And Rain
(Help It Along – 1974)

First Date
(Now You See Me, Now You Don't – 1982)

From A Distance
(From A Distance The Event – 1990)

Get On Board Little Children
(Good News – 1967)

Go Where I Send Thee
(Good News – 1967)

God Rest Ye Merry Gentlemen
(Carol Singers – 1967)

Going Home
(Small Corners – 1978)

Good News
(Good News – 1968)

Good On The Sally Army
(Small Corners – 1978)

Hava Nagila
(His Land – 1970)

**Have Yourself A Merry Little
Christmas**
(Together With Cliff Richard –
1991)

He's Everything To Me
(His Land – 1970)

Help It Along
(Help It Along – 1974)

Hey Watcha Say
(Small Corners – 1978)

Higher Ground
(Help It Along – 1974)

His Execution And Death
(About That Man – 1970)

His Land
(His Land – 1970)

I Love
(Small Corners – 1978)

I Wish We'd All Been Ready
(Small Corners – 1978)

I've Got News For You
(Small Corners – 1978)

In The Bleak Midwinter
(Carol Singers – 1967)

It Has To Be You It Has To Be Me
(Now You See Me, Now You
Don't – 1982)

It Is No Secret
(Good News – 1967)

Jerusalem Jerusalem
(His Land – 1970)

Jesus
(Single – 1972)

**Jesus Addresses The Crowd On
The Hillside**
(About That Man – 1970)

Jesus Is Betrayed And Arrested
(About That Man – 1970)

Jesus Loves You
(Help It Along – 1974)

**Jesus Recruits His Helpers And
Heals The Sick**
(About That Man – 1970)

**John The Baptist Points Out
Jesus**
(About That Man – 1970)

Joseph
(Small Corners – 1978)

Just A Closer Walk With Thee
(Good News – 1967)

Keep Me Where Love Is
(His Land – 1970)

Little Town
(Now You See Me, Now You
Don't – 1982)

**Mary What You Gonna Name
That Pretty Little Baby**
(Good News – 1967)

**May The Good Lord Bless And
Keep You**
(Good News – 1967)

Mistletoe And Wine
(Together With Cliff Richard –
1991)

Mr Businessman
(Help It Along – 1974)

Narration And Hallelujah Chorus
(His Land – 1970)

Now You See Me Now You Don't
(Now You See Me, Now You
Don't – 1982)

O Little Town Of Bethlehem
(Carol Singers – 1967)

Over In Bethelehem
(His Land – 1970)

Peace In Our Time
(Single – 1993)

Reflections
(About That Man – 1970)

Saviour's Day
(Together With Cliff Richard – 1991)

Scarlet Ribbons
(Together With Cliff Richard – 1991)

Silent Night
(Together With Cliff Richard – 1991)

Sing A Song Of Freedom
(Single – 1971)

Son Of Thunder
(Now You See Me, Now You Don't – 1982)

Sweet Little Jesus Boy
(Single – 1967)

Take My Hand Precious Lord
(Good News – 1968)

The Birth Of John The Baptist
(About That Man – 1970)

The Christmas Song (Merry Christmas To You)
(Together With Cliff Richard – 1991)

The First Easter – The Empty Tomb
(About That Man – 1970)

The Holly And The Ivy
(Single – 1991)

The King Of Love My Shepherd Is
(Good News – 1967)

The New 23rd
(His Land – 1970)

The Only Way Out
(Now You See Me, Now You Don't – 1982)

The Trial Of Jesus
(About That Man – 1970)

The Twelve Days of Christmas
(Single – 1991)

The Visit Of The Wise Men And The Escape Into Egypt
(About That Man – 1970)

The Water Is Wide
(Now You See Me, Now You Don't – 1982)

Thief In The Night
(Now You See Me, Now You Don't – 1982)

This New Year
(Together With Cliff Richard – 1991)

Unto Us A Boy Is Born
(Carol Singers – 1967)

Up In Canada
(Small Corners – 1978)

Venite (O Come All Ye Faithful)
(Together With Cliff Richard – 1991)

We Shall Be Changed
(Good News – 1968)

We Should Be Together
(Together With Cliff Richard – 1991)

What A Friend We Have In Jesus
(Good News – 1967)

When I Survey The Wondrous Cross
(Good News – 1967)

Where Do We Go From Here
(Now You See Me, Now You Don't – 1982)

Where Is That Man
(About That Man – 1970)

While Shepherds Watched
(Carol Singers – 1967)

White Christmas
(Together With Cliff Richard – 1991)

Why Me Lord
(Small Corners – 1978)

Why Should The Devil Have All The Good Music
(Small Corners – 1978)

Yes He Lives
(Small Corners – 1978)

Yesterday Today Forever
(Single – 1988)

SONGS WITH CLIFF AS PRODUCER

Better Day
(Stronger – 1989)

Brother To Brother
(Cliff Richard The Album – 1992)

Bulange Downpour
(Single – 1992)

Carrie
(Single – 1978)

Carrie (Live)
(Dressed For The Occasion –
1982)

Carrie (Re-recording)
(My Kinda Life – 1990)

Christmas Alphabet
(Together With Cliff Richard –
1991)

Christmas Never Comes
(Together With Cliff Richard –
1991)

Cities May Fall
(Rock 'n' Roll Juvenile – 1978)

Clear Blue Skies
(Stronger – 1989)

Devil Woman (Live)
(Dressed For The Occasion –
1982)

Doing Fine
(Rock 'n' Roll Juvenile – 1978)

Everybody Knows
(Stronger – 1989)

Falling In Love
(Rock 'n' Roll Juvenile – 1978)

Forever You Will Be Mine
(Stronger – 1989)

Galadriel (Live)
(Dressed For The Occasion –
1982)

Going Home
(Small Corners – 1976)

Good On The Sally Army
(Small Corners – 1976)

Green Light (Live)
(Dressed For The Occasion –
1982)

Handle My Heart
(Cliff Richard The Album – 1992)

**Have Yourself A Merry Little
Christmas**
(Together With Cliff Richard –
1991)

Healing Love
(Cliff Richard The Album – 1992)

Heart User
(The Rock Connection – 1984)

Hey Watcha Say
(Small Corners – 1976)

Hold Us Together
(Cliff Richard The Album – 1992)

Hot Shot
(Rock 'n' Roll Juvenile – 1978)

Human Work Of Art
(Cliff Richard The Album – 1992)

I Love
(Small Corners – 1976)

I Need Love
(Cliff Richard The Album – 1992)

I Still Believe In You
(Cliff Richard The Album – 1992)

I Will Follow You
(Single – 1984)

I Wish We'd All Been Ready
(Small Corners – 1976)

I've Got News For You
(Small Corners – 1976)

Joanna
(Stronger – 1989)

Joseph
(Small Corners – 1976)

Keep Me Warm
(Stronger – 1989)

La Gonave
(The Rock Connection – 1984)

Language Of Love
(Rock 'n' Roll Juvenile – 1978)

Lean On You
(Stronger – 1989)

Learning How To Rock 'n' Roll
(The Rock Connection – 1984)

Lindsay Jane II
(Single – 1990)

Little Mistreater
(Cliff Richard The Album – 1992)

Love Is The Strongest Emotion
(Cliff Richard The Album – 1992)

Lovers And Friends
(The Rock Connection – 1984)

Love's Salvation
(Cliff Richard The Album – 1992)

Maybe Someday (Live)
(Dressed For The Occasion – 1982)

Miss You Nights (Live)
(Dressed For The Occasion – 1982)

Mistletoe And Wine
(Single – 1988)

Monday Thru Friday
(Rock 'n' Roll Juvenile – 1978)

More To Life
(Single – 1991)

Moving In
(Single – 1980)

My Luck Won't Change
(Rock 'n' Roll Juvenile – 1978)

Never Let Go
(Cliff Richard The Album – 1992)

Only Angel
(Cliff Richard The Album – 1992)

Over You
(The Rock Connection – 1984)

Peace In Our Time
(Cliff Richard The Album – 1992)

Ragged
(Single – 1992)

Rock 'n' Roll Juvenile
(Rock 'n' Roll Juvenile – 1978)

Saviours Day
(Single – 1990)

Scarlet Ribbons
(Together With Cliff Richard – 1991)

Sci-Fi
(Rock 'n' Roll Juvenile – 1978)

Share A Dream
(Stronger – 1989)

Shooting From The Heart
(The Rock Connection – 1984)

Silent Night
(Together With Cliff Richard – 1991)

Small World
(Single – 1984)

Softly As I Leave You (Live)
(Dressed For The Occasion – 1982)

Somebody Loves You
(Single – 1991)

Stronger Than That
(Stronger – 1989)

The Best Of Me
(Stronger – 1989)

The Christmas Song
(Together With Cliff Richard – 1991)

There's No Power In Pity
(Single – 1992)

Thief In The Night (Live)
(Dressed For The Occasion – 1982)

This New Year
(Together With Cliff Richard – 1991)

Tiny Planet
(It's A Small World – 1984)

Treasure Of Love (Live)
(Dressed For The Occasion – 1982)

True Love Ways (Live)
(Dressed For The Occasion – 1982)

Up In Canada
(Small Corners – 1976)

Up In The World (Live)
(Dressed For The Occasion – 1982)

Venite
(Together With Cliff Richard – 1991)

Walking In The Light
(Single – 1978)

We Don't Talk Anymore
(Live)
(Dressed For The Occasion – 1982)

We Should Be Together
(Single – 1992)

When I Survey The Wondrous Cross
(Small Corners – 1976)

Whenever God Shines His Light
(Single – 1989)

White Christmas
(Together With Cliff Richard – 1991)

Who's In Love
(Stronger – 1989)

Why Me Lord
(Small Corners – 1976)

Willie And The Hand Jive
(The Rock Connection – 1984)

Yes He Lives
(Small Corners – 1976)

Why Should The Devil Have All The Good Music
(Small Corners – 1976)

Yes He Lives
(Small Corners – 1976)

You Know That I Love You
(Rock 'n' Roll Juvenile – 1978)

You Move Heaven
(Cliff Richard The Album – 1992)

SONGS WITH CLIFF AS WRITER, CO-WRITER, ARRANGER

And Me (I'm On The Outside Now)
Bachelor Boy
Big News
Bulange Downpour
Don't Talk To Him
Fireside Song
Hold Us Together
I Love You So
I Will Follow You
I'll Love You Forever Today
Jesus Loves You
La Gonave
Lindsay Jane
Lindsay Jane II
Lonely GirlLove And A Helping Hand
Love's Salvation
Moving In

Nothing To Remind Me
On The Beach
Our Love Could Be So Real
Over You
Questions
Reflections
Rock 'n' Roll Juvenile
Silent Night
Small World
The 31st Of February Street
(Opening)
The 31st Of February Street (Closing)
The Winner
There's Now Power In Pity
There You Go Again
Tiny Planet
Two A Penny
Where You Are
Without You
Yesterday's Memories
Yesterday, Today, Forever
You, Me And Jesus

ARTISTS WITH WHOM CLIFF SANG A DUET OR AS PART OF A GROUP

Andrew Mezek
To A Friend – 1990

Aswad
Share A Dream – 1989

Dallas Boys
Oh Boy Medley – 1989
The Girl Can't Help It – 1989
Medley – 1989

Elton John
Slow Rivers – 1984

Hank Marvin
Throw Down A Line – 1969

Helen Hobson
The Wedding – 1996

Helen Shapiro
We Being Many – 1995

Janet Jackson
Two To The Power – 1984

Kalin Twins
Oh Boy Medley – 1989 (Live)

Olivia Newton-John
Don't Move Away – 1970
Suddenly – 1980
Had To Be —1995
Dream Tomorrow – 1995
I Do Not Love You Isabella (with
   Kristina Nichols) – 1995
Choosing (When It's Too Late) –
   1995

Marked With Death – 1995

Phil Everly
She Means Nothing To Me –
   1983
All I Have To Do Is Dream –
   1994
When Will I Be Loved – 1994

Sarah Brightman
All I Ask Of You – 1986

Sheila Walsh
Drifting – 1983

Tammy Wynette
This Love – 1995

The Young Ones
Living Doll – 1986

Van Morrison
Whenever God Shines His Light –
   1989

Vernon Girls

Oh Boy Medley – 1989
Sea Cruise – 1989
Medley – 1989

MUSIC TRIVIA

● Cliff has spent 432 weeks on the EP charts. The only act to be placed higher was the Shadows with 461 weeks.

● In 1981 Cliff released Dreaming with Dynamite as the B side. At the same time teenage American disco star Stacy Lattishaw released a single with an A side called Dynamite and a B side titled Dreaming.

● Placed 17 EPs in the top ten.

● Two EPs, Carol Singers and Congratulations, were released after the charts ceased in 1968.

● In 1991 EMI released a Christmas EP which featured two tracks that had not appeared on the Carol Singers EP in 1967.

● Has spent 731 weeks on the LP chart.

● Had 48 hit albums.

● Love Songs spent 43 weeks on the chart.

● Had 13 number one Singles.

● Had 7 number one Albums.

● Released over 110 singles in the United Kingdom.

● Spent more than 1077 weeks in the British Singles Charts.

● Congratulations was number one in the UK, Belgium, Norway, Sweden, Spain, Malaysia, Holland and Singapore.

● Spent a total of 78 weeks in the British Singles Chart in 1960.

● Cliff had the 7th best selling record in the 50s with Living Doll.

● Spent 100 weeks on the EP charts in 1960, 96 weeks in 1961, 109 in 1962 and 79 in 1963

● Has had 23 hits on the EP charts.

● Has had over 112 hits in the singles chart.

● Achieved 26 consecutive top ten hit singles.

● Spent 43 weeks at number one in the Singles Chart.

● Cliff's biggest gap between number one singles was 11 years (1968–1979)

● The Young Ones is the only Cliff Richard single to enter the charts at number one.

● The Young Ones had advanced orders of over 500,000 copies by the day of release.

- Cliff's best selling record in Germany was Lucky Lips which spent 10 weeks at number one and sold more than 500,000 copies.

- Cliff was replaced at number one three times by the Shadows.

- Had 4 number one EPs.

- The 14th best selling single in the sixties was The Young Ones.

- Spent 10 weeks at number one on the EP charts.

- Cliff's worst selling record was Honky Tonk Angel.

- Cliff Richard – The Album was originally going to be call Access All Areas.

- Cliff is the only artist to enjoy British Top Thirty hits with new material in the 50s, 60s, 70s, 80s and 90s.

- Devil Woman was Cliff's biggest selling single in America.

- The Performing Rights Society has over 600 different songs on file entitled I Love You making it by far the most common of all titles. The only one of this name to reach number one was written by Bruce Welch and recorded by Cliff in 1960.

- In July 1963 the cost of a Cliff album went up from £1 10s 11d to £1 12s 0d. Singles went up by 5d and EPs by 8d to 10s 9d.

- Cliff is the only artist to successfully complete a return to the top of the singles and albums charts after gaps of more than 10 years.

- Cliff has had more than thirty hits in Australia. Only Elvis and the Beatles had more.

- Every single released by Cliff between Mean Streak and The Minute You're Gone reached the Top Ten.

- Cliff had more hits on the Columbia label than any other artist. When his records were switched to the EMI label he, again, had more hits on that label than anyone else.

- Cliff had more UK hits (43 singles) in the sixties than any other artist.

- Cliff is the only artist in the history of the charts to have two singles return to the number one position after dropping from the summit – Please Don't Tease (1960) and Summer Holiday (1963)

- Cliff's best year in Australia was 1962 when he had three number ones – When The Girl In Your Arms, Do You Wanna Dance and The Young Ones.

- We Don't Talk Anymore and Mistletoe And Wine were the 35th and 12th biggest selling singles in the 70s and 80s respectively.

- Cliff holds the record for the most appearances on Top Of The Pops. Including live and video appearances he has been seen over 90 times since 1964.

● Cliff, best known for his singing, played bongos on the Shadows number one hit Apache.

● Summer Holiday was played to Soviet Cosmonauts by ground control in the sixties.

RECORDS THAT REPLACED CLIFF AT NUMBER ONE

SINGLES

Livin' Doll was replaced at number one by Only Sixteen (Craig Douglas)

Travellin' Light was replaced at number one by What Do You Want (Adam Faith)

Please Don't Tease was replaced at number one by Apache (the Shadows)

I Love You was replaced at number one by Poetry in Motion (Johnny Tillotson)

The Young Ones was replaced at number one by Can't Help Falling In Love (Elvis Presley)

The Next Time/Bachelor Boy was replaced at number one by Dance On (the Shadows)

Summer Holiday was replaced at number one by Foot Tapper (the Shadows)

The Minute You're Gone was replaced at number one by Ticket To Ride (the Beatles)

Congratulations was replaced at number one by Wonderful World (Louis Armstrong)

We Don't Talk Anymore was replaced at number one by Cars (Gary Numan)

Living Doll was replaced at number one by A Different Corner (George Michael)

Mistletoe And Wine was replaced at number one by Especially For You (Kylie Minogue)

Saviours Day was replaced at number one by Take Your Daughter To The Slaughter (Metallica)

ALBUMS

21 Today was replaced at number one by **Another Black And White Minstrel Show** (George Mitchell Minstrels)

The Young Ones was replaced at number one by **Rot Luck** (Elvis Presley)

Summer Holiday was replaced at number one by **Please Please Me** (the Beatles)

40 Golden Greats was replaced at number one by **Never Mind The XXXXXXX Here's The Sex Pistols** (the Sex Pistols)

Love Songs was replaced at number one by **The Official BBC Album of the Royal Wedding**

Private Collection was replaced at number one by **Now That's What I Call Music 13** (Various)

Cliff Richard – The Album was replaced at number one by **Automatic For The People** (REM)

THE CLIFF POLL 1973–1995

with thanks to William Hooper

Since 1973 William Hooper, Editor of *Constantly Cliff* and President of The Gloucester and Oxford Fan Club, has produced a Cliff Poll of fans favourite songs and, in 1976 added favourite albums. Listed below are the top 5 results of these polls for the years 1973–1995 along with 23 year points table for songs and a 20 year points table for albums. Cliff fans the world over vote in this Annual Poll in *Dynamite International*.

1973
Songs
1. THE DAY I MET MARIE — 1043
2. The Young Ones — 618
3. Sing A Song Of Freedom — 498
4. The Next Time — 496
5. Living Doll — 392

1974
Songs
1. THE DAY I MET MARIE — 832
2. You Keep Me Hangin' On — 819
3. The Young Ones — 541
4. Power To All Our Friends — 520
5. The Next Time — 476

1975
Songs
1. THE DAY I MET MARIE — 807
2. You Keep Me Hangin' On — 743
3. Visions — 728
4. It's Only Me You've Left Behind — 669
5. The Young Ones — 408

1976
Songs
1. DEVIL WOMAN — 1052
2. Miss You Nights — 1037
3. I Can't Ask For Anymore Than You — 489
4. Visions — 472
5. The Day I Met Marie — 423
Albums
1. I'M NEARLY FAMOUS — 192
2. 31st Of February Street — 48
3. The Best Of Cliff Volume 2 — 14
4. Help It Along — 13
5. More Hits By Cliff — 11

1977
Songs
1. DEVIL WOMAN — 889
2. Miss You Nights — 841
3. My Kinda Life — 738
4. When Two Worlds Drift Apart — 702
5. It Must Be Love — 454

Albums
1. EVERY FACE TELLS A STORY — 141
2. I'm Nearly Famous — 103
3. 31st Of February Street — 26
4. Help It Along — 22
5. Two A Penny — 17

1978
Songs
1. DEVIL WOMAN — 922
2. Miss You Nights — 895
3. Why Should The Devil Have All The Good Music — 519
4. Yes He Lives — 511
5. Visions — 342
Albums
1. SMALL CORNERS — 137
2. Every Face Tells A Story — 95
3. I'm Nearly Famous — 71
4. 40 Golden Greats — 58
5. 31st Of February Street — 29

1979
Songs
1. DEVIL WOMAN — 838
2. Miss You Nights — 779
3. Green Light — 689
4. Can't Take The Hurt Anymore — 624
5. Why Should The Devil Have All The Good Music — 435
Albums
1. GREEN LIGHT — 182
2. Thank You Very Much — 73
3. Small Corners — 47
4. I'm Nearly Famous — 38
5. 31st Of February Street — 21

1980
Songs
1. WE DON'T TALK ANYMORE — 1466
2. Carrie — 978
3. Miss You Nights — 712
4. Devil Woman — 693
5. Dreamin' — 657

Albums

1. ROCK 'N' ROLL JUVENILE	582
2. I'm Nearly Famous	297
3. Green Light	284
4. Small Corners	115
5. 31st Of February Street	89

1981

Songs

1. WE DON'T TALK ANYMORE	1121
2. Miss You Nights	837
3. Dreamin'	759
4. Devil Woman	678
5. Carrie	672

Albums

1. I'M NO HERO	547
2. Rock 'n' Roll Juvenile	423
3. I'm Nearly Famous	202
4. Green Light	175
5. 31st Of February Street	73

1982

Songs

1. DADDY'S HOME	972
2. Miss You Nights	855
3. We Don't Talk Anymore	718
4. Wired For Sound	640
5. Summer Rain	371

Albums

1. WIRED FOR SOUND	482
2. Love Songs	244
3. I'm No Hero	193
4. I'm Nearly Famous	136
5. Small Corners	129

1983

Songs

1. DADDY'S HOME	906
2. True Love Ways	783
3. Miss You Nights	729
4. We Don't Talk Anymore	649
5. Devil Woman	441

Albums

1. NOW YOU SEE ME, NOW YOU DON'T	417
2. Wired For Sound	304
3. I'm No Hero	169
4. I'm Nearly Famous	145
5. Dressed For Occasion	144

1984

Songs

1. OCEAN DEEP	938
2. Please Don't Fall In Love	699
3. Miss You Nights	652
4. We Don't Talk Anymore	650
5. Daddy's Home	621

Albums

1. SILVER	524
2. Wired For Sound	261

3. Now You See Me, Now You Don't	182
4. Dressed For The Occasion	126
5. I'm No Hero	98

1985
Songs

1. OCEAN DEEP	852
2. We Don't Talk Anymore	733
3. Miss You Nights	686
4. La Gonave	615
5. Heart User	579

Albums

1. SILVER	443
2. The Rock Connection	387
3. Wired For Sound	315
4. Now You See Me, Now You Don't	179
5. I'm No Hero	112

1986
Songs

1. OCEAN DEEP	809
2. We Don't Talk Anymore	687
3. It's In Everyone Of Us	652
4. Born To Rock 'n' Roll	574
5. She's So Beautiful	563

Albums

1. SILVER	416
2. Wired For Sound	332
3. The Rock Connection	291
4. From The Heart	224
5. Now You See Me, Now You Don't	205

1987
Songs

1. OCEAN DEEP	733
2. My Pretty One	721
3. We Don't Talk Anymore	654
4. Born To Rock 'n' Roll	547
5. Miss You Nights	519

Albums

1. SILVER	357
2. Wired For Sound	293
3. The Rock Connection	249
4. Now You See Me, Now You Don't	186
5. I'm No Hero	142

1988
Songs

1. SOME PEOPLE	1061
2. Ocean Deep	682
3. We Don't Talk Anymore	527
4. My Pretty One	494
5. Miss You Nights	459

Albums

1. ALWAYS GUARANTEED	584
2. Silver	293
3. Wired For Sound	177
4. Now You See Me, Now You Don't	119
5. I'm No Hero	82

1989
Songs

1. OCEAN DEEP	753
2. Some People	728
3. The Best Of Me	709
4. We Don't Talk Anymore	512
5. Miss You Nights	461

Albums

1. ALWAYS GUARANTEED — 515
2. Private Collection — 307
3. Wired For Sound — 189
4. Silver — 131
5. Dressed For The Occasion — 96

1990

Songs

1. OCEAN DEEP — 882
2. Miss You Nights — 645
3. The Best Of Me — 561
4. Some People — 520
5. From A Distance — 383

Albums

1. STRONGER — 603
2. Always Guaranteed — 392
3. Private Collection — 274
4. Silver — 162
5. I'm Nearly Famous — 85

1991

Songs

1. OCEAN DEEP — 829
2. From A Distance — 671
3. Miss You Nights — 624
4. The Best Of Me — 597
5. Some People — 338

Albums

1. FROM A DISTANCE — 577
2. Stronger — 467
3. Always Guaranteed — 293
4. Private Collection — 179
5. Now You See Me, Now You Don't — 96

1992

Songs

1. OCEAN DEEP — 925
2. All The Time You Need — 630
3. Miss You Nights — 552
4. The Best Of Me — 538
5. Some People — 373

Albums

1. STRONGER — 516
2. Always Guaranteed — 481

3. From A Distance — 410
4. Private Collection — 195
5. Together With Cliff — 122

1993

Songs

1. OCEAN DEEP — 792
2. Peace In Our Time — 648
3. Some People — 541
4. Healing Love — 517
5. Miss You Nights — 485

Albums

1. THE ALBUM — 681
2. Stronger — 273
3. Always Guaranteed — 225
4. From A Distance — 168
5. Silver — 130

1994

Songs

1. OCEAN DEEP — 746
2. Peace In Our Time — 611
3. Miss You Nights — 563
4. The Best Of Me — 532
5. Some People — 507

Albums

1. THE ALBUM — 562
2. Always Guaranteed — 427
3. Stronger — 269
4. From A Distance — 193
5. Private Collection — 136

1995

Songs

1. OCEAN DEEP — 874
2. Some People — 619
3. The Best Of Me — 587
4. Peace In Our Time — 543
5. Misunderstood Man — 496

Albums

1. THE ALBUM — 543
2. Always Guaranteed — 367
3. Stronger — 284
4. The Hit List — 259
5. Silver — 165

23 YEAR SONGS POINTS TABLE

	Year	Total Points	Highest Position
1. MISS YOU NIGHTS	1975	12767	2
2. Devil Woman	1976	9972	1
3. We Don't Talk Anymore	1979	9826	1
4. Ocean Deep	1983	9815	1
5. The Young Ones	1962	7515	2
6. Daddy's Home	1981	5449	1
7. The Next Time	1963	5377	4
8. Visions	1966	4854	3
9. Some People	1987	4687	1
10. The Day I Met Marie	1967	4553	1
11. The Best Of Me	1989	3877	3
12. Move It	1958	3558	12
13. Wired For Sound	1981	3434	4
14. Dreamin'	1980	3348	3
15. Carrie	1980	3323	2
16. Constantly	1964	3271	6
17. True Love Ways	1983	3022	2
18. Why Should The Devil …	1978	2645	3
19. All The Time You Need	1988	2637	2
20. From A Distance	1989	2625	2
21. Thief In The Night	1982	2552	8
22. My Pretty One	1987	2517	2
23. Summer Holiday	1963	2411	12
24. (You Keep Me) Hangin' On	1974	2408	2
25. Born To Rock 'n' Roll	1986	2320	4
26. Please Don't Fall In Love	1983	2316	2
27. When Two Worlds Drift Apart	1977	2248	4
28. Hey Mr Dream Maker	1976	2195	11
29. Never Say Die	1983	2167	9
30. Living Doll	1959	2125	5
31. Remember Me	1988	1873	12
32. Peace In Our Time	1993	1802	2
33. It's In Everyone Of Us	1985	1730	3
34. Can't Take The Hurt Anymore	1978	1652	4
35. Power To All Our Friends	1973	1651	4
36. Two Hearts	1988	1629	7
37. Sing A Song Of Freedom	1971	1547	3
38. La Gonave	1984	1501	4
39. Baby You're Dynamite	1983	1480	6
40. The Only Way Out	1982	1435	6
41. Such Is The Mystery	1976	1417	11
42. Bachelor Boy	1963	1371	11
43. A Little In Love	1981	1305	6
44. Healing Love	1993	1288	4
45. Wind Me Up	1965	1260	12
46. My Kinda Life	1977	1256	3
47. Mistletoe And Wine	1988	1255	6
48. She's So Beautiful	1985	1232	5
49. Stranger Than That	1989	1227	12
50. The Water Is Wide	1982	1166	7

20 YEAR ALBUM POINTS TABLE

	Year	Total Points	Highest Position
1. ALWAYS GUARANTEED	1987	3284	1
2. Silver	1983	2885	1
3. Wired For Sound	1981	2742	1
4. Stronger	1989	2412	1
5. I'm Nearly Famous	1976	1996	1
6. I'm No Hero	1980	1953	1
7. Now You See Me, Now You Don't	1982	1820	1
8. The Album	1993	1786	1
9. Rock 'n' Roll Juvenile	1979	1755	1
10. From A Distance – The Event	1990	1481	1
11. Private Collection	1988	1246	2
12. The Rock Connection	1984	1110	2
13. Green Light	1978	1109	1
14. Small Corners	1978	1034	1
15. Dressed For The Occasion	1983	982	4
16. 31st Of February Street	1974	830	4
17. Love Songs	1981	824	2
18. Every Face Tells A Story	1977	670	1
19. 40 Golden Greats	1977	502	4
20. Thank You Very Much	1979	452	2

POP POLL TRIVIA

- Even though it was never placed at number one in the annual poll Miss You Nights is the top song.

- Miss You Nights has been runner-up no less than seven times.

- Devil Woman won four years in a row – 1976 to 1979.

- In the 1980 poll We Don't Talk Anymore scored the highest amount of points with 1466. This has not been beaten.

- Ocean Deep has topped the poll more times than any other song, eleven times between 1984 and 1995.

- Although voted by the fans as their favourite song Ocean Deep was only the B-side of Baby You're Dynamite, a No. 27 chart hit in 1984.

- The most regularly placed 'oldie' is The Young Ones.

- The highest placed 'non-single' in the Points Table was Why Should The Devil Have All The Good Music, narrowly ahead of All The Time You Need, the highest placed 'non-single' in the poll and runner-up in 1992.

- The album Silver has won the poll four times, the most wins in the album section to date.

- Ocean Deep should be runner up to Miss You Nights in the points table after the 1996 Cliff Poll results.

- Cliff fans have voted in this Poll from the following countries: America, Australia, Austria, Canada, Chile, Denmark, England, Finland, France, Germany, Greece, Hong Kong, Hungary, Iceland, India, Indonesia, Ireland, Japan, Malaysia, Malta, New Zealand, Netherlands, Norway, Philippines, Poland, Portugal, Scotland, Singapore, South Africa, Spain, Sri Lanka, Sweden, Switzerland, Yugoslavia and Wales.

SHEET MUSIC

(Title/Publisher/Original Price)

Move It
B. F. Wood Music 2/-

High Class Baby
Kalith Music Ltd 2/-

My Feet Hit The Ground
Kalith Music Ltd 2/-

Mean Streak
Kalith Music Ltd 2/-

Never Mind
Kalith Music Ltd 2/-

Worry-Go-Luck-Me
Chappell & Co Ltd 2/-

(Sheet music for this song, intended for the film *Expresso Bongo* was printed and published with Cliff's picture on the cover announcing 'from the film', although a recording of the title has not yet been found.)

Living Doll
Peter Maurice Music Co Ltd 2/-

Mad About You
Peter Maurice Music Co Ltd 2/-

No Turning Back
Peter Maurice Music Co Ltd 2/-

Apron Strings
June Music Ltd 2/-

Travellin' Light
Aberbach (London) Ltd 2/-

Dynamite
Kalith Music Ltd 2/-

Don't Be Mad At Me
Aberbach (London) Ltd 2/-

Fall In Love With You
Kalith Music Ltd 2/-

Please Don't Tease
Belinda (London) Ltd 2/-

Nine Times Out Of Ten
Aberbach (London) Ltd 2/-

Thinking Of Our Love
Belinda (London) Ltd 2/-

I Love You
Belinda (London) Ltd 2/-

Theme For A Dream
Eugene Music 2/-

Gee Whiz It's You
Belinda (London) Ltd 2/-

A Girl Like You
Francis/Day/Hunter 2/6

Now's The Time To Fall In Love
Belinda (London) Ltd 2/-

When The Girl In Your Arms, Is The Girl In Your Heart
Eugene Music 2/6

The Young Ones
Harms Witmark 2/6

I'm Looking Out The Window
Chappell 2/-

It'll Be Me
Aberbach (London) Ltd 2/6

Since I Lost You
Shadows Music/Belinda (London) Ltd 2/6

The Next Time
Elstree 2/6

Lucky Lips
Belinda (London) Ltd 2/6

I Wonder
Belinda (London) Ltd/Shadows Music 2/6

It's All In The Game
Canadian Music 2/6

Your Eyes Tell On You
Shadows Music 2/6

Don't Talk To Him
Belinda (London) Ltd/Shadows
Music 2/6

Say You're Mine
Belinda (London) Ltd 2/6

I'm The Lonely One
Eugene Music 2/6

**Watch What You Do With
My Baby**
Joaneline 2/6

Constantly
Worldwide Music 2/6

True True Lovin'
Shadows Music/Belinda (London)
Ltd 2/6

**I Could Easily Fall In Love
With You**
Shadows Music 2/6

The Minute You're Gone
2/6

Look In My Eyes Maria
Belinda (London) Ltd 2/6

The Time In Between
Shadows Music 2/6

All By Yourself In The Moonlight
Cambell 2/6
(Sheet music exists for this song,
apparently recorded by Cliff
Richard, although the title cannot
be traced anywhere on record)

Shooting Star
Shadows Music 3/-

Blue Turns To Grey
Essex Music 2/6

Visions
Joaneline 3/-

Time Drags By
Shadows Music 3/-

La La La Song
Shadows Music 3/-

In The Country
Shadows Music Ltd 3/-

Finders Keepers
Shadows Music Ltd 3/-

The Day I Met Marie
Shadows Music 3/-

Congratulations
Peter Maurice Music Co Ltd 3/-

I'll Love You Forever Today
Joaneline/Carlin Music 3/-

Don't Forget To Catch Me
Shadows Music 3/-

Throw Down A Line
Shadows Music Ltd 3/-

With The Eyes Of A Child
Abacus 3/-

The Joy Of Living
Shadows Music/Belinda (London)
Ltd 3/-

Goodbye Sam, Hello Samantha
Intune Ltd -15p

Silvery Rain
Shadows Music -20p

Sing A Song Of Freedom
Big Secret -20p

Jesus
Burlington -20p

Power To All Our Friends
Big Secret -20p

Take Me High
Coronado -25p

(You Keep Me) Hangin' On
Petro -25p

It's Only Me You've Left Behind
ATV Music -25p

My Kinda Life
Cam-Al Music -30p

True Love Ways
Southern Music -75p

Never Say Die
Chappell

Heart User
Chappell

Living Doll (w. The Young Ones)
EMI

My Pretty One
£1.95

Some People
£1.95

Mistletoe And Wine
Southern Music £1.50

The Best Of Me

I Just Don't Have The Heart
£1.95

Saviours Day
Clouseau Music

MUSIC BOOKS

CLIFF RICHARD SONGS FROM THE FILM ALBUM
Living Doll
Mad About You
No Turning Back
Chinchilla
Peter Maurice Music Co Ltd, 3/-

JUKE BOX FAVOURITES
High Class Baby
My Feet Hit The Ground
Danny
Livin' Lovin' Doll
Steady With You
Kalith Music/Belinda (London) Ltd, 3/-

GOLDEN GREATS
Bachelor Boy
Congratulations
Constantly
Devil Woman
A Girl Like You
I Can't Ask For Anymore Than You
Living Doll
Miss You Nights
Move It
The Next Time
On The Beach
Summer Holiday
Wind Me Up
The Young Ones

NEW ANTHOLOGY
Bachelor Boy
Carrie
Congratulations
Daddy's Home

Devil Woman
Little In Love
Living Doll
Locked Inside Your Prison
Miss You Nights
Move It
Never Say Die
Now You See Me, Now You Don't
On The Beach
Power To All Our Friends
Summer Holiday
True Love Ways
We Don't Talk Anymore
Young Ones

IT'S A SMALL WORLD
Tiny Planet
Small World
Devil Woman
Movin' In
It Has To Be You, It Has To Be Me
La Gonave
I Will Follow You
The Only Way Out
Rock 'n' Roll Juvenile
Where Do We Go From Here

ALADDIN
Emperor Theme
Me Oh My
I Could Easily Fall (In Love With You)
Little Princess
This Was My Special Day
I'm In Love With You
There's Gotta Be A Way
Ballet
Dance Of The Warriors
Friends
Dragon Dance
Genie With The Light Brown Lamp
Make Ev'ry Day A Carnival Day
Widow Twankey's Song
I'm Feeling Oh So Lovely

I've Said Too Many Things
Evening Comes
Havin' Fun
Shadows Music, 7/6

ESTABLISHED 1958
Don't Forget To Catch Me
Voyage To The Bottom Of The Bath
Not The Way That It Should Be
Poem
The Dreams I Dream
The Average Life Of A Daily Man
Somewhere By The Sea
Banana Man
Girl On The Bus
The Magical Mrs Clamps
Ooh La La
Here I Go Again Loving You
What's Behind The Eyes Of Mary
Maggie's Samba
Shadows Music, 7/6

CLIFF RICHARD'S BOOK OF SONGS & CAROLS
Auld Lang Syne
Away In A Manger
Bachelor Boy
Congratulations
Dancing Shoes
Flying Machine
Get On Board Little Children
God Rest Ye Merry Gentlemen
Good Christian Men Rejoice
Good King Wencelas
Greensleeves
Holy Night
Home On The Range
I Dream Of Jeanie
I Got A Rose
I'll Take You Home Again Kathleen
I'm Lookin' Out The Window

In The Country
I Saw Three Ships
It'll Be Me
Jingle Bells
Living Doll
Michael Row The Boat Ashore
My Grandfather's Clock
O Come All Ye Faithful
Oh Dear! What Can The
    Matter Be?
Old Macdonald Had A Farm
Please Don't Tease
Silvery Rain
Some Folks Like To Sigh
Summer Holiday
Swing Low, Sweet Chariot
The Blue-Tail Fly
The Day I Met Marie
The Next Time
The Young Ones
Travellin' Light
Visions
We Three Kings
Your Eyes Tell On You

An 8-page pull-out-and-keep book
with song lyrics presented with
Woman magazine on 27 November,
1971.

RECOMMENDED RECORDS TO UNDERSTAND CLIFF'S ERA

PAT BOONE: *Love Letters In The Sand*
FRANK SINATRA: *Fly Me To The Moon*
DEAN MARTIN: *Everybody Loves Somebody*
All are absolute 'musts' showing the similarity of Cliff's orchestral arrangements on the 'Listen To Cliff' and 'Love Is Forever' LPs.

RAY CHARLES: *What'd I Say* shows the earlier influences of R&B on rock 'n' roll.

BILL HALEY & HIS COMETS: *Rock Around The Clock* shows the influences of country music on rock 'n' roll.

ELVIS PRESLEY: *Heartbreak Hotel* shows the influence of Elvis's style on Cliff's early work.

BUDDY HOLLY: *That'll Be The Day*. A definite influence in the chord progression of Cliff's 'Gee Whiz It's You'.

CLIFF RICHARD: *Cliff*. Debut LP recorded at Abbey Road studios in front of a live audience, was a startling vote of confidence from Columbia in Cliff's abilities as a performer. Sixteen rock 'n' roll tunes paid tribute to the rock 'n' roll stars and the songs that made them famous. Includes the first known live version of his own hit 'Move It', and a couple of solo performances by the Drifters. A truly remarkable record.

CLIFF RICHARD: *Nine Times Out Of Ten*. Allegedly written for Elvis and shows the similarity of Cliff's early style to Presley's.

CLIFF RICHARD: *Please Don't Tease*. The song the fans chose to be a hit in 1960. A must for all fans!

WEST SIDE STORY: Made in the same year, there are clear similarities in parts to 'The Young Ones'.

HERMANS HERMITS: *Silhouettes*. A fine sample of sixties dowop.

CLIFF RICHARD: *Cliff's Hit Album*. Fourteen of Cliff's early, great hits. A must for all listeners.

THE BEATLES: *Rubber Soul*.
THE BEATLES: *Revolver*.
THE BEATLES: *Sergeant Pepper's Lonely Hearts Club Band*. All are absolute required listening. These were the albums that changed British pop, from choosing original material to recording without the supervision of a producer, and the introduction of all-night sessions.

ELVIS PRESLEY: *How Great Thou Art*. Eleven religious songs that gave Presley his first Grammy award for the music he loved. A must for all listeners.

CLIFF RICHARD: *Congratulations*. Cliff's first Eurovision outing which probably now ranks as popular as 'Happy Birthday' and has become an essential ingredient for just about every celebration imaginable. Keep a copy handy!

THE SHADOWS: *20 Golden Greats*. A collection of the best of the Shadows. Interesting to listen to the group that created the backing sound for Cliff and how, without him, this set of recordings still has that unique and instantly recognizable sound. A must for all Cliff and Shadows fans.

CONWAY TWITTY: *Honky Tonk Angel*. A hard to find record that was covered by both Elvis and Cliff, although Cliff withdrew his single because he was not happy with the lyrical content. Worth a listen.

SHAKIN' STEVENS: *This Ole House*. An excellent re-working of the Rosemary Clooney hit. It was probably the best British rock 'n' roll record since 'Move It', and marked a return to rock roots and influences. Great boppin' music!

KYLIE MINOGUE: *I Should Be So Lucky*.
RICK ASTLEY: *Never Gonna Give You Up*.
Both these show the influence on Cliff's 'I Just Don't Have The Heart' from the Eighties' dance craze records produced by Stock, Aitken & Waterman.

CLIFF RICHARD: *Together With Cliff Richard*. Thirteen seasonal tunes including 'O Come All Ye Faithful', 'White Christmas' and 'Silent Night' among the traditional numbers, and 'Mistletoe And Wine', and 'Saviours Day'

from Cliff's own hits. A good seasonal listening experience.

CLIFF RICHARD: *The Hit List*. A double compact disc set that contains an incredible collection of Cliff's best songs of top five hits over a period of thirty-five years.

LONNIE DONEGAN: *Rock Island Line*. A good example of how skiffle influenced early rock 'n' roll.

TOMMY STEELE: *Rock With The Caveman*. The first hit from the first British rock 'n' roll star. Some fine boogie piano.

THE FIVE CHESTERNUTS: *Teenage Love*. Hank Marvin and Bruce Welch's first record. Pure Buddy Holly innocence that introduces rock 'n' roll to a generation to whom it would become a way of life. Very hard to find, but worth the hunt.

MARTY WILDE: *Endless Sleep*. A monster guitar riff, a fantastically quivering vocal and superb back-up vocals all add up to a classic teenage melodrama. Great stuff!

JERRY LEE LEWIS: *Great Balls Of Fire*. An incredible listening experience, showing the dynamic breadth, strength, and sponteneity of one of the best 'rockabilly' artists.

CLIFF RICHARD: *Move It*. The birth of British rock 'n' roll and Cliff Richard. Nothing more need be said!

CLIFF RICHARD: *Travellin' Light*. Originally written for Elvis to sing in 'King Creole', this early sixties recording by Cliff allows him to explore country influences. Should have been a good qualifier for the American Country charts.

CLIFF RICHARD: *Summer Holiday*. A great pop song which seems to have worked its way into our musical culture. There were more hits from the film than any other. Essential listening for the holidays!

BILLY FURY: *That's Love*. The opener from one of the finest British rock albums *The Sound Of Fury* in that it is a totally convincing homage to the Elvis Sun sound. A 'rockabilly' pop classic. Irresistible!

ADAM FAITH: *Made You*. The standout song from the film, *Beat Girl*. Listen out for the Eddie Cochran 'Something Else' soundalike guitar riff.

THE SHADOWS: *Wonderful Land*. A fine example of the perfect pop tune of the period. A gorgeous tune, great guitar tone, light bouncy rhythm, and a sweeping horn and string arrangement. It still sounds impossibly fresh and unbearably innocent.

JOE BROWN: *A Picture Of You*. An energetic vocal, fine female back-ups and snappy guitar work make this one to play and play again.

HELEN SHAPIRO: *Walkin' Back To Happiness*.
JOHNNY KIDD AND THE PIRATES: *Shakin' All Over*.
CRAIG DOUGLAS: *Our Favourite Melodies*.
JOHN LEYTON: *Johnny Remember Me*.
All perfect slices of sixties pop.

SHEP & THE LIMELIGHTS: *Daddy's Home*. From Cliff's own juke box collection of favourites. One of the best dowop ballads from the fifties.

CLIFF RICHARD: *Small Corners* shows the influences of gospel music, but a rocking 'Why Should The Devil Have All The Good Music' gives it a kick.

OLIVIA NEWTON-JOHN: *If Not For You* shows the earlier influences on Olivia of American country music. A must!

VIDEOS

The videos in this section are chronologically listed according to their original issue date, and re-issues are noted at the end of the relevant entries.

Two A Penny
Catalogue Number: Worldwide Home Video
Released: 1978 Running Time: 65 minutes

For synopsis and credits please see the appropriate entry in the Movie Section

The Young Ones
Catalogue Number: EVM 20242 (Beta version)
Released: 1981 Running Time: 104 minutes
For synopsis and credits please see the appropriate entry in the Movie Section
Also released as EMI TXC 90 0242 4 Beta version in 1983 and Warner Home Video PES 38075 in June 1988

It's A Small World
Catalogue Number: Tear Fund. Greenleaf Films (BETA version)
Released: 1984 Running Time: 32 minutes

Together – Cliff & The Shadows 1984
Catalogue Number: PMI MVP 991008 2
Released: December 1984 Running Time: 78 minutes
Tracks: Move It/Don't Talk To Him/Please Don't Tease/It's All In The Game/Lucky Lips/Wonderful Land/The Theme From The Deerhunter (Cavatina)/F.B.I./Living Doll/Bachelor Boy/Summer Holiday/The Young Ones/I Love You/The Day I Met Marie/The Twelfth Of Never/Congratulations/Let Me Be The One/Power To All Our Friends/On The Beach/I Could Easily Fall In Love/Do You Wanna Dance/We Don't Talk Anymore/Visions/We Don't Talk Anymore (Reprise)
In 1984 Cliff and the Shadows joined for a short UK tour that took in London and Birmingham. This show, recorded at the National Exhibition Centre in Birmingham, features a selection of their early hits and solo releases.
Also released as MXP 9910084 Beta version

Together – Cliff & The Shadows 1984
Catalogue Number: Music Club MC 2124
Released: UNKNOWN Running Time: 78 minutes
Same tracks as featured on the PMI release.

The Video Connection
Catalogue Number: PMI MVP 9910402
Released: October 1984 Running Time: 55 minutes
Tracks: My Kinda Life/Wired For Sound/A Little In

Tracks: End Of The Show (Thank You Very Much)/
Turn Me Loose/Love/The Young Ones/Move It/
Summer Holiday/The Look Of Love/We Say Yeah/
When I'm Sixty Four/Do You Wanna Dance/The Day
I Met Marie/F.B.I./Let Me Be The One/Willie And
The Hand Jive/Move It/Up In Canada/Yes He Lives/
Miss You Nights/All Shook Up/Devil Woman/Why
Should The Devil Have All The Good Music/End Of
The Show (Thank You Very Much)

March 1978, and for two weeks Cliff and the Shadows
were reunited on stage for the first time in 10 years to
recreate 20 years of that special magic. This video
features footage from this reunion as well as other rare
film from their early career and comments from Cliff,
Hank Marvin, Bruce Welch, Olivia Newton-John, Adam
Faith and other fellow musicians.
Also released as MXP 9910134 Beta version

Thank You Very Much
Catalogue Number: Video Collection PM 0003
Released: May 1987 Running Time: 52 minutes
Same tracks as featured on the PMI release.

Thank You Very Much
Catalogue Number: Music Club MC 2012
Released: April 1989 Running Time: 52 minutes
Same tracks as featured on the PMI release.
Also released as TVE 9003292 Beta version in 1982

Rock In Australia
Catalogue Number: PMI MVN 9911302
Released: December 1986 Running Time: 70 minutes
Tracks: I'm Nearly Famous/Wired For Sound/
Learning How To Rock 'n' Roll/Dreamin'/Donna/
The Only Way Out/Love Stealer/Miss You Nights/
Shooting From The Heart/Devil Woman/Lucille/
Under The Gun/Where You Are/Lovers & Friends/
Ocean Deep/Thief In The Night/Living Doll/Summer
Holiday/Bachelor Boy/We Don't Talk Anymore

This show was recorded at the Sydney Entertainment
Centre during Cliff's 'Rock Connection' tour in 1984 and
featured tracks from his recent albums Silver and The
Rock Connection as well as firm favourites like Miss You
Nights and Living Doll.
Also released as MXN 9911304 Beta Version in 1985

Love/Hey Mr Dream Maker/Summer Holiday/Miss
You Nights/Devil Woman/Baby You're Dynamite/
Please Don't Fall In Love/Never Say Die/Carrie/The
Young Ones/Dreamin'/Daddy's Home/We Don't
Talk Anymore

In the eighties promotional videos were the norm and
this video release collected thirteen of Cliff's videos
from 1975 to 1984. Also included were clips from the
films Summer Holiday and The Young Ones.
Also released as TXE 9019604 Beta version in 1983

The Video Connection
Catalogue Number: Music Club MC 2081
Released: March 1992 Running Time: 55 minutes
Same tracks as featured on the PMI release.

Thank You Very Much
Catalogue Number: PMI MVP 9910132
Released: June 1986 Running Time: 52 minutes

Rock In Australia

Catalogue Number: Music Club MC 2056

Released: March 1991 Running Time: 70 minutes

Same tracks as featured on the PMI release.

Mine To Share

Catalogue Number: Bagster Video (no number)

Released: 1987 Running Time: 35 minutes
(Tape 1)/35 minutes (Tape 2)

We Don't Talk Anymore

Catalogue Number: Gold Rushes PM 0025

Released: March 1987 Running Time: 8 minutes

Tracks: We Don't Talk Anymore/Miss You Nights

Take Me High

Catalogue Number: Warner Home Video PES 38074

Released: 1988 Running Time: 87 minutes

For synopsis and credits please see the appropriate
entry in the Movie Section

Always Guaranteed

Catalogue Number: PMI MVS 9900743

Released: March 1988 Running Time: 17 minutes

Tracks: My Pretty One/Some People/Remember Me/
Two Hearts

Released as a companion to the Always Guaranteed
album this video featured the four singles released from
the album.

Summer Holiday

Catalogue Number: Warner Home Video PES 38073

Released: June 1988 Running Time: 103 minutes

For synopsis and credits please see the appropriate
entry in the Movie Section

*Also released as TXJ 9022054 Beta version in 1983
with running time of 105 minutes*

Wonderful Life

Catalogue Number: Warner Home Video PES 38076

Released: June 1988 Running Time: 109 minutes

For synopsis and credits please see the appropriate
entry in the Movie Section

*Also released as TXJ 9009704 Beta version in 1983
with running time of 104 minutes*

Live And Guaranteed

Catalogue Number: PMI MVP 9911793

Released: February 1989 Running Time: 60 minutes

Tracks: Remember Me/Always Guaranteed/Two
Hearts/Devil Woman/All The Time You Need/Living
Doll/The Young Ones/Miss You Nights/Some
People/UFO – Thief In The Night/I Wish We'd All
Been Ready/We Don't Talk Anymore

This follow-up to 'Rock In Australia' was filmed during
the European leg to Cliff's 'Always Guaranteed' World
Tour in 1988. The tracks were mainly recent singles
and album material from Always Guaranteed. The video
included exclusive backstage interviews and footage.

Live And Guaranteed

Catalogue Number: SAV 49113753

Released: March 1995 Running Time: 60 minutes

Re-issued as a CD/Video Double Pack on Sound and
Vision (PMI) the video contained the same tracks as the
original issue.

Private Collection 1979–1988

Catalogue Number: PMI MVP CR1

Released: November 1988 Running Time: 57 minutes

Tracks: Some People/Wired For Sound/Carrie/
Remember Me/Dreamin'/A Little In Love/Daddy's
Home/Never Say Die/The Only Way Out/Please
Don't Fall In Love/My Pretty One/She's So
Beautiful/Two Hearts/We Don't Talk Anymore/
Where Do We Go From Here/Mistletoe And Wine

As with The Video Connection this featured a selection
of recent promotional videos covering a ten-year period.

From A Distance – The Event

Catalogue Number: PMI MVP 4910413

Released: November 1990 Running Time: 124 minutes

Tracks: (Tape 1) Oh Boy Medley/Zing! Went The
Strings Of My Heart/Always/When/The Glory Of
Love/Hoots Mon/Don't Look Now/The Girl Can't
Help It/Sea Cruise/Medley

(Tape 2) Wired For Sound/Dreamin'/Daddy's Home/I
Could Easily Fall In Love/Some People/We Don't
Talk Anymore/Two Hearts/Move It/Shake, Rattle
And Roll/Joanna/Remember Me/Stronger Than
That/Silhouettes/Good Golly, Miss Molly/Miss You

Nights/Summer Holiday/I Just Don't Have The Heart/Fighter/Thief In The Night/The Best Of Me/From A Distance

A two video set featuring the Oh Boy Section and Cliff's own set from his two sell-out performances at Wembley Stadium, better known as 'The Event'.

An Evening With Cliff Richard

Catalogue Number: UNKNOWN
Released: 1990 Running Time: UNKNOWN

This video was taped during a gospel concert at Monash University in Melbourne, Australia in January 1989.

Knebworth – The Event Volume 1

Catalogue Number: CMP 6006
Released: 1990 Running Time: 60 minutes
Tracks: On The Beach/Do You Wanna Dance/Good
    Golly Miss Molly/Living Doll/We Don't Talk Anymore

Volume One of a three video set recorded during the 1990 Knebworth concert in aid of the Nordoff-Robins Music Therapy Clinic. Along with Cliff this video also includes Tears For Fears, Phil Collins and Paul McCartney.

Together With Cliff Richard

Catalogue Number: PMI MVC 9913233
Released: November 1991 Running Time: 55 minutes
Tracks: Have Yourself A Merry Little Christmas/
    (Venite) O Come All Ye Faithful/White Christmas/
    Christmas Alphabet/Mistletoe And Wine/I Love
    You/Saviour's Day/Scarlet Ribbons/The Christmas
    Song/Christmas Never Comes/We Should Be
    Together/Silent Night/This New Year

Released to coincide with his first Christmas album this set contains 12 seasonal tracks, specially recorded before a live audience, along with his other Christmas, non-seasonal, number one, I Love You.

Expresso Bongo

Catalogue Number: Virgin VVD1014
Released: 1992 Running Time: 101 minutes
For synopsis and credits please see the appropriate
    entry in the Movie Section

The Event

Catalogue Number: PMI MVP 491D413
Released: 1992 Running Time: 90 minutes

This is a re-issue of Cliff's set from the From A Distance – The Event double video.

When The Music Stops

Catalogue Number: WORD WV9000
Released: September 1992 Running Time: 57 minutes

In this video Cliff is faced by over 50 teenagers who question him about his faith. Cliff responds to their questions and, although you may not agree with his answers, it is obvious that his Christian faith has made a large impact on his life.

When The Music Stops

Catalogue Number: Wienerworld WNR 2035
Released: 8 March 1993 Running Time: 57 minutes
Straight re-issue of the Word video release.

Oh Boy

Catalogue Number: Music Club MC 2132
Released: 1993 Running Time: 39 minutes

This is a re-issue of the Oh Boy segment from the From A Distance – The Event double video

The Young Ones/Summer Holiday

Catalogue Number: Warner Home Video S038696
Released: 1993 Running Time: 104 minutes
    & 103 minutes
For synopsis and credits please see the appropriate
    entry in the Movie Section

Wonderful Life/Take Me High

Catalogue Number: Warner Home Video S038697
Released: 1993 Running Time: 109 minutes
    & 86 minutes
For synopsis and credits please see the appropriate
    entry in the Movie Section

Compassion Has The Heart

Catalogue Number: Tear Fund. Greenleaf Films
Released: 7 January 1993 Running Time: 32 minutes

Access All Areas – The Tour 1992

Catalogue Number: PMI MVB 4911123

Released: 5 April 1993 Running Time: 51 minutes
(Tape 1)/83 minutes (Tape 2)

Tracks: (Tape 1) Move It/The Young Ones/Summer
Holiday/Love On/It's All In The Game/Silhouettes/
That's Alright Mama/Free/Daddy's Home/Please
Don't Tease/On The Beach

(Tape 2) From A Distance/Monday Thru Friday/Some
People/Little Mistreater/Devil Woman/Miss You
Nights/Willie And The Hand Jive/Love Is The
Strongest Emotion/Silvery Rain/I Still Believe In
You/We Don't Talk Anymore/Mistletoe And Wine/
Human Work Of Art/Handle My Heart/Wired For
Sound/My Kinda Life/Peace In Our Time

This two video set contains a complete concert from
Cliff's successful 'Access All Areas' tour in late 1992.
The first video featured the acoustic set and the second
Cliff's set with his band.

The Story So Far

Catalogue Number: PMI MVD 4911883

Released: 15 November 1993 Running Time: 135
minutes

This video traces Cliff's career through exclusive
interviews with family, friends and colleagues as well as
clips from his movies, rare concert clips and private
footage.

The Hit List

Catalogue Number: PMI MVD 4913453

Released: 3 October 1994 Running Time: 85 minutes

Tracks: Move It/Living Doll/Travellin' Light/Voice In
The Wilderness/Fall In Love With You/Please Don't
Tease/Nine Times Out Of Ten/I Love You/Theme
For A Dream/Gee Whiz It's You/When The Girl In
Your Arms Is The Girl In Your Heart/The Young
Ones/Do You Wanna Dance/I'm Looking Out The
Window/Bachelor Boy/Summer Holiday/The Next
Time/Constantly/The Minute You're Gone/Wind
Me Up (Let Me Go)/Lucky Lips/Congratulations/
Power To All Our Friends/We Don't Talk Anymore/
Wired For Sound/Some People/Mistletoe And
Wine/The Best Of Me/I Just Don't Have The Heart/
Saviour's Day

Released as a limited edition companion to the Hit List
double CD and cassette this video brings together 30
film, television and video performances of which 26
have never been released before. Cliff introduces many
of the clips himself.

Christmas With Cliff Richard

Catalogue Number: Wienerworld WNR 2046

Released: December 1994 Running Time: 43 minutes

Tracks: Sweet Little Jesus Boy/We're All One/You
Can't Get To Heaven By Livin' Like Hell/Jesus Is
The Answer/Thief In The Night/I Wish We'd All Been
Ready/Everyman/Song For Sarah/The Rock That
Doesn't Roll/O Little Town Of Bethlehem/Silent
Night/ In The Bleak Mid Winter/Away In A Manger

Recorded before a specially invited audience this classic
concert from 1980 features a seasonal selection high-
lighting his Christian beliefs.

The Hit List Live

Catalogue Number: PMI MVD 4914673

Released: 16 October 1995 Running Time: 145 minutes

Tracks: Wired For Sound/Lucky Lips/Constantly/ Power To All Our Friends/Carrie/Gee Whiz It's You/ Nine Times Out Of Ten/Some People/When The Girl In Your Arms Is The Girl In Your Heart/A Girl Like You/Theme For a Dream/It'll Be Me/Don't Talk To Him/It's All In The Game/The Best Of Me/Do You Wanna Dance/Daddy's Home/Wind Me Up (Let Me Go)/Fall In Love With You/A Voice In The Wilderness/When Will I Be Loved/Move It/Summer Holiday/Congratulations/Travellin' Light/The Young Ones/The Minute You're Gone/Living Doll/Bachelor Boy/The Next Time/I Love You/Please Don't Tease/(All I Have To Do Is) Dream/Mistletoe And Wine/Saviour's Day/Miss You Nights/Dreamin'/We Don't Talk Anymore

Recorded in Sheffield on 15 December 1994 during the 'Hit List' tour this video contains the complete concert with the exception of the three songs featured on the tour from Heathcliff.

These last few video releases are placed here as no accurate release date could be found.

Serious Charge

Catalogue Number: Odyssey ODY131

Released: UNKNOWN Running Time: 90 minutes

For synopsis and credits please see the appropriate entry in the Movie Section

Thunderbirds Are Go

Catalogue Number: MGM/UA SCV 50231

For synopsis and credits please see the appropriate entry in the Movie Section

His Land

Catalogue Number: World-Wide Home Video

Released: UNKNOWN Running Time: 67 minutes

For synopsis and credits please see the appropriate entry in the Movie Section

Cliff In Kenya

Catalogue Number: Tear Fund

Released: UNKNOWN Running Time: 55 minutes

Journey Into Life

Catalogue Number: Sunrise Video

Released: UNKNOWN Running Time: 25 minutes

PART 4
THE PERFORMER

FEATURE FILMS

Nowadays, if a pop artist releases a single there is almost always a pop video to accompany it. It is expected. Some would say it's vital. But in 1958, when Cliff made his first film, the notion of the pop video was decades away, so the next best thing if you couldn't see him in person was to watch and enjoy Cliff's every cinematic moment when he would come to life on the giant screen. It was so much better than a photograph. At least fans could see their idol and hero 'singin' dancing' and swingin' at their local picture house.

For Cliff, the rise from television to cinema screen was almost as meteoric as his rise from obscurity to fame as the pioneer of British rock 'n' roll. As Hollywood had done with Elvis Presley, British film makers sensed that Cliff would be a box office sensation in the right vehicles. In fact, it was a British Elvis that Micky Delamar was looking to cast in *Serious Charge*, and probably the same could be said of Val Guest, who cast Cliff's second film *Expresso Bongo*. Both characters could be loosely identified with the roles Elvis had played in his second and third movies. Curley Thompson, like Elvis's Vince Everett in *Jailhouse Rock*, was a juvenile rebel, and Bongo Herbert resembled Elvis's Deke Rivers in *Loving You*, who was a manipulated teenage idol.

During the sixties, Elvis made 'beach movies', and Cliff went from supporting roles to debut as a leading man in the first of a trilogy of films that would become known as the Cliff Richard musicals. The idea had been developed by film producer Kenneth Harper who had seen Cliff live on stage during one of his gruelling one-nighter tours that for the most part were staged at cinemas with at least two shows a night. What Harper discovered was that Cliff was filling cinemas on a Sunday night when films left them empty, consequently he knew that Cliff was the person to make a film with. The initial problem, however, was finding a story to turn into a musical. The most obvious would have been to do *The Cliff Richard Story*, but that was abandoned in favour of an original musical, and *The Young Ones* set the pattern for the next few films. Elvis continued his 'beach movie' formula and Cliff, his youth orientated 'fun' films – *Summer Holiday*, *Wonderful Life*, and *Finder's Keepers* all fell into the archetypal 'Cliff Richard musical' category. The latter was not quite as successful as its predecessors, but *Wonderful Life* did well, even though it had strong competition from the Beatles' first film *A Hard Day's Night* which had been released in the same month and year.

By the late sixties, the pop movie had become less popular. They were being replaced by documentary films like the Beatles' *Let It Be*, *Woodstock* and then, in the early seventies, *Elvis On Tour*. Cliff made a couple more films during this period. *Two A Penny* was probably the only film in which Cliff truly aspired to become a serious actor, while *Take Me High* returned to the musical category, although most of the songs were heard on the soundtrack rather than being performed on screen. Cliff only made seven films for major cinema release against Elvis' thirty-three. The Beatles made even fewer. But no matter how many films Cliff starred in, we must remember that every one was commercially successful and are still enjoyed by people of all ages via cable, satellite and video.

SERIOUS CHARGE

Alva Films. 1959. A Mickey Delamar Production. Certificate X. Running time: 99 minutes. Length: 8929 ft. Cliff's first film.

CAST

Howard Phillips	ANTHONY QUAYLE
Hester Peters	SARAH CHURCHILL
Larry Thompson	ANDREW RAY
Mrs Phillips	IRENE BROWNE
Mr Thompson	PERCY HERBERT
Mr Peters	NOEL HOWLETT
Police Sergeant	WENSLEY PITHEY
Mary Williams	LEIGH MADISON
Probation Officer	JUDITH FURSE
Almshouse Matron	JEAN CADELL
Verger	WILFRED BRAMBELL
Mrs Browning	OLIVE SLOAN
Fishmonger	GEORGE RODERICK
and	
Curley Thompson	CLIFF RICHARD
Michelle	LILLIANE BROUSSE

CREW

Screenplay	GUY ELMES & MICKY DELAMAR
Director of Photography	GEORGE PERINAL
Editor	REGINALD BECK
Art Director	ALLAN HARRIS
Assistant Director	ADRIAN PRYCE-JONES
Camera Operator	DENYS COOP
Sound	GERRY TURNER & J B SMITH
Dubbing Editor	GORDON DANIEL
Make-up	PHIL LEAKEY
Wardrobe	CHARLES GUERIN
Special Effects	TOM HOWARD
Production Supervisor	T S LYNDON-HAYNES
Producer	MICKEY DELAMAR
Director	TERENCE YOUNG
From 'Serious Charge' by	PHILIP KING
Music composed and conducted by	LEIGHTON LUCAS

Cliff Richard songs:
'No Turning Back', 'Living Doll', 'Mad' by LIONEL BART
Theme: 'Chinchilla' by Randy Starr and Dick Wolf

SONGS

1. 'No Turning Back' – sung at the Church Youth Club to Cliff's friend of the evening Lulubell (Juliette Nisson) while others jive to the disapproval of Anthony Quayle.

2. 'Living Doll' – sung at the coffee bar, prior to Andrew Ray being summoned to Anthony Quayle's house.

3. 'Mad About You' – sung on the soundtrack as Jess Conrad and others look out from the coffee bar on Anthony Quayle crossing the High Street.

4. 'Chinchilla' – played by the Drifters is heard as incidental music on the soundtrack.

THE STORY

When the Rev. Howard Phillips, ex-army padre, arrives in the town of Bellingham he is faced with a problem – juvenile delinquency. His attempts to attract the juvenile population to his Youth Club receive the wholehearted support of Hester Peters, daughter of the former vicar, and the bitter hostility of Larry Thompson, leader of a gang of crazy teenagers who have been causing havoc in the town.

When Larry's young brother Curley is charged with wanton destruction. Howard pleads on his behalf, and is given a week in which to investigate the boy's background before he is brought to trial. The Magistrate's decision is regarded as weakness by Larry and his gang. Curley, who now respects the parson is deeply embarrassed when the gang call at the Youth Club to see Michelle, the latest object of Larry's affections. They are obliged to leave after Larry has unsuccessfully tangled with the brawny vicar.

Hester calls at the vicarage, in Howard's absence, and tries to make a favourable impression on his mother. Howard returns late and is obliged to drive Hester home. She interprets this as a sign of his dawning affection for her. Arriving home, she tells her father that she loves Howard and hopes to marry him. Before Mrs Phillips leaves on holiday she warns her son that Hester is in love with him, and that he should be careful how he treats her.

The following week, the Probation Officer collects Howard and Curley for the second hearing of the case. The Magistrate decides to quash the case if Howard can persuade the shopkeepers whose windows have been smashed to withdraw their charges, and if he will stand surety for Curley's good behaviour.

Shopping in the High Street, Howard finds Mary Williams in tears. She rejects his offer of help and Howard tells her to come to the vicarage if she changes her mind. Taking him up on his offer, Mary confesses to Howard that she is pregnant and that Larry Thompson is responsible. Howard comforts her with a promise to break the news to her parents. They are interrupted by the arrival of Hester, and Mary leaves. All too soon, Howard finds his mother's prophecy correct and is forced to reject Hester's embarrassing proposal of marriage. On her way home from the vicarage Mary discovers Larry and Michelle in a passionate embrace. She is numb with despair and does not notice an oncoming truck as she steps to her death in the road. After the inquest, Howard summons Larry to the vicarage hoping to make him realise his responsibility. Larry refuses to listen and Howard threatens to disclose the truth to the boy's father. Hearing footsteps outside, Larry conceives a vicious plan to discredit the vicar and so save his own skin. He wrecks the room, and runs dishevelled towards the door, sobbing wildly. Hester enters, and despite Howard's protestations of innocence, her hurt pride induces her to believe Larry's story of the attack made on him by the vicar. She resigns from all her parish duties.

Unable to get any sense out of his daughter, Mr Peters visits the Thompson home and such is Larry's fear of his father's wrath that he sticks resolutely to his story. Mr Thompson, accompanied by the police sergeant, visits the vicarage and confronts Howard with Larry's story. Howard counters the charge with the truth about Mary's pregnancy, which Larry denies. Thompson cannot quite believe that the vicar's story is a fabrication until Hester confirms Larry's version of the facts.

Social ostracism begins for Howard with many annoyances culminating in a fight with Thompson and Michelle being withdrawn from the vicarage by her employment agent.

Mrs Phillips returns from holiday to find that her son has decided to send his resignation to the bishop. Her determination to clear Howard of the serious charge provides the dramatic climax for this topical and powerful story.

PRODUCTION NOTES & TRIVIA

● *Serious Charge* opened nationally on 29 June 1959. The companion feature in most areas was *Man Mad*.

● Filming began in December 1958 at the MGM Studios in Borehamwood. Exteriors were shot in the new town of Stevenage.

● *Serious Charge* was based on the stage play of the same name. The part Cliff played as Curley Thompson was not a character of the stage version, but was added for the film.

● All the songs for *Serious Charge* were composed by Lionel Bart who went on to write the musicals *Fings Ain't Wot They Used T'be*, *Oliver!*, *Blitz!* and *Maggie May*. He reportedly wrote 'Living Doll' for the film in ten minutes while reading the *Sunday Pictorial* in October 1958.

● As performed on the soundtrack of the film 'Living Doll' was a fast song in four-four time which Cliff hated singing, so when it came to re-recording the songs for record release, Bruce Welch suggested having it as a country song, and that's how it was recorded in April 1959.

● The Americal title of *Serious Charge* was *A Touch Of Hell*.

● In some overseas areas, the film was titled *Immoral Charge*.

● *Serious Charge* carried an X certificate, which meant fans under the age of 16 were unable to see it.

● Singer Tommy Steele, then the reigning King of British rock 'n' roll with eleven top thirty hits visited Cliff on the set at Borehamwood during filming.

● Cliff had to have his hair curled for his part every morning before shooting began.

● Jess Conrad had a small bit part. He can be seen playing the leader of the local gang that disrupts the vicar's youth club.

● Director Terence Young went on to direct the early James Bond films *Dr No*, *From Russia With Love* and *Thunderball*.

● It was Lionel Bart and music publisher Jimmy Phillips who recommended Cliff for the part of Curley in the film.

● Sarah Churchill, who played the part of Hester Phillips, was the daughter of Sir Winston Churchill. She later committed suicide.

● Andrew Ray called the film 'a poor man's *The Wild Ones* set in Stevenage.'

● *Serious Charge* was one of two films in which Cliff did not receive top billing. The other was *Expresso Bongo*.

● Actress Lilliane Brousse made her screen debut in *Serious Charge*.

● Some of the ad lines for the film included: 'A Vile Accusation That Started With A Whisper!', 'A Provocative Theme As Topical As Today's Headlines!', and 'An Adult Picture That Young People Will Enjoy!'

● Reviews of the film included 'Cliff Richard will please those of his fans old enough to see the film', and that he had 'the voice of a young Presley.' Generally the critics thought the film was 'sincere and intelligent', and most reviews praised Anthony Quayle's performance, judging it the best and most likeable of his career.

● Blooper: the quad-crown movie poster for *Serious Charge* listed the songs that Cliff sang in the film. *Mad About You* became *Mad*, and the Drifters' instrumental 'Chinchilla' became one of the songs Cliff sang.

● A specially written 7500 word serialisation of the film was made available for local newspapers, but could not be published before Monday 20 July 1959, nor any announcement made about the publication of the serial before 13 July.

● In April 1963, *Serious Charge* was re-released nationally.

EXPRESSO BONGO

Britannia Films Distributors 1959. A Val Guest Production. Certificate A. Running time: 111 minutes. Length: 10011 ft. Filmed in Dyaliscope.
Cliff's second film.

CAST

Johnny Jackson	LAURENCE HARVEY
Maisie King	SYLVIA SIMS
Dixie Collins	YOLANDE DONLAN
Bongo Herbert	CLIFF RICHARD
Mayer	MEIER TZELNIKER
Lady Rosemary	AMBROSINE PHILLPOTTS
Leon	ERIC POHLMANN
Gilbert Harding	GILBERT HARDING
Penelope	HERMOINE BADDELEY
Rev Tobias Craven	REGINALD BECKWITH
Mr Rudge	WILFRED LAWSON
Kakky	MARTIN MILLER
Mrs Rudge	AVIS BUNNAGE
Beast Burns	BARRY LOWE
Charlie	KENNETH GRIFFITH
Cynthia	SUSAN HAMPSHIRE
Cynthia's Boyfriend	PETER MYERS
Edna Rudge	SUSAN BURNET
Mayer's Secretary	NORMA PARNELL
Miss Collins' Chauffeur	ROY EVERSON
Woman Columnist	PATRICIA LEWIS
Toastmaster	COPELAND LAWRENCE
Chinese Rose	LISA PEAKE
Alma	KATHERINE KEETON
Drusilla	CHRISTINE PHILLIPS
Intime Girl (Dancer)	SYLVIA STEELE
Intime Girl (Dancer)	PAULA BARRY
Intime Girl (Dancer)	RITA BURKE
Intime Girl (Dancer)	MAUREEN O'CONNOR
Intime Girl	PATTY DALTON
Intime Girl	PAMELA MORRIS

CREW

Associate Producer	JON PENINGTON
Art Director	TONY MASTERS
Choreography	KENNETH MACMILLAN
Sound Mixer	BERT ROSS
Film Editor	BILL LENNY
Sound Editor	CHRIS GREENHAM
Production Manager	PATRICK MARSDEN
Make-up	ERNEST GASSER
Assistant Director	PHILIP SHIPWAY
Camera Operator	MORAY GRANT
Hairdressing	BARBARA RITCHIE
Continuity	PAMELA DAVIES
Musical Direction	ROBERT FARNON
Music & Lyrics	ROBERT FARNON
	VAL GUEST
	NORRIE PARAMOR
	BUNNY LEWIS
	PADDY ROBERTS
Numbers From Original Show	JULIAN MORE
	MONTY NORMAN
	DAVID HENNEKER
Director of Photography	JOHN WILCOX
Screenplay	WOLF MANKOWITZ
Costumes	BEATRICE DAWSON
Yolande Donlan's Dresses	PIERRE BALMAIN, Paris
Producer & Director	VAL GUEST
Based on 'Expresso Bongo' by	WOLF MANKOWITZ & JULIAN MORE

SONGS

1. 'Bongo Blues' – played by the Shadows on the stage of a jazz cellar that Laurence Harvey and Sylvia Sims visit, and later at the Tom Tom expresso coffee bar.

2. 'Love' – sung at the same jazz cellar after Cliff is encouraged to sing and play the bongos by the regulars.

3. 'A Voice In The Wilderness' – sung at the Tom Tom expresso coffee bar.

4. 'The Shrine On The Second Floor' – sung during the Dixie Collins Show at a London theatre.

'Worry Go Lucky Me' a song written by Val Guest and Robert Farnon for the film was not used.

THE STORY

Johnny Jackson – a drummer by trade and a slick, fast-talking, sympathetic shark of an agent by confession – has been making a bare living out of show business for too many years to have a generous nature. He is known intimately by all the shady, unsavoury characters who inhabit Soho. But Johnny still wears his professional smile. He is not licked yet.

There are two important reasons why Johnny's head remains above the surface of the Soho muck-pond. The first is the love of Maisie, a soubrette in a local strip show. The second reason is Johnny's irrepressible confidence in himself. He is certain that the day will come when he will be sitting on a cloud with a British Elvis Presley bringing fame, fortune and luxury to the drab Johnny Jackson life.

Although Soho teems with people of questionable character, there is always the odd person willing to make a near-honest living. Such a man is Leon, a coffee-bar owner. Leon and Johnny are always bickering but underneath there is a firm friendship. And it is this that brings about the unexpected realisation of Johnny's dreams.

Johnny is hunting for a presentable teenage singer to entertain the younger patrons of Leon's coffee bar and, together with Maisie, visits a jazz cellar where he witnesses teenage hysteria induced by a young singer with the unlikely name of Bert Rudge. Johnny is not slow in realising the youngster's monetary potential and immediately signs Rudge as his personal property – changing his name to Bongo Herbert. Johnny's hopes as an agent – for so long frustrated – now show promise of materialising. He browbeats his way through television appearances, brazenly lies to the Press and eventually secures a recording contract. Bongo becomes an overnight success and Johnny – who has given himself fifty per cent of his artist's earnings – quickly cashes in.

But success such as this cannot last. The turning point comes when Bongo's recording company brings Dixie Collins, a fading American musical star, to London. Dixie, sexually attracted to the much younger Bongo, and appalled by the way in which he is exploited by his manager, sets out to have Johnny's contract nullified. Dixie succeeds and Johnny finds himself squeezed out of the big time. With his newly made star taken from him, Johnny is back where he started – at the bottom. But he's not despondent. There are plenty more stones to be turned over – and any might hide another Bongo Herbert.

PRODUCTION NOTES & TRIVIA

● *Expresso Bongo* premiered in London at the Carlton Cinema on 20 November 1959. It opened nationally on 11 January 1960. In America the film opened at the Sutton Theatre, New York on 15 March 1960.

● Filming began in September 1959 at Shepperton Studios, and was completed by October.

● *Expresso Bongo* was originally created as a satire on the Tommy Steele phenomenon and had previously been a West End play starring Paul Schofield in Laurence Harvey's part, and James Kenny in Cliff's role.

● Ad line for *Expresso Bongo*: 'Johnny Never Had It So Good – Or Lost It So Fast!'

● *Expresso Bongo* was first published in book form in 1960 by Ace Books, written by Wolf Mankowitz.

● Most memorable line from the film has to be Sylvia Sims to Laurence Harvey: 'That boy's got more sex than age' after hearing Cliff sing 'Love'.

● The Coffee Bar and Cellar sequences were filmed based on the famous 2i's coffee bar – where Tommy Steele and Terry Dene were discovered, and Cliff started out from.

● Peter Sellers was originally considered for the part of Johnny Jackson.

● Laurence Harvey's character of Johnny Jackson was modelled on that of Larry Parnes, Marty Wilde's manager.

● Reviews included 'A really brilliant musical. It's witty, tuneful, well acted', 'A film to see', 'A British musical to applaud', and 'A British film-musical America may well envy', 'First rate, directed at a spanking pace.'

● Producer/Director Val Guest later worked on Olivia Newton-John's debut film 'Tomorrow' directing for producer Harry Saltzman who would later become one of the producers for the James Bond movies.

● Marty Wilde was originally considered for the role of Bongo Herbert, but standing at six feet three inches was thought 'too big to feel sorry for.' Another reason that Wilde lost out on the role is thought to have been because he had pulled out of appearing on the 'Oh Boy!' show.

THE YOUNG ONES

Associated British Corporation 1961. An Elstree Film Production. Certificate U. Running time: 108 minutes. Technicolor. A Cinemascope Picture. Cliff's third film.

CAST

Nicky	CLIFF RICHARD
Hamilton	ROBERT MORLEY
Toni	CAROLE GRAY
Ernest	RICHARD O'SULLIVAN
Jimmy	MELVYN HAYES
Chris	TEDDY GREEN
Barbara	ANNETTE ROBERTSON
Dorinda	SONYA CORDEAU
Eddie	SEAN SULLIVAN
Dench	HAROLD SCOTT
Watts	GERALD HARPER
Chauffeur	ROBERT HARE
Woman in Market	RITA WEBB
The Shadows	THE SHADOWS

DANCERS

Wendy Barry	Alan Angel
Burda Cann	Bernie Boyd
Pat Cassie	Lindsay Dolan
Annette Clair	Terry Gilbert
Leander Feden	John Howard
Pamela Hart	Ken Martyne
John McDonald	Pat McIntyre
Derina House	Eithne Milne

CREW

Original Story & Screenplay	PETER MYERS & RONALD CASS
Director of Photography	DOUGLAS SLOCOMBE
Art Director	JOHN HOWELL
Editor	JACK SLADE
Production Manager	JOHN D WILCOX
Scenario Editor	FREDERICK GOTFURT
Casting Director	ROBERT LENNARD
Assistant Director	FRED SHARK
Camera Operator	CHIC WATERSON
Sound Recordists	C HITCHCOCK
	LEN SHELTON
Music Recordist	LESLIE HAMMOND
Dubbing Editor	JAMES SHIELD
Music Cutter	DEVERIL C GOODMAN
Assistant Dubbing Editor	GORDON DAVIE
Fashion Consultant	ALAN SIEVE WRIGHT
Continuity	H WHITSUN
Make-up	S FREEBORNE
Hairdressing	I EMMERTON
Wardrobe Mistress	JACKIE BREED
Assistant Casting Director	JUDITH JOURD
Assistant to the Choreographer	CHRISTINE LAWSON
Music & Lyrics	PETER MYERS & RONALD CASS
Additional Songs & Music	ROY BENNETT
	SID TEPPER
	SHIRLEY WOLFE
	SY SOLOWAY
	BRUCE WELCH
	HANK B MARVIN
	PETER GORMLEY
	NORRIE PARAMOR
	STANLEY BLACK
Background Score, Orchestrations and Musical Direction	STANLEY BLACK
Played by	THE ASSOCIATED BRITISH STUDIO ORCHESTRA WITH THE MICHAEL SAMMES SINGERS

Musical Supervision of
Cliff Richard and the Shadows   NORRIE PARAMOR
Recording Director   A W LUMKIN
Associate Producer   ANDREW MITCHELL
Dances and Musical
Numbers Staged by   HERBERT ROSS
Producer   KENNETH HARPER
Director   SIDNEY J FURIE

SONGS

1. 'Friday Night' – sung over the opening credits.

2. 'Got A Funny Feeling' – sung on the stage of the youth club.

3. 'Peace Pipe' – played by the Shadows on the stage of the youth club as Cliff dances with Carole Gray.

4. 'Nothing Is Impossible' – sung as a duet with Carole Gray outside the youth club after Cliff and Carole share a bag of chips.

5. 'The Young Ones' – sung to Carole Gray at the boating and water sports lake, and its surrounding area.

6. 'All For One' – sung at the youth club after Cliff has the idea for a fund-raising show at a theatre.

7. 'Lessons In Love' – sung at the youth club so the others can hear what Cliff has in mind for a duet with Carole Gray for the show.

8. 'Lessons In Love' (second version) – sung as a duet with Carole Gray at the youth club during a rehearsal in front of Sonya Cordeau's character of American singing star Dorinda Merell.

9. 'Lessons In Love' (third version) – sung to Cliff by Sonya Cordeau as Dorinda Merell during the youth club rehearsal.

10. 'No One For Me But Nicky' – sung by Carole Gray outside the youth club immediately after Cliff

romantically kisses Dorinda (Sonya Cordeau) as the ending to their 'Lessons In Love' song routine.

11. 'What Do You Know We've Got A Show' – sung on the stage at the Empire theatre by Cliff and cast in a vaudeville routine sequence.

12. 'When The Girl In Your Arms' – sung at the youth club as Melvyn Hayes makes a tape recording, and later played back as the voice of the mystery singer from a fruit market barrow.

13. 'The Savage' – played by the Shadows on the stage of the Empire Theatre at the youth club's fund-raising show.

14. 'We Say Yeah' – sung on the stage at the Empire Theatre immediately after the audience hear the voice of the mystery singer singing a few lines of 'When The Girl In Your Arms'.

15. 'What Do You Know We've Got A Show' (second version) – sung at the end of the film as the grand finale with Cliff, Robert Morley and other cast members on stage at the Empire Theatre.

16. 'The Young Ones' (second version) – sung over the closing credits.

'Outsider' was recorded for *The Young Ones* but not used. Instead it was used on the album '21 Today'.

THE STORY

Nicky is the leader of a Youth Club which makes its headquarters in a ramshackle hut in a shabby London neighbourhood. Here, Nicky, his girlfriend Toni and other youngsters can escape from the narrow and disapproving adult world in their games and let off steam through their rock 'n' roll music. Hamilton Black, a millionaire property owner, plans to buy up the land on which the club stands to build a modern office block. Unknown to the other club members, Black is in fact Nicky's father, a fact of which Nicky is not particularly proud.

The youngsters discover that there is an escape clause in the lease of the property and they tackle Black about it. He tells them they can have the land – if they can find five years' rent in advance, a matter of fifteen hundred pounds. At the same time, he discovers that his son is a member of the club and while he admires Nicky for putting up a fight, tells him he cannot win. But Nicky and his gang have other ideas. They rent a dilapidated theatre, renovate and decorate it in order to put on a fund-raising show. With an old radio transmitter they broadcast the date of their show over the national television network.

When Hamilton Black hears of their plans he attempts to buy the theatre before the show gets under way. The gang plan to waylay him in order to prevent this eleventh-hour move. Nicky is appalled and tries to stop them, but the boys and girls of the club have discovered Nicky's secret and stand guard over him until the time comes for him to go on stage. Nicky escapes, however, finds his father, releases him, and together they hurry back to the theatre just in time to hear the audience beginning to demand its money back.

Nicky immediately goes onto the stage and begins to sing, his singing talent captures the noisy audience and he finishes to tremendous applause. He leaves the stage to find his delighted father offering to build them a big new club!

The gang accept the offer and Nicky returns to the clamouring audience for a grand finale.

PRODUCTION NOTES & TRIVIA

● The Gala World Premiere of *The Young Ones* took place at London's Warner Theatre in Leicester Square on Wednesday 13 December 1961 at 8.30pm. The film opened nationally on 22 January 1962. The companion feature in most areas was *The Sinister Man*.

● Filming began on 29 May 1961 at Elstree, and was completed on 13 August. The vaudeville finale was shot at the Finsbury Park Empire Theatre.

● Film rehearsals for *The Young Ones* were due to start on 20 May but was postponed due to the death of Cliff's father. This was the second delay in production.

- *The Young Ones* was Cliff's first colour film.

- Although the film is considered to be Carole Gray's film debut, she had made one previous film appearance – a brief dancing sequence in 'The Prince And The Showgirl' with Laurence Olivier and Marilyn Monroe. Carole had previously captured stage roles in 'The Boyfriend' and 'West Side Story'. She was not the first actress offered the co-starring role of Toni. It was first offered to Annette Robertson who was later given the part of Barbara.

- The American title to *The Young Ones* was *It's Wonderful To Be Young*, and a new opening sequence using the audio track was shot by Paramount Pictures. This footage was also extensively used in the US trailer.

- Stanley Holloway was originally considered for the part of Hamilton Black, and Doris Day for the part of Dorinda Merell.

- Cliff and Carole were not meant to link arms with Robert Morley at the end of the film during the grand finale on the stage at the Empire Theatre, but they thought it was the most natural way to help Morley with his dance routine, which he had trouble remembering.

- The LP cover of Dorinda Merell – Dorinda Sings For You can be seen on the top of the youth club's stage.

- Cliff sang a duet with Carole Gray on 'Nothing's Impossible', and Carol sang her own solo 'No One For Me But Nicky', but the vocals for these were done by Grazina Frame.

- The first clip from *The Young Ones* was shown on BBC TV's *Picture Parade* on 19 December 1961.

- *The Young Ones* was heralded by the critics as 'The best musical Britain has ever made – and the finest screen entertainment produced for a long time – anywhere!'

- In America, one review of *The Young Ones* by the San Francisco Chronicle said 'Richard has all the requisites for idolisation – big brown eyes, wavy hair, a pretty boy face, a certain magnetism and an undistinguished voice.'

- Ad line for the film: 'That Joyous, Jumping, Jubilant Musical.'

- The first screening on British television was on 27 December 1969 by London Weekend Television.

- The budget for the film was £230,000 (£100,000 under the original estimate).

- On 6 April 1962, a print was sent to Princess Margaret at Clarence House.

- *The Young Ones* caused a 'row' involving Cliff and Connie Francis in November 1961 when Connie recorded a cover version of 'When The Girl In Your Arms' substituting 'Boy' for 'Girl' in the lyrics. Cliff complained that it was unethical for Connie to 'jump the gun' before the film had hit the screens.

- For the year 1962, *The Young Ones* was ranked number two in the list of top grossing films. The top movie was *The Guns Of Navarrone*.

SUMMER HOLIDAY

Associated British Picture Corporation 1962.
An Elstree Film Production. Certificate U. Running time: 109 minutes. Technicolor. A Cinemascope Picture. Cliff's fourth film.

CAST

Don	CLIFF RICHARD
Barbara	LAURI PETERS
Cyril	MELVYN HAYES
Sandy	UNA STUBBS
Steve	TEDDY GREEN
Angie	PAMELA HART
Edwin	JEREMY BULLOCH

Mimsie	JACQUELINE DARYL
Stella	MADGE RYAN
Jerry	LIONEL MURTON
Annie	CHRISTINE LAWSON
Orlando	RON MOODY
Magistrate	DAVID KOSSOFF
Shepherdess	WENDY BARRY
Wrightmore	NICHOLAS PHIPPS
The Shadows	THE SHADOWS

DANCERS

Lindsay Dolan	Wendy Barry
Richard Farley	Anne Briley
Terry Gilbert	Leander Fedden
Vincent Logan	Sarah Hardenberg
Ian Kaye	Derina House
John McDonald	Eithne Milne
Leon Pomeranetz	Sheila O'Neill
Ben Stevenson	Joan Palethorpe
Pat McIntryre	

CREW

Original Story & Screenplay	PETER MYERS & RONALD CASS
Director of Photography	JOHN WILCOX
Editor	JACK SLADE
Production Manager	JOHN D WILCOX
Art Director	SYD CAIN
Casting Director	ROBERT LENNARD
Fashion Co-ordinator	CYNTHIA TINGEY
Shoes	DOLCIS
Mens Sportswear	JOHN MICHAEL
Paris Model Dresses	BALMAIN
Contemporary Dresses Supplied and Designed	DAVID GIBSON FASHION GROUP
Assistant Director	FRANK ERNST
Camera Operator	TONY WHITE
Sound Recordists	WALLY MILNER LEN SHILTON
Dubbing Editor	JIMMY SHIELDS
Music Editor	ROY NEVILL
Continuity	HELEN WHITSON
Make-up	JOHN O'GORMAN
Hairdresser	EILEEN WARWICK
Wardrobe Mistress	JACKIE BREED
Assistant Casting Director	JUDITH JOURD
Special Effects	GEORGE BLACKWELL
Music and Lyrics	PETER MYERS & RONALD CASS
Additional Songs and Music	BRUCE WELCH BRIAN BENNETT HANK MARVIN CLIFF RICHARD MIKE CONLIN BUDDY KAYE PHILIP SPRINGER
Background Score, Orchestrations and Musical Direction	STANLEY BLACK
Played by	THE ASSOCIATED BRITISH STUDIO ORCHESTRA
Additional Orchestrations	MALCOLM LOCKYER & ROLAND SHAW
Musical Supervision of Cliff Richard and the Shadows	NORRIE PARAMOR
Recording Director	A W LUMKIN
Choreography and Musical Numbers Directed by	HERBERT ROSS
Associate Producer	ANDREW MITCHELL
Producer	KENNETH HARPER
Director	PETER YATES

SONGS

1. 'Summer Holiday' – sung over the opening credits and later in the film when Cliff is driving the bus through France.

2. 'Seven Days To A Holiday' – sung at the bus depot while converting the double decker to a 'travelling hotel'.

3. 'Let Us Take You For A Ride' – sung at the roadside after running Una Stubbs' car off the road.

4. 'Round And Round' – played by the Shadows at a nightclub in France.

5. 'Les Girls' – played by the Shadows in the nightclub while Teddy Green and Una Stubbs go through a dance routine.

6. 'Foot Tapper' – played by the Shadows on the sound-track is heard on a portable radio as Cliff drives and the others dance on the bus after leaving the nightclub.

7. 'A Stranger In Town' – sung while stopping en route to buy some postcards to send home.

8. 'Orlandos Mime' – played by the Associated British Orchestra while Cliff and team, and Ron Moody and his travelling entertainers perform some dance and mime routines for the magistrate (David Kossoff).

9. 'Bachelor Boy' – sung after filling the bus radiator with water, immediately after discovering the 'boy' stowaway is a girl.

10. 'A Swinging Affair' – sung by Cliff and Lauri Peters on the restaurant patio after taking the bus over the mountains into Switzerland.

11. 'Really Waltzing' – sung after eating dinner at a restaurant in Austria.

12. 'All At Once' – sung to Lauri Peters outside the restaurant.

13. 'Dancing Shoes' – sung to a shepherdess (Wendy Barry) after losing their way in Yugoslavia.

14. 'Yugoslav Wedding' – played by the Associated British Orchestra as Cliff attempts to escape the Yugoslav villagers after the Shepherdess (Wendy Barry) thinks he wants to marry her.

15. 'The Next Time' – sung overlooking Athens after being arrested for the alleged kidnapping of Lauri Peters.

16. 'Big News' – sung to everyone at a press conference.

17. 'Summer Holiday' (second version) – sung at the

end of the film over the closing credits with other cast members joining in.

THE STORY

Four London Transport mechanics, Don, Cyril, Steve and Edwin, persuade London Transport to lend them an old bus, and turn it into a mobile home for a travelling holiday across Europe. The idea is that if they make the trip without a major hazard, they will get more old buses and form themselves into a company catering for 'do-it-yourself' holidays. Their original destination is the South of France, but these plans are soon shattered when, on the way to Paris, they accidentally crash into a rickety old car driven by the three attractive singers – Mimsie, Angie and Sandy. The car is a write-off, so the boys offer to take the girls to Athens, where they have a singing engagement. Passing through Paris, the bus takes on another passenger. This is Barbara, an internationally famous singing star who is being driven to the point of desperation by her ambitious mother, Stella. Barbara has been promised a holiday after her Paris engagement, and when her agent, Jerry, announces a big new contract for a summer television series, Barbara flees from the theatre dressed as a boy, stows away aboard the bus and persuades the others to take her with them. Taken in by her appearance, Don warns her in a moment of confidence never to get mixed up with girls.

Meanwhile, Stella and Jerry realise that Barbara's disappearance can be put to immense publicity advantage. Accordingly, they plan to hamper the journey of the bus while at the same time extracting the maximum coverage from the story. They have the bus held up in a French town on a charge of vagrancy, but the youngsters manage to escape with the help of Orlando, an old-time entertainer who helps them to convince the magistrate that they are all professional performers.

Inevitably, Barbara's true identity comes out, and after she convinces Don that she is not using them all for publicity, she and Don realise they are fast falling in love.

Stella's next step is to plant a bracelet on the bus and advise the guards at the Yugoslav border that there is stolen property on board. But Barbara manages to talk her way out by identifying the bracelet, and showing the police her picture inside a locket. Eventually the bus reaches Athens and they are all taken immediately into custody – charged by Stella with kidnapping her daughter. The boys are really in trouble until Don and Barbara work out a plan: Don appears at Stella's press reception to announce he and Barbara are in love. Stella, convinced he is lying, exclaims melodramatically that her daughter could not possibly want to marry him – but that if she did, Stella would not stand in her way. At that moment, Barbara appears, released by Don from the hotel room where her mother had locked her in, to say she and Don are engaged. Stella eventually sees reason, Barbara delightedly accepts Don's proposal of marriage, and the bus and its passengers prepare to make the journey home, having received a cable from London Transport that they are prepared to accept the scheme of 'holidays on wheels'. Stella gleefully realises that she may have a rich son-in-law after all. The bus rolls out of Athens in a blaze of sunshine and the biggest 'summer holiday' of all is about to begin.

PRODUCTION NOTES & TRIVIA

● *Summer Holiday* was premiered at the Warner Theatre in Leicester Square, London on 11 January 1963. It opened nationally on 18 February and broke all previous box-office records for a British film. The companion feature in most areas was *Black Gold*.

● Interiors were filmed at Elstree studios.

● Exteriors were shot on location in and around Athens. A camera crew was also sent to Paris for location shooting to use as atmosphere in the film.

● Filming began on 25 May 1962. The 'Bachelor Boy' scene was shot after the film had been completed.

● Before filming *Summer Holiday*, Cliff had reduced his weight from 12 to 11 stone.

● Blooper: in the 'Really Waltzing' sequence, Cliff

dropped Lauri Peters at the end of their dance routine, which can be seen only on the big screen version.

● Cliff and Melvyn Hayes personally chose Una Stubbs for the part of Sandy at the casting auditions.

● Actor Jeremy Bulloch was not the first choice for the part of clumsy Edwin. It was originally offered to Richard O'Sullivan who had played Ernest in *The Young Ones*. Richard was unable to accept the role.

● Lauri Peters sang a duet with Cliff on 'A Swinging Affair' but the voice actually heard was that of Grazina Frame.

● The opening sequence of the film was shot in black and white as a teaser, but changed to colour after the opening credits and Cliff arrives at the bus depot driving a red double-decker.

● Reviews included one critic saying 'I wouldn't have believed that such a first-class musical could have been made in this country – the film will provide all the amenities of a real holiday – with the exception of the tan.'

● Ad line for *Summer Holiday* was '*The Young Ones* Have Gone Abroad!'

● Another review compared the film to Elvis in *Girls! Girls! Girls!* 'I'm not praising *Summer Holiday* out of patriotism but it's simply a fact that it has more freshness and zest than *Girls! Girls! Girls!*'

● Although three double-decker buses were purchased for the filming of *Summer Holiday*, only one was featured in the film. The registration number was WLB 991. The vehicle came from Cricklewood Garage – its depot code can be seen on the side, but it is unknown whether the registration was fictitious, as there was a Routemaster with the registration of WLT 991.

● During filming in Greece, a rumour reached Fleet Street that Cliff had been seriously hurt in an accident, but the incident in the film when Cliff's bus and the old car driven by Una Stubbs get involved in a pile-up with a lorry was treated as real by a passer-by!

● *Melody Maker* described *Summer Holiday* as 'first class throughout. The story-line and tone of acting, plus some haunting tunes will endear it to millions.'

● Cliff was coached by London Transport at the Chiswick depot for the film.

● Cliff arrived on location in Greece on 27 May, while the Shadows arrived there on 16 June.

● While filming, Cliff and cast hired a cabin cruiser to visit the Greek isle of Hydra.

● American actress Lauri Peters made her film debut in 'Mr Hobb Takes A Train' with James Stewart. *Summer Holiday* was her second film. She was married to Jon Voight who later starred in *Midnight Cowboy* with Dustin Hoffman.

● One of the songs in *Summer Holiday*, 'Big News' was written in a few minutes in Cliff's washroom. Director Peter Yates told Cliff that they were short of a song, so Cliff and road manager Mike Conlin got to work during a break at Elstree. They played the song over the phone to producer Kenneth Harper in Paris for his approval.

● Originally *Summer Holiday* was to have been directed by Sidney Furie, who had directed Cliff in *The Young Ones*, but he was working on *The Boys* starring Jess Conrad, the music for which was written by the Shadows.

● For the year 1963, *Summer Holiday* was ranked number two in the list of top grossing films.

WONDERFUL LIFE

Elstree Distributors, 1964. An Ivy Film Production.
Certificate U. Running time: 112 minutes.
Length: 10080 ft. Technicolor. Techniscope.
Cliff's fifth film.

CAST

Johnnie	CLIFF RICHARD
Lloyd Davis	WALTER SLEZAK
Jenny	SUSAN HAMPSHIRE
Douglas Leslie	DEREK BOND
Jerry	MELVYN HAYES
Edward	RICHARD O'SULLIVAN
Barbara	UNA STUBBS
Carmelita	ALIZIA GUR
Miguel	JOSEPH CUBY
The Shadows	THE SHADOWS

CREW

Original Story & Screenplay	PETER MYERS & RONALD CASS
Director of Photography	KENNETH HIGGINS
Production Manager	JOHN D WILCOX
Editor	JACK SLADE
Camera Operator	CHIC WATERSON
Production Designer	STANLEY DORFMAN
Casting Director	ROBERT LENNARD
Spanish Co-ordinator	ROBERTO ROBERTS
Art Director	HERBERT SMITH
Assistant Director	FRED SLARK
Sound Recordists	LES HAMMOND
	LEN SHILTON
Dubbing Editor	CHARLES CRAFFORD
Music Editor	BARRIE VINCE
Assistant Editor	LOIS GRAY
Continuity	HELEN WHITSON
Make-up	BOB LAWRENCE
Hairdresser	DAPHNE MARTIN
Wardrobe Mistress	JACKIE JACKSON
Assistant Casting Director	JUDITH JOURD
Costumes by	BERMANS
Costumes Designed by	CYNTHIA TINGEY
Sound	RCA SYSTEM
Music and Lyrics	PETER MYERS & RONALD CASS
Additional Songs and Music	HANK B MARVIN
	BRUCE WELCH
	CLIFF RICHARD
	BRIAN BENNETT

Background Score, Orchestrations and Musical Direction	STANLEY BLACK
Recording Director	A W LUMKIN
Choreography	GILLIAN LYNNE
Musical Supervision of Cliff Richard and the Shadows	NORRIE PARAMOR
Associate Producer	ANDREW MITCHELL
Producer	KENNETH HARPER
Director	SIDNEY J FURIE

SONGS

1. 'Wonderful Life' – sung over the opening credits.

2. 'A Girl In Every Port' – sung as Cliff, the Shadows, Melvyn Hayes and Richard O'Sullivan follow Susan Hampshire from the port.

3. 'Home' – sung by Cliff, Melvyn Hayes and Richard O'Sullivan after seeing a mirage of a ship in the sand dunes, and imagine they are on deck.

4. 'A Little Imagination' – sung to Susan Hampshire at the restaurant in a surrealistic imagination sequence.

5. 'On The Beach' – sung on the beach film set.

6. 'In The Stars' – sung as a duet between Cliff and Susan Hampshire on top of the sand dunes at the beach film set.

7. 'We Love A Movie' – sung at the film studios using a number of props and scenes to tell the 'History of the Movies' through song and dance.

8. 'Do You Remember' – sung as a duet with Susan Hampshire in the restaurant as Melvyn Hayes and Richard O'Sullivan film the song through a disguised camera in a cake.

9. 'What've I Gotta Do' – sung at the movie viewing theatre.

10. 'All Kinds Of People' – sung on the film set after

having their camera and film taken away from Walter Slezak, but discover 'Miguel' (Joseph Cuby) has a loaded movie camera.

11. 'A Matter Of Moments' – sung to Susan Hampshire as they ride through the mountains on a horse and carriage.

12. 'In The Stars' (second version) – sung by Cliff, Susan Hampshire and Derek Bond in the sand dunes at the end of their film.

13. 'Youth And Experience' – sung at the end of the film by Cliff and Walter Slezak on the stage of the cinema where their film is premiered.

'Walkin' and 'Theme For Young Lovers' – played by the Shadows is heard as incidental music in the film.

THE STORY

Aboard a luxury liner in the Mediterranean, Johnnie, and his friends Hank, Bruce, Brian and John are entertaining the dining-room customers with Victorian ballads, encouraged by two young waiters, Jerry and Edward, who are chums of theirs. Late at night, after the diners have retired, the boys bring out the guitars and, despite Jerry's warnings that they are overloading the power, plug in all their amplifiers. There is a blinding flash, and the ship grinds slowly to a halt. On a vast expanse of sea, Johnnie, Edward, Jerry and the Shadows are doing their best to operate a life raft, very annoyed at the captain for kicking them off the ship. In the far distance, they spot land and, using their guitars as paddles, head for the coastline.

On land, the boys plod across a desert towards what they hope is civilisation. They are startled to see a camel galloping past, with a girl tied across its back. Johnnie dashes into action, pulls up the camel and cuts down the girl. Instead of being grateful, however, the girl (Jenny) tells him he has ruined the best shot in the picture.

Over the horizon comes Film Director, Lloyd Davis, livid with rage. Following him is the leading man Douglas Leslie, a once-famous juvenile lead who has been a juvenile too long. Leslie tells Davis not to get too mad; if the young man is so athletic he can be a stunt man for

the film – they have already been through two!

In the weeks that follow, Johnnie settles in as stunt man; the Shadows are hired by the eccentric Davis to play mood music; Jerry becomes friendly with the continuity girl, Barbara. A bright young Spanish cameraman reporter, Miguel, has joined the gang, and poor Jenny gets more and more depressed as she realises that Director Davis is giving her no help whatsoever. Johnnie is aware of this, and calls the gang together. They decide to make their own film, using Jenny without her knowledge. Enlisting the aid of Miguel, they arrange for camera and sound. Barbara and Jerry manage to 'find' the film stock. Johnnie, pretending to rehearse Jenny in her lines, acts as leading man. After various misadvantures, Davis finishes his film and Johnnie his. Both are mediocre. However, Davis's action scenes are marvellous, and Johnnie has drawn a wonderful performance from Jenny. Johnnie confesses to Davis what he has done, and the Director decides to cut the two films together. Youth has combined with experience to produce a terrific film. The premiere is a huge success, and Johnnie and Jenny are joined by the whole gang as they proudly come on stage to take their bows.

PRODUCTION NOTES & TRIVIA

● *Wonderful Life* was premiered at the Empire Theatre in Leicester Square, London on 2 July 1964 in the presence of HRH Princess Alexandra and the Hon. Angus Oglivy in aid of the National Association of Youth Clubs Expansion Fund. A second premiere took place in Manchester on 13 July. The film opened nationally on 7 September. The companion feature in most areas was *A Woman's Privilege*.

● Location filming in the Canary Islands began on 2 December 1963.

● Interior scenes were shot at Elstree studios during February and March, 1964.

● *Wonderful Life* was the third of Cliff's films with the Harper, Cass and Myers team, and the second to be directed by Sidney Furie.

- The American title was *Swinger's Paradise*.

- The July 1964 edition of *Photoplay* featured Cliff and Susan Hampshire on the cover in a scene from *Wonderful Life*.

- Cliff and Susan Hampshire had worked together previously in *Expresso Bongo*. Susan played the small bit part she had had in the stage show.

- Some scenes were filmed aboard the gigantic *Queen Mary* liner which stopped at Las Palmas during its winter cruise. Passengers aboard the liner missed going ashore sightseeing so they could watch Cliff and Susan filming some song and dance routines for the movie.

- While filming *Wonderful Life*, Cliff, the Shadows, Susan Hampshire, Una Stubbs, Melvyn Hayes, Richard O'Sullivan, Derek Bond, Walter Slezak, Kenneth Harper and Sidney Furie stayed at the Santa Catalina Hotel in Las Palmas.

• To film in the Canaries, the film company used four location sites, including Las Palmas, Gran Canaria, Mas Palomas and Castelromana; 138 extras; 50 tons of filming and recording equipment; and 39 vehicles.

• The dance routines were choreographed by Gillian Lynne, the first female choreographer to arrange routines for a major feature film. Her previous work had included the brilliant dance revue 'Collages' which had been enthusiastically received at the 1963 Edinburgh Film Festival and later in London.

• During the first week of filming, Cliff slashed his hand open scrambling over rocks during one of the scenes for the movie. Nurse Jennifer Gretton, who was attached to the film unit during their ten-week stay in the Canaries, attended to the wound.

• During production, Melvyn Hayes broke a bone in his foot, and had to return to England for an operation before completing the 'Home' dance sequence which was filmed two months after the film had been completed. The sequence was shot aboard a ship on the River Thames.

• The original story for *Wonderful Life* was written by Peter Myers and Ronnie Cass, who also wrote seven of the musical numbers; 'A Girl In Every Port'; 'Home'; 'Imagination'; 'In The Stars'; 'The History Of The Movies'; 'All Kinds Of People' and 'Youth And Experience'.

• 'A Matter Of Moments' was filmed inside an extinct volcanic crater situated near Las Palmas at Terjira.

• Reviews included 'No one will be able to say they haven't had their money's worth, there's everything in it but the kitchen sink' and 'Cliff improves with every picture he makes. Not only is his acting ability much more convincing but he also displays considerable talent as a light comedian and impressionist.'

• For one scene, director Sidney Furie planned to take down the advertisements of the current film showing at the Warner Cinema in Leicester Square, and replace them with neons for the premiere of the film's film 'Daughter Of The Sheik' but police refused permission for filming.

• The Shadows took riding lessons for their part in the film in July 1963.

• While filming *Wonderful Life*, Cliff became romantically linked with Una Stubbs.

• Director of Photography, Kenneth Higgins, had previously filmed the prize-winning documentary *Terminus*, and the comedy *French Dressing*.

• Ad line for *Wonderful Life*: 'Cliff's Back! He's Swinging, Singin', Livin' and Dancing to a Dozen Hit Tunes.'

• For the year 1964, *Wonderful Life* was ranked number five in the list of top grossing films.

THUNDERBIRDS ARE GO

United Artists, 1966. Certificate U. Running time: 92 minutes. Gerry Anderson Century 20 Cinema Production. Technicolor and Techniscope. Supermarionation.
Full length feature version of TV series produced for the cinema which incorporated puppet replicas of Cliff and the Shadows. The film is not regarded as a major Cliff Richard film vehicle.

CHARACTER VOICES

Lady Penelope Creighton-Ward	SYLVIA ANDERSON
John Tracy	
The Hood	RAY BARRETT
Controller Glenn Field	
Greg Martin	ALEXANDER DAVION
Jeff Tracy	PETER DYNELEY
Tin-Tin	
Brains	CHRISTINE FINN
Gordon Tracy	
Parker	DAVID GRAHAM
Paul Travers	PAUL MAXWELL
Dr Pierce	NEIL McCALLUM
Brad Newman	BOB MONKHOUSE

Scott Tracy	SHANE RIMMER
Dr Grant	
Public Relations Officer	CHARLES TINGWELL
Angry Young Man	
Virgil Tracy	JEREMY WILKIN
President Exploration Centre	
Alan Tracy	MATT ZIMMERMAN
Messenger	

CREW

Producer	SYLVIA ANDERSON
Director	DAVID LANE
Screenplay	GERRY & SYLVIA ANDERSON
Supervising Art Director	BOB BELL
Art Director	GRENVILLE KNOTT
Music Composer and Director	BARRY GRAY
Editor	LEN WALTERS
Martian Sequences filmed by	CENTURY 21 SPACE LOCATION UNIT
'Shooting Star' sung by	CLIFF RICHARD
Written and Accompanied by	THE SHADOWS
Instrumental 'Lady Penelope'	
Written and Played by	THE SHADOWS

The Producers gratefully acknowledge the co-operation of: SPACE COLONEL HARRIS of the Martian Exploration Centre, Cape Johnson.
COMMANDER CASEY – Commander-in-Chief, Glenn Field.
JIM GLENN – President of the NEW WORLD AIRCRAFT CORPORATION. Designers and manufacturers of the ZERO X craft, without whose help this motion picture would not have been possible.

SONGS

1. 'Lady Penelope' – played by the Shadows on the stage of the Swinging Star Nightclub while Lady Penelope and Alan Tracey watch the cabaret.

2. 'Shooting Star' – sung on the stage of the Swinging Star Nightclub and in surrealistic sequences immediately after the Shadows finish their instrumental, and Cliff Richard Junior is introduced as the 'biggest star in the universe'.

THE STORY

It is the 21st Century. Five astronauts who attempt a space flight to Mars are sabotaged by a sinister intruder called The Hood. They land safely in the sea after ejection but their space vehicle Zero X is destroyed.

Two years later, after a special board of inquiry has demanded that 'International Rescue' be present, a new manned flight in a new Zero X is launched. This time, The Hood is foiled and eliminated just before the flight, and the spacemen are launched successfully.

On Mars, the rocks suddenly come to life when the men attempt to take a few specimens, and they leave the planet hurriedly, determined that the red planet is uninhabitable. As they approach Earth, part of their mechanism goes haywire and a collision seems inevitable. The emergency call for help reaches 'International Rescue' and a team of Thunderbirds (manned rescue missiles) leap into action. With only seconds to spare, the chief pilot of the Thunderbirds, through dangerous and intricate manoeuvres; saves the space travellers as another Zero X plunges to a fiery end.

PRODUCTION NOTES & TRIVIA

● *Thunderbirds Are Go!* had a World Charity premiere in aid of Dr Barnardo's at the London Pavilion on 12 December 1966 at 8.30pm in the presence of a star-studded audience which included Cliff and the Shadows, International Rescue's famous Tracy family, Lady Penelope and Parker!

● *Thunderbirds Are Go!* opened nationally on 23 December 1966. The companion feature in most areas was *Namu The Killer Whale.*

● Ad lines: 'Their First Big Screen Adventure In Colour!', 'Streak Through Unchartered Worlds of Adventure', and 'Excitement is Go! Adventure is Go! Danger is Go! Go Where You've Never Been Before with the Incredible Tracy Family!'

● Posters carried the warning: 'Adults over 16 should be accompanied by children.'

FINDERS KEEPERS

United Artists, 1966. An Interstate Film in association with Ivy Productions. Certificate U. Running time: 94 minutes. Eastman Colour. Cliff's sixth film.

CAST

Cliff	CLIFF RICHARD
The Shadows	BRUCE WELCH
	HANK B MARVIN
	BRIAN BENNETT
	JOHN ROSTILL
Colonel Roberts	ROBERT MORLEY
Mrs Bragg	PEGGY MOUNT
Emelia	VIVIANE VENTURA
Burke	GRAHAM STARK
Mr X	JOHN LE MESURIER
Commander	ROBERT HUTTON
Junior Officer	GORDAN RUTTAN
Grandma	ELLEN POLLACK
Air Marshall	ERNEST CLARK
Pilot	BURNELL TUCKER
Priest	GEORGE RODERICK
GI Guard	BILL MITCHELL
Drunk	RONNIE BRODY

CREW

Lighting Cameraman	ALAN HUME
Editor	TRISTAN CONES
Art Director	JACK SHAMPAN
Production Manager	FRANK BEVIS
Assistant Director	STEWART FREEMAN
Camera Operator	BRIAN WEST
Continuity	DORIS MARTIN
Sound Editor	LES WIGGINS
2nd Unit Director	JAN DARNLEY-SMITH
Costume Designer	CYNTHIA TINGYE
2nd Unit Cameraman	RONNIE TAYLOR
Choreographer	MALCOLM CLARE
Assistant to Choreographer	AUDREY BAYLEY
Musical Number Created by	HUGH LAMBERT
Music & Lyrics	THE SHADOWS

Musical Direction	NORRIE PARAMOR
Screenplay	MICHAEL PERTWEE
From An Original Story by	GEORGE H BROWN
Producer	GEORGE H BROWN
Director	SIDNEY HAYERS

SONGS

1. 'Finders Keepers' – sung over the opening credits while Cliff and the Shadows travel through Spain on top of a train.

2. 'Time Drags By' – sung in the reception of the Hotel Bellamar.

3. 'Washerwoman' – sung to Viviane Ventura on a secluded river bank during the wash day parade.

4. 'La La La Song' – sung to Viviane Ventura and children in the town square outside the Hotel Bellamar.

5. 'My Way' – sung by the Shadows at the Café Del Mar.

6. 'Oh Senorita' – sung at the Café Del Mar after Cliff disguises himself as a waiter to take a note to the Commander in a hamburger.

7. 'Oh Senorita' (second version) – sung by the Shadows and patrons of the Café Del Mar as Cliff takes a second note to the Commander in a hamburger.

8. 'This Day' – sung to Vivian Ventura as Cliff rows her on a dinghy through an old pirate's grotto.

9. 'Spanish Music' – played by the Shadows is heard on the soundtrack as Cliff, disguised as a waiter, leads the Commander and Junior Officer to the alleged bomb in the old pirate's grotto.

10. 'Paella' – sung to Vivian Ventura at her grandmother's cottage.

11. 'Time Drags By' (second version) – sung in the wine cellar of the Cafe Del Mar after Cliff and the Shadows have been locked up by the Commander,

and they create a 'noise' to escape from the watchful Junior Officer.

12. 'Fiesta' – sung at the town fiesta while running through the crowds.

13. 'Finders Keepers/My Way/Paella/Fiesta' – played by the Shadows is heard on the soundtrack during the dance sequences at the town fiesta.

THE STORY

Somewhere over Spain one fine day, there was an almighty calamity. An American aircraft on a delicate secret mission drops one of its load of Mighty Mini bombs – by accident, of course. A few thousand feet below, a sugar cane train trundles towards the seaside town of San Carlos with an illicit cargo of five musical stowaways from London, Cliff Richard and the Shadows. One of the local hoteliers, fellow Engishman, Colonel Ronald Roberts has booked Cliff and the group to help entertain the tourists. Jumping off the train after being spotted by a guard, Cliff and the boys hitch-hike the rest of the way to San Carlos. The reception there is not quite what they expected. San Carlos is not a swinging town any more – not since a Mighty Mini plopped into the ocean, a few yards from the shore, and sank without trace. The publicity has done little for the tourist image, and San Carlos is now a garrison town, manned to the hilt by swarms of uniformed Americans. While their search for the bomb goes on, the sea has been declared off-limits both to bathers and to the local fishermen; the holiday makers have fled; there's a shortage of food and even the goats don't feel like producing much milk.

The Colonel's henchman, a bundle of misery named Burke breaks it to Cliff and the boys that without tourists they have no audience and no money. Roberts, in the meantime, has had a visit from a sinister Mr X, representing a foreign power eager to grab the bomb before the Americans locate it. Under a long-standing obligation, the Colonel agrees to 'bug' all bedrooms at the Bellamar Hotel and keep a sharp look out for an undercover British agent known to be operating in the neighbourhood. Determined to make the best of a glum

stay in San Carlos, Cliff and the boys try charming the natives. They discover a group of girls on a US servicemen's wash day parade on a secluded river bank. One of them (Emilia) responds by giving Cliff a sharp crack on the head with a rock followed by a ducking. When the girls realise that Cliff and the boys are nothing to do with the bomb, just penniless entertainers, Emilia tells them that the traditional Fiesta, when the fishing boats are blessed, is threatened by the bomb scare. Cliff decides that entertaining the Americans might lull them into allowing the Fiesta to take place.

The boys are smuggled into the base in the girls' laundry baskets. Once inside they are confronted by the irate commander in charge of the Find The Bomb operation, who explains that it is Washington's directive not to allow the festival to go on, even though the fishermen are superstitious. The unhappy Burke, meanwhile, has got himself entangled with the Colonel's burly Cockney housekeeper, Mrs Bragg. She has overheard Burke testing one of the Colonel's bugging machines in Cliff's bedroom by reading extracts from a rather suggestive book. In his panic, Burke pretends he was practising a passionate speech to her. But Mrs Bragg is also up to something. Unbeknown to the Colonel, she has been sending out her own messages (to the British Secret Service).

The boys, now resolved to help Emilia and the fisher folk have their Fiesta, try another hair-raising scheme – to lure the American Navy out of the way by reporting the 'discovery' of the bomb. Managing to elude the nosy Colonel and his assistant, Cliff, in heavy disguise, hides in the restaurant where the American Commander is giving his official explanation to the locals, and inserts a note inside his hamburger, whereupon it is blithely swallowed by a junior officer.

In one hectic spy scramble, Mrs Bragg, disguised as a desirable Spanish mystery woman, and the Colonel, spot the Commander with a note (this time successfully delivered). The Colonel is momentarily put out of action by a karate blow from Mrs Bragg in mistake for a lovelorn drunk.

Cliff's ruse has begun to work like a charm. Acting on his note the American Navy is making haste out of San Carlos bay, watched by cheering Spaniards, to a point some miles away where the boys have arranged to meet the Commander, their rendezvous being an old pirates' grotto. By the time the deception – in the shape of a rusty old cistern – is discovered, San Carlos will have had its Fiesta.

The Colonel and the redoubtable Mr X continue searching the bay, aided by a team of deep sea divers, but the real bomb isn't in the bay – Emilia's old grandmother has it in her kitchen. But for Cliff's speedy action, on returning hastily from the grotto, she would be bashing it with a hammer to make it work, thinking it was another gas cylinder. Leaving Emilia behind at the cottage to make sure the old lady doesn't give the bomg another bash, Cliff tears round to the Colonel and unwittingly blurts out the truth. The wily Colonel prevents him from telephoning the American base and, as soon as Cliff has left, phones the news himself to Mr X – overheard by Mrs Bragg. X orders Burke and the Colonel to recover the bomb immediately and take it to a transfer point five miles outside San Pedro. They rush off in their car, complete with excess baggage – Mrs Bragg, who has locked herself securely in the boot. Cliff in the meantime has located the commander, who treats the latest 'news' with disdain and, for their pains, locks the five boys in a wine cellar despite their protests that this time they are telling the truth.

They escape by singing a number loud enough to drown the noise of their window breaking. Rescuing a dishevelled Mrs Brass from the boot of the Colonel's car, after her captors have transferred to Burke's van, Cliff races towards Emilia's grandmother. But the Colonel and Burke have already got there. Pretending to Emilia that Cliff has deputed them to collect the bomb they 'kidnap' her, leaving her grandmother sound asleep, and make for Rendezvous X. They arrive just in time for the start of the Fiesta. The streets are crammed full of gaily coloured floats with mounted effigies and Spaniards in carnival costume. The van cannot get through. And Cliff and his friends are not far behind.

One of the floats symbolising 'Peace', festooned with flowers and doves joins the line: Burke driving, the Colonel an exquiste 'angel'.

But Cliff, the boys and Mrs Bragg are in close pursuit. Finding the van abandoned, they stop a band of student singers and borrow their clothes and instruments. Meanwhile the 'Peace' float is all set to charge the barrier at the end of the street and make its getaway. Then the Colonel has a last minute change of heart – why not double-cross Mr X, collect the ten thousand pounds for the bomb, and sneak to the authorities?

Trying a last desperate ruse, Cliff, who has caught sight of Emilia, grabs an imitation bomb which is on the side of one of the decorated floats representing the search for the bomb, carries it to the float where Emilia is, warns her of the Colonel's treachery, and substitutes the cylinder for the bomb. Suddenly, the float roars forward, throwing the couple into the road. But Mr X has already forestalled the Colonel. At the transit point, thinking he at last has the bomb, he forces Roberts and Burke to fly with him out of the country. In the air, X stares incredulously at the words 'Gas Butane' while the real bomb, now safely in police hands, is dispatched to San Carlos leaving Cliff and Emilia contentedly in each others arms. Burke and the Colonel escape from the plane by parachute. Not far behind, floating forlornly in mid-aid is Mr X who has decided to retire to the Colonel's hotel.

PRODUCTION NOTES & TRIVIA

● *Finders Keepers* premiered at the Odeon Leicester Square on 8 December 1966. Cliff attended, escorting Pippa Steel. The film opened nationally on 6 January 1967.

● Production began on 27 May 1966 and lasted nine weeks.

● Although several locations were photographed in Spain, Cliff did not travel to the country. All his scenes were shot at Pinewood Studios and on the south coast of England.

● The soundtrack album had 10 'New Smash Hits' including the single 'Time Drags By' which was the runner-up in the Film Song Of the Year category in the Ivor Novello Awards presented in March 1967.

- Ad lines for *Finders Keepers*: 'It's A Songful, Colourful, Wonderful Romp Through Swinging Singing Spain', 'Find Out What Fun Is!!! Get Rhythm and With 'Em! Get Singing And Swinging!', and 'The Beat Is the Wildest! The Blast Is the Craziest! And The Fun Is Where You Find It!'

- Auditions began on 9 May 1966 and lasted four days.

- Cliff's leading lady was Vivian Ventura because her South-American looks gave her the Spanish looking qualities for the part. She became engaged when wealthy property developer Frank Duggan interrupted filming at Pinewood Studios to propose.

- *Finders Keepers* was the first film that gave the Shadows equal billing with Cliff, and in which they had major co-starring roles.

- It was announced in August 1965 that *Finders Keepers* would go into production on 1 November and would be 'altogether more sophisticated than Cliff's last pictures.'

- Reviews included one by Derek Johnson who said 'Most people regard *Finders Keepers* as Cliff's worst film to date. This is an opinion I do not share, but as I appear to be in the minority one can only say that it must be due to the hurried hotch potch fashion in which it was put together. A pity for Cliff Richard who had previously set an all-time high in the standard of British film musicals.'

- *Finders Keepers* was the second of two films in which Robert Morley co-starred with Cliff (the first was *The Young Ones*).

- Doubles were used for the long shots of the opening showing Cliff and the Shadows singing on top of a train.

- 'This Day' and 'Time Drags By' were Cliff's two favourite songs from the film.

- In some areas, 'spot the difference' newspaper contests were held to publicise *Finders Keepers* by using an illustration of a scene from the film. Prizewinners won a bottle of Perelada, the Spanish sparkling wine. Other newspaper contests included a colouring block for children, and a 'Miss Mini-Bombshell' contest that had the finalist winning mini-skirts and outfits as prizes.

- For the year 1966, *Finders Keepers* was ranked the top musical of the year in the list of top grossing films.

TWO A PENNY

World Wide Films 1967. Running time: 98 minutes. Cliff's seventh film.

CAST

Jamie Hopkins	CLIFF RICHARD
Ruby Hopkins	DORA BRYAN
Carol Turner	ANN HOLLOWAY
Mrs Burry	AVRIL ANGERS
Alec Fitch	GEOFFREY BAYLDON
The Vicar	PETER BARKWORTH
Hubert	NIGEL GOODWIN
Dr Berman	DONALD BISSETT
Jenkins	EDWARD EVANS
Mrs Duckett	MONA WASHBOURNE
Gladys	TINA PACKER
The Verger	EARL CAMERON
Dennis Lancaster	NOEL DAVIS
Rev. Allison	CHARLES LLOYD PACK
As himself	BILLY GRAHAM

CREW

Lighting Cameraman	MICHAEL REED
Art Director	PETER WILLIAMS
Production Supervisor	BASIL APPLEBY
Editors	ANN CHEGWIDDEN
	EUGENE PENDLETON
Camera Operator	ALEC MILLS
Assistant Director	GORDON GILBERT

Unit Manager	BERNARD HANSON
Assistant Art Director	MARTIN ATKINSON
Continuity	KAY RAWLINGS
Sound Mixer	GORDON EVERETT
Script Consultant	DAVID WINTER
Second Unit Camera	DICK LEDERHAUS
Sound Recording	MICHAEL STRONG
Make-up	BUNTY PHILLIPS
Hairdressing	PAT GRANT
Special Stills	RUSS BUSBY
Wardrobe	HARRY & TINA HAYNES
Production Assistant	SHEILA COLLINS
Original Story & Screenplay	STELLA LINDEN
Executive Producer	FRANK R JACOBSON
Director	JAMES F COLLIER
Music Composed and Conducted by	MIKE LEANDER
Color by	EASTMANCOLOR

SONGS

1. 'Two A Penny' – sung over the opening credits.

2. 'Twist And Shout' – sung on the stage of 'The Drum' pub.

3. 'I Love You Forever Today' – sung on the soundtrack after Carol (Ann Holloway) is found after running away and returns home with Cliff to his mother's (Dora Bryan) house.

4. 'Questions' – sung at the end of the film following a discussion between Cliff and Ann Holloway.

THE STORY

Jamie Hopkins, a product of the mod, materialistic sixties, regards his widowed mother Ruby and his 'bird' Carol Turner as easy money sources for his 'get rich quick' schemes – the latest, a start in the dope running racket, ends in a punch up when Jamie attempts to use the pusher's dough for his own scheme. Jamie's ego is gently pushed back into shape by Carol and they tip-toe upstairs to Carol's room, past the sleeping landlady, ex-show girl Deidre Burry. As Jamie pursues his bird, she scuffles with him and the landlady appears, telling him the only rule is 'don't get caught'.

Jamie, swallowing his pride, visits the pusher for another chance. Fitch, when reassured that Jamie is ready for anything, asks for the keys to the doctor's office where his mother works. Dr Berman, a psychologist, is experimenting with psychedelic drugs. Jamie readily agrees, quite upset for overlooking this opportunity himself.

Meeting Carol in their usual lunch spot, she mentions the tickets she was given to see Billy Graham that evening and her plans to invite Mrs Burry. Jamie suggests that she takes Billy Graham to see Mrs Burry, 'then you might have something'. He decides it might be a giggle, and agrees to go. He visits his mother at the doctor's office and manages to extract the office key from her purse, so he can make a duplicate. Gradually, though, he realises that Fitch will end up with most of the money while he takes all the risk. Switching the tactics, he phones the doctor and sets up an appointment during his mother's lunch hour. He asks the doctor for any kind of work, washing up the bottles perhaps, in order to help his mother put him through school.

Dropping by later to pick up Carol, he runs into Mrs Burry who has set her sights on him. Refusing to wait for Carol in front of the Billy Graham meeting, he fast-talks himself inside and on to the speaker's platform. As he listens to Graham he comments to himself on the strange message and, to his horror, sees Carol among the members of the audience who are going up to the front in answer to Graham's call to commitment.

Stopping at his local, Jamie does a take-off of Graham for the patrons, while Carol pensively makes her way home. As Mrs Burry is out, Jamie talks her into letting him come in and confronts her with her commitment. He grabs for her and she pulls away, running out of the house past Mrs Burry to a nearby church. He taunts her, and when she walks away, decides there's 'plenty more where she came from'.

Carol returns to her room, where Mrs Burry forces her to move out within twenty four hours. Miserable, Carol wanders about London the next evening, looking for a place to stay. Jamie changes his mind and calls by for her, but can't imagine where she's got to. Finally, thinking of their noontime meeting place, he seeks for, and finds her there. They rush into each other's arms and Jamie takes over, herding the frightened sparrow home. The song, 'I Love You Forever, Today', expresses Jamie's thoughts on their relationship.

Ruby takes the girl in 'for the night', but later decides she can stay on as a roomer. Carol is invited to a youth meeting by a vicar, where she meets Gladys, the girl that gave her the Graham tickets. Attending the meeting starts a running battle with Jamie, but finally he attends one evening, with the predictable result – Jamie's rejection of what he hears. After a stroll along the Thames that evening, Carol again scrambles away from him, as his advances become rougher. 'Sex is natural when two people are supposed to be in love, Miss Dolly', he angrily retorts.

Having tried to peddle some of the drugs he's been able to lift from the doctor's medicine cabinet, and met with a blunt, 'I thought you knew I only deal with Finch', Jamie decides to remove Fitch from the scene. He gives him the key to the office and then informs the police of the planned burglary. But first he removes the most valuable drugs for his own plans, knowing that their loss will be blamed on Fitch. From a nearby rooftop he watches in vain for the attempted break-in, and even the police seem uninterested. Waking at dawn, he realises that his plan has backfired and he's the one they'll be looking for when the drugs are missed. Frantic, Jamie attempts to get the key back from Fitch. Wrestling with Fitch, Jamie's struck down by Hubert, Fitch's assistant. Jamie then dashes home to borrow his mother's keys and return the drugs before the doctor arrives. Carol hears him come in and when the packet of pills spill, Ruby is wakened by the commotion. Disowning her son and turning him out of the house, she takes the pills back.

Jamie then attempts to bounce back again with another wild scheme, but Carol fears that he will always rush away from reality. Finally, forced to take a good look at himself, Jamie begins to realise that the first step towards changing his life for the better doesn't have to be a very big step.

PRODUCTION NOTES & TRIVIA

● *Two A Penny* premiered at the Prince Charles Cinema in London on 20 June 1968.

● Filming began in June 1967 at Goldhawk Studios in Shepherds Bush and was completed in July.

● Halliwell's Film Guide called *Two A Penny* a 'naive religious propaganda sponsored by the Billy Graham movement and featuring the evangelist in a cameo. A curiosity.'

● Reviews of the film included one by Alan Smith who said 'Attempted rape, the seduction of a young man by an older woman, drug trafficking and Billy Graham with the word of God. In some respects it's the best Cliff's ever made – as he says himself, he's no Sir Laurence, but at least he gets the chance to act in a serious and straightforward story. Rave versions by Cliff of 'Twist And Shout' plus three catchy numbers 'Two A Penny', 'I Love You Forever Today' and 'Questions'. Another review in the *Los Angeles Times* said '*Two A Penny*, quite flatly, is an outstanding film in all aspects. The entire cast is excellent.'

● Director James F Collier had previously worked on *Alfie* starring Michael Caine.

● A week before its premiere *Two A Penny* was screened for the religious press.

● Production Supervisor, Basil Appleby, had previously worked on *Khartoum*, starring Charlton Heston.

● *Two A Penny* was made by Worldwide Pictures of Burbank, California, a division of Billy Graham's worldwide organisation, with a £150,000 budget. All proceeds from the film were donated to charity.

● Cliff's salary for the film was £40 a week, the minimum payment Cliff could earn, as stipulated by Equity, the actors union, but Cliff insisted that his salary was paid over to charity.

- In August 1968, Billy Graham worked on German and Japanese versions of the film.

- Ann Holloway made her film debut in the film. She later went on to star in the 'Father Dear Father' television series.

- Cliff wrote three songs for *Two A Penny*: the title song, 'Questions' and 'I'll Love You Forever Today', which became his 42nd single in 1968.

- *Two A Penny* is the only movie in which Cliff appears unshaven.

- At the end of the film, Cliff arrives at a recording studio as himself to talk about his own experience and invites the audience to complete a souvenir card to find their answers. This footage has been cut from the version later released on video.

HIS LAND

Worldwide Pictures, 1970. Certificate U.
Running time: 65 minutes. Cliff's eighth film.

CAST

Cliff Richard	CLIFF RICHARD
Cliff Burrows	CLIFF BURROWS

CREW

Production Supervisor	BASIL APPLEBY
Photography	PAUL LOHMANN
Second Unit Photography	RICHARD LEDERHAUS
	PETER ROHE
Production Assistant	YERAH COVER
Assistant Director	JACOB HAMEIRI
Location Manager	SAM BECKER
Chief Electrician	AVRAHAM LIEBMAN
Music Composed & Directed by	RALPH CARMICHAEL
Music Supervisor	LEE GILLETTE
Conductor	HY LESNICK
Editors	EUGENE PENDLETON
	DOLF RUDEEN
Music Editor	ED NORTON
Sound	MICHAEL STRONG
	LEE KISLING
Continuity	KENETTE GFELLER
Montage Editor	CARLO LODATO
Montage Stills	RICHARD LEDERHAUS
	FRANK RAYMOND
Montage Research	WOODY BOOSEY
Editorial Assistant	STEVE BOBEK
Our thanks to	HOLYLAND HOTEL
	GOVERNMENT FILM SERVICE
	YAD VASHEM MEMORIAL
	GUIDING STAR TOURIST AGENCY
Executive Producer	FRANK R JACOBSON
Written & Directed by	JAMES F COLLIER

SONGS

1. 'Dry Bones' – sung over the opening credits.

2. 'His Land' – sung overlooking Tel Aviv after on-screen narration by Cliff Burrows.

3. 'His Land' (second version) – sung as Cliff walks through crops in the Hooda Valley in Israel.

4. 'His Land' (third version) – sung on soundtrack as film shows landscape views of Israel.

5. 'Jerusalem, Jerusalem' – sung at various locations around Jerusalem.

6. 'Hava Nagalia' – sung by the crowds during street celebration in Tel Aviv.

7. 'Over In Bethlehem' – sung as a duet with Cliff Burrows at a location outside Bethlehem.

8. 'He's Everything To Me' – sung as a duet with Cliff Burrows at an open-air fireside gathering in Galilee.

9. 'Keep Me Where Love Is' – sung walking through locations surrounding Galilee, and while rowing a dinghy.

10. 'Hallelujah' – sung at the end of the film over montage following narration by Cliff Burrows.

THE STORY

His Land is an award-winning documentary film that has been described as a 'musical journey into the soul of a nation'. It is a compelling and colourful tour of Israel, filled with the sights and sounds of a vibrant country. The film visits many of the places where our Lord's earthly ministry unfolded, and discovers how the prophecies of the Old Testament were fulfilled with His coming. The film reminds us anew of that day yet to be – when His triumphant return will signal the dawning of a new age.

His Land is a truly memorable film experience hosted by Cliff Burrows of the Billy Graham team, and Cliff Richard.

PRODUCTION NOTES & TRIVIA

● *His Land* was never released nationally through cinemas in Great Britain. The film was shown in youth clubs and church halls.

● The working title was *Fire In Zion*.

● Location filming in Israel began on 11 June 1969 in the Holy Land and lasted for three weeks.

● Ad line for *His Land*: 'A Musical Journey Into The Soul Of A Nation!'

● *His Land* was the second Cliff Richard film to be made by Worldwide Pictures of Burbank, California – a division of the Billy Graham organisation.

TAKE ME HIGH

Anglo EMI Films, 1973. A Kenneth Harper Production. Certificate U. Running time: 90 minutes. Length: 8096 ft. Cliff's ninth film.

CAST

Tim Matthews	CLIFF RICHARD
Sarah	DEBBIE WATLING
Sir Harry Cunningham	HUGH GRIFFITH
Bert Jackson	GEORGE COLE
Hugo Flaxman	ANTHONY ANDREWS
Sir Charles Furness	RICHARD WATTIS
Vicki	MADELINE SMITH
Molly	MOYRA FRASER
Sam	RONALD HINES
Hulbert	JIMMY GARDNER
Paul	NOEL TRAVERTHEN
Boardman	GRAHAM ARMITAGE
Alderman	JOHN FRANKLIN-ROBBINS
Grandson	PETER MARSHALL
Waitress	ELISABETH SCOTT
Receptionist	POLLY WILLIAMS

CREW

Story & Screenplay	CHRISTOPHER PENFOLD
Based on an original idea by	KENNETH HARPER
Music & Lyrics	TONY COLE
Musical Director	DAVID MACKAY
Conductor	BARRIE GUARD
Musical Co-ordinator	PETER GORMLEY
Editor	RICHARD BEST
Art Director	EDWARD MARSHALL
Production Manager	JOHN WILCOX
Location Manager	DEREK GIBSON
Assistant Director	NICHOLAS GRANBY
Camera Operator	NEIL BINNEY
Sound Recordists	LES HAMMOND
	BILL ROWE
Music Recordist	TONY CLARK
Dubbing Editor	VERNON MESSENGER
Assistant Art Director	JOHN LAGEU
Set Dressing	MICHAEL FORD
Make-up	BOB LAWRENCE
Hairdressing	GORDON BOND
Wardrobe Supervisor	BRENDA DABBS
Casting	MAUDE SPECTOR

Continuity	GLADYS GOLDSMITH
Publicity	JEAN GARDIOCH
Director of Photography	NORMAN WARWICK
Producer	KENNETH HARPER
Director	DAVID ASKEY

SONGS

1. 'It's Only Money' – sung over the opening credits.

2. 'Midnight Blue' – sung in Cliff's mini after he has been kicked out of his home by his girlfriend.

3. 'Winning' – sung on the soundtrack as Cliff walks around Birmingham looking for somewhere to live.

4. 'The Anti-Brotherhood Of Man' – sung on the soundtrack as Cliff, Anthony Andrews and Debbie Watling argue in Cliff's office.

5. 'Why' – sung on the soundtrack as a duet with Anthony Andrews in his car during their getaway from Hugh Griffith's estate after being shot at.

6. 'Life' – sung on the soundtrack as Debbie Watling takes a look around Cliff's barge.

7. 'Life' (second version) – sung on the soundtrack as Debbie Watling takes Cliff's barge along the river.

8. 'Hover' – instrumental played on the soundtrack as Cliff drives a hover-boat along the river, and Anthony Andrews' car radiator overheats.

9. 'The Game' – sung in Cliff's barge while accompanying himself on guitar.

10. 'Brumburger Duet' – sung as a duet with Debbie Watling in Cliff's barge as Debbie cooks a brumburger.

11. 'Driving' – sung on the soundtrack as Cliff and Debbie Watling drive through the country to watch the hunt led by Hugh Griffith.

12. 'Driving' (instrumental version) – played on the soundtrack as the fox gets into Cliff's mini, and Cliff, Debbie and fox move to meet up with Hugh Griffith while leading his hunting party.

13. 'Driving' (second version) – sung on the soundtrack after meeting Hugh Griffith immediately after Cliff and Debbie let the fox out of Cliff's mini.

14. 'Take Me High' – sung on the soundtrack as Cliff and Debbie walk romantically through 'Gardens' before kissing each other.

15. 'Join The Band' – sung on the soundtrack as Cliff and Debbie travel through Birmingham City Centre in a procession to celebrate their Brumburger.

16. 'The World Is Love' – sung at the Brumburger restaurant as Debbie prepares some ingredients.

17. 'Brumburger' (Finale) – sung at the end of the film at the Brumburger restaurant and over the closing credits.

THE STORY

Tim Matthews is a successful and ambitious young financier working for a London Merchant Bank. He is not particularly disturbed at being thrown out by Vicki, one of his many girlfriends, but he is astonished when his Chairman, Sir Charles Furness, sends him to Birmingham instead of the promised New York posting. However, his custom-built mini threads its way through Spaghetti Junction towards the Company's head-quarters in the British Midlands. There he meets his rival, Flaxman, a suave, smooth talking young man who appears to run his business life by his pocket-size astrological calculator. Both men are now competing for a seat on the Birmingham Board of Directors. Yet it is Matthews, smiling and cynically lighthearted, whose razor sharp mind for finance begins to take over the running of things. Disdaining a penthouse, Matthews buys an old barge and converts it into a luxurious home. His neighbours are the people he bought it from, Sam and Molly. And their daughter is Sarah, who has opened a French restaurant in the city on money raised for her by Flaxman. When she needs a further loan it is refused by Tim whom she first met as a complaining customer at her restaurant. Sarah is disillusioned with bankers – all bankers.

Meanwhile Bert Jackson, a Left-wing City Councillor, needs a mere ten million pounds for a new scheme. Blandly unmoved by the fact that the eccentric local millionaire tycoon, Sir Harry Cunningham, has been publicly denounced by Jackson on television. Tim wheels and deals to finally bring off the most unlikely of financial 'marriage' coups. On the hunting field he swerves his Mini into the midst of the local upper crust hunting set in order to offer Sir Harry the best deal he's ever had – and a promise of a great reputation as a City benefactor. In the local bowling alley he intimates that Jackson needs that City Cross deal to get under way to keep his place on the council. And where else could the council get ten million pounds?

Meanwhile, he has got to know and like Sarah since she dropped in on the new owner of the barge, little suspecting that it would belong to the banker, Tim Matthews. While their friendship deepens, they take *The Sophie* through the canals, stopping for a picnic of hamburgers. Discovering them to be quite inedible, the young couple suddenly decide they'll produce their own hamburger. It will be called a Brumburger – something new and different for the people to enjoy at a special restaurant. (Brum is short for Birmingham).

At a lunch to celebrate the financial 'marriage' of Left and Right, Sir Harry and Bert Jackson are introduced to Sarah and her Brumburger. Made from her own secret recipe, it will be Britain's answer to the hamburger. Jackson agrees to provide planning permission for a derelict building to be redesigned as The Brumburger and Sir Harry is persuaded to finance the proposition – which he proceeds to do with all his usual ballyhoo. A cavalcade parades through the Birmingham streets to the music of two bands marching behind banners bearing the legend 'The Brumburger – the biggest little mouthful in the land'. A somewhat disgruntled Flaxman now urgently impresses upon Sir Charles the desirability of sending young Matthews to New York. But for Matthews, a changed man since living among the people of Birmingham and falling for the lovely Sarah, New York is the last place he wants to go. Indeed, if Sir Charles is adamant, then Matthews will be forced to leave the Company and take the Cunningham account with him. Tim then thrashes his Mini through traffic-laden streets and the screech of brakes as he lands on the Council House steps and stops Sir Harry, who is about to make the pronouncement on the new City deal. Instead, he changes his mind, pushes his chauffeur from the driving seat of his Rolls and, with Tim and Bert Jackson holding on to their coat tails in the back seat, roars off to open The Brumburger. Pressmen, television cameras and police cars eventually catch him up as he arrives at the new restaurant. 'The biggest little mouthful in the land' is off to a rousing start. And Tim and Sarah are happy – launched in business and in love.

PRODUCTION NOTES & TRIVIA

● *Take Me High* opened nationally on 26 December 1974. The companion feature in most areas was *Wolfshead – The Legend Of Robin Hood*.

● *Hot Property* was first considered as the film's title and, in fact, was used in America.

● In Thailand the film was released under the title *The Heavenly Sounds*.

● *Take Me High* was filmed during June and July 1973 entirely on location in Birmingham.

● Ad line for the film: 'Cliff's Back! In The Bubbling, Champagne Film Musical of '74.'

● *Take Me High* was the first film in which most of the songs were used as soundtracks rather than Cliff performing staged and choreographed sequences.

MOVIE
MISCELLANEA

Cliff made two films in black and white:
1. *Serious Charge*
2. *Expresso Bongo*

Kenneth Harper produced four Cliff films:
1. *The Young Ones*
2. *Summer Holiday*
3. *Wonderful Life*
4. *Take Me High*

Movies in which Cliff sang a duet:
1. *The Young Ones:*
   'Nothing's Impossible' with Carole Gray
   'Lessons In Love' with Carole Gray
2. *Summer Holiday:*
   'A Swinging Affair' with Lauri Peters
3. *Wonderful Life:*
   'In The Stars' with Susan Hampshire
   'Do You Remember' with Susan Hampshire
4. *His Land:*
   'Over In Bethlehem' with Cliff Burrows
   'He's Everything To Me' with Cliff Burrows
5. *Take Me High:*
   'Why' with Anthony Andrews
   'Brumburger Duet' with Debbie Watling

Cliff's feature films in Chronological order:
1. *Serious Charge* (1959)
2. *Expresso Bongo* (1959)
3. *The Young Ones* (1961)
4. *Summer Holiday* (1962)
5. *Wonderful Life* (1964)
6. *Finders Keepers* (1966)
7. *Two A Penny* (1967)
8. *His Land* (1970)
9. *Take Me High* (1973)

Film Production Companies:
Alva Films: *Serious Charge*
Britannia Films: *Expresso Bongo*
Associated British Picture Corporation: *The Young Ones;*

Summer Holiday
Ivy Films: *Wonderful Life*
United Artists: *Finders Keepers*
World Wide Films: *Two A Penny; His Land*
Anglo EMI Films: *Take Me High*

The most popular film stars of 1962
(compiled by the Motion Picture Herald)
1. CLIFF RICHARD
2. Elvis Presley
3. Peter Sellers
4. Kenneth More
5. Hayley Mills
6. Doris Day
7. Sophia Loren
8. John Wayne
9. Frank Sinatra
10. Sean Connery

The most popular film stars of 1963
(compiled by the Motion Picture Herald)
1. CLIFF RICHARD
2. Peter Sellers
3. Elvis Presley
4. Sean Connery
5. Hayley Mills
6. Elizabeth Taylor
7. Marlon Brando
8. Albert Finney
9. Dirk Bogarde
10. Norman Wisdom

German Movie Titles:
1. Die Schamlosen (Serious Charge)
2. Bongo-Boy (Expresso Bongo)
3. Hallo Mr Twen (The Young Ones)
4. Hollifay Fur Dich Und Mich (Summer Holiday)
5. Kub Mich Mit Musik (Wonderful Life)
6. Finders Keepers (Same)
7. Take Me High (Same)
8. Bin Kein Mr Niemand (Two A Penny)
9. Sien Land (His Land)

SHORT SUBJECT
FILMS

Why Should The Devil Have All The Good Music
This was a 16mm Eastman colour film with a running time of 50 minutes. It was produced by Colin Rank of Abba Productions. Direction was by James Swackhammer. Cliff starred along with a number of well-known Jesus Music artists, including Larry Norman, Judy McKenzie and Dave Cooke, Malcolm and Alwyn, Graham Kendrick, the Arts Centre Group director, and actor Nigel Goodwin, and pop singer Dana. It was a documentary of the 1972 London Festival for Jesus, basically a celebration of Christian beliefs.

A World Of Difference
This was a 16mm colour documentary for Tear Fund centring on the Fund's director, George Hoffman. Cliff contributed to the film.

Loved Into Life and Love Never Gives Up
Two Tear Fund filmstrips about Cliff's visit to Bangladesh.

Cliff – Flipside
This was filmed at Cliff's Tear Fund concert at the Royal Albert Hall, 1979, and also at his home. He talks about his faith. The director and scriptwriter was Mike Pritchard. Intamedia produced the film for International Films. It runs for 30 minutes and is a 16mm colour presentation.

A Day With Cliff
As the title indicates, the film follows Cliff through a day. It was made by Dutch Television in the early seventies.

Come Together
A film of the popular religious musical by American Jimmy Owens. Cliff is interviewed by Pat Boone. The film is 16mm colour. International Films.

Let's Join Together
Cliff plus Johnny Cash and Choralerna. The music and message of the Spree Festival, London 1973. International Films.

Greenbelt Live!
Some of the highlights of the major British religious festival held in 1979 where music is an important ingredient. Cliff gives a brief interview, is glimpsed from time to time, and has one stage song 'Yes He Lives'. Also in the film, among many, are Garth Hewitt, After The Fire, Randy Stonehill, and Larry Norman. A Tony Tew film for Grenville Film Productions in association with Marshalls Publishing.

Judge For Yourself
This Scripture Union filmstrip deals with basic religious questions like 'Does it make sense?', 'Does it work?', 'Does it fit in with what I know!', 'Can it be applied to God's message?'

London Crusade
Documentary in which Cliff makes an appearance. 1966. Worldwide Films.

I'm Going To Ask You To Get Out Of Your Seats
Richard Causton's documentary on Billy Graham for BBC TV. Cliff makes an appearance.

Rhythm 'n' Greens
The Shadows starred in this 1964, 32 minute film. Cliff played the part of King Canute.

THEATRICAL
APPEARANCES

In this section we have listed Cliff's theatrical appearances from his first dramatic role in *Five Finger Exercise* to his first major musical role as *The Rock Star* in *Time*.

Some information is scarce. For instance, very little could be traced on Cliff's stage debut in *Five Finger Exercise* apart from what is already known; Cliff played his first straight acting role as Clive in this Peter Schaeffer play, his co-star was Pamela Denton, and it had a three-week run at Bromley New Theatre in May 1970.

Information for *A Midsummer Night Dream* is just as scarce. We know that Cliff played Bottom in a production that was performed by the Riversmead School Dramatic Society who were made up of past and present pupils, it was produced by Jay Norris, and opened the same day that Olivia Newton-John opened a season in Vegas!

Full details of Cliff's second play *The Potting Shed*, and his first West End musical *Time* including cast lists, stage credits, scene changes, theatre and play dates have been well documented.

We have included the information currently available for *Heathcliff*. The shows were postponed from 1994 to 1996 as more rehearsal time was needed. For Cliff, the idea to adapt Emily Brontë's classic *Wuthering Heights* into a musical has been both a professional and personal ambition. He first read the book as a schoolboy. Then and later, as an adult, he found himself impressed and intrigued with Heathcliff's character. He was amazed at the darker side. To ensure authenticity, Cliff visited the Brontë Parsonage Museum in Haworth to research the necessary background which promises to make the *Heathcliff* spectacular just that.

FIVE FINGER EXERCISE

Bromley New Theatre, 11 May 1970.

THE POTTING SHED

Opening on 17 May 1971 for one week at the Sadler's Wells Theatre, Cliff appeared in Graham Greene's play

The Potting Shed. Originally scheduled to have opened on 10 May at the Bromley New Theatre for three weeks, the production had to be re-scheduled due to a fire destroying the theatre on 6 May.

Cliff played the role of James Calliger – the unwanted member of the family who is denied a bedside place at the death of his father. Trying to find out the reasons through a psychiatrist, his mother, a widow, and a drunk priest, he finally discovers something that happened to him in the potting shed when he was a teenager at fourteen, which solves his problem.

In the original production of the play twenty years previously, Cliff's part was written for a man in his mid-forties, and the actor who played the part was Sir John Gielgud. For Cliff's role, the age was altered to suit a man of thirty. Together with the other members of the cast, Cliff earned better press reviews than the original production did. The fire at the Bromley New Theatre provided Cliff with the opportunity to make his acting debut at a West End theatre, and although the play only had a week's run, the box office receipts exceeded any other production staged for longer periods at the Bromley Theatre.

CAST

Dr Frederick Baston	GEOFFREY WINCOTT
Anne Callifer	PATSY BLOWER
Sara Callifer	MARGO JENKINS
Mrs Callifer	MARGOT THOMAS
John Callifer	DONALD GEE
James Callifer	CLIFF RICHARD
Dr Kreuzer	BILL WIESENER
Coroner	DEAN HARRIS
Mrs Potter	CONSTANCE FRASER
Miss Connolly	EDNA DORE
Father William Callifer	PATRICK BARR

CREDITS

Director	PATRICK TUCKER
Designer	PAUL MAYO
Lighting Designer	NEVILLE CURRIER

FOR BROMLEY THEATRE TRUST LTD

Production Manager	FRANK JERRAM
Stage Manager	VERONICA GRIFFITHS
Deputy Stage Manager	PAUL FARMER
Assistant Stage Managers	CARMEL COLGAN
	JOHN GAINES
	ELIZABETH MOOREFIELD
	ALAN MUNDAY

Master Carpenter	DAVID NICOL
Chief Electrician	CHRISTOPHER BAZELEY
Design Assistant	CHRISTINA JONES
Workshop Assistant	LAWRENCE GOBLE
Production Photographs	JOHN JORDAN
Incidental Music	THE MUSIC SHOP (A.T. Furlong & Son) 25 Thomas Street, Woolwich
Lighters by	RONSON
Telephones by	THE POST OFFICE
Miss Jenkins' clothes by	NICHOLSON'S of Bromley
Spectacles by	CLIFFORD BROWN of Bromley
Loose-Leaf Binders by courtesy of	KALAMANZOO LTD
Books kindly loaned by	BROMLEY PUBLIC LIBRARY
Typewriter by	BROMLEY OFFICE SUPPLIES
Christmas tree by	THE BROMLEY PARKS DEPT
Mars bars by	MARS LTD
Glasses by	PETER DOMINIC
Sets specially constructed for the New Bromley Theatre at Sadlers Wells Theatre by	BRUNSKILL & LOVEDAY

ACT ONE

Scene 1 – The living room of the Callifer's house, Wild Grove, in what was once the country.
Scene 2 – The same. Evening, two days later.

ACT TWO

Scene 1 – James Callifer's lodgings in Nottingham, four weeks later.
Scene 2 – Father William Callifer's presbytery, somewhere in East Anglia. Evening, the next day.

INTERVAL

ACT THREE

The living room at Wild Grove, the next evening.
Time – the present.

A MIDSUMMER NIGHT'S DREAM

Riversmead School, Cheshunt.
3 July – 12 July 1974.

TIME – THE MUSICAL

Dominion Theatre, London. 9 April 1986 – 11 April 1987.

Cliff's 12-month run in *Time* saw him surrounded by hi-tech wizardry never before witnessed in a West End show. Nearly 2,000 people packed out the Dominion theatre to see Cliff play alongside the giant visual projection of his co-star and revered acting legend Laurence Olivier.

Dave Clark's epic musical told how rock star Chris Wilder (Cliff) challenged and won over all-powerful god-like time lords bent on destroying the earth. Earth, viewed as a corrupt and decadent planet by the time lords, is put on trial for its life as evidence unfolds on an intergalactic scale. They beam up a representative of the planet to defend it and Cliff finds himself in the dock thanks to a teleportation error. But he eventually triumphs, and earth survives to witness the rock star's concerts.

CAST (in order of appearance)

The Rock Star, Chris Wilder	CLIFF RICHARD
Louise	JODIE WILSON
Babs	DAWN HOPE
Carol	MARIA VENTURA
The Rock Group	NEIL GOW-HUNTER
	SIMON SHELTON
	SPARKEY
	IAN STEWART

Akash, The Ultimate Word In Truth	LAURENCE OLIVIER
Judge Morgua	DILYS WATLING
Judge Trigon	BERNARD LLOYD
Judge Lagus	DAVID TIMSON
Lord Melchisedic, The Time Lord	JEFF SHANKLEY
Lord Melchisedic's Retinue	WAYNE ASPINALL
	GARY CO-BURN
	NEIL GOW-HUNTER
	STEVE MONDEY
	GARRY NOAKES
	TOM SEARLE
	SIMON SHELTON
	DAVE TREVORS
Captain Ebony	LINTON DERRICKS-CARROLL
Captain Ebony's Retinue	LINDA-MAE BREWER
	ROBIN CLEAVER
	ROSEMARIE FORD
	HEATHER ROBBINS
	SPARKEY
	IAN STEWART

THE ORCHESTRA

Production Musical Director/ Keyboards	MIKE MORAN
Musical Director/Keyboards	ALLAN ROGERS
Assistant MD/Keyboards	PETER LEE
Drums	BRETT MORGAN
Bass	ALAN JONES
Guitar	RAY RUSSELL
Guitar	CHRIS RAE
Keyboards	DAVE ARCH
Percussion	FRANK RICOTTI
Percussion	GARY KETTEL
Alto Sax/Flute	ANDY MACKINTOSH
French Horn/Wagner Tuba	BARRY CASTLE

BACK-UP SINGERS

Sonia Jones, Valerie McKenna, Michael Mullins, Keith Murrell, Phil Nicoll

SPECIAL STANDBY

The Rock Star	JOHN CHRISTIE
Lord Melchisedic	JOHN CHRISTIE

UNDERSTUDIES

Captain Ebony	DANNY JOHN JULES
Judge Trigon/Lord Melchisedic	GARY MARTIN
Judge Morgua	ROSEMARIE FORD
Judge Lagus	IAN STEWART
Louise	ALEXANDRA WORRALL
Babs	ROBIN CLEAVER
Carol	LINDA-MAE BREWER

SWINGS

Janett Rolle, Alexandra Worrall, Wayne Anthony, Vince Debano

STAGE MANAGEMENT

Company Manager	TIM RICHARDS
Stage Manager	BILL SIMON
Deputy Stage Manager	HENRIETTA BOXER
Assistant Stage Managers	SARAH OVEREND
	MARGARET SUTHERLAND

PRODUCTION STAFF FOR *TIME*

Production Manager	PAUL MACKAY for IMAGINATION
Assistant to Arlene Phillips	HEATHER SEYMOUR
Musical Associate/Orchestrator	KEVIN TOWNSEND
Casting	LEONIE COSMAN
Production Photographer	NOBBY CLARKE
Assistant Production Manager	NICHOLAS FRASER
Assistant Designer	SUE JENKINSON
Chief Production Electricians	HOWARD EATON
	MICHAEL ODAM
Costume Supervisor	KIM BAKER
Production Theatre Services	ROBERT KNIGHT COMPLETE THEATRE SERVICES

	CHRIS ORGAN
	JOHN LEONARD
Production Electricians	JONATHAN BADGER
	GREG HAMLIN
	NICK JONES
	ENEAS MACKINTOSH
Chief Design Engineers	MIKE BARNETT
	ROGER HARDWICK
Projection Consultants	HAVE FACILITIES
Animatronics Designed by	MALCOLM CLARKE &
	PETER BROOKS
Assistant to John Napier	BENEDICT HILLIARD
Assistant To Mr Bridge	SIMON BRUXNER-RANDALL
Editing	JIM GROOM
Head Sculptor	IRENE DREXLER
Production Riggers (URC)	STEVE COLLEY
	ANDY TOWNSEND
	DEREK HAY
	RORY McKEOWN
	COLIN RABY
	STEVE BOOKHAM
	ALAN JACOBI
Production Site Engineer	JOHN MUGFORD for KW LTD
Make-up Consultant	NAOMI DONNE
Make-up Artist	LOUISE CONSTAD
Costume Supervision Assistants	SARAH DENNY
	JOHN COWELL
Rehearsal Body Popping Coach	VENOL JOHN

STAFF FOR *TIME*

Assistant to Larry Fuller	TONY EDGE
1st Sound Engineer	PERRY MORGAN
2nd Sound Engineer	TIMOTHY LYNN
Dance Captain	ALEXANDRA WORRALL
Wig Mistress	MARION STREET
Wardrobe Master	DAVID HOY
Chief Electrician	PAUL TAYLOR
Lighting Operator	ANDREW OLSEN
Varilite Operator	TIM TURNER
Electrician	DAVID SMITH

Chief Follow Spot Operator	MIKE CORDINA
Projectionists	GRAHAM PHILLIPS
	MARTIN PURSEY
Laser Operator	JIM HEPPLEWHITE
Master Carpenter	CHRIS BARRON
Deputy Master Carpenter	LEE ELD
Stage Dayman	NORMAN BAILEY
Scenery Control Operator	MIKI JABLKOWSKA
Hydraulics Assistant	ANDREW HOLLEY
Throne Operators	RUSSELL BOSTRIDGE
	NICOLA BARCLAY
	CAROLLA KRONFELD
	WILLIAM SMEE
1st Sound Assistant	ADAM REED
2nd Sound Assistant	CHRIS BRACK
PA to Tim Richards	CAROLINE HEYWOOD
	FOR THE RIGHT TIME PRODUCTION CO. LTD
Producer	DAVE CLARK
Production Executive and PA to Dave Clark	ROGER BROWN
Production Consultant	DAVID COLE
Accounts Administrator	COLIN NEWMAN
Newman & Company Solicitor	JOHN COHEN
Assistant to Dave Clark	BOBBY BANNERMAN
Secretary to Dave Clark	ANTHEA GRAVES
Consultant	PATRICK O'DONOVAN
Sound Consultant	ASHLEY HOWE
Press Representation	PETER THOMPSON ASSOCIATES
Advertising & Graphics	DEWYNTERS LTD
General Management	ANDREW TREAGUS ASSOCIATES LTD

FOR THE ANDREW TREAGUS ASSOCIATES LTD

General Manager	ANDREW TREAGUS
Associate General Manager	ALISTAIR SMITH
Production Administrators	JOHN RAE-SMITH
	CLARE LINDSAY
Production Assistant	HELEN NICHOLSON
Office Assistant	AMANDA SOFTLY
Production Management	IMAGINATION

ADDITIONAL MUSIC AND LYRICS

John Christie, Hans Poulsen, David Pomeranz,
Jessica St. John

ACT ONE

Now that man is venturing to the stars and has already
walked on the Moon, 'Melchisedic', the Time Lord, has
decided that the time has come to examine the earth's
people to determine whether they shall be an asset or
a threat to Universal peace. The time is now.

'Time Talkin'	The Rock Star: Chris Wilder, Louise, Babs and Carol
'Born To Rock 'n' Roll'	Chris
'Time'	Chris
'The Music of the Spheres' Part 1 – The Ascension Part 2 – The Arrival	Orchestral
'Law Of The Universe'	The Judges: Trigon, Lagus and Morgua
'The Time Lord Theme'	Lord Melchisedic: The Time Lord
'The Charge'	The Judges: Trigon, Lagus and Morgua
'One Human Family'	Chris, Louise, Babs and Carol
'Your Brother In Soul'	Captain Ebony and his Retinue
'Case For The Prosecution'	Lord Melchisedic and his Retinue
'Time Will Teach Us All'	Chris
'If You Only Knew'	Chris and Captain Ebony
'I Object'	Lord Melchisedic
'In My Dance'	Chris

ACT TWO

'Move The Judge'	Captain Ebony and his Retinue
'What On Earth'	Louise
'I Don't Like You'	Lord Melchisedic and Captain Ebony
'She's So Beautiful'	Chris, Louise, Babs and Carol
'We're The U.F.O.'	Lord Melchisedic and his Retinue
'The Theme from Time'	Akash
'Harmony'	Lord Melchisedic, Chris, Captain Ebony and Company
'The Return'	Orchestral
'Time' (Reprise)	Chris
'It's In Every One Of Us'	Chris and Full Company

HEATHCLIFF

Birmingham Academy (NIA) 16–31 October, 1–2
November and 14–19 December, 1996.
Edinburgh Playhouse 5–16 November and 2–7
December, 1996
Manchester Palace Theatre 7–25 January, 1997
London, Labbatt's Apollo Hammersmith 12–28
February, 1–8 March and 24 March–5 April, 1997

The world premiere production of the musical version of
Emily Brontë's *Wuthering Heights*, with Cliff playing the
lead role in this musical re-telling of the hard-bitten tragic
tale of star-crossed love, passion, betrayal, romance
and revenge set against a desolate North Yorkshire
moorland landscape in the early nineteenth century.

CAST

Heathcliff	CLIFF RICHARD
Cathy	HELEN HOBSON

CREDITS

Director	FRANK DUNLOP
Music	JOHN FARRAR
Lyrics	TIM RICE
Presented by	THE CLIFF RICHARD ORGANISATION

PANTOMIMES

In this section we have listed each of Cliff's three pantomime seasons. Information is scarce on the first; 1959 at the Stockton Globe. No details could be traced on the co-stars of *Babes In The Wood* apart from the Shadows of course. We couldn't even establish the exact performance dates and times. However, full details of Cliff's second and third pantos include full cast lists, stage credits, songs performed, theatre, and play dates. Although rare today, in the sixties, a pantomime with one of Britain's hitmakers was almost expected. Apart from Cliff and the Shadows, Tommy Steele and Frank Ifield were among the others treading the boards to portray children's favourite panto characters.

For Cliff, a pantomime was like a movie. He would follow the same procedure of recording a soundtrack album with maybe fourteen tracks or more, including the

usual Shadows instrumentals, the orchestral set pieces, a hit single, and an EP of 'Hits From…' There would also be the usual cast of good supporting actors and actresses, while the Shadows and Norrie Paramor provided the musical score. The ingredients couldn't fail.

From the very successful box-office pantomime seasons at the London Palladium, the idea of making a film version of *Aladdin* was developed, but never really got out of pre-production stages, and the idea of staging *Pinocchio* as Cliff's fourth panto vehicle at the Palladium was also dropped. Both became unrealised projects and are detailed in that section of our book.

BABES IN THE WOOD

Stockton Globe, December 1959.

ALADDIN AND HIS WONDERFUL LAMP

London Palladium December 1964 – April 1965
Presented by Leslie A MacDonnell & Leslie Grade
in association with Bernard Delfont

CAST (in order of appearance)

Abanazar	ALAN CURTIS
Genie of the Ring	WENDY BARRY
Grand Vizier (Chamberlain to the Emperor)	MICHAEL HENRY
Town Crier	BILLY TASKER
Chief Inspector Bathrobe	CHARLIE CAIROLI
Sergeant Pork	PAUL KING
PC Noodles	LITTLE JIMMY
PC Boodles	HENRY LYTTON
Patrol Cops	JOHNNY VOLANT FIVE
Widow Twankey (Aladdin's Mother)	ARTHUR ASKEY
Friends of Aladdin:	
Wishie	BRUCE WELCH
Washee	HANK MARVIN
Noshee	BRIAN BENNETT
Poshee	JOHN ROSTILL
Aladdin	CLIFF RICHARD

Ladies-in-Waiting to the Princess:	
So-Shy	JOAN PALETHORPE
Tai-Ping	AUDREY BAYLEY
Emperor of China	TOM CHATTO
Princess Balroubadour (His Daughter)	UNA STUBBS
Slave of the Lamp	DAVID DAVENPORT

The Pamela Devis Dancing Girls:

Valerie Barrett	Louise Clarke
Rosalind Early	Diane Eldridge
Ingrid Gregoriceva	Gillian Gregory
Janet Gosling	Bernadette Hill
Gabrielle Murrow	Vivienne Roberts
Kaye Rogers	Jennifer Rufus
Joanna Short	Wendy Stewart
Wendy Thornley	Brigitte Verinder
Diane Waring	

The Pamela Devis Dancing Boys:

Rod Barratt	Ray Cornell
Hal Davis	David Eavis
John Harmer	Russell Leachman
Barry Lines	Eric Wilson
Steve Cornell	

The Shepherd Singers:

Sheila Bruce	Ann Lester
Liz Newell	Angela Shade
Ron Davies	William Daw
Ken Fraser	Johnny Johnson
Gee Kenny	Tony Menery
Alan Starkey	David York

Specialists:

The Johnny Volant Five   The Seven Lukacs

MUSICAL NUMBERS

'Pekin Scene'	Ensemble
'Me Oh My'	Wishie, Washee, Poshee & Noshee
'I Could Easily Fall'	Aladdin
'Emperor's Processional'	Emperor's Ensemble
'Princess's Processional'	Princess's Ensemble
'This Was My Special Day'	Princess & Ladies
'I'm In Love With You'	Aladdin
'Friends'	Aladdin, Wishie, Washee, Noshee & Poshee
'There's Gotta Be A Way'	Aladdin
'Jewel Dances'	Dancing Ensemble
'Warrior's Dance'	The Dancing Boys
'Festival of Lanterns – Dragon Dance'	Ensemble
'Genie With The Light Brown Lamp'	The Shadows
'Make Ev'ry Day A Carnival Day'	Aladdin
'Widow Twankey's Song'	Widow Twankey & Emperor
'I'm Feeling Oh So Lovely'	Princess & Ladies
'I've Said Too Many Things'	Aladdin
'Evening Comes'	Aladdin
'Havin' Fun'	Aladdin, Wishie, Washee, Noshee & Poshee

ACT ONE

Prologue
(a) 'The Four Seasons' (b) 'Abanazar's Den'
THE CITY OF PEKIN IN OLD CHINA
MARKET PLACE
ENTRANCE TO THE ROYAL BATHS
ANOTHER PART OF THE CITY
OUTSIDE THE POLICE STATION
THE POOL IN THE ROYAL BATHS
OUTSKIRTS OF PEKIN
WIDOW TWANKEY'S LAUNDRY

ON THE WAY TO THE CAVE
OUTSIDE THE MOUNTAIN CAVE
INTERIOR OF THE CAVE
THE JEWEL BALLETS
(a) Rubies (b) Emeralds (c) Sapphires (d) Diamonds
(e) The Warrior's Dance (f) Gold and Silver Cascade

INTERVAL

ACT TWO

FESTIVAL OF THE LANTERNS
THE EMPEROR'S AUDIENCE CHAMBER
CHIEF INSPECTOR BATHROBE'S DWELLING
ANOTHER PART OF THE CITY
THE PRINCESS'S BOUDOIR
THE EMPEROR'S PALACE
The Wedding Reception
The Entertainers: THE SENSATIONAL LUKACS
INSPECTOR BATHROBE'S DILEMMA
ALADDIN'S PALACE
(a) Pekin (b) In The Desert (c) Back in Pekin
THE HALL OF SCREENS
ALADDIN'S RECEPTION

CREDITS

Music and Lyrics	THE SHADOWS
Orchestrations	NORRIE PARAMOR
Ballet Master	SEAMUS GORDON
The London Palladium Orchestra Conducted by	BILLY TERNENT
Flying Effects	KIRBY'S FLYING BALLETS
Special Sound Effects	TALKING PICTURES
Film Sequence	IVY PRODUCTIONS
Scenery Designed by	TOD KINGMAN
Scenery Painted by	KEY STUDIOS
Costumes Designed by	CYNTHIA TINGEY
Costumes Executed by	MESSRS BERMANS of London & Hollywood
Properties by	KEY STUDIOS ELIZABETH HETHERINGTON & GEORGE &

Shoes by	DENNIS PERRY GAMBA, ANELLO & DAVIDE
Nylon Stockings by	KAYSER
Wigs by	WIG CREATIONS
Widow Twankey's Sweets by	BARKER & DOBSON

CINDERELLA

London Palladium. December 1966 – April 1967
Presented by Leslie A MacDonnell & Leslie Grade
in association with Bernard Delfont

CAST (in order of appearance)

The Town Crier	BILL TASKER
Baron Hardup	JACK DOUGLAS
Cinderella (His Daughter)	PIPPA STEEL
Buttons (His Page)	CLIFF RICHARD
Teresa (Cinder's Step Sister)	TERRY SCOTT
Eunice	HUGH LLOYD
(Cinder's Other Step Sister)	
The Brokers Men	THE SHADOWS:
	BRUCE WELCH
	HANK MARVIN
	JOHN ROSTILL
	BRIAN BENNETT
The Vicar of Stoneybroke	BILL TASKER
The Old Lady	ROSALIND EARLY
The Prince	PETER GILMORE
Dandini (The Prince's Equerry)	TUDOR DAVIES
Cinderella's Guardian Fairy	PATRICIA MERRIN
The Major-Domo	JACK FRANCOIS
Mistress Maybelle	AVRIL YARROW
The Inn-Keeper	JACK FRANCOIS
The Footmen	THE BEL CANTO SINGERS
The Pages	THE AIDA FOSTER CHILDREN

The Pamela Devis Dancing Girls

Mary-Ann Barham	Zilpha Beckett
Susan Cartman	Rosalind Early
Denise Fone	Kim Fraser
Carol Gerrie	Salli Hale
Deidre Laird	Susan Lamb
Lorna Nathan	Gillian Pearl
Tracey St. Claire	Lynn Waller
Diane Waring	Regina Watson
Sandra Williams	

The Pamela Devis Dancing Boys:

Nigel Bars	Jimmy Bell
Brian Evans	Clive Davis
Harry Higham	John Lane
Russell Leachman	Andrew Morrison
Ettienne Pettiford	Brian Rogers
Jack Webster	

The Bel Canto Singers:

Derry Bebbington	Jacky Mitchell
Margaret Webster	Rosemary Williams
Mark Allan	Davie Allen
Peter Gee	Gerry Gerrard
Michael Hartley	Tony Lane
Roger Miles	David Richmond
David York	Scott Young

The Aida Foster Children:

Pamela Barker	Joanne Gilbert
Lesley Liebert	Janet Mansell
Nadine Marzell	Lindsay Morris
Shelley Parker	Drina Pavlovic

ACT ONE

ONCE UPON A TIME – A PROLOGUE
THE TOWN OF STONEYBROKE
THE COURTYARD OF STONEYBROKE HALL
THE LIBRARY OF STONEYBROKE HALL
THE FOREST
MEANWHILE AT THE PALACE
THE PRINCE RECEIVES A PRESENT
THE LIBRARY
THE SISTERS' BOUDOIR
THE LIBRARY
THE KITCHEN OF STONEYBROKE HALL
A BALLET FOR ALL SEASONS
SPRING featuring Susan Lamb

SUMMER featuring Zilpha Beckett
AUTUMN featuring the Shadows and the Dancers
Regina Weston and Ettienne Pettiford
WINTER featuring Patricia Merrin
TABLEAUX
CINDERELLA GOES TO THE BALL featuring The Crystal
Coach, The Douglas George Ponies and Ensemble

INTERVAL

ACT TWO

ENTRANCE TO THE ROYAL PALACE
THE BALLROOM OF THE PALACE
CINDERELLA'S FLIGHT
ON THE WAY HOME
THE INN
THE SEARCH FOR PRINCESS CRYSTAL
THE LIBRARY
THE PRINCE'S RECEPTION
   with guests from: SWITZERLAND
                          SCOTLAND
                          INDIA
                          SPAIN
                          AFRICA
                          GERMANY
                          RUSSIA
                          HUNGARY
                          CHINA

CREDITS

Music & Lyrics by	THE SHADOWS
Devised & Produced by	ALBERT J KNIGHT
Choreography	PAMELA DAVIS
Decor by	TOD KINGMAN
Costumes Designed by	CYNTHIA TINGEY
and executed by	BERMANS of London and Hollywood
Book by	DAVID CROFT
Musical Supervision	NORRIE PARAMOR
Orchestrations by	NORRIE PARAMOR & BILLY TERNENT
The London Palladium Orchestra Conducted by	BILLY TERNENT
Film Sequence by	TALKING PICTURES LTD
Special Sound Effects by	E J ASHBY & TALKING PICTURES LTD
The artists in this production use radio microphones powered by	EVER READY BATTERIES
Ballet Mistress	DENISE SHAUNE
Assistant to the Choreographer	DAVID TOGURI
Speciality by	TANYA presented by JENDA SHAMA
'Happy Lad' & The Douglas George Ponies are staying with their friends at	THE WHITBREAD STABLES

CLIFF RICHARD – IN CONCERT

1958–1995

Touring has always been a major part of Cliff's career and through the years there have been many changes in the format and style of these tours. In the early days, Cliff could be found touring the length and breadth of the country on a bill that would include artists such as Wee Willie Harris and The Kalin Twins as well as the Shadows. The early tours usually played to the cinema and theatre circuits that included the ABC chain of venues. For the artists the fifties and sixties were not a time of luxury travel between venues nor did they have the help of roadies to manhandle equipment to and from the often beat up vans that were used as tour buses in those days! Often it would be the responsibility of the artists themselves to ensure that they arrived at the venues on time, set up their equipment for that evening's performance and dismantle it all again at the end of the evening, repeating the process at the next venue, more often than not several hundred miles across the country. The format of those early shows followed a set pattern: supporting acts; a comedian, who sometimes also acted as compere for the evening; the Shadows, who would perform their own set; and then Cliff, whose show would last about 20–30 minutes and would be a mix of recent hits and rock 'n' roll standards. The early tours would last about twenty or thirty days, with only a day off here and there. No sooner would they be back after a gruelling tour than they would have to prepare for the next round of concerts. As his success spread worldwide, so did the concert tours. In 1961, Cliff toured America as part of a package and the same year saw a short trip to Australia.

The early to mid-seventies found Cliff making several trips to the Far East where he was extremely popular. By this time, the Shadows had disbanded and he was now backed by several different groups including Marvin, Welch and Farrar. It was during this period that Cliff first worked with Olivia Newton-John. Recordings were made during a number of these Far East tours, finding release in their respective territories, as well as becoming available on import in the UK.

A return visit to the USA in 1981 kept his stateside fans happy and helped push his then current singles into the top 100.

In the eighties, Cliff's concerts became more like theatrical shows with the advent of laser-lights, smoke machines and the incredible lighting effects that were now available to artists. Gone were the days of Cliff and the Shadows, plus equipment,

piling into a van – the whole show would be transported by means of up to five trucks. Many companies were now involved in these tours – companies that dealt specifically with trucking, lighting, sound and catering, as well as the merchandisers, printers, and promoters. The logistics of these mammoth tours necessitated a large band of people just to make it all happen. Add to them the film crews and recording technicians and you begin to see the work that went into the immensely successful Event concerts held at Wembley Stadium in July 1989.

By playing at venues such as Wembley Arena and the National Exhibition Centre in Birmingham, artists such as Cliff could present not just one show but a series of shows, as with the From A Distance tour in 1990 when Cliff sold out the Arena for an incredible seventeen nights. This avoided the need to transport large volumes of equipment around the county although, on the minus side, it did prevent many fans from the smaller towns from seeing him in concert.

Throughout the seventies, eighties and into the nineties Cliff also undertook Gospel Tours. These tours, with the proceeds going to the TEAR Fund, featured Cliff performing gospel tracks, talking to the audience about Christianity and a question and answer session with Bill Latham.

The following list is a complete list of every known live appearance and Gospel tour Cliff undertook from 1958 through to the present day.

1958

May 3	Regal Ballroom, Ripley
October 5	Victoria Hall, Hanley
October 6	Odeon, Blackpool
October 7	Ritz, Wigan
October 8	St. Andrews Hall, Glasgow
October 10	Free Trade Hall, Manchester
October 12	Empire, Liverpool
October 14	De Montfort Hall, Leicester
October 15	City Hall, Sheffield
October 16	City Hall, Newcastle
October 17	Town Hall, Birmingham
October 18	Rialto, York
October 19	Colston Hall, Bristol
November 17	Metropolitan, Edgware, London

1959

January	Free Trade Hall, Manchester
January	Plaza, Bedford
January	Odeon, Romford
January	Dome, Brighton
January	Gaumont, Ipswich
January	Gaumont, Salisbury
January 24	Rialto, York
February 1	Gaumont, Ipswich
February 2	Lyceum, Strand
February 3	Lyceum, Strand
February 4	Lyceum, Strand
February 5	Lyceum, Strand
February 6	Lyceum, Strand
February 7	Lyceum, Strand
February 8	Gaumont, Salisbury
February 11	Cecil Theatre, Hull
February 12	Ritz, Wigan
February 13	City Hall, Newcastle
February 14	City Hall, Sheffield
February 15	Regal, Edmonton
February 21	Town Hall, Birmingham
February 22	Gaumont, Cheltenham
February 23	Granada, Kettering
February 24	Granada, Grantham

February 25	Granada, Hansfield
February 26	Granada, East Ham
February 27	Granada, Dartford
February 28	Granada, Tooting
October	Scandinavian tour
	(No further details available)

1960

January 22	The Forum, Montreal
January 23	Community War Memorial Auditorium, Rochester
January 24	Armoury, Pennsylvania
January 25	Maple Leaf Gardens, Toronto
January 26	Kitchner Memorial Auditorium, Kitchner, Ontario
January 27	Indiana Theatre, Indianapolis
January 28	Veteran's Memorial Auditorium, Columbus
January 29	Stanbaugh Auditorium, Youngstown, Ohio
January 30	North Side Gym, Elkhart, Indiana
January 31	Olympia Stadium, Michigan
February 1	Coliseum, Indiana
February 2	Armoury, Kentucky
February 3	Syria Mosque, Pittsburgh
February 4	The Mosque, New Jersey
February 5	Sports Arena, Hershey Pennsylvania
February 6	Municipal Auditorium, Virginia
February 7	The Mosque, Virginia
February 8	Memorial Coliseum, Winston-Salem
February 9	Memorial Auditorium, Greenville
February 10	Coliseum, North Carolina
February 11	Memorial Auditorium, North Carolina
February 12	Township Auditorium, South Carolina
February 13	Will Rogers Memorial Auditorium, Fort Worth, Texas
February 14	Sam Houstone Coliseum, Houston, Texas
February 15	Municipal Auditorium, San Antonio, Texas
February 16	Memorial Auditorium, Dallas, Texas
February 17	Coliseum, Lubbock, Texas

February 18	Municipal Auditorium, Oklahoma City
February 19	The Forum, Wichita, Kansas
February 20	Arena-Civic Auditorium, Kansas City
February 21	Civic Auditorium, Omaha, Nebraska
February 26	Kiel Opera House, St Louis, Missouri
February 27	Mikwaukee Auditorium Arena, Milwaukee
March 22	Royal Albert Hall, London
April 4	Empire, Glasgow
April 5	Empire, Glasgow
April 6	Empire, Glasgow
April 7	Empire, Glasgow
April 8	Empire, Glasgow
April 9	Empire, Glasgow
April 10	Empire, Glasgow
April 11	Theatre, Coventry
April 12	Theatre, Coventry
April 13	Theatre, Coventry
April 14	Theatre, Coventry
April 15	Theatre, Coventry
April 16	Theatre, Coventry
April 17	Opera House, Blackpool
April 18	Lyceum, Sheffield
April 19	Lyceum, Sheffield
April 20	Lyceum, Sheffield
April 21	Lyceum, Sheffield
April 22	Lyceum, Sheffield
April 23	Lyceum, Sheffield
April 24	Lyceum, Sheffield
April 24	Gaumont, Worcester
April 25	Granada, Dover
April 27	Troxy, Portsmouth
April 28	Essoldo, Norwich
April 29	Gaumont, Bradford
April 30	Danilo, Cannick
May 1	Gaumont, Derby
May 2	Lonsdale, Carlisle
May 4	City Hall, Newcastle
May 5	Cecil, Hull
May 6	Odeon, Manchester
May 7	Essoldo, Stoke
May 8	Empire, Liverpool
May 9	Town Hall, Birmingham
May 10	Colston Hall, Bristol
May 11	Savoy, Exeter

May 12	Colston Hall, Bristol
May 13	Regal, Cambridge
May 14	Essoldo, Clacton
May 15	Gaumont, Ipswich
June 30	Palladium, London ('Stars In Your Eyes' – six month run)

1961

February 5	Hippodrome, Birmingham
February 6	Gaumont, Derby
February 7	Globe, Stockton
February 8	Green's, Glasgow
February 9	Usher Hall, Edinburgh
February 10	City Hall, Newcastle
February 11	City Hall, Sheffield
February 12	Empire, Liverpool
February 14	Colston Hall, Bristol
February 15	Gaumont, Cardiff
February 16	Gaumont, Southampton
February 17	Odeon, Southend
February 18	Gaumont, Lewisham
February 19	Gaumont, Ipswich
February 20	Guildhall, Portsmouth
February 21	Gaumont, Wolverhampton
February 22	Gaumont, Doncaster
February 23	Gaumont, Chester
February 24	Rialto, York
February 25	Gaumont, Bradford
February 26	Gaumont, Worcester
March	SOUTH AFRICA/AUSTRALIA/ NEW ZEALAND/SINGAPORE AND MALAYA tour (No further details available)
March 15	Colosseum, Johannesburg
April 9	Empire, Liverpool (2 shows)
April 10	Apollo, Manchester (2 shows)
April 11	ABC, Hull (2 shows)
April 12	City Hall, Newcastle (2 shows)
April 14	Gaumont, Cardiff (2 shows)
April 15	Gaumont, Cheltenham (2 shows)
April 16	Odeon, Plymouth (2 shows)
August 15	Stockholm
August 16	Stockholm

August 17	Tivoli Gardens, Stockholm
August 18	Stockholm
August 19	Furuvik, Sweden
August 21	Stavanger, Norway
August 23	Oslo, Norway
August 28	Opera House, Blackpool (6-week run)
October	Australia/Far East tour
October 19	Sydney
October 20	Sydney
October 21	Sydney
October 22	Sydney
October 25	Melbourne
October 26	Melbourne
October 27	Melbourne

1962

January 21	Liverpool
January 28	Gaumont, Derby
January 29	ABC, Chesterfield
January 30	ABC, Huddersfield
January 31	Lonsdale, Carlisle
February 1	Odeon, Glasgow
February 3	Usher Hall, Edinburgh
February 4	Odeon, Leeds
February 6	Essoldo, Brighton
February 7	Gaumont, Bournemouth
February 8	ABC, Exeter
February 9	ABC, Plymouth
February 10	Gaumont, Lewisham
February 11	Gaumont, Southampton
February 13	ABC, Lincoln
February 14	ABC, Cleethorpes
February 15	City Hall, Sheffield
March 7	ABC Theatre, Kingston (2 shows)
October 25	Memphis
November 1	Houston
November 2	St. Louis
November 3	Detroit
November 6	Toronto
November 7	Buffalo
November 8	New Orleans

1963

January	Port Elizabeth
January	Johannesburg
January	Durban
January	Bulawayo
January	Salisbury
January	Cape Town
February 23	Sophia Gardens, Cardiff
February 24	Birmingham
February 27	Cambridge
February 28	Northampton
March 1	Romford
March 2	Portsmouth
March 3	Plymouth
March 4	Exeter
March 6	Croydon
March 7	ABC, Kingston
March 10	Liverpool
March 11	Newcastle
March 12	Manchester
March 13	Huddersfield
March 14	Carlisle
March 15	Glasgow
March 16	Edinburgh
March 17	Stockton
March 19	Cleethorpes
March 20	Chesterfield
March 21	Lincoln
March 22	Odeon, Leeds
March 23	De Montfort Hall, Leicester
March 24	Gaumont, Ipswich
March 26	ABC, Dover

March 27	ABC, Hastings	May 10	Antwerp
March 28	Odeon, Southend	May 12	Munich
March 29	Gaumont, Watford	May	Stadhalle, Vienna
March 30	Walthamstow	May	Berlin
March 31	Coventry	May 15	Grugahalle, Essen
April 2	Hull	May 19	Olympia, Paris
April 3	York	May 20	Olympia, Paris
April 4	Wolverhampton	May 21	Olympia, Paris
April 5	Cheltenham	May 22	Olympia, Paris
April 6	Astoria, Finsbury Park	May 23	Olympia, Paris
April 7	Brighton	May 24	Olympia, Paris
June–September	ABC, Blackpool (Summer season)	May 25	Olympia, Paris
September 29	Tel Aviv, Israel	May 27	Falkoner Centret, Copenhagen (2 shows)
		June 8	Falkoner Centret, Copenhagen (2 shows)

1964

		October 18	Gaumont, Derby
March 28	ABC, Southampton	October 19	ABC, Luton
March 29	Gaumont, Bournemouth	October 20	ABC, Chesterfield
March 30	Astoria, Finsbury Park	October 21	ABC, Chester
March 31	ABC, Harrow	October 22	Gaumont, Wolverhampton
April 1	ABC, Romford	October 23	Odeon, Southend
April 2	ABC, Kingston	October 24	Colston Hall, Bristol
April 3	ABC, Luton	October 26	Wembley Stadium, London (Charity show)
April 4	Capitol, Cardiff		
April 5	Hippodrome, Birmingham	October 27	ABC, Dublin
April 6	Colston Hall, Bristol	October 28	ABC, Dublin
April 7	ABC, Exeter	October 29	ABC, Belfast
April 8	ABC, Plymouth	October 30	ABC, Belfast
April 9	Gaumont, Cheltenham	October 31	ABC, Wigan
April 11	Guildhall, Portsmouth	November 1	De Montfort Hall, Leicester
April 12	Coventry Theatre, Coventry	November 3	Odeon, Glasgow
April 13	Odeon, Nottingham	November 4	ABC, Edinburgh
April 14	City Hall, Sheffield	November 5	ABC, Stockton
April 15	ABC, Edinburgh	November 6	ABC, Hull
April 16	Odeon, Glasgow	November 10	ABC, Manchester
April 17	City Hall, Newcastle	November 11	ABC, Huddersfield
April 18	ABC, Stockton	November 15	Odeon, Lewisham
April 19	Odeon, Leeds	November 17	ABC, Gloucester
May 5	Amsterdam	November 18	ABC, Exeter
May 6	Scheveningen	November 19	ABC, Plymouth
May 7	Leeuwarden/Blokker	November 20	ABC, Southampton
May 8	Liege	November 21	Odeon, Hanley
May 9	Brussels		

1965

July 7	Frejus
July 8	Vienna
July 9	Biarritz
July 10	Marseilles
July 11	Valbonne
July 12	Casablanca
July 14	Zurich
July 15	Colmar
July 16	Geneva
July 26	Odeon, Southend
July 27	Odeon, Southend
July 28	Odeon, Southend
August 2	Gaumont, Bournemouth
August 3	Gaumont, Bournemouth
August 4	Gaumont, Bournemouth
August 6	Spain/France/Switzerland (Vienna, Marseilles, Casablanca, Zurich, Geneva) (No further details available)
September 2	ABC, Northampton
September 24	ABC, Northampton
September 25	ABC, Northampton
September 26	ABC, Northampton
October 3	Gaumont, Derby
October 11	Roma Theatre, Warsaw
November 10	Odeon, Newcastle
November 11	Odeon, Leeds
November 12	Odeon, Manchester
November 24	Capitol, Cardiff
November 25	Odeon, Cheltenham
November 26	Gaumont, Southampton
December	Lisbon

1966

January 31	Talk Of The Town, London (4-week Cabaret season)
April 3	Empire Pool, Wembley

1967

October	Tokyo

1968

May 13	Talk Of The Town, London (4-week season)
August	Butlins, Clacton (20 Day season)
Sep 19–Dec 14	Palladium, London (Variety season)

1969

March 9–12	Italy
March 21–22	Holland
October 7	Shinjuku Kosei-Nenkin Hall, Tokyo
October 8	Osaka Kosei-Nenkin Hall, Osaka
October 9	Osaka Festival Hall, Osaka
October 11	Kyoto Hall, Kyoto
October 12	Sankei Hall, Tokyo (2 concerts)
October 13	Chuninchi Theatre, Nagoya
November 5	Guildhall, Portsmouth
November 6	Fairfield Hall, Croydon
November 7	Finsbury Park Astoria, London
November 8	Odeon, Birmingham
November 12	City Hall, Newcastle
November 13	City Hall, Sheffield
December 5	Empire, Liverpool (Re-scheduled from November 14)
December 20	Odeon, Manchester (Re-sheduled from November 15)

1970

April 6	Batley Variety Club, Yorkshire
April 7	Batley Variety Club, Yorkshire
April 8	Batley Variety Club, Yorkshire
April 9	Batley Variety Club, Yorkshire
April 10	Batley Variety Club, Yorkshire
April 11	Batley Variety Club, Yorkshire
April 12	Batley Variety Club, Yorkshire

June 11–12	Romania & Czechoslovakia
	(No further details available)
September 28	Talk Of The Town London
	(4-week season)
November 11	Odeon, Newcastle
November 12	ABC, Stockton
November 13	ABC, Hull
November 14	Odeon, Manchester
November 18	Odeon, Birmingham
November 19	Capitol, Cardiff
November 20	Winter Gardens, Bournemouth
November 21	Odeon, London

1971

March 26	De Doelen, Rotterdam
March 27	Falkoner Centret, Copenhagen
March 28	Concertgebouw, Amsterdam
March 29	Kuppelsaal, Hannover
March 30	Stadthalle, Bremen
March 31	Meistersingerhalle, Nurnberg
April 1	Deutsches Museum, Munchen
April 2	Sportpalast, Berlin
April 3	Jahrhunderthalle, Frankfurt
April 4	Musikhalle, Hamburg
April 5	Liederhalle, Stuttgart
April 6	Vienna
April 7	Zurich
April 8	Antwerp
June 13	Palladium, London
	(A Night With The Stars)
September	Fiesta, Stockton
September 20	Fiesta, Sheffield
September 21	Fiesta, Sheffield
September 22	Fiesta, Sheffield
September 23	Fiesta, Sheffield
September 24	Fiesta, Sheffield
September 25	Fiesta, Sheffield
September 26	Fiesta, Sheffield
October 11–30	Palladium, London (Season)
November 17	ABC, Gloucester
November 18	Capitol, Cardiff
November 19	Gaumont, Hanley
November 20	Odeon, Derby

November 22	The Dome, Brighton
November 24	Winter Gardens, Bournemouth
November 26	Empire, Liverpool
November 29	Fairfield Hall, Croydon
November 30	Guildhall, Portsmouth
December 1	New Theatre, Oxford
December 2	New Theatre, Oxford
December 3	Odeon, Birmingham

1972

September 5	Istora Senayan, Djakarta
September 14	Festival Hall, Osaka
September 15	Festival Hall, Osaka
September 16	Aichi Bunkakaikan Hall, Nagoya
September 18	Kaikan Hall, Kyoto
September 20	Kawasaki Sangyo Kaikan Hall,
	Kanagawa
September 21	Shinjuku Kosei-Nenkin Hall, Tokyo
September 22	Shinjuku Kosei-Nenkin Hall, Tokyo
September 23	Shinjuku Kosei-Nenkin Hall, Tokyo
September 24	Shibuya Public Hall, Tokyo
September 30	Falkoner Centret, Copenhagen
	(2 shows)
October 18	New Theatre, Oxford
October 19	Theatre Royal, Nottingham
October 20	Theatre Royal, Nottingham
October 21	Odeon, Birmingham
October 25	Philharmonic, Liverpool
October 26	Floral Hall, Southport
October 27	Odeon, Manchester
October 28	City Hall, Sheffield
November 1	City Hall, Newcastle
November 2	Gaumont, Wolverhampton
November 3	Odeon, Cheltenham
November 4	Gaumont, Hanley
November 8	Odeon, Edinburgh
November 9	Caird Hall, Dundee
November 10	Kelvin Hall, Glasgow
November 11	Kelvin Hall, Glasgow
November 13	Guildhall, Portsmouth
November 14	Colston Hall, Bristol
November 17	Fairfield Hall, Croydon
November 18	Winter Gardens, Bournemouth

November 23	ABC, Stockton
November 24	Gaumont, Doncaster
November 25	Gaumont, Derby
November 30	Gaumont, Ipswich
December 1	ABC, Peterborough
December 2	ABC, Peterborough
December 11	Batley Variety Club, Yorkshire
December 12	Batley Variety Club, Yorkshire
December 13	Batley Variety Club, Yorkshire
December 14	Batley Variety Club, Yorkshire
December 15	Batley Variety Club, Yorkshire
December 16	Batley Variety Club, Yorkshire
December 17	Batley Variety Club, Yorkshire
December 18	Batley Variety Club, Yorkshire
December 19	Batley Variety Club, Yorkshire
December 20	Batley Variety Club, Yorkshire
December 21	Batley Variety Club, Yorkshire
December 22	Batley Variety Club, Yorkshire
December 23	Batley Variety Club, Yorkshire

1973

January	Talk Of The Town, London (3-week season)
September 17	Royal Festival Hall, London
September 27	Birmingham
September 28	Central Hall, Chatham
September 30	Falconer Theatre, Copehagen
October 6	Ipswich
October 11	Odeon, Manchester
October 12	Floral Hall, Southport
October 13	Floral Hall, Southport
November 14	Apollo Theatre, Glasgow
November 15	Caird Hall, Dundee
November 16	Odeon, Edinburgh
November 17	Odeon, Edinburgh
November 19	Dome, Brighton
November 22	Fairfield Hall, Croydon
November 23	Gaumont, Southampton
November 27	Lakeside Country Club, Camberley
November 28	Lakeside Country Club, Camberley
November 29	Lakeside Country Club, Camberley
November 30	Lakeside Country Club, Camberley
December 1	Lakeside Country Club, Camberley

December 3	The Golden Garter, Manchester
December 4	The Golden Garter, Manchester
December 5	The Golden Garter, Manchester
December 6	The Golden Garter, Manchester
December 7	The Golden Garter, Manchester
December 8	The Golden Garter, Manchester
December 10	Fiesta Club, Sheffield
December 11	Fiesta Club, Sheffield
December 12	Fiesta Club, Sheffield
December 13	Fiesta Club, Sheffield
December 14	Fiesta Club, Sheffield
December 15	Fiesta Club, Sheffield

1974

March 31	Lakeside Country Club, Surrey
April 17	Palladium, London
October 5	Sun Plaza Hall, Tokyo
October 7	Kosei Nenkin Hall, Tokyo
October 8	Kosei Nenkin Hall, Tokyo
October 9	Sumpu Kaikan, Shizuoka
October 10	Festival Hall, Osaka
October 11	Festival Hall, Osaka
October 12	Yubin Chokin Hall, Hiroshima
October 13	Shimin Kaikan Hall, Fukuoka
October 14	Kaikan Hall, Kyoto
October 15	Bunka Tailiku-kan, Yohohama
October 27	Palladium, London (Benefit Gala)
November 7	Odeon Theatre, Birmingham
November 8	Colston Hall, Bristol
November 9	Central Hall, Chatham
November 13	Double Diamond Club, Caerphilly
November 14	Double Diamond Club, Caerphilly
November 15	Double Diamond Club, Caerphilly
November 16	Double Diamond Club, Caerphilly
November 20	New Theatre, Oxford
November 21	New Theatre, Oxford
November 22	New Theatre, Southport
November 23	New Theatre, Southport
November 27	Guildhall, Portsmouth
November 28	Fairfield Hall, Croydon
November 29	Congress Theatre, Eastbourne
November 30	Winder Gardens, Bournemouth
December 4	City Hall, Sheffield

December 5	De Montfort Hall, Leicester	November 14	New Theatre, Southport
December 6	Talk of the Midlands, Derby	November 15	New Theatre, Southport
December 7	City Hall, St. Albans	November 18	Coventry Theatre, Coventry
December 11	Free Trade Hall, Manchester	November 19	Fiesta Club, Sheffield
December 12	Town Hall, Leeds	November 20	Fiesta Club, Sheffield
December 13	Empire Theatre, Sunderland	November 21	Fiesta Club, Sheffield
December 14	City Hall, Hull	November 22	Empire Theatre, Sunderland
December 19	Odeon, Hammersmith		
December 20	Odeon, Hammersmith		
December 21	Odeon, Hammersmith		

1975

October 31	Central Hall, Chatham
November 1	Gaumont Theatre, Ipswich
November 5	De Montfort Hall, Leicester
November 6	Talk Of The Midlands, Derby
November 7	Fairfield Hall, Croydon
November 8	Winter Gardens, Bournemouth
November 12	Civic Theatre, Halifax
November 13	New Theatre, Southport

1976

April 3	Tivoli's Koncertsal, Copenhagen (2 shows)
April 5	Hamburger Bors, Stockholm
April 6	Hamburger Bors, Stockholm
April 7	Hamburger Bors, Stockholm
April 8	Hamburger Bors, Stockholm
April 9	Hamburger Bors, Stockholm
April 10	Scandinavian Stadium, Gothenburg
April 11	Herning Hallen, Herning
April 12	Fyens Forum, Odense
June 21	Sun Plaza Hall, Tokyo

June 22	Kaikan, Kyoto
June 23	Kokusai Kaikan, Kobe
June 24	Shimin Kaikan, Fukuoka
June 25	Mainichi Hall, Osaka
June 26	Kosei Nenkin Hall, Tokyo
June 27	Kenmin Hall, Yokohama
June 29	Kosei Nenkin Hall, Sapporo
June 30	Kenmin Kaikan, Sendai-Miyagi
July 1	Kokaido Shibuya, Tokyo
July 2	Kanko Kaikan, Kanazawa
July 3	Kenmin Kaikan, Niigata
July 12	New York
July 14	Boston
July 15	Dallas
July 16	Atlanta
July 19	Detroit
July 20	Chicago
July 21	Los Angeles
July 22	Los Angeles
October 22	Odeon, Birmingham
October 23	Odeon, Birmingham
October 27	Cliff's Pavilion, Southend
October 28	Fairfield Hall, Croydon
October 29	Fairfield Hall, Croydon
October 30	Winter Gardens, Bournemouth
November 3	Free Trade Hall, Manchester
November 4	New Theatre, Southport
November 5	New Theatre, Southport
November 6	Civic Theatre, Halifax
November 10	Coventry Theatre, Coventry
November 11	Coventry Theatre, Coventry
November 12	Grand Theatre, Leeds
November 13	Grand Theatre, Leeds
November 17	Jollees Club, Stock-on-Trent
November 18	Jollees Club, Stock-on-Trent
November 19	Jollees Club, Stock-on-Trent
November 20	Jollees Club, Stock-on-Trent
November 22	Royal Albert Hall, London
November 25	Usher Hall, Edinburgh
November 26	Apollo Theatre, Glasgow
November 27	Apollo Theatre, Glasgow
December 7	Kalamandir Auditorium, New Delhi
December 8	Kalamandir Auditorium, New Delhi

1977

May 2–25	Australasia tour
May 13	Regent Theatre, Sydney
May 14	Regent Theatre, Sydney
May 17	Regent Theatre, Sydney
September 9	Vejlby Riiskov Hallen, Aarhus
September 10	Thyhall, Thisted
September 11	Tivoli's Koncertstal, Copenhagen (2 shows)
September 13	Congresscentrum, Hamburg
September 14	Philipshalle, Dusseldorf
September 15	Congresgebouw, Den Haag
September 16	Philipsszaal, Eindhoven
September 17	Kon Elizabeth Zaal, Antwerp
September 19	Olympia, Paris
September 21	Jahrhunderthalle, Frankfurt
September 22	Zirkus Krone, Munich
November 9	Gaumont, Southampton
November 11	Odeon, Birmingham
November 12	Odeon, Birmingham
November 16	Town Hall, Middlesborough
November 17	Apollo Theatre, Glasgow
November 18	Apollo Theatre, Glasgow
November 19	Apollo Theatre, Glasgow
November 23	New Theatre, Oxford
November 24	Fairfield Hall, Croydon
November 25	Fairfield Hall, Croydon
November 26	Winter Gardens, Bournemouth
December 1	Apollo Theatre, Manchester
December 2	New Theatre, Southport
December 3	Opera House, Blackpool
December 5	Royal Albert Hall, London
December 7	Closton Hall, Bristol
December 8	De Montfort Hall, Leicester
December 9	Cliff's Pavilion, Southend
December 10	Cliff's Pavilion, Southend
December 12	Town Hall, Watford

1978

March 11	Palladium, London
March 15	Film Trust Arena, Johannesburg

March 16	Film Trust Arena, Johannesburg		October 2	Halle Munsterland, Munster
March 17	Film Trust Arena, Johannesburg		October 3	Mozartsaal, Mannheim
May 12	Hong Kong Stadium, Hong Kong		October 4	Eilenriedehalle, Hannover
May 13	Hong Kong Stadium, Hong Kong		October 5	Liederhalle, Stuttgart
May 14	Hong Kong Stadium, Hong Kong		October 6	Philipshalle, Dusseldorf
May 18	Regent Theatre, Sydney		October 8	Maintalhalle, Wurzburg
May 19	Regent Theatre, Sydney		October 9	Circus Krone, Munchen
May 20	Festival Hall, Brisbane		October 12	Koningin Elisabeth Zaal, Antwerp
May 22	Canberra Theatre, Canberra		October 13	Doelen, Rotterdam
May 23	Canberra Theatre, Canberra		October 14	Jaap Edenhal, Amsterdam
May 25	Festival Hall, Melbourne		October 15	Meistersingerhalle, Nurnberg
May 27	Apollo Stadium, Adelaide		October 16	ICC, Berlin
May 29	Entertainment Centre, Perth		October 17	Stadthalle, Braunschweig
November 1	Gaumont Theatre, Southampton		October 18	Grugahalle, Essen
November 3	Odeon Theatre, Birmingham		October 19	Congresscentrum, Hamburg
November 4	Odeon Theatre, Birmingham		October 20	Stadthalle, Bremen
November 8	Usher Hall, Edinburgh		October 21	Eurogress, Aachen
November 9	Usher Hall, Edinburgh		October 22	Sporthalle, Koln
November 10	Town Hall, Middlesbrough		October 23	Jahrhunderthalle, Frankfurt
November 11	Town Hall, Middlesbrough		November 1	New Theatre, Oxford
November 15	City Hall, Sheffield		November 2	New Theatre, Oxford
November 16	City Hall, Sheffield		November 3	New Theatre, Oxford
November 17	New Theatre, Oxford		November 6	Odeon, Birmingham
November 18	Centre, Brighton		November 7	Odeon, Birmingham
November 22	De Montfort Hall, Leicester		November 8	Odeon, Birmingham
November 23	Colston Hall, Bristol		November 9	Empire, Liverpool
November 24	Winter Gardens, Bournemouth		November 10	Empire, Liverpool
November 25	Winter Gardens, Bournemouth		November 14	Cliff's Pavilion, Southend
November 29	Fairfield Hall, Croydon		November 15	Cliff's Pavilion, Southend
November 30	Fairfield Hall, Croydon		November 16	Winter Gardens, Bournemouth
December 1	Cliff's Pavilion, Southend		November 17	Winter Gardens, Bournemouth
December 2	Cliff's Pavilion, Southend		November 22	Apollo, Glasgow
December 6	Apollo Theatre, Manchester		November 23	Apollo, Glasgow
December 7	Apollo Theatre, Manchester		November 24	Apollo, Glasgow
December 8	Opera House, Blackpool		November 28	De Montfort Hall, Leicester
December 9	Opera House, Blackpool		November 29	De Montfort Hall, Leicester
December 11	Royal Albert Hall, London		November 30	The Centre, Brighton
December 12	Dominion Theatre, London		December 1	The Centre, Brighton
December 13	Trentham Gardens, Stoke		December 5	Apollo, Manchester

1979

			December 6	Apollo, Manchester
			December 7	Apollo, Manchester
May 14–26	Palladium, London		December 13	Odeon, Hammersmith
October 1	Cologne, Germany		December 14	Odeon, Hammersmith
			December 16	Odeon, Hammersmith
			December 18	The Theatre, Coventry

1980

February 20	City Hall, Durban
February 21	City Hall, Durban
February 22	City Hall, Durban
February 23	City Hall, Durban
February 25	Feathermarket Hall, Port Elizabeth
February 26	Feathermarket Hall, Port Elizabeth
February 28	Three Arts Theatre, Cape Town
February 29	Three Arts Theatre, Cape Town
March 1	Three Arts Theatre, Cape Town
March 5	Colosseum Theatre, Johannesburg
March 6	Colosseum Theatre, Johannesburg
March 7	Colosseum Theatre, Johannesburg
March 8	Colosseum Theatre, Johannesburg
March 10	Colosseum Theatre, Johannesburg
March 11	Colosseum Theatre, Johannesburg
September 5	Brondby Hallen, Copenhagen
October 14	Apollo Theatre, London
October 15	Apollo Theatre, London
October 16	Apollo Theatre, London
October 17	Apollo Theatre, London
October 18	Apollo Theatre, London

1981

March 3	Paramount Theatre, Seattle
March 4	Royal Theatre, Victoria
March 5	Q.E. Theatre
March 7	Jubilee Auditorium, Calgary
March 8	Jubilee Auditorium, Edmonton
March 9	Centre of the Arts, Regina
March 10	Centre of the Arts, Regina
March 11	Centennial Auditorium, Winnipeg
March 12	Centennial Auditorium, Winnipeg
March 15	Guthrie Theatre, Minneapolis
March 17	Chester Fritz Auditorium, Grand Forks
March 19	Ft. Williams Gardens
March 20	The Gardens, Sault St. Marie
March 21	Arena, Sudbury
March 23	National Arts Centre, Ottawa
March 24	Hamilton Place, Hamilton

March 26	Arena, Kingston
March 27	Circle In The Square, Kitchener
March 28	Alumni Hall, London
March 30	O'Keefe Centre, Totonto
March 31	St. Dennis Theatre, Montreal
April 2	Savoy, New York
April 3	Emerald City, Philadelphia
April 4	Painters Mill, Baltimore
April 6	Front Row, Cleveland
April 7	Palace, Cincinatti
April 8	Palace Theatre, Columbus
April 9	Park West, Chicago
April 10	PAC Centre, Milwaukee
April 12	Uptown Theatre, Kansas City
April 14	Rainbow Theatre, Denver
April 15	Kinsbury Hall, Salt Lake City
April 17	Foxwarfield, San Francisco
April 18	Santa Monica Civil Auditorium, Los Angeles
November 2	Apollo, Glasgow
November 3	Apollo, Glasgow
November 4	Apollo, Glasgow
November 5	Playhouse, Edinburgh
November 6	Playhouse, Edinburgh
November 7	Playhouse, Edinburgh
November 11	Apollo, Manchester
November 12	Apollo, Manchester
November 13	Apollo, Manchester
November 14	Apollo, Manchester
November 18	Centre, Brighton
November 19	Centre, Brighton
November 20	Centre, Brighton
November 21	Centre, Brighton
November 25	Odeon, Birmingham
November 26	Odeon, Birmingham
November 27	Odeon, Birmingham
November 28	Odeon, Birmingham
December 2	Hammersmith Odeon, London
December 3	Hammersmith Odeon, London
December 4	Hammersmith Odeon, London
December 5	Hammersmith Odeon, London
December 9	Winter Gardens, Bournemouth
December 10	Winter Gardens, Bournemouth
December 11	Winter Gardens, Bournemouth
December 12	Winter Gardens, Bournemouth

December 16	Coliseum, St. Austell
December 17	Coliseum, St. Austell
December 18	Coliseum, St. Austell
December 19	Coliseum, St. Austell

1982

February 1	Blazers, Windsor
February 2	Blazers, Windsor
February 3	Blazers, Windsor
February 4	Blazers, Windsor
February 5	Blazers, Windsor
February 6	Blazers, Windsor
February 12	Queen Elizabeth Hall, Hong Kong
February 13	Queen Elizabeth Hall, Hong Kong
February 15	Hua Mark Stadium, Bangkok
February 16	Hua Mark Stadium, Bangkok
February 18	Negara Stadium, Kuala Lumpur
February 19	Singapore
February 22	Entertainment Centre, Perth
February 24	Apollo Stadium, Adelaide
February 25	Apollo Stadium, Adelaide
February 27	Festival Hall, Melbourne
February 28	Festival Hall, Melbourne
March 3	Festival Hall, Brisbane
March 5	Horden Pavilion, Sydney
March 6	Horden Pavilion, Sydney
March 9	Town Hall, Christchurch
March 10	Town Hall, Christchurch
March 12	Logan Campbell Centre, Auckland
March 13	Logan Campbell Centre, Auckland
March 15	The Country Club, Los Angeles
March 16	The Country Club, Los Angeles
March 17	New York
March 18	New York
July 10	Concord, San Francisco
July 12	The Greek, Los Angeles
July 13	Queen Elizabeth Centre, Vancouver
July 15	Coliseum, Edmonton
July 16	Sportsplex, Lethbridge
July 17	Centre Of The Arts, Regina
July 18	Centennial Auditorium, Saskatoon
July 19	Centennial Auditorium, Saskatoon

July 21	Playhouse Theatre, Winnipeg
July 22	Playhouse Theatre, Winnipeg
July 25	Alumni Hall, London
July 26	O'Keefe Centre, Toronto
July 27	Camp Fortune, Ottawa
July 28	Place Des Arts, Montreal
July 29	Centre In The Square, Kitchener
July 30	Hamilton Place, Hamilton
October 10	Hannover
October 11	Berlin
October 12	Hamburg
October 13	Vejlby Riiskov Hallen, Aarhus
October 14	Aalborg Hallen, Aalborg
October 16	Helsinki
October 18	Oslo
October 19	Falkoner Theatre, Copenhagen
October 20	Falkoner Theatre, Copenhagen
October 22	Rotterdam
October 23	Essen
October 24	Mozartsaal, Manheim
October 26	Frankfurt
October 27	Frankfurt
October 28	Munich
October 30	Brussels
October 31	Dusseldorf
November 1	Munster
November 23	Royal Albert Hall, London

1983

January 20	Blazers, Windsor
January 21	Blazers, Windsor
January 22	Blazers, Windsor
January 23	Blazers, Windsor
January 24	Blazers, Windsor
January 25	Blazers, Windsor
January 26	Blazers, Windsor
February 3	National Theatre, Singapore
February 4	National Theatre, Singapore
February 6	Welfare Centre, Bangkok
February 7	Welfare Centre, Bangkok
February 9	A C Hall, Hong Kong
February 10	A C Hall, Hong Kong
February 11	A C Hall, Hong Kong

February 13	Manila Hotel, Manila
February 14	Manila Hotel, Manila
February 15	Folks Art Centre, Manila
February 18	Festival Hall, Melbourne
February 19	Festival Hall, Melbourne
February 20	Festival Hall, Melbourne
February 21	Festival Hall, Melbourne
February 23	Bruce Stadium, Canberra
February 24	Bruce Stadium, Canberra
February 26	Festival Hall, Brisbane
February 27	Festival Hall, Brisbane
March 1	Horden Pavillion, Sydney
March 2	Horden Pavillion, Sydney
March 3	Horden Pavillion, Sydney
March 4	Horden Pavillion, Sydney
March 7	Apollo Stadium, Adelaide
March 8	Apollo Stadium, Adelaide
March 9	Apollo Stadium, Adelaide
March 12	Entertainment Centre, Perth
March 13	Entertainment Centre, Perth
April 9	Lisbon, Portugal
April 13	Barcelona, Spain
April 15	Stuttgart, Germany
April 16	Hof, Germany
April 19	Grughalle, Essen, Germany
April 20	Siegen, Germany
April 22	Malmo, Sweden
April 23	Gothenburg, Sweden
April 26	Rotterdam, Holland
April 27	Antwerp, Holland
April 28	Brussels, Belgium
October 5	Apollo, Oxford
October 6	Apollo, Oxford
October 7	Apollo, Oxford
October 8	Apollo, Oxford
October 11	Apollo, Glasgow
October 12	Apollo, Glasgow
October 14	Playhouse, Edinburgh
October 15	Playhouse, Edinburgh
October 19	Apollo, Manchester
October 20	Apollo, Manchester
October 21	Apollo, Manchester
October 22	Apollo, Manchester
October 26	Odeon, Birmingham
October 27	Odeon, Birmingham

October 28	Odeon, Birmingham
October 29	Odeon, Birmingham
Nov 3–Dec 10	Apollo, Victoria, London
(ex. Sundays)	

1984

July 2	Wembley Arena, London
July 3	Wembley Arena, London
July 4	Wembley Arena, London
July 5	Wembley Arena, London
July 7	N.E.C., Birmingham
July 8	N.E.C., Birmingham
July 9	N.E.C., Birmingham
July 10	N.E.C., Birmingham
July 11	N.E.C., Birmingham
October 8	Blazers, Windsor
October 9	Blazers, Windsor
October 10	Blazers, Windsor
October 11	Blazers, Windsor
October 12	Blazers, Windsor
October 13	Blazers, Windsor
October 20	Amphitheatre, Darwin
October 25	Entertainment Centre, Perth
October 26	Entertainment Centre, Perth
October 30	The Showgrounds, Cairns
October 31	The Showrounds, Townsville
November 2	The Showground, Mackay
November 3	Musicbowl, Rockhampton
November 5	Festival Hall, Brisbane
November 6	Festival Hall, Brisbane
November 9	Entertainment Centre, Sydney
November 10	Entertainment Centre, Sydney
November 12	Bruce Stadium, Canberra
November 13	Bruce Stadium, Canberra
November 14	Entertainment Centre, Melbourne
November 15	Entertainment Centre, Melbourne
November 16	Entertainment Centre, Melbourne
November 18	Apollo Stadium, Adelaide
November 19	Apollo Stadium, Adelaide
November 20	Apollo Stadium, Adelaide
November 21	Apollo Stadium, Adelaide
November 24	Mount Smart, Auckland
November 26	Michael Fowler Centre, Wellington

| November 27 | Michael Fowler Centre, Wellington |

1985

October 4	Grugahalle, Essen
October 5	Forest National, Brussels
October 7	Ahoy, Rotterdam
October 8	Munsterlandhalle, Munster
October 9	Stadthalle, Bremen
October 10	Herninghalle, Herning
October 11	Vejlby-Risskov Halle, Aarhus
October 13	Concert House, Stockholm
October 15	Ice Hall, Helsinki
October 17	Drammen Hall, Oslo
October 18	Falkoner Theatre, Copenhagen
October 19	Falkoner Theatre, Copenhagen
October 20	Falkoner Theatre, Copenhagen
October 21	Aalborg Hall, Aalbórg
October 23	CCH, Hamburg
October 24	CCH, Hamburg
October 25	Jahrhunderthalle, Frankfurt
October 26	Jahrhunderthalle, Frankfurt
October 28	Sporthalle, Cologne
October 29	Stadion Sporthalle, Hanover
November 5	Hammersmith Odeon, London
November 6	Hammersmith Odeon, London
November 7	Hammersmith Odeon, London
November 8	Hammersmith Odeon, London
November 9	Hammersmith Odeon, London
November 13	Apollo Theatre, Manchester
November 14	Apollo Theatre, Manchester
November 15	Apollo Theatre, Manchester
November 16	Apollo Theatre, Manchester
November 20	Playhouse, Edinburgh
November 21	Playhouse, Edinburgh
November 22	Playhouse, Edinburgh
November 23	Playhouse, Edinburgh
November 27	Centre, Brighton
November 28	Centre, Brighton
November 29	Centre, Brighton
November 30	Centre, Brighton
December 4	International Centre, Bournemouth
December 5	International Centre, Bournemouth
December 6	International Centre, Bournemouth
December 7	International Centre, Bournemouth
December 10	N.E.C., Birmingham
December 11	N.E.C., Birmingham
December 12	N.E.C., Birmingham
December 13	N.E.C., Birmingham
December 14	N.E.C., Birmingham

1987

September 25	Wimbledon Theatre, London
September 26	Wimbledon Theatre, London
September 27	Wimbledon Theatre, London
September 28	Wimbledon Theatre, London
October 1	Berlin
October 2	Stadhalle, Wolfsburg
October 4	C.C.H, Hamburg
October 5	C.C.H, Hamburg
October 6	Kuppelsaal, Hanover
October 8	Stadthalle, Bremen
October 9	Grugahalle, Essen
October 10	Forest National, Brussels
October 12	De Doelen, Rotterdam
October 13	De Doelen, Rotterdam
October 15	Halle Munsterland, Munster
October 17	Sporthalle, Cologne
October 18	Mozartsaal, Mannheim
October 19	Stadthalle, Karlsruhe
October 20	Saarlandhalle, Saarbrucken
October 22	Siegerlandhalle, Siegen
October 24	Festhalle, Frankfurt
October 25	Hallen Stadion, Zurich
October 26	Stadthalle, Freiburg
October 28	Oberschwabenhalle, Ravensburg
October 29	Deutsches Museum, Munich
October 30	Deutsches Museum, Munich
October 31	Stadthalle, Vienna
November 2	Hall Spodek, Katowice
November 3	Hall Spodek, Katowice
November 4	Sporthall, Budapest
November 5	Sporthall, Budapest
November 6	Sporthall, Budapest
November 8	Hala Tivoli, Ljubliana
November 9	Dom Sportova, Zagreb
November 10	Hala Pionir, Belgrade

November 13	Carl Diem Hall, Wurzburg	March 2	Entertainment Centre, Sydney
November 14	Eissporthalle, Kassel	March 5	Velodrome, Launceston
November 15	Stadthalle, Osnabruck	March 6	KGV Stadium, Hobart
November 18	Grieghall, Bergen	March 9	Entertainment Centre, Melbourne
November 19	Drammens Hall, Oslo	March 10	Entertainment Centre, Melbourne
November 20	Liseberg Hall, Gothenburg	March 11	Entertainment Centre, Melbourne
November 21	Solna Hall, Stockholm	March 12	Bruce Stadium, Canberra
November 23	Ice Hal, Helsinki	March 13	Bruce Stadium, Canberra
November 25	Valby Hall, Copenhagen	March 17	Dean Park, Townsville
November 26	Valby Hall, Copenhagen	March 19	Amphitheatre, Darwin
November 27	Aalborg Hall, Aalborg	May 8	Skedsmo Hall, Oslo
November 28	Skive Hall, Skive	May 9	Valby Hall, Copenhagen
November 30	Herning Hall, Herning	May 10	Fyns Forum, Odense
December 1	Vejlby Risskov Hall, Aarhus	May 11	Cologne
December 2	Vejlby Risskov Hall, Aarhus	May 12	Cologne
December 8	N.E.C., Birmingham	May 13	Ahoy, Rotterdam
December 9	N.E.C., Birmingham	May 14	Eberthalle, Ludwigshafen
December 10	N.E.C., Birmingham	May 15	Schleyerhalle, Stuttgart
December 11	N.E.C., Birmingham	May 16	Frankenhalle, Nurenburg
December 12	N.E.C., Birmingham	May 17	Philipshalle, Dusseldorf
		May 18	CCH, Hamburg

1988

		May 21	Ostseehalle, Kiel
		May 22	Fyns Forum, Odense
February 2	Logan Campbell Centre, Auckland	September 25	R.D.S., Dublin
February 3	Logan Campbell Centre, Auckland	September 26	R.D.S., Dublin
February 4	Logan Campbell Centre, Auckland	September 27	R.D.S., Dublin
February 6	Michael Fowler Centre, Wellington	September 29	King's Hall, Belfast
February 7	Michael Fowler Centre, Wellington	September 30	King's Hall, Belfast
February 8	Michael Fowler Centre, Wellington	October 1	King's Hall, Belfast
February 9	Michael Fowler Centre, Wellington	October 4	Hammersmith Odeon, London
February 10	Town Hall, Christchurch	October 5	Hammersmith Odeon, London
February 11	Town Hall, Christchurch	October 6	Hammersmith Odeon, London
February 12	Town Hall, Christchurch	October 7	Hammersmith Odeon, London
February 13	Town Hall, Christchurch	October 8	Hammersmith Odeon, London
February 14	Town Hall, Christchurch	October 11	City Hall, Sheffield
February 16	Entertainment Centre, Perth	October 12	City Hall, Sheffield
February 17	Entertainment Centre, Perth	October 13	City Hall, Sheffield
February 20	Apollo Stadium, Adelaide	October 14	City Hall, Sheffield
February 21	Apollo Stadium, Adelaide	October 19	Playhouse, Edinburgh
February 22	Apollo Stadium, Adelaide	October 20	Playhouse, Edinburgh
February 23	Apollo Stadium, Adelaide	October 21	Playhouse, Edinburgh
February 26	Entertainment Centre, Brisbane	October 22	Playhouse, Edinburgh
February 27	Entertainment Centre, Brisbane	October 26	Apollo, Manchester
March 1	Entertainment Centre, Sydney	October 27	Apollo, Manchester
		October 28	Apollo, Manchester

October 29	Apollo, Manchester		November 30	Conference Centre, Brighton
November 2	Newport Centre, Newport		December 1	Conference Centre, Brighton
November 3	Newport Centre, Newport		December 2	Conference Centre, Brighton
November 4	Newport Centre, Newport		December 3	Conference Centre, Brighton
November 5	Newport Centre, Newport		December 7	N.E.C., Birmingham
November 9	Coliseum, St Austell		December 8	N.E.C., Birmingham
November 10	Coliseum, St Austell		December 9	N.E.C., Birmingham
November 11	Coliseum, St Austell		December 10	N.E.C., Birmingham
November 12	Coliseum, St Austell			
November 16	Bournemouth International Centre, Bournemouth			

1989

November 17	Bournemouth International Centre, Bournemouth		April 18	Caesar's Palace, Luton
November 18	Bournemouth International Centre, Bournemouth		April 19	Caesar's Palace, Luton
			April 20	Caesar's Palace, Luton
November 19	Bournemouth International Centre, Bournemouth		April 21	Caesar's Palace, Luton
			April 22	Caesar's Palace, Luton
November 23	Empire, Liverpool		April 25	Savvas Club, Usk
November 24	Empire, Liverpool		April 26	Savvas Club, Usk
November 25	Empire, Liverpool		April 27	Savvas Club, Usk
November 26	Empire, Liverpool		April 28	Savvas Club, Usk

April 29	Savvas Club, Usk
May 2	Blazers, Windsor
May 3	Blazers, Windsor
May 4	Blazers, Windsor
May 5	Blazers, Windsor
May 6	Blazers, Windsor
May 9	Blazers, Windsor
May 10	Blazers, Windsor
May 11	Blazers, Windsor
May 12	Blazers, Windsor
May 13	Blazers, Windsor
June 16	Wembley Stadium, London
June 17	Wembley Stadium, London

1990

February 3	Michael Fowler Centre, Wellington
February 4	Michael Fowler Centre, Wellington
February 5	Michael Fowler Centre, Wellington
February 6	Michael Fowler Centre, Wellington
February 7	Michael Fowler Centre, Wellington
February 8	Michael Fowler Centre, Wellington
February 9	Michael Fowler Centre, Wellington
February 12	Logan Cambell Centre, Auckland
February 13	Logan Cambell Centre, Auckland
February 14	Logan Cambell Centre, Auckland
February 15	Logan Cambell Centre, Auckland
February 16	Logan Cambell Centre, Auckland
February 17	Logan Cambell Centre, Auckland
February 20	Town Hall, Christchurch
February 21	Town Hall, Christchurch
February 22	Town Hall, Christchurch
February 23	Town Hall, Christchurch
February 25	Town Hall, Dunedin
February 26	Town Hall, Dunedin
February 27	Town Hall, Dunedin
March 3	Entertainment Centre, Perth
March 4	Entertainment Centre, Perth
March 7	Apollo Stadium, Adelaide
March 8	Apollo Stadium, Adelaide
March 9	Apollo Stadium, Adelaide
March 10	Apollo Stadium, Adelaide
March 13	Tennis Centre, Melbourne
March 14	Tennis Centre, Melbourne

March 17	Derwent Entertainment Centre, Hobart
March 18	Silverdome, Launceston
March 21	Entertainment Centre, Sydney
March 22	Entertainment Centre, Sydney
March 24	Canberra
March 25	Canberra
March 27	Entertainment Centre, Brisbane
March 28	Entertainment Centre, Brisbane
March 31	Amphitheatre, Darwin
May 1	Ice Hall, Helsinki
May 3	Globe, Stockholm
May 5	Fyens Forum, Odense
May 6	Vejlby Riiskov Hallen, Aarhus
May 7	Cirkelhallen, Herning
May 9	Valby Hallen, Copenhagen
May 10	Valby Hallen, Copenhagen
May 11	Valby Hallen, Copenhagen
May 15	Eilenriedehalle, Hanover
May 16	Munsterlandhalle, Munster
May 17	Ostseehalle, Kiev
May 19	Vorst National, Brussels
May 20	Ahoy, Rotterdam
May 22	Philipshalle, Dusseldorf
May 27	Teatro Smeraldo, Milan
May 29	Schleyerhalle, Stuttgart
May 30	Festhalle, Frankfurt
May 31	Olympiahalle, Munich
June 1	Stadthalle, Vienna
June 3	Sporthalle, Linz
June 5	Hallenstadion, Zurich
June 7	Zenith, Paris
June 30	Knebworth
November 1	N.E.C., Birmingham
November 2	N.E.C., Birmingham
November 3	N.E.C., Birmingham
November 5	N.E.C., Birmingham
November 6	N.E.C., Birmingham
November 7	N.E.C., Birmingham
November 9	N.E.C., Birmingham
November 10	N.E.C., Birmingham
November 11	N.E.C., Birmingham
November 13	N.E.C., Birmingham
November 14	N.E.C., Birmingham
November 15	N.E.C., Birmingham
November 17	Exhibition Centre, Aberdeen

November 18	Exhibition Centre, Aberdeen
November 19	Exhibition Centre, Aberdeen
November 20	Exhibition Centre, Aberdeen
November 21	Exhibition Centre, Aberdeen
November 22	Exhibition Centre, Aberdeen
November 28	N.E.C., Birmingham
November 29	N.E.C., Birmingham
December 2	Wembley Arena
December 3	Wembley Arena
December 4	Wembley Arena
December 7	Wembley Arena
December 8	Wembley Arena
December 10	Wembley Arena
December 11	Wembley Arena
December 12	Wembley Arena
December 14	The Point, Dublin
December 15	The Point, Dublin
December 18	King's Hall, Belfast
December 19	King's Hall, Belfast
December 28	Wembley Arena
December 29	Wembley Arena
December 30	Wembley Arena

1991

January 1	Wembley Arena
January 2	Wembley Arena
January 3	Wembley Arena
January 5	Wembley Arena
January 6	Wembley Arena
January 7	Wembley Arena
September 16	Savvas Club, Usk
September 17	Savvas Club, Usk
September 18	Savvas Club, Usk
September 19	Savvas Club, Usk
September 20	Savvas Club, Usk
September 21	Savvas Club, Usk
October 14	Logan Campbell Centre, Auckland
October 15	Logan Campbell Centre, Auckland
October 16	Logan Campbell Centre, Auckland
October 17	Logan Campbell Centre, Auckland
October 18	Logan Campbell Centre, Auckland
October 19	Logan Campbell Centre, Auckland
October 21	Michael Fowler Centre, Wellington

October 22	Michael Fowler Centre, Wellington
October 23	Michael Fowler Centre, Wellington
October 24	Michael Fowler Centre, Wellington
October 25	Michael Fowler Centre, Wellington
October 26	Michael Fowler Centre, Wellington
October 27	Michael Fowler Centre, Wellington
October 28	Town Hall, Christchurch
October 29	Town Hall, Christchurch
October 30	Town Hall, Christchurch
October 31	Town Hall, Christchurch
November 1	Town Hall, Christchurch
November 2	Town Hall, Christchurch
November 3	Town Hall, Christchurch
November 9	Perth
November 10	Perth
November 13	Adelaide
November 14	Adelaide
November 16	Launceston
November 17	Hobart
November 19	Melbourne
November 20	Melbourne
November 21	Melbourne
November 23	Canberra
November 24	Canberra
November 27	Brisbane
November 28	Brisbane
November 30	Sydney
December 1	Sydney

1992

August 24	Savvas Club, Usk
August 25	Savvas Club, Usk
August 26	Savvas Club, Usk
August 27	Savvas Club, Usk
August 28	Savvas Club, Usk
August 29	Savvas Club, Usk
October 1	N.E.C., Birmingham
October 2	N.E.C., Birmingham
October 3	N.E.C., Birmingham
October 5	N.E.C., Birmingham
October 6	N.E.C., Birmingham
October 7	N.E.C., Birmingham
October 9	N.E.C., Birmingham

October 10	N.E.C., Birmingham
October 11	N.E.C., Birmingham
October 13	N.E.C., Birmingham
October 14	N.E.C., Birmingham
October 15	N.E.C., Birmingham
October 17	N.E.C., Birmingham
October 18	N.E.C., Birmingham
October 22	Arena, Sheffield
October 23	Arena, Sheffield
October 24	Arena, Sheffield
October 25	Arena, Sheffield
October 27	Arena, Sheffield
October 29	S.E.C.C., Glasgow
October 30	S.E.C.C., Glasgow
October 31	S.E.C.C., Glasgow
November 2	Wembley Arena
November 3	Wembley Arena
November 4	Wembley Arena
November 10	Wembley Arena
November 11	Wembley Arena
November 12	Wembley Arena
November 14	Wembley Arena
November 15	Wembley Arena
November 16	Wembley Arena
November 18	Wembley Arena
November 19	Wembley Arena
November 20	Wembley Arena
November 27	Wembley Arena
November 28	Wembley Arena
November 29	Wembley Arena
December 7	King's Hall, Belfast
December 8	King's Hall, Belfast
December 10	The Point, Dublin
December 11	The Point, Dublin
December 12	The Point, Dublin

1993

October 16	Diplomat Hotel, Bahrain
October 18	Marine Club, Abu Dhabi
October 20	Leisureland Ice, Dubai
October 21	Dubai Hotel, Dubai
October 29	Ostseehalle, Kiel
October 30	Seidenstickerhalle, Bielefeld

October 31	Kuppelsaal, Hannover
November 2	I.C.C., Berlin
November 3	Alte Oper, Frankfurt
November 4	Philipshalle, Dusseldorf
November 6	Le Zenith, Paris
November 7	Ahoy, Rotterdam
November 8	Stadthalle, Bremen
November 11	Hallenstadion, Zurich
November 12	Sedlmayerhalle, Munich
November 14	Austria Centre, Vienna
November 15	Oberfrankenhalle, Bayreuth
November 17	C.C.H., Hamburg
November 18	Valby Hallen, Copenhagen
November 19	Valby Hallen, Copenhagen
November 20	Idrattens Hus, Vejle
November 22	Solnahallen, Stockholm
November 24	Skive Hallerne, Skive
November 25	Fyns Forum, Odense
November 26	Circle Hall, Herning
November 28	Forest National, Brussels

1994

November 8	N.E.C., Birmingham
November 9	N.E.C., Birmingham
November 11	N.E.C., Birmingham
November 12	N.E.C., Birmingham
November 13	N.E.C., Birmingham
November 15	N.E.C., Birmingham
November 16	N.E.C., Birmingham
November 18	Wembley Arena, London
November 19	Wembley Arena, London
November 20	Wembley Arena, London
November 22	Wembley Arena, London
November 23	Wembley Arena, London
November 25	Wembley Arena, London
November 26	Wembley Arena, London
November 27	Wembley Arena, London
November 29	Wembley Arena, London
November 30	Wembley Arena, London
December 4	S.E.C.C., Glasgow
December 5	S.E.C.C., Glasgow
December 6	S.E.C.C., Glasgow
December 8	Exhibition Centre, Aberdeen

December 9	Exhibition Centre, Aberdeen
December 10	Exhibition Centre, Aberdeen
December 13	Arena, Sheffield
December 14	Arena, Sheffield
December 15	Arena, Sheffield
December 16	Arena, Sheffield

1995

January 23	Queen Elizabeth Stadium, Hong Kong
January 24	Queen Elizabeth Stadium, Hong Kong
January 26	Indoor Stadium, Singapore
January 28	Town Hall, Christchurch
January 29	Town Hall, Christchurch
January 30	Town Hall, Christchurch
January 31	Town Hall, Christchurch
February 2	Superdrome, Auckland
February 3	Superdrome, Auckland
February 4	Bowl of Brooklands, Plymouth
February 9	Entertainment Centre, Brisbane
February 11	Entertainment Centre, Newcastle
February 12	Entertainment Centre, Newcastle
February 14	Flinders Park, Melbourne
February 15	Flinders Park, Melbourne
February 17	Bruce Indoor Stadium, Canberra
February 18	Bruce Indoor Stadium, Canberra
February 20	Entertainment Centre, Sydney
February 21	Entertainment Centre, Sydney
February 22	Entertainment Centre, Sydney
February 24	Entertainment Centre, Adelaide
February 25	Entertainment Centre, Adelaide
February 28	Entertainment Centre, Perth
March 1	Entertainment Centre, Perth
April 12	St. George's Park, Port Elizabeth
April 15	Kingsmead Cricket Stadium, Durban
April 17	Loftus Vesveld, Pretoria
April 19	Springbok Park, Bloemfontein
April 22	Newlands Cricket Stadium, Cape Town

Throughout the eighties and nineties many of the tours had a central theme or title and below we have listed the titles along with the dates they apply to:

THE SILVER TOUR
(October–December 1983)

TOGETHER
(July 1984)

THE ROCK CONNECTION – AUSTRALIA/NEW ZEALAND
(October–November 1984)

THE ROCK CONNECTION – EUROPE
(September–December 1985)

ALWAYS GUARANTEED – EUROPE
(October–November 1987)

ALWAYS GUARANTEED – NEW ZEALAND/AUSTRALIA
(February–March 1988)

ALWAYS GUARANTEED – EUROPE
(May 1988)

30th ANNIVERSARY TOUR
(September–December 1988)

STRONGER
(February–March 1990)

STRONGER OVER EUROPE
(May–June 1990)

FROM A DISTANCE – UK
(November 1990–January 1991)

FROM A DISTANCE – AUSTRALIA/NEW ZEALAND
(October–December 1991)

ACCESS ALL AREAS
(October–November 1992)

THE HIT LIST – UK
(November–December 1994)

THE HIT LIST – FAR EAST/AUSTRALIA/SOUTH AFRICA
(January–April 1995)

GOSPEL TOURS

The following is a complete list, as far as is known of every Gospel concert tour.

1972

April 14	Philarmonic Hall, Liverpool
April 15	Central Hall, Liverpool
April 18	Stadt-Casino, Basel
April 19	Palais des Beaux Arts, Brussels
April 20	Roma, Antwerp
April 21	Pleyel, Paris
April 22	Theatre de Foire au Vin, Colmar
April 23	Harmonie Hall, Heilbronn
April 24	Messingerhalle, Nuremburg
April 27	Colston Hall, Bristol

1973

April 17	Concert Hall, Perth
April 19	Apollo Stadium, Adelaide
April 21	Hordern Pavilion, Sydney
April 22	Canberra Theatre, Canberra
April 23	City Hall, Hobart
April 25	Festival Hall, Melbourne
April 28	Festival Hall, Brisbane
September 20	Alhambra, Bradford
September 21	City Hall, Sheffield
September 22	Central Hall, Coventry
September 26	Civic Hall, Guildford
October 5	Winter Gardens, Bournemouth
November 24	Festival Hall, Paignton

1974

October 23	Music Hall, Aberdeen
October 24	Usher Hall, Edinburgh

October 25	Kelvin Hall, Glasgow
October 26	Caird Hall, Dundee
October 27	Palladium, London
October 30	King George's Hall, Blackburn
October 31	King's Hall, Stoke
November 1	Afan Lido, Port Talbot

1975

October 9	The Pavilion, Hemel Hemptead
October 10	Assembly Hall, Tunbridge Wells
October 15	Albert Hall, Nottingham
October 16	Mountford Hall, Liverpool
October 17	Town Hall, Leeds
October 18	City Hall, Hull
October 22	New Theatre, Oxford
October 23	Festival Hall, Corby
October 24	Town Hall, Birmingham
October 25	University Great Hall, Exeter
October 30	Odeon, Hammersmith

1976

October 1	RDS Concert Hall, Dublin
October 2	Wellington Hall, Belfast
October 6	Town Hall, Watford
October 7	Gaumont, Southampton
October 8	Town Hall, Middlesborough
October 9	City Hall, Newcastle
October 13	Central Hall, Chatham
October 14	Colston Hall, Bristol
October 15	Town Hall, Reading
October 16	Congress Theatre, Eastbourne

1977

October 7	Carn Brae Leisure Centre, Redworth
October 8	Festival Hall, Paignton
October 12	New Theatre, Cardiff
October 13	Trentham Gardens, Stafford
October 14	Free Trade Hall, Manchester
October 15	University Hall, York

October 19	Dome, Brighton
October 20	ABC, Ilford
October 21	Kelsey Kerridge Sports Hall, Cambridge
October 22	Gaumont, Ipswich
October 24	Rotterdam

1978

May 31	Bankstown Town Hall, Sydney
June 1	Mt. Kurring-Gai Town Hall, Sydney
June 2	Brisbane
June 3	Melbourne
June 4	Melbourne
June 5	Hobart
June 7	Adelaide
June 9	Perth
October 3	Market Assembly Hall, Carlisle
October 4	Usher Hall, Edinburgh
October 5	Glasgow
October 6	Music Hall, Aberdeen
October 9	Royal Albert Hall, London
October 10	Royal Albert Hall, London
October 13	Southport Theatre, Southport
October 14	Astra Theatre, Llandudno

1979

January 17	Wellington Hall, Belfast
January 19	National Stadium, Belfast
January 23	University Great Hall, Exeter
January 24	Leisure Centre, Gloucester
January 25	De Montfort Hall, Leicester
January 26	Leisure Centre, Bletchley
January 30	Town Hall, Birmingham
January 31	Town Hall, Leeds
February 1	Philharmonic Hall, Liverpool
February 2	ABC Theatre, Peterborough

1980

January 19	National Stadium, Dublin
January 23	University Great Hall, Exeter

January 24	Leisure Centre, Gloucester
January 25	De Montfort Hall, Leicester
January 26	Leisure Centre, Bletchley
January 30	Town Hall, Birmingham
January 31	Town Hall, Leeds
February 1	The Philharmonic Hall, Liverpool
February 2	ABC Theatre, Peterborough
November 7	Colloseum, Johannesburg
November 8	Colloseum, Johannesburg
November 10	Colloseum, Johannesburg
November 11	Colloseum, Johannesburg
November 12	Colloseum, Johannesburg
November 13	Colloseum, Johannesburg
November 14	Colloseum, Johannesburg
November 15	Colloseum, Johannesburg
November 18	Feathermarket Hall, Port Elizabeth
November 20	Three Arts Centre, Cape Town
November 21	Three Arts Centre, Cape Town
November 22	Three Arts Centre, Cape Town
November 25	City Hall, Durban
November 26	City Hall, Durban
November 27	City Hall, Durban
November 28	City Hall, Durban

1981

January 22	Cliff's Pavilion, Southend
January 23	Odeon, Hammersmith
January 24	Odeon, Hammersmith
January 28	The Hexagon, Reading
January 29	Congress Theatre, Eastbourne
January 31	Guildhall, Portsmouth
February 4	City Hall, Newcastle
February 5	City Hall, Sheffield
February 6	Apollo, Manchester
February 7	Assembly Rooms, Derby

1982

December 3	Apollo, Glasgow
December 4	Playhouse, Edinburgh
December 8	St George's Hall, Bradford
December 9	Guildhall, Preston

December 10 Trentham Gardens, Stoke
December 11 Royal Bath and West Showground, Wells
December 15 City Hall, Hull
December 16 St. David's Hall, Cardiff
December 17 Oasis Leisure Centre, Swindon
December 18 Centre, Brighton

1983

April 10 Colloseum, Lisbon
April 12 Palcio Municipal de los Deportes, Barcelona
April 15 Messenhalle, Sindelfingen
April 16 Freiheitshalle
April 17 CCH, Hamburg
April 19 Grugahalle, Essen
April 20 Siegerlandhalle, Siegen
April 22 Baltiska Hallen, Malmo
April 23 Scandinavium, Gothenburg
April 26 Ahoy, Rotterdam
April 27 Queen Elizabeth Hall, Antwerp
April 28 Vorst National, Brussels
April 30 Apollo, Manchester

1984

September 11 Gaumont, Southampton
September 13 Coliseum, Cornwall
September 14 Coliseum, Cornwall
September 15 Colston Hall, Bristol
September 18 Royal Centre, Nottingham
September 19 Royal Centre, Nottingham
September 20 Empire Theatre, Liverpool
September 21 Empire Theatre, Liverpool
September 22 Apollo Theatre, Coventry
September 25 Gaumont Theatre, Ipswich
September 26 Gaumont Theatre, Ipswich
September 27 Odeon, Hammersmith
September 28 Odeon, Hammersmith
September 29 Odeon, Hammersmith

1985

July 9 Conference Centre, Harrogate
July 10 Conference Centre, Harrogate
July 11 Apollo, Manchester
July 12 Apollo, Manchester
July 13 Odeon, Birmingham
July 15 Beau Sejour Centre, Guernsey
July 16 Beau Sejour Centre, Guernsey
July 18 Fort Regent, Jersey
July 19 Fort Regent, Jersey

1987

June 9 Newcastle
June 10 Playhouse, Edinburgh
June 11 Playhouse, Edinburgh
June 12 Playhouse, Edinburgh
June 13 Playhouse, Edinburgh
June 16 Centre, Brighton
June 17 Centre, Brighton
June 19 Arena, Wembley
June 20 Arena, Wembley
June 25 N.E.C., Birmingham
June 26 N.E.C., Birmingham
June 27 N.E.C., Birmingham

1989

July 19 City Hall, Newcastle
July 20 Town Hall, Leeds
July 21 Trentham Gardens, Stoke
July 22 De Montfort Hall, Leicester
July 27 The Hexagon, Reading
July 28 Leisure Centre, Gloucester
July 29 Colston Hall, Bristol
July 30 Colston Hall, Bristol
August 2 Civic Center, Guildford
August 3 Leisure Centre, Harrow
August 4 Brentwood Centre, Brentwood
August 5 Mayflower Theatre, Southampton

1991

March 13	Temple Park Centre, South Shields
March 14	The Sands Centre, Carlisle
March 15	Opera House, Blackpool
March 16	Free Trade Hall, Manchester
March 20	Cornwall Coliseum, St Austell
March 21	The Plaza, Exeter
March 22	Newport Centre, Newport
March 23	Apollo Theatre, Oxford
March 27	Assembly Rooms, Derby
March 28	Arts Centre, University of Warwick, Coventry
March 29	Congress Theatre, Eastbourne
March 30	Royal Albert Hall, London

1993

March 30	The Point, Dublin
March 31	Dundonald International Ice Bowl, Belfast.
April 1	Dundonald International Ice Bowl, Belfast.
April 2	Scottish Exhibition Centre, Glasgow
April 3	Exhibition and Conference Centre, Aberdeen
April 7	International Conference Centre, Harrogate
April 8	Royal Centre, Nottingham
April 9	Kings Park Centre, Northampton
April 10	Symphony Hall, Birmingham
April 14	The Pavilions, Plymouth
April 15	International Centre, Bournemouth
April 16	Centre, Brighton
April 19	Hammersmith Apollo, London

TELEVISION
APPEARANCES

The following list gives dates, titles and TV companies for Cliff's appearances on television. It would be virtually impossible to have included every appearance but this list does show the scope and amount of work undertaken during his career. It should be noted that the dates given (in most cases) are for the broadcast of a programme and not the date of recording.

1958

13 September	Oh Boy! (ABC)
20 September	Oh Boy! (ABC)
11 October	Oh Boy! (ABC)
18 October	Oh Boy! (ABC)
25 October	Oh Boy! (ABC)
1 November	Oh Boy! (ABC)
8 November	Oh Boy! (ABC)
15 November	Oh Boy! (ABC)
22 November	Oh Boy! (ABC)
29 November	Oh Boy! (ABC)
6 December	Oh Boy! (ABC)
20 December	Oh Boy! (ABC)

1959

17 January	Oh Boy! (ABC)
31 January	Oh Boy! (ABC)
7 February	Oh Boy! (ABC)
7 March	Oh Boy! (ABC)
28 March	Oh Boy! (ABC)
2 May	Oh Boy! (ABC)
23 May	Oh Boy! (ABC)
30 May	Oh Boy! (ABC)

1 November	Sunday Night At The London Palladium (ATV)
25 December	Hughie Green's Christmas Day Special

1960

16 January	Sunday Night At The London Palladium (ATV)
21 January	Pat Boone Show (USA)
21 February	Sunday Night At The London Palladium (ATV)
19 March	Saturday Spectacular (ATV)
31 March	Crackerjack (BBC)
13 April	Me and My Shadows (ATV)
16 May	Royal Variety Show
21 May	Saturday Spectacular (ATV)
31 July	Saturday Spectacular (ATV)
1 October	Oh Boy! (ABC)
16 October	Birthday Honours (ATV)

1961

19 January	Crackerjack (BBC)
1 March	Parade Of The Pops (BBC)

8 April	Juke Box Jury (BBC)
26 April	Parade Of The Pops (BBC)
20 May	Thank Your Lucky Stars
25 June	Billy Cotton Band Show (BBC)
7 October	Thank Your Lucky Stars (ITV)
10 December	Sunday Night At The London Palladium (ATV)
26 December	All Kings Of Music (ATV)
31 December	Sunday Night At The London Palladium (ATV)

1962

5 May	Thank Your Lucky Stars (ITV)
8 September	Billy Cotton Show (BBC)
21 October	Ed Sullivan Show (USA)
29 October	Royal Variety Show
25 December	Christmas Fare (ATV)

1963

24 February	Billy Cotton Band Show (BBC)
28 April	Cliff TV Special (BBC)
May	Ed Sullivan Show (USA)
13 June	Sunday Night At The London Palladium (ATV)
10 August	Thank Your Lucky Stars (ITV)
20 October	Ed Sullivan Show (USA)
3 November	Sunday Night At The London Palladium (ATV)
30 November	Thank Your Lucky Stars (ITV)
25 December	Sounds And Sweet Airs (ATV)

1964

25 April	Thank Your Lucky Stars (ITV)
May	German TV Show, Munich
12 July	The Best Of Both Worlds (BBC)
15 July	ATV Spectacular (ATV)

1965

14 March	Sunday Night At The London Palladium (ATV)
13 June	Sunday Night At The London Palladium (ATV)
August	Thank Your Lucky Stars (ABC)
15 September	Cliff Richard And The Shadows Special (ATV)
16 September	Live at Forum, Liege, Belgium (Belgium TV)
22 September	Cliff Richard And The Shadows (ATV)
29 September	It's Cliff
29 September	Cliff Richard And The Shadows (ATV)
5 November	Thank Your Lucky Stars (ITV)
December	Wish Upon A Wishbone (ITV)
25 December	Cliff Richard's Christmas Cheer (BBC)

1966

22 March	Pop Inn
26 March	Thank Your Lucky Stars (ITV)
8 April	Stars Organisation for Spastics Special Star Show (BBC)
15 April	Show Of The Week (BBC)
30 April	The ABC Of ABC (ABC)
4 June	Saturday Club (BBC)
9 October	Sunday Night At The London Palladium (ATV)
December	Christmas Show

1967

13 May	Juke Box Jury (BBC)
24 May	ATV Spectacular (ATV)
	Cliff Richard Show
	Cliff and the Shadows (German TV)
September	Top Of The Pops (BBC)
October	Japanese TV Special
26 December	Top Of The Pops '67 (BBC)

1968

27 February	The Golden Show (German TV)
5 March	Cilla (BBC)
24 March	Dee Time (BBC)
31 March	Morecambe and Wise Show (BBC)
April	Top Of The Pops (BBC)
1 April	A Matter Of Diamonds
6 April	Eurovision Song Contest (BBC)
5 May	The Big Show (ATV)
June	After Ten Fellas – Ten! (ITV)
22 June	Billy Cotton Show (BBC)
23 June	The Big Show (ITV)
28 June	Cliff Richard At The Talk Of The Town (ITV)
17 July	Juke Box Jury (BBC)
21 September	Cliff Richard at the Movies (LWT)
25 December	Top Of The Pops (BBC)
25 December	Morecambe And Wise Christmas Show (BBC)

1969

19 February	Cilla Black Show (BBC)
27 February	Top Of The Pops (BBC)
March	Rolf Harris Show (BBC)
19 March	Top Of The Pops (BBC)
3 April	Top Of The Pops (BBC)
12 May	Sooty Show (BBC)
7 June	Dee Time (BBC)
8 June	Top Of The Pops (BBC)
14 June	Top Of The Pops (BBC)
6 July	Liberace
UNKNOWN	After Ten Fellas (ITV)
UNKNOWN	Life With Johnny 1 (Johnny Come Home) (Tyne Tees)
UNKNOWN	Life With Johnny 2 (Johnny Faces Facts) (Tyne Tees)
UNKNOWN	Life With Johnny 3 (Johnny Up The Creek) (Tyne Tees)
UNKNOWN	Life With Johnny 4 (Tyne Tees)
UNKNOWN	Life With Johnny 5 (Tyne Tees)
UNKNOWN	Life With Johnny 6 (Tyne Tees)

4 September	Top Of The Pops (BBC)
25 September	Top Of The Pops (BBC)
7 November	Cliff In Scotland (Danish TV)
28 November	French TV
24 December	Cilla Black Show
31 December	Pop Goes The Sixties (BBC)

1970

3 January	It's Cliff Richard (BBC)
10 January	It's Cliff Richard (BBC)
17 January	It's Cliff Richard (BBC)
24 January	It's Cliff Richard (BBC)
31 January	It's Cliff Richard (BBC)
7 February	It's Cliff Richard (BBC)
14 February	It's Cliff Richard (BBC)
21 February	It's Cliff Richard (BBC)
28 February	It's Cliff Richard (BBC)
7 March	It's Cliff Richard (BBC)
14 March	It's Cliff Richard (BBC)
21 March	It's Cliff Richard (BBC)
28 March	It's Cliff Richard (BBC)
1 May	Personal Cinema
7 June	Roy Castle Show
31 August	The Cliff Richard Show
October	Sing A New Song (BBC)
24 December	Cliff Richard Special (BBC)
26 December	Cliff In Scandinavia

1971

16 January	It's Cliff Richard (BBC)
23 January	It's Cliff Richard (BBC)
24 January	Lollipop Tree (The World About Us) (BBC)
30 January	It's Cliff Richard (BBC)
6 February	It's Cliff Richard (BBC)
13 February	It's Cliff Richard (BBC)
20 February	It's Cliff Richard (BBC)
27 February	It's Cliff Richard (BBC)
6 March	It's Cliff Richard (BBC)
13 March	It's Cliff Richard (BBC)
15 March	Cliff In Berlin (German TV)

20 March	It's Cliff Richard (BBC)
27 March	It's Cliff Richard (BBC)
3 April	It's Cliff Richard (BBC)
10 April	It's Cliff Richard (BBC)
11 April	Cliff Live at Skansen (Swedish TV)
18 June	It's Cliff (BBC)
30 August	Getaway with Cliff (BBC)
6 November	Cilla (BBC)
24 December	Cliff Christmas Eve Special (BBC)

1972

UNKNOWN	It's Cliff Richard (BBC)
15 January	It's Cliff Richard (BBC)
22 January	It's Cliff Richard (BBC)
19 August	Lulu Show (BBC)
2 September	The Case (Swedish TV)

1973

2 January	Cliff In Scotland (BRT TIV)
10 January	Cilla Black Show (BBC)
19 January	They Sold A Million (BBC)
27 January	Cilla (BBC)
7 April	Eurovision Song Contest (BBC)

1974

4 May	Mike Yarwood Show (BBC)
9 May	Nana Mouskouri Show (BBC)
24 May	The Eddy Go Round Show (Dutch TV)
24 August	It's Cliff Richard (BBC)

1975

28 March	The Eddy Go Round Show (Dutch TV)
3 April	The Eddy Go Round Show (Dutch TV)
9 April	Shang-A-Lang (ITV)

19 September	Saturday Scene
26 April	Cliff in Copenhagen
July	Jim'll Fix It
6 September	It's Cliff and Friends
13 September	It's Cliff and Friends
UNKNOWN	Hits a go go/Hit Spot
20 September	Supersonic (ITV)
October	Today (ITV)
10 October	Russell Harty
13 October	Men Neme TV (Dutch TV)
21 October	Look Alive
27 December	It's Cliff and Friends (BBC)
30 December	Adamo Show (Belgium TV)

1976

3 January	It's Cliff and Friends (BBC)
10 January	It's Cliff and Friends (BBC)
17 January	It's Cliff and Friends (BBC)
19 January	Studio B
24 January	It's Cliff and Friends (BBC)
31 January	It's Cliff and Friends (BBC)
7 February	It's Cliff and Friends (BBC)
7 February	A Popstar and his Jesus (German TV)
14 February	It's Cliff and Friends (BBC)
14 February	Supersonic (ITV)
15 June	Eddy Go Round Special (Dutch TV)
19 June	Supersonic (ITV)
26 June	Supersonic (ITV)
24 July	Cliff In Concert (BBC)
6 September	Nationwide (BBC)
30 December	Adamo Special (Belgian TV)
31 December	A Jubilee Of Music (BBC)

1977

8 January	Multi-Coloured Swap Show (BBC)
26 February	Supersonic (ITV)
11 March	Een van de act (Dutch TV)
19 March	Kwistig met Muziek (Dutch TV)
April	Top Of The Pops (BBC)
2 July	Saturday Scene (ITV)

September	Cliff Gospel Concert
UNKNOWN	Cliff in Utrecht (Dutch TV)
UNKNOWN	Gospel Concert in Holland (Dutch TV)
1 October	Michael Parkinson Show (BBC)
9 October	Cliff (German TV)
12 November	Tiswas (ITV)
17 December	Swap Shop Christmas Show (BBC)

1978

15 February	Pebble Mill At One (BBC)
23 February	Cliff Live At The Film Trust Arena
UNKNOWN	Thank You Very Much
August	Val Doonican Show (BBC)
21 September	Star Parade (German TV)
30 October	Australian Music To The World (Australian TV)
December	Little And Large Christmas Show (BBC)

1979

13 February	Pop Quest (BBC)
17 February	Swap Shop (BBC)
6 March	Pop Quest (BBC)
8 June	50 Jaar NJHC, Utrecht, Holland (Dutch TV)
12 June	Avro Gala Special (Dutch TV)
27 August	Greenbelt (BBC)
September	Kolner Treff (WDR 3TV)
11 October	Star Parade (German TV)
December	Cliff in Concert (BBC)

1980

1 January	Little And Large Show (BBC)
8 January	Dinah Shore and Friends (USA)
January	Mike Douglas Show (USA)
16 February	Thank You For The Music
20 February	Pop Shop Special
March	Pop Gospel (ITV)

14 April	Hollywood Nights (USA)
June	Midnight Special (USA)
22 June	Greenbelt Live (BBC 1)
27 October	Swap Shop (BBC)
13 December	Michael Parkinson Show (BBC)
December	Cliff in London (Danish TV)
19 December	Cliff in Chichester (ITV)

1981

4 January	Cliff Richard Sings Gospel (SA SATV)
4 January	John Kelly Show (USA)
5 January	The John Davidson Show (USA)
6 January	Dionne Warwick Solid Gold Show (USA)
7 January	The Merv Griffin Show (USA)
March	Midnight Special (USA)
20 March	Cliff In London (BBC)
10 September	Top Of The Pops (BBC)
27 November	Royal Variety Performance
28 November	Tiswas (ITV)
30 November	Cliff – Rock 'n' Roll Juvenile (BBC)
7 December	Cliff – Why Should The Devil Have All The Good Music (BBC)
14 December	Cliff – Travelling Light (BBC)
21 December	Cliff – My Kinda Life (BBC)
27 December	Everyman
December	Pop Quiz (BBC)

1982

UNKNOWN	Everyman
23 November	Dressed For The Occasion
27 November	Noel Edmonds Late, Late Show (BBC)
23 December	Top Of The Pops (BBC)

1983

31 March	Wogan (BBC)
21 April	TV Hour (Finland)

11 June	Pop Quiz (BBC)
1 July	Time Of Your Life (BBC)
28 October	Show Business

1984

17 February	I kvall (Swedish TV)
21 March	Eldorado (Danish TV)
25 March	Fiesta Continual (Portugal TV)
21 April	Cliff Richard (Finland TV)
UNKNOWN	Rock In Australia
23 December	Rock Gospel (BBC)

1985

25 January	The Tube (Channel 4)
UNKNOWN	Together (Danish TV)
UNKNOWN	Face to Face I (Australian TV)
UNKNOWN	Face to Face II (Australian TV)
UNKNOWN	The Rock Gospel Show
2 February	Aspel and Friends (ITV)
7 February	Good Morning Britain (ITV)
9 February	Saturday Superstore (BBC)
7 April	Cliff Richard And The Shadows Together (ITV)
5 May	40 Years of Peace
24 August	Momarkedet (Norway TV)
26 August	Wogan (BBC)
28 September	Saturday Superstore (BBC)
23 November	TX (ITV)
1 December	Pebble Mill At One (BBC)
3 December	Open To Question (BBC)
11 December	Pebble Mill (BBC)
21 December	Saturday Superstore (BBC)

1986

22 February	Aspel and Friends
26 February	TV Times Awards Show (ITV)
5 March	Reporting London (Thames TV)
22 March	Saturday Superstore (BBC)
7 April	Rockspell

22 April	Good Morning America (NBC)
29 August	Wogan (BBC)
11 October	Saturday Superstore (BBC)
27 December	From The Hip (Channel 4)

1987

19 January	Wogan (BBC)
19 March	After Nine – part one
26 March	After Nine – part two
19 June	The Grand Knockout Tournament
UNKNOWN	Mine To Share I
UNKNOWN	Mine To Share II
22 June	Wogan (BBC)
23 June	Get Fresh
June	Top Of The Pops (BBC)
June	Midlands Today (BBC)
June	Wogan (BBC)
July	Edna Everage TV Show (LWT)
July	Hold Tight
23 July	ARD Wunschkonzert
1 August	Summertime Special (BBC)
19 August	Hold Tight (ITV)
25 August	The Roxy
September	Top Of The Pops (BBC)
12 September	OBS '87
12 September	The Dame Edna Experience (LWT)
24 September	All Our Yesterdays (Thames Television)
5 October	Thank You Very Much (ITV)
16 October	Rockline
28 October	Ohne Filter
28 December	Cliff from The Hip (Channel Four)

1988

January	Wogan (BBC)
5 February	A Night of Comic Relief (BBC)
July	Saturday Night (ITV)
8 October	30 ar pa toppen – Cliff Richard in Odense
November	Des O'Connor Show (ITV)
16 November	Wogan (BBC)

21 November	Royal Command Performance
November	Jimmy Tarbuck Show
December	Top Of The Pops (BBC)
26 December	Cliff Richard – 30 ar i spotlight

1989

14 January	An Evening With Cliff Richard
13 February	B.P.I. Prisuddeling
11 March	Europa Europa
UNKNOWN	Dame Edna Experience (LWT)
April	On The Waterfront
14 May	Going Live (BBC)
9 September	Saturday Matters (ITV)
12 October	Top Of The Pops (BBC)
October	Ehren Lowe (RTL TV)
20 October	Record Breakers (BBC)
20 October	Eleva2ren (Danish TV)

21 October	Motormouth
25 October	Des O'Connor Show (ITV)
25 November	Late, Late TV Show
28 November	Sacre Soiree (French TV)
8 December	Wogan (BBC)
9 December	Wetten Das (German TV)
14 December	Top Of The Pops (BBC)

1990

20 January	The Event (ITV)
UNKNOWN	The Event (ITV)
UNKNOWN	The Event – Oh Boy! (ITV)
12 April	Eddie Skoller Show
30 June	Knebworth Concert (ITV)
18 September	What's That Noise (BBC)
20 September	Galla For Englands Bedstemor (Danish TV)

6 October	Going Live (BBC)
14 October	From A Distance (ITV)
23 November	Children In Need (BBC)
26 November	Wogan (BBC)
1 December	Motormouth
6 December	Top Of The Pops (BBC)
12 December	Des O'Connor (ITV)
22 December	Going Live (BBC)
December	Cliff At Christmas

1991

13 April	Wetten Das In Berlin (German TV)
15 June	World Music Awards (ITV)
UNKNOWN	The Event in a Tent
31 August	World Music Award '91
September	Top Of The Pops (BBC)
12 December	Top Of The Pops (BBC)
12 December	Des O'Connor (ITV)
13 December	This Morning (ITV)
23 December	Jul med Cliff Richard

1992

January	Top Of The Pops (BBC)
28 February	Wogan (BBC)
March	40 Minutes (BBC)
April	The Word (Channel Four)
April 20	Culture Rock (French TV)
8 May	Eleva2ren (Danish)
12 May	Gloria Hunniford Show
28 June	National Music Day (BBC)
11 July	World Music Award '92
14 October	Good Morning Show (BBC)
1 December	Pebble Mill (BBC)
4 December	Wogan (BBC)
22 December	Joy To The World

1993

11 March	Top Of The Pops (BBC)
20 March	Wetten Dab (ZDF TV)

22 March	This Morning (ITV)
18 May	Staatsloterijshow
22 May	Flitterabend (German TV)
30 May	Surprise, Surprise (ITV)
31 May	Goldene Eins (German TV)
5 June	Naturschutzgala
7 June	Bruce Forsyth's Guest Night (ITV)
26 July	Cliff Live (Japan NHK BS-2)
29 July	Michael Ball (ITV)
25 September	The Cilla Black Celebration Show (ITV)
26 September	Sunday Morning (Anglia)
31 October	Songs Of Praise (BBC 1)
8 December	Top Of The Pops (BBC)
22 December	Songs Of Praise
22 December	Des O'Connor Show
24 December	Joy To The World

| 24 December | South Bank Show Special (The Story So Far) (ITV) |
| 27 December | Cliff Richard In Concert (Carlton) |

1994

5 June	Surprise, Surprise
2 October	Top Gear
25 September	Paul Merton's 'Palladium Story' (BBC)
9 November	GMTV
10 November	This Morning (Granada)
11 November	Pebble Mill (BBC)
15 November	Good Morning (BBC)

6 December	Prince's Trust Gala
12 December	Surprise, Surprise (ITV)
17 December	Hit List Live (Channel Four)
26 December	The Prince's Trust Gala (BBC 1)

1995

16 January	This Morning (Granada)
February	Barrymore (ITV)
12 March	Songs of Praise (BBC)
8 May	VE Day Celebrations (BBC)
20 October	Eleva2ren (Danish TV)
25 November	Royal Variety Performance

CLIFF ON
RADIO

Throughout his career Cliff has made numerous radio broadcasts and to compile a complete list of every show on which he has appeared is beyond the scope of this book. However, we will take a look back at some of the highlights and will include details on many of the shows on which Cliff contributed on a regular basis.

SATURDAY CLUB
Cliff made his firt appearance on this BBC Light
Programme on 25 October 1958

RADIO LUXEMBOURG BROADCASTS
   June 1960–December 1961
   January 1963–April 1963
Recorded at the London Studios of Radio Luxembourg
these shows were 15 minutes long and usually featured
two songs by the Shadows and three by Cliff. Titled Me
And My Shadows the shows featured a mix of current
hits and several songs not recorded in the studio for
commercial release.

LIVE CONCERT BROADCASTS
During the seventies, eighties and nineties several
concerts were broadcast on radio and below is a list of
some of these performances.
   November 1977
Live recordings from the Fairfield Halls, Croydon
   December 1979
Live recordings from the Hammersmith Odeon, London
   December 1988
Highlights from the 30th Anniversary Concert at the
Brighton Centre
   June 1990
Cliff's appearance at the Nordoff-Robbins Charity
concert at Knebworth broadcast on Radio One
   January 1991
From A Distance Tour live broadcast from Wembley
Arena of the complete concert
   November 1992
Highlights from the Access All Areas tour taped at
London's Wembley Arena
   April 1993
Highlights from An Evening With Cliff Richard Gospel
Concert
   1995
The Hit List. A complete concert from Sheffield Arena
during the Hit List Tour

Selection of other appearances with dates
where known

SATURDAY CLUB (throughout the fifties and early sixties)
PARADE OF THE POPS (Sixties)
EASY BEAT (Sixties)
TEEN BEAT (1961)
CALLING TO YOUTH (1961)
MONDAY SPECTACULAR – Radio Luxembourg (1961)
ABC OF THE STARS – Radio Luxembourg (1962)
POP INN (1963)
EUROPE ONE (1963)
THE CLIFF RICHARD STORY (1965)
LET THE GOOD TIMES ROLL (1966)
FIVE TO TEN (1967)
OFF THE RECORD (1968)
DAVE CASH PROGRAMME (1968/1969)
PETE'S SATURDAY PEOPLE (1969)
OPEN HOUSE (1969)
LET'S GO WITH CLIFF (1969)
CLIFF RICHARD STORY (1970)
MUSIC FOR SUNDAY (1971)
TOP TWELVE (1973)
PAUSE FOR THOUGHT (1974)
CHRISTMAS DAY SPECIAL (1975)
GOSPEL ROAD (1976)
INSIGHT (1976)
20 GOLDEN YEARS (1978)
GREENBELT (1979)
TWO SIDES OF CLIFF (1979)
STAR SPECIAL (1979)
REFLECTIONS (1980)
TALKABOUT (1982)
A CELEBRATION OF CHRISTMAS (1984)
GOOD MORNING SUNDAY (1986)
EMI 90TH BIRTHDAY SHOW
SINGLED OUT (1989)
MY TOP TEN (1990)
WIRED FOR SOUND: THE CLIFF RICHARD STORY
   (6-part series) (1992)

RADIO INTERVIEWS
Throughout his career Cliff has granted many
interviews, not only in the UK but also Australia,
America and Germany. It would be impossible to
compile a list of every interview Cliff has ever given.

TENNIS

Cliff's involvement with tennis goes back to the early eighties and he has been a regular visitor to Wimbledon Fortnight in July each year and many of the smaller tennis tournaments throughout the UK.

The Cliff Richard Tennis Trail, which has charitable status, works to boost the popularity of tennis amongst schoolchildren and to provide support, not only with coaching but also financially, the children who have what it takes and the desire to become an international tennis player. The Tennis Trail takes the sport directly to the schools, and during these visits many thousands of children are seen by some of the top tennis coaches. The trail has also provided equipment to various schools throughout the country. If, during these visits, any child shows promise they are invited to their local sports complex for a thorough testing and, if successful, are known as 'Cliff Richard Trailblazers' and are financially assisted through their tennis programme. Family Tennis Extravaganza Weekends are also held where whole families can test their skills with a racquet. Amongst the sponsors who have supported the Tennis Trail over the years are The Mortgage Corporation, Direct Line Insurance, The Royal Bank of Scotland, Wilson Short Tennis and The East London Bus Company. The Trail has visited many cities throughout the UK including Sheffield, Solihull, Newcastle and Birmingham. In 1983 the first Christmas Pro-Celebrity Tennis Tournament was held at the Brighton Centre and in 1992, on the tenth anniversary, the venue moved to the National Indoor Arena in Birmingham. These events bring together well-known tennis stars and celebrities in an evening of tennis and humour, especially from some of the celebrities, and ends in a Christmas sing-along with the audiences being urged to join in.

PRO-CELEBRITY TENNIS TOURNAMENTS
1983–1995

Date: Monday 19th December 1983
Time: 7.30pm
Venue: The Brighton Centre
Master of Ceremonies: Bill Latham
Host: Gerald Williams
THE PLAYERS
Cliff Richard and Sue Barker
Hank Marvin and Sue Mappin
Trevor Eve and Anne Hobbs
Mike Read and Jo Durie
THE FINAL
Cliff Richard and Sue Barker vs Trevor Eve and Anne Hobbs
THE WINNERS
Trevor and Anne
Man of the Match: Mike Read

Proceeds To: Lawn Tennis Association (L.T.A.)
Umpires: Jeremy Shales and Bob Jenkins

Date: Saturday 15th December 1984
Time: 5.30pm
Venue: The Brighton Centre
Master of Ceremonies: Bill Latham
Host: Mike Read
Guest: John Feaver
THE PLAYERS
Cliff Richard and Sara Gomer
Hank Marvin and Sue Mappin
Terry Wogan and Annabel Croft
Mike Yarwood and Julie Salmon
THE FINAL
Cliff Richard and Sara Gomer vs Hank Marvin and Sue Mappin
THE WINNERS
Cliff and Sara
Man of the Match: Mike Yarwood
Umpires: Jeremy Shales and Bob Jenkins

Date: Saturday 21st December 1985
Time: 6.30pm
Venue: The Brighton Centre
Master of Ceremonies: Bill Latham
Host: Jimmy Hill
THE PLAYERS
Cliff Richard and Sara Gomer
Mike Read and Anne Hobbs
Hank Marvin and Virginia Wade
Shakin' Stevens and Annabel Croft
THE FINAL
Cliff Richard and Sara Gomer vs Hank Marvin and
Virginia Wade
THE WINNERS
Cliff and Sara
Man of the Match: Shakin' Stevens
Sponsors: American Express
Umpires: Jeremy Shales and Gerry Armstrong
Songs: Hark The Herald Angels Sing/Silent Night/
    O Come All Ye Faithful

Date: Saturday 21st December 1986
Time: 5.30pm
Venue: The Brighton Centre
Master of Ceremonies: Bill Latham
Host: Mike Read
Guest: Sue Mappin and youngsters
THE PLAYERS
Cliff Richard and Sue Barker
Peter Cook and Annabel Croft
Sebastian Coe and Virginia Wade
Ronnie Corbett and Sara Gomer
THE FINAL
Cliff Richard and Sue Barker vs Sebastian Coe and
Virginia Wade
THE WINNERS
Cliff and Sue
Man of the Match: Pete Cook and Ronnie Corbett (tie)
Sponsors: American Express
Umpires: Jeremy Shales and Georgina Clark
Songs: O Come All Ye Faithful/Silent Night/Living Doll/
    Hark The Herald Angels Sing

Date: Saturday 19th December 1987
Time: 5.30pm
Venue: The Brighton Centre
Master of Ceremonies: Bill Latham
Host: Mike Read
Guest: Sue Mappin and youngsters
THE PLAYERS
Cliff Richard and Sue Barker
Emlyn Hughes and Annabel Croft
Mike Yarwood and Sara Gomer
Elton John and Virginia Wade
THE FINAL
Emlyn Hughes and Annabel Croft vs Elton John and
Virginia Wade
THE WINNERS
Emlyn and Annabel
Man of the Match: Mike Yarwood
Sponsors: Mortgage Corporation
Umpires: Jeremy Shales and Georgina Clark
Songs: Hark The Herald Angels Sing/Another Christmas
    Day/Silent Night/O Come All Ye Faithful/Little Town/
    Living Doll/O, Come All Ye Faithful (Reprise)

Date: Saturday 17th December 1988
Time: 5.30pm
Venue: The Brighton Centre
Master of Ceremonies: Bill Latham
Guest: Sue Mappin and youngsters
THE PLAYERS
Cliff Richard and Anne Hobbs
Aled Jones and Julie Salmon
Jimmy Tarbuck and Annabel Croft
Mike Read and Virginia Wade
THE FINAL
Mike Read and Virginia Wade vs Aled Jones and Julie
Salmon
THE WINNERS
Mike and Virginia
Man of the Match: Jimmy Tarbuck
Proceeds: Search For A Star/Lawn Tennis Association
(L.T.A.)
Umpires: Georgina Clark and Mike Sertin
Songs: O, Come All Ye Faithful/Hark the Herald Angels
    Sing/Move It/Another Christmas Day/Silent Night
    (duet with Mike Read)/Little Town/Mistletoe and Wine

Date: Saturday 16th December 1989
Time: 5.30pm
Venue: The Brighton Centre
Master of Ceremonies: Bill Latham
Guest: Sue Mappin and youngsters
THE PLAYERS
Cliff Richard and Anne Hobbs
Mike Read and Virginia Wade
Roy Castle and Jo Durie
Jason Donovan and Clare Wood
THE FINAL
Cliff Richard and Anne Hobbs vs Jason Donovan and
Clare Wood
THE WINNERS
Cliff and Anne
Man of the Match: Roy Castle
Proceeds: Search For a Star
Sponsors: Mortgage Corporation
Umpires: Jeremy Shales and Georgina Clark
Songs: Hark The Herald Angels Sing/Sweet Little Jesus
    Boy/Dream (duet with Mike)/Move It (with Mike)/Carol
    (with Mike and Roy)/Mistletoe and Wine (with Roy)/
    O Come All Ye Faithful

Date: Saturday 16th December 1990
Time: 5.30pm
Venue: The Brighton Centre
Master of Ceremonies: Bill Latham
Guest: Sue Mappin and youngsters
THE PLAYERS
Cliff Richard and Sara Gomer
Jeremy Irons and Clare Wood
Paul Daniels and Jo Durie
Bruce Forsyth and Virginia Wade
THE FINAL
Cliff Richard and Sara Gomer vs Bruce Forsyth and
Virginia Wade
THE WINNERS
Cliff and Sara
Man of the Match: Jeremy Irons
Proceeds: Search For A Star
Sponsors: Mortgage Corporation
Umpires: Jeremy Shales and Georgina Clark
Songs: O Come All Ye Faithful/Mistletoe And Wine/All
    Shook Up/Do You Wanna Dance/Silent Night/
    Saviours Day

Date: Saturday 14th December 1991
Time: 5.30pm
Venue: The Brighton Centre
Master of Ceremonies: Bill Latham
Guest: Sue Mappin and youngsters
THE PLAYERS
Cliff Richard and Sara Gomer/Amanda Barrie
Alvin Stardust and Clare Wood
Bill Roache and Virginia Wade
Mike Read and Jo Durie
Des O'Connor and Jo Durie
THE FINAL
Cliff Richard and Sara Gomer vs Des O'Connor and Jo
Durie
THE WINNERS
Cliff and Sara
Man of the Match: Alvin Stardust
Proceeds: Search For A Star
Sponsors: Mortgage Corporation
Umpires: Jeremy Shales and Georgina Clark
Songs: I Love You/On The Beach (with Alvin and Mike)/
    Do You Wanna Dance (with Alvin and Mike/Oh Boy

(with Alvin and Mike)/Mistletoe and Wine/O Come All
Ye Faithful/Silent Night/Saviour's Day/Hark The
Herald Angels Sing

Date: Saturday 19th December 1992
Time: 5.30pm
Venue: National Indoor Arena, Birmingham
Master of Ceremonies: Bill Latham
Guest: Sue Mappin and youngsters/Michael Ball/Tennis
Comedians
Santa: Roy Barraclough
THE PLAYERS
Cliff Richard and Gloria Hunniford
Roy Castle and Jo Durie
Frank Bruno and Virginia Wade
Mike Read and Clare Wood
THE FINAL
Cliff Richard and Jo Durie vs Mike Read and Clare Wood
THE WINNERS
Cliff and Jo
Man of the Match: Roy Castle
Proceeds: Search For A Star
Sponsors: Direct Line Insurance
Umpires: Jeremy Shales and Georgina Clark
Songs: Mary's Boy Child (with Michael, Mike and Roy)/
    Silent Night/Mistletoe And Wine/Little Town/O Come
    All Ye Faithful/Hark The Herald Angels Sing/Saviour's
    Day

Date: Saturday 18th December 1993
Time: 5.30pm
Venue: National Indoor Arena, Birmingham
Master of Ceremonies: Bill Latham
Guest: Sue Mappin and youngsters
Santa: Rosemary Ford
THE PLAYERS
Cliff Richard and Clare Wood/Jeremy Bates
Jasper Carrott and Virginia Wade
Tommy Cannon/Bobby Ball and Roger Taylor
Tim Rice and Jeremy Bates
Mike Read and Clare Wood
THE FINAL
Cliff Richard and Jeremy Bates vs Jasper Carrott and
Virginia Wade
THE WINNERS

Cliff and Jeremy
Man of the Match: Jasper Carrott
Proceeds: Search For A Star
Sponsors: Direct Line
Umpires: Jeremy Shales and Georgina Clark
Songs: All Shook Up/Whole Lotta Shakin' (with Jasper)/
Singing The Blues (with Jasper and Mike)/Some
People (with Hackney School Steel Band)/In The Bleak
Mid-Winter/O Come All Ye Faithful/Mistletoe And Wine/
Hark The Herald Angels Sing/Saviour's Day/Little Town

Date: Saturday 18th December 1994
Time: 5.30pm
Venue: National Indoor Arena, Birmingham
Master of Ceremonies: Bill Latham
Guest: Sue Mappin and youngsters/Jeremy Bates/Chris
Bailey
Santa: Nick Owen
THE PLAYERS
Cliff Richard and Julie Salmon
Hank Marvin and Virginia Wade
Brian Conley and Jeremy Bates
Mr Motivator and Chris Bailey
THE FINAL
Cliff Richard and Julie Salmon vs Hank Marvin and
Virginia Wade
THE WINNERS
Cliff and Julie
Man of the Match: Brian Conley
Sponsors: Direct Line Insurance

Umpires: Jeremy Shales
Songs: Living Doll (with Hank)/Travellin' Light (with Hank)/
Move It (with Hank)/Willie And The Hand Jive
(with Hank)/Have Yourself A Merry Little Christmas
(with band)/White Christmas (with Hackney School
Steel Band)/O Come All Ye Faithful/Mistletoe And
Wine/Hark The Herald Angels Sing/Silent Night/
Saviour's Day

Date: Saturday 16th December 1995
Time: 5.30pm
Venue: National Indoor Arena, Birmingham
Master of Ceremonies: Bill Latham
Guest: Sue Mappin and youngsters and Jill Dando
Santa: Gary Wilmot
THE PLAYERS
Cliff Richard and Virginia Wade
Michael Barrymore and Jo Durie
Hank Marvin and Greg Rusedski
Michael Ball and David Lloyd
Sponsors: Direct Line Insurance
Umpires: Jeremy Shales and Georgina Clark
Songs: Summer Holiday (with Hank Marvin)/All Shook Up
(with Hank Marvin)/Living Doll (with Hank Marvin)/
Move It (with Hank Marvin)/Dream (with Michael Ball/
Travelling Light (with Hank Marvin)/The Young Ones
(with Hank Marvin)/Oh Come All Ye Faithful/Mistletoe
And Wine/Hark The Herald Angels Sing/Away In A
Manger/Silent Night/Saviour's Day

PART 5

COLLECTING CLIFF

Cliff Richard

Cliff Richard

Cliff Richard

Cliff Richard

MEMORABILIA

Cliff Richard, Elvis Presley, and the Beatles are probably the most collected or collectable entertainers in the history of popular music. Their music and their personalities have captured the hearts of millions of fans throughout the world. Elvis is probably more popular today than when he was alive. From very early on in their careers, manufacturing companies were granted merchandising licences to develop products with both Elvis's and Cliff's image on them. Everything from 2/6d photo books to 5/11d pillowcases.

THE EARLIEST MEMORABILIA (FROM 1959)

The earliest Cliff memorabilia became available in 1959, but was available only through 'Mirabelle' as a special offer. For 2/6d, readers could obtain the first ever Cliff Richard Gold Pendant and Chain that featured a head and shoulders pic in a square pendant. The following year came The Cliff Richard Silver Pendant and Chain which this time was oval in shape and featured what must be regarded as one of the earliest holograms, the two pics of Cliff from the 'Oh Boy!' TV show would change with a slight movement of the pendant. One pic featured Cliff in close-up, while the other was a full-length shot. This pendant was available at Woolworths for the price of £1. In the same year (1960), another magazine 'Boyfriend' was giving away Cliff Richard Wall Panels. For 1/6d per week, readers could collect four different wall panels in as many weeks of Cliff in four different poses per panel which were printed on a pink and grey striped background complete with 'typical of the period' microphones graphics. 'Boyfriend' designed a new set of wall panels

two years later in 1962. This time the four photos of Cliff came from 'Summer Holiday', and the background pattern had changed from stripes to diamonds with palm tree graphics, but this time they were slightly more expensive. Now the magazine was costing 1/9d.

By the summer of 1961, ABC Bubblegum had introduced Cliff Richard Bubblegum Cards. There were fifty different pictures of Cliff printed in black-and-white with a caption, and cost 2d per pack and were the only bubblegum cards ever produced, anywhere. We have listed the complete set of numbers and captions except where the caption is unknown, we have stated such.

1. Unknown
2. With Sammy Samuels and Freddy Cannon
3. Cliff has a go on the drums
4. Listening to a recording at the studios
5. This is for you
6. Cliff telephones and interviews at the same time
7. With The Shadows and Freddy Cannon
8. Cliff portrait
9. Relaxed mood
10. Some fun at the fair
11. Cliff phones his mother from Palladium
12. A Star on the Palladium dressing room door

13. Cliff with his fans at EMI studios
14. Candid shot at a party
15. Rehearsing with Cherry Wainer
16. Cliff with Tito Burns, Mum and Dad, Norrie Paramor, his recording manager
17. Cliff shows a silver disc to Russ Conway and Billy Dainty
18. Cliff with his new car mascot
19. Cliff records a new record
20. Cliff is met at London Airport from America
21. Cliff on TV
22. Unknown
23. Unknown
24. Rehearsing with Norrie Paramor, his recording manager
25. Cliff in pensive mood
26. Cliff resting in his dressing room
27. Cliff in action
28. Outdoor shot
29. Cliff sings
30. Presented with another silver disc at Palladium
31. Cliff with Cherry Wainer on TV
32. Cliff rehearsing
33. Cliff in action
34. Cliff with some fans in North London
35. Cliff portrait
36. With five silver discs
37. Cliff with his recording manager
38. Listening to some tapes in his dressing room
39. Signing autographs at radio show
40. Cliff during an LP recording
41. Cliff sings
42. Happy mood on stage
43. Fitting his golden mascot on his new car
44. Xmas spirit
45. Dig this (on stage)
46. With some of the Shadows
47. Party mood
48. Cliff in the make-up department of TV
49. Cliff recording
50. Unknown

Collectable magazines with Cliff on the cover include a couple from the many New Musical Express 'Cliff' front covers: 12 August 1959: 'as you will see him in the film Expresso Bongo'; 13 October 1961: 'Cliff and Carole Gray' plus four-page 21st Birthday tribute. A four-page tribute had previously appeared in NME on 25 September 1959. All the Pop Weekly magazines are rare, but look out for the issues from 31 August 1962 and 6 April 1963. The latter featured a picture of Cliff, Laurie Peters and the St Bernard dog from 'Summer Holiday'. The July 1964 issue of Photoplay featured Cliff and Susan Hampshire on the cover in a scene from 'Wonderful Life', and the July 1965 edition of Rave also had Cliff on the cover. Other magazines to feature Cliff covers included, ABC Film Review, Photoplay, Fab 208, Woman's Own, Show Time, Star International, Mirabelle, Roxy, Boyfriend, TV Times, and countless others. It would be impossible to list all the individual issues of these and other magazines that have been published over the years simply because there have just been too many, but a few other magazines that we tracked down include a couple of personally

No. 32   **CLIFF RICHARD**
rehearsing

No. 19   **CLIFF RICHARD**
Cliff records a new record

No. 11   **CLIFF RICHARD**
'phones his mother from Palladium

No. 33   **CLIFF RICHARD**
Cliff in action

No. 42   **CLIFF RICHARD**
Happy mood on stage

No. 49   **CLIFF RICHARD**
recording

written articles by Cliff published in the 17 March 1961 and 1 April 1963 issues of Hit Parade. An interview and article in Newsweek (1 March 1963), and in the American '16' magazine (March 1963). Other printed publications of interest around this period were the 'Cliff Richard Picture Parade Book' with around 120 pictures which was sold for 3/6d in October 1959, and 'Life with Cliff Richard' also for 3/6d in May 1963 and a year later at the same price in July 1964 'Cliff And His Wonderful Life' was published by Go magazine.

Other souvenirs being marketed were the 'Cliff Richard Two-Way Shirt' in black and white for 32/6; a Cliff necklet and heart locket, and a five-inch high figurine for 10/6d; photo postcards of Cliff in typical poses from the fifties and sixties in colour, and in black-and-white; and the 'Cliff Richard Pillowcase' was advertised as the item 'you will never lose'.

THE LATEST MEMORABILIA (FROM 1988)

In 1988, official Cliff Richard merchandising of all Cliff related product, not including records, was granted to Adrian Hopkins and Jo Chester of Adrian Hopkins Merchandising. Their first collection of items were produced for Cliff's 30th anniversary tour and included two different T-shirts, designer sweat shirt, a tour brochure with a colour glossy photo inserted, a mug, a VIP key-ring, a limited edition Cliff brooch, a guitar badge, an embroidered sweat shirt, tour jacket and cardigan jacket. For the Spring 89 tour and the 'Event', the range consisted of T-shirts, embroidered striped rugby and polo shirts, a heart badge and key-ring, a limited edition guitar badge, and the 'Event' brochure. In 1990, the product remained much the same, the only difference being the name change of the tour, although some unusual items from the 90 and 91 tours included a 'Star' enamel badge, a set of six photo postcards, and a weekend bag. By this time Adrian Hopkins Merchandising had become Theatre Franchise UK. Much of the same memorabilia was again produced for the 'Access All Areas' tour. The 'Hit List' tour in 1994

added some never before items such as the picture CD clock, the Coral gold plated brooch, a 1995 diary, fibre tip pens, and a fridge magnet. Most of the merchandise carried the 'Hit List' juke box logos. By now Theatre Franchise had become Chester Hopkins International and in the same year had been granted the licensing rights for the official Cliff Richard calendar which had previously been produced by Danilo Printing since 1982. Although the official calendar is the recognised product, a company called Culture Shock who later changed their trading name to Oliver Books have been producing an 'unofficial' one since 1989. Apart from the official merchandising by Hopkins and Chester there are a number of fans who have sold photographs, fridge magnets, key-rings, watches, mirrors and stickers donating the proceeds of these items to Cliff's charitable trust. Other items from pre-1988 tours have included a white fringed full length scarf, a 'Rock 'n' Roll Juvenile'

poster and button badge, and 'Every Face Tells A Story' and 'Roll 'n' Roll Juvenile' mirrors. Rare and unusual items to have appeared during the eighties have been the souvenir photo menus from Blazers nightclub in Windsor and the Savvas club in Wales. Although not intended as Cliff Richard merchandise the 'Cliff Lights' American blend cigarettes from Germany, and the Cliff shower gel from Denmark have become a popular item simply because they carry the name 'Cliff'. Kelloggs Corn Flakes and EMI Germany marketed a special pack of facts, info, and pictures from 'The Event' album. In the UK the product bearing Cliff's name continued with a 'Bathtime Musical Fun Sponge' which played an instrumental version of a 'Congratulations', two-inch badges, some with pictures, and some with the 'Every Face Tells A Story' or 'Time' logos, others with 'Making History – 30 Years at the Top' and 'I Love Cliff'. There seems to be an endless list of picture badges in all different shapes and sizes. Pens with 'Cliff Fan Club', or 'Cliff's One Human Work of Art', or 'Move It with Cliff' and 'There's More To Life with Cliff' printed on them. Jigsaw puzzles range from everything from 'The Young Ones' record sleeve to colour photos from the eighties and nineties, and more record sleeve mirrors include the cover art of the albums, 'Thank You Very Much', and 'I'm Nearly Famous'. 'Cliff Richard's Search For A Star' T-shirt with logo and 'sponsored by the Mortgage Corporation' wording were only available at the Brighton Centre during Cliff's 1990 pro-celebrity tournament there. There was a silver pendant and chain with an eighties pic of Cliff available from Wembley market around 1994, and in 1995, the Birmingham fan club produced a canvas shopping bag, and 'Cliff Rug', both with photos printed on.

SELLERS OF CLIFF MEMORABILIA

The only official source of purchasing Cliff memorabilia is through Chester Hopkins International Ltd, PO Box 1492, London W6 9PD, but be sure to send a stamped addressed envelope if making enquiries of details of merchandise that is available.

To buy photographs and other fan produced items refer to the various fan club newsletters and publications, or send a stamped addressed envelope for lists.

Other sources worth checking out are the many Record and Collector fairs up and down the country, and there is of course the various pop auctions.

MOVIE MEMORABILIA

To promote Cliff's films, the distributor prepared publicity material for front of house and foyer display. The most common items included movie posters: quad crown (30 x 40 inches), double crown (20 x 30 inches) four-sheet (80 x 60 inches). Stills were studio 10 x 8 prints illustrating scenes from a film (black-and-white, some in colour). Lobby cards and exhibitors stills were made in sets of eight, featuring different film scenes in full colour. Window cards were 14 x 22 inches. Insert cards were 14 x 36 inches, and lobby photos were 22 x 28. On some occasions other gimmickry to encourage audiences to rush to cinemas to purchase tickets were used, and these have all been detailed in the listing below.

SERIOUS CHARGE (1959): quad-crown movie poster, double-crown posters of Andrew Ray and Sarah Churchill, Lilliane Brousse and Anthony Quayle, Cliff

Richard; composite quad-crown poster for theatres playing 'Serious Charge' and 'Man Mad' as a programme; set of eight exhibitors stills; set of three stills of Liliane Brousse; set of three stills of Cliff Richard; set of three stills of three scenes from the film; set of five 'Rock 'n' Roll' stills featuring dance scenes from the film; a three-panel unit for front of house and foyer display featuring movie poster and six stills from the film; Cliff Richard postcard giveaways (3 x 5 inches) featuring autographed photo printed on card with details of film credits, theatre and playdate on reverse side; music cut out discs (22 inches in diameter) printed in colour on stout card and strutted; window stickers (15 x 5 inches) for film and record tie-ups.

EXPRESSO BONGO (1959): quad-crown movie poster; teaser double-crown poster of Laurence Harvey, Sylvia Syms, Cliff Richard; set

of eight exhibitors stills; photographic montage (10 x 8 inches; 11 x 14 inches; 20 x 30 inches; 22 x 28 inches; 30 x 40 inches); blow-ups and star portraits of Laurence Harvey, Sylvia Syms, Cliff Richard, Yolande Donlan, Sylvia Syms and Laurence Harvey (same sizes as photographic montage); paper bags featuring four inch DC ad and 'Did You Know' quiz block; Cliff Richard fan postcards.

THE YOUNG ONES (1961): quad-crown movie poster; set of eight exhibitors stills in colour.

SUMMER HOLIDAY (1962): quad-crown movie poster; set of eight exhibitors stills in colour.

WONDERFUL LIFE (1964): quad-crown movie poster; set of eight exhibitors stills in colour; tie-up stills and enlargements in black-and-white (10 x 8 inches, 11 x 14 inches, 20 x 30 inches, 30 x 40 inches) poster (18 x 24 inches) of Cliff and Susan Hampshire dancing on the beach as incorporated on the album sleeve and movie poster; hanging cards for film and Pepsi-Cola tie-ups.

FINDERS KEEPERS (1966): quad-crown movie poster (two different versions), sixteen-sheet movie poster; lobby card (22 x 28 inches); set of eight exhibitors stills in colour; art still; photographic enlargements (10 x 8 inches, 11 x 14 inches, 20 x 30 inches, 30 x 40 inches) featuring scenes from the film.

THUNDERBIRDS ARE GO (1966): quad-crown movie poster; three-sheet movie poster; lobby card (22 x 28); insert card; window card; set of eight lobby cards (11 x 14 inches); set of eight exhibitors stills in colour; a 24 x 82 inches title display in brilliant da-glo which converts to 24 x 60 inches by folding back the pictorial sidepiece.

TWO A PENNY (1967): quad-crown movie poster; set of eight exhibitors stills

TAKE ME HIGH (1973): quad-crown movie poster; double-crown movie poster; set of eight exhibitors stills in colour.

RARE RECORDS

This section details the singles, albums and EPs which frequently fetch these prices at record and collectors fairs etc. These prices are accurate at the time of going to press.

SINGLES

OVER £50

Fall In Love With You/Willie And The Hand Jive
(Columbia DB 4431 – 78rpm)

£41–£50

Livin' Lovin' Doll/Steady With You
(Columbia DB 4249 – 78rpm)
Mean Streak/Never Mind
(Columbia DB 4290 – 78rpm)
A Voice In The Wilderness/Don't Be Mad At Me
(Columbia DB 4398 – 78rpm)

£21–£30

Move It/Schoolboy Crush
(Columbia DB 4178 – Black Label)
Move It/Schoolboy Crush

(Columbia DB 4178 – 78rpm)

High Class Baby/My Feet Hit The Ground
(Columbia DB 4203 – Black Label)

High Class Baby/My Feet Hit The Ground
(Columbia DB 4203 – 78rpm)

Livin' Lovin' Doll/Steady With You
(Columbia DB 4249 – Black Label)

Mean Streak/Never Mind
(Columbia DB 4290 – Black Label)

Living Doll/Apron Strings
(Columbia DB 4306 – Black Label)

Travellin' Light/Dynamite
(Columbia DB 4351 – 78rpm)

This Was My Special Day/I'm Feeling Oh So Lonely
(Columbia DB 7435)

£10–£20

Move It/Schoolboy Crush
(Columbia DB 4178 – Green Label)

High Class Baby/My Feet Hit The Ground
(Columbia DB 4203 – Green Label)

Livin' Lovin' Doll/Steady With You
(Columbia DB 4249 – Green Label)

Mean Streak/Never Mind
(Columbia DB 4290 – Green Label)

Travellin' Light/Dynamite
(Columbia DB 4351 – 78rpm)

Living Doll/Apron Strings
(Columbia DB 4306 – 78 rpm)

EXTENDED PLAYS

OVER £50

Cinderella
(Columbia SEG 8527)

£41–£50

Cliff No. 1
(Columbia ESG 7754 – Stereo Issue)

Cliff No. 2
(Columbia ESG 7769 – Stereo Issue)

Cliff Sings No. 1
(Columbia ESG 7788 – Stereo Issue)

Cliff Sings No. 2
(Columbia ESG 7794 – Stereo Issue)

Cliff Sings No. 3
(Columbia ESG 7808 – Stereo Issue)

Cliff Sings No. 4
(Columbia ESG 7816 – Stereo Issue)

Time For Cliff And The Shadows
(Columbia ESG 7887 – Stereo Issue – Turquoise Label)

Love Songs
(Columbia ESG 7900 – Stereo Issue)

Hits From 'When In Rome'
(Columbia SEG 8378)

Thunderbirds Are Go
(Columbia SEG 8510)

£31–£40

Me And My Shadows No. 1
(Columbia ESG 7837 – Stereo Issue)

Me And My Shadows No. 2
(Columbia ESG 7841 – Stereo Issue)

Me And My Shadows No. 3
(Columbia ESG 7843 – Stereo Issue)

Listen To Cliff No. 1
(Columbia ESG 7858 – Stereo Issue)

Dream
(Columbia ESG 7867 – Stereo Issue)

Listen To Cliff No. 2
(Columbia ESG 7870 – Stereo Issue)

Time For Cliff And The Shadows
(Columbia ESG 7887 – Stereo Issue – Blue/Black Label)

Holiday Carnival
(Columbia ESG 7892 – Stereo Issue)

Hits From 'Summer Holiday'
(Columbia ESG 7896 – Stereo Issue)

More Hits From 'Summer Holiday'
(Columbia ESG 7898 – Stereo Issue)

Wonderful Life
(Columbia ESG 7902 – Stereo Issue)

Wonderful Life No. 2
(Columbia ESG 7903 – Stereo Issue)

Hits From 'Wonderful Life'
(Columbia ESG 7906 – Stereo Issue)

£21–£30

Serious Charge
(Columbia SEG 7895)
Cliff No. 1
(Columbia SEG 7903 – Mono Issue)
Cliff No. 2
(Columbia SEG 7910 – Mono Issue)
Cliff Sings No. 1
(Columbia SEG 7979 – Mono Issue)
Cliff No. 2
(Columbia SEG 7987 – Mono Issue)
Cliff No. 3
(Columbia SEG 8005 – Mono Issue)
Cliff No. 4
(Columbia SEG 8021 – Mono Issue)
Cliff's Palladium Successes
(Columbia SEG 8320)
Look In My Eyes Maria
(Columbia SEG 8405)
Angel
(Columbia SEG 8444)
Love Is Forever
(Columbia SEG 8488)
La, La, La, La, La
(Columbia SEG 8517)
Carol Singers
(Columbia SEG 8533)
Congratulations
(Columbia SEG 8540)

£10–£20

Expresso Bongo
(Columbia SEG 7971 – Mono Issue)
Cliff's Silver Discs
(Columbia SEG 8050)
Me And My Shadows No. 1
(Columbia SEG 8065 – Mono Issue)
Me And My Shadows No. 2
(Columbia SEG 8071 – Mono Issue)
Me And My Shadows No. 3
(Columbia SEG 8078 – Mono Issue)
Listen To Cliff
(Columbia SEG 8105 – Mono Issue)

Dream
(Columbia SEG 8119 – Mono Issue)

Listen To Cliff No. 2
(Columbia SEG 8126 – Mono Issue)

Cliff's Hit Parade
(Columbia SEG 8133)

Cliff Richard
(Columbia SEG 8151)

Hits From The 'Young Ones'
(Columbia SEG 8159)

Cliff Richard No. 2
(Columbia SEG 8168)

Cliff's Hits
(Columbia SEG 8203)

Time For Cliff Richard And The Shadows
(Columbia SEG 8228 – Mono Issue)

Holiday Carnival
(Columbia SEG 8246 – Mono Issue)

Hits From 'Summer Holiday'
(Columbia SEG 8250 – Mono Issue)

More Hits From 'Summer Holiday'
(Columbia SEG 8263 – Mono Issue)

Cliff's Lucky Lips
(Columbia SEG 8269)

Love Songs
(Columbia SEG 8272 – Mono Issue)

When In France
(Columbia SEG 8290)

Cliff Sings 'Don't Talk To Him'
(Columbia SEG 8299)

Wonderful Life
(Columbia SEG 8338 – Mono Issue)

A Forever Kind Of Love
(Columbia SEG 8347)

Wonderful Life No. 2
(Columbia SEG 8354 – Mono Issue)

Hits From 'Wonderful Life'
(Columbia SEG 8376 – Mono Issue)

Why Don't They Understand?
(Columbia SEG 8384)

Cliff's Hits From 'Aladdin And His Wonderful Lamp'
(Columbia SEG 8395)

Take Four
(Columbia SEG 8450)

Wind Me Up
(Columbia SEG 8474)

ALBUMS

OVER £50

About That Man
(Columbia SCX 6408)
His Land
(Columbia SCX 6443)

£41–£50

Me And My Shadows
(Columbia SCX 3330 – Stereo Issue)
Listen To Cliff
(Columbia SCX 3375 – Stereo Issue)
21 Today
(Columbia SCX 3409 – Stereo Issue)
32 Minutes And 17 Seconds With Cliff Richard
(Columbia SCX 3436 – Stereo Issue)

£31–£40

Cliff
(Columbia 33SX 1147 – Green Label)
Cliff Sings
(Columbia 33SX 1192 – Green Label)
The Young Ones
(Columbia SCX 3397 – Stereo Issue)
Cliff Richard
(Columbia SX 1709 – Mono Issue)
Cliff Richard
(Columbia SCX 3546 – Stereo Issue)
Kinda Latin
(Columbia SCX 6039 – Stereo Issue)

£21–£30

Cliff
(Columbia 33SX 1147 – Black Label)
Cliff Sings
(Columbia 33SX 1192 – Black Label)
Me And My Shadows
(Columbia 33SX 1261 – Mono Issue)

Listen To Cliff
(Columbia 33SX 1320 – Mono Issue)
21 Today
(Columbia 33SX 1368 – Mono Issue)
32 Minutes And 17 Seconds With Cliff Richard
(Columbia 33SX 1431 – Mono Issue)
Summer Holiday
(Columbia SCX 3462 – Stereo Issue)
When In Spain
(Columbia SCX 3488 – Stereo Issue)
Wonderful Life
(Columbia SCX 3515 – Stereo Issue)
When In Rome
(Columbia SX 1762)
Love Is Forever
(Columbia SCX 3569 – Stereo Issue)
Kinda Latin
(Columbia SX 6039 – Stereo Issue)
Finders Keepers
(Columbia SCX 6079 – Stereo Issue)
Cinderella
(Columbia SCX 6103)
Don't Stop Me Now
(Columbia SCX 6133)
Two A Penny
(Columbia SCX 6262 – Stereo Issue)
Cliff In Japan
(Columbia SCX 6244 – Stereo Issue)
Sincerely
(Columbia SCX 6357 – Stereo Issue)
Tracks And Grooves
(Columbia SCX 6435)
Take Me High
(EMI EMC 3016)

CLIFF ITEMS
SOLD AT AUCTION

SOTHEBY'S
Striped Jacket   £320
Cliff + Shadows signed photo   £200
Power To All Our Friends Silver Disc   £250
Everybody Needs Someone To Love test pressings £40

Localpost (UK) Limited
Head Office
136 Main Street
Halton, Runcorn
Cheshire
WA7 2PW

Poster for Finders Keepers film 1965	£30	2 Rock 'n' Roll juvenile photos	£100
7 South African 78s on Columbia	£80	2 sets of 1960s lobby cards	£30
Signed photo album – early 1960s	£200	4 U.S. film posters	£55
Various signatures	£130	Promotional poster for Palladium show	£45
Wonderful Life film poster	£143	3 U.S. film posters	£30
		2 U.K. film posters	£35
		Framed Dezo Hoffmann photo	£30
CHRISTIES		Dezo Hoffmann photo with Hank Marvin	£20
Honky Tonk Angel & Take Me High		Concert programmes and posters	£40
acetates + photos/ magazines	£275	Stage jacket, with note from Cliff	£120
Expresso Bongo EP + magazines	£130	3 signed items	£50
I'm Willing To Learn + Fall In Love With You		4 Dezo Hofmann photos	£140
2-side acetates	£160	Various items	£200
Mistletoe And Wine gold disc	£220	2 concert posters	£40
Signed photos and card	£30	5 unreleased one-sided acetates	£320
2 signed photos	£60	23 one-sided acetates	£360
Cliff Richard posters	£28	2 early 7" discs	£60
3 early contracts	£240	10 45s, 2 EPs, 1 LP	£30
One-sided Summer Holiday LP acetate	£80	Cliff Richard Peter Tosh LP artwork	£90
Wonderful Life double LP – limited edition	£300	2 signed LPs	£80
Summer Holiday double LP – limited edition	£300	4 unpublished black/white negs	£130
		42 songsheets 50s–70s	£140
PHILLIP'S		Signed B/W photo + handbill	£45
2 LPs + book (signed) + 4 1960s photos	£85		
240 publicity postcards	£55		

BOOKS
ON CLIFF

Cliff Around The Clock, Bob Ferrier
(Daily Mirror Publications, 1959)

Driftin' With Cliff, Jet Harris
(Charles Buchan, 1959)

Cliff Richard
(Fan Star Library, 1959)

Cliff Richard: Baron Of Beat, Jack Sutter
(Valex Products, 1960)

The Wonderful World of Cliff Richard, Bob Ferrier
(Peter Davies, 1960)

Cliff Around The Clock, Bob Ferrier
(Daily Mirror Publications, 1961)

The Wonderful World Of Cliff, Bob Ferrier
(Peter Davies, 1964)

New Singer, New Song, David Winter
(Hodder & Stoughton, 1967)

From Cliff To You, Janet Johnson
(International Cliff Richard Movement – for
    members only)

The Cliff Richard Story, George Tremlett
(Futura, 1975)

Two A Penny, film story by David Winter and Stella Linden
(Hodder & Stoughton, 1978)

Visions
(Cliff Richard Fan Club of London, 1980)

Cliff, Pat Doncaster and Tony Jasper
(Sidgwick & Jackson, 1981)

Silver Cliff, Tony Jasper
(Sidgwick and Jackson, 1982)

25 Years of Cliff, John Tobler
(W H Smith, 1982)

*Cliff Richard and The Shadows – Around The World In
Pictures by Dezo Hoffman*, Norman Jopling
(Virgin, 1985)

The Cliff Richard File, Mike Read
(Roger Houghton, 1986)

Survivor, Tony Jasper
(Marshall Pickering, 1989)

Cliff – A Celebration, Theresa Wassif
(Hodder & Stoughton, 1989)

*Cliff Richard – The Complete Recording Sessions
1958–1990*, Peter Lewry and Nigel Goodall
(Blandford/Cassell, 1991)

Cliff In His Own Words, Kevin St John
(Omnibus, 1981, revised 1992)

Cliff, Gale Barker
  (Marshall Pickering, 1992)

Cliff Richard – The Biography, Steve Turner
  (Lion, 1993)

Cliff Richard – The Complete Chronicle, Mike Read,
Nigel Goodall and Peter Lewry
  (Hamlyn, 1993)

Cliff Richard – The Biography, Steve Turner – Read
by Paul Jones
  (Chivers Audio Books, 1995)

BOOKS
BY CLIFF

It's Great To Be Young
  (Souvenir, 1960)

Me and My Shadows
  (Daily Mirror Publications, 1960)

Questions
  (Hodder & Stoughton)

The Way I See It
  (Hodder & Stoughton, 1968)

Which One's Cliff with Bill Latham
  (Hodder & Stoughton, 1978, re-issued and
    updated, 1990)

Happy Christmas from Cliff
  (Hodder & Stoughton, 1980)

You, Me And Jesus
  (Hodder & Stoughton, 1985)

Single Minded
  (Hodder & Stoughton, 1988)

Jesus, Me And You
  (Hodder & Stoughton, 1988)

*Cliff Richard's Favourite Bible Stories Retold For
Children*, Sue Shaw
  (Conrad-Octopus, 1993)

BOOKS
THAT MENTION CLIFF

Big Beat Scene, Royston Ellis
  (Four Square, 1961)

The Shadows By Themselves, Royston Ellis
  (Consul, 1961)

The Golden Disc, Frank Clews
  (Brown, Watson, 1963)

Love Me Do: The Beatles' Progress, Michael Braun
  (Penguin, 1964)

Crusade '66, John Pollock
  (Hodder & Stoughton, 1966)

Awopbopaloobop Alopbamboom, Nik Cohn
  (Weidenfeld & Nicholson, 1969)

Revolt Into Style, George Melly
  (Allen Lane, 1970)

Land Aflame, Flo Dobbie
  (Hodder & Stoughton, 1972)

Spre-e '73, David Coomes
  (Coverdale House, 1973)

Rock 'n' Roll, Chris May
  (Socion, 1974)

Celluloid Rock, Philip Jenkinson & Alan Warner
  (Lorrimer, 1974)

Jesus In A Pop Culture, Tony Jasper
(Collins, 1975)

The Guitar Greats, John Tobler and Stuart Grundy
(BBC Publications, 1983)

The Story Of The Shadows, Mike Read
(Elm Tree Books, 1983)

Rock Solid, Tony Jasper
(Word, 1986)

Days In The Life, Jonathan Green
(Heinemann, 1988)

Rock 'n' Roll – I Gave You The Best Years Of My Life,
Bruce Welch
(Viking, 1989)

Feel So Real, Tony Jasper
(Marshall Pickering, 1991)

Moments Of Truth, Tony Jasper
(Marshall Pickering, 1991)

God Put A Fighter In Me, Sheila Walsh
(Hodder & Stoughton)

My Faith, Mary Elizabeth Callen
(Hodder & Stoughton)

NME Rock 'n' Roll Decades 60 – The Sixties
(W H Smith, 1992)

Funny Old World: John Henry Rostill, Rob Bradford
(Rob Bradford, 1992)

BOOKLETS BY CLIFF

Your Date Book By Cliff Richard
(A Honey Special, 1960)

Mine Forever
(Hodder & Stoughton, 1989)

Mine To Share
(Hodder & Stoughton, 1984)

BOOKLETS ABOUT CLIFF

Meet Cliff Richard Star Special No. 2
(Charles Buchan Publications)

Meeting Cliff In Wonderful Life Star Special No. 24
(Charles Buchan Publications)

Life With Cliff
(Charles Buchan Publications)

Cliff Richard Introduces
(Mirabelle Library)

Have Spare Time Fun With Cliff
(Mirabelle Library)

Visions
(Cliff Richard Fan Club)

Cliff With The Kids In America
(Empire Records, Leicester)

Congratulations Cliff – 30th Anniversary
(Starbitz)

Cliff Richard – A 30th Anniversary Souvenir
(Lionbound)

Cliff Special – Photo Mags
(ICRM)

Music Collector Cliff Specials January–March 1991

ANNUALS

Valentine Pop Special No.3
(Fleetway Publications, 1960)

Top Numbers Book of the Stars No.1, Compiled &
Edited by John Oliver
(Tolgate Press, 1960)

Top Pop Stars, Edited by Ken Simmons
(Purnell, 1960)

ATV Television Star Book, Joan Griffiths
(Purnell, 1960)

ATV Television Star Book, Harry Darton
(Purnell, 1960)

Valentine Pop Special No.4
(Fleetway Publications, 1961)

Top Numbers Book of the Stars No.6, Compiled by
John Oliver
(Tolgate Press, 1961)

Top Pop Stars, Edited by Ken Simmons
(Purnell, 1961)

Film Show Annual Edited by Ken Simmons
(Purnell & Sons, 1962)

Top Pop Stars, Edited by Ken Simmons
(Purnell, 1962)

Valentine Pop Special No.5
(Fleetway Publications, 1962)

The Radio Luxembourg Book of Record Stars No.2,
Edited by Jack Fishman
(Souvenir Press, 1963)

Film Show Edited by Ken & Sylvia Ferguson
(Purnell, 1963)

ATV Television Star Book
(Purnell, 1963)

Cliff Richard's Top Pops, Patrick Doncaster
(Daily Mirror Newspapers Ltd, 1963)

Girl Television & Film Annual 1963, Edited by
Maud Miller
(Longacre Press)

Who's Who In Show Biz
(Purnell, 1963)

Boyfriend 63 Book
(City Magazines Ltd)

Radio Luxembourg Official Book of Record Stars No.3,
Introduced by Cliff. Edited by Jack Fishman
(Souvenir Press, 1964)

Boyfriend 64 Book
(City Magazines Ltd)

Radio Luxembourg Record Stars Book No.4, Edited by
Jack Fishman
(Souvenir, 1965)

Radio Luxembourg Record Stars Book No.2, Edited by
Jack Fishman
    (Souvenir, 1965)

Girl Television & Film Annual 1965, Edited by
Shirley Young
    (Odhams)

Radio Luxembourg Record Stars Book No.5, Edited by
Jack Fishman
    (Souvenir, 1966)

Boyfriend Book 1966
    (City Magazines Ltd)

Star TV & Film Annual 1967
    (Odhams)

Top Pop Stars, Edited by Ken Ferguson
    (Purnell, 1969)

Pop Stars of the 50s, 60s, 70s & 80s Portraits, Harry
Hammond & Gerad Mankowitz
    (Treasure Press, 1984)

PART 6

MISCELLANEA

AWARDS

Starting in 1958 the RIAA (Recording Industry Association of America) began certifying million-sellers and awarding Gold Discs for albums that had sold one million dollars worth of albums in value (wholesale price) based on one third of the list price, a figure that represented much less than 1 million actual units sold. The qualifying sales figure was changed to half a million in 1975 and also represented singles. It would be a long time before a British system of awards was introduced and in 1959 Gerald Marks, the then editor of *Disc*, began a scheme that would be the equivalent of the American system. Basing his system on the fact that the population of the UK was approximately a quarter of that in the States it was decided to award a Silver Disc for sales of 250,000 units. To claim an award the record company had to notify the editor of *Disc*. As there was no audit carried out, these claims were taken on trust. In 1959 only four record companies claimed Silver Discs including Columbia and Decca. With the demise of *Disc* in the seventies, the certification of records and presentation of awards fell to the British Phonographic Industry. The basic design of these awards has changed little over the years.

The BPI were not the only organisation making these awards though, many were presented by the Record Companies themselves (In-House Awards), which differed from the BPI awards as the BPI initials would be missing. At this time, awards were not only being presented to the artists but also to companies, producers and engineers. With vinyl becoming a thing of the past, today's awards feature reproductions of the cassettes and compact discs along with the covers. Multiple awards are often represented with reproductions of the covers, the quantity of these covers based on the volume sold. Below are the qualifying figures for awards from the BPI (as at December 1993):

SINGLES		SINGLES		ALBUMS	
(up to December 1988)		(after January 1989)			
Silver	250,000	Silver	200,000	Silver	60,000
Gold	500,000	Gold	400,000	Gold	100,000
Platinum	1,000,000	Platinum	600,000	Platinum	300,000

BPI CERTIFIED AWARDS

SINGLES

Gold:
  We Don't Talk Anymore (1979)
  Daddy's Home (1981)
  Living Doll (1986)
  Mistletoe And Wine (1988)

Silver:
  Carrie (1980)
  Dreamin' (1980)
  Wired For Sound (1981)
  Please Don't Fall In Love (1983)
  All I Ask Of You (1986)
  The Best Of Me (1989)
  I Just Don't Have The Heart (1990)
  Saviours Day (1990)
  Some People (1987)

ALBUMS

Multi-Platinum:
  Private Collection (1989) (4 x Platinum)

Double Platinum:
  From A Distance – The Event (1991)

Platinum:
  40 Golden Greats (1977)
  Love Songs (1981)
  Wired For Sound (1981)
  Always Guaranteed (1987)
  Stronger (1989)
  Together (1991)
  The Hit List (1994)
Gold:
  I'm Nearly Famous (1976)
  The Cliff Richard Story (1976)
  Rock 'n' Roll Juvenile (1979)
  Thank You Very Much (1979)
  I'm No Hero (1980)
  Now You See Me, Now You Don't (1982)

Silver (1983) (includes Box Set)
The Best Of Cliff Richard And The Shadows (1987)
The Album (1993)

Silver:
  Live (1977)
  The Rock Connection (1985)
  Dressed For The Occasion (1983)

IN-HOUSE AWARDS

Silver:
  Living Doll
  Travellin' Light
  A Voice In The Wilderness
  Fall In Love With You
  Please Don't Tease
  Nine Times Out Of Ten
  I Love You
  Theme For a Dream
  A Girl Like You
  When The Girl In Your Arms Is The Girl In Your Heart
  The Young Ones
  I'm Looking Out The Window
  It'll Be Me
  The Next Time
  Summer Holiday
  Lucky Lips
  It's All In The Game
  Don't Talk To Him
  Constantly
  On The Beach
  I Could Easily Fall
  The Minute You're Gone
  Wind Me Up
  Congratulations
  Goodbye Sam, Hello Samantha
  Power To All Our Friends
  Devil Woman
  We Don't Talk Anymore
  Carrie
  Dreamin'
  Wired For Sound
  Daddy's Home

Please Don't Fall In Love
Living Doll (w. The Young Ones)
Some People
The Best Of Me
From A Distance
Saviour's Day

Gold:
Living Doll
The Young Ones
The Next Time
Congratulations
We Don't Talk Anymore
Wired For Sound
Daddy's Home
Living Doll (w. The Young Ones)
Mistletoe And Wine

POP POLLS

Throughout the fifties, sixties and seventies the main music papers (New Musical Express, Disc, Melody Maker and Record Mirror) held yearly pop polls where readers could vote for their favourite artists, records or TV Pop Programmes. The following list details those awards:

NEW MUSICAL EXPRESS: The most popular Pop Polls were held by this weekly paper and Cliff was a constant winner throughout the life of the Polls. In 1959 he won the Best New Singer award following this in 1960 with Top British Male Singer, an award he would win every year from 1960 to 1966, Top Singles Artist in Britain, and came second in both the World Male Singer and British Vocal Personality categories. A fifth place in World Musical Personality rounded of a successful year in the NME awards. In 1961 he came second in the World Male Singer Category and British Vocal Pesonality moving up to fourth in World Musical Personality. The same positions were reached in the 1962 awards and the following year he achieved World's Most Outstanding Singer whilst taking second place in British Vocal Personality and Worlds Outstanding Music Personality. 1964 found Cliff with first place in Top British Vocal Personality and third in both World Male Singer and

World Musical Personality. As well as being placed in both World and British Vocal Personality during the 1965 Polls Cliff also came fifth in the Best New Disc Of The Year with The Minute You're Gone. Throughout 1966, 1967 and 1968 he stayed in the top three for World Musical Personality while winning Top British Vocal Personality. With his TV Shows this gave Cliff another category to appear in and in 1970 and 1971 he came third in the Best TV/Radio Show with It's Cliff Richard.

MELODY MAKER: Between 1960 and 1967, with the exception of 1966, Cliff won the Top British Male Singer award and twice won the Single Of The Year, in 1960 with Living Doll and 1962 with The Young Ones.

RECORD MIRROR: For three years running, 1964–1966, Cliff was Top British Male Singer and in 1964/5 was awarded the Best Dressed Singer (World) award.

DISC: Another paper that voted Cliff Top British Male Singer, this time in 1965, 1966. Awards were given under many different categories and Cliff's wins included the Mr Valentine Award (1970), Best Dressed Male Star (1968 and 1970), Top Male TV Artist (third and second in 1968 and 1969 respectively.

OTHER AWARDS

As well as numerous Silver and Gold Discs presented for record sales and awards bestowed by the Music Press over the past thirty-seven years Cliff has also received countless awards from other sources. Early in his career the Variety Club of Great Britain presented Cliff with their 'Show Business Personality of the Year-1962' award and the following year he received an award for 'Most Promising Singer' from the US magazine *16*. The British daily tabloid the *Sun* voted Cliff 'Top Male Pop Personality' three years running from 1972 to 1974. Cliff has also been honored by various sectors of the Music Business – in 1974 he was the recipient of a 'Silver Cleff' from the Music Therapy Committee, three years later, in 1977, he received both a BPI Britannia Award for 'Best British Male Solo Artist' and a 'Gold Badge Award' from the Songwriters Guild of Great Britain. Another tabloid, the *Daily Mirror*, presented Cliff with the 'Nationwide Golden Award–Best Family Entertainer' and in a reader's poll held by the *Sunday Telegraph* came 'Top Pop Star–1981'. *Music Week*, the industry journal, awarded both Cliff and the Shadows an award for twenty-five years as major recording artists in 1983. The TV listings magazine *TV Times* regularly held a readers' poll and at the awards ceremony, broadcast on television, Cliff has been a regular, winning awards that have included the 1986 'Top Singer Award'. More honours were forthcoming in 1989 including a 'Lifetime Achievement Award' from the British Phonographic Industry and a 'Lifetime Achievement Diamond Award' from Diamond Awards. Whilst all these mean a great deal to Cliff the two most prestigious awards came in 1980 and 1995 respectively. In the 1980 New Years Honours list Cliff received his OBE and in 1995 became the first pop star to receive a Knighthood.

This article does not pretend to be a complete list of awards and presentations made to Cliff and there is no doubt that in the coming years he will be the recipient of many more.

THE KNIGHTHOOD

The crowds are usually there to catch a glimpse of the Queen, but on Wednesday 25 October 1995, it was Cliff who held court outside Buckingham Palace with the hundreds of fans who had gathered as the singer arrived for his 10.30am formal investiture as Knight Bachelor. Even the royal staff, who are used to welcoming a stream of famous visitors, peered excitedly through the Palace curtains. Cliff, dressed in an evergreen morning suit, was accompanied by his three sisters, Jacqui, Joan and Donna, who watched their brother receive his knighthood as the Queen touched a sword to his shoulders during the brief ceremony held in the Palace ballroom.

After the ceremony, Cliff was photographed by the press in the courtyard of the Palace as he showed off the medal inscribed 'Knight Bachelor' and declared 'It's very apt. What I am proud of is that I have received this for nothing to do with politics, commerce, or even rock 'n' roll'. The knighthood was in fact awarded in the Queen's Birthday Honours for his dedication to charity, 'Like many in showbusiness I have worked for many charities over the years – it is something really worthwhile'.

STUDIOS
USED DURING CLIFF'S CAREER

ABBEY ROAD STUDIOS, London
Formerly known as the EMI Studios it became internationally famous when the Beatles called their last album Abbey Road. Used regularly by Cliff throughout the fifties, sixties and into the mid-seventies.

EMI STUDIOS, Barcelona
The EMI studios in Spain were, appropriately, the location of the recording of the When In Spain tracks.

JUBILEE HALL, Blackpool
In 1963 a handful of tracks for EP release were recorded during Cliff's season in Blackpool.

ESTUDIOS VALENTIM DE CARVALHO, Lisbon
This foreign studio was used in the mid-sixties to record the backing tracks for When In Rome.

IBC STUDIOS, London
Cliff only used this studio a couple of times during the last sixties.

ADVISION
In the late sixties-early seventies Cliff recorded in a number of different studios for just one or two sessions. Advision was one such studio used in the early seventies.

CHAPPELL STUDIOS, London
This London studio was used on a few occasions throughout 1968–1971.

MORGAN STUDIOS, London
Cliff's live album, Help It Along, was recorded at this London studio along with a number of album tracks and singles.

PATHE MARCONI, Paris
These studios were used to record the basic tracks for what was to become the Rock 'n' Roll Juvenile album in 1979.

RG JONES, Wimbledon
Studio used regularly throughout the late eighties and nineties. Among the albums recorded at this studio are Always Guaranteed, Stronger and The Album.

RIVERSIDE STUDIOS, London
Tracks that appears on the I'm No Hero album along with some B-sides were recorded at this London studio.

GALLERY STUDIOS, Chertsey
Studio owned by Phil Manzanera where Cliff recorded the Wired For Sound tracks in the early 1980s.

STRAWBERRY STUDIOS SOUTH, Dorking
Now closed down this studio was used extensively in the early eighties. Most of the Silver and Rock 'n' Roll Silver tracks were recorded here.

EDEN STUDIOS, London
Studio used for the recording of the 1983 Cliff and Phil Everly duets She Means Nothing To Me and I'll Mend Your Broken Heart

AIR RECORDING STUDIOS, London
This Oxford Street studio was used for a handful of tracks including the Mike Batt produced Please Don't Fall In Love.

MAYFAIR RECORDING STUDIOS, London
This studio was utilised extensively in the eighties for overdubbing and mixing, particularly on the tracks that made up the Always Guaranteed album.

THE 'SOL' STUDIO, Kent
Studio used for the recording of the Elton John duet Slow Rivers.

ROUNDHOUSE STUDIOS, London
Cliff's vocals for She's So Beautiful were recorded at Roundhouse.

MARCUS STUDIOS, London
Another studio that was used for only a handful of sessions in the mid-eighties.

MASTER ROCK STUDIOS
Stuart Colman produced the number one single Living Doll with Cliff and The Young Ones at this London studio.

BATTERY STUDIOS, London
Only one track was recorded by Cliff at this London studio, the Aswad duet Share A Dream.

PWL STUDIOS, London
The famous studios owned and operated by Stock, Aitken and Waterman. Responsible for many dance records in the eighties Cliff turned to SAW and their studios when he recorded his dance track Just Don't Have The Heart.

BLACK BARN STUDIOS, Surrey
Everybody's Got A Crisis In Their Lives was the only track recorded at this studio. Cliff provided vocals on this charity record.

THE TOWNHOUSE, London
London studio mainly used for remixing and mastering of Cliff product in the eighties.

JFM STUDIOS, Twickenham
A couple of Dave Cooke penned numbers were recorded at this studio.

WESTSIDE STUDIOS
Three Bruce Welch produced tracks that found release on Cliff Richard – The Album were recorded here.

THE HIT FACTORY
One track from Cliff Richard – The Album was recorded at this studio.

NOMIS STUDIOS
As with the Hit Factory this studio produced just one track featured on Cliff Richard – The Album.

SARM WEST, London
Mainly used for mixing and re-mixing of material. The Event album was mixed and mastered here.

VENUES

WHERE CLIFF HAS BEEN RECORDED LIVE

ABBEY ROAD STUDIOS, London
In 1959 Cliff recorded his debut album before a specially invited audience of 200 at these famous studios.

ABC THEATRE, Kingston, Surrey
During Cliff and the Shadows' 1962 hectic touring schedule recordings were made at this theatre for future record release. As detailed elsewhere these recordings never found an official release.

SHIBUYA PUBLIC HALL, Tokyo, Japan
In 1967 this venue was the location of Cliff's first real live album.

TALK OF THE TOWN, London
In the late sixties Cliff appeared at this popular London venue many times and in May 1968 three shows were taped for future release.

KOSEINENKIN HALL, Tokyo, Japan
In 1972 and 1974 live recordings were made at this Far East venue.

MORGAN STUDIOS, London
As with Cliff's debut album a specially invited audience attended the three-day taping of the Help It Along album in 1973.

PALLADIUM, London
This well-known London Theatre had seen many successes for Cliff and the Shadows – pantomimes, cabaret and variety seasons – and was the venue for the 20th anniversary reunion concerts given by Cliff and the Shadows in 1978.

HAMMERSMITH ODEON, London
Cliff's appearance in 1981 at the Hammersmith Odeon was featured in the four-part TV series and a handful of tracks made it on to vinyl.

ROYAL ALBERT HALL, London
This famous concert hall was the setting for Cliff's appearance with the London Philharmonic Orchestra in 1983 resulting in the Dressed For The Occasion album.

WEMBLEY STADIUM
This giant arena, with a capacity of over 72,000 and more famous for its sporting events than rock concerts, was sold out for both of Cliff's Event concerts in 1989.

KNEBWORTH
In 1990 Cliff and the Shadows appeared at this annual festival in aid of the Nordoff-Robbins Music Therapy Clinic.

WEMBLEY ARENA, London
One of London's main rock/pop venues. In the 1990s several Cliff concerts were recorded for radio and record release.

CLIFF-RELATED SIGHTS

FOR FANS AND TOURISTS

1. The 2i's Coffee Bar where Cliff regularly appeared and met Hank Marvin and Bruce Welch is located at 57–59 Old Compton Street in London. It re-opened as the Dome Bar Cafe on 5 October 1995.

2. Abbey Road Recording Studios is located in St Johns Wood, North London where Cliff and the Shadows began their recording careers under the direction and supervision of producer Norrie Paramor.

3. The Empire Theatre where 'Oh Boy!' was broadcast live every Sunday is located in Hackey, and is now a bingo club.

4. Gas Street Basin where Cliff filmed scenes for 'Take Me High' among the narrow boats is located in Birmingham. The narrow boat converted into a floating home as seen in the film is moored in Gas Street Basin.

5. Filopapou Hill overlooking the Acropolis just outside Athens where Cliff in string vest filmed 'The Next Time' for 'Summer Holiday'.

6. CBS Television City where Cliff filmed his appearance on 'The Ed Sullivan Show' is located at Fairfax Avenue, and Beverly Boulevard, Los Angeles.

7. Elstree Film Studios where Cliff filmed 'The Young Ones' is located in Borehamwood High Street, Hertfordshire. The studios have not been used since 1990, and were placed on the market for sale in 1993. Most of the stages have become derelict and in need of repair.

8. MGM film studios in Borehamwood where Cliff began his film career were demolished in 1986 and redeveloped as office blocks.

9. Pinewood Film Studios where Cliff filmed 'Finders Keepers' is located at Ivor Heath in Buckinghamshire.

10. Shepperton Film Studios where Cliff filmed 'Expresso Bongo' is located at Studios Road, Shepperton in Middlesex.

11. The recording studio that was located over the HMV record shop in Oxford Street (near Bond Street) where Cliff recorded his demo tape of 'Lawdy Miss Clawdy' and 'Breathless' in the summer of 1958 closed down, although HMV still runs one of their own Oxford Street stores from the same site.

12. Harley House South where the Cliff Richard Organisation were formerly located is situated in Portsmouth Road, Esher overlooking the Sandown race course. A small ground floor studio was used for rehearsals, and for recording some B sides and speech only recordings.

13. Cheshunt Secondary Modern School later renamed Riversmead, then, Bishops Lee, closed down around 1986, but reopened as Cheshunt School around 1992 and is located in College Road. The main teaching block where Cliff's classroom was situated still remains.

UNREALISED PROJECTS

The Cliff Richard Show 1962

Recordings made at the ABC Kingston were to be issued as a live album featuring both Cliff's and the Shadows performance from two shows given at the venue in March 1962. The project had proceeded as far as finished lacquers being made before the project was dropped. The album would have featured the following Cliff tracks: Do You Wanna Dance/Dim, Dim The Lights/My Blue Heaven/Razzle Dazzle/Roving Gambler/Save My Soul/When The Girl In Your Arms Is The Girl In Your Heart/I Got A Woman/Medley: Lessons In Love–Got A Funny Feeling–The Young Ones–We Say Yeah

Hide My Eyes

In 1960 it was announced that the Margery Allingham novel Hide My Eyes would be adapted as Cliff's third film. American actress Carol Lynley was to be Cliff's co-star and Cliff would have sung at least three songs in the movie. The idea was dropped in favour of The Young Ones.

Aladdin

Following on from the successful pantomime season Cliff was due to star in a movie version of Aladdin. Due to other commitments by both Cliff and supporting artists, the project was dropped.

Pinnochio

Following on from his other successes in pantomime plans were made to star in Pinnochio. The idea never materialised probably due to Cliff's hectic schedule of touring and filming.

Sing-A-Song Of Disney 1965

In November 1965 Cliff recorded four tracks for possible inclusion on an album/extended play release provisionally titled 'Sing A Song Of Disney'. The tracks; Sooner Or Later/A Spoonful Of Sugar/Chim Chim Cheree and Zip-A-Dee-Do-Dah were all songs made famous in Disney productions. For unknown reasons the idea was dropped and these tracks remain unissued.

Xanadu

In 1971 it was announced that Cliff's sixth film was to be Xanadu, based on the story by Alan Plater. The idea was postponed indefinitely and by 1973 Cliff had begun work on Hot Property (Take Me High). In the 1980 film and soundtrack album from Xanadu, which starred Olivia Newton-John and Gene Kelly, Cliff sang Suddenly as a duet with Olivia.

Cliff – The Early Years

This 'best of' compilation of early tracks was scheduled for release in February 1980 but cancelled for reasons unknown. Track listing was to be as follows: Please Don't Tease/Willie And The Hand Jive/'D' In Love/High Class Baby/Mean Woman Blues/Nine Times Out Of Ten/My Feet Hit The Ground/Apron Strings/Livin' Lovin' Doll/Never Mind/Schoolboy Crush/It'll Be Me/Gee Whiz It's You/Choppin' 'n' Changin'/Blue Suede Shoes/Dynamite/Mean Streak/She's Gone/I Cannot Find A True Love/Move It

Concert Run in London's West End 1990

Following on from Cliff's successful two appearances at Wembley Stadium in June 1989 (The Event) plans were made to stage a concert/theatrical show in the West End. At the time Cliff said: 'I am going to open with a concert in the West End. I've always wanted to do a concert where I was settled in one theatre for a period of time, so I'll be there for a minimum of three months, possibly six months, at the London Dominion Theatre, Tottenham Court Road. I'll do a concert style performance specially built for London. I hope it will be exciting and different because being in one theatre for a length of time means I can go overboard with effects and things as you don't have to pull them down every night.' Artwork for the concert posters/fliers was prepared and eventually altered to promote the From A Distance tour.

CLIFF'S FAVOURITE
BIBLE STORIES FOR CHILDREN

The Old Testament:
1. God creates the world
2. Adam and Eve
3. Noah and his ark
4. Abraham's journey
5. Abraham and Isaac
6. Joseph's coat of many colours
7. Joseph sees his family again
8. God chooses Moses
9. Moses saves the Israelites
10. Moses teaches God's law
11. Rahab and the red cord
12. The battle of Jericho
13. Achan steals from God
14. God calls to Samuel
15. David fights Goliath
16. King Solomon
17. Daniel in the lion's den
18. Elijah prays for rain
19. Esther saves her people
20. Isaiah learns a new king

The New Testament:
21. Jesus is born
22. The shepherds go to Bethlehem
23. The three wise men visit Jesus
24. Jesus is found in the temple
25. Jesus is baptised and tested
26. Jesus calls his first disciples
27. Jesus calms the storm
28. Jesus heals the paralysed man
29. The loaves and the fishes
30. Jesus teaches the people
31. The good Samaritan
32. The lost son
33. Zaccheus listens to Jesus
34. Jesus enters Jerusalem
35. Jesus is angry in the temple
36. Jesus' last night.
37. Jesus dies on the cross
38. Jesus lives again
39. Jesus goes to heaven
40. God sends his Holy Spirit
41. Peter escapes his prison
42. Paul turns to God

CLIFF'S FAVOURITE
BIBLICAL QUOTE

Philippians 4:13:
'I can do all things through Christ who strengthens me.'

CLIFF'S LIFELINES

1958 & 1992

CLIFF'S LIFELINES (as published in New Musical Express on 14 November 1958)

First public appearance Youth fellowship dance in Cheshunt in 1954.

Dislikes Insincere people; putting on a false smile for photographers; smoking.

Favourite food Indian curry and rice.

Favourite guitarists Duane Eddy, Al Casey, Hank Marvin.

Favourite band Glenn Miller.

Favourite female singers Connie Francis, Julie London, Helen Shapiro.

Favourite male singers Elvis Presley, Ricky Nelson, Ray Charles.

Hobbies Collecting Elvis records; playing badminton.

Greatest ambition To meet Elvis.

Musical education Taught guitar by his father.

Former job Office clerk.

Educated Stanley Park Road School, Carshalton. Cheshunt Secondary Modern.

Sisters Donella, Jacqueline and Joan.

20 CRUCIAL CLIFF FAX (as published in 'Cliff Behind The Legend!' magazine 1992)

Full Name Harry Rodger Webb.

Born 14 October 1940.

Place Lucknow, India.

Family Parents Rodger and Dorothy Webb, sisters Donella, Jacqueline, Joan.

Height 5ft 10.5ins.

Weight 10st 9lb.

Eyes Dark brown.

Starsign Libra

Primary Schools Stanley Park Road Primary, Carshalton, Surrey and Kings Road Primary, Waltham Cross, Herts.

Secondary School Cheshunt Secondary Modern, Herts.

School Sports Played football for Herts under 14's, school javelin record.

Exams Passed O level English.

First Girlfriend Elizabeth Sayers.

First Job Accounts clerk, Atlas Lamps, Enfield.

First Record 'Heartbreak Hotel' by Elvis.

First Car Sunbeam Alpine.

Food Likes condensed milk sandwich (urgh!), curry and rice, porridge, egg beans chips and spotted dick with custard.

Worst Habit Sucking teeth.

Hates Rude children.

Honours Awarded an OBE.

FAN CLUBS

Although there is no official Cliff Richard fan club, there is the very efficiently operated International Cliff Richard Movement (ICRM) which has gained the approval and co-operation of the Cliff Richard Organisation.

The ICRM publishes a bi-monthly club paper 'Dynamite International'. The club headquarters and their regional clubs, are listed below.

ICRM HEADQUARTERS

ANTON HUSMAN JNR
International Cliff Richard Movement
Postbox 94164
1090 GD
Amsterdam
Netherlands

GENERAL ICRM INFORMATION

INTERNATIONAL CLIFF RICHARD MOVEMENT
PO Box 2BQ
London W1A 2BQ

(All mail is distributed to respective fan club or to Cliff)

REGIONAL ICRM FAN CLUBS IN THE UK

MRS ANTHEA JANSEN
Cliff Richard Fan Club of **Birmingham**
1 Aldis Road
Walsall WS2 9AY

MRS MAUREEN NEATHWAY and
JACKIE HIMBURG
Cliff Richard Fan Club of **Bristol** and **Somerset**
22 Trent Close
Yeovil
Somerset BA21 5XQ

RITA DOWDING
Cliff Richard Fan Club of **Derbyshire** and **Nottinghamshire**
173 Pym Street
Nottingham NG3 2FF

MRS JUDY BREWIN
Cliff Richard Fan Club of **Beds** and **Herts**
No. 8 Lloyd Court
15 The Crescent
Beds MK40 2RT

MRS SUE COLLIER
Cliff Richard Fan Club of **Devon** and **Cornwall**
205 Hemerdon Heights
Chaddlewood
Plymouth
Devon PL7 3TJ

FREDA HECTOR and MAUREEN WAKEFIELD
Cliff Richard Fan Club of **Dorset**
22 Benmoor Road
Creekmoor
Poole
Dorset BH17 7DS

MRS SUSAN DAVIE
Cliff Richard Fan Club of **Edinburgh**
8 Neidpath Court
Craigievar Wynd
Edinburgh
Scotland EH12 8UF

MRS EVANE WHITE
Cliff Richard Fan Club of **Strathclyde**
2 Beechwood Road
North Caebrain
Scotland G67 2NW

WILLIAM HOOPER
Cliff Richard Fan Club of **Gloucestershire** and
Oxfordshire
17 Podsmead Road
Tuffley
Gloucester GL1 5PB

MRS MARION CUNNINGHAM
Cliff Richard Fan Club of **Hampshire**
66 Park Road
Freemantle
Southampton
Hants S15 3DE

NICKY PIERCY
Cliff Richard Fan Club of **Hereford** and **Worcester**
12 Monks Way
Peopleton
Pershore
Worcs WR10 2EH

HELEN JONES
Cliff Richard Fan Club of **Kent**
29 Wren Road
Sidcup, Kent DA14 4LY

KATHLEEN FEREDAY
Cliff Richard Fan Club of **Lancashire** and **Cumbria**
46 Rydal Road
Lancaster
Lancs LA1 3HA

MRS L MOWE
Cliff Richard Fan Club of **Leicestershire** and
Northants
148 Roston Drive
Hinckley
Leics LE10 0XP

MRS JULIE LEIGHTON
Cliff Richard Fan Club of **Lincolnshire** and
Humberside
3 Folkingham Road
Billingborough
Lincs NG34 0NT

JANET MANLEY
Cliff Richard Fan Club of **London** and **Surrey**
78 Portland Road
Kingston Upon Thames
Surrey KT1 25H

SANDRA HOUGH
Cliff Richard Fan Club of **Manchester**
4 Dawlish Avenue
Cheadle Hulme
Greater Manchester SK8 6JF

WENDY LEFTWICH
Cliff Richard Fan Club of **Merseyside** and **Cheshire**
2 The Green
Caldry
Wirral
Merseyside L48 2LA

MRS S P HANDS
Cliff Richard Fan Club of **Middlesex** and
Buckinghamshire
11 Southview
Downley
High Wycombe HP13 5UL

MRS ANN THOMPSON
Cliff Richard Fan Club of **Northern Ireland**
409 Ballysillan Road
Belfast
Northern Ireland BT14 6RE

MISS MAUREEN WINN
Cliff Richard Fan Club of **NE England**
29 Rodsley Avenue
Gateshead
Tyne And Wear NE8 4JY

MRS SANDRA MCGREISH
Cliff Richard Fan Club of **East Anglia**
133 George Lambton Avenue
Newmarket
Suffolk CB8 0BN

MRS CAROLE DAVIS
Cliff Richard Fan Club of **Sussex**
18 Westlake Gardens
Worthing
West Sussex BN13 1LF

MRS DAWN NOTT
Cliff Richard Fan Club of **Isle of Wight**
5 Park Road
Kings Town Estate
Brading
Isle of Wight PO36 0HU

SARAH MULLINS
Cliff Richard Fan Club of **Wiltshire** and **Berkshire**
St Teresas Cottage
Church Street
Tisbury
Salisbury
Wiltshire

MRS JENNIFER CHATTEN
Cliff Richard Fan Club of **Yorkshire**
26 Wentworth Drive
Harrogate
Yorkshire HG2 7LA

MRS WENDY ASHBY
Cliff Richard Fan Club of **Warwickshire**
51 Shenstone Avenue
Rugby CV22 5BL

ANGELA J KING
Cliff Richard Fan Club of **Wales**
1 Ffordd Penrhwylfa
Prestatyn
Clwyd
North Wales LL19 8AD

ANGELA THOMPSON
Cliff Richard Fan Club of **Ireland**
50 Castlefarm
Shankill
Co. Dublin
Ireland

ICRM FANS CLUBS OVERSEAS

PETRA WICHMANN
Cliff Richard Fan Club of **Austria**
Zieglergasse 12/14
1.1070 Vienna
AUSTRIA

GWENDA HUGHES
Cliff Richard Movement of **Australia**
33 Lance Drive
Mt Warren Park
4207 Queensland
AUSTRALIA

MISS MARLEEN SUYKERBUYK
Cliff Richard Fan Club of **Belgium**
Korte Damstraat 15
9180 Moerbeke-Waas
BELGIUM

DENISE MAGI
Cliff Richard Fan Club of **Canada**
PO Box 124 – Station F
Con-May 2L4
Toronto Ont.
CANADA

JYTTE MATHIASEN
Cliff Richard Fan Club of **Denmark**
Ostergarden 42 3th
DK-2635 Ishoej
DENMARK

MR BERNARD BROCHE
Cliff Richard Fan Club of **France**
10 Rue Edouard Rouviere
F-38450 Vif
FRANCE

MICHAELA SELLHOFF
Cliff Richard Fans of **Germany**
Leithestr. 56
D-44866
Bochum
GERMANY

MRS KATRINA RICHARDS
Cliff Richard Movement of **New Zealand**
29 Cotton Street
St Johns
Auckland 6
NEW ZEALAND

HELLE KJENOLLE
Cliff Richard Fan Club of **Norway**
Hoffsveien 30
N-0275 Oslo
NORWAY

MARIANNE KNUTSON
Cliff Richard Fan Club of **Sweden**
Tyringegatan 3
S-252 52 Helsingborg
SWEDEN

MR ALBIN HOGMANN
Cliff Richard Fan Club of **Switzerland**
Birchstrasse 231
CH–8032 Zurich
SWITZERLAND

GILL ATKINS
Cliff Richard Movement of **South Africa**
63 Franschoek Road
Durbanville Hills 7550
Cape Province
SOUTH AFRICA

MARY POSNER
Cliff Richard Movement of **America**
8916 N Skokie Blvd
USA 60077 Skokie
Illinois
USA

INDEPENDENT
CLIFF RICHARD FAN CLUBS

CLIFF RICHARD GRAPEVINE
PO Box 55
Colchester
Essex CO4 3XJ

GRAPEVINE issues a quarterly magazine-format
newsletter. The club raises funds through the sale
of photographs, stationery, sweatshirts and other
memorabilia which is donated to Cliff's charitable trust.
The club is run by Veronica Owen, Diana Duffet, Judith
Abbott and Gordon Donaldson

CLIFF UNITED FAN CLUB
28 Blenheim Road
Sutton
Surrey SM1 2PX

The CLIFF UNITED FAN CLUB is operated by Christine
Whitehead and emphasises Cliff's Christian activities.
The club membership offers an extensive magazine as
well as the organisation of many and varied events.

INTERNATIONAL
CLIFF WEEK

International Cliff Week is annually held during the week of Cliff's birthday (14 October), during which time all members of the International Cliff Richard Movement bombard their local radio stations with requests for Cliff's music to be played.

THE CLIFF RICHARD
CHARITABLE TRUST

The Cliff Richard Charitable Trust was set up and established so that Cliff had a convenient channel for his support of the many charities with which he sympathises. The trust makes a series of donations every quarter, and all recipients have to be registered charities, and appeals from individuals cannot and are not considered. The trust makes no public appeal for funds and is essentially a channel for Cliff's own personal donations, however both individual fans and fan clubs such as the International Cliff Richard Movement, Cliff United and Grapevine do make donations to the trust.

BIBLIOGRAPHY

During our research we made use of the following books:

It's Great To Be Young, Cliff Richard
  (Souvenir Press, 1960)
The Cliff Richard Story, George Tremlett
  (Futura, 1975)
Which One's Cliff?, Cliff Richard
  (Hodder & Stoughton 1977 and 1990)
Cliff – A Biography, Tony Jasper and Patrick Doncaster
  (Sidgwick & Jackson, 1981 and 1992)
Cliff Richard and the Shadows, Dezo Hoffman
  (Virgin, 1985)
Abbey Road, Brian Hall
  (Patrick Stephens, 1985)
Cliff, Jorgen Mylius
  (Mallings, 1986)
Rock 'n' Roll – I Gave You The Best Years Of My Life, Bruce Welch
  (Viking, 1989)
Elvis His Life From A–Z, Ferd L Worth & Steve D Tamerius
  (Corgi, 1989)
The NME Rock 'n' Roll Years
  (Hamlyn, 1990)
Cliff Richard In His Own Words, Kevin St John
  (Omnibus, 1991)
The Top Twenty Book 1955–1990, Tony Jasper
  (Blandford, 1991)
Cliff Richard: The Complete Recording Sessions 1958–1990 Peter Lewry & Nigel Goodall
  (Blandford, 1991)

The Complete Beatles Chronicle, Mark Lewisohn
  (Pyramid, 1992)
Cliff Richard: The Complete Chronicle, Mike Read, Nigel Goodall & Peter Lewry
  (Hamlyn, 1993)
Cliff Richard – The Biography, Steve Turner
  (Lion, 1993)
Cliff Richard's Favourite Bible Stories Retold For Children, Sue Shaw
  (Conrad-Octopus, 1993)
Hollywood Rock, Marshall Crenshaw
  (Plexus, 1994)
The Ultimate Elvis: Elvis Presley Day By Day, Patricia Jobe Pierce
  (Simon & Schuster, 1994)
British Hit Albums, Paul Gambaccini, Tim Rice & Jonathan Rice
  (Guinness Publishing, 1994)
Guinness Book of Rock Stars, Dafydd Rees & Luke Crampton
  (Guinness, 1994)
British Hit Singles, Paul Gambaccini, Tim Rice & Jonathan Rice
  (Guinness Publishing, 1995)

We also consulted the following periodicals, magazines and newspapers during our research:

New Musical Express, Melody Maker, Music Week, Rolling Stone, Billboard, Record Collector, Now Dig This, Music Collector, Boyfriend, Mirabelle and Bournemouth Evening Echo.

PICTURE ACKNOWLEDGEMENTS

Every effort has been made to trace the copyright holders of the photographs in this book, but one or two were unreachable. We would be grateful if the photographers concerned would contact us.

Page No

iii Cliff, early 1960s (Rex Features)

vi Cliff, early 1960s (Rex Features)

x Bruce Welch (Paolo Battigelli)

PART 1

14 Cliff, 1964 (Rex Features)

16 Clockwise from centre: Cliff, Donna Webb, Tito Burns, Joe Lee (chauffer), Hank Marvin, Tony Meehan, Bruce Welch, Jet Harris, Len Saxon (road Manager), George Ganjou, Dorothy Webb (Hulton Deutsch)

17 Front row, left to right: Cliff, unkown, John Foster, Ian Samwell, Terry Smart. Back row, left to right: unknown, Alex Most, Bruce Welch, Clem Cattini (courtesy of Tricia Hercoe)

18 Cliff at Hampton Court, 1994 (Sue Andrews)

20 Cliff at The Album launch, 1993 (John McGoran)

22 Cliff, 1994 (John McGoran)

23 Cliff, 1964 (Rex Features)

24 Dorothy Webb, Cliff, unkown – early 60s (Rex Features)

25 Cliff, 1950s (Gary Cards)

26 Cliff, 1964 (Colette Williams Collection)

27 (top right) Publicity photo of Cliff from the early 1960s (Klasik Cards – from Colette Williams Collection)

27 (bottom left) Expresso Bongo Publicity picture, 1959 (Colette Williams collection)

31 Publicity photo from Wonderful Life, 1963

35 Cliff and Claudia Lombard, competitors for the Eurovision Song Contest, 1964 – Cliff sang 'Congratulations' and Claude sang 'When the World Was Mine' for Belgium (Hulton Deutsch)

36 Cliff, late 1960s (Denisa Nova)

37 Cliff, early 1970s (Denisa Nova)

39 Cliff with Russell Harty and members of London Symphony Orchestra, 1979 (Hulton Deutsch)

40 Cliff, 1979 (Hulton Deutsch)

41 Cliff receiving Daily Mirror Readers' Award, 1980 (Syndication International)

23 Cliff, 1965 (Rex Features)

46 Cliff, 1992 (Tricia Hercoe)

47 Cliff at Birmingham Heathcliff launch, 1994 (Mary Corbett)

PART 2

50 Left to right: Debbie McGhee, Gloria Hunniford, Cliff, Annabella Croft, Sue Barker and Angel Rippon at the launch of Cliff's Tennis Trail, 1992 (John McGoran)

59 Cliff on stage with Hank Marvin, 1995 (Sue Andrews)

60 Hank Marvin (Unkown)

62 Cliff and Frank Bruno, 1992 (Sue Andrews)

63 Cliff and Sue Barker, 1991 (Tricia Hercoe)
Cliff and Gloria Hunniford, 1993 (Sue Andrews)
Cliff and Hank Marvin, 1994 (Sue Andrews)

67 Cliff with Tim Rice at Heathcliff press conference, 1996 (Samantha Esplin)

72 Cliff, 1992 (Rex Features)

77 Cliff and Cilla Black, early 1960s (Rex Features)

78 Cliff and Una Stubbs in Wonderful Life, 1963 (Hulton Deutsch)

PART 3

80 Cliff, New Zealand, 1990 (Tricia Hercoe)

81 Cliff and the Shadows with their Gold Disc Award, 1968 (Hulton Deutsch)

87 Bubblegum Card – 'No. 21: Cliff on TV' (Colette Williams Collection)

90 Bubblegum Card – 'No. 45: Dig this (on stage)' (Colette Williams Collection)

95 Bubblegum Card – 'No 41: Cliff Sings' (Colette Williams Collection)

100 Bubblegum Card – 'No. 15: Rehearsing with Cherry Wainer' (Colette Williams Collection)

104 Bubblegum Card – 'No.10: Some fun at the fair' (Colette Williams Collection)

111 Bubblegum Card – 'No. 4: Listening to a recording' (Colette Williams Collection)

115 Cliff, 1970s (Unknown)

120 Cliff at the Boys Brigade Top Squad Night, mid-seventies (Michael Wilson Collection)

131 Cliff, 1950s (unknown)

135 Cliff backstage at the Greenbelt Festival, 1993 (Christine Whitehead)

141 Cliff, 1970 (Michael Wilson Collection)

145 Cliff, Wembley 1990 (Tricia Hercoe)

152 Cliff, Liverpool 1988 (Lisa Gray)

153 Cliff, New Zealand 1995 (Tricia Hercoe)

158 Cliff, Wembley 1990 (Tricia Hercoe)

165 Cliff, Wembley 1990 (Tricia Hercoe)

168 Cliff, Gospel Tour 1989 (Sue Andrews)

175 Cliff, mid-eighties (Mary Liprino)

178 Cliff, New Zealand 1990 (Tricia Hercoe)

184 Cliff, New Zealand 1990 (Tricia Hercoe)

193 Mid-seventies Bootleg LP cover

197 Cliff, South Africa 1995 (Tricia Hercoe)

200 Cliff, 30th Anniversary Concert, 1988 (Sue Andrews)

201 Cliff, New Zealand 1990 (Tricia Hercoe)

204 Cliff, From a Distance Tour 1990 (Sue Andrews)

205 Cliff, New Zealand 1990 (Tricia Hercoe)

209 Cliff, New Zealand 1990 (Tricia Hercoe)

212 Cliff, From a Distance Tour 1990 (Sue Andrews)

213 Cliff, Stronger Tour 1990 (Sue Andrews)

216 Cliff, Gospel Tour 1991 (Sue Andrews)

217 Cliff, European Tour 1993 (Sue Andrews)

219 Cliff with Olivia Newton John, 1971 (Hulton Deutsch)

220 Cliff, Stronger Tour 1990 (Sue Andrews)

221 Cliff, European Tour 1993 (Sue Andrews)

224 Cliff in Time: The Musical, 1986 (Sue Andrews)

225 Cliff, New Zealand 1990 (Tricia Hercoe)

228 Cliff with Olivia Newton John and Elaine Paige during the finale of the Royal Variety Performance, 1995 (Tricia Hercoe)

229 Cliff, South Africa 1995 (Tricia Hercoe)

232 Cliff in concert, 1990s (Caron Merrick)

233 Cliff, Hit List Tour, 1994 (Sue Andrews)

236 Cliff, South Africa 1995 (Tricia Hercoe)

237 Cliff, Wembley 1990 (Tricia Hercoe)

240 Cliff, South Africa 1995 (Tricia Hercoe)

241 Cliff, European Tour 1993 (Sue Andrews)

PART 4

244 Heathcliff Launch, 1994 (Rex Features)

246 Publicity photo for Sumer Holiday, 1962

248/9 Publicity photo ror Wonderful Life, 1964 (Rex Features)

252 Publicity photo for Serious Charge, 1959

256 Cliff and Carole Gray in The Young Ones, 1961

260/1 Cliff, Director Peter Yates and Lauri Peters on location for Summer Holiday, 1962 (Michael Wilson Collection)

266 Cliff and Susan Hampshire on location for Wonderful Life, 1964 (Hulton Deutsch)

279 Cliff and the Shadows, 1966 (Nordfoto)

284 Cliff and Pamela Denton rehearsing for Five Finger Exercise, 1970 (Hulton Deutsch)

289 Cliff and Helen Hobson at Heathcliff launch, 1996 (Sue Andrews)

290 Cliff, early 1960s (Rex Features)

298/9 Cliff postcard, 1958 (Harry Hammond)

301 Cliff backstage, early 1960s (Colette Williams Collection)

303 Cliff 'live', early 1960s (London Features International)

307 left to right: Jimmy Tarbuck, Fiona Castle and Cliff at charity concert For the Love of Roy [Castle], London Palladium 1995 (Sue Andrews)

315 Cliff and Rosemary Ford singing 'Devil Woman', 1988 (Mogens Troeisen)

318 Cliff, South Africa 1995 (Tricia Hercoe)

384 Cliff, 1970s (Rex Features)

325 Cliff, New Zealand 1990 (Tricia Hercoe)

333 left to right: Des O'Connor, Cliff and Ronni Corbett, early 1990s (unkown)

334 Cliff with Ruby Wax on Joy To The World, 1993 (Sue Andrews)

335 Cliff with Olivia Newton John in the Royal Variety Performance, 1995 (Tricia Hercoe)

336 Cliff, early 1960s (Star Pictures)

337 Cliff at the Dreamworld Press Conference, Australia early 1990s (Unknown)

340 Cliff, 1994 (Tricia Hercoe)

341 Cliff and Michael Barrymore, 1995 (Sue Andrews)

342 Cliff at a tennis tournament, 1990s (Sheilagh Middleton)

343 Cliff with Jasper Carrot, 1993 (John McGoran)

344 Cliff, 1991 (Sue Andrews)

345 Cliff, 1988 (Sue Andrews)

347 Cliff, 1993 (Sue Andrews)

PART 5

350 Very rare early postcards of Cliff (Colette Williams Collection)

352 Advertisement for Serious Charge, 1959

363 Very rare bubblegum cards featuring Cliff (Colette Williams Collection)

354 1996 Cliff Memorabilia (Chester Hopkins International Ltd)

355 Official Cliff Richard Fan Club 1964 Calendar

356 Advertisement for Expresso Bongo, 1959

357 Amercian poster for Summer Holiday, 1962 (Michael Wilson Collection)

358 Extremely rare acetate of 'Summer Holiday' signed by Cliff

360/1 Pictures from mid-seventies bootleg LP

362 Cliff in concert, early 1960s (Colette Williams Collection)

363 Richard O'Sullivan, Cliff, Melvyn Hayes and Una Stubbs on location for Wonderful Life, 1964 (Rex Features)

364 Cliff, signing Time programme backstage, 1986 (Mary Liprino)

365 First Day issue of Cliff Richard stamps, 1996

368 Cliff at book signing, 1988 (Sue Andrews)

369 Cliff, early 1960s (Colette Williams Collection)

371 Cliff, early 1960s (Star Pictures – Colette Williams Collection)

372/3 Cliff and wax model at Rock Circus, early 1990s (Sue Andrews)

PART 6

276 Cliff, 1984 (Unknown)

379 Cliff with Silver Disc Award, late 1950s (Rex Features)

381 Cliff at Buckingham Palace following his knighthood, 1995 (Rex Features)

383 Cliff at Docklands Press Conference for Access All Areas Tour, 1992 (Tricia Hercoe)

384 Cliff, Wembley 1990 (Tricia Hercoe)

388 Cliff at the Hampton Court Flower Show, 1995 (Tricia Hercoe)

390 Cliff, 1970s (Hulton Deutsch)

392 Joy To The World concert, 1995 (Sue Andrews)

397 Heathcliff launch, 1994 (John McGoran)

398 Cliff opening the Virgin Megastore in Oxford Street, 1994 (Sue Andrews)

PART 7

UPDATE 1996–1997

(Picture by Sue Andrews)

CHRONOLOGY OF CLIFF

1996–1997

10 June 1996 – Cliff took part in a Royal Gala Concert at the NEC Birmingham.

3 July 1996 – Cliff gives an impromptu spontaneous live performance to cheer up rain-soaked crowds on the centre court at Wimbledon. He sings eight songs backed by eight of the top female tennis players in the world.

22 July 1996 – In his first in-store appearance in central London for several years, a huge crowd welcomes Cliff to Tower Records in Piccadilly.

19 August 1996 – The *Cliff Richard At The Movies 1959-1974* album is released.

29 August 1996 – Rehearsals for *Heathcliff* begin.

10–11 October 1996 – The first public rehearsals of *Heathcliff* are held on an improvised stage at Earls Court in London.

16 October 1996 – The opening night of *Heathcliff* at the Academy Theatre (NIA) in Birmingham. EMI record the show for release as the live cast album.

21 October 1996 – The *Cliff At The Movies* video is released.

24 October 1996 – Press launch for the *Cliff At The Movies* video in Birmingham.

28 October 1996 – Helen Hobson's debut album *Hobson's Choice* is released, including a new arrangement of 'If Ever I Would Leave You' in a duet with Cliff.

2 December 1996 – The full-cast album *Starring Cliff Richard: Heathcliff Live (The Show)* is released.

8 December 1996 – Cliff sang a duet with Claudia Jung on German television show.

21 December 1996 – Cliff's annual pro-celebrity tennis tournament took place at the National Indoor Arena in Birmingham. Guests included Darren Day, Philip Schofield, Jo Pasquale and Jasper Carrott.

13 January 1997 – 'Be With Me Always' and three songs from Cliff's live performance at Centre Court Wimbledon is released as the new single.

12 February 1997 – The opening night of *Heathcliff* in London at the Hammersmith Labatts Apollo.

24 February 1997 – Darren Day's soundtrack album of *Summer Holiday – The Musical* is released featuring a collection of 23 songs from the show.

9 June 1997 – *Cliff Richard – The Rock 'n' Roll Years* box set is released.

4 July 1997 – *Summer Holiday – The Musical* opens in London at the Hammersmith Labatts Apollo.

DISCOGRAPHY

SINGLES – CD

Be With Me Always/Summer Holiday (live)**/The Young Ones** (live)**/Bachelor Boy** (live)
CDEM 453 January 1997

SINGLES – CASSETTE

Be With Me Always/Congratulations (live)
TCEM 453 January 1997

COMPACT DISCS

Heathcliff Live
CDEMD 1099 December 1996
(Act I): Overture *(Gordon Giltrap)* / A Misunderstood Man *(Cliff Richard/The Elements)* / Funeral Cortege *(Gordon Giltrap/Helen Hobson/The Company)* / The Sleep Of The Good *(Cliff Richard)* / Gypsy Bundle *(Jimmy Johnston/The Company)* / The Grange Waltz *(The Company)* / Each To His Own *(Helen Hobson/Cliff Richard)* / Had To Be *(Cliff Richard/Helen Hobson/Darryl Knock)* / Mrs Edgar Linton *(Helen Hobson/Friends of Cathy)* / The Journey: Africa-India-China *(The Company)* / When You Thought Of Me *(Cliff Richard/The Company)* /
(Act II): Overture (reprise)-Entr'acte Music *(Gordon Giltrap)* / When You Thought Of Me (Reprise) *(Cliff Richard/The Company)* / Dream Tomorrow *(Cliff Richard/Helen Hobson)* / I Do Not Love You Isabella (Bridge) *(Sara Haggerty/Gordon Giltrap)* / The Gambling Song *(Cliff Richard/Jimmy Johnston/The Company)* / I Do Not Love You Isabella *(Cliff Richard/Helen Hobson/Sara Haggerty/Darryl Knock/The Company)* / Isabella (Reprise) *(Sara Haggerty)* / Choosing When It's Too Late *(Cliff Richard/Helen Hobson/Darryl Knock/Sara Haggerty)* / The Madness Of Cathy *(Helen Hobson)* / Marked With Death *(Cliff Richard/Helen Hobson)* / Be With Me Always *(Cliff Richard/The Company)* / The Nightmare *(Cliff Richard/Helen Hobson/Sara Haggerty/Darryl Knock/Jimmy Johnston/Gordon Giltrap)* / Be With Me Always (Reprise) *(Helen Hobson)* / Overture (Reprise) *(Gordon Giltrap)* / A Misunderstood Man (Reprise) *(The Entire Company)* / Music For Curtain Calls

The live recording of Heathcliff was taped at Earls Court in London and The Academy, National Indoor Arena in Birmingham. Five new songs were featured on the album which came in a slip case with accompanying 40-page booklet with lyrics, a Heathcliff Diary, The Cliff Richard Heathcliff Interview and many photos.

BOX SETS

Cliff Richard The Rock 'n' Roll Years 1958-1963
CD CLIFF 001/TC CLIFF 001 June 1997
CD1 – 1958–1959: Schoolboy Crush/High Class Baby/My Feet Hit The Ground/Don't Bug Me Baby/ King Creole/TV Hop/Rockin' Robin/I'll Try/High School

(Picture by Rosie Troughton courtesy of Upbeat Recording)

Confidential/Early In The Morning/Somebody Touched Me/Livin' Lovin' Doll/Mean Streak/Never Mind/Steady With You/My Babe/Move It/That'll Be the Day/Danny/Whole Lotta Shakin' Goin' On/One Night/Apron Strings/Dynamite/I Gotta Know/The Snake And The Bookworm/Here Comes Summer/Twenty Flight Rock/Blue Suede Shoes

CD2 – 1959 (continued)–1960: Mean Woman Blues/Pointed Toe Shoes/I'm Walkin'/Don't Be Mad At Me/Willie And The Hand Jive/Nine Times Out Of Ten/Thinking Of Our Love/Evergreen Tree/She's Gone/Tell Me/Where Is My Heart/Lamp Of Love/I'm Gonna Get You/I Cannot Find A True Love/Working After School/You And I/I'm Willing To Learn/We Have It Made/Choppin' 'n' Changin'/It's You/Now's The Time To Fall In Love/I Love You/'D' In Love/Catch Me/True Love Will Come To You/First Lesson In Love/I Want You To Know/Blue Moon

CD3 – 1961 (continued)–1962: Tough Enough/Mumblin' Mosie/Fifty Tears For Every Kiss/Unchained Melody/What'd I Say/Forty Days/Without You/Shame On You/Spanish Harlem/Do You Remember/I'm Looking Out The Window/You Don't Know/Take

Special Care/Do You Wanna Dance/Since I Lost You/Dim, Dim The Lights/Save My Soul/I'm Walking The Blues/Summer Holiday/The Next Time/Blueberry Hill/A Forever Kind Of Love/Razzle Dazzle/Reelin' And Rockin'/It's All In The Game

CD4 – Rare and Rockin': Lawdy Miss Clawdy/Breathless/Twenty Flight Rock/Jailhouse Rock/Money Honey/Heartbreak Hotel/Turn Me Loose/Who's Gonna Take You Home/Let's Stick Together/What'd I Say/Forty Days/Got A Funny Feeling/Rosalie (Come Back To Me)/Me And My Shadows/Lessons In Love/We Say Yeah/Hang Up Your Rock And Roll Shoes/Dancing Shoes/It'll Be Me/Summer Holiday Advertising EP/Cliff's Personal Message To You

This highly anticipated follow-up to *Cliff Richard At The Movies 1959-1974* was once again compiled and co-ordinated by the authors of this book, and contained original master takes released during the period and many rare and previously unreleased performances. The set was packaged in a 12 x 12 box with a 48-page booklet of rare photos and memorabilia from fans' collections plus full supporting recording data, discography and chronology.

As with *The Rock 'n' Roll Years 1958-1963*, EMI (UK) are expected to release a retrospective set of the years 1963 to 1972 during Cliff's 40th anniversary year of 1998. It is believed that previously unreleased recordings will again be present on this package.

MISCELLANEOUS

Claudia Jung/Winter Träume

EMI 8 54849 2 November 1996

Cliff duets on Weihnachszeit (Mistletoe and Wine) and Saviour's Day

Helen Hobson/Hobson's Choice

Upbeat URCD124 December 1996

Cliff duets with Helen on If Ever I Would Leave You and The Wedding Song

Darren Day/Songs from Summer Holiday

RCA 74321456162 February 1997

Cliff provides backing vocals on the following tracks: In The Country/Do You Wanna Dance/(I Could Easily) Fall In Love With You/On The Beach/The Summer Holiday Megamix

BOOTLEGS

Oh Boy!

This two CD set contained the complete original *Oh Boy!* album that featured Cliff on: TV Hop/ Rockin' Robin'/High School Confidential/Early In The Morning/King Creole/I'll Try/Somebody Touched Me, as well as a second show that included Cliff performing Turn Me Loose/Three Cool Cats (with Marty Wilde and Duffy Power)/Early In The Morning (with Billy Fury and Marty Wilde) and a Rock 'n' Roll Medley (with Billy Fury, Duffy Power and The Dallas Boys)

(Art and design by Peacock)

THEATRICAL
APPEARANCES

HEATHCLIFF

Birmingham Academy (NIA) 16 October – 2 November
  14 – 19 December 1996
Edinburgh Playhouse Theatre 5 November –
  7 December 1996
Manchester Palace Theatre 7 January – 8 February 1997
London Labatts Apollo 12 February – 17 May 1997

(Picture by Sue Andrews)

Heathcliff was the realisation of Cliff's life-long personal dream to stage a major new musical based on the characters from Emily Brönte's romantic novel, *Wuthering Heights*. The world premiere production with Cliff in the lead role, and Helen Hobson opposite him as Cathy, took four years to reach the stage as a spectacular musical that combined the best of dramatic and musical theatre with a re-telling of the tragic tale of star-crossed love, passion, betrayal, romance, and revenge, set against a desolate North Yorkshire moorland landscape in the early nineteenth century. The show ran successfully for eight months at four different venues with extra performances by public demand extending the original play dates.

CAST

Narrator/Heathcliff	CLIFF RICHARD
Cathy	HELEN HOBSON
Earnshaw/Hindley	JIMMY JOHNSTON
Edgar	DARRYL KNOCK
Isabella	SARA HAGGERTY
Troubadour	GORDON GILTRAP
Elements	GEOFF DAVID
	CHRIS HOLLAND
	SONIA JONES
	NIKI KITT
	SUZANNE PARRY
Dancers	ANDREW CARROLL
	PHYLLIDA CROWLEY-SMITH
	SAMUEL HALL
	JACQUI JAMESON
	LIZZIE LEIGH

(Picture by Tricia Hercoe)

Swing

	DAVID OBINYAN
	ANDREA SMART
	BRYN WALTERS
Swing	RICHARD JOSEPH
Vocalists	DAVID COMBES
	JOHN PERRY
	MICK WILSON

Musicians:

MD/Keyboards	ALAN PARK
Keyboards	BOB NOBLE
Keyboards	KEITH HAYMAN
Guitar	JOHN CLARK
Bass	STEVE STROUD
Drums	PETE MAY

CREDITS

Lyrics	TIM RICE
Music	JOHN FARRAR
Book by	CLIFF RICHARD &
	FRANK DUNLOP
Inspired by	EMILY BRÖNTE'S
	WUTHERING HEIGHTS
Choreography	BRAD JEFFRIES
Production Musical Director	MIKE MORAN
Production Design	JOE VANEK
Lighting Design	ANDREW BRIDGE
Sound Design	MIKE LOWE
	COLIN NORFIELD
	JOHN JAMES
Director	FRANK DUNLOP
Presented by	THE CLIFF RICHARD
	ORGANISATION

PRODUCTION STAFF

Resident Director	BRAD JEFFRIES
Assistant Choreographer	MICHELLE PAPOUIS
Fights Devised by	DEREK WARE
Company & Stage Manager	DAVID FFITCH
Deputy Stage Manager	STEVE GILL
Assistant Stage Managers	TWIG CLARK
	MARINA KILBY
Automation Operator	WILL SLATTER
Sound Engineer	COLIN NORFIELD

(Picture by Tricia Hercoe)

Monitor Engineer	JOHN JAMES
Sound Technician	PAUL JOHNSON
Radio Sound Technician	VINCE SHARPE
Sound Technician	MARIA MAZARRACIN
Set Technician	TONY RAVENHILL
Backline Technician	DEREK HAGGAR
Lighting Crew Chief & Board Operator	GERRY MOTT
Lighting Crew	GEORGE OSBORNE
Vari lite Programmer	DEREK JONES
Vari lite Technician	AIDEN McCABE
Projection Operator	ANDY JOYES
Projection Technician	JACK MIDDLEBROOK
Wardrobe Mistress	REBECCA AUSTIN-THOMAS
Deputy Wardrobe Mistress	FIONA PORTEOUS
Wardrobe Assistant/ Dresser to Miss Hobson	MURRAY LANE
Wig Mistress	SHARON SUCKLEY
Assistant Wig Mistress	KENDALL WATSON

FOR HEATHCLIFF

Production Executive	DICK PARKINSON

(Picture by Tricia Hercoe)

Lighting Design Assistant	ALISTAIR GRANT
Design Researcher	NORMAN COATES
Make-Up	JACKIE SHREEVE

ACKNOWLEDGEMENTS

Set Painter	TONY BANFIELD
	OLLY JAMES
	CHRIS CLARK
Set Texturing	RUSSELL BECK
Set Sculpturing	CHRISTINE ANGUS
Model Makers	COLMAN CORISH
	TONY BANFIELD
Props & Furniture	HELEN PETTITT
	ROLF DRIVER &
	VIKKI HERON
	HOT PROPS
	NICK REDGRAVE
	STEPHEN PYLE
	WORKSHOPS
	MICHAEL WHITELEY
	ASSOCIATES
	HOWARD EATON
	LIGHTING
	RUSSELL BECK
	STUDIO
	JOHN NEVILLE
	BOWER WOOD
	SCENERY
	KEN CREASEY LTD
	WALLIS GROUP
Shoe Buying by	CLARE HARTLEY
Cliff Richard's Costumes made by	HENRIETTA WEBB
Miss Hobson's Costumes made by	CAROL MOLYNEUX
Costume Dying & Painting by	PENNY HADRILL
	NICOLA KILLEEN
	GABRIELLE FIRTH
Costumes made by	CHERYL MAW
	LIZ JONES
	LYNN CLARKE
	BILL BUTLER
	DEE SHEEHAN &
	JO HALL

Set Production Manager	ALEX REEDIJK
Production Manager	STEVE JONES
Assistant Production Manager	MIKE GROVE
Production Assistant	DEBBIE BRAY
Costume Supervisor	WENDY GRIFFITHS
Costume Supervisor's Assistant	EMMA MARSHALL
Properties Supervisor	JANE SLATTERY
Assistant Properties Buyer	GABRIELLE BRIDGES
Wig Supervisor	DANUTA BARSZCZEWSKA
Projection Realisation	PAUL CHATFIELD
Orchestration	SEAN CALLERY
Musical Associate & Additional Orchestration	KEVIN TOWNEND
Solo Guitar Adaptions	GORDON GILTRAP
Vocal Coach & Musical Rehearsal Co-ordinator	ALAN ROGERS
Repetiteur Piano	ROB ALDERTON
Rehearsal Drummer	BRIAN GREENE
Music Preparation	RON SHILLINGFORD & JOHN BAKER
Rigger	JON BRAY
Production Electrician	NICK JONES

KEITH WATSON
ANN MATHERSON
JENNY CAREY
DAVID PLUNKETT
HILARY PARKINSON
DENISE & SHIRLEY
   FITZGERALD
KEITH BISH
ROBBIE GORDON
JUDITH DARRACOTT
JACKIE KENNEDY
JUDITH CANNAN
VIV CHAMPION
JANET CHRISTMAS
ACADEMY COSTUMES
SALLY PAYNE

Hats made by	SANDRA KIERANS
Masks by	RUSSELL CRAIG
Flying Theatre Grid	UNUSUAL RIGGING
Ancillary Rigging	SUMMIT STEEL
Lights	THEATRE PROJECTS
Moving Lights	VARI LITE EUROPE LTD
Set Construction	BRILLIANT DECISIONS
Sound Systems	BRITANNIA ROW PRODUCTIONS LTD
Projection	CREATIVE TECHNOLOGY LTD
Hotels and Flights	TRINIFOLD TRAVEL LTD
Catering	SAUCERY
Trucking	REDBURN TRANSFER
Lasers	LASER CREATIONS INTERNATIONAL LTD
Radio Microphone Systems	SENNHEISER UK LTD
In-ear Monitoring	HANDHELD AUDIO/ GARWOOD COMMUNICATIONS
Merchandise	PAUL MAXWELL & JASON GOODE for CHESTER HOPKINS INTERNATIONAL LTD
Brochure Photography	PAUL COX
Photograph of Helen Hobson	IAN HOOTON
(Reproduced with kind permission of Upbeat Recordings)	
Brochure Art Direction	VIC POWER
Brochure Print	MIKE PLOSKER for

Also thanks to   PRINTERS INC & DESIGN
SYSTEM WORKSHOP
FORMULA SOUND LTD
PACKHORSE CASE COMPANY
HANGMAN DRAPES
LONDON COMMUNICATIONS
BOOTLEG MUSIC
MOLESEY REFRIGERATION
LINDA BARROW and everyone at THE ACADEMY & NEC GROUP PAUL GREGG & SAM SHROUDER and everyone at APOLLO LEISURE GROUP

FOR THE CLIFF RICHARD
ORGANISATION

Management	MALCOLM SMITH
	DAVID BRYCE
	BILL LATHAM
	ROGER BRUCE
	RITA PEASGOOD
	DIANE SANDERS
	JOHN SEYMOUR
	GILL SNOW

CHARACTERS

Heathcliff, a foundling, born 1764, died 1802
Earnshaw, owner of Wuthering Heights, died 1777
Hindley Earnshaw, born 1757, died 1784
Cathy Earnshaw, born 1765, died 1784
Edgar Linton of the Grange, born 1762, died 1801
Isabella Linton, born 1765, died 1797
Hareton, son of Hindley, born 1778
Catherine, daughter of Edgar and Catherine, born 1784
Linton, son of Isabella and Heathcliff, born 1784, died 1801

ACT ONE

The tale begins in the year 1771 when the foundling child, Heathcliff, is brought to Wuthering Heights.

The passionate but tangled love of the brooding Heathcliff and the troubled Cathy unfolds with Heathcliff leaving to travel the world. Heathcliff returns a wealthy man and the story continues until its tragic conclusion on the snow covered moors…

Overture	Troubadour
A Misunderstood Man	Storyteller
	Elements
Funeral Cortege	Troubadour
	The Company
The Sleep Of The Good	Heathcliff
Gypsy Bundle	Earnshaw
	Old Servants
	The Company
The Grange Waltz	
(The Seduction of Cathy)	The Company
Each To His Own	Cathy
	Heathcliff
Had To Be	Heathcliff
	Cathy
	Edgar

(Picture by Tricia Hercoe)

Mrs Edgar Linton	Cathy
	Isabella
	Friends of Cathy
The Journey: India/Africa/China	The Company
When You Thought Of Me	Heathcliff
	The Company

ACT TWO

Entr'acte	Troubadour
	The Company
When You Thought Of Me	
(Reprise)	Heathcliff
	The Company
Dream Tomorrow	Heathcliff
	Cathy
Isabella (Link)	Isabella
The Gambling Song	Heathcliff
	Hindley
	The Company
I Do Not Love You Isabella	Heathcliff
	Cathy
	Isabella
	Edgar
	The Company
Isabella (Reprise)	Isabella
	Heathcliff
Choosing When It's Too Late	Heathcliff
	Cathy
	Edgar
	Isabella
The Madness Of Cathy	Cathy
Marked With Death	Heathcliff
	Cathy
Be With Me Always	Heathcliff
	The Company
Funeral Cortege (Reprise)	The Company
The Nightmare	Heathcliff
	Cathy
	Isabella
	Edgar
	Hindley
	Troubadour
Be With Me Always (Reprise)	Cathy
Finale	The Company

SUMMER HOLIDAY – THE MUSICAL

Blackpool Opera House 6 June – 9 November 1996

The world premiere of the long-awaited stage version of Cliff's *Summer Holiday* movie grossed an amazing £3.8 million in six months during its run in Blackpool, and was received with critical acclaim. The *Daily Mirror* called it a 'spectacular show with a fabulous cast and huge sets and every song a hit', while the *Blackpool Evening Gazette* said it was 'a winner with a tried and tested hit song every few minutes. A family outing with sunshine guaranteed'. Cliff gave the show his blessing and was delighted at the prospect of the film being revived as a stage musical: 'Although I've never driven a bus or been to Athens since, those *Summer Holiday* memories remain vivid. Somehow the film captured a little of the mood of the sixties. I can't wait to see it and hear those songs again.' Cliff took to the stage for a duet encore on the opening night as well as adding backing vocals to the album of songs from the show.

(Picture by Sue Andrews)

CAST

Principals:

Don	DARREN DAY
Barbara Winters	CLARE BUCKFIELD
Stella Winters, her mother	FAITH BROWN
Wally H Spencer III	ROS KING
Alma	MARISSA DUNLOP
Steve	DANIEL HINCHLIFFE
Angie	JANE HOUSLEY
Edwin	MARK McGEE
Mimsie	TAMZIN OUTHWAITE
Cyril	RENE ZAGGER

Ensemble:

JANE ANDERS-MILLER	JOSEPH BARR
NICK BOURNE	DAVID CHRISTOPHER
LEE WILLIAM DAVIS	JOANNE ELLERY
TOM KANAVAN	RYAN LAIGHT
LOUISA LANDON	SARAH LIDDLE
MIRANDA RICHARDS	DAVID RUFFIN
PATRICIA VILLA	IRENE WARREN

CREDITS

Stage Adaption by	MARK HADDIGAN & MICHAEL GYNGELL
Lighting Designed by	HOWARD HARRISON
Sound Designed by	ALPHA AUDIO SYSTEMS
Musical Director	ANDY RUMBLE
Musical Consultant	BRIAN BENNETT
Musical Arrangements by	ANDY RUMBLE
Co-Executive Producers	ANITA LAND & ADRIAN LEGGETT
Choreographed by	QUINNY SACKS
Directed & Designed by	ULTZ
Special thanks to	THE JAMES GRANT MEDIA GROUP
Presented by	APOLLO LEISURE (UK) LTD & BARRY CLAYMAN CONCERTS

(Picture by Sue Andrews)

Production Photographs   CLIVE BARDA
Souvenir Brochure   DEWYNTERS

SUMMER HOLIDAY – THE TOUR

Manchester Opera House 3 March–12 April 1997
Bristol Hippodrome 16 April–21 June 1997
Hammersmith Labatts Apollo 4 July–20 September 1997
Birmingham Alexandra 6 October–13 December 1997
Oxford Apollo 17 December 1997–24 January 1998
Edinburgh Playhouse from 11 February 1998

Summer Holiday – The Musical took to the road
around the UK for a fifteen month tour that kicked off
at the Manchester Opera House in March 1997 with
some minor cast changes to the principals and
ensemble. The credits for the show remained the
same as in Blackpool.

CAST

Principals:

Don	DARREN DAY
Barbara Winters	CLARE BUCKFIELD
Stella Winters, her mother	HILARY O'NEIL
Wallace	ROSS KING
Steve	DARREN J BENNETT
Mimsie	LUCIE FENTUM
Edwin	MARK McGEE
Angie	MIRANDA RICHARDS
Alma	JO SHERWOOD
Cyril	RENE ZAGGER

Ensemble:

THERESA COLLETTE	JENNIE DALE
CHARLOTTE GRISLEY	GAVIN HATCHER
MATHIEU JACOB	TOM KANAVAN
RYAN LAIGHT	BETH O'BRIAN
MARK PETTITT	HOLLY ROOK
DAVID SELLINGS	GAIL-MARIE SHAPTER
TIM STANLEY	SIMONE WALLER